IN OFFICE

IN OFFICE

Norman Lamont

LITTLE, BROWN AND COMPANY

le, Brown Book

First published in Great Britain in 1999
by Little, Brown and Company

Copyright © 1999 by Norman Lamont

The moral right of the author has been asserted.

A CIP catalogue record for this book is
available from the British Library

ISBN 0 316 64707 1

Typeset in Sabon by M Rules
Printed and bound in Great Britain by
Clays Ltd, St Ives plc

Little, Brown and Company (UK)
Brettenham House
Lancaster Place
London WC2E 7EN

For Rosemary, James and Sophie

Contents

Introduction   1

1 The Leadership Election, 1990   6

2 A Hurried Budget, 1990–91   31

3 Russia   64

4 False Dawn – The Recovery That Kept
  Disappearing   89

5 Maastricht – Britain Tries to Square the
  Circle, 1990–91   110

6 The Recovery Stalls   137

7 The 1992 Budget and the General Election   155

8 How Victory Turned to Dust, April–
  September 1992   191

9 The Glidepath Towards Disaster   220

10 Black or White Wednesday?   246

11 Rebuilding – Policy Out of the Ashes   267

12 Autumn Statement 1992   299

13 Muddling On   313

14 The 1993 Budget – The Day of Reckoning   333

15 Resignation and Exit from the Government   359

16 The ERM and the 1990–93 Recession   385

17 Return to the Backbenches   396

18 A Vote Against My Party and a
     Leadership Election   424

19 Why I Am Against the Single Currency   448

20 The Countdown – The Wasted Years, 1995–7   461

21 Adoption at Harrogate and Defeat   477

22 The Major Years, 1990–97   493

23 After the 1997 General Election   505

     The Resignation Speech   518

     Bibliography   525

     Appendix: Tables

     1 UK Base and Exchange Rates   526

     2 National Income 1990–93   527

     3 Manufacturing Output and Retail Sales   528

     4 Retail Prices Index   530

     5 Discount and Lombard Rates of
         Bundesbank   531

     6 Deutschmark–Sterling Real Exchange Rate   532

     7 The Popularity of the Conservative Party   533

     8 Monthly Unemployment Count for the
         UK 1990–93   536

     Index   539

Introduction

Much of this book has been written in a room in the Treasury. When an ex-Minister wishes to consult the departmental papers of his time he has to return to his department and is only allowed to study them there. They don't quite lock you in a room, but very nearly.

I found it a strange thrill to return to the austere surroundings of the Treasury, with its uncarpeted floors and wide corridors, which always used to remind me of a Soviet psychiatric hospital. When I was Chancellor I was always expecting to bump into a patient being wheeled on a trolley towards me in one of the gloomier hallways. Although my time at the Treasury was a very stormy one, and a period of great stress, probably as difficult as any Chancellor has ever experienced, I enjoyed it enormously. No matter what the pressures, once I had closed the doors behind me in that office and started to read the papers about dual resident companies or some tax proposal for the budget or once I engaged in argument with the mandarins of the Treasury, somehow I felt protected from all the assaults of the outside world. I felt a curious security in No. 1 Great George Street.

Going back to the Treasury and rereading my papers allowed me to relive many of the arguments and dramas. To read again those elegant and learned submissions put before me brought back all the excitement. Sometimes, when I reread a paper, I thought perhaps I should have come to a different conclusion. Sometimes odd paragraphs would strike me, and I would wonder, but not be able to remember, whether I had fully taken on board a particular point.

The Treasury building, a fine underappreciated one designed by John McKean Bryden, is always untidy. In the elegant circular courtyard there always seem to be piles of building materials or mysterious planks of wood left lying around. The interior also suffers from what I call 'notice pollution'. There isn't a wall in the building not plastered with notices saying 'Save energy, switch it off', 'Emergency zone assembly point' or 'black alert'. When you come through the side entrance opposite the Foreign Office a notice tells you the precise width and height of the entrance. One day someone ought to get round to cleaning and smartening up the building.

To write this book I was given a room in a distant corridor where there were two filing cabinets and a table. After my first visit and after I had been given a Treasury pass, I couldn't find the room the next time. When I did, I wasn't sure it was the right room. Because there was no furniture I couldn't identify it. For all I knew I could have been in the Lubyanka. Fortunately I noticed the clock on the wall had stopped at 3.10 and that is how I identified it in future.

On one occasion, alone in the room in the Treasury, I looked at some of the papers relating to one of my Budgets. The words I was trying to read lost their focus. My mind wandered. I dreamt I was Chancellor of the Exchequer again. I did all the things that I had wanted to do, but never did, like reforming Capital Gains Tax. I dreamt that we were never in the ERM, that there was no Black Wednesday. The Budget was more or less in balance, and all my colleagues were supportive in controlling public expenditure. Above all, I never had any quarrel with the Prime Minister. I pulled myself together. This book is not about what might have been. It is about the hard, stubborn facts, however difficult they are for me to set down.

The Treasury is a most impressive department. It is, as they say, a Rolls-Royce machine. No Minister could have been, nor ever will be, as loyally and as well served as I was by the officials there. But there is one respect in which the Treasury is less than impressive. Its records and filing system are terrible. This is no reflection on the conscientious civil servants who in vain tried to find for me records of the Maastricht monthly meetings or the mysteriously missing records of certain meetings between myself and the Prime Minister. I did go into the Foreign Office to try to find some of the Maastricht papers, and I have to say that, for once, the Treasury has much to learn from the Foreign Office. The Treasury's idea of finding a particular paper for you is to give you three files, three feet high, and say, 'There you are.' In the Foreign Office, if you ask for a paper they hand you the specific file.

This book is not an autobiography. It is merely an account of my time at the Treasury, which happened to be, I believe, a particularly interesting one. I have never myself found autobiographies with accounts of how people went to school with no shoes or how they and all their contemporaries were a brilliant generation at university very gripping.

My purposes in writing this book are several. I wanted simply to describe what it was like, day by day, to live through a momentous and very difficult period. I wanted to describe the pressures and the juxtaposition, as so often happened, of the highly dramatic with the sometimes farcical.

It is frequently said that political memoirs are boring because they are full of self-justification. Certainly no one is entitled to write their own school report. I hope I have not tried to do that.

But inevitably I have tried to describe why certain decisions were made while I was Chancellor. With the exception of Selwyn Lloyd, who also presided over a difficult recession, no Chancellor was as unpopular or as highly criticised as I was. Sometimes the reasons for certain harsh decisions seem to me somewhat misunderstood. I hope I might at least be allowed to explain why, even when mistakes were made, decisions went in one direction rather than another.

I have attempted to be as dispassionate as I can about the events and my role in them. I have also tried to reveal my own uncertainties. In doing so, I realise I run the risk that I may make myself appear indecisive. But collective responsibility and the nature of Cabinet Government all the time involve compromise.

I have tried throughout to rely on the records of official meetings, and the recollections of colleagues. When there has been no official confirmation or record of a meeting, and when I have relied only on my memory, I have specifically said so.

The Appendix at the end of the book contains a series of economic tables. The careful reader will notice that these do not necessarily always correspond to all the figures given in the text. This is because I have used in the text the figures I had at the time, whereas those in the tables have subsequently been revised, sometimes several times. This of course illustrates one of the probelms of economic management – do you have accurate statistics?

Perhaps unusually for a book of this kind, this one is entirely my own work. There have been no great teams of researchers or writers. It is my story as I saw it. Nonetheless my thanks and gratitude are due to the following:

Wendy Garthwaite, my secretary, has painstakingly typed up innumerable versions of the manuscript. My chosen method of working could not be more obsolete and invites hilarious disbelief from my journalistic friends: writing by hand, dictating and then correcting. Wendy has been extremely patient.

Rupert Darwall has made very many excellent suggestions and many amendments.

Kieran Carne helped me to retrieve papers in the Treasury's chaotic archives, and Jonathan Collett to locate newspaper articles and information.

Judy Bachrach corrected much of my inelegant grammar and made many valuable editorial changes.

Nancy Miller Jong provided helpful comments on the jacket.

Caroline North has been a meticulous editor.

As well as helping me with the facts, Lord Burns, Sir Nigel Wicks, Robert Culpin, Jeremy Heywood, Alastair Ross Goobey and David Cameron were all highly valued and deeply loyal colleagues to me during my time in the Treasury, and I shall always be grateful to them. They have all read parts of the manuscript dealing with various events. Needless to say, that does not mean that they agree with my account, let alone any conclusions. They almost certainly don't.

The great sadness for me is that while I have been writing this book, my wife, Rosemary, and I were in the process of divorcing. The burden of that knowledge has certainly meant the book is not the one I wanted to write. But I would like to record my deep thanks to Rosemary and my children for all the support they gave me the whole time I was in No. 11. I know that in many ways they did not greatly enjoy the experience and had to put up with many intrusions into their lives. But they were wonderful to me. I shall always be in their debt and I shall never be able to repay them.

1

The Leadership Election, 1990

On the idle hill of summer,
Sleepy with the flow of streams,
Far I hear the steady drummer
Drumming like a noise in dreams.
                    A. E. Housman

'You do know you will soon be the most unpopular man in the country.' That was how Sir Terence Burns, Chief Economic Advisor to the Government, greeted me in the long, dark room that is the Chancellor's office in the Treasury, on Wednesday 29 November 1990, minutes after I had become Chancellor of the Exchequer. I thought I knew what he meant. After all, I had seen Nigel Lawson have some rough times as Chancellor. His successor, John Major, had also experienced a difficult time, although he was anticipating easier ones. But my mind was on other things. And I doubt if even Terry Burns really knew quite how tough things were going to be.

Appointment

To be Chancellor of the Exchequer was the peak of my ambition. Almost all my Ministerial experience had been in economic jobs.

I had been in the Treasury both as Financial Secretary to the Treasury under Nigel Lawson, in charge of the Inland Revenue and privatisation, and as Chief Secretary to the Treasury under John Major, in the Cabinet in charge of controlling public expenditure – a really gruelling job if ever there was one. Sarah Hogg, the head of the PM's Policy Unit, was kind enough to say that no one had come to the job so well qualified. It wasn't remotely true, but it was kind of her to say it. Nonetheless I was somewhat daunted at the prospect.

John Major appointed me Chancellor in his small, upstairs sitting room in No. 10. The appointment had already been widely trailed in the newspapers. 'The markets will like it, and the Party will like it,' he said. I went out through the front door of No. 10 into the street, which was packed with photographers. The flashlights went as I climbed into the Chancellor's Jaguar and was driven the few hundred yards back to the Treasury to start work. At least I knew my way round. I knew what a Chancellor was meant to do, having after all seen two of them do the job.

The next day a piece in the *Financial Times* by Philip Stephens caught my eye. In an article about me he described the post of Chancellor as 'a poisoned chalice'. He wrote that I was no doubt pleased at this moment, but he wondered if in a year's time I would still be quite so pleased. He pointed out the looming problems: the stubbornly high rate of inflation, the continuing need for high interest rates, and the fears of recession and rising unemployment. I did not give it too much thought, but the article stuck in my mind.

If someone had told me a few months earlier that I was just about to become Chancellor, I would not have believed them. It had happened unexpectedly as a result of a series of extraordinary events.

Britain's entry into the ERM

Eight weeks earlier Margaret Thatcher and John Major had taken Britain into the Exchange Rate Mechanism. At the time, as Chief Secretary, I had my hands full dealing with the autumn spending round and fighting off the claims of Cabinet colleagues for more money. Outsiders may find it surprising, but I played no part and was not involved in the decision to join the ERM. That was how the Treasury operated with John Major and Nigel Lawson before him. Big macro-economic decisions were taken by the Chancellor alone or by the Chancellor and the PM.

During my time in Cabinet there were no discussions about the ERM. John Major had a brief discussion with me a few days before the announcement was made. It was obvious the decision had been made, and I raised no objection. I did say to one senior Treasury official, 'What have we done this for?' He replied, 'It's politics.' I said, 'I don't think I would have given up the flexibility of the exchange rate.' Little did I realise that this decision would have such huge consequences for the country, for him, and indeed for myself.

Although I had not been involved in the decision I was wheeled out to support the Government and the decision in the debate in the House of Commons to approve our entry. I did so very much in terms of counter-inflation policy.

Some years later, when asked about joining the ERM, I realised I couldn't remember in which year it happened. Was it 1989? No, it must have been 1990, the same year I became Chancellor – that is a measure of how remote the decision to join was from me. It seemed to belong to a different era, but in fact it occurred only eight weeks before I became Chancellor.

Membership of the ERM, though much criticised subsequently, at the time was greeted by many people with acclaim. Many newspapers that would become highly critical gave it a warm welcome, as did the CBI and most of industry. Dissenting voices were a minority. One immediate effect was a huge boost to the standing of John Major, particularly in the House of Commons. I remember saying to him that I thought the decision would be the political making of him. After all, he had persuaded Mrs Thatcher to do something she did not want to do, and he had succeeded where Geoffrey Howe and Nigel Lawson had both failed. Quite how he achieved it I never understood or discovered, but it increased his reputation as a man of consummate political skill.

In politics the unexpected always happens. Our decision to

join the ERM had been a surprise to me. But what happened next was even more unexpected. A whole series of events, from Geoffrey Howe's resignation as Deputy Prime Minister to Michael Heseltine's leadership bid, were to cause Margaret Thatcher to resign and John Major to stand for the leadership of the Conservative Party. And I found myself in the role of John Major's Campaign Manager.

The fall of Mrs Thatcher

Much has been written about the resignation of Mrs Thatcher and John Major's leadership campaign. There have been allegations of plots against Mrs Thatcher, including manoeuvring by John Major and his supporters. Most of these stories have been refuted, rightly so, since they were largely the invention of journalists.

When Michael Heseltine announced on 14 November that he was going to stand for the leadership against Mrs Thatcher, my reaction was one of dismay. I liked Michael personally, but I disagreed with him on a wide range of issues. I had been one of his Junior Ministers in the Ministry of Defence and though I had not enjoyed the MOD, I very much liked working for him. He is a person of flair, charm and determination. But his views on economics, particularly industry and Europe, were very different from mine. After his resignation I once took him out to lunch and told him that, much as I liked him, if he ever stood for the leadership of the Party unfortunately he would not have my support because of his position on Europe. He expressed surprise and said that when people worked together differences between them disappeared. I believe that is what he thought, and in my experience that is certainly how he operated as a Minister. Nevertheless I told him that I thought Europe was the fundamental issue, and that he would never become Leader of the Conservative Party if he persisted in holding the views that he did.

Michael had basically been campaigning for the leadership for several years, waiting for the moment. He did a lot of speaking in MPs' constituencies. His assiduous nature was once brought home to me by a conversation I overheard between two backbench MPs in the Smoking Room. One said to the other, 'I had Michael Heseltine to stay when he spoke for me.' 'So did I. But did he give you advice on your garden?' 'No, but did he give you a tree?' Michael was well known for his arboretum at Thenford. I hadn't realised his hobby had political uses too.

During the first round of the election I threw myself into Mrs Thatcher's campaign, but it wasn't easy. Several times I rang Peter Morrison, her Campaign Manager, MP for Chester, and offered to call any wavering backbenchers. Trying to get names from him was like extracting blood from a stone. Usually I was told all was under control. Then I started to ring with the names of waverers that I had discovered. One example was Andrew Mitchell, MP for Gedling, assumed to be a Thatcher supporter, but who I discovered was intending to vote for Michael Heseltine. Another was Michael Knowles (Nottingham East), whom I knew well as Leader of Kingston Council in my constituency. When I passed this information to Peter Morrison he was surprised. But I kept finding more. From then on I asked William Hague, my Parliamentary Private Secretary, to help me check the names of people we thought might be secretly doubtful. Although I still thought Mrs Thatcher would win, I became more and more nervous about the outcome.

My opposition to the single currency

On 15 November I made a speech to the Bruges Group, supporting Mrs Thatcher's policies on Europe and attacking the idea of a European single currency. She needed to be defended. Ironically, one of the criticisms made about Mrs Thatcher by some Conservative MPs was that she was too strident in her criticisms of Europe. In a few years' time most Conservatives would long for a Leader to say 'No, No, No', but at that time 'No, No, No' was regarded by many as too uncompromising.

I saw matters differently. In my speech I strongly supported Mrs Thatcher's opposition to the single currency and said that the issues involved went 'to the heart of Government' and that the subject was the most important constitutional issue to face Britain since it first joined the Community in 1973. I said there were few examples in history of a currency union without a political union, and that 'a single currency means a single government'. That was what I believed then and what I have continued to believe ever since. Anyone who thinks my Euroscepticism only developed after I left the Government has only to read that speech to see that this is not so.

I also argued for widening the EU to include the former Communist countries. At that time this was not the conventional wisdom, though it has become so since. I felt that expansion was necessary to help the Eastern Europeans, but it would also mean that Europe was likely to become a looser association of nation states. Michael Heseltine, for the opposite reason, was fiercely opposed to wider membership of the EU; he thought it would threaten closer integration in Europe.

My speech was reported, along with other statements by Ministers, on the front page of the *Evening Standard* under the headline 'The Leadership Fights Back'. Curiously, Treasury officials had tried to prevent me making the speech and John Major himself, perhaps prompted by officials, had expressed doubts, asking if it was really necessary for me to make the speech. It was, he explained, not that he disagreed, 'I just wouldn't put it that way myself.' What did he mean? I never found out. What other way was there to put it? I was determined to make the speech, because I felt it would help Mrs Thatcher. It was well received by an audience that included Conrad Black, proprietor of the *Daily Telegraph*, and we had an enjoyable lunch afterwards in Salomon Brothers' dining room.

John Major was absent for much of the time during the leadership election. Weeks previously, he had decided to go into hospital to have a wisdom tooth operation over the weekend beginning Friday 16 November. Later, journalists suggested that the operation was an excuse so that he could avoid campaigning for Mrs Thatcher. This is nonsense. His behaviour was scrupulous. In fact I suggested to him that, in view of the leadership election, perhaps he ought to postpone his operation. If anything went wrong for Mrs Thatcher he would have to be a candidate. But he was adamant that he would not postpone the operation. Any such move would be misunderstood. Everyone would think he was expecting something to go wrong, and returning to take advantage of the situation. So he had his operation as planned.

He came out of hospital on the Sunday, and returned home to convalesce and sleep. On the Monday he took few calls, but I did discuss with him my anxieties about the election. From then on, as his deputy in the Treasury, I was in regular contact with him, keeping him in touch with developments.

On Monday night, the evening before the first ballot, I was standing in Speaker's Court, at the back of the Chamber, waiting for my Ministerial car. Peter Morrison arrived and said, 'It will be all right tomorrow. Unless I am much mistaken she will get at least 220 to 240 votes.' I wondered to myself, but said nothing.

The next day, Tuesday 20 November, was a tense one. Voting began in the morning and went on all day. The result was to be announced at 6.30 p.m. in Room 12 on the Committee Corridor on the first floor of the House of Commons. I went up and found it absolutely packed. It had a very excited atmosphere. We waited and we waited for the announcement, but it didn't come. Then John Gorst, the MP for Hendon, popped his head around the door and said to the assembled 300 MPs, 'The press are saying they have got the result.' I have never seen a crowded room erupt with so much anger. MPs were outraged and all their pent-up resentment exploded; how outrageous it was that the Press should be told the result before MPs!

In the end the result, announced by Cranley Onslow, Chairman of the 1922 Committee, turned out to be:

Margaret Thatcher	204
Michael Heseltine	152
Abstentions	16

Mrs Thatcher had the most votes, but under the constitution of the Conservative Party they were not enough. If she had received 4 more she would have been declared the winner then and there. A second ballot was now inevitable.

For an incumbent Prime Minister with an international reputation who had been in power for eleven years it was a poor result. I was disappointed, but my feeling was still that she would fight on and win. That opinion was quickly to be reassessed.

The House of Commons was in turmoil. Everywhere there were groups of people in corners talking. Both Michael Heseltine and Mrs Thatcher announced they would fight in the second round.

As the hours went by it became more and more apparent that the situation was not as might have been expected. Some people were saying that Mrs Thatcher would get fewer votes in the second round than in the first. Early that evening, Rob Hayward, the MP for Kingswood, who is something of an expert on elections, thought that about forty people would withdraw their support from Mrs Thatcher. William Hague told me he had come across many people who said they had voted for Mrs Thatcher out of loyalty but now felt that her credibility had been irretrievably damaged. They were not prepared to vote for her again. 'If nearly half our Parliamentary colleagues can vote against the Prime Minister as leader, how can we possibly expect a majority in the country to re-elect her?' was how one MP had put it. William's view was confirmed by many others. Michael Jopling, the former Chief Whip, also told me that Mrs Thatcher's support was shrinking.

Some commentators have doubted whether Mrs Thatcher's vote would actually have fallen in a second round. There have even been suggestions that Michael Heseltine's supporters were pretending they had voted for Mrs Thatcher and saying that they would not do so in the second round. Some may have engaged in such Machiavellian tactics, but far too many people were saying that they could not support Mrs Thatcher again. I have no doubt that her vote would have fallen. Other Thatcherites in the Cabinet, such as Michael Howard and Peter Lilley, without talking to me came to the same conclusion. That night in the Division Lobby Alan Clark, MP for Plymouth, Sutton, said to me, 'It's magnificent. She is a kamikaze pilot. She is not just going to crash the plane, she is determined to sink the battleship.' He was referring to the damage to the Party if she fought on as she intended.

The Catherine Place meeting

In the afternoon I bumped into Tristan Garel-Jones, Minister of State for the Foreign Office, who suggested I came round to have a chat at his house after the 10 o'clock division. He said there would be one or two other colleagues there. I passed this information on to Peter Lilley, Secretary of State for Trade and Industry, and suggested that he came too. Peter subsequently told me that he was more or less told by Tristan not to come. I am not sure why this was the case.

The meeting at Tristan's flat in Catherine Place has been written about as though it was some kind of plot against Mrs Thatcher. It was nothing of the sort. It was simply a meeting of politicians to discuss what should be done, as often happens on such occasions. No one guided or steered the discussion in any particular direction. Almost certainly, similar meetings were taking place all over the House of Commons at the same time.

When I arrived at Tristan's I found the meeting larger than I had expected. There were about twelve people present, all but one of them Ministers. They included Tony Newton, Malcolm Rifkind, Chris Patten, John Patten, Douglas Hogg, Alan Clark, Alan Howarth and William Waldegrave. Most were from the left of the Party and were not likely to agree with anything I might say. The general view was much in line with what William Hague had told me. Support for Mrs Thatcher was ebbing away and people felt she was finished. A number said she should resign. No one dissented. There was then a discussion about who should be Leader.

Most of those present argued for Douglas Hurd, the Foreign Secretary. Alan Clark suggested Tom King, Secretary of State for Defence. This was rather surprising, not least since his own diaries subsequently showed what a low opinion he had of him. There was little support for Michael Heseltine, and several people were sharply critical of him. Since I liked Michael as a person, I made some observations about what I saw as his good qualities. These comments were wrongly interpreted by Alan Clark as implying I might support Michael for the leadership. I can't think how he ever got that idea, since I stated clearly I believed Major was the man we should back. No one supported me. I was rather taken aback by the strong opposition of William Waldegrave and Douglas Hogg. Both had been Foreign Office Ministers when John was Foreign Secretary. Douglas Hogg said it was too soon for him. William Waldegrave was virulent and scathing, and implied that John Major had not been up to the job of Foreign Secretary. I was not the only person shocked at the tone of his remarks.

I had come to the view some time ago that when Mrs Thatcher eventually decided to step down John Major would be the most suitable successor. He had been a successful Chief Secretary to the Treasury and built up a reputation as a brilliant negotiator, which I saw in action when I was Chief Secretary and he was Foreign Secretary, and I had to negotiate the Foreign Office Budget with him. He had left the Treasury only a few weeks previously; to my discomfort I discovered that he remembered the Treasury brief better than I had learnt it, and he ran circles around me. To me he was plainly a highly intelligent man. But strangely I always felt he was more comfortable as Chief Secretary than as Chancellor. He preferred figures and budgets to concepts, analysis and logical argument. As Chancellor he was popular with the Parliamentary Party and the press. He was certainly thought of as 'the coming man'. I was also impressed that in a Party of public school- and Oxbridge-educated people, he gave no impression of chippiness at all about his own background. As he said, he had been educated in the 'University of Life', having left school at an early age. Although not well known in the country, he appeared to combine dry economics with an emollient style, natural good manners and considerable political shrewdness. He seemed an ideal person to consolidate the achievements of the last decade into 'a kinder gentler Thatcherism'. But to me the most important point, indeed the most important by far, was that, compared with Hurd and Heseltine, he appeared to be cautious about Europe and the single currency.

He also had steel. Judith Chaplin, his Political Secretary, later MP for Newbury, summed him up well in her diary. 'He is certainly tough enough. It is possible to understand [him] if you recognise every decision is taken on how it affects and promotes him. This doesn't mean he is not a very nice man, as everyone says he is, but he is ruthless.'

I felt fairly certain John wanted to be Leader, although he was to tell me that he wasn't sure. I had noticed, as others did, that when he was Chief Secretary he spoke in an enormous number of MPs' constituencies. He was always rushing off to speak at some dining club in the North of England at the request of a backbench MP. Often I noticed he wrote to the MP afterwards saying how much he had enjoyed it. It showed remarkable energy when the burden of the job of Chief Secretary was so crushing.

Contrary to what has been alleged, there had been no canvassing for John Major at this stage. Until the last few days I had expected Mrs Thatcher to lead us into the next Election. But conversations about the succession were not unknown in the House of Commons. Chris Patten once remarked to me, 'One day you will be stepping into your car after lunch and your driver will suddenly say to you, "Have you heard the news, Minister?" That is how you will learn she has resigned.'

The only consensus of the Catherine Place meeting was that people should tell the Whips their views about the dangers of Mrs Thatcher standing in the second round, and later that evening Malcolm Rifkind, Tony Newton and I duly went together to see Tim Renton, the Chief Whip, and expressed our view. At the same time, John MacGregor, the Leader of the House, was canvassing all members of the Cabinet. He asked me my opinions, which I gave him. I understand the Cabinet's view, by 12 to 5, was that Mrs Thatcher should stand down.

Although I expressed my support for John Major at Catherine Place, the only discussions I had ever had with him on this matter had been very tentative. At the very start of the leadership election, I had said to him, 'It is possible it will all go wrong for Margaret and you may have to hold yourself ready.' He had made a non-committal reply, but I guessed he was interested. I had returned to the subject on another occasion. He said he wasn't sure that he wanted to be Prime Minister, and that even if he did he wasn't sure that he was ready for it now. I wasn't sure whether I really believed him. I was to press him more in the days ahead.

A meeting with Mrs Thatcher

The next day, Wednesday, I was informed by John MacGregor's office that all the Cabinet were to see Mrs Thatcher one by one. The meetings took place in the evening, over several hours. It was not an interview that I was looking forward to at all. I had made up my mind that she could not win and that therefore she should consider standing down in favour of someone who would continue her policies. Looking back at that meeting today, I am rather aghast at my presumptuousness in daring to tell her any such thing. How could I have said such a thing to the greatest Leader of the Conservative Party since Winston Churchill? But at the time I felt I had to do so. When I saw Mrs Thatcher I said it was my clear view that she would be defeated and Michael Heseltine would win. I made it very plain that if she took a different view and fought on I would energetically and publicly do all I could to support her. But I felt it was all over. The danger was that everything that she had achieved on the economy would be placed in danger, and then there was also the prospect of a much more pro-European policy.

Other Cabinet Ministers were said to have been fairly brutal and to have threatened to resign if she did not stand down. But that was not my position.

At the time I thought it the most difficult meeting of my life. She was very upset by what I said, presumably because it came from someone who was one of her strongest supporters. I felt wretched saying it, yet I thought it was necessary. Then she changed and started to talk about who would succeed her. I said, in my view, John Major was the man most likely to preserve her legacy. She agreed but talked about the need not to split the vote. She thought there ought to be one candidate only in order to defeat Michael Heseltine. I was not at all keen on this, as I feared it would be Douglas Hurd. He was a civilised and intelligent man, whom I liked, but I did not feel that he had much grasp of economics and he was still very much a Heath man. I also thought he would be beaten by Michael Heseltine. My view was that two candidates, far from splitting the vote, might attract more votes away from Michael.

After the Cabinet Ministers had been seen, other individual MPs gave her their views as well. Some were for fighting on, but the majority view was that she could not win. There is no doubt that this view was gaining ground everywhere.

I telephoned John Major and told him what I had said to Mrs Thatcher. He seemed surprised I had been so direct, and described it as 'very brave'. I thought his tone implied it was not something he would have done. However, I told him I now thought Mrs Thatcher would definitely drop out of the next round, and that if we were to stop Heseltine he must stand. This time he did not dissent. He talked a little about having a unity ticket with Douglas Hurd, but seemed to come down against it. I was now confident he would stand.

Events were moving fast. I was not at all surprised when Peter Morrison telephoned me that night. He was oblique, but I got the message: there was a distinct possibility that Mrs Thatcher would resign the next day. I passed this news on to John Major. To my surprise he already knew, and his intention to stand still seemed firm.

On the morning of Thursday 22 November I received a telephone call from my friend Woodrow Wyatt, a former Labour MP and now a cross-bench peer, who urged that Mrs Thatcher should fight on. I told him that I thought the decision had been made, and almost certainly there would be an announcement later that morning. He was very angry, and refused to believe it.

Cabinet had been brought forward that morning. If the Wednesday-night meeting with Mrs Thatcher had been difficult, this was even worse. Before Cabinet everyone hung around outside the Cabinet room in a gloomy mood. Margaret arrived and we all trooped in behind her. She referred to the events of the last few days and to the advice she had had from 'so many of you' that she could not win and should not fight on. The way she put it implied that she did not agree and thought us spineless. Suddenly the tears flooded, the voice broke, then she recovered her composure and read a resignation statement.

The Lord Chancellor, James Mackay, and Douglas Hurd both made eloquent apposite tributes to her. Douglas referred to 'this whole wretched business', which is exactly what everyone felt. The rest of the Cabinet agenda was completed in a few minutes, then we sat around in the Cabinet Room drinking coffee. No one dared move or give any indication of wanting to leave. It would have been indecent to do so. But I caught Michael Howard's eye. I could tell that, like me, he was anxious to get away. All the time we were sitting there, time was being wasted. Michael Heseltine was already out there campaigning. He had the momentum. We could not afford to waste a minute since we had so much work to do. Eventually Margaret seemed to see what we were thinking and told us all to leave and to stop Heseltine.

Getting organised

Michael Howard, the Secretary of State for Employment, Peter Lilley, John Gummer, Minister of Agriculture, and I immediately went round to the Treasury to John Major's office. He still had not returned from Huntington and John Gieve, his private secretary, was not prepared to let us use his office in his absence, so we went round to my office, where we were joined by Terence Higgins (MP for Worthing and a former Minister), William Hague, Robert Atkins (MP for Ribble South), Francis Maude, a Foreign Office Minister, and Major's PPS, Graham Bright. This spontaneous meeting was the start of the campaign.

Our first task was to have John Major nominated as a candidate. There wasn't much time as nomination forms had to be in by 12 o'clock that day. Initially the view was that it was best for John to be nominated by backbenchers rather than Cabinet Ministers, with Terence Higgins as the proposer. While we talked about this, the minutes were ticking by, and John still hadn't arrived from Huntington. I was beginning to get anxious. Eventually he turned up, and after further discussion it was decided that he should be nominated by Cabinet colleagues. Various combinations of names were put forward. The Home Secretary, David Waddington, was approached and declined. In the end, the Proposer and Seconder were myself and John Gummer. It was felt that this provided the right balance between left and right.

We needed a campaign headquarters. We couldn't use No. 11, John's official residence, and offices in the House of Commons were far too small. William Hague said that he had a friend, Alan Duncan, with a house in Gayfere Street that he thought he might be willing to lend. I did not know Alan Duncan at that time, though he subsequently became a good friend. His house turned out to be ideal, within walking distance of the House of Commons, and it had the added advantage that Alan, an oil trader, had recently installed no fewer than six telephone lines for his own business purposes. Later on, newspapers were to see the number of telephone lines already installed as evidence that the Major campaign had started before Mrs Thatcher had resigned, reinforcing the stories of a plot. Again, this was nonsense. But the telephone lines were a great advantage.

The key point about the election that I kept emphasising from the beginning was that the only people who mattered were Conservative MPs. The most important thing was to talk to 'the voters', and the only people who had votes were MPs. Press conferences, speeches, interviews on television were all very well, but they were only relevant if they influenced MPs. There was a tendency to waste time on press interviews, while it was more important to contact doubtful MPs and to convert them.

We did have the lists of MPs that the Thatcher team had compiled, but since these had proved inaccurate we had to check the names all over again. It did not follow, of course, that everyone who had backed Mrs Thatcher would necessarily support John Major and, as we were to find out, there were some curious defections to the Heseltine camp. We were fortunate in having a number of Whips and ex-Whips in our team, and they had a lot of information about MPs' grudges and enthusiasms. They also had ways of checking on MPs' views without the MPs themselves knowing. Francis Maude and Richard Ryder, both former Whips, and Rob Hayward began work on the lists immediately. Right from the start, MPs were phoning in with their support and we were pleasantly encouraged by the numbers.

Major's Campaign Manager

The Major campaign was generally regarded as highly professional and well organised, but initially it was far from that. At first there was no Campaign Manager. We held meetings at which there was no chairman, though people did ask me to sum up. John Major himself had said to me, 'I don't want a Campaign Manager. I don't want anybody to feel excluded or shut out.' That was rather an extraordinary view, not to mention an impractical one, but it was what he wanted.

After a day of chaos John Major's PPS, Graham Bright, came and begged me to get myself made Campaign Manager. 'No one is making decisions,' he said. 'No one is in charge.' I repeated John's own words, but then other people in the campaign team came and said much the same. In this way I became the Campaign Manager at the request of the team. John was informed, and acquiesced. I myself had in fact earlier approached the MP for Sutton Coldfield, Norman Fowler, to do the job, but he had declined because, he said, he was already committed to Michael Heseltine.

Much has been made of the fact that I was John Major's Campaign Manager. When describing my subsequent relationship with John, journalists frequently referred to me as his 'former Campaign Manager' and people assumed that he and I were very close. That was not true. It was really an accident that I became his Campaign Manager; in fact I was not chosen by him.

At one point John said to me, 'I am surprised that you are backing me so strongly. After all, we haven't always agreed.' He was quite right. We had several strong disagreements in the Treasury on economic matters. I discovered I was well to the right of John in my economic views, particularly on tax cuts against public spending. At one point when he was Chancellor and the post for Secretary of State for Industry became vacant, John had suggested to me that I might want to leave the Treasury and move to the DTI. But I was much more interested in being the No. 2 in the Treasury than being the No. 1 in Industry. I never knew whether he had made that suggestion because he was uncomfortable with me or because he genuinely thought it would be a good move for me. I suspect the former.

Certainly relations between us had not always been good but, since I was his deputy, I had been extremely careful to keep that as well-kept a secret as possible. Philip Stephens, the *Financial Times* reporter, who had unusually good sources in the Treasury, had told me several times that he had learned my relations with Major were strained. I had to deny this. It would have been very bad for the Treasury if such rumours had circulated, and I must have sounded sufficiently convincing since, to the best of my knowledge, Philip Stephens never wrote about it.

The campaign starts

From the beginning the tide was going strongly in our direction. However, I tend by nature to be something of a pessimist, so I took nothing for granted and tried to make sure that we left little to chance.

I arranged that we should have a campaign team meeting every day at 8 a.m., usually in No. 11 Downing Street. The team consisted of a small number of people, but each day more and more supporters wanted to join. I decided to let anyone who wanted to do so attend and I began to see what John Major meant by saying that we mustn't 'exclude' or 'offend' anyone. Not for the first time John Major's political antennae proved more sensitive than mine.

At the meetings we discussed the latest information about supporters and opponents. When the name of a waverer cropped up, we would discuss who knew him best and how to approach him. As often as we could we would also try to identify a way of getting a second opinion. The mistakes of the Thatcher campaign had made us well aware that in these circumstances many MPs commit themselves to more than one name. We needed realistic lists. After discussing names we would then tell the meeting the campaign messages for the day – what to say to journalists, what to say in the Tea Room, what to say about the other candidates.

Every day more and more people came to the meetings. Since the TV and press were always outside No. 11 they could see the momentum of our campaign increasing. The meetings also flattered MPs by allowing them to state that they were part of the campaign team. After a few days these meetings were attended by more than thirty people. Many months later, when John Major gave a 'thank you' dinner for the team in the large, downstairs dining room in No. 10 normally used for Government occasions, we could hardly accommodate all those who claimed to have been part of the campaign team.

These meetings, though a useful sounding board, were impractical for making decisions. So I formed a smaller group of Richard Ryder, Francis Maude and myself, meeting at the even earlier time of 7.15 each morning. Not normally an early riser, I didn't find this very congenial. We decided the real issues and the strategy. John Major was never present, but I reported to him every few hours on how we saw things and what we were doing. Secrecy was important, and we also had to guard against infiltration. I knew from experience that such things happen.

I was particularly worried about Alan Clark, who kept drifting into Gayfere Street and asking questions. While I knew he was against Michael Heseltine I wasn't at all sure whether he was part of Douglas Hurd's team or that he wouldn't switch to Douglas if he thought Douglas was going to win. Alan kept trying to barge into the room downstairs – what we called the bunker – where Francis Maude and Richard Ryder kept the lists, but I had made it a rule that nobody was allowed to go in there to disturb them. People could hand in information, but they weren't allowed to see the list. I am not sure that Francis Maude even showed me the real figures.

But John Major also had his own list. There were a number of important people and waverers whom he saw on his own and their names were added to our lists after he had seen them. But I rather think that he kept one or two names to himself. It was difficult otherwise to explain his complete self-confidence throughout the campaign.

Intelligence came from many sources: MPs, Party workers, even journalists. One very surprising and important source of information emerged when a senior figure at ITN telephoned Richard Ryder and asked him if he would like to see the results, name by name, of a confidential ITN poll of Tory MPs who had been asked on strict assurances of confidentiality how they were intending to vote in the election. I can never understand why MPs participate in such polls. Perhaps they are flattered to be asked? Very wisely a number of MPs had declined to take part, but the results covered over half the Parliamentary Party. I was astonished that this person at ITN was prepared to divulge confidential information that had been obtained on an explicit understanding. Whenever I had been asked by television companies or newspapers to participate in polls that I was assured were confidential I never believed it, but now I knew. Be that as it may, the information was certainly very valuable.

While the canvassing went on hourly in the Smoking Room, the Tea Room, the corridors and other parts of the House of Commons, we also had to wage the campaign in the press and on television. When he was not meeting MPs John Major gave interviews to the media and most of them went extremely well. Most journalists were charmed and also impressed by his expressed determination to carry on with Thatcherite policies. A conspicuous exception was Charles Moore, then the editor of the *Sunday Telegraph*. I was in No. 11 when Charles emerged looking not very happy. John Major came out from the flat white with anger, and said he had never been so patronised in his life. I was surprised. Although Charles Moore has a different political outlook from John Major, he is a traditional Tory and a mild-mannered man. I could not imagine what he had said, but I had seldom seen John so worked up. He retained his dislike of Charles Moore, and Charles never overcame his innate suspicion of Major.

Every day we held a press conference, which I chaired. At intervals we released figures of the pledges of support we had received. In circumstances like these politicians will often exaggerate. My impression was that our opponents were exaggerating their support in the hope of creating a bandwagon effect. We did the opposite. Since we were doing surprisingly well, we decided we could afford to understate our pledges, enabling us each day to announce increased numbers so that a real bandwagon was shown to exist anyway. On the first day I revealed the number of our pledges, we had in fact considerably more.

The first whiff of success

I was not at all sure how the media or the opposing camps would react to our figures. In the event I was enormously encouraged by the reaction of the Heseltine team. Indeed, it was the first moment at which I began to realise that we were probably going to win. Neil Macfarlane, MP for Sutton and Michael Heseltine's Campaign Manager, denounced our figures as grossly inflated and said we were plainly exaggerating. At the same time he refused to give any figures of his own, and appeared badly rattled. I knew then we had them on the run.

But we had to keep up the pressure on MPs. Newspaper and TV interviews were all very well, but it was the MPs that mattered. I told John that, even though MPs were away, we could not afford to lose the weekend. We needed to keep telephoning the doubters. We acquired all the weekend telephone numbers of MPs from the Whips' Office, and made a list of those whom we still needed to contact. All the telephoning was done over the weekend from the Chancellor's study in No. 11, but after the campaign we made sure that the bill was paid by the campaign fighting fund.

In order to reach as many people as possible, helpers in the outer office telephoned ahead, arranging times for us to ring back. Sometimes I actually dialled the number. All John had to do was to speak when the phone was handed to him. Initially he resented this approach, and complained a little when I stood over him and got the numbers for him. But it was necessary and it was time well spent.

During one of these sessions in No. 11 David Shaw, the MP for Dover, arrived. He had insisted on having a personal interview with John to discuss policy. I was rather startled when he arrived at the door of No. 11 carrying a baby, whom he brought into John's room, and then he proceeded to ask John to guarantee that, if he was elected leader, Dover would have its much needed bypass. No one could say that David Shaw didn't work hard for his constituency, but his request was politely fended off.

Another person who came to see John Major was John Redwood, then a junior Minister at the DTI. I told John that Redwood was more interested in the European single currency than any other issue, and that was how it turned out. Redwood questioned him extremely closely. Major did not commit himself absolutely, but indicated his lack of sympathy for the single currency. Redwood wasn't happy. He thought Major could have been clearer, though in the end I believe he voted for Major.

An unfortunate row with Nigel Lawson

Events such as leadership elections can test the best of friendships. Listening to TV one night I learnt that Geoffrey Howe and Nigel Lawson had made a public declaration of support for Michael Heseltine. Geoffrey's response was to be expected, but Nigel astonished me; in fact I felt even more strongly than that. I thought it was a snub by Nigel to someone who had worked loyally for him and that it was a denial of all Nigel's lifelong political beliefs. Michael Heseltine was an interventionist in industrial policy, a high spender, a fierce critic of Mrs Thatcher and a European federalist. On all these issues Nigel's and Michael's views were diametrically opposed and I did not see how Nigel could possibly support Michael, even though Michael had unexpectedly come out in favour of independence for the Bank of England, an issue that was of great interest to Nigel. Perhaps this had swayed him and perhaps it was a cunning move by Heseltine. Civil servants in the Treasury were just as astonished as I was.

I had worked for Nigel for several years, and I greatly admired and respected him, but at the time I felt outraged on John Major's behalf. Impetuously I picked up the telephone, got through to Nigel, and in far too emotional terms protested to him. I suggested that he was abandoning his own beliefs, then put the phone down and refused to take Nigel's call when he phoned back.

My behaviour was inexcusable and after the leadership election I realised that I had been extremely rude. I regretted what I had done and wrote to Nigel apologising for my behaviour and intemperate language. I owed Nigel a huge amount and felt that an old friendship should not be strained in this way. Generously, he accepted my apology.

Major scores on TV

All three candidates gave TV interviews over the weekend, and all of them performed well. Douglas Hurd suffered from press comment about his background, which he tried to brush aside. I thought Michael Heseltine came across as sympathetic and persuasive, though I was dismayed when I heard him say that right-wingers such as Edward Leigh were supporting him. Edward, the MP for Gainsborough, was a strong Thatcherite who, I assumed, would support John Major. But he was one of several MPs misled by newspaper stories of plots who felt that Mrs Thatcher had been badly let down and that there had been intrigue against her. I realised other Thatcherites probably had similar feelings. Heseltine had skilfully used the names of Edward Leigh and Neil Hamilton, who had worked for him, to appeal to the right wing.

Fortunately Mrs Thatcher herself magnanimously came to the rescue, giving a lunch for the No Turning Back Group and strongly pleading with doubters like Michael Forsyth and Michael Brown to vote for John Major. Not all did, but undoubtedly she turned some votes, and she was very active in telephoning and talking to other waverers.

Skilful as Michael Heseltine and Douglas Hurd were on TV over the weekend, it was John Major who enjoyed the greatest success. Until the leadership election, he was not well known in the country. Heseltine, by contrast, had been campaigning for the leadership for several years, was extremely well known and had considerable support. Yet within a few days of Major's standing for the leadership, the polls began to show a sharp increase in support for him and soon he was the public's first choice. This was a remarkable achievement in a few days and showed that his charm and modesty had come across to people on television. This made a great impact on MPs who concluded that such appeal on TV would be a great asset in a Party Leader.

As we entered the final stages I increasingly felt that Douglas Hurd was out of the race. The last forty-eight hours were spent putting the squeeze on Douglas's supporters. Preparations were begun for the next round, which we assumed might be necessary.

We began to research the second preferences of Douglas's supporters to see which would go to Heseltine and which would come to us. In the final hours before the vote we actually began to canvass people in the Hurd camp for the next round.

To the best of my knowledge John Major never offered anyone who came to see him any job or any incentive to vote for him. I know the same could not be said of the other candidates. One female Thatcherite backbencher told me that she had never spoken to Michael Heseltine until the day before the vote, when she was suddenly telephoned and asked to come and see him. He began his conversation with the words, 'There is so much unused talent in this party. We desperately need more people from your intake.' Michael's tactics showed occasional signs of desperation. William Hague, my PPS, was publicly known to be part of the Major campaign team, but outside the loo in the division lobby he was approached by Michael, who asked if he would support him. Michael even approached me saying, 'Whatever you say publicly, you are going to support me in the secrecy of the ballot box, aren't you?' It is one of Michael's most endearing characteristics that he always believes that everyone is on his side.

Our canvassing efforts continued right up to the closing of the ballot box. Our figures showed that we were ahead of the other two, but could we be sure that they were more reliable than the previous figures of Margaret Thatcher's team?

Victory

On the afternoon of Thursday 27 November we retreated to No. 11 Downing Street and discussed possible tactics for the next round. John Major at this stage was absolutely exhausted. Although a leadership election does not make the physical demands of a General Election, with all the travel that involves, the pressure had been unrelenting and the stakes were high. He had been astonishingly calm and composed throughout the whole campaign. He told me he wanted to go and rest in No. 11; I was to come and get him when the result was due.

Richard Ryder, Francis Maude and I were all in the upstairs reception room called the State Room, outside the entrance to the flat at the top of No. 11. Shortly before the result was announced I went into the flat to get John Major. I called out, but there was no reply. I eventually found him stretched out, fast asleep on his bed. I had some difficulty waking him up.

When we went back to the State Room, I gave John three cards with notes prepared by Richard Ryder for three different speeches. The first, which I hoped we would not need, was the speech for a defeat. The second, which I thought the most likely to be used, was a speech if another round was necessary. The third was for an outright victory. John smiled, and said he wouldn't need the first two. He appeared completely confident.

Then the telephone rang. We learnt the result was:

John Major	185
Michael Heseltine	131
Douglas Hurd	56

It was convincing. John had not got over 50 per cent, but he was so far ahead of Michael that it was obvious that he would easily win the next round. Within minutes Michael telephoned to concede defeat and to congratulate John. Michael's public announcement was made, as I saw on television, with enormous style and generosity.

Immediately people started to arrive at the State Room in No. 11. I had been expecting members of the campaign team, but all sorts of hangers-on appeared from nowhere. One was the chairman of a well-known public company, who strolled confidently into the room completely uninvited. I had not seen him once during the campaign and I was quite sure that if Michael Heseltine had won he would have been marching into his office and congratulating him. I was not at all surprised to read recently that this same businessman has been actively wooing New Labour.

Then Mrs Thatcher arrived, kissed John and congratulated him. By this time there was a vast crowd of TV crews and cameras outside.

The celebrations went on and gradually people left. I went into the flat with John. We sat down and talked, not really a serious chat, just enjoying the situation and relishing the result. He asked me what job I thought he should give Michael Heseltine. I said Home Secretary, which was what I assumed he wanted. John said that perhaps he should get his teeth stuck into the Ministry of Health. I was surprised at this suggestion and said that I thought it would appear insulting. Later Michael told me he had been offered the Home Office but declined it. He said that at the time he regarded it as a trap to discredit him. I didn't understand why Michael was so suspicious. We weren't thinking like that at all.

John Major asked me about various other people. I suggested that Richard Ryder should be made Chief Whip since that was what he had told me he wanted to do. John thought it was a good idea. I have to confess that the unworthy thought occurred to me that henceforth I would have a friend and supporter in the Chief Whip, and that was reassuring. We did not discuss my position. Obviously I had wondered what he had in mind, but we never discussed it at any time until the next day, when he asked me to be Chancellor.

2

A Hurried Budget, 1990–91

Reaction to my appointment was generally not unfavourable. A few papers suggested I had been made Chancellor as a reward for managing John Major's campaign, but most recognised that I had long Ministerial experience in the Treasury. I was pleased to get a note from John Smith, the Shadow Chancellor, congratulating me and wishing me luck 'on a personal basis'.

My Ministerial team in the Treasury was a strong one. David Mellor became Chief Secretary and my deputy, with a seat in the Cabinet. He was not my choice and initially I had reservations about him, but he quickly demonstrated his quick mind and he relished the intellectual challenge of the job. I think he even ended up quite liking the Treasury. Francis Maude, an able free-market man, became Financial Secretary, John Maples, previously my PPS, Economic Secretary, and Gillian Shephard, as Minister of State, was the first woman Minister in the Treasury. John was extremely keen to have a woman Minister in the Treasury because he felt sensitive about the criticism that he had no women in his

Cabinet. It was indeed odd that he unwittingly appointed the first all-male Cabinet for over twenty-four years. Whatever the motive I was delighted to have Gillian on my team.

William Hague continued as my PPS, a role he had assumed in 1990. He was thought young to be a PPS to a Cabinet Minister, but he quickly demonstrated his shrewdness and justified the high reputation he had on entering Parliament. I inherited from John Major his Private Secretary, John Gieve, who had also been Private Secretary to Nigel Lawson and thus was Private Secretary to three Chancellors in succession. But the plan was for John to stay on only until after the Budget. One of the Gieves of Gieves and Hawkes, he had a whimsical sense of humour that was to be invaluable in the months ahead.

In addition to junior Ministers and Private Offices, every Cabinet Minister also had a team of Political Advisors. These were people from outside the Civil Service, who, because they were not Ministers or MPs, would spend time working with civil servants and making sure that Ministers' political aims were understood.

My political advisors were Alastair Ross Goobey who brought great expertise from the City, Warwick Lightfoot and, for a short while, Mark Call. Warwick had worked for Nigel and John. Later on I recruited Bill Robinson, a taxation expert, from the Institute of Fiscal Studies. I also informally involved Andrew Tyrie, who had resigned as an advisor on becoming a Parliamentary candidate.

My office as Chief Secretary had been on the Parliament Square side of the building. I had occupied that office for five years, both as Financial Secretary and Chief Secretary. It was not a very elegant room, but I had grown rather fond of it and installed my own paintings. Now had to move round to the immensely large office of the Chancellor on the Foreign Office side of the building. I didn't much like it. Apart from its size – it was big enough to practise putting – it was dark, with panelled walls and forbidding Dutch paintings apparently nailed to them. Perhaps the Treasury was worried the Chancellor might steal them? The huge conference table in the room could comfortably sit thirty people. At the end, behind the Chancellor's desk, was a concealed loo within an alcove. I remember once being in the room when Nigel Lawson totally vanished to reappear unexpectedly from a panel in the wall.

On the desk at the far end of the office I found a folder waiting for me from Terry Burns, the Chief Economic Advisor, since the Permanent Secretary, Sir Peter Middleton, was away in New Zealand. Inside there was a note addressed to 'the new Chancellor'. Its first words were 'Welcome to the Treasury'. It had obviously been written before they knew the identity of their new boss. Perhaps they had not expected me to become Chancellor?

The folder contained a few observations about the economy, EMU (European Monetary Union) and the state of the public finances. It also had a diary from December to December of next year informing me of all the international meetings such as Ecofin (the Committee of European Finance Ministers) and G7 that I would have to attend. There were also details of an imminent EMU meeting, and the paper outlined some options.

Reviewing the economy

One of my first meetings was with Sir Peter Middleton, Terry Burns and the team of Treasury forecasters to discuss the economy. As Chief Secretary, although not involved in economic policy, I had seen the economic forecast documents that were circulated to all Ministers and produced three times a year. The last of these had appeared in July. The Treasury at that point had not foreseen any recession and neither, it should be added, had the vast majority of independent forecasters, even at that late stage. By the autumn things were looking different, and there were signs that the world economy was weaker than expected before the sharp rise in oil prices caused by the crisis in the Gulf had depressed the prospects for trade. We had also since then joined the ERM, although even before that the Treasury had concluded that the economy was 'probably' in a period of falling GDP that would probably last for three or four quarters. The origianal forecasts had been more pessimistic, but John Major revised them upwards.

Major had been very reluctant to utter the word 'recession'. In fact he refused to use it all. He had also said that any downturn would be 'short and shallow'. I do not think he can be criticised for this, because it was indeed what the Treasury had forecast.

In the 1974 recession output had fallen for four quarters. In the 1980–81 recession it had fallen for five quarters and by a total of 5 per cent. Conditions in 1990 were in many ways different. Although inflation in 1990 was high it was lower than the very high rates of the early 1970s or 1980s (inflation in the 1970s reached 27 per cent, and in the 1980s, 22 per cent). This meant the degree of disinflation required to return to a tolerable inflation level was less. So the Treasury expected a short recession, with a total fall in GDP of about 1.25 per cent spread across three quarters. Recovery would be led by the consumer; confidence would revive as inflation fell.

Inflation was a real problem. Almost on the day I became Chancellor it had reached the uncomfortable rate of just under 11 per cent. For a Government that had, in Nigel Lawson's words, claimed that inflation was 'judge and jury', the verdict looked likely to be 'guilty'. Inflation had been gradually rising since 1987, the year of the stock market crash, when Nigel had cut interest rates. He was later to say with hindsight that he had overreacted, but he was hardly to be criticised. As Financial Secretary at the time, I remembered how the press and business were unanimous that interest rates must come down drastically or there would be a slump.

Inflation had also increased because the economy had grown unexpectedly strongly in 1989 and 1990 and, as it turned out, more rapidly than the official statistics indicated at the time. Nigel could only base his policy on the economy as shown by statistics. Someone once remarked that trying to make policy on the basis of current statistics is like trying to drive a car by the rearview mirror. He might have added that the mirror is so cracked and so dirty you can't even see where you have been.

The situation called for a difficult judgement: inflation was high, which required a continuation of high interest rates, and we also needed to maintain our position in the ERM. On the other hand there were clear signs that the economy was deteriorating, and we had already had interest rates at 15 per cent for a year, so there was already considerable disinflation in the pipeline. I formed the view that we needed to cut rates, but carefully, so as not to endanger our ERM membership. But how quickly could we move?

Inheriting the ERM

My own relations with John Major appeared very relaxed. Like everyone else, I appreciated the more consensual style of conducting business compared with Margaret's. Occasionally I was startled by the odd remark. Once, very early in his Premiership, he remarked to me that he thought we should organise a seminar on 'what we believed in'.

I also didn't much care for his remark about being 'at the very heart of Europe'. People often quote the phrase without the 'very'. The speech in which he made it was in many ways excellent but, since he professed to be sceptical about the single currency, how could we be 'at the very heart of Europe'? And if he was against political union, as he repeatedly said, how could we be 'at the very heart of Europe'? I did query the phrase when he read me part of the speech, but he and Sarah Hogg the head of his Policy Unit, were obviously keen on it.

Every week I had a 'bilateral' meeting with the Prime Minister. Often only a Private Secretary was present to take notes, but sometimes Sarah also attended. My first meeting was on 5 December, just a few days after I had become Chancellor. I gave my preliminary views on the economy to the Prime Minister and said that there was a need to reduce interest rates at an early opportunity. However, I had to make the point that we had only just joined the ERM at the PM's own initiative and I too had just become Chancellor, so the markets were carefully watching the actions and words of both of us. When we had joined the 'European snake', a precursor of the ERM, in the 1970s, we had left after a few weeks. Many wondered whether our commitment would be stronger this time. If we were to get interest rates down, we had first to build up our own credibility within the ERM. Without that we would not be able to get interest rates even further down in the future as we both wanted. So we had to move carefully.

Many people who supported the ERM did not appreciate how it was meant to work when it was put into practice. Interest rates remained the main tool of monetary policy, but now the overriding factor in setting them was to meet the UK's ERM obligations and to keep the pound close to its central rate against the other ERM currencies. This was not some additional optional discipline but a complete regime for interest rates.

The consequence was that for a high inflation country like the UK, interest rates would have to be higher until our inflation rate moved into line with that of the best, which was usually that of Germany, the anchor of the system. From the moment we joined the ERM our interest rates were inevitably heavily influenced by those of Germany. One of the problems was that, as a result of German reunification in 1989, Germany was beginning to have its own inflation problems, although they were nothing like as great as our own. Because of reunification, Germany was experiencing a boom just at the time Britain was going into recession. This meant that the needs of the two economies were strikingly different.

It was always possible that there might be occasions when domestic conditions and ERM obligations conflicted. Domestic conditions might point to interest rates lower than those permitted by ERM obligations. But it was hoped those occasions would prove to be the exception rather than the rule. In the years since 1978, that had been the case for the existing members of the ERM. It was also argued that any loss of control over our own interest rates was generally likely to be compensated for by a marked improvement in inflation performance, increased market confidence and in the long run therefore lower interest rates.

As I have already explained I had played practically no part in the decision to join the ERM. Whatever my view, I had no option but to implement the policy. It was hardly open to me to reverse a decision made by the Prime Minister, the previous Prime Minister and the Foreign Secretary.

I was personally agnostic about the ERM. When Nigel Lawson had resigned in 1989, partly over his relations with Mrs Thatcher and partly over the ERM, I had written to him urging him not to resign because the ERM was not worth it. When I had been asked in the Commons by Giles Radice, MP for Durham North, why I had not resigned with Nigel Lawson, I had made it clear that I did not share his enthusiasm for the ERM. I personally would not have taken the decision to join the ERM, but nonetheless once I became Chancellor I saw no reason why it should not continue to operate with the same smoothness as it had since it had started in 1979. I had no doubt it was my job to implement the settled policy of the whole Government and maintain Britain's position in the ERM.

In the autumn of 1990 it was obvious that there was a lot of bad news building up in the economy. On 15 November, just two weeks before I became Chancellor, there had been the biggest monthly rise in unemployment in over four years when the seasonally adjusted figure rose by 32,000 to pass the 1.7 million mark. The *Financial Times* commented, 'There is a growing consensus among City economists that the latest data make the Treasury forecast that the current slowdown would be both shallow and short-lived unrealistic.'

To me it seemed pointless to deny, as John Major had done, that the economy was now in recession. In my first appearance in the House as Chancellor I took the opportunity to use the 'R' word. When I appeared before the Select Committee on the Autumn Statement on 5 December, I wanted to strike a realistic note, but at the same time I did not want to contradict what my predecessor had recently said. Asked whether I agreed with John Major that the recession would be 'short and shallow', I replied that 'there are reasons why one could believe that it will be relatively short-lived and relatively shallow'. I said what the reasons were, but my words were qualified. Despite my conspicuous caution the words 'short and shallow' were subsequently remorselessly quoted back at me, as though they were my own.

I have always had an innate suspicion of both official statistics and economic forecasts. This is no criticism of the Treasury, which in Britain has one of the better records, if the word 'better' means anything in this context, but the performance of economies depends upon the decisions of millions of individuals, and since individual human beings are not programmed computers, forecasts are never likely to be accurate as long as human beings remain free. Indeed, it is positively reassuring that forecasting never gets it right, because it means human beings are free spirits, not machines. I told the Treasury and Select Committee that 'the one thing we know about forecasts is that they are always wrong'. In many ways I would have preferred to have published no forecasts whatsoever. I discussed that possibility with officials, feeling that a belief in the ability to predict short-term developments in the economy was a harmful human addiction. But it was quickly pointed out to me that the Industry Act placed a legal obligation on me as Chancellor to lay forecasts once a year before Parliament. Later on I made another attempt to defuse the mystique of forecasting by publishing a raft of different forecasts, private sector as well as Treasury, to show the wide variation in expectations of the future.

Because professional forecasts are so often wrong, many people react by wrongly suggesting that policy-makers should listen more to businessmen. A cursory glance at company chairmens' statements at their Annual General Meetings shows that businessmen are no more able to foresee the future accurately than anyone else. Businessmen in their economic views tend to go in and out of fashion like other people go through revolving doors. Businessmen tend to talk their own book and always favour lower interest rates unless, very unusually, they happen to be in a sector that benefits from higher interest rates.

Nevertheless it is useful to have as accurate a picture as one can of what is currently happening in the economy. I was impressed by the way in which Alan Greenspan, the Chairman of the Federal Reserve Board, and probably the world's most highly regarded central banker, made use of a large amount of data from firms or sometimes even individual factories to help him make decisions about American monetary policy. Eventually I too came to the view that it was not sufficient to rely on official statistics on retail sales, industrial production or manufacturing. These were often presented to me as preliminary estimates and then revised several times, and frequently the revisions were greater than the initial estimated changes. Later on, with the help of Terry Burns and Alastair Ross Goobey, we devised a whole series of weekly databases for different parts of the economy. Alastair Ross Goobey's knowledge from his investment days was extremely useful.

Preparing the Budget

My immediate priority on becoming Chancellor was to start preparing for the next Budget. I was conscious that there was a very short time available, and in effect I had about eight to ten weeks in which to draft it. It wasn't quite as bad a prospect as it might have seemed since I had watched and participated in the preparation of four Budgets, under both Nigel Lawson and John Major. In fact, John had already begun thinking about the Budget, but his preparation had been interrupted by the political events of the autumn.

The framing of a Budget is an immense task, normally covering five or six months of work. The Chancellor, helped by his Ministers, has to look at many complicated different options on tax policy, all of which are costed and analysed in detail. A vast array of technical anti-avoidance measures are always put forward by the Inland Revenue and Customs and Excise; individual lobbies put forward their thoughts; and then ministers have their own suggestions for tax reform. In the end many ideas are discarded after months of work by officials. Then at the last stage a huge amount of documentation has to be designed, written, approved and printed. Much of the detail has to be settled weeks before Budget day, yet members of the public and sometimes business lobbies carry on making representations to the Chancellor long after it is possible for them to have any impact.

It would be an exaggeration to say that as soon as one Budget is finished the preparation for the next begins, but it is not a great exaggeration. Nigel Lawson used to start thinking about his next Budget in the summer and he was always well advanced in his thoughts by October.

Much of the work for the Budget was done at weekly overview meetings attended by the Chancellor, all the Treasury Ministers, the Permanent Secretary, the Chief Economic Advisor, the Head of the Inland Revenue, the Head of Customs and Excise, a number of other senior civil servants and also the Chancellor's Political Advisors. A Private Secretary would attend as note-taker and each meeting would last some two and a half to three hours. The agenda would consist of different potential items for the

Budget and teams of civil servants would come in to the meeting to discuss particular items such as corporation tax, VAT or PEPs. At any one time there might be twenty to thirty people at the meeting. After one item had been discussed, one team would withdraw to be replaced by the next one.

I would conclude each meeting by evaluating the leading candidates for inclusion in the Budget. Each week a 'score card' would be compiled showing the costing of each possible measure and the total of the draft Budget measures. In between the weekly overviews there would be smaller meetings to discuss the economy and public finances and sometimes sessions with other departments who might be affected by individual measures. Nearer the date of the Budget many meetings would go through the text, diagrams and charts in the Budget documents. Nigel Lawson always gave virtuoso performances at such meetings, frequently querying obscure footnotes or definitions in appendices with officials.

Apart from dealing with the Budget, my other aim was to form a view about the economy. As Chief Secretary I had not been exercising my mind much about whether the UK was or was not entering a recession. Outsiders may find this strange, perhaps not understanding the gruelling and demanding nature of the job of Chief Secretary. Until the autumn I had been completely immersed in the public expenditure round, holding meetings with spending Ministers and doing deals with them on their budgets. A large part of my negotiations had been at the Conservative Party Conference, where I had been a rather invisible figure as I had spent much of the time in Bournemouth hotels in secret negotiations. But Mrs Thatcher had pointedly referred to me in her final speech in the Conference in which she said, 'Many of the best speeches have not been made in the Conference Hall. They have also been very brief speeches consisting simply of the words "No, No"'. As Chief Secretary I always knew I could rely on Mrs Thatcher's support for controlling public expenditure. Since John Major himself had been Chief Secretary, I had no reason to think it would be any different with him.

Despite the worsening economic climate and our inability, because of the ERM, to respond with immediate cuts in interest rates, things continued to go well politically for the Government. There undoubtedly had been an increase in the Party's popularity after the change in leadership. *The Sunday Times* on 27 January 1991 had the headline 'Major's rating rivals Churchill', saying he enjoyed a personal satisfaction rating as high as the highest recorded by Margaret Thatcher during the Falklands War, and 'the biggest surge in support for any Prime Minister since Winston Churchill took over from Neville Chamberlain in 1940'.

Rates down to 13.5 per cent, but it's not so easy

At the beginning of January 1991 domestic conditions clearly needed a reduction in interest rates, but we still had not made the cut. There was a new problem. There were indications that the Germans would put up interest rates. Moving British rates in the opposite direction to those of Germany was going to be difficult inside the ERM and the PM and I felt we must wait until after the Bundesbank meeting later in the month. A cut followed by a forced increase would be disastrous, perhaps forcing us to leave the ERM only a few weeks after we had joined. On 1 February the Germans did, as expected, raise both their key interest rates, the Lombard rate and the discount rate, by 0.5 per cent to 9 per cent and 6.5 per cent. We waited until 13 February before cutting interest rates by 0.5 per cent to 13.5 per cent.

Many people felt we had waited too long. It seemed a long time to me too, but it was only eleven weeks since I had become Chancellor and it was essential to show the markets that we would fight inflation and take no risks with the ERM. It was the first cut since the 1 per cent reduction made when Britain had joined the ERM in October, and sterling reacted strongly, moving up nearly a pfennig against the mark to DM 2.904 and edging higher against the dollar to $1.9925.

The reaction in the press was muted. *The Times* thought it was too little. There was also a disagreement between those who thought German rates had now peaked and those who thought they would rise further. Our strategy may have been cautious, but it had worked. By holding back and waiting we had built up credibility and the currency had strengthened. Our longer-term objective, of course, was to achieve more significant reductions in rates. On 27 February we cut rates by another 0.5 per cent, so rates had now come down 2 per cent since we had joined the ERM to 13 per cent.

Our difficulties were compounded by the fact that conditions both domestically and internationally were now deteriorating quickly. The US and Canadian economies had joined us in recession and growth in France and Italy had slowed markedly. Growth for G7 as a whole was expected to slow to 1.5 per cent, the slowest growth since 1982.

The Treasury economists produced a new forecast, this time predicting a longer and deeper recession – much more so than in the October forecast. Non-oil GDP was expected to fall by a total of 2.25 per cent spread over four quarters to mid 1991, compared with the previous predicted fall in output of 1.25 per cent spread over three quarters. But it was still their view that recovery would start in the second half of 1991, led by a revival of consumer spending.

Getting rid of the Poll Tax

As well as preparing for the Budget, much of my time was taken up with Michael Heseltine's work to find an alternative to the Community Charge or Poll Tax. Michael had built much of his opposition to Mrs Thatcher on his criticism of the tax. During the leadership election he had said he would abolish it but gave no alternative, merely saying, 'Nothing is ruled in and nothing ruled out.' During the leadership election I had persuaded John Major to match Heseltine's pledge and he would certainly not have won the leadership election if he had not done this.

When Major appointed Heseltine to the Environment post, one which, to my surprise, he actually wanted, the Prime Minister perhaps assumed that Heseltine by now had some clear idea of how to replace the Community Charge. But he had no such fixed idea at all. Not that John or I were in any position to be critical. We were no clearer.

As Financial Secretary and Chief Secretary I had watched the saga of the Poll Tax unfold. Margaret Thatcher had good reasons for introducing the Poll Tax, particularly the escalating expenditure of local authorities and an absence of any awareness of this fact among most of the electorate. The tax was designed to bring home to voters the cost of local government. To many Conservatives rates appeared to be an unfair tax paid by a relatively small number of people. Whatever the merits of the Poll Tax, Nigel Lawson from the start had made no secret of his view that a flat, universal tax of this kind would inevitably be a political disaster. That Nigel made his views clear, even in private, was revealing. He was the most loyal of colleagues and all the time I worked for him, with the exception of the Poll Tax, he never let drop a hint of any disagreement between himself and the Prime Minister. But his views on the Poll Tax were known to all his Treasury colleagues. Nigel, like all Chancellors of the Exchequer, was frequently accused of being non-political, but on this occasion, as on others, his political instincts were acute.

I had other reservations about the Poll Tax. It was extremely expensive and difficult to collect. Its unpopularity was such that successive measures to make it more equitable absorbed some £10 billion of relief over two years. Over half those due to pay the tax were having their payments reduced through reliefs and in 1991 a quarter of those liable to pay had not done so by March. It was also a fatal mistake to require those on benefit to pay the tax, and to relax capping of local authorities.

Conservative MPs were equally unclear about what they wanted to replace the Poll Tax. Some merely wanted yet more reliefs to make the Poll Tax more palatable, others wanted a local income tax. There were several varieties of a property tax that differed from rates. Some wanted the responsibility for certain local government services such as Fire and Police and even Education transferred to central government.

To me, more reliefs seemed to get the worst of all worlds. We would have less revenue and forgo the advantage of the tax – its universality. I was also against the idea of a local income tax which, as well as running counter to a long-term aim of the Conservative Party, would also be extremely bureaucratic.

The problems of a property tax were further complicated by the whole question of the need for a rating revaluation of every house in the country. The Government had landed itself in a nasty mess by delaying a rating revaluation, which was required for water rates. In the meantime property values had diverged and increased, so any new property tax was going to throw up some nasty surprises; any property tax based on ratable values would be unpopular. It was a problem of the Government's own making. Conservative MPs by and large emphatically did not want a return to rates, which were very unpopular with Conservative supporters. Was there a property tax that could be devised which avoided the disadvantages of the rating system?

It was a problem that was not going to be solved quickly, but John Major and I decided that we had to find some way to take the sting out of the Poll Tax immediately.

Most of the credit, if credit it is, for the idea of switching part of the burden of local taxation to central government belongs to John Major. It was he who suggested it to me, although the idea had been around in the Treasury for some time and had already been mentioned to me. But the original idea of John and Sarah Hogg was that we ought to reduce the Poll Tax by a central government grant, paid for by an increase in income tax, of perhaps 2 or 3 pence. I considered that, but was not keen on the idea of increasing income tax. The Conservative Party had expended much effort in getting income tax rates down to encourage the supply side of the economy, and to sharpen incentives. It would have been a huge reverse to have put up income tax in order to facilitate the abolition of the Poll Tax. That would have been to compound our earlier error. I had already told John that I did not think we should ditch the Conservative Party's pledge to reduce income tax to 20 pence. On one occasion I put the idea of a switch to income tax to Michael Heseltine and he replied with remarkable understatement, 'I don't think the Party is quite ready for that yet.' I am sure he was right. The Party would have hated another 2 or 3 pence on income tax.

I preferred a switch from the Poll Tax to VAT. We would have to introduce a bill to give extra grant to local authorities to reduce the Poll Tax and in order to pay for it we would have to put up

VAT from 15 per cent to 17.5 per cent. It was one thing to provide the money to enable local authorities to cut the Poll Tax, but it was quite another for the local authorities to cut it rather than spend the money themselves. In order to make sure the money was used as we intended we had to introduce 'universal capping' of all local authorities. This was exceedingly complicated and somewhat draconian, but unavoidable.

I was anxious about the distributive effects of the Budget, but the increase in VAT was not so regressive as is popularly imagined, because items on which the poor spend proportionally more, such as transport, food and children's clothes, are zero-rated for VAT. An increase in the standard rate of VAT affects the poor less than many other income groups. The VAT increase would enable us to switch £4.25 billion away from the local tax base to central government. It would be the biggest switch in taxation for over a decade, and would knock £140 per head off the Poll Tax.

The Budget takes shape: reducing mortgage relief

The rest of the Budget preparation was by now relatively advanced. Our labours with the weekly overview meetings were beginning to yield fruit and the shape of the Budget was emerging. I was particularly keen to tackle what I thought was one of the root causes of the British economy's historic instability: mortgage tax relief. In Britain for many years savers had been encouraged by mortgage tax relief to put the main part of their savings into housing. The results had been repeatedly inflated house prices, and instability in the housing market.

Mortgage relief may have served a purpose after the Second World War when the few people who owned their own houses were taxed for the privilege, but in my view it had had its day. Nigel Lawson shared this view, and would have liked to reduce mortgage relief, but Mrs Thatcher was always strongly opposed.

I decided to abolish mortgage relief against the higher rate of tax. Henceforth it would only be available against the basic rate. I saw this as the first step towards abolishing it completely. In order not to create losers from the limitation of mortgage relief I increased the threshold for the higher rate of tax from £20,700 to £23,700, £1,000 more than required to match inflation.

I also felt it was important in the Budget that we were seen to do what we could to ease the burden on industry. The economy was beginning to worsen and we continued to be constrained on interest rates because of the ERM. It was in my opinion particularly important to help smaller businesses, so we were working on a package that allowed the self-employed and sole traders to pay income tax and National Insurance quarterly and reduced the number of businesses that had to account for VAT. For larger businesses I had in mind to reduce the corporation tax rate both for the current year and the next year. However, I could only do this for the current year because corporation tax is paid in arrears.

To finance the business package it was necessary to seek revenue somewhere else. I did this with a combination of raising tobacco and alcohol duties by more than the rate of inflation and by extending Employers' National Insurance to company cars. Obviously the latter was never going to be popular but as a Junior Minister in the Treasury I had long ago come to the view that since we were reducing tax rates, particularly for the higher paid, it made no sense for employers to go on paying people benefits in kind that were taxed less heavily than income. Benefits in kind as a method of remuneration perhaps made sense in the socialist world of 98 per cent income tax, but they had no place in the new low-tax environment we wanted to create.

I decided to increase sharply the scale charges on company cars. As part of the attack on benefits in kind I also decided to introduce a scale tax on employer-provided mobile telephones. This was not, as people later believed, a tax on mobile phones themselves, but only on the provision of mobile phones by employers as benefits in kind for their employees.

Other measures included a reduction in the age at which people could claim retirement relief, and be exempt from Capital Gains Tax when they sold their businesses. This was one way of offsetting my decision not to reform Capital Gains Tax in this Budget. In my opinion, part of the harm caused by Capital Gains Tax was that done to entrepreneurs and those who started their own businesses. I hoped to return to the matter again in future Budgets.

Government borrowing starts to rise

The recession and the Gulf War, whose build-up began in the autumn, were already beginning to eat into the national finances. Tax revenues were slowing down, recession meant that expenditure was rising and as a result so was Government borrowing. In the Autumn Statement John Major, as Chancellor, had predicted that there would be a surplus of £2 billion in the Government's finances for the year 1990/91. By January 1991 this had vanished, to become merely a predicted balance in the Budget. This was disappointing, but not enough to cause serious worry at that stage. It was a small change compared to what was to come.

No. 11 and the IRA attack

All the time the Budget was being prepared I continued to live in our Notting Hill house. We had not moved into No. 11 Downing Street, the traditional home of Chancellors of the Exchequer, partly because it was so near Christmas and partly because we were uncertain whether we would be there long enough to justify the move; it was quite possible there might be an election within a few months. We eventually decided to make the move and did so on 8 March.

Although we were not sure how long we would be there, we were thrilled to have the opportunity to live at No. 11. The accommodation, on two floors, is often described as a flat, but it is more like a house, and it is spacious. My son James, then seventeen, away at school in Canterbury, and my daughter Sophie, then fourteen, at school in London, were delighted to have much bigger bedrooms than in our Notting Hill home. James and I were also delighted there was a table for table tennis on the top floor. I can quite understand why Gordon Brown and Tony Blair decided that it made more sense for the

Blairs, as a family of five, to live in No. 11 and for a bachelor Chancellor to live in the much smaller single-storey flat 'above the shop' at No. 10.

The flat in No. 11 is on the first floor, although the Chancellor has a study on the ground floor, which I used only occasionally, for meetings. Outside the flat there is the State Room, a large public reception room, hung with Gainsboroughs and paintings from different galleries, some of which were selected by Rosemary.

The No. 11 flat is arranged around a hall with a circular staircase reaching to the upper floor. We put Sophie's piano below the stairs, and as the flat was so open the sound of her playing could be heard almost everywhere in the building.

The second day after we moved in, Rosemary was still unpacking cases when the IRA launched a mortar attack on Downing Street. One of the furniture removers was standing by a back window when the first mortar went off. He was unhurt as the broken glass was caught by the lead-weighted safety curtains, but he was badly shaken and had to go home. Strangely, the night before John Gieve and I had been sitting in that very room and discussed the possibility of an IRA mortar attack. I had declared my intention to remove the safety curtains because they ruined the view of Horseguards. It was very lucky I had done nothing about it.

At the time of the attack the Cabinet was discussing the situation in Iraq. There was the noise of an explosion as the mortar landed in the garden, but to me it did not sound at all close. I thought perhaps it was a car bomb in Horseguards. Sir Robin Butler, the Cabinet Secretary, however, was better trained, and quietly told everyone to lie down on the floor, which we did. We waited for a second explosion, which duly came, although it missed the garden, went over the garden wall and landed near the statue of Lord Mountbatten on the edge of St James's Park. A third mortar failed to go off.

Robin Butler told us all to go immediately to a room in the basement of the Cabinet Office. I was worried about Rosemary and Sophie but had to go down with the others. The meeting continued in a state of some excitement.

We were not allowed upstairs for some time and when we

emerged from below we had no idea what damage had been caused. I was still anxious about both Sophie and Rosemary, but was not allowed by the security men into No. 11. Eventually I was told that they were safe. Gus O'Donnell, John Major's Press Secretary, by this time had managed some contact with the outside world. I overheard the PM say to him, 'Do the press know how close the bomb was to me?'

Once allowed through to No. 11, I was deeply shocked to discover how extensive the damage was. The Cabinet Room where our meeting had been held had reinforced windows that had withstood the blast so I did not appreciate what had happened elsewhere. There was extensive damage everywhere. Every window in No. 11, including those on the Downing Street side of the building, even those facing on to an inner court, had been blown in. A door leading off the State Room on to the balcony had been blown off its hinges, landing on top of Sophie's guinea pig's cage. This was duly reported in a Sunday newspaper and I received letters of support from guinea pig owners from as far afield as New Zealand. Miraculously, the guinea pig survived long enough to return to Notting Hill in 1993.

That day I was meant to be having lunch with Robert Maxwell. I have to confess that, like many others who won't now admit it, I enjoyed his company. Nonetheless I was always careful not to say anything confidential to him. I was interested to talk to him because of his knowledge of Russia and the Eastern Bloc. My Private Secretary telephoned him to say he could not now come to lunch. He replied, 'I'm not going to let those bastards stop me coming to lunch.' He was told that the police would not let me out and were unlikely to let him in. I believe he still tried.

Maxwell came to lunch on a subsequent occasion. I remember it vividly because the sofa completely collapsed under his weight. He was something of a bomb himself.

That night we had nowhere to sleep, but Kenneth Baker kindly offered us a bed in his house. Unfortunately there was a power cut that night so his normally warm house was slightly colder than usual. We were very grateful to both him and Mary, though by this point we felt a little beleaguered.

It was partly because of the IRA attack that Sophie decided she did not like living at No. 11 and wanted to go away to be at the same school as her brother. Her bedroom was badly damaged by the bomb, and not long afterwards another taxi bomb went off at the bottom of Downing Street when Sophie was alone in the flat. Both she and Rosemary found the security in Downing Street oppressive. Each time Rosemary drove Sophie to Godolphin School and then returned with her in the afternoon, the police insisted on opening not just the boot but the bonnet of the car. In vain Rosemary would point out she had not got out of the car. The police would say, 'But the IRA are very ingenious.' It was not designed to make a young girl feel reassured.

Decisions on child benefit

We decided to increase child benefit, which had been frozen for several years under the Conservative Government. Child benefit was an unpopular benefit with the Conservative Party. Under Mrs Thatcher it was generally assumed that freezing it would finally result in it being phased out. Mrs Thatcher preferred child tax allowances to cash benefits, but tax allowances were of no help to people on low incomes.

As Chief Secretary I had been forced to rethink child benefit because of advice that a continued freeze might put us in breach of our statutory obligations and leave us open to legal challenge. The choice was to abolish the benefit or to revert to increasing it. In fact we decided to give an extra increase and to make a commitment to update it annually in line with inflation.

The more I thought about it the more I became convinced that the atavistic dislike in the Tory Party for child benefit was wrong. As a benefit it had many advantages. For a start it was paid to those in and out of work, and so did not have the same disincentives as income-related benefits. Furthermore the correct way to look at child benefit was as part of the overall tax and benefit system. Many people forget that child benefit was originally introduced as the first instalment of a wider tax credit system that had been planned by Tony Barber and Arthur Cockfield during the Heath Government. Child tax allowances had been abolished and replaced by child benefit, which was not a social security benefit, but a tax credit. There is no country in the world that I know of that has a tax and benefit system which does not recognise the needs of children and families. Child benefit seems a much more effective way of helping them than a tax allowance.

At the same time I was suspicious of the utility of the married couples allowance in the tax system. Why should there be a special tax allowance for married couples, even when they have no children? Often both partners in a marriage will be working. The major 'cost' of most marriages is children, and it is to them that the tax and benefit system should be directed. For that reason, hand in hand with the increase in child benefit, I decided that the married couples allowance should itself be frozen in cash terms with a view to one day eliminating it.

This decision has subsequently been criticised as 'an attack on marriage' and I regret that William Hague made the reduction in the married couples allowance one of the points of the Major Government for which he felt he had to apologise when he became Leader of the Conservative Party. It seems to me absurd to suggest that couples without children are more likely to stay married if they are given a tax allowance worth a few pounds a week. Far better, I would argue, to help couples and indeed single parents with children.

Of course the tax and benefit system must recognise marriage. It would be difficult to devise a system that failed to do so, and the correct way to achieve this is through help for children. And the best way to do that is a non-means-tested benefit. I still believe that today, and I maintain that it is a more coherent view than all the mumbo jumbo of the Conservative Party about not 'taxing marriage'.

I also decided to increase the premium on benefit for the first child. This change seemed well merited since the greatest expense often comes with the first child because that is when most mothers give up work.

Eleven days before the Budget, on 8 March, the Tory Party received a message from the electorate that emphasised the importance of the Budget. In the Ribble Valley by-election a Tory majority of 19,528 was converted into a Liberal Democrat majority of 4,601. Nigel Evans, the defeated Tory candidate said that the cause of the Tory defeat was 'the Poll Tax first, second and last. It didn't matter what we did.'

On 10 March a story in the *Independent* told how Michael Heseltine was drawing up a plan for a £4.4 billion package of reforms of the Poll Tax. John Major was furious and made his views clear to Michael Heseltine. Rightly or wrongly he believed that this was an attempt by Heseltine to pre-empt the Budget. It was an interesting example of how much distrust and suspicion existed between the two at that time. I was sceptical myself that Michael would have deliberately leaked the plan. My experience was that he was always very reliable on these matters and never leaked for personal advantage.

Budget Day, 19 March

Budget Day itself is a strange experience for a Chancellor, and particularly so the first time. All the work has been done and the speech has been prepared. One has to spend the morning doing nothing very much. Traditionally the Chancellor is photographed walking around St James's Park, watching the ducks like Neville Chamberlain or Sir Edward Grey. No doubt Peter Mandelson subsequently found something more interesting for Labour Chancellors to do, but I was less imaginative, and for the rest of the morning sat around in Downing Street nervously wondering how the Budget would be received and whether I had made the right decisions.

Traditionally during the Budget speech Chancellors have been allowed to have whisky in a glass by the dispatch box. I asked William Hague to make sure that I had some of Orkney's famous Highland Park whisky mixed with Highland Spring water. There are no legal distilleries in Shetland or I would have had whisky from there, but Orkney had the nearest distillery to my Shetland birthplace. I also rather liked Highland Park whisky.

William later told a *Spectator* Parliamentarian of the Year lunch, itself sponsored by Highland Park, that in order to smuggle the whisky into the Commons I put a bottle in the Gladstone Budget box, which I, like every other Chancellor, held up before the country's cameras on the steps of No. 11. He suggested the box might have opened and the bottle tumbled out. It was a good story, but actually it was William himself who took the whisky to the House of Commons. Gladstone's Budget box is far too small to carry anything the size of a bottle of whisky, unless it was a miniature.

It is difficult to describe the feelings of a Chancellor as he walks out of No. 11 to face the press before a Budget. The whole exercise has to be timed to the last second. Behind the closed door a crowd of civil servants with mobile telephones is co-ordinating it all, the door-keeper standing ready to swing the door open at the right moment. I emerged to face the photographers, who were not on the road but on a tiered stand like a mini football stadium. One of the papers carried a picture of the photographers photographing Rosemary and myself in front of No. 11. We appeared as two tiny dots in front of this huge mass of photographers.

We stood there for a few minutes. Rosemary was more than a little nervous and the minutes seemed like hours. I may not have been the best ever Chancellor, but she was certainly the most beautiful Chancellor's wife to stand there. After the Budget there were innumerable requests for interviews with her. Editors tried to coax her with bouquets of flowers, but she turned down all requests for interviews the whole two and a half years we were in Downing Street.

We made the short journey by Jaguar to the Commons. I had wanted to walk, as I knew Chancellors had done before the War, but I was strongly advised that it would be a security risk and cause traffic chaos, so I abandoned the idea. But I always regretted it, not least when I saw that Tony Blair managed to walk to his first State Opening of Parliament.

In the House of Commons I went first to my office and waited while John Major continued to answer Prime Minister's Questions. Then I hovered for a few minutes behind the Speaker's Chair and entered the Chamber just before the end of Prime Minister's Questions. During moments like this one wonders whether something might go wrong. I particularly remembered the year when Nigel Lawson found while delivering his Budget speech that one page was in the wrong place, which led momentarily to some confusion.

The Budget speech

Nervously I entered the Chamber to a huge cheer. I thought I had never seen the Chamber so packed. Certainly I had never spoken to such a crowded Chamber. While nervous I was not particularly conscious that the event was being televised live to the whole country. As I read out the speech I continually compared in my mind the reaction in the Chamber with what I had anticipated it would be. Sometimes the reaction to particular sentences was completely unexpected.

During the Budget speech the Chair in the House of Commons is taken by the Deputy Speaker in his capacity as Chairman of Ways and Means. On this occasion it was Harold Walker, the veteran 'old Labour' MP for Doncaster. In calling the House to order Harold accidentally referred to 'the Mother of all Parliaments'. Saddam Hussein and his threat of the 'Mother of all battles' was still on everyone's mind.

Budget speeches were normally in two distinct sections. The first part is a necessarily abbreviated description of the economic background, both domestic and international. The House of Commons banters and tries to put the Chancellor off with many off-stage comments not always picked up by TV, leaving viewers at home puzzled by what is so amusing to the House. Traditionally the Chancellor signals the second part of the speech to the House with the words, 'I now turn to my tax proposals.' After that you can hear a pin drop. No one knows what is coming, at least you hope they don't, and they certainly don't want to miss anything.

I had never believed a Budget speech had to be without lightness of touch. I began by saying that I had read there had been a huge amount of speculation about the Budget, and I had learnt a few things. 'For example, I was surprised to learn last Wednesday that I was almost as well known as Desert Orchid' –

the legendary racehorse. I added, 'And I haven't yet run in the Gold Cup.' I went on, 'Actually Desert Orchid and I have a lot in common. We are both greys. Vast sums of money are riding on our performance, the Opposition hopes we will fall at the first fence, and we are both carrying too much weight.'

I went on to thank Nigel Lawson for all that I had learned from him. I was very conscious that both he and Mrs Thatcher were sitting behind, and I hoped it was a Budget of which they would not disapprove.

I made it clear that I saw no scope for an overall reduction in taxes but that I saw it as my job to encourage and help business through the recession. After sketching in the gloomy international and domestic background I pointed out that recession had come after an unprecedented period of eight years of growth, but as a result firms and individuals had become overborrowed.

Expectations on inflation and growth

I emphasised that the most important objective was the reduction of inflation from its unacceptably high level. That was essential for our competitiveness and therefore for longer-term employment. Inflation had already come down by 2 percentage points, and I predicted it would fall to an average of 4 per cent in the last quarter of the year. We expected it to fall to 3.75 per cent by mid-1992. With hindsight, the rapid deceleration in inflation that occurred in 1991–4 now seems inevitable. But it didn't seem so obvious or inevitable then, and indeed initially inflation did not come down quite as fast as forecast.

This was an ambitious target and an unprecedented deceleration in inflation. It was obviously going to be tough, but in my view it was better to get it over with quickly. I knew this would be greeted with scepticism, as it was. In the whole of the 1980s we had only briefly got inflation below 4 per cent, and then it had quickly risen again. My aim was to narrow that inflation gap with our competitors but to keep it there permanently.

I wanted people to be under no illusion that getting inflation down would be painful and cause unemployment to rise. There

would indeed be a 'price' for reducing inflation. 'Squeezing inflation out means higher interest rates, frustrated hopes, bankruptcies
and lost jobs.' I could not have hammered the point much more
emphatically: 'Regrettably, unemployment is likely to go on rising
for a while yet, even after the recovery has started.' I knew this was
unfortunately true, and I just hoped people would listen.

I knew that the part of my speech that would be most carefully
analysed was my view about the recovery and I took great care to
stress the qualification. 'One of the lessons I have learned from
years of grappling with statistics is that it is difficult to be certain
about the past, let alone the future. And it is difficult to predict
the timing of turning points in the economy.'

The Treasury's best estimate remained that they expected
recovery would begin around the middle of that year, although
initially it would be slow. As in the past, falling inflation would
revive consumer spending, so additions to stockbuilding would
slow. The United Kingdom would also benefit from the expected
recovery in the United States.

I expected output to increase by about 2 per cent over the twelve
months to the first half of 1992. Looking further ahead, we saw
growth of about 3 per cent a year as the economy recovered further.
Other forecasting bodies such as the Organisation for Economic
Co-operation and Development (OECD) and the International
Monetary Fund (IMF) were making similar predictions.

I went on to link John Major's decision to join the ERM with
lower inflation. It promised 'a secure framework for combating
inflation'. That was 'its real significance'. I added, 'We committed
ourselves to that discipline after lengthy debate and our decision
was widely supported on both sides of the House and in the country at large.' There was not a murmur of dissent.

Borrowing and the automatic stabilisers

On the public finances I announced that I was expecting a Public
Sector Borrowing Requirement (PSBR) of £8 billion (1.25 per
cent of GDP for 1991/92) and a somewhat larger one for the
following year. It was the first deficit for four years. This deterio-

ration was worse than the markets expected, but not catastrophically so. 1990/91 had ended with a small net repayment of £750 million.

What was significant was my explanation of the fiscal policy I intended to follow. We were in deficit while we were in recession, but that was not inconsistent with Budget balance over the whole of the cycle. 'It is one of the more reliable laws of economics, not that there are many, that the Budget balance varies markedly over the economic cycle. When activity is growing strongly, tax revenues rise relative to income and lower unemployment brings lower social security payments . . . These forces go into reverse when the economy slows down. This is why the budget surplus has shrunk over the last two years.' I said that I thought it right to tolerate the larger deficit in 1992/93 because it would take time for the efforts of lower activity to feed through fully to revenue.

I called my fiscal stance 'prudent'. In order to support it the Budget was neutral in revenue terms for the immediate year and designed to produce an increase in revenue of £1.8 billion for the following year, 1992/93. It was quite a tough Budget for a recession and to have gone further in tightening fiscal policy at that time would have been wrong.

I explained the economic significance of these 'automatic stabilisers': 'These cyclical swings in the Budget can play a useful role in offsetting the swings in private sector borrowing and in stabilising the economy.' But they had a further usefulness: 'They come about automatically without the need for difficult judgements about the state of the economy and it is entirely consistent with the medium-term approach I have already outlined to tolerate these swings in the fiscal position. But I am not persuaded of the case for going beyond that.' They were the most important words in the speech, even though they were probably lost on 99 per cent of the audience in the House and on TV.

In the early 1980s Geoffrey Howe had cut expenditure, put up taxes despite the recession and simultaneously cut interest rates. Some Conservatives would have liked me to do the same, but we were now in a different world. The ERM meant that I could not cut interest rates quickly, and because we were constrained it made sense to allow the non-discretionary parts of Government spending, such as unemployment costs, to rise without making cuts elsewhere. The corollary was that the deficit would correct itself as the economy recovered, and that the underlying budget deficit would be close to zero. This was neither a fiscal activism nor a Keynesian stimulus. It was a policy that seemed reasonable and was widely accepted at the time.

The tax proposals

The taxes on benefits, particularly on company cars, were received in silence on our side of the House and met ironic cheers from Labour. *Bien pensants* on both sides nodded wisely when I announced the reduction in mortgage tax relief. When I came to my modest proposal on mobile phones, perhaps rather rashly I referred to the mobile telephone as 'one of the scourges of modern life'. I had always disliked the noise of mobile telephones disrupting the calm of railway journeys. After announcing my proposal I quipped, 'As a result restaurants will be quieter and roads safer.'

I rattled through the changes in the excise duty a bit too quickly. This was a mistake, because for many people watching on TV the increases in excise duty are the important parts of the Budget. Beer was put up 2 pence per pint, cigarettes by 16 pence per pack and spirits by 56 pence a bottle.

When I came to income tax I could sense the House listening more intently than ever. I repeated the longer term commitment to a basic rate of 20 pence, but I announced that for this year there would be no change in income tax.

At this stage the House was getting restless and some people were leaving, thinking it was all over bar a few concluding remarks. At this point I added, 'Any Budget would not be complete if it did not address one other issue which has attracted a certain amount of attention.' I said that Michael Heseltine would be announcing very soon our review of local government taxation. In the meantime, I said, 'I have concluded that local taxes are being asked to bear too large a burden, and the level of the Community Charge is still too high.' I then announced the switch from local to central government taxation. At this point our side were cheering strongly. Some of them in their enthusiasm forgot that this switch would have to be financed, but their cheering subsided a bit when I said I proposed to increase VAT by 2.5 per cent to 17.5 per cent. On average the headline Community Charge – the average charge without any reliefs – in both England and Scotland would fall from about £390 to about £250.

The speech was seventy-six minutes long and had included an unusually large number of specific tax changes. There were loud cheers when I sat down. I looked up at the Gallery and saw from Rosemary's expression that she thought it had gone well. Our Argentinian friend Rosario de Mandat-Grancey, with characteristic Latin American enthusiasm, stretched out her long arms in a victory gesture. I was worried she would be removed from the gallery by the attendants for making a demonstration.

Immediately after a Budget there is a packed round of engagements. I felt there was too much duplication. I could never see the point of giving a press conference immediately after a Budget speech that has been drafted with immense care to explain what one is doing and why one is doing it. All too often the press conference merely spoiled the effect of the first presentation. However, my meeting with the lobby went off smoothly.

There was also a meeting with the 1922 Committee, which is an opportunity to give Conservative MPs a more political gloss on the Budget. There I received a warm welcome from the Parliamentary Party, who were relieved that the sting had been taken from the Community Charge. They did not seem to be at all alarmed by the switch to VAT. Then came the finishing touches to the Budget Broadcast, which is an attempt to explain to the country in five minutes the main points of the Budget. We had rehearsed some parts a few days earlier, but now we had to add the detailed measures to the 'voice-overs'.

When I arrived back at No. 11, I found waiting for me a porcelain replica of Desert Orchid, sent by a friend who was the managing director of Royal Doulton, as well as a solitary orchid from a member of the public.

Reaction to the Budget

The next day's press was generally favourable. Most of the attention was focused on the reduction in the Community Charge, which was enthusiastically welcomed. The *Express* had as its headline: '£140 off, Storming Norman massacres Poll Tax, but up goes VAT'. They called the Budget 'a bold debut'.

The *Financial Times* described the Budget as the 'slaughter of sacred cows . . .' adding, 'Mr Norman Lamont played a difficult hand bravely and skilfully.' *The Times* was more critical, referred to my 'fearful orthodoxy' and focused on the economy in its editorial headline 'Recession Unrelieved'. It asked: 'What does the Budget do to encourage [this] recovery? Mr Lamont appears to feel that recovery will take place largely unaided by him. Precisely why it should is unclear.' The *Independent* had as its headline 'Lamont clears way to June General Election' and went on, along with other papers, to say that the Budget marked a new departure in its economic philosophy. It saw the point of what I had said about 'the automatic stabilisers' and explained: 'He put the emphasis on maintaining a cyclically adjusted balanced budget. This means allowing the so-called "automatic stabilisers" to do their work in full which is a very different approach to that of the original MTFS (Medium Term Financial Strategy).' The *Independent* summed up the Budget by saying the 'social market takes shape', a phrase used by David Owen in the Budget debate.

I certainly did not intend the Budget as a rejection of Thatcherism. I saw measures such as the ending of mortgage tax relief and the reinstatement of property taxes as ones that removed distortions and facilitated the working of market mechanisms. They were truly Thatcherite measures, even if Mrs Thatcher disapproved of them. Equally the increase in child benefit was part of a truly integrated view of the benefit and tax system.

The phrase 'social market' was not one that had any unfavourable connotations for me, even though it was widely misunderstood by Conservative MPs. They thought it had to do with social democracy. I remembered how frequently the phrase had been used by Keith Joseph, echoing Ludwig Erhard, the Conservative architect of Germany's post-war economic miracle.

The *Daily Telegraph* called the Budget 'prudent for Britain, but bold enough to win'. It said: 'Mr Lamont deserves the gratitude of his Party for doing his utmost with a very restricted compass for manoeuvre to create the conditions in which Britain can win.' Tim Congdon wrote that I had a hard task uniting my Party and preserving Thatcherite rectitude, and had come 'close to meeting this impossible challenge'.

I was grateful to receive a note immediately after the Budget from Nigel Lawson, congratulating me but adding pointedly, 'Pity about the last five minutes.' He had not liked the shift from central to local government because he feared this would become a permanent switch, leaving local authorities financing too little of their expenditure from their own resources. Perhaps he was right. Sam Brittan remarked: 'The Government might as well abolish local authorities and move over to the French system of centrally appointed Prefects.' Mrs Thatcher, I know, was also upset by the reductions in mortgage relief, but as I have said, I did not regard this as inconsistent with her own philosophy.

Two days after the Budget Michael Heseltine, on his fifty-eighth birthday, made a Commons statement on the review of the Poll Tax, which was meant to constitute the last rites for this controversial and much disliked innovation. Unfortunately some observers noted that in his statement the certainties of backbench rebellion had been replaced by a marked absence of clear-cut solutions. Michael was, however, able to say that the new tax would combine a property tax with a personal element. That was indeed the basis of the new Council Tax which replaced the Poll Tax.

There were complaints from the users of mobile phones. My measure simply meant that mobile phones would be taxed, just as the provision of company cars and flats is taxed. Nonetheless I was accused of taxing yuppies, those representatives of Thatcherism, and of exposing lone women to the risk of rape on motorways.

One subtle aspect of the Budget passed most people by, and that was the way the increase in VAT did not put up inflation. I was able to do that because of a statistical quirk.

When the Poll Tax was introduced the Central Statistical Office (CSO) had insisted, to the fury of Mrs Thatcher, on including it in the Retail Price Index (RPI). Despite repeated efforts by Nigel Lawson and others, the CSO, which is of course independent, maintained that position. To most of us this seemed odd. The Poll Tax also had innumerable reliefs and rebates, so much so that a large part of the population did not pay the full tax. Even more oddly, these reliefs were also ignored by the CSO in calculating the impact of the Poll Tax on the RPI. No matter how these reliefs were increased by the Government, it was the full headline Poll Tax that scored in the RPI. The only way that the RPI could be affected was to change the headline Poll Tax. So the £140 per head across the board reduction dramatically cut inflation and offset the rise that would follow from the increase in VAT.

When Geoffrey Howe had increased VAT in 1979, the impact quickly worked through to inflation, which rose in six months from 10.3 per cent to 17.4 per cent. Contrary to what many people feared, my increase in VAT did not put up inflation and indeed, six months after the Budget, remarkably, inflation had almost halved.

Interest rates cut again

What the Budget had not delivered but was designed to bring about, was a reduction in interest rates. I wanted to deliver the Budget first, and to make the markets wait. I needed to see the reaction not only to the Budget but also to the inflation figures published on the following Thursday, which I knew would be disappointing. The headline rate of inflation fell to 8.9 per cent but the underlying rate, the Retail Prices Index less the effects of mortgage interest payments, rose for the first time since October to 7.5 per cent from 7.4 per cent. Once the markets had the figures and were able to examine them against the bold inflation forecast I had made in the Budget speech, I thought I would probably still be able to make the cut. I did so with the third cut since mid-February, bringing rates down to 12.5 per cent. Sterling reacted by rising to DM 2.9400 from DM 2.9350 and on the trade-weighted index the pound closed 0.2 higher at 92.6.

It was the end of a momentous week, which had seen the biggest ever switch between local and central taxation combined with another cut in interest rates. But what few people noticed on the day of the Budget was a speech at a meeting of the European Parliament's Committee on Economic and Monetary Union made by Karl Otto Pohl, President of the Bundesbank. He described as 'a disaster' the monetary union now taking place between East and West Germany. If he was right, that event would have more effect on the UK economy than anything in the Budget.

3

Russia

One issue that occupied a surprising amount of my time at the Treasury was Russia and its economic problems. I did not begrudge it, since Russia was undoubtedly the most important issue facing the world. It was a more important issue than the single currency that took up so much time.

My period as Chancellor coincided with dramatic changes in Russia that increasingly involved the West. Events followed upon each other so swiftly that at the time their significance was not always easy to see.

Mikhail Gorbachev

I first met Mikhail Gorbachev in 1984 when I was a Junior Minister at the DTI. Although we had only spoken briefly I had been surprised how much he knew about the British motor industry, which was then one of my Ministerial concerns. I was impressed by his quickness and willingness to debate issues. Usually Russian leaders simply lectured one, spouting rather frightening propaganda.

My curiosity was aroused, and subsequently I keenly read and followed Gorbachev's speeches. Once I sat next to David Owen, the former Foreign Secretary, at a dinner given by Arco, the American oil company, and we argued over Gorbachev and his significance for the West. I felt that Gorbachev was a completely new, different sort of Russian leader and was impressed by a remarkable speech on disarmament Gorbachev had made that day to the United Nations. David was very dismissive: 'He is just an old-fashioned Leninist.' In a sense he was right but in another sense we both were. Gorbachev was a communist and remained a communist, but he was a very new sort of communist.

Western views of Gorbachev may have been naive. They were certainly enthusiastic. Wherever he went in the West there were crowds and standing ovations. Gorbymania swept all before it, but Gorbachev was no social democrat.

It is difficult to convey the extraordinary impact of Gorbachev's charm and personality. It had something to do with his wide eyes, open expression, energy and warmth. Like everyone else I immediately liked him. I could understand Mrs Thatcher's rapport and fascination with him, but I could also understand why he didn't get on so well with Ronald Reagan, who would not have relished the long, sometimes didactic debates about fundamentals.

However, Gorbachev seemed to me to be muddled in many of his economic views, and he was sometimes dogmatic. He was unable to understand the true nature of privatisation and purported to believe that it meant handing over utilities to billionaires. Ironically that was what subsequently happened with Russian privatisation, but it was not inevitable. It is difficult for people who have grown up in societies where private property and profit are familiar concepts to understand how difficult it is for someone who has lived in a totally different system to take on board these alien concepts. At one time, plenty of Western intellectuals purported to have difficulty in understanding the concepts of profit and private property.

But Gorbachev had an undoubted humanity and sincerity. His

politics were often improvised, but he did try to make the Russian system more humane, genuinely believing in openness and freedom of speech. I observed his distaste for force. Commentators can call that 'weakness', if they like, but do we in the West not have cause to be grateful that Gorbachev did exist?

At the end of 1990 an economic dialogue had begun between the West and Russia. Even then Gorbachev's reform policies were increasingly seen to have failed. *Perestroika* had not delivered economic benefits, and innumerable laws on state enterprises had failed to galvanise the vast state corporations. Output was falling steeply, and the balance of payments was in massive deficit. Unemployment, which in theory had never existed, was beginning to be visible. There was now a growing financial crisis. Talk of a possible complete collapse of the Soviet economy did not seem exaggerated. The gravity of the situation was confirmed by an IMF study that landed on my desk immediately I became Chancellor.

Gorbachev appealed for Western help. His motives may have been mixed. Clearly he wanted, and indeed needed, to reform the Soviet economy. But he was also engaged in a major tactical effort to link the West into rescuing the Soviet economy.

These remarkable events were a challenge. We could not let the Soviet Union collapse with totally unknowable consequences, yet what was the appropriate response? There were many influential voices, including that of Jacques Attali, the newly appointed President of the European Bank for Reconstruction and Development (EBRD), calling for a new Marshall Plan and a massive injection of funds by the West. But aid without successful reform would have been pointless. The system was flawed and there had to be fundamental change, which Gorbachev had so far avoided.

These issues were discussed in a number of different international forums. The most valuable discussions were in the G7, where meetings were attended by Michel Camdessus, the Managing Director of the IMF, which seemed to me the right body to oversee reform of Soviet finances.

Various other organisations were always trying to get in on the act. The EBRD, recently set up in London, had a role, but Jacques Attali had excessively grand ideas and was not prepared to defer to the United States. Attali, a French Algerian, was a curious, colourful, visionary character, as interested in poetry as politics and economics. I once asked him how he first met President Mitterrand, and he told me it was in a night club. I was not altogether surprised when his tenure at the EBRD was ended by scandal over lavish expenditure, but I was sorry to see him go.

The European Union also wanted a leading role. Whenever I pointed out that much of what we were doing was already being carried out by the IMF, I was always told, 'But Europe must act, or Europe will have no role.'

In 1991 the European Union drew up an unnecessary and expensive 1.5 billion ecu plan for food aid for the Soviet Union. Later that year, when it transpired that the Soviet harvest was not nearly so bad as had been expected, I suggested that we should reconsider the plan. Again the response was, 'How can we do that? Europe must be seen to have a role.' I am quite sure that much of the EU food aid went to the Mafia or rotted in trains. After the EU food programme had been implemented, I suggested we might do a study of its effectiveness. Needless to say there was no enthusiasm for that either.

Another issue was Soviet membership of the IMF and the World Bank. It seemed to me that membership would lock the Soviet Union into a programme of real reform, put it in regular contact with expert policy advisors and be a symbol of the Soviet Union as part of the global economy. The issue was by no means straightforward, since the US Congress would have to agree an increase in IMF quotas before the Soviet Union could join, but I was excited by the prospects.

Gorbachev had announced his intention of attending the G7 Summit in July 1991, when Britain was to be the host. The announcement caused a great stir. It was unprecedented for the leader of the greatest Communist power on Earth to attend a meeting of the leading capitalist economies of the world. On 12 July Yevgeni Primakhov, then Gorbachev's Foreign Policy advisor, came to see me to deliver Gorbachev's views on the Soviet economy for consideration by the G7. Primakhov was very much the professional diplomat and looked like a pocket version of Leonid Brezhnev. The document outlining Gorbachev's views had some promising points, for example on the liberalisation of prices, but it was, on the whole, disappointing, trying to find a middle way between the views of Grigori Yavlinksy, Gorbachev's Economic Advisor, and Valentin Pavlov, the anti-reform Prime Minister.

The Summit began on Monday 15 July with the arrival of Heads of Government. There was great excitement in London at the imminent appearance of Gorbachev, though he was not in fact due until the last day of the Summit. On the Monday I went out to RAF Northolt and greeted President Mitterrand, having had a meeting with Ryutaro Hashimoto, then Japanese Finance Minister, and chaired a meeting of the G7 Finance Ministers.

On Tuesday the Summit began in earnest. In the morning I had a meeting with Nick Brady, the US Treasury Secretary. A Wall Street investment banker, he had played a key role in easing the problems of the Third World debt in the late 1980s. He also read the world recession of the early nineties very accurately. Brady could sometimes be difficult, but he was frequently underestimated. He made no secret to me that he thought that it was in everyone's interest for the Soviet Union to disintegrate and he was one of the few people to dare to say such things. 'Gorbachev will end up alone in the Kremlin with a dozen Hussars,' he told me, but he acknowledged that this was not George Bush's view.

Later that morning John Major, Douglas Hurd and I went to Lancaster House and waited for the heads of government to arrive. Gradually they all came one by one, with the exception of President Mitterrand. By convention the President of the United States is the last to arrive, but President Mitterrand regarded himself as the senior statesman and was determined to arrive last, so everyone was kept waiting. That morning there was a plenary session involving heads of government and Finance Ministers. I had to make a report on the views of the G7 Finance Ministers on the world economy as well as the prospects for reform in the Soviet Union. My nervousness was much increased when something I said caused Chancellor Kohl to grunt and heave and shake his head. He began to mutter under his breath and his huge frame shook. I didn't know what had offended him, but I realised how physically intimidating a man he was. Not for nothing had he been called 'Bismarck in a cardigan'.

In my report I said that Gorbachev's message to the Summit, while it had some good points, lacked concrete measures to restore stability. There was distinct fuzziness on the issues of privatisation and private property and his message on agriculture had been particularly depressing. It said: 'People must be free to decide on their own whether they want to continue working on a profitable collective or state-owned farm or to go private and work their own plot of land.' Gorbachev also asked for a restructuring of Soviet external debt. It would have been inappropriate to have had a semi-public discussion of that subject, so I suggested that for the moment our first priority was to urge the Soviet authorities to step up reform.

After the plenary session, in the coffee break I went to the loo. I discovered President Mitterrand there with a miniature, high-tech electric razor, carefully cutting the hairs in his nostrils. I wondered whether he had a lunchtime date. Apparently even his late arrival had not allowed him adequate time for his preparations. Then I bumped into Chancellor Kohl, who seemed to have surmounted our earlier disagreement. He addressed me non-stop in German, of which I did not understand a word, but thanks to his gestures and the odd word in English I got the gist. He was saying it was very important that John Major be re-elected and that he would do all he could to help him. John deserved his support, he said, because he was so much more constructive on Europe than Mrs Thatcher.

Then we all walked round the corner for lunch at the huge house of the Greek shipping millionaire, John Latsis, on the edge of St James's Park. It was a very hot summer day and we drank champagne on the lawn. All the Heads of Government were greeted by the ginger-haired Mr Latsis who was wearing a baggy, bright blue suit. Inside the house a pianist in a white dinner jacket tinkled a white piano in a vast marble hall. I did wonder whether we had got the tone quite right.

That evening there was a reception and dinner in the Portrait Gallery at Buckingham Palace. Barbara Bush came up to Rosemary laughing loudly and said, 'I have just watched something absolutely hilarious. That man over there came up to George and said, "Do you work for British Airways?" And

George had to say, "Actually I am the President of the United States."' Afterwards there was a spectacular display of fireworks which we all watched from a Palace balcony.

The next day was the event for which everyone had been waiting. Gorbachev arrived and came to address the Heads of Government. Each of them replied and then Gorbachev spoke a second time. Finance Ministers were not present, but I read Gorbachev's speech. Much of it was a repetition of the points he had made in the document passed to me via Primakhov. Read today, his speech sounds pretty commonplace, but at the time it was difficult to believe that it was really being said. He did give a warning which I heard him repeat on several occasions that large parts of the population in Russia were not prepared to embrace the market economy.

The main weakness of the speech was its continued emphasis on centralised controls on industry. But he did say that 70 per cent of all prices should be liberalised by the end of 1991 and he gave a commitment to privatise 80 per cent of retail outlets by the end of 1992. But would he really do it?

Gorbachev talked about transferring large state-owned manufacturing businesses into joint-stock companies and workers' collectives. This hardly amounted to privatisation. When I visited the Soviet Union I was to discover that what the Russians meant by privatisation was very different from our interpretation. He also made a request for a huge food aid programme. There was no understanding shown of the fundamental reasons for the shortages.

Most significantly he spent time discussing his new Union Treaty and the division of powers between the Central Government and the individual republics of the Soviet Union. This was a vital issue not only politically but also financially because of the risk that individual republics might default on Soviet debts. At this time Gorbachev was still hoping that through his Union Treaty he could keep the Soviet Union together. He was to be deeply disappointed.

The communiqué from the Summit called on the international institutions, the EBRD as well as the IMF and the World Bank, to work together to support the Soviet Union. It also proposed a special association of the Soviet Union with the IMF and the World Bank. This was somewhat less than the full membership which Gorbachev wanted, but it was a start.

The next day I gave a breakfast in No. 11 for Vladimir Shcherbakov, one of Gorbachev's Deputy Prime Ministers, who had responsibility for privatisation. He was rather too much of an old-style Communist to be a convincing reformer, but he was an engaging character. He turned up at No. 11 for breakfast with his tie loosened, smelling slightly, I thought, of alcohol and carrying a single rose, which he presented to Rosemary. Over breakfast he told me that he believed that most businessmen in the Soviet Union were basically criminals, and that was why privatisation couldn't happen more rapidly.

That morning John Major had meetings with Gorbachev which I joined. I was able to report to Gorbachev the views of the G7 Finance Ministers from a meeting the night before. Gorbachev suggested that I should go to visit the Soviet Union in the next few weeks to continue the discussions as Chairman of the G7 group of Finance Ministers. Strictly speaking, there was no such thing as a Chairman of the G7 – Britain just happened to be the host country at that time – but I was keen to do it and the rest of the G7, apart from a slightly grudging Nick Brady, were enthusiastic. The announcement of the visit led to some predictably cynical comments in the House of Commons. John Smith remarked that since I couldn't run the British economy, what was I doing going off to advise the Russians?

That evening the Gorbachevs, John and Norma Major, Sir Roderick Braithwaite, our Ambassador in Moscow, Lady Braithwaite, Rosemary and I all went to Covent Garden for a performance of Rossini's *La Cenerentola*. Gorbachev was given a standing ovation. Afterwards we had dinner at Admiralty House, where John Major was living while renovations were being made to No. 10 after the IRA attack. Rosemary sat next to Gorbachev and enjoyed talking to him about seventeenth-century Scottish architects in Leningrad. I sat opposite Raisa. Watching them, it was obvious they were a close couple. Raisa said to me, 'You don't know the danger my husband is facing. There could be a coup in the Soviet Union any time.'

I asked Gorbachev why he did not privatise agriculture. Surely, I argued, it would be the most basic privatisation of all and would help to solve food shortages and give the peasants the feeling that they had a stake in the new society. Gorbachev became very excited and started to raise his voice. 'You obviously know nothing about Russian history. What you are proposing would lead to murder and bloodshed.' Although he appeared excited, I could tell from the twinkle in his eyes that he really enjoyed a good argument. John Major became extremely nervous and kept kicking me under the table, feeling I had gone too far. I have to say I was amused at his nervousness. Gorbachev was not really annoyed and was putting some of it on. Years later I asked Gorbachev whether my impression was right. He laughed and nodded.

The next day Rosemary and I went to see the Gorbachevs off at Heathrow. There was a huge party from the Russian Embassy, the Foreign Office and other parts of the Government. Both Roderick Braithwaite and Boris Pankin, the Russian Ambassador to London, were there. William Astor, Lord-in-Waiting, was representing the Queen.

When the Gorbachevs arrived and we sat down to have a cup of coffee, he immediately started discussing the issues all over again. We walked out with him to the huge plane on the runway, and as it taxied away the Gorbachevs put their hands flat against the glass of two windows as a goodbye gesture.

Visit to Moscow

My visit to Moscow was eventually fixed for 31 July–4 August, immediately before my planned holiday and also immediately before Mr Gorbachev's own holiday, though his was to be the more eventful.

During my visit I wanted to see as wide a range of people as possible, including many outside the Government. The Embassy was very helpful and arranged an imaginative programme.

One evening was spent talking with a group of Soviet entrepreneurs. I felt something must be going right if Moscow now had a 'millionaire's club'. Today Russian billionaires are not unknown, but these were people who had made their fortunes under communism. The stories of some of those present were remarkable. Some had owned mines, supermarkets, small businesses or hotels and several had spent years in labour camps. I recalled Shcherbakov's remark in London about businessmen being criminals.

One interesting character was Dr Fyodorov, an eye surgeon who had pioneered laser operations and performed them in Birmingham. I was puzzled how a person living in a communist country could become a millionaire performing private medical operations in National Health Service theatres in the United Kingdom. He presumably hired the NHS facilities and then charged his patients for them. We talked about the privatisation of small businesses. He explained to me that it was very difficult to sell off small shops or cafes. A private shop was only an effective business if it had access to a supply of goods. While the Soviet government was happy to sell off shops, it wanted to keep control of their wholesale supply, so ownership was unattractive. Most of the businessmen were very cynical about Gorbachev.

There was another dinner for Soviet economists where I met Grigori Yavlinsky, a remarkable figure whom I was to get to know better. A brave, outspoken advocate of economic reform, with political ambitions of his own, he was an advisor first to Gorbachev, then to Yeltsin, and eventually stood against Yeltsin in the Presidential Election. I formed a great admiration for him, as I did for Yegor Gaidar, later Prime Minister. Both of them had summoned up the courage to move from the world of academic economics into the dangerous maelstrom of Soviet politics. I wanted to do everything I could to support them.

The night I arrived I had dinner with Shcherbakov. Again he was intransigent. I asked him why the road haulage industry couldn't be privatised and he said the population was against the privatisation of transport. The number of people wanting to own their own lorries was falling. The privatisation of taxis had gone badly. He alleged there were now fewer cabs in Moscow than before. This was manifestly untrue.

I was anxious to find out how the IMF Mission in Moscow were getting on with their task. Largely staffed by British Treasury officials, it was headed up by John Odling-Smee, who had been Deputy Chief Economic Advisor to the Treasury. Britain was developing a close relationship with the Soviet Government. David Peretz, the Treasury's man in Washington, did much work on their behalf, too. We were regarded as their friends in dealing with international institutions, and they increasingly turned to us for advice. Odling-Smee said one problem holding up agreement on IMF membership was the absence of proper financial statistics about the public finances. We needed to persuade the Soviets to reveal the full extent of their gold holdings. I promised to pursue this matter with Shcherbakov.

The next day I had a meeting with Pavlov, the Soviet Prime Minister. He was a sinister, tubby figure with dark glasses and a high-pitched voice who had surrounded himself with gun-touting bodyguards. He took a sour view of the IMF and was well known for his anti-reform views. He started off by saying that he did not want to hear anything about the G7, only my personal views. After I had given them he said that I was the sort of person who would refuse a drowning man a rope and instead throw him a swimming manual.

He said my ideas threatened the whole fabric of Russian society. According to him the Soviet people believed that if industry was privatised it would end up in the hands of either thieves or foreigners. When I said something that displeased him he replied that the next time I came to the Soviet Union he must make sure that I visited the tundra. It was one of the chilliest meetings I ever attended, even without visiting the tundra.

At a meeting with Shcherbakov I pressed him for more information about the government's finances. He kept saying I could have all the information I wanted, and he waved a document in front of me. As I was leaving he handed it to me. When I passed it to an official in the car it turned out simply to be an old document with out-of-date information. Why did he do this? He must have known that the moment I was out of the meeting I would discover that he had completely misled me. It seemed pointless.

On 1 August I had my meeting with Gorbachev. It was an

extraordinary experience to find oneself in a Rolls-Royce with a Union Jack pennant, representing the capitalist world, being driven into the Kremlin. I suppose it was less extraordinary than the scene I had seen on television when Mr Gorbachev had driven up to Windsor Castle in his official Zil to be greeted by the Queen and the Duke of Edinburgh.

I was accompanied by Sir Nigel Wicks and we were escorted through meandering corridors past innumerable guards. Gorbachev met us in a small room with modern furniture, red carpets and brightly coloured fabrics. He was accompanied only by an interpreter and a note-taker.

I noticed that he always had the same interpreter. Interpreters in the Soviet Union were powerful and influential people who can also take extraordinary risks. When I visited the Soviet Union in 1979 I had been seen off at the airport by a Russian Minister for Electricity who did not speak a word of English. The Minister started to tell me various stories about Pushkin, his love life and his duels. The interpreter duly translated these stories, but suddenly said, 'Mr Lamont, please tell the Minister I am a good interpreter . . . and then Pushkin took aim and was ready to fire . . . Mr Lamont I have a wife and two children . . . but Pushkin's shot missed . . . Mr Lamont I desperately need more money.' Gorbachev's interpreter was not at all like that. He obviously had the confidence of his boss and was discreet, though perhaps one day we will read his memoirs.

The Foreign Office had asked me to deliver an official protest about the shooting of Lithuanians by Russian soldiers. It was right that this should be done, though I was anxious that it should not get in the way of our main business. Gorbachev did not take offence, but replied that he in no way condoned the killings; indeed, he deeply regretted them. He said he could not personally control every action of Soviet soldiers in the Baltic States, and that he was already investigating the matter. Cynics would have been unimpressed. I was inclined to take his statement at face value.

Gorbachev was in relaxed, expansive form. He felt progress was being made on the Union Treaty. This time he talked more about the need to encourage privatisation of small businesses to bring about a change in attitudes. I explained to him the difficulties that we were having in obtaining financial information, and he promised that figures for gold holdings would be made available.

Meeting with Yeltsin

The next day I had my first meeting with Boris Yeltsin, at that time the President of the Russian Federation, whom I met at the White House, a vast concrete and glass palace with marble halls. The atmosphere could not have been more different from the Gorbachev meeting. Yeltsin was accompanied by a vast team of advisors and Ivan Silaev, the Prime Minister of the Russian Federation, sat on his right. But no one else spoke.

I did not see then how Yeltsin was using Russian nationalism to undermine Gorbachev's position as President of the Soviet Union. I did not instinctively warm to Yeltsin as I did to Gorbachev. I could not help remembering what Guido Carli, the Italian Finance Minister, had once said to me when he described Yeltsin as 'a Slavic Mussolini'. However strange Yeltsin's Siberian looks, there was no denying that his policies over privatisation and economic reform were more radical than anything ever said by Gorbachev.

Yeltsin said that he had been pleased with the outcome of the London Summit, and claimed that Gorbachev had followed his advice on the line he had taken. He stated he had advised Gorbachev not to go with a begging bowl and said he was determined to promote the growth of private farming. That was very different from Gorbachev.

He also talked about Gorbachev's new Union Treaty, but put a very different gloss on it. The West, he said, had seriously underestimated the degree to which the Republics would now have their own sovereignty. This would become clear once the Treaty was signed. The Russian Federation and Kazakhstan would be the first signatories. On all this he was quite correct.

Yeltsin was obviously keen for something to announce to the press. He kept pressing me for specific support for farming, food processing, and poultry feedstuffs. Eventually we agreed to set up a joint working group to examine the possibilities of co-operation. I did this rather reluctantly as I knew that such joint working groups rarely produced anything of value, but they were a favourite device of communist countries for extracting information about Western technology. Then Yeltsin escorted me out to a large press conference with TV cameras. He beefed up this very modest proposal about the food industry and no doubt he got some press coverage.

I went back to London, half elated and half disappointed by what I had seen. The political transformation really was just beginning, but there was a yawning gap between what the Soviets said they were doing and what was really happening. Gorbachev and Yeltsin said they were committed to market reforms, yet I wondered whether they fully understood their goal, still less how to get to it.

Holiday and an attempted coup

After returning to London I went on holiday with Rosemary and the children to Italy. We had been invited, as for several years past, to spend some days with Woodrow and Varushka Wyatt at Port Ercole on the coast of Tuscany. We had, as always, a delightful time, swimming, going out in boats, eating too much pasta, and Woodrow and I had our usual vigorous political arguments.

I told Woodrow about my visit to Russia. I was strongly of the view, and it was one I had unsuccessfully tried on John Major, that because of the changes in Russia we could now reduce defence spending. Other countries in the West were cutting more than we were. One day Woodrow and I strongly disagreed about the subject. 'You bloody fool,' were the last words I remember him saying before I went to bed. The next morning (19 August) I was woken up by the sound of Woodrow outside my bedroom in his swimming trunks wearing his hat with an MCC ribbon, singing 'God Save the Queen', and shouting, 'Gorbachev's been overthrown. I told you we couldn't cut defence spending. You bloody fool, you wouldn't listen.' I gathered that Gorbachev and his wife Raisa had been held captive in their dacha in the Caucasus while a coup was being mounted in Moscow. I was shocked. It was only two weeks since I had seen Gorbachev.

It was not easy to follow exactly what was happening from Italian television. Unable to get much sense, I rang up the Duty Clerk at the Foreign Office, who told me it all looked very bad indeed. Yeltsin was resisting forlornly, and in a few hours would be overthrown and probably killed. As always, the Foreign Office got it wrong. Yeltsin not only resisted successfully but turned events decisively in his own favour. I gathered that the plotters included Pavlov and, according to some reports, Shcherbakov as well. We learned from the TV that the plotters were in an aircraft heading in a south-easterly direction to an unknown destination. The Villa Safir had a vast library with excellent atlases and Woodrow, curious as always, dug some maps out. We followed the route of Mr Pavlov and the other conspirators all the way to Khrgystan.

To this day Gorbachev's own precise role in these events remains mysterious. Edouard Shevarnadze, Gorbachev's former Foreign Minister, went so far as to imply that Gorbachev had been part of the coup. Others suggested that at least he should have foreseen it. Grigori Yavlinsky later told me that even he, an admirer of Gorbachev, was not at all sure what his position had been.

It was the beginning of the end for Gorbachev. It fatally weakened him and Yeltsin did not hesitate to humiliate him publicly. At the joint press conference between the two, Gorbachev played his hand badly. Events were now out of his control. The best that could be said was that the Soviet Union had entered a period of co-presidency between him and Yeltsin, but it was clear that Yeltsin was calling the shots and moving his men into the Russian Parliament. Gorbachev was obliged to endorse recent decrees of the Russian Federation, including one giving independence to the Baltic States. Russia was emerging as the dominant force, with Gorbachev being pushed aside.

On 25 August Gorbachev resigned as General Secretary of the Communist Party, recommending the dissolution of its Central Committee and ordering the confiscation of its property and the abolition of its activities in the army and the KGB. He also sacked the Cabinet in its entirety for collaborating with the coup. He appointed a Committee to manage the national economy, headed by Silaev, the Russian Prime Minister. Yavlinksy became one of the Deputy Prime Ministers. Yeltsin was moving towards abolishing Gorbachev's position and dissolving the Soviet Union, but that took a few more months.

The IMF Meeting, autumn 1991

My next involvement with the Soviet Union was at the IMF meeting in Bangkok in mid-October. We were still in the dark about the Soviet Government's financial requirements. No one in the West knew what the gold holdings were, but it was generally assumed that they must be large and could be used by the Soviets as collateral.

A meeting was set up between myself and Grigori Yavlinsky and I was told that I would be presented with all the details there. We met in a room in the Conference Centre. I was accompanied by Andrew Crockett from the Bank of England and Jeremy Heywood, my new Private Secretary, Yavlinsky by Viktor Geraschenko, the Governor of Gosbank, the central bank of the Soviet Union. Yavlinsky immediately handed me an envelope, which I opened. It had only a couple of pages with some figures on it. The total holdings of Soviet gold were a mere 240 tonnes. This figure was a complete surprise and far below the estimates of Western so-called experts and organisations such as the CIA. My immediate reaction was to wonder whether it was a true figure.

At the end of the meeting Yavlinksy asked if he could see me alone. He said he wanted to explain how gold had been handled in the pre-coup Soviet Union. Gold came from all the republics of the Soviet Union into a special department in the Ministry of Finance and one solitary official dealt with and approved all transactions and decisions, including any use of gold. The truth was that Gosbank never had any gold. In 1937 it had received from the Ministry of Finance a piece of paper stating that it had 375 tonnes of gold, but it had never seen that gold and it had never had any control over it.

When Yavlinsky had said that he intended to announce the figure of 240 tonnes there had been consternation all round.

Geraschenko was worried, because this did not square with the Bank's published accounts and Gorbachev was concerned because he was sure he would be accused of stealing it.

I asked Yavlinsky whether he thought he had been told the truth. He said that he never could be sure he had been told the truth in the way a Chancellor of the Exchequer could be sure that he knew the true facts about the gold and foreign exchange reserves, but he believed 240 tonnes was the correct figure. He said that Gorbachev had telephoned him in a high state of anxiety; some people were saying that Gorbachev should be taken to court. If Gorbachev had known there was more gold he would certainly have said so. If the figure of 240 tonnes was wrong, Gorbachev had not been told and neither had the Head of the KGB. If neither of those knew, nobody did.

Yavlinsky added that in the last few years there had also been a massive rundown in Soviet gold holdings to finance consumer goods and food for the population. What had been revealed at the meeting was astonishing, but at least now we had the figures.

I had one other chance encounter with Yavlinsky before I left Bangkok, when I asked him about the events of the summer. I commented that people were beginning to say that the future lay with Yeltsin and Russia, and that he only represented the Union and Gorbachev, both of which were on the way out. Yavlinsky said that he had a good relationship with both Yeltsin and Gorbachev; he was a member of Gorbachev's committee of advisors and was close to him. But both Yeltsin and Gorbachev were Communists and both were therefore liable to bend with the popular wind. Yavlinsky said that Gorbachev was a good man who had done many things that he had not needed to do. He had freed prisoners and allowed free speech. Yavlinsky himself had spent a period in a prison for intellectuals, and also had been in a psychiatric hospital. Nonetheless, he trusted Gorbachev and felt he trusted him in return. He made one strange observation. He said that in meetings everyone always wanted to touch Gorbachev, but Gorbachev and Yavlinsky were always careful to sit at the bottom of the table, out of reach.

Yavlinsky said that Gorbachev had expressed surprise to him that I had not chaired the G7 meetings in Bangkok. Gorbachev had a point. Nicholas Brady had become rather insecure about his own position and kept reminding us that in reality there was no such thing as a Chairman of the G7. Gorbachev had said that the United States was trying to run the G7 using other people's money.

Yavlinsky observed that people such as Geraschenko were playing their own games, which was why he had found my cross-examination on the Soviet finances helpful. He welcomed questions because they forced his people to produce the answers. He suggested I should provide my analysis of the Soviet external position. This could be given to him and he could publish them as his own assessment.

I asked Yavlinksy whether he ever felt that seventy years of communism meant that all signs of enterprise and initiative had been extinguished in the Russian people. He replied, 'Mr Lamont, to ask that question shows you do not understand what a struggle it is for ordinary people to survive every day in Russia. You need enterprise merely to get a loaf of bread.'

At the plenary session of the IMF I chose to make my speech about economic reform in the Soviet Union and Eastern Europe, which seemed to me natural. I had been asked to take a lead on behalf of the G7, and it was in my opinion by far the most important problem facing the Western world. I was, however, criticised in the British press for not devoting my speech to the United Kingdom.

Russian membership of the IMF did not come about until the spring meeting in Washington, on 27 April 1992. There Russia was represented by Yegor Gaidar, another ardent liberal reformer who had now been made Finance Minister of the Russian Federation. I was asked if I would do the honours and introduce Russia into the IMF which meant I had to walk beside Mr Gaidar into the plenary session, where he was to be recognised by the Managing Director. I was flattered to be asked. It was like introducing a new Member into the House of Commons after a by-election. New Members are usually introduced by friends. To me it was an important and symbolic moment, but it went unreported in the British press.

I was impressed by Gaidar's knowledge of market economics.

I found it difficult to understand how someone educated at a
state university in a communist country could have such a clear
understanding. He could usefully have given Gorbachev a few
tutorials. He told me that he had learnt economics while sitting at
the back of the lecture hall pretending to study mathematics.

The next G7 Meeting was in Munich on 6–8 July 1992. By this
time much had happened. Gorbachev had resigned, the Soviet
Union had been dissolved, and the Commonwealth of Independent
States (CIS) had been created. Yeltsin attended as President of
Russia. It was the first time I had ever visited Munich and I found
it a city with a certain sweetness in the atmosphere. It was difficult
to believe that here, among the churches, libraries and museums,
Hitler had begun his rise to power. On the second night of the
Summit we visited a Bavarian Schloss where Chancellor Kohl had
assembled on the lawns the massed brass bands of hundreds of
villages. They looked rather incongruous in their lederhosen,
carrying their weighty tubas, trumpets and exotic alpine instruments, but it was a moving occasion to listen to the mixture of
brass and yodelling followed by the Bavarian national anthem.

Yeltsin made the best of the position, but there was no doubt-
ing that things had yet again worsened. Nonetheless the Munich
Summit was significant, because it agreed that the first tranche of
the IMF standby credit could be released to Russia. It also completed the first official rescheduling of debt. The work of the last
year and a half was now coming together. It may not have added
up to the great stabilisation package originally demanded by
Gorbachev and economists such as Jeffrey Sachs, but it was significant. Anything more, as Yavlinksy himself said, would have
run the risk of holding back reform.

Yeltsin's visit to London

In early November Yeltsin made a state visit to London accompanied by Kozyrev, the Foreign Minister. By this time he was
under immense pressure on both the political and economic
fronts. Political opposition was mounting and there was intense
criticism of Gaidar, who was now Prime Minister. Industrial

output was 25 per cent lower than a year earlier, the annual rate of inflation was expected to rise to around 2,200 per cent, and if that was not bad enough the budget deficit was about 20 per cent of GDP. The Russians had not honoured the commitments given at Munich in exchange for the release of the first IMF credit tranche. The slippage in economic performance did Russian credibility immense harm.

It was the first state visit to the United Kingdom by a Russian President. Before his arrival there had been discussion among Ministers whether Yeltsin should lay a wreath at the Cenotaph on Armistice Day. John Major thought this might offend people, so the wreath-laying ceremony took place in Westminster Abbey instead.

I had to meet Yeltsin off the plane and we travelled into London together. He was curiously silent in the car until I made some criticism of Gorbachev's reluctance to privatise agriculture. Immediately he sprang to life, held out his hands, rubbed his thumb and fingers together as though handling soil, and said, 'Give people earth and it will change everything.' I congratulated him on the liberalisation of prices in the shops. Yeltsin replied that he had been told his reforms would work in six months. That seemed highly optimistic. I wondered how much he really understood.

Yeltsin's arrival was the week after the crucial paving vote in the House of Commons on Maastricht. When he arrived Yeltsin said to John Major that they ought to have greeted each other with the words, 'How's your crisis?' He said the three people who had given the Government their majority in the House should be called 'the three wise men'.

In the discussions Yeltsin said that he would have to ask for the resignation of some his Ministers, but his main objective was to keep Gaidar and the core of his team. He stressed there was no constitutional procedure that Congress could use to get rid of him. He was popularly elected, so the political struggle had focused on Gaidar and Kozyrev.

He recalled Churchill's Fulton speech, in which Churchill had prophesied the collapse of communism. The seventy-fifth anniversary of the Revolution had just passed. In the old days millions used to take to the streets to celebrate, but this year throughout the whole of Russia only just over 100,000 had done so. Major presciently asked Yeltsin if, were he forced to take up a position against Congress, he would have the support of the armed forces, and would they allow him to suspend the constitution? Yeltsin replied he was not thinking of suspending it but of adopting a new one by referendum.

At lunch I sat next to Yeltsin. I noted that he drank nothing at all. I thought no one would believe me if I told them this. He told me that one of the problems with the Soviet economy was that there was no bankruptcy law. The supreme Soviet would shortly adopt one and so there would be more bankruptcies. This was serious tough talking. He also said that an 'Inland Revenue' had been set up. This move had met with resistance because it was an entirely new phenomenon in Russia, but also because an investigative arm had been created with 30,000 officers recruited from the armed forces. There was no doubt that much of what Yeltsin said, whether calculated or not, was what we had wanted to hear. It all appeared something of a contrast to Gorbachev.

One of the problems I discussed with Yeltsin was the Russian banking system. Many banks were insolvent or close to collapse; and there were far too many of them. A large-scale write-off of bad debts was required.

A sound banking system is basic to capitalism, and Russia badly needed more people trained in finance. I had arranged for the Bank of England to give some advice to the banking sector, and also increased the Government's technical assistance. I would like to have initiated a much larger programme of training for young people, but the costs would have been unaffordable. Then it occurred to me that I might be able to get British private-sector financial institutions to train young people if the Government paid the costs of bringing them here. The companies could then pay a modest training allowance and teach them the skills for banking, stockbroking and investment. There would also be advantages for British companies.

I asked the Treasury to work up the details of a scheme, then wrote several hundred letters to chairmen of banks, insurance companies and merchant banks. The result was encouraging, and

I felt that we would be able to launch a scheme. I told all this to Yeltsin, who was pleased. We announced it together at the press conference in the afternoon.

Some months later Rosemary and I held a reception in No. 11 for the first trainees. It was moving to hear their hopes for their short stay in the United Kingdom. They were all deeply grateful for the opportunity. When I returned to Rothschild's in the City, I found that my old firm had been one of the first to participate, recruiting an able young Russian for their Treasury Department. He subsequently returned to Moscow and became Rothschild's representative. This was just the kind of result I hoped the scheme would produce.

Russia: a country without hope?

Looking back at these events six years on, it might seem that little in Russia has improved. Some of the changes have been for the worse. The Russian people have had an extremely hard time. There may be more goods in the shops, but many people can't afford to buy them. For vast numbers of people, particularly the elderly, economic reforms have meant that living standards have fallen. Life expectancy has fallen for the whole population. Unemployment has risen; beggars and criminals roam the streets.

The economy has continued to shrink. Each year is promised as the one in which the economy will grow. Of course the shrinkage is a consequence of cutting out industrial production that had no value, but the bottom never seems to be reached.

On the political front there have been reverses too, but Yeltsin has shown extraordinary resilience, particularly when he resisted a second attempted coup in October 1993. Then the coup was mounted by a democratically elected communist-dominated Parliament. Yeltsin's actions may have been of questionable legality, but they have helped to keep Russia on the path of democracy.

I recently attended a lecture in Washington by a British expert on Russia. He could not have been more pessimistic. He felt the outlook was extremely grim, pointing to the breakdown in law and order and the dominance of the Mafia everywhere. I asked him how Russia differed from Italy after the war. In 1945 the Italian economy had collapsed and all the circumstances the lecturer ascribed to Russia applied to Italy then, but Italy came through the crisis and established both democracy and free enterprise.

Free markets and capitalism need civic virtues such as trust and the rule of law, and institutions such as private property, all of which communism set out to destroy. In some cases, the legacy of communism will take more than a generation to repair. In Romania, young children roaming the streets of Bucharest are the living consequences of President Ceausescu's campaign to destroy the family. By contrast, of all the countries of the former Communist Bloc, Poland withstood the worst moral consequences of communism because of the strength of the Catholic Church. But nations such as Spain and Portugal show that it is better to avoid communism altogether. A Franco or a Salazar are far less damaging.

The years after 1989 were the ones where hopefully the West helped to make the changes in Russia irreversible. Russia's membership of the IMF was an important step in integrating Russia into the global economy, and the consequences of opening Russia up to foreign economic influences can hardly be overstated. I am sure the West was right not simply to pour money into Russia, even though considerable sums were given or written off. More money would not have solved the problems.

Russia has been fortunate in having had a remarkable number of young economic reformers such as Yavlinsky and Gaidar. And when they have sometimes had to be temporarily sidelined for political reasons, others like Chubais or Nemstov have emerged. There seems to be an endless supply of brilliant young men prepared to fight for reform. Yeltsin, at least in his early years, deserves credit for backing them most of the time.

And what of Gorbachev's role? Commentators write how the 'weakness' of Gorbachev led to the disintegration of the Soviet Union and its empire. According to them, Gorbachev's attempts at *glasnost* and *perestroika* were flawed because they were attempts to run a repressive system without repression. When the screws are loosened the system explodes, so reform never could have worked. If Gorbachev had only had the 'courage' to use troops the West would not have interfered and the Soviet Union might still exist today. According to these followers of realpolitik he didn't know what he was doing but was an improviser and the West owes him little. Change happened in spite of him, not because of him. I do not think this is fair.

There is a dramatic contrast between the view of Gorbachev within Russia and the view held by many all over the rest of the world. Russians to this day have a low opinion of Gorbachev. In the Presidential Election, in which he sadly insisted on standing, he attracted a derisory vote. One explanation for this is that Gorbachev presided over the disintegration of the Soviet Union. Russians took pride in the Soviet Union, although it was not, as George Bush once called it, 'a country'. Although Gorbachev provided freedom and opportunity for Soviet citizens to speak their minds, law and order deteriorated, chaos ensued, and living standards did not improve.

Gorbachev was not inevitable. What is remarkable is that a system as brutal as the Soviet Union's produced a Gorbachev at all. A different man might well have responded differently to the demand for change. If Mr Alyev, now the President of Azerbaijan, had become General Secretary instead of Gorbachev, he might have used force, as was done in Hungary in 1956 and in Czechoslovakia in 1968. Would the West have intervened this time? It did nothing in 1989 when Deng Xiaoping boasted 'a million is not a large number' as demonstrators were shot in Tienanmen Square.

George Lichtenberg once wrote: 'The great of this world are often blamed for not doing what they could have done. They can reply: just think of the evil that we could have done, and have not done.' That is the least one could say of Gorbachev. Whether he knew where he was going or not, he started the process of change by his commitment to openness and his instinct for basic decencies. The admiration and gratitude felt in the West are well justified. One day he will be recognised in his own country.

Russia has had a difficult time in the last few years. The abolition of the planned economy has not led to free markets, but to *nomenklatura* capitalism and massive corruption. Sadly, reform has brought chaos and yet another period of pain and suffering. And yet I do not believe there was any alternative to the changes. A 'middle way', or gradualism, would have produced its own problems. A more transparent competitive economy will eventually evolve from today's robber-baron capitalism, but it will need a civic framework of law if institutions of the kind that communism did so much to destroy are to be recreated.

Against the evidence I remain stubbornly optimistic about Russia. In some ways Russians seem well suited to Parliamentary democracy. Gorbachev isn't the only Russian who loves talking. They all love talking. In the end the market economy and democracy correspond to deep needs in human nature. Russians are no different from the rest of us.

4

False Dawn – The Recovery That Kept Disappearing

Nothing prevents recovery as effectively as fear of political action; nothing promotes it as does firm and sober handling of the existing situation under the existing conditions.

Joseph Schumpeter

The financial crisis was over before the year was out, but roughly three years of depression followed. Here is a case which exemplifies how much basis there is for the belief in the recuperative powers of capitalism. For Government did next to nothing beyond permitting, at the height of the financial strain, the issue of one-pound and two-pound notes by the Bank of England. Although the masses did not suffer in silence and their riots, if nothing else, should have been sufficient motive for public action, things were allowed to take their course. And business did recover. Losses had to be taken, South American investments to be written off, prices had to find their levels, what was unable to adapt itself had to be eliminated. All this took time. But as soon as it was done, an upward swing set in by itself.

Schumpeter on England and the crash of 1824

In the Budget I had presented a Treasury forecast that pointed to a recovery in the second half of 1991. As far as the media were concerned, I had nailed my colours to that forecast. As I have explained, I have always been deeply sceptical about economic forecasts, and have always known that they are usually wrong. But it is human nature to demand to know the future. No matter how I qualified the statements, the qualifications were never noticed. Even though the question 'of when the recession would end' could not be answered, British public opinion demanded to know when it would happen, and so did the Conservative MPs who were deeply worried about the General Election.

Recessions are inevitable in capitalist economies, an inherent part of the capitalist system of evolution and innovation. Nigel Lawson once presciently remarked near the top of the 1980s boom, 'Not even a Conservative Government can abolish the trade cycle.' The recession of the early 1990s was unavoidable after the boom of the 1980s and double digit inflation. The *Financial Times* before 1990 even suggested a recession was necessary and that it would be a good thing, criticising John Major for seeking to put off the recession needed to correct the errors of the late 1980s. The British situation was similar to that of Australia, where a runaway boom had been followed by a period of negative growth. Paul Keating, the Treasurer and later Prime Minister of Australia, found himself in trouble when he remarked of the Australian recession, 'This was the recession we had to have.' On 16 May I made a similar remark, 'Rising unemployment and the recession have been the price we have had to pay to get inflation down. That price is well worth paying.' That unfortunate moment of truth-telling landed me in hot water too.

I wanted lower unemployment as much as anyone. But employment would only be maximised if we first achieved low inflation, and there was no way that could be done without unemployment rising temporarily. Of course the price would be worthwhile if inflation really was tamed permanently and didn't just burst out again, as had happened so often in the past. That would be a real change.

But the public was in no mood for such arguments. Of course public opinion was quite right to be critical about the recession, since it originated in the excess growth of the late eighties. In saying that I make no criticism of Nigel Lawson, since few people saw the need to tighten policy then, including those who were critical of the policy of shadowing the Deutschmark.

It was one of John Major's political successes that he managed to persuade people to think of his Government as a wholly new administration that had nothing to do with the policy decisions under Mrs Thatcher. The public were nonetheless impatient for an end to the recession and demanded lower interest rates, which the newspapers told them would 'kick start' the recovery. The hard truth was that even if Britain had been outside the ERM, with headline inflation in double digits, in November 1990, it would have been wrong to cut rates quickly before there was real evidence that inflation was coming down. The fact that we had joined the ERM made it impossible. That did not prevent newspapers, like *The Sunday Times*, which had campaigned strongly for Britain to join the ERM, from calling for deep cuts immediately. As one senior mandarin wryly remarked to me, 'The Murdoch press have two objectives: to bring down interest rates, and the Monarchy.'

The recession of the early 1990s was frequently described as being the 'deepest since the 1930s' and sometimes is to this day. Reading the descriptions you would hardly think that, according to the latest statistics for GDP at constant market prices, the total loss in GDP during the recession was 1.5 per cent, compared with over 3 per cent in the early 1980s. But several features of the 1990 recession made it different. Significantly, it affected parts of the country not normally touched by recession, with a disproportionate impact in the South and the service economy. Its effect was also severe on the property and housing sectors. Conservative supporters, used to applauding speeches urging blue-collar workers in the North to get 'on their bikes', were startled when such advice was directed at them. This all added to the political pressure and the belief that the economy must be capable of being manipulated to bring the recession to an end.

Many people who were old enough to know better seemed to believe there must be some magical way to cure our economic ills at a stroke, if only the Chancellor of the Exchequer was bright enough to think of it. But life was not so simple. There was no such solution.

Conservative Central Office, various aides in No. 10 and sometimes even the Prime Minister suffered from a different illusion.

They believed words could end the recession, and were desperate to hear the words 'The recession has ended' or 'The recovery has started'. The whole time I was Chancellor I was engaged in a battle to prevent the Prime Minister and other Ministers from uttering them and myself from being bullied or cajoled into using them prematurely. The fact that I would not do so meant that in their eyes I became the problem: I was thought to be too cautious with my words, and therefore to be hampering recovery.

Sometimes it was difficult to avoid having words put in one's mouth. On one occasion, in an interview on *The Frost Programme* I was asked about the prospects for recovery. I referred in an inelegant phrase to 'faint stirrings in the housing market' and added that I thought the housing market would be the first sector to recover. On the last point I was dramatically wrong, but it was nonetheless true that in early 1991 there were signs of increased orders being placed by housing developers, even though house prices themselves remained depressed.

Returning to No. 11 after the interview, I turned on the lunchtime news and saw my comments were being broadcast by the BBC as the lead item. 'The Chancellor has announced the recovery has started,' said the newscaster. I was alarmed, and then made a bad error. I personally telephoned the editor of the programme to tell him that I had not announced the beginning of the recovery. To my astonishment he replied, 'I heard what you said and I am not going to alter my programme.' What I had said was nothing like what had been reported. The incident illustrated the wider problem.

In May Sir Peter Middleton retired from the Treasury and departed for pastures new in the City. I was sorry to see him go. In my experience when they get to the top, many Permanent Secretaries are absorbed in the administration of their department and seem to know less about less and less. Peter was not at all like that. One could always rely on him to be in the front line, fighting. Whenever there was a crisis he would be there. The Prime Minister and I agreed that Terry Burns should succeed him. I had great respect for his judgement and was delighted to have him. He had been in the Treasury since 1980, when he joined from the London Business School, shortly after Geoffrey Howe and Nigel Lawson arrived. He was an integral part of the Thatcherite revolution, which was one reason why the Labour Party was suspicious of him. Terry was replaced as Chief Economic Advisor by Alan Budd from Barclays Bank. I had already been consulting him, so he fitted naturally into the vacant slot.

A bizarre incident

On Saturday 13 April, not long after the Budget, I was in the large sitting room in No. 11 that overlooks Horseguards, talking to Peter Fullerton, a Cambridge friend who was then working as a lawyer in America and had come to visit us. Just as we were having tea, the Treasury Duty Press Officer telephoned with a bizarre message. Apparently the *News of the World* was intending to lead with a front-page story that my house in Notting Hill had been rented to 'a sex therapist', one Sara Dale, who became known to the national press as 'Miss Whiplash'.

The next day whole pages of the *News of the World* were given over to lurid descriptions of Miss Dale's flourishing sex therapy business, which was being run from my home. Miss Dale denied being a prostitute, but the newspapers described how she stripped naked while massaging clients and fulfilled their sexual fantasies.

The *News of the World* was careful to say that I had never met Miss Dale. The flat had been let by an estate agency who had been provided with impeccable references, including one from a firm of solicitors.

I engaged Carter-Ruck to evict Miss Dale and her business partner, who surprisingly turned out to be someone who had been at Cambridge at the same time as me, a point that newspapers followed up vigorously. A number of journalists later wondered why I had engaged Carter-Ruck, who were primarily known as libel lawyers, and expensive. There were a number of reasons. First of all, David Mellor knew a lawyer there, Andrew Stephenson, whom he strongly recommended to me. Secondly, the Treasury had received a series of anonymous tip-offs from someone in Fleet Street that there was going to be an attempt in a

national newspaper to smear me. These warnings had been given
in telephone calls, and I had already notified both the Permanent
Secretary to the Treasury and the Cabinet Secretary about them.

Although the story was not serious, it was embarrassing and
not exactly the sort of publicity one welcomed as a member of the
Cabinet. The view in Whitehall was that it was essential that I
succeeded in getting the woman evicted as quickly as possible.
That was not quite as easy or as straightforward as it might have
seemed. It was necessary to get evidence about my tenant's activities and I was advised that newspaper accounts were not sufficient
evidence.

At this point Carter-Ruck unexpectedly received a telephone
call from Sara Dale's Brazilian maid, who said the newspapers
and my tenant were working in a conspiracy to embarrass me.
My solicitors then tried to take a statement from the maid, but
found she had gone to Heathrow where they caught up with her
surrounded by 'heavies' from News International, and about to
get on a plane to Brazil. Rupert Murdoch himself later admitted
to the PM that that was true. However, before she left she managed
to slip a statement to my solicitors. And Andrew Knight, then at
News International, also told Rosemary that money had changed
hands.

The solicitor acting for me was suspicious that this whole incident was not just an accident. A stunt? But created by whom?
While there was some evidence to support that idea, no one was
able to prove it.

Many people thought that I overreacted to the incident, and
perhaps they were right. However, my family, particularly my
children, found it deeply distressing as the story dominated the
front pages of the tabloids for what seemed like an eternity.

Eviction proceedings can be lengthy, so I was advised to get
leave from a court to get expedited proceedings. My solicitors
also had to deal with a huge number of newspaper enquiries,
many of them hinting at dark allegations. As a result, after my
tenant was evicted I was left with a hefty legal bill of £23,000,
which I had scant means of paying.

Shortly after the publicity died down, Peter Middleton, the
Permanent Secretary, approached me and said that it was the

considered view of the Treasury that it would be right for the Treasury to pay my legal bill. He said that if I had been a private citizen I would certainly not have had the cost of an expedited hearing, and indeed I would probably not have bothered to evict my tenant at all, who was on a short-term lease. In addition my solicitor had had to handle a huge amount of press enquiries that would normally have been dealt with at the taxpayers' expense by the Treasury Press Office. At no time had I raised the idea or in any way suggested to the Treasury that they should pay my bill. It was entirely the Treasury's initiative.

A few months later, when Terry Burns took over as Permanent Secretary, he decided that the Treasury should not pay the total bill, only the costs of the expedited hearing and dealing with press enquiries. The matter was referred to Sir Robin Butler, the Head of the Civil Service, and the Prime Minister. By this time I was keen to get the matter settled. Further discussions took place between Robin Butler and Chris Patten, as a result of which it was decided that the Treasury contribution would be only £4,700 and Central Office would pick up the rest of the £23,000 bill. I assumed this was in order as it had been suggested in the first instance by the then Permanent Secretary and approved by the Cabinet Secretary and the Prime Minister.

Public spending: problems loom

I had other problems on my mind, especially public spending. The fiscal position of the Government was becoming more and more precarious. In the Budget I had forecast a PSBR for 1991/92 of 1.25 per cent of GDP. I was not aware then that the Treasury forecasts on the revenue side would prove so overoptimistic, particularly for corporation tax receipts, but I knew in this pre-Election period there were immense pressures on public expenditure which, if not resisted, would push public borrowing to even more dangerous levels. There were also the unavoidable costs of the war in the Gulf.

On 24 April I had a meeting with the Prime Minister and David Mellor, the Chief Secretary, to discuss the forthcoming public expenditure round. I informed the PM that early indications from spending Ministers were extremely worrying. It seemed they were likely to submit bids for their departments totalling £15 billion for the next year, which was way above what could be afforded. Colleagues did not seem to realise that the recession itself was already increasing Government spending and borrowing.

Just a few months into the new financial year the Treasury had already admitted that General Government Expenditure (GGE) – the widest definition of public spending, including local authorities – was likely to overshoot by £1.5 billion because of rising unemployment and falling income from the nationalised industries.

David Mellor explained that British Rail was going to overshoot its cash limit by £700 million and there was a worrying escalation of the estimated capital costs of the extension to the Jubilee Line and expenditure connected with the Channel Tunnel. Only the public sector could have contrived to have an overrun on a construction project in the middle of what was said to be the deepest ever recession in the construction industry. The Department of Employment were putting forward large bids for 'initiatives' to reduce unemployment every few weeks and quite often they were backed by No. 10. These wheezes were usually schemes that would have little lasting effect on unemployment and David Mellor had exposed many areas where there was room for economy in the Department of Employment budget. But Michael Howard had put forward a large bid and on top of this we knew there would be an inevitable uprating of social security benefits and more demands for money for local authorities to keep down the Community Charge, which would be strongly supported by the Scottish and Welsh Offices.

I told the Prime Minister that, based on any realistic appreciation of the sort of settlement David Mellor was likely to be able to achieve, there would be a large, real terms (i.e. after inflation) increase in public spending. Furthermore, the ratio of public spending to GDP would increase significantly.

The PM's initial reaction was that the Treasury was being unduly alarmist, as it always was. He sometimes revealed, for an ex-Chancellor, an astonishing hostility to the Treasury, believing it had an inbuilt bias towards the hair shirt. He pointed out that much of the overrun for 1991/92 was higher than forecast unemployment, which was unavoidable and temporary. For the coming year he thought the projections were at the worst end of the spectrum, which was true. But I pointed out that our gloomy forecasts were made after we were only a few weeks into the new financial year, and there were likely to be other unforeseen contingencies.

Despite the PM's misgivings, it was agreed that the Chief Secretary should circulate a strong minute to the Cabinet pointing out the seriousness of the situation and the need to keep as close as possible to existing plans. That was fine, as far as it went, but such notes were fairly routine and in my experience had little effect on colleagues. The date of the Public Expenditure Cabinet was later fixed for 18 July, and it was agreed that the Prime Minister would reinforce the message at that meeting.

Arguments with the PM over the banks

About this time another issue produced some friction between myself and the Prime Minister and perhaps illustrated a difference in our temperaments. *The Sunday Times* ran a series of articles about the behaviour of the banks towards their small business customers, alleging that banks were charging very high interest rates and often withdrawing facilities from small businesses without notice. At a time of recession the article struck a chord and there were cries for the Government to act.

The Prime Minister became angry. He was convinced it was the banks that were causing rising unemployment and bankruptcies, and wanted me to intervene. I was reluctant to do so. Banks were businesses, not government departments, and operated in a competitive environment. In a recession they themselves were exposed to the risk of making losses and having their balance sheets weakened. It was all too easy to turn on the banks in a recession and blame them. But they had their own problems. I vividly remembered how, in the recession of the early seventies, some of the clearing banks had come perilously close to financial difficulty.

Nevertheless, I talked to the Governor of the Bank of England, Robin Leigh-Pemberton, asking him to pass on the Prime Minister's concern to the chairmen of the banks, but that was not sufficient for the PM. I have to say the Governor was not very pleased with me either, since he felt the banks should not be made scapegoats for the recession. He did not know that I very much sympathised with his view.

Public concern, however, continued and backbenchers became vocal. In response to pressure for action from No. 10, the Treasury received all the correspondence from *The Sunday Times* and went through all the letters. This was extraordinarily time-consuming and a bit of a waste of time. At the PM's request, I then spoke personally to the chairmen of the banks. I also considered the possibility of referring the lending practices of the banks to the Office of Fair Trading for investigation, but was informed by the DTI that there was no evidence of any anti-competitive behaviour. The Governor continued to feel that I was whipping up public feeling against the banks, passing the buck for the recession to them. Christopher Fildes in the *Daily Telegraph* wrote a strong piece attacking me as an interventionist old-fashioned corporatist. I could not say that I blamed him or disagreed with a word he wrote.

The Treasury's investigation of the letters sent to *The Sunday Times* revealed little to justify the strident criticism. On closer examination, many of the stories relayed to the newspaper turned out to be very different. Many of the so-called 'hard cases' were people who had exceeded their overdraft limits despite repeated warnings. Unsurprisingly, the banks often put up their rates to call a halt to this. Ninety per cent of the loans to small businesses were linked to base rate at a margin of around 3 per cent. Lloyds, on the other hand, had widened their margins, and about half their small business customers were on a managed rate basis. The Prime Minister asked me to impress on the chairmen the need to tell their managers to show greater awareness of the need to handle their customers sensitively. I did so with some embarrassment, but was relieved when I was able to conclude the whole matter with a written statement summarising my talks with the chairmen and giving the findings of our investigations.

Recovery around the corner: or so it seemed

These were diversions from my main concern – the progress of the economy. Much depended on how far we could cut rates. At the time of the Budget the Treasury forecast assumed that rates might fall to around 10 per cent by the year end. On 12 April rates were cut again to 12 per cent, but further progress depended on other countries. By the middle of May, Italy had cut its interest rates by 1 per cent to marginally just below the UK's, and it looked as though France might also cut by a quarter and the Danes follow. But Germany remained a problem, as there were more indications that German rates might rise again. Eventually the French did cut rates by 0.25 per cent on 24 May and I agreed we would cut our rates again, by 0.5 cent to 11.5 per cent, with a co-ordinated cut on the same day.

By June it still looked as though the economy was moving broadly in line with the Budget. There had been a slight improvement in the CBI and Institute of Directors surveys of business confidence. From the figures for industrial production and retail sales it looked as though the recession was bottoming out. There were even a few encouraging signs of recovery. Orders to building contracting companies were recovering and there was an increase in housing starts, though these were soon to be reversed. Imports of capital goods were rising and the three-monthly and six-monthly annualised rates for M0 (narrow money, notes and coins in circulation) and M4 (broad money, largely bank deposits) were showing signs of acceleration.

Nonetheless it proved impossible to reduce rates further that June. The markets were becoming sceptical about the Government's anti-inflation resolve. The rate on ten-year Government bonds was drifting up again and the spot exchange rate was not far removed from its effective ERM floor. No other member of the ERM group seemed likely to reduce interest rates for the time being. The short-term interest rate differential against the Deutschmark was 2.4 per cent and the long-term was now 2.2 per cent.

In July the PM and I received the next Treasury quarterly economic forecast. Comfortingly, this was unchanged from the

Budget. The recession was thought to be 'petering out at the moment' and recovery was still expected to get under way in the second half of the year. The recovery it forecast might be slow at first, and it would not be enough to avoid a fall of 1.75 per cent in GDP for 1991 compared to 1990 as a whole.

Inflation prospects had improved since Budget time, and it was expected that Retail Price Inflation could be 3.5 per cent in the fourth quarter. But this was a somewhat flattering illusion since the underlying rate of inflation (the RPI minus mortgage interest payments) was coming down more slowly.

Why was the Treasury so convinced recovery was on its way? One of the key points was that the personal sector and individuals were back in financial surplus, which was expected to be the largest since 1982. In layman's tems this simply meant individuals had repaid much of the debt they had enthusiastically built up during the boom. The savings ratio had risen from its low point of 4.75 per cent in mid-1998 to around 10.75 per cent but was stabilising and expected to fall. It was therefore reasonable to expect consumption to rise as confidence, shown by numerous surveys to be recovering, was restored.

Nonetheless the forecasters stressed the uncertainties. Modestly they admitted that a year before, even though we had been on the immediate threshold of the recession, 'Neither we nor any other major forecaster perceived such a prospect. If anything the latest demand and activity at the time were pointing to renewed and unexpected buoyancy.' They couldn't have been much more wrong. But the Treasury were not alone in not foreseeing the downturn. In fact recessions frequently come out of the blue. In 1997, the year of the great Asian crash, the IMF had been predicting a continued boom and for countries like Malaysia and Indonesia to grow by around 7 per cent.

As recently as February 1991, the consensus of independent forecasters was for a fall of UK GDP of only 0.75 per cent. It had been quickly revised to a fall of 1.75 per cent as more data appeared. That was one of the luxuries enjoyed by independent forecasters. Frequently brokers and banks could adjust their forecasts in the middle of the year in the light of what the Treasury said.

I discussed the forecast in lengthy meetings with the PM, Terry Burns and Peter Middleton. The risks were clearly on the downside, but the view of the future seemed reasonable.

It was an attitude shared by many influential voices. Gavyn Davies, close to Gordon Brown and John Smith, wrote an article in the *Sun* on 16 July under the heading 'Five Signs That the Slump is Over'. He added, 'The recession has been hyped up and not enough attention has been paid to what is really happening.'

Public spending bids come in: colleagues show no restraint

I continued to be worried about the public expenditure position. The bids were even higher than the £15 billion I had predicted. Colleagues had ignored all the warnings from David Mellor and submitted bids of nearly £20 billion. Of these about £5.5 billion were in my opinion more or less irresistible. A number would have to be conceded. Unless David was successful in cutting the bids by more than 50 per cent, which was unlikely, there would be a major increase in the planning total and in real terms across all programmes.

The July economic forecast had indicated that the PSBR might reach some £20.75 billion in 1992/93, much more than the modest increase I had forecast in the Budget. Only a third of the increase would be attributable to lost revenue; most of it could come from the spending increases that now looked likely, including those caused by the recession. The ratio of GGE to GDP, a key indicator, would touch 42.75 per cent, up from the 38 per cent reached in 1988/9. This was very disappointing and would be seen as a reversal of the Government's policy of reducing the ratio of Government spending in the economy.

Nevertheless the PM was worried about the Health Service. He insisted we could not go through a winter before a General Election with the closure of wards in hospitals. He saw an attraction in a commitment to a 3 per cent real increase in health expenditure indefinitely. I was disappointed that this was his view, but in the end I accepted it as politically inevitable this side of the Election.

If the Prime Minister held this view I did not feel that I was likely to get support from other colleagues.

Another danger area was local authority expenditure. I proposed to restrict it to a 7 per cent increase which, with underlying inflation expected to be around 5 per cent next year, would allow a 2 per cent real increase. This was quite generous, but again in an Election year would no doubt be greeted with angry denunciation by local authorities. It was agreed the Lord President, John MacGregor, Chairman of EA (LA), the Cabinet Sub-Committee dealing with Local Government Finance, should be informed.

We decided to follow much the same procedure for the public spending negotiations as in previous years, but thought it best for David Mellor to avoid having to do too much of his negotiation at the Party Conference, which had tended to result in leaks and distracting publicity. I remembered vividly in 1989 as Chief Secretary being chased by reporters from one Blackpool Hotel to another where I had appointments with colleagues, usually in some dark curtained-off section of a dance floor in a none too luxurious hotel. We also agreed there was a case for the Prime Minister and myself seeing individual colleagues and explaining to them the seriousness of the situation.

Anxiety about unemployment, but interest rates come down again

Despite the increasing confidence we felt inside the Treasury, this was not how it appeared to many outside. On 8 July the CSO announced that the fall in retail sales finally reported for May was worse than the preliminary estimate. As Gavyn Davies pointed out, this still left retail sales higher than the low point, but it led to calls from retailers for sharp cuts in interest rates.

There was little relief. Ten days later the growth in unemployment was estimated at 59,700 on top of 67,000 the month before. Conservative MPs' anxiety was increased by the fact that London and the South-East experienced one of the largest rises in the whole country. This was the fifteenth monthly increase in a row and took the adjusted total to 2.3 million, or 8.1% of the workforce. On top of this a report from the European Community warned of further sharp increases that would take unemployment to 3 million by 1992.

The PM and I agreed another interest rate cut of 0.5 per cent for 11 July. On 10 July I had told the PM there was a danger that the Bundesbank might increase the Lombard rate by 25 basis points the next day. In those circumstances it would look odd and be risky for the UK to cut base rates simultaneously, and I proposed to delay our cut. There was also still a risk that the inflation figures to be published that day would be badly received by the markets. I intended to make it clear that there was every expectation that in the following month there would be a drop in both the headline and underlying rates.

The Prime Minister's disappointment showed in his face. I pointed out that it was only a twenty-four-hour delay and that I was looking for two more half-point reductions by Christmas. They might be difficult, but once our inflation had dropped dramatically, as we expected, after the August figure was announced in September, there might be more scope. The key was Germany. Once German interest rates were seen to peak, as we expected to happen soon, it would be easier. In fact on this occasion Germany didn't increase rates, and therefore the Bank of England cut rates on the 12 July to 11 per cent. It was the sixth cut that year and sterling strengthened in the expectation of more to come.

It is important to emphasise that up to this point I had had few serious disagreements with the Prime Minister over interest rate policy. We both wanted to get rates down and both agreed the level at which we were aiming. The PM was later to claim to Paul Dacre of the *Daily Mail* that every interest rate cut had had to be imposed by him on the Treasury. I didn't think that was true. Occasionally we might disagree over the precise timing of a cut. All Prime Ministers are inclined to think that their Chancellors are a bit cautious, and John Major was always asking me when I thought the next cut could be. Occasionally I worried that we might seem to be overeager or grasping at cuts and that the pound would consequently weaken in the ERM.

Despite the rate cuts, the press was becoming more stridently critical all the time. The *Sun* was typical of many when it declared

on 9 July: 'Norman Lamont says he has spied recovery on the
horizon. Maybe he should lend us his telescope, we cannot see it.'
The same day *The Times* commented in an editorial: 'Mr Lamont
should be reaching for the accelerator . . . the greatest danger at
this point in the economic cycle is not that of overstimulating the
economy, but of persisting for too long with deflation and thereby
needlessly prolonging the slump.'

The mood of the critics was most forcefully put in an editorial
in the *Evening Standard* on 19 July written by Christopher
Monckton, formerly a member of Mrs Thatcher's policy review
staff in Downing Street. It summed up what many other commentators were writing:

> There is only one respectable reason for high real interest
> rates: the control of inflation. Yet money supply is falling.
> Besides companies, shoppers and house buyers are no
> longer in the mood to borrow or to spend . . . It would
> accordingly be possible for the Chancellor to reduce inter-
> est rates by 2 or 3 percentage points without the slightest
> risk of stoking up inflation.
>
> Yet Mr Lamont fails to act. Why? Solely because the
> pound is in the Exchange Rate Mechanism and he cannot
> countenance the political embarrassment of the devalua-
> tion.
>
> Every indicator shows that monetary policy is far too
> restrictive. The Government should bring interest rates
> swiftly and sharply down, even if a devaluation within the
> ERM were to result. The devaluation would, indeed, be a
> relatively small one if the Chancellor made it plain that
> interest rates would rise if there was the slightest sign of an
> impending resurgence in inflation. But it would be
> economically perverse, morally wrong, and electoral
> suicide to continue to sacrifice thousands of British
> industries and millions of British jobs to the false god of
> the exchange rate stability. You cannot buck the market.

The article would have been more persuasive if it had followed
its own logic and advocated leaving the ERM. It was wrong to

assume lower interest rates would be combined with a devaluation within the ERM. The opposite would have been more likely. The only real alternative was leaving the ERM.

All this was mild stuff compared with the blast from *The Sunday Times* that called for me to be dismissed and replaced by Chris Patten, the Chairman of the Conservative Party, the first of many such articles in that newspaper. From the attacks on the ERM and myself, no one could have dreamt that *The Sunday Times* had been one of the strongest supporters of joining the ERM.

Despite these problems, at the end of the Parliamentary session John Major gave an upbeat assessment of the situation in his end-of-term address to MPs. They were delighted by his statement that the Government would not be railroaded into accepting a single European currency at the Maastricht Summit and he pointed out that there was quite a long time before the Government needed to go to the country. He held up the prospect of inflation being below the Budget forecast of 4 per cent by Christmas, as a landmark on the road to Election victory. He predicted a slowing in the rate of unemployment as the world came out of recession. He added: 'Our tough measures have shown that we are not going to play around with the economy for our short term interests. The public still believes that we handle the economy better than Labour, and that will be the basis of our re-election.' It was a claim that we were then still able to make.

While I was on holiday in Italy the Bundesbank on 16 August made the rate increase I had expected the previous month, increasing the discount rate by 1 per cent to 7.5 per cent and the Lombard rate by 0.25 per cent to 9.25 per cent. This was unwelcome, if not unexpected, but we hoped that this was the peak of German rates and that the market would now settle down.

Green shoots?

After the summer break there seemed to be a change in perception about the prospects for recovery. The first data, concerned with

retail sales and credit, had all been consistent with growing consumer confidence. A CBI survey published on 1 September
showed that most companies, across eighteen business sectors,
expected sales and profits to recover from the previous year's
levels. The survey had always in the past been an excellent indicator of the trends in output. Dr Andrew Sentance, CBI Economic
Affairs Director, said, 'It looks like 1992 will be the year of recovery for the British economy.' The *Daily Mail*'s headline was
'Recovery by Christmas say Chiefs of Industry'.

And opinion polls put the Conservative Party in the lead for the
first time for months. The PM's personal ratings over Neil
Kinnock increased and the *Daily Telegraph*, impressed by the
improvement in the economy, even attacked John Smith for calling for further cuts in interest rates. Parts of the press now seemed
convinced that recovery was imminent. Commentators such as
Gavyn Davies, Sam Brittan and Hamish McCrae stated that the
recession was coming to an end.

Of course the word recovery itself is ambiguous. Recessions
do not normally stop by things getting better, but with an end to
things getting worse. That is normally the first sign. But is that
recovery? Or does recovery occur when the economy significantly improves from its lowest point? Or does recovery only
happen when the output lost in the recession has been recovered
in the next upturn? The last definition seemed to me absurd; the
appropriate definition was the middle one, with recovery occur-
ring when total output of the economy has moved off the
bottom and turned positive. By the autumn of 1991 there was
plenty of evidence that things had stopped getting worse and
that positive growth would resume. This situation appeared
consistent with the economic forecast both in June and at the
time of the Budget.

The pressure from the Prime Minister and other colleagues on
me to say 'The recovery has started' became immense, but I was
determined to resist it until it had actually happened. At times
some colleagues overstepped the mark and made announcements
themselves, but the press paid little attention to their utterances. I
devised many circumlocutions to try to satisfy Conservative
Central Office: 'We are at or near the turning point', 'The recession

is bottoming out', 'We are on the road to recovery', 'The clouds of recession are beginning to lift'.

The Treasury forecast in the Budget had suggested 2 per cent growth between the second half of 1991 and the second half of 1992. That still seemed possible in the autumn of 1991, provided the bottoming out gradually metamorphosed into an upturn and then accelerated the following year.

On 4 September, after consultations with the Bank of England, I cut interest rates again by another half point, to 10.5 per cent, near to our year-end target. We had got rates down close to our target, and to the level the Treasury thought sufficient to bring about recovery. The markets had been strengthening because of the improved position of the Government in the opinion polls, but in the days after the cut the pound weakened again. I suggested to the Prime Minister the following week that this would probably have to be the last cut for some time, and that we should dampen expectations of another cut. But little did I think, as I said it, that we would not cut rates again for eight months.

Even the bad news sometimes could be interpreted as good news. On 12 September it was announced that unemployment had risen in August. On the one hand it was the second largest August increase since records began, but on the other it was the second lowest monthly increase since January and the three-monthly average increase had declined. Michael Howard, the Employment Secretary, felt able to say that the figures showed 'the recession was coming to an end'.

There was the biggest fall in average earnings growth for nine years. The annual rise in earnings fell half a point to 7.5 per cent, still a high figure. According to the press the City was shocked. But it was central to the economic discipline imposed by the ERM that earnings growth should fall to levels comparable with the rest of Europe. Lower earnings growth was good news for future jobs.

The key indicators were business surveys which showed gradually growing optimism. This wasn't just a case of amplifying businessmen's vague sense of optimism but was more scientific. CBI surveys were regarded by economists as a 'leading indicator'. Alas, as Professor Charles Goodhart has observed, once an economic indicator is targeted it often ceases to behave as it did previously.

Housing: in the doldrums

Despite the encouraging signs elsewhere in the economy, one unrelieved blackspot was the housing market. Economic trends seldom go in straight lines. When is a trend a trend? Small upturns may transform themselves into a trend, though on other occasions they have a habit of petering out for no explicable reason. Whatever positive signs there had been in the housing market earlier in the year were no longer there in the autumn. My 'faint stirrings' had ceased to exist.

From June 1991 to September 1991 a record 36,610 homes were repossessed and 220,000 home-owners had not paid their mortgages for six months. The Council of Mortgage Lenders did not provide mortgage data for mortgages less than six months in arrears, but the number was substantial; even Conservative estimates suggested it might be 500,000. This was much worse than in the 1980s recession.

One of the initial mistakes I made was to underestimate the effect of the housing crisis. I expected the cuts in interest rates to be more effective in stimulating the market than they were. Many people were frightened and determined not to borrow money again, even when interest rates came down. The fall in house prices had an impact on consumption through its effect on people's wealth, but it also had a much wider effect on confidence.

Having taken the first step towards removing mortgage relief in my 1991 Budget, and with a continuing crisis in the housing market, I did not want to consider a further step in my 1992 Budget. The time was clearly not right. Indeed I was under pressure from backbenchers to reverse the step I had already taken and some people advocated the doubling of mortgage relief to £60,000, despite the fact that the cuts in mortgage relief had been substantially outweighed by falls in interest rates.

However, there was continuing good news on the inflation front. On 13 September the headline inflation rate fell from 5.5

per cent to 4.7 per cent, the lowest level for more than three years. This was the tenth consecutive month that inflation had fallen and prompted suggestions that the headline figure might drop even below the 4 per cent figure I had forecast in the Budget.

The Governor of the Bank of England now joined the optimists and said in a speech, 'I am confident we are now coming out of recession. The picture is undeniably improving.' For this expression of optimism, the Governor was attacked by both John Smith and Margaret Beckett, Shadow Chief Secretary, who accused him of 'doing his bit for the Conservative Government who appointed him'.

This growing optimism was summed up in the *Independent* on 14 September in an editorial entitled 'Something has changed'. It accurately mirrors what we then felt. 'In economics perceptions are sometimes as important as reality. The performance of an economy is in large measure a function of the confidence of the industrialists, financiers and consumers who make up that economy. As evidence mounts that the bottom of our recession has been reached, confidence is creeping back as it must, as without it, recovery cannot be sustained.' The article went on to refer to the CBI surveys, the improved retail sales, the better August for the motor trade and the rise in share prices to record levels. It pointed out that the growth in unit labour costs had been contained. 'The broad conclusion is that the pound's membership of the ERM has worked. It has forced a rapid and painful adjustment on the country. But in less than a year that adjustment is secure, if not yet complete. There is now little talk of the pound having joined the ERM at too high a level. Instead there is increasing confidence (within the Labour Party as well as the Government) that were the EC to move rapidly to a single currency, Britain would be strong enough to join the club.' It ended 'We now have a functioning market economy, and it has taken a recession to show it.'

5

Maastricht – Britain Tries to Square the Circle, 1990–91

There is a path which no fowl knoweth, and which the eye of the vulture hath not seen.

Book of Job

The Maastricht Treaty became synonymous with John Major's administration, but few foresaw at the outset the problems it would cause.

The forthcoming Maastricht negotiations were one of the first issues I discussed with John Major on becoming Chancellor. He had given a lot of thought to the subject as Chancellor. On one occasion he had remarked to me that he was convinced that there was a way in which Britain could sign a Treaty on monetary union. Since I knew that Margaret Thatcher, the PM at the time was, like myself, wholly opposed to a single currency, I was intrigued. But John was the person who had persuaded her, against all her apparent instincts, to join the ERM, so obviously he knew something that I didn't.

John Major's views on EMU

I discovered subsequently that as Chancellor John Major had been turning over in his mind the idea put to him by Nigel Wicks,

Second Permanent Secretary to the Treasury, that Britain might have an 'opt-out' from any treaty on monetary union. The idea was that Britain would sign the Treaty, like every other country, but that we, and possibly other countries, would retain the freedom to decide by a Parliamentary vote at a later date whether we wished to join the single currency. John Major believed that this opt-out would keep Britain involved at the heart of Europe but avoid any definite commitment and thus keep the Party united. The latter point was his main concern.

Opinion in the Conservative Party on Europe was certainly volatile. At the time of Margaret Thatcher's resignation Conservative Parliamentary opinion was different from that which emerged in the course of the Maastricht debates. After the European Summit in Naples in Autumn 1990, Mrs Thatcher felt that she had been bounced by Giulio Andreotti, the Italian Prime Minister, into accepting the principle of monetary union embodied in the Delors Report. Reporting to the House of Commons, however, she had emphatically declared, 'No, No, No,' meaning 'No' to more powers for the European Parliament, 'No' to a federal Europe and 'No' to a single currency. At that time many Conservative MPs felt that Mrs Thatcher's approach was too dogmatic and privately said so. I did not share that view, and wholly supported her approach, but many MPs felt that our position in Europe was being damaged by intransigence. In my opinion it was a fatal error to believe there was a way of reconciling Britain's view of Europe with those of other countries. That delusion was longstanding, and is one of the mistakes made by Tony Blair also.

John Major was inclined to sympathise with those who felt a more emollient, constructive negotiating style would be more productive. At the same time he, as a Whip, must have known that part of the Conservative Party would oppose any proposal for a single European currency, but these divisions were not so obvious then as now. The idea of a single currency seemed a very distant and theoretical prospect to Conservative MPs. For John the opt-out was the way in which the Party could be kept united.

Of course, the opt-out was always only an expedient that was time-limited. Sometimes supporters of the opt-out forgot that. Eventually Britain would have to decide one way or the other, for or against the single currency. But John Major frequently made clear to me that he did not believe that the single currency would actually happen, 'I believe it will collapse before we ever get there,' he remarked to me on one occasion, a view that he continued to hold against all the evidence, right up to the point at which the decision was made to go ahead with the single currency. His view was that he would never have to make a decision.

My own view on the single currency was one of strong opposition. Very shortly after I first entered the House of Commons in 1972, I was horrified when Ted Heath announced to the House that Britain had accepted the principles of the original Werner Plan for monetary union in Europe. Fortunately the oil crisis soon put paid to that plan. In the eighteen years since, my views had remained unchanged. I felt that a single currency would inevitably lead to a common taxation policy and necessitate the creation of a European government and a European state. I had repeated my views in the speech I made to the Bruges Group in the middle of the Leadership Election before I became Chancellor.

John Major and I discussed the general approach to the forthcoming Maastricht negotiations shortly after he became PM. I respected his reputation as a negotiator, but I too was attracted by the Treasury's idea of the opt-out. I felt stronger hostility to the idea of a single currency than the PM, but I was reassured by his conviction that the whole project would disintegrate. At least that indicated that he wasn't a wild enthusiast. I was never in any doubt myself that if it came to Britain having to make the choice I would be on the side of those against the single currency. But I felt reassured that the PM's instincts were in the right place.

The hard ecu: a good idea that no one wanted

As Chancellor, John Major had also been working up ideas for a completely different approach to monetary union, which embodied the idea of a 'hard ecu'. Strictly speaking, the hard ecu was not a single European currency but a common, or parallel, currency, to be used in competition with national currencies. It would only develop if there was a real need and demand for it. It was called the hard ecu because it was designed so that it could not be devalued. If the value of any of the national currencies making up the ecu increased, then its weighting in the basket that made up the ecu would be increased, making the ecu 'hard' and different from the conventional ecu. It would be a credible store of value and for that reason might be attractive to businesses. Above all it meant that monetary union would only develop in an evolutionary way.

The British proposals for the hard ecu had first been put forward by John Major when he was Chancellor in a speech to the German Industry Forum in June 1990. On 8 January 1991 I published a detailed plan in the form of proposed amendments for the Inter-Governmental Conference (IGC) on EMU. The UK proposals would have created a European Monetary Fund that would manage the hard ecu to make sure it was never devalued against other EU currencies, requiring the EMF to pursue a monetary policy at least as tight as the most rigorous national monetary policy in the EU. Ecus would only be issued in exchange for national currencies so that the creation of hard ecus would never result in an increase in the EU's aggregate money supply.

John Major was right. The hard ecu would have been a more realistic evolutionary approach than the rigid, grand blueprint that had been drawn up by the Committee, chaired by Jacques Delors. Unfortunately it was that report that formed the basis of the Maastricht negotations.

The hard ecu was well received by Conservative backbenchers, but it was always doomed. John Major had tried to interest other governments in the idea, but it was not visionary enough for them. The Germans also felt the management of their own currency would become more difficult if they had to cope with a parallel currency. But John insisted that I keep on trying to sell the hard ecu.

One of my first attempts was with Pierre Bérégovoy, the French Finance Minister, a key figure in the Maastricht negotiations and very effective at all international financial meetings. He was of Ukrainian origin, a trade unionist, and a close associate of

President Mitterrand. Despite his background, he had developed orthodox financial views on public spending and inflation. He later went on to become Prime Minister but led the Socialist Party to their crushing defeat in the Parliamentary elections in 1993. After that debacle, Bérégovoy shocked the world by shooting himself. No one ever knew whether this was because of his depression at the election or whether it was because of accusations of corruption made against him. I found the latter suggestion unlikely. He always wore cheap suits and smoked small cheroots. Bérégovoy seemed a man of modest tastes.

We agreed to meet in the French Consulate in New York at the time of a G7 Meeting on 19 January 1991. There was deep snow on the ground at the time and we had difficulty slithering around in our official cars from meeting to meeting. I wondered whether I would find the French Finance Minister hostile to the UK's rather grudging approach to monetary union, but Bérégovoy initially displayed some interest in the hard ecu. He summed up its merits well, observing, 'It would be better to increase progressively the credibility of the ecu rather than to bring it in by decree on the first day of Stage 3 of monetary union.' He asked me many questions about it without revealing his hand. He was extremely courteous, though I had the impression of being circled and examined by a wary, curious, slightly suspicious Bérégovoy. Subsequently I came to like him a lot.

I continued to push the hard ecu, as the Prime Minister wanted, at our monthly negotiating sessions on the Maastricht Treaty. At times the French and Spanish took an interest, but it became clear that there was little real enthusiasm. I had great difficulty in persuading John Major to let me scrap the idea. Every time we decided to drop it, he came back a few weeks later and urged me to float it again. I suspected pride of authorship was part of the reason.

Subsidiarity: a blind alley

Another difficult issue was that of so called 'subsidiarity'. This was an ugly word for an attractive idea. The theory of subsidiarity was that in Europe decisions would only be made at the European level when they needed to be; otherwise, decisions would be taken at a national level. When this concept was first discussed in Whitehall a number of members of the Cabinet were sceptical. Michael Howard in particular felt that it was a two-edged weapon that could be used by the Commission to achieve more centralisation. I felt that the drift towards centralisation was so strong that writing a provision like this into the Treaty might help.

I pushed the idea of subsidiarity hard, both with the Prime Minister and the Cabinet, and eventually it did become a British objective and was incorporated into the Treaty.

But I could not have been more wrong about its effectiveness. It achieved absolutely nothing, but was endlessly used by the Government to illustrate they were winning the argument in Europe!

Negotiations begin

The negotiations for the Maastricht Treaty began in earnest at the end of 1990 and lasted a year. On the monetary and economic parts of the Treaty, the negotiations took the form of monthly meetings between the Finance Ministers of all the EU countries. As Chancellor I was responsible for negotiating the monetary element, while Douglas Hurd conducted parallel negotiations on other aspects of the Treaty that covered foreign affairs, security, employment and social policy, together with the role of the European Parliament. Both of us were, of course, under the Prime Minister's direction, reporting to both him and the Cabinet after every monthly meeting.

The first meeting of the Inter-Governmental Conference was held in Rome on 15 December 1990 when the Commission submitted formal amendments to the Treaty of Rome designed to bring economic and monetary union into effect. A number of Governments expressed doubts about the Commission's proposals. I made it clear at this first session that the UK could not accept the imposition of a single currency, quoting Karl Otto Pohl as saying Germany's experience with reunification was an object lesson in the need for the convergence of economies before a currency union could be established. I added, 'I remain unconvinced that the potential benefits of a single currency are as great as its supporters allege.'

On 14 January I minuted the Defence and Overseas Policy Committee of the Cabinet (DOP) on our negotiating objectives. My objectives were three. Firstly to secure our opt-out from having to join the single currency. Secondly, to make sure the opt-out was watertight and valid, that Britain's discretion to determine its own economic policy remained. Thirdly, to make sure that even in the period of preparation for the single currency there should be no binding obligations on Britain. I wanted to be able to stand up in the House of Commons and say that as long as we had made no decision to join the single currency, there was nothing in the treaty that interfered in any way with our freedom to set our own interest rates and pursue our own fiscal and taxation policies. For that reason, I was against legally binding controls on countries' fiscal deficits.

I concluded that I was optimistic that, provided we negotiated constructively, there was a realistic chance of achieving an outcome that met our needs as well as those of our Community partners.

The negotiations normally took place on the same date as the monthly Ecofin meeting, which was regularly held by Finance Ministers and took place in the Charlemagne Building in a very large conference room with dark brown walls and a huge oblong table. The room was as dark as it was dreary.

At one end sat Jacques Delors and Henning Christophersen, the EU Commissioners, along with the Ministers of the country that held the EU Presidency. For the first six months of 1991 the Presidency was held by Luxembourg, and in the second half by the Dutch. All round the table were the Ministers and one official from each participating country. Other officials were allowed to sit behind Ministers, but not at the table. All together, with interpreters, officials, and hangers-on from national delegations there were at least 100 people in the room. I was always accompanied by Nigel Wicks from the Treasury, and Sir John Kerr, our Ambassador to the EU, who alternated sitting at the table.

With fifteen delegations all wanting to make their points, the meetings could hardly be called intimate. On one occasion, when we had an Ecofin meeting attended by the Finance Ministers of new countries wanting to join the EU, I felt I needed binoculars to see my fellow Ministers at the other end of the room. I often wondered how so many different technical problems could be negotiated in this way. No doubt there was quite a lot of finessing of the minutes by officials, as is common in meetings in Whitehall. But there were many other meetings of officials, and Francis Maude did much valuable work as well.

Sometimes the meetings went on late into the night with adjournments for cappuccinos and huge baguettes stuffed with tomato and mozzarella cheese. Overnight I used to stay at the residence of Sir John Kerr. He had a rather grand town house as his Embassy. Some have claimed it was the place where the Duchess of Richmond held her ball on the eve of Waterloo. John was a very political civil servant, albeit an able one. He once summed himself up to me thus: 'There are two sorts of civil servants. Those who do what they are told, and those who try to save Ministers from their folly. I am the second.' Of course opinion may differ as to what constitutes 'folly'.

The first few meetings were devoted to general principles. We had as our framework the Delors Report on a single currency, which had incurred the scorn and wrath of Mrs Thatcher. She had every reason to feel that she had been bounced. The Report was the work of a committee of central bankers, chaired by Jacques Delors. This was curious enough, since Jacques Delors himself was not a central banker, but what infuriated Mrs Thatcher was that the committee had been set up to examine not the principle of a single currency but how one would be designed and administered if it ever came into existence, which made it difficult for the British to oppose the establishment of the committee. But inevitably, with Delors as Chairman, the conclusions of the committee were taken to mean that a monetary union in Europe was desirable as well as practical. Mrs Thatcher had hoped that Robin Leigh-Pemberton, the Governor of the Bank of England, might be able to stop the Report himself or dissent from its conclusions, but he certainly was unable to do the first and was not inclined to do the latter.

The conclusions of the Delors Report had recommended a single European currency and European Central Bank modelled closely on the Deutschmark and the Bundesbank. If the committee had recommended any other model Karl Otto Pohl, then President of the Bundesbank, probably would not have endorsed the Report. Mrs Thatcher fought a rearguard action at the Naples Summit in October 1990, but while making her own difference of opinion clear she did not veto the conclusions. This left it open to the European Union to proceed.

Economic convergence and the single currency

One of the key issues for Ministers in the Maastricht negotiations was the agreement of convergence criteria for the single currency. It was argued that it would be impossible to have a single currency without some 'convergence' of economic conditions in the participating countries. Otherwise how could you have a single interest rate for different economies? In 1991 the lack of convergence in the EU was spectacular: inflation varied from 2 per cent to 23 per cent, short-term interest rates from 9 per cent to 19 per cent, unemployment from 1 per cent to 16 per cent and budget deficits from 3 per cent to 19 per cent of GDP. When we discussed these matters there was much wringing of hands by the Italians and the Greeks, but the Germans were firm. The strict financial convergence criteria in the Maastricht Treaty were logical if there was to be a single currency. Many Eurosceptics in Britain got this wrong when they opposed the idea of low Budget deficits simply because they were aims of the Maastricht Treaty.

I felt that if there was to be an EMU, even if Britain was not part of it, it was important that it was as financially sound as possible, without unduly fettering national discretion. So I firmly supported strong convergence criteria, economic as well as financial.

What mattered most for the Germans was the convergence of countries' indebtedness, both annually and cumulatively. It was not difficult to see how high deficits in one country might mean that interest rates would be forced up throughout the single currency area. Germany was also afraid that a default by any overindebted country would mean that it might have to stand behind it, a danger that might be reduced by strict limits on annual deficits (normally 3 per cent of GDP) and total debt (normally 60 per cent of GDP). These were the rules for qualifying to join the euro.

I was, however, as I had stated to the House of Commons, opposed to legal controls or fines on countries with excessive deficits. That seemed to me to rob national governments of an important responsibility and function. In fact I think most Finance Ministers were, like me, initially opposed to controls, but the Germans were adamant and in the end got their way. For me the most important point was that these controls, and multilateral surveillance, should not have any binding effect as long as Britain remained outside the single currency. The fact that joining the single currency would have meant the acceptance of controls over a country's right to determine for itself its own level of borrowing merely confirmed to me that the single currency inevitably entailed a real loss of sovereignty. But none of this applied to Britain as long as it was outside.

The Germans were represented by Theo Waigel, the German Finance Minister, who was as passionate for the interests of Bavaria as he was for Germany. When he showed me round his beloved Munich I had to drink white beer and eat Bavarian sausages at breakfast. As I got to know Theo better I discovered that he too had some private reservations about the idea of a single currency. In our meetings he sometimes managed to sound pretty Eurosceptical, but when he came back to Ecofin after his meetings with Chancellor Kohl he always initially had greater enthusiasm for the single currency. Nonetheless I had the impression that if the convergence criteria had not been agreed then even Germany might have vetoed the single currency, because German public opinion would not have accepted it.

Ironically when the convergence criteria were finally brought into play in 1998 for the purpose of determining which currencies qualified to join the euro, the Germans along with the Commission and everyone else acquiesced in fudging the figures.

Every country other than Greece was judged to have qualified, even though several countries, notably Belgium and Italy, had either annual deficits or total indebtedness massively beyond the limits set by Maastricht. The reality was that Germany was determined to have the euro for political reasons, even if it meant the inclusion of countries such as Italy about which there were real reservations.

Central Bank independence

Another early issue was the degree of independence of the European Central Bank. The Delors Report had been clear about the need for complete independence along Bundesbank lines. After all, it had been written by central bankers. Increasingly I found it difficult to see how the Bank could be organised on any other lines if it was to exist at all. If it was controlled by individual countries, or if the Directors of the Bank were simply delegates of national governments, then it could hardly operate as a European institution; indeed, it would be unworkable. Nonetheless the issue remained of whether the Bank might in some limited way be accountable, either to national Parliaments or perhaps to the European Parliament.

Initially one of the opponents of European Central Bank independence was Pierre Bérégovoy, who wanted the Bank to be accountable to Ecofin, which would form an economic strategy for Europe and the beginnings of what he called 'an economic government for Europe.' Although I came to the conclusion that independence for the European Central Bank was the only realistic option, initially I was content to explore this issue with an open mind and to listen to the French. However, just at the moment when the French looked as though they might make some progress, Bérégovoy mysteriously dropped the idea. As always, one never quite knew with the French, but I suspected there had been some bilateral deal with the Germans.

At one point I wanted to tell the House of Commons that we accepted the need for the European Central Bank to be independent, but John Major did not want me to volunteer that opinion, while saying that if I was asked the question I should not avoid answering it!

Although it seemed inevitable that the ECB would ultimately have to be independent, Major did not want to be compelled to make the Bank of England independent in the run-up to the single currency. However, the final Treaty stated that any country wanting to join the single currency had to make its Central Bank independent first, which seemed logical. France, to some people's surprise did just that, showing again how really determined it was to join. The Conservative Government in its dying days in 1997 found itself, to its considerable embarrassment, caught out by this matter. At that time the Government wanted to maintain its 'wait and see' policy on the single currency but found that keeping the option open of joining the single currency would require it to draw up plans to make the Bank independent, which John Major did not want to do.

For the purposes of the Treaty, it was agreed that the ECB in Stage 3, when the single currency was in existence, should be completely independent and free of all political influence.

Part of the discussion about the European Central Bank was conducted after the informal Ecofin meeting held on 11 and 12 May under the Luxembourg Presidency. I remember we had an excursion on a boat on the Moselle and I sat next to Karl Otto Pohl who said to me, 'Don't ever underestimate Helmut Kohl. He is a skilled survivor and he will be there after you and I have gone.' He was right.

Sometimes I grew depressed with the negotiations. Wearied by the procedures at the informal Ecofin in Luxembourg, I wandered outside for a breath of fresh air and a walk in the garden. I have always been a keen birdwatcher and I was thrilled to see my first ever black redstart, singing in a tree in front of the conference centre. As the name implies, a black redstart is a rather nondescript little black bird with a red tail. It is common in Luxembourg, but very rare in England. I had to suppress my excitement but returned to the negotiations in a much better mood.

The opt-out: essential for Britain

I made it clear from the very start that Britain would require an opt-out, and that if we did not have one we would not be able to sign the Treaty. Initially other countries refused to accept this. Although the achievement of the opt-out was later to be hailed as a great triumph for British diplomacy, the reality was that the other governments could never in practice have denied the British Government what it wanted. We simply would not have signed the Treaty without an opt-out, and a Treaty without Britain would have looked incomplete. Futhermore, the other countries would have had difficulty in going ahead on their own since they could not have amended the Treaty of Rome without our vote. The others desperately wanted us to sign, even if we did so without being committed to moving to the single currency. So all the talk of this great achievement of obtaining the opt-out was a bit of a sham.

Initially I argued that we did not want specific arrangements for Britain, but that every country should be required by the Treaty to put the decision to move to a single currency, when conditions were right, to a vote of its national Parliament. This would have meant that Britain would have been covered by the Treaty in exactly the same way as other countries, and that every country would only make a final decision on moving to a single currency shortly before it was to happen. I am not sure whether I truly believed that this rather more general version of the opt-out was ever really likely to be acceptable to other countries. It didn't seem very revolutionary, but there was a fierce reaction against it from the other EU countries, terrified their Parliaments might behave in an unexpected way.

Often when there was a tricky issue in the negotiations on which agreement proved elusive, it would be decided to refer the matter to lunch. The lunches during Maastricht were always extraordinarily lavish occasions, preceded by cocktails and rounded off with cigars and liqueurs. No doubt it was thought that the convivial atmosphere was more conducive to agreement. The other great advantage of the lunches as a mechanism for reaching agreements was that national Civil Servants were not usually allowed to attend. No doubt it was reasoned Finance Ministers were more likely to reach a compromise if they were not bothered by tiresome Civil Servants reminding them of the difficulties of whatever the Commission wanted.

The question of whether Parliaments should have the right to a vote on the move to a single currency was referred to one such lunch. We had drunk a 1979 Château Yon Figeac St-Emilon. I continued to argue the point, but other Ministers were adamant that once the Maastricht Treaty itself had been approved by Parliaments it was simply up to the Commission and governments to decide whether individual countries qualified for the single currency and then to make the decision to go ahead. Wim Kok, then the Dutch Finance Minister and later Prime Minister, astonished me by saying, 'If we let Parliaments interfere in this matter then they may vote against the single currency and Europe will never find its destiny.' I tried to contain my impatience and said that if Europe really had a historic destiny, it must surely be based on the will of the people and Parliaments of Europe, but the sense of the lunch was overwhelmingly against me. Although I continued to maintain my position I knew that this was a point on which ultimately I would have to give way.

Ironically, when the decision on the single currency actually came in 1998, the Bundestag insisted on voting on the issue. That was not in accordance with the Treaty of Maastricht that was negotiated and casts an interesting light on the rule of law within the European Union and the fact that Germany is prepared to regard its laws as superior to European law.

My own reservations on the euro

The longer the negotiations went on, the deeper the reservations I felt about the whole venture. All my political life I had supported our membership of the European Union. When I had been selected as the Conservative candidate for the Kingston by-election in 1972 I had been chosen partly because I was more pro-European than my rivals. I had even made my Maiden Speech in support of the Third Reading of the European

Communities Bill, which set the seal on British membership of
the EEC. But I had always seen the European Union essentially as
an economic venture, though accompanied by increasing political co-operation. While there was some political language in the
preamble to the Treaty of Rome, I had never taken those words
seriously. In my lifetime pro-Europeans had always assured one
that they meant little. I had never believed that Europe would
ever become anything resembling a country called Europe or a
European state.

During the negotiations of the Maastricht Treaty, for the first
time I heard European politicians openly and enthusiastically
arguing for the creation of a European state. They never actually
used that phrase in public, but it was quite clear that that was
what they meant. Europe was something to be constructed, to be
built, to be united. Anything that contributed to that cause was
good; anything that delayed it was bad. I was startled one day
when Bérégovoy, whom I regarded as a realistic man, had said
that he did not think he would live to see it, but he was convinced
that his children would live under a European government.

I felt that I could justify to myself my participation in the negotiations since my task was to make sure that Britain retained the
freedom to decide for itself. Whatever commitments other countries might make, I was simply negotiating for the British
Parliament to have the right to say 'Yes' or 'No' at the appropriate time.

I had many fierce, heated arguments with Treasury officials
about all this. I am not referring to formal advice about the details
of Maastricht, but to late-night chats, often over a drink, where
we would argue about whether the single currency could ever
work, or whether it was consistent with the continued existence
of Britain as an independent country.

In discussions about the theory of the single currency, some of
my friends argued that the single currency was a modern version
of the gold standard. Britain, they argued, had too often devalued
in the past to make its economy competitive, which was a soft
option leading nowhere. We should adjust our productivity to
our exchange rate rather than the other way round. Those who
regarded the single currency as a modern version of the gold

standard argued that the single currency was no more a threat to the British government's freedom than the gold standard had been. Furthermore, monetary sovereignty was an illusion – 'You take the interest rate you are given' was their view. Some of the advisors to whom I was closest personally were also worried that my own hostility to the idea of the single currency would damage me personally. They kept reminding me that, whatever my personal views, the single currency was going to happen. I must be careful, they suggested, not to find myself on the wrong side of history.

If I ever gave history a thought I worried that I would be remembered as the man who had negotiated away Britain's right to be an independent self-governing country. Such a thought literally made me feel physically ill.

I agreed with those who argued that in a world of global capital flows governments did not have complete freedom to do everything they wanted on interest rates. That was not necessarily a bad thing, but it did not mean that we had no room for manoeuvre in British monetary policy. Subsequently our exit from the ERM and the interest rate reductions showed how wrong the Europhile argument was.

I also agreed that devaluation was fools' gold, obviously. It was far better to increase one's productivity than to devalue, though that is easier said than done. There are times when alterations in the external value of a country's exchange rate are inevitable. To give up the right to adjust the exchange rate of a country is to give up a fundamental tool of policy.

But my main fear about the euro was that ultimately it would lead to the creation of a European government and state. I could not see that there was any evidence to suggest that Britain would be better governed under such an arrangement. Furthermore democracy in a multi-national state is, as history shows, not an easy thing to operate.

I do not take the view of the Duke of Wellington that the British constitution is incapable of improvement, but before one destroys one set of institutions and substitutes another for them, it seems common sense that one must first be satisfied that this will be an improvement. Whatever else may be said about Britain, it has, compared with most countries, an enviable record both of stability and as a successful functioning democracy. It also inspires loyalty, which the institutions and idea of Europe do not.

In spite of my own reservations, my relations with my opposite numbers in other countries remained, for the most part, excellent. I had a few difficulties with Philippe Maystadt, the Belgian Finance Minister, who never missed an opportunity to make an anti-British point, and I found Wim Kok prickly. But with my other colleagues relations were easy; several of them, such as Piero Barucci, who succeeded Guido Carli as Italian Finance Minister, and Effdhimios Christodoulou, the Greek Minister, remain friends to this day. Occasionally there was a hint of condescension about my opposition to the single currency and they would tease me. 'You say these things but when the time comes you will be there' was Effdhimios Christodoulou's line.

There were also very many points of common ground between me and other European Finance Ministers on the precise conditions for a successful single currency. I have already said that on many issues I felt in strong agreement with the position taken by the Germans, but sometimes agreement surprisingly went much further. At one Ecofin meeting I found myself having a late-night drink with a senior official from one of the European countries most enthusiastic for the single currency. I shall not embarrass him as he is still in the same senior position today, but after a few drinks he told me that he agreed with almost every economic point that I made against the single currency, but I should recognise that it was going to happen and Britain would be forced to join. On another occasion Giscard d'Estaing said to me, 'The points you make are good, but it's going to happen.' I found this an unconvincing argument.

The ERM as a treaty obligation: a narrow escape

One of the suggested convergence criteria for the euro that worried me was the idea that membership of the ERM should become a Treaty obligation. I accepted the stipulation that if a country wanted to join the single currency eventually it ought to have a track record of two years' stability in the ERM, which was common sense. If you can't have exchange rate stability you do not have the underlying foundations on which a single currency could be built and made to work. But the requirement that all countries signing the Treaty, whether they intended to join the single currency or not, must by law be members of the ERM caused me much heart-searching. As Chancellor I was, of course, in the front line, publicly supporting our membership of the ERM. We were already in the ERM, not as a matter of law but as a result of a voluntary and reversible decision by the British Government, and not necessarily for ever. For that reason it would have been wrong for us to bind both ourselves and any successor Government, converting a discretionary policy decision into an irreversible Treaty obligation.

All this was in my mind at a time well before the subsequent currency crisis, when there was no question of our leaving the ERM. An early version of the Dutch Treaty included this idea, and I did not like it at all. At a meeting with the Prime Minister and the Foreign Secretary in the Cabinet Office to review progress on Maastricht, I explained my reservations. They were unsympathetic. Douglas Hurd said, 'I can't see what you are so worked up about. We are in the ERM. What difference does it make if it is in the Treaty?' I had also found no support from my civil servant advisors on this point. They too thought my worries theoretical. For me the problem was profound.

The Prime Minister and the Foreign Secretary suggested that I should calm down and get on with more important matters in the negotiations. But I wasn't prepared to do that, and I decided to ignore them. At the next Maastricht meeting I made it clear that I was not prepared to accept this, and at my insistence it was removed. Membership of the ERM ceased to be a Treaty obligation. I felt very much happier. Little did I realise that had I not insisted on this point it would have been highly embarrassing for the UK Government, as events that I did not foresee subsequently showed. My former Private Secretary clearly recalls my concern and my reaction on returning to the Treasury after the meeting.

There was one curious interlude in the Maastricht negotiations.

In Summer 1991, after visiting Gorbachev and Yeltsin, I dropped into Ukraine, where I had seen the President and the Prime Minister in Kiev. I discovered that the Ukrainians were planning to abandon the rouble and develop their own currency. Curiously the Ukrainians were passionately interested in the arguments in Britain about the single currency, particularly its relationship to what they called 'economic space'. The issues in their mind were almost a mirror image of those in the Maastricht debate, except they were wanting to go back to their own national currency in order to strengthen their independence. We discussed these issues late into the night, and I told them my view that if they really wanted independence from Russia they must have their own currency.

At lunch at Ecofin I was asked by Delors to bring EU Ministers up to date with developments in the Soviet Union. Among other things I mentioned my visit to Ukraine and their plan for their own currency. This provoked outrage around the table; Ukraine was destroying 'the single market of the Soviet Union', I was told. Then Delors let the cat out of the bag. 'If they do go ahead with their idea of a national currency, the case for the European single currency will be undermined.' In vain I pointed out that if Ukraine was determined to recapture its independence after several hundred years, lectures from the European Union would hardly prevent them, and I felt we had no right to try to dissuade them. The feeling of Ministers was that we should stop them.

In July the Dutch took over the Presidency from Luxembourg, and Wim Kok, the Dutch Finance Minister took over as Chairman of Ecofin from Jean-Claude Juncker, the Luxembourg Finance Minister. Both men went on to become Prime Ministers of their countries, but there the similarity stopped. Whereas Jean-Claude Juncker was sympathetic, charming and understanding of British difficulties, Wim Kok was awkward and difficult and seldom missed an opportunity to make life difficult for us, usually with some unhelpful interview on the BBC news. If you had put a Belgian there, he couldn't have been worse.

The Dutch held an informal Ecofin at Apeldoorn on 20–22 September. One of the issues raised was when to set up the ECB.

I did not want it set up too early. We managed to head off an attempt to establish the European Central Bank in the transitional phase to a single currency, and instead agreed to the setting up of a European Monetary Institute as a precursor to the Central Bank.

In November the Dutch produced a draft Treaty text, which had some provisions that we could not accept and to which the Dutch knew we could not agree. Many of them were ironed out at a meeting in the Hague on 30 November and in Brussels on 2 December.

The last meeting of the Inter-Governmental Conference prior to the final meeting at Maastricht took place on 3 December. There was an important discussion on how the question of excessive deficits, those exceeding 3 per cent of GDP, should be handled in Stage 3 when the euro came into existence. I was keen that some flexibility should be built into the procedure. It would, in my opinion, have been quite wrong to have drafted a Treaty in which a country in the euro zone would, for example, be fined by the EU if its Budget deficit exceeded the 3 per cent rule simply because of a recession. Fortunately in the end common sense prevailed.

However, Kok showed his true colours and revealed just how unhelpful he could be by suggesting that if I pursued this point, the earlier agreement that the law on excessive deficits would not apply in Stage 2, before the start of the euro, might be reconsidered.

On the question of the opt-out the PM and I agreed that we would argue for a clause of general application to all countries, that is to say no country would join the single currency without a specific vote by Parliament. We would only consider a UK-specific protocol when we got to Maastricht.

There was also a highly important change made to the draft Treaty on the initiative of the French. The draft Treaty had suggested that to move to the single currency in 1997 it should be necessary to have a minimum number of nine countries. But Bérégovoy suggested that if the European Council could not agree in 1997 to go ahead with the single currency, then in 1999 all the countries that qualified would automatically move to form a

single currency, whatever their number, but subject to a qualified
majority decision by the Council.

This new approach, which was adopted, had several consequences. Firstly, it allowed more time and, as events turned out,
that was wise. Secondly, it guaranteed that even if a majority of
countries didn't qualify, probably some countries would, and the
single currency was almost bound to happen.

Kok declared the IGC complete to general congratulations on
3 December. Much had indeed been agreed but the outstanding
issues for the final meeting at Maastricht included the transition
to Stage 3, the cohesion fund, of great importance to Spain, and
the absence of a no-compulsion clause, which was of great importance to the United Kingdom.

The draft Treaty

The draft Maastricht Treaty divided progress towards the single
currency into three stages. Stage 1 was the completion of the
single market, and the removal of capital controls. That was more
or less the world as it was. Eurosceptics got worked up about
aspects of Stage 1, but there was nothing to it. Stage 2 was the
period when countries prepared for the single currency in accordance with convergence criteria by reducing deficits and public
debt and showed they could remain within the narrow bands of
the ERM. The European Monetary Institute was to be set up to
prepare the way for the European Central Bank. Finally, Stage 3
would be the point at which all participating countries would
substitute the euro for their national currencies and the European
Central Bank would come into existence.

My objectives for the final stage were much the same as I had
outlined to the Defence and Overseas Policy Committee. By this
time it was clear that Stage 2 would not impose any legal obligations on Britain. I also had little doubt we would get an
opt-out. The important point was to make sure it was right in all
its detail.

The meeting at Maastricht

The final negotiation of the Treaty took place on 9–10 December in the Dutch town of Maastricht, which has long been associated with D'Artagnan of *The Three Musketeers*. I am told that the town has attractive, historic parts, but I saw little of them from either the conference hall or the uninspiring hotel where we stayed.

The final stages of the negotiations were divided into two. In one room there were Heads of Government, Prime Ministers and Foreign Ministers, who were negotiating the foreign affairs, security and home affairs aspects of the Treaty. The Finance Ministers met separately in a large circular room rather like an old-fashioned Odeon cinema; one half-expected a woman to come round with an ice cream tray. Obviously the Finance Ministers' negotiations were subject to final approval or veto by the Heads of Government. Occasionally I had to slip from the Finance Ministers' meeting into the other one, as points in that meeting about the structural and cohesion funds had financial implications the PM wanted me to consider.

I decided that the best way to design the opt-out was to draw up a protocol that listed all those parts of the Treaty from which Britain wanted exemption. At the Finance Ministers' Meeting I gave this protocol to Wim Kok, who immediately said that the meeting of Ministers would want to consider it. I said that I understood Ministers would wish to discuss the issue of a British opt-out, but he should be in no doubt that if we did not get one we would not sign the Treaty. Furthermore, the protocol was our minimum demand, and was designed to be watertight. It had no effect on other countries. It only applied to Britain and so its detail was not negotiable.

We had a number of other points to consider first, but when the time came to consider the British opt-out, the first thing that Wim Kok said was that he proposed that the meeting go through my draft protocol line by line. I protested. He persisted and said that the meeting might wish to amend the document. I responded again that the opt-out affected no country other than Britain and was not negotiable.

Wim Kok started to put the protocol line by line to the meeting, so I rose from my seat and walked out. It ought to be said that at meetings like this people are coming and going all the time, even when matters affecting their own country are under discussion. Nigel Wicks was still in the UK seat. But I was angry. I tried hard to slam the door, but it was a heavy, thick door that only moved very slowly in a gradual, creaky way. I learned later that the officials said I had gone to the loo.

I was quite sure that Kok had done this deliberately. I did not hurry back. A long time later Tristan Garel-Jones, the Foreign Office Minister, who played no part in the negotiations on the single currency but who was there to report back to the Whips' Office, suggested that I had endangered the opt-out by walking out and that the negotiation had to be rescued by John Major. He even invented a story that he has repeated several times that he had to keep me out of a meeting with John Major.

The truth is that while I was out of the meeting I did discuss the situation with John Major, who was having a bilateral meeting with Ruud Lubbers, the Dutch Prime Minister. I did have to wait until they had finished whatever they were previously discussing, and then I told him and Lubbers exactly where we were. At no stage did John Major express the slightest concern. Far from endangering the negotiations, I am quite sure the walk-out had exactly the desired effect. When I returned to the room I was informed by Nigel Wicks that the opt-out had in my absence been accepted without any amendment. If I had stayed there I am sure I would have been bogged down in line-by-line discussion and that would have been risky.

We had achieved our objectives. Stage 2 would be entirely voluntary, both for Britain and other countries. And then the opt-out applied to Britain for Stage 3. The result was that unless Britain decided that it wished to join the single currency it could pursue its own monetary policy and have its own interest rate, only joining the single currency after a separate vote of the British Parliament at the appropriate time.

I had no great enthusiasm for Maastricht, but I believed it was acceptable. We had not sold out on anything and, if John Major was right – though I had doubts – and the whole project floundered, we would have the best of all possible worlds.

What of the other parts of the Treaty? The Prime Minister and Douglas Hurd succeeded in making the proposals for moving to a common foreign policy into an inter-governmental agreement, the so-called 'twin pillars', rather than a Treaty obligation.

On the Social Chapter, too, an opt-out was secured, but that was very much the result of Michael Howard's determination. He had insisted that he would not remain Employment Secretary if the proposals on employment policy and social policy were not withdrawn. At one point John had asked me to telephone Michael to find out whether he really meant it. My recollection is that he said he would resign. He was telephoned again by Sir John Kerr, who asked him whether he would accept a diluted version of the Social Chapter rather than an opt-out, and he replied that he didn't think that was acceptable. Sir John said to him, 'The Prime Minister won't be pleased to hear that.' Michael replied, 'Well, that is up to him, but I am just giving you my opinion.' Much political credit was subsequently claimed by the PM for the Social Chapter opt-out, but it really belongs to Michael. The PM followed him when he would not give way.

I was also involved in another part of the negotiations about the so-called Cohesion Fund which came outside the monetary part of the Treaty and was negotiated by the Heads of Government meeting. The Cohesion Fund was just another name for extra regional assistance that Spain demanded as a quid pro quo for support of the single currency. At John Major's request I came into that meeting in place of Douglas Hurd to put our case. I didn't enjoy slipping into a meeting where Kohl, Mitterrand, Gonzales and Lubbers were in full flow and I didn't know what had transpired beforehand. I didn't do very well, and we ended up with a Cohesion Fund provision that was too generous.

One point of the Treaty that left me particularly uncomfortable was that part dealing with citizenship and passports. I did not like the concept of 'a citizen of the European Union', nor was I keen to abandon the traditional British passport. To me this seemed to confirm we were taking another step towards the creation of a European state. Others, such as Malcolm Rifkind, then Transport Secretary argued at Cabinet meetings that there were so many different types of British citizenship already, what difference did one more make? I continued to feel uneasy, but it was not my immediate responsibility and I had quite enough issues with which to deal.

I also didn't like even the relatively small increases in the powers of the European Parliament. I had fiercely resisted any expansion of these in the EMU text. But in other parts of Maastricht there were some regrettable increases in the power of the European Parliament.

The return from Maastricht

The general reaction in the press to the Maastricht Treaty that was secured was an overwhelmingly favourable one. John Major received a very warm welcome in the House of Commons. The Eurosceptics grumbled, but not in a very outspoken way. The majority feeling in the House was that the Prime Minister, once again, had shown himself a brilliant negotiator, squaring the circle and succeeding where Mrs Thatcher had failed, both in safeguarding British interests and in maintaining good relations with our Continental neighbours. He indeed deserved the credit. He had negotiated skilfully and patiently and achieved his objectives. I didn't like the aims of the Treaty, but felt we had built in all the necessary safeguards on the economic front. It wouldn't do harm.

I was disappointed that after the draft Treaty was first publicly revealed a number of Eurosceptics and lawyers claimed that the Maastricht Treaty still did impose obligations on Britain. It is true that we had subscribed to aims such as running low deficits and keeping national debt down, but these were good conservative aims that were not legally binding and, contrary to what was frequently claimed, there was no possibility of the Commission being able to fine us if we exceeded any target. England was free to be as drunk as it wanted. I insisted emphatically in House of Commons debates and in Maastricht that nothing in the Treaty interfered with Britain's freedom to form its own policy as long as we remained outside the single currency.

A long time afterwards I discovered that the statements I made so confidently were not 100 per cent correct, and as regards one small technical point were wrong. It transpired that officials had overlooked an obscure part of the Treaty dealing with the Bank of England's open market operations, the so-called 'warehousing' of gilts, which did slip through and become a legal obligation in the Treaty. I was furious with the officials for having missed this, even though it was a point of no practical significance. I felt very disappointed because I had not wanted to concede one single point to the power of Brussels.

However, some of the rhetoric of the Prime Minister worried me. It was not my experience that we were 'winning the argument in Europe'. Also the claim that Europe would now be a decentralised Europe seemed overdone. That plainly wasn't true.

I wondered what the future would hold. From what I had seen of my Finance Minister colleagues, other European countries did not seem likely to abandon the single currency, as John Major believed. I knew that I would not be Chancellor when the decision whether to join or not would have to be made. For that I felt relieved, as I would not have wanted anything to do with a recommendation to join.

When I came back to the UK from Maastricht a friend said to me, 'Congratulations.' I replied, 'Congratulations on what? I feel quite miserable about it.'

A few days later, I was sitting next to Michael Heseltine in the first Cabinet Meeting after Maastricht and he muttered in my ear, 'I envy you'.

'Why?'

'Because you are part of history,' he said.

I replied, 'It was a part of history from which I would willingly be excluded.'

The Maastricht Treaty was due to be signed in February 1992. I received a note from Jeremy Heywood informing me of the administrative arrangements for the ceremony and the signing. I could imagine what it would be like. There would be gold pens, a bank of flags and an impressive array the European *nomenklatura*. After our morning prayers meeting I was talking to Francis Maude, the Financial Secretary, and said, 'I just wish I didn't have to go over to Holland and sign the Maastricht Treaty.

I can't bear the thought that my signature will forever be on that Treaty.' Francis replied, 'Really? I am very happy to go if you want.'

And so it happened. That is why the British signatures on the Maastricht Treaty are the Rt Hon. Douglas Hurd, Foreign Secretary, and the Rt Hon. Francis Maude, Financial Secretary to the Treasury.

6

The Recovery Stalls

Of all human follies prophecy is the most gratuitous.
Fyodor Dostoyevsky

Monday 16 September 1991 was a key date with figures both for retail sales and production. Many felt that if both sets of statistics were favourable, the end of recession could be announced.

The figures were mixed. Retail sales in August had dropped 1.4 per cent, a sharp drop, depressing expectations about a consumer-led upturn. On the other hand manufacturing output grew 0.8 per cent between June and July and showed the first rise in the three-month average since the recession started. This suggested the low point of the manufacturing recession had probably passed, but it was still not an unambiguous 'end to the recession'.

The better news, albeit a little ambiguous, led some Cabinet colleagues to suggest to the Prime Minister an autumn or November Election, but Chris Patten, John MacGregor and I continued to press the case for holding on until next year. Douglas Hurd was open-minded. Kenneth Baker, the Home Secretary, had given a lunch for the Prime Minister at Dorneywood and reacted to the polls giving the Conservative Party a lead by urging John Major to wait and see what happened over the next few weeks.

This was a period of intense political activity. An outside observer might have been forgiven for thinking that the General Election had already started. Every economic statistic was analysed endlessly on *Newsnight*, the *Nine O'clock News* and *News at Ten*, and claims and counter claims were made. I doubt if there has ever been a time when monthly economic indicators have featured so much on television. Every month's figures for retail sales, exports, unemployment, credit expansion and industrial production became a subject for debate. The Treasury was asked almost every day to make a Treasury Minister available to comment in a debate on some statistic that in less frenetic times would have been completely ignored. Few of the discussions shed much light. It was difficult to keep a cool head and to encourage others not to make exaggerated claims.

The public spending round: pressure from colleagues continues

The grind of the public expenditure round continued. David Mellor had been hard at work over the summer break. I had my reservations about David, but he had set about the task with energy and his natural quick wit and forensic skills were great assets. But it was an uphill task, since in a pre-election period Cabinet colleagues were desperate to protect their own programmes and to be able to announce increases to the voter. I was somewhat dismayed by the Treasury's attitude, which to me was rather defeatist. The view was that many of the bids were unavoidable. I insisted that the target outcome for the round be made more ambitious. It was for politicians, not civil servants, to say if bids were 'politically unavoidable'.

Michael Howard was among those who had submitted a large bid and David Mellor countered by suggesting cuts, providing examples of many wasteful programmes. There is no doubt there was scope for economies in the Department of Employment's programmes but, when unemployment was rising, it was difficult to persuade colleagues. David's proposed cuts would have saved some £1 billion over three years, but in the end Michael Howard got a £470 million increase. At Health, William Waldegrave, who was offered a generous settlement, as the Prime Minister insisted, continued fighting to the end, and threatened to take his case to Cabinet if he was not given even more money.

Despite these difficulties I was able to report to the Prime Minister at the end of October that, following a re-examination of debt interest and local authority self-financed expenditure, the forecast increase in General Government Expenditure had been slightly revised downwards and that I expected the year-on-year increase to 1992/93 to be 3.75 per cent in real terms. This was provided we held the reserve to £3.5 billion rather than £4 billion and also brought forward some EU contributions into this financial year. Although the outcome was on the generous side, it reflected two exceptional influences: the recession and the 'automatic stabilisers'.

Party Conference

The Party Conference took place in Blackpool in the second week of October. Party members were in a state of great excitement. Some thought the Prime Minister might announce a General Election there and then, so the Conference was looking for guidance and a call to battle. Once again the pressure on me to announce that the recovery had started was intense, and it came not just from Central Office. John Wakeham, the Minister responsible for the presentation of government policy, wrote me a letter saying that if I said there was a recovery then there would be a recovery. 'It is as simple as that,' he said.

Many people thought the recovery had started. The *Economist* had pronounced on 4 October, 'The economy has begun a weak recovery.' In its October forecast the Treasury estimated that 'non-oil GDP rose by 0.25 per cent in the third quarter, and will rise at a similar rate in the fourth quarter'. Nonetheless Terry Burns strongly advised me not to utter the words 'The recovery has started' and I agreed with him.

The Prime Minister demanded to see my speech before I delivered it to the Conference. The Prime Minister disliked what I wanted to say about Europe and reluctantly agreed that I could keep it in, but it was on the wording of the recovery that there was most argument. Successive redrafts were delivered page by page to the PM's suite.

My speech was to be on the Wednesday morning. It was the first time I had made a major speech at a Party Conference. As Chief Secretary at the previous Conference, my role had been off stage and I had been highly invisible. I had watched enough of Nigel Lawson's very carefully prepared and crafted Conference speeches to know that a warm reception was not guaranteed.

I did receive applause when I said that I would not allow a single currency to be imposed on Britain, but the thunderous applause came when I uttered the very words to which John Major had objected: 'We have to ensure that the decisions about the economy of this country are taken where they should be – in Britain . . . Unlike the Labour Party we do not want laws to be made and taxes to be raised in Brussels for which the British people have not voted.'

I defended my cautious approach to interest rates: 'Step by step I have brought them down. Each time there have been shouts for larger cuts and quicker cuts. I fear that some memories have been as short as the voices have been shrill . . . We have cut interest rates eight times whilst in Germany they have been rising.' Inflation was now better than forecast in the Budget and I told the Conference, 'Soon I will be the first Chancellor of the Exchequer in nearly a quarter of a century who will be able to stand before you and say that Britain has lower inflation than Germany'.

The words that I used about recovery were ones that had been carefully negotiated with John Major. 'Economies are like tides, they ebb and flow. The turn of the tide is sometimes difficult to discern.' Referring to rising optimism, 'That is not just my opinion, it is the verdict of the IMF, the CBI, the Institute of Directors and numerous surveys of businessmen and consumers up and down the country.' I then went on to utter words that were later misquoted and hurled back in my face, 'What we are seeing is the return of that vital ingredient – confidence. The green shoots of economic spring are appearing once again.'

'Green shoots' was my latest formulation. Read in its context it is quite clear that it referred to confidence and surveys of business opinion, and not to any actual recovery. I was rather pleased with the formulation. Others were more doubtful. The best argument against it had been put by Rosemary: 'You don't get green shoots in the autumn.'

Although the phrase subsequently became notorious, it was not picked up much by the press at the time. No papers suggested I had been overexuberant. The *Guardian* described my speech as 'a noticeably cautious assessment'. Michael White even added, 'Mr Lamont avoided talking up what he called "the green shoots of economic spring".' Nonetheless the myth grew up that I had talked about the 'green shoots of recovery' and the incorrect version of my remarks even appeared in a dictionary of quotations.

I was cautious about income tax and, according to some reports, disappointed the Conference by saying it might take two Parliaments to reduce the standard rate from 25 pence to 20 pence. Nonetheless, I reaffirmed the objective of a 20 per cent basic rate.

My speech was well if not rapturously received. Chris Buckland wrote in the *Daily Express*: 'And if Mr Lamont was looking cheerful, he had every right . . . the critics have been proved wrong.'

Another person who claimed he welcomed my speech was John Smith, who said it indicated 'very clearly the choice before the British electorate'. He went on to say that we could not afford to reduce the standard rate of income tax because the money was needed for health and public services generally. I regarded Smith's words as sheer bravado and wondered whether he really welcomed the challenge for the General Election.

My speech and the reference to 'green shoots' was heavily influenced by the information I was receiving about what the next CBI survey was likely to show. When it was published on 29 October it exceeded people's expectations. The survey involved 1,203 companies and accounted for about half the manufacturing workforce in exports. It showed that manufacturing output was likely to rise slightly. Two per cent more people were optimistic than pessimistic. This was dramatically different from July, when 26 per cent more people had been pessimistic than optimistic. This was the biggest rise in business optimism for seventeen years. I was careful in my response publicly and merely said, 'There could be little doubt the economy was coming out of recession.' *The Times* the next day commented: 'The Government's public response [to the survey] was carefully modulated . . . [Norman Lamont] has yet to respond to the urgings of his neighbour in Downing Street to proclaim recovery underway.'

The next important speech was on 30 October, the 'Mansion House Speech,' which that year was to be delivered at the Guildhall because the Mansion House was being refurbished. The speech was undoubtedly too 'bitty'. In the Mansion House Speech Chancellors had normally spoken about some technical aspect of monetary policy. Because monetary policy along with the ERM was now on auto-pilot, I decided instead to cover a number of subjects, including supervision of the banking system and Russia. For the first time I floated in public the idea I had developed of the UK financial sector giving help to train young people from Russia. But I repeated much of what I had said at Blackpool.

If I had said nothing the press did not seem entirely dissatisfied. The *Daily Telegraph* said I was 'a Chancellor with the courage to do nothing'. *The Times* said: 'For all his past misjudgements, the Chancellor deserves to enjoy a modicum of self-satisfaction.'

The Mansion House Speech was followed by the Autumn Statement. By this time I had received and discussed with the Prime Minister the next Treasury economic forecast, which again claimed to be little different from the Budget. Output, it repeated, had stopped falling and recovery had 'probably' started. Non-Oil GDP was forecast to rise by 0.25 per cent to 0.5 per cent in the second half of the year. If this was true then recovery had definitely started. The PSBR was likely to be £10 billion compared with the £8 billion forecast at the Budget. The forecast had concluded unambiguously, 'nonetheless we do believe the recovery has started.'

Even on housing the report said: 'The decline in the house price earnings ratio and improvements in consumer confidence were expected to generate a slow recovery in turnover through the next year. This would include a modest rise in prices of up to 3% in the year to the fourth quarter 1992.'

The road to Budget deficit is paved with good causes

So the prospects still looked as though they might soon improve. On the eve of the Autumn Statement the *Independent* said: 'Norman Lamont is paying for the sins of his predecessors. So outrageous was the overconfidence of Lawson, so seductive Major's assurance the recession would be avoided that few people are now willing to believe the present Chancellor when he says the economy is beginning to recover. But for the first time in several years, hardly a decimal of the Treasury's economic forecast will need to be changed. Credit where it is due.'

The Autumn Statement on public spending was on 5 November, an appropriate date. Until the system was changed this was the most important economic day in the Parliamentary year after the Budget. The Statement used to consist of two parts: a review of the economy and then a statement of the outcome of the public expenditure negotiations between departmental Ministers and the Chief Secretary. In many ways it would have been more appropriate if the statement had been made by the Chief Secretary, since he handled all the negotiations with individual Ministers.

It had been a gruelling series of negotiations, with a huge number of meetings. But undoubtedly the increases of £11 billion that I announced were large, coming on top of the hefty year-on-year increases already built into the existing plans. Much of the extra increase was because of the recession and its impact on unemployment and the finances of the nationalised industries. Nearly half was accounted for by four programmes: transport, social security, employment and health, where the PM had insisted a generous increase was essential. Health was given £1.65 billion more than planned for 1992/93, making an increase, year on year, after inflation of 5 per cent; £4.2 billion had to be allocated to social security, reflecting an assumption that unemployment would rise further, and £1.4 billion was given to the nationalised transport industries, reflecting the recession.

In my statement I said, 'The rise in no way could be described as some sort of cynical give-away.' I did mean it and it certainly didn't feel like a give-away at the time. I had reservations about the increase in health, which I did feel was overgenerous. There was no cyclical reason for rising health spending, and if a 5 per cent increase wasn't throwing money at a problem, what was? However, as the subsequent Election was to show, health was an acutely sensitive political subject.

I had also decided that, in a recession where my freedom for manoeuvre was so limited, it was right to let the 'automatic stabilisers' work and not to cut programmes where the increases in expenditure had been caused by the recession. I had referred to this in the Budget speech as well. The theory was that these temporary increases, for example, the cost of unemployment, would cancel themselves out as the economy recovered, and at the same time the extra spending would help to stabilise the fall in output. This was particularly important now that we were in the ERM. The effects would be that borrowing would increase in the short run, but would come down over the cycle as a whole. This was our ERM fiscal policy.

The Autumn Statement predicted a PSBR for 1991/92, the current year, of £10.5 billion, up £2 billion from the Budget estimate. As usual no figure was published for the next year, 1992/93, but the Autumn Statement document revealed an assumption 'of a PSBR of around 3 per cent of nominal GDP'. As there was a forecast for GDP it was easy to work out that I foresaw a PSBR of around £19 billion (up about £6 billion). The vanishing recovery was beginning to affect the Government's finances through lower revenues and pressure on spending.

If the Treasury's forecast of a rise in output in 1991 of 0.5 per cent had been met the PSBR would have been much as forecast in the Budget, and there was as yet no great sense of danger. Our fiscal position still compared very favourably with most EU countries. Germany was borrowing about 5 per cent of GDP, substantially higher than the UK figure. And it was our intention to balance the Budget over the cycle.

Nonetheless the figures were embarrassing and clearly the risks were there. For the fourth year running the Government had been forced to abandon its once dearly held political tenet that government spending as a proportion of GDP should shrink year by year. However, when the economy itself was shrinking this was an inevitable result.

On the economy I was able to give a moderately encouraging report in line with the Budget. Echoing the Treasury forecast, I said, 'The economy may have already started to pick up.' I was soon to find out that was too optimistic. On inflation we had already reached the 4 per cent target. The Treasury expected inflation to rise and then flatten out to 4 per cent again. Here the Treasury was too pessimistic; we were to do better than that.

The reaction of the tabloids was favourable, though the broadsheets were more cautious and commentators on their inside pages more cynical. Christopher Huhne in the *Independent* wrote: 'The Chancellor's main message in the Autumn Statement was that the Conservatives can now be trusted with the NHS.' Philip Stephens in the *FT* called it 'the triumph of politics over ideology'. Nick Ridley in *The Times* pointedly asked, 'But who pays, Mr Lamont?' He went on: 'The difficulty in a rise in the level of spending is that it would be hard to claw back in later years, and will leave people inevitably worse off as a result. Whether that would happen before or after the Election we must wait and see.' They were prophetic words.

The Autumn Statement budgeted for an overall increase in General Government Expenditure of 3.75 per cent in real terms. That was higher than the growth in the economy, both in the short run and the longer run. On the other hand, as I have said, it recognised the reality of the recession. There is no doubt that Treasury officials themselves believed it to be the best outcome that could be obtained. Indeed it was tighter than the outcome they themselves predicted and initially recommended to Ministers.

Looking back at the figures for public spending in 1992 reveals that the actual increase in GGE was not the 3.75 per cent that was planned, but actually nearer 6 per cent in real terms. How did this dangerously high increase happen? The answer is complex.

Firstly, inflation in 1992/93 turned out again to be lower than expected, thus increasing the increase in real terms. Public expenditure is planned in cash terms – if inflation falls, there is more to spend, and the value of any Budget increases in real terms. Secondly, local authorities' self-financed expenditure – what they spent from their own resources, including Poll Tax receipts – increased sharply. This was largely beyond the control of Central Government. And thirdly, the interest cost of government debt was higher than forecast because the budget deficit was higher because the recession was longer than expected. This was truly an 'unvirtuous circle'.

I regard the 1991/92 public expenditure round as the feature of my Chancellorship about which I feel most defensive. It was not meant as a give-away, and it was conducted in difficult circumstances, but we should have been tougher. In addition, as I later suggested to the PM, we should have cut public expenditure when inflation turned out to be much lower than predicted. Departments then could afford cuts.

Whatever reservations I may have today about the 1991 Autumn Statement, I had no reason to feel that Labour had any right to criticise the Statement. They wanted to increase public spending by £35 billion on top of the increases I announced in the Autumn Statement. I made this point when I wound up the four-day debate in a noisy finale. It was a typical 9.30 p.m. occasion in the House, with MPs fresh from the dining rooms cheering and counter-cheering. I waded into John Smith's attitude towards interest rates. Every time I cut rates he demanded another cut while at the same time claiming to be an enthusiastic supporter of the ERM. 'The truth is that if he were ever to become Chancellor the only thing he would be doing would be putting them up quickly,' I said, 'Mr one percent cut would become Mr one percent rise.'

The green shoots wither away

I had been waiting for 19 November, the day the first estimates for GDP in the third quarter would be published. As I have already said, the Treasury forecast had given me their opinion that non-oil GDP and GDP had increased in the third quarter and I was anticipating that now I would at last be able to utter the magic words 'The recovery has started'. Unfortunately the figures were a disappointment. Total GDP, the whole economy, had indeed increased by 0.3 per cent, but excluding oil and gas production GDP had fallen by 0.3 per cent. The whole of the quarter's growth came from a once and for all rise in North Sea oil production. Oil is, of course, part of the economy and I was able to declare the recession technically over, but it was heavily qualified good news. The sense of disappointment after all that waiting was acute.

A package for the housing market

The economic news was indeed grim. Somewhat belatedly I had become convinced that one of the reasons why the economy was not responding as predicted was the crisis in the housing market, with large amounts of negative equity and mounting repossessions. Prices were falling, making potential buyers stand back, and transactions were decreasing in number. The obvious answer should have been lower rates of interest, but throughout the world they remained high. And, of course, we were constrained by the ERM.

Since we could not cut rates, we were forced to think about other meaures. For some months I had been considering with both Treasury officials and the Prime Minister a targeted package aimed specifically at the housing market. In the 1980s Conservative Governments had very much prided themselves on not producing mini budgets as Denis Healey had frequently done. I was concerned that a special package might appear to be ineffective tinkering and also undermine confidence by making it seem that I myself had lost confidence in the prospects for recovery. I was conscious I was the prisoner of my own words.

There were a number of possibilities. One was designed to reduce future repossessions for those on low incomes if the Government would make possible the direct payment of interest to the building societies by the Department of Social Security on behalf of those people on income support who had mortgages paid by the DSS. Often these DSS payments were not passed on to the building societies, with the result that repossessions then took place. This change would require legislation, which would be controversial and run the risk of amendments. In exchange the Government was looking to the building societies for measures that would reduce the number of repossessions straight away. It had to be a joint initiative.

On 16 December I chaired a huge meeting with the Council of Mortgage Lenders, led by the chief executive of the Abbey National. It was a constructive meeting and the lenders said they were prepared, each on an individual basis, to announce schemes along the lines I wanted. They would undertake not to repossess where they were receiving direct income support and transfer these mortgages into interest-only ones. With other low-income earners they said they would do everything they could to take a softer line, as long as there were some repayments, but the lenders also said they needed increased confidence in the economy and asked me to consider abolishing stamp duty on houses.

Total abolition was too radical and too expensive, but I was prepared to consider suspending stamp duty for most transactions for a period. I remained worried that it would look like tinkering and ultimately be ineffective. Ministers and officials were divided. Michael Portillo and John Maples were against, while Francis Maude and Bill Robinson were in favour. In the end we decided to go ahead with the package, as agreed with the building societies, and to raise the threshold for stamp duty (1 per cent on the value of a house) to £250,000 for nine months.

I was able to find the money for this measure because of the delay in the Stock Exchange's computerised dealing system, which meant that the abolition of stamp duty on shares had been postponed. So I could present the change as a switch between stamp duty on houses and equities. It was important to present it not as a macro-economic measure, but as a specific housing sector one designed to deal with its problems. On 18 December I decided to make the announcement the next day.

That evening Rosemary was giving a party in the State Room at No. 11 for various officials, journalists and MPs. Richard

Ryder, the Chief Whip, told Terry as he arrived for the party that he had discovered a number of important procedural problems, in particular that we would have to have a special Ways and Means resolution that would take up most of the day in the House. This would endanger the second day of the European debate, infuriating the Eurosceptics. Finally the procedure would also require MPs to be present at short notice on a Friday, which would annoy the rest of the Party.

After the reception we had to have a marathon session with Richard Ryder, Murdo Maclean, Private Secretary to successive Chief Whips, Conservative and Labour, officials from the Inland Revenue and Parliamentary Counsel. Richard Ryder opposed the measure because of the disruption to Government business, and we began to think about dropping it. It had been a close call, and if it was going to result in Parliamentary chaos it would completely lose its point. Richard Ryder went to bed, and we carried on. Eventually we thought we had found a way through by splitting the legislation into several parts. Parliamentary Counsel were exceedingly nervous, but thought it would be possible. We didn't finish the meeting until 2 a.m., and decided to proceed if no further problems emerged the following morning.

The next day at 8.45 a.m. I discussed the issue with the PM and Sarah Hogg and we were later joined by Chris Patten. We decided to go ahead that afternoon. The Inland Revenue then discovered some further technical problems at 9.15 a.m., but these were resolved. I had a final meeting with the Council of Mortgage Lenders later that morning.

In the afternoon, to a surprised House of Commons and press I announced the package, including the stamp duty element. The total rescue package put together by the building societies came to a supposed £750 million. It was no small measure. Its merit was that without further cost to the taxpayer it had leveraged in substantial money from the private sector to target an acute problem. It received a mixed reception. Conservative MPs warmly welcomed it, but commentators felt that although ingenious it was small in relation to the market, and probably, as I suspected, only amounted to tinkering. Only time would tell whether it would have an effect. It might not be quite enough, but what was the alternative?

The alternative, of course, was deep cuts in interest rates. I wholly accepted the need for that, but it simply was not possible.

German interest rates go up

I had originally hoped that we would reduce rates to about 10 per cent by the end of the year, but it had not proved possible.

However, the gap between the UK's base rate and the German Lombard rate had now fallen by almost 5.75 percentage points over the past year, which was remarkable. Although this was the most encouraging feature of our experience in the ERM, the room for manoeuvre in December now looked very small unless German rates fell. The *Financial Times* thought that by June next year short-term interest rates might only be half a point lower. And yet our real short-term rates (i.e., after inflation), at just under 5 per cent were still high. I was beginning to learn the hard way that the idea that there might indeed be a conflict between the external demands of the ERM and the needs of the domestic economy was not a remote one.

The difficulties that we were up against, not just in the housing market but more generally, were unexpectedly underlined by the decision of the Bundesbank to raise both the Lombard rate and the Discount rate by half a per cent to 7 per cent and 9.25 per cent. There was pressure on us to follow and this development, at a stroke, wiped out all hope of lower British interest rates in the near future. Indeed the reaction of the foreign exchange markets was an indicator of greater problems to come. Against that background the housing package now looked even less likely to succeed.

On Sunday 22 December I learned that the French were going to increase their rates to put themselves just above the Germans. It was to be announced at 8.30 a.m. the next day. The problem was exacerbated by the United States, which had cut rates by a full point. Alan Greenspan had rung on Friday to say they had to move because of the domestic weakness of the US economy, but they were ready and willing to intervene to support the dollar.

Lower American rates were particularly bad news for sterling because they would mean a weaker dollar and therefore a stronger Deutschmark, putting more pressure on the pound's position within the ERM. The French were angry at what they saw as a lack of international co-operation on the world economy, and the chances were that the Italians would also follow the French, leaving the pound even further exposed.

On Sunday evening I called a meeting at No. 11 with Terry Burns, Nigel Wicks and Ian Plenderleith from the Bank of England. We discussed between ourselves whether, in view of the conflicting pressures, we should explore whether the Germans wanted a realignment and whether that would deliver lower rates, but the general feeling was that this would not have much effect on German interest rates. We would need to persuade the Bundesbank that an even higher DM should be an alternative to raising rates. At one point I suggested we should perhaps indicate to the Germans that we would consider leaving the ERM. I said I wanted to use the next G7 Meeting to explore the possibility of a co-ordinated reduction in interest rates, but in the meantime I decided to talk to Pierre Bérégovoy.

The next morning, Monday 23 December, most of the country was thinking about Christmas, going to office parties and doing last-minute Christmas shopping as we tried to stave off the incipient crisis for the pound in the foreign exchange markets. The French franc, despite the rate increase, was back at the bottom of its band. Sterling interbank market rates were above 11 per cent. The Spanish also increased rates and the Bank of England thought the chances that we would avoid a rate increase no better than 30 per cent. That would have been catastrophic.

I was keen to see whether the French might perhaps accept a 6–8 per cent revaluation of the Deutschmark. I wondered whether this would give the Germans the excuse to lower interest rates to reflect the tightening of policy. If that didn't work, it seemed to me that, given the direness of the domestic situation, the question of whether putting up interest rates was really better than leaving the ERM should be asked.

I asked Terry whether officials could sound out the French about a realignment. He thought it was unlikely that the French would agree and was anxious about letting officials discuss such sensitive matters. He felt there was a risk the approach would be leaked with catastrophic consequences for sterling. Only an approach by myself to Bérégovoy would do. I did not believe Pierre would allow any conversation I had with him to leak. He and I got on well while he was Finance Minister and he continued to ring me up occasionally after he became Prime Minister. I trusted him more than any other French politician. He was a real friend to this country, always conscious of our position and never wanting to see us isolated. I decided to take the risk and telephone him to ask whether the revaluation of the Deutschmark upwards would lead to a similar revaluation of the Franc or whether a de facto devaluation would be accepted.

At 11.30 a.m. I spoke to Bérégovoy. He did not think a G7 Meeting would move the Germans, but he was prepared to have a smaller meeting with myself and Theo Waigel, the German Finance Minister. But the main point was that Bérégovoy was completely against a revaluation of the Deutschmark. 'Absolutely unthinkable' was his phrase. He said that if the mark were revalued the French franc would move along with it. I said I felt we were getting into a very difficult situation in Europe. The policy needs of different countries were opposed to each other. I would be willing to attend any meeting.

My phone call was then followed by a meeting with officials, including Robin Leigh-Pemberton, the Governor of the Bank of England, and Ian Plenderleith and Mervyn King, also from the Bank. The Governor was able to bring better news. At noon sterling was up and showing commendable steadiness. One-month interest rates, which had opened at 11.25 per cent were now 11.125 per cent, thanks to skilful dealing by the Bank. They thought it was now more likely that we would get through the immediate crisis without a rate increase.

I asked the Governor how long he thought the Germans would keep up rates. He thought possibly three months, but more likely six months. The professionals at the Bundesbank, aware of the international pressure, had wanted a smaller increase but the representatives of the Lander had insisted on a full half point. Professor Dr Helmut Schlesinger, the President of the Bundesbank, had listened to the central bankers at Basle, but had to be noncommittal in view of the attitude of the full Council. He thought if the Germans had known about the size of the US reduction they might have gone up by less. It all seemed to underline that we needed to understand each other's situations more thoroughly and to talk to each other, but my own doubts about whether we should be in the ERM, and so constrained, were beginning to grow.

That evening, on *Channel Four News*, I was asked about differences between myself and John Major. Naturally I denied them. Indeed, I wasn't aware that there were any serious ones then. But someone somewhere obviously thought otherwise.

We needed more international co-operation, but none of our international meetings, I have to say, contributed much towards easing our problems. Following my conversation with Bérégovoy a European G4 meeting – Waigel, Bérégovoy, Carli, the Italian Finance Minister, and myself – was arranged for 7 January 1992 in Paris. It was also hoped that it would help us to prepare a common European line for the G7 Meeting in January.

The meeting was planned in the greatest secrecy. I was flown to a French military base then taken by car to Paris, where I was to be transferred by boat to the Trésor. The secrecy was somewhat punctured when at the Place de la Concorde I was spotted by a British tourist who immediately whipped out his camera and photographed me getting on to the Trésor launch. Fortunately he did not sell his pictures to the *Sun* and start a run on sterling.

The Paris meeting, however, produced little beyond the familiar entrenched positions. I decided not to press for a German realignment, as I knew the French position, but instead to emphasise the problems that stemmed from high German rates. John Major had simultaneously written to Kohl in much the same vein. However, the Germans themselves raised the subject, though the French ruled it out. Sometimes I had the impression from the Germans that their rate increase resulted from their dislike of EMU and that expressions of concern from the French or ourselves just made them more determined. However, Schlesinger said he thought interest rates might have just peaked.

The G7 Meeting in Washington on the weekend of 24 January was even worse than the Paris one. There was a good presentation from Michel Camdessus Managing Director of the IMF, and a brief round-table discussion followed by a short dialogue on the Soviet Union. The rest of the time was literally spent arguing about the communiqué which, as always at international meetings, was stretched to cover several different positions. A cynic might have said we had spent several hours deciding to do nothing about the world economy and half an hour deciding to do nothing about the Soviet Union.

By the end of 1991, I had become increasingly convinced that the ERM was constraining my ability to have a monetary policy to accommodate economic recovery. The Treasury, myself included, had underestimated the sensitivity of the economy to interest rates. In part this was because the ratcheting up of interest rates had taken so long to have any effect on the economy. The recession was not just a result of the need to bring inflation down. The private sector, particularly households, had over-borrowed in the good times and now needed to retrench. The necessary adjustment of household balance sheets was bound to be painful. Stabilising asset prices, particularly the property market, and the return of confidence were important for sustained recovery.

When I told the party conference that Britain might soon have lower inflation than Germany, few realised that this was making our membership of the ERM increasingly unworkable. Rapid disinflation meant British rates should fall. If inflation in Britain was lower than in Germany, British interest rates needed to be lower than German rates, which was impossible inside the ERM. Instead, ERM membership embroiled me in sensitive financial diplomacy which yielded nothing positive, although it might have stopped things getting worse for the time being. Ironically, by internationalising monetary policy, the ERM created disputes between members which would have disappeared if countries had been free to pursue their own policies. These disputes became even more tense as the negotiations over the Maastricht Treaty intensified.

7

The 1992 Budget and the General Election

Lord, may my words be ever soft and low for I may have to eat them.

The Politician's Prayer, *quoted by former Congressman Mo Udall*

F rom the moment John Major became Prime Minister the imminence of the General Election dominated Ministers and newspapers alike. When John Major entered No. 10 there were only eighteen months until the last possible date on which an Election could be called, so time was pressing on. On subjects such as the Poll Tax we knew we had to sort out our policy well in advance of the Election. At other times the prospect of the Election seemed like a race against the economy. The recession had started almost on the very day that John Major became Prime Minister and I became Chancellor. As the recession worsened, anxiety about how long it could last, and when it would end, increased. For the whole of 1991 the pressure on me, from both the Prime Minister and Central Office, to talk up the economy was never far away.

When to hold the Election?

At the beginning of October 1990 the Conservative Party, under

Mrs Thatcher, was well behind Labour in the polls. Undoubtedly one factor that led MPs to vote against her was the belief that she could not win the Election. Sadly, I have to say that to this day I think that belief was right. Mrs Thatcher seldom let the mask slip, but even she, I suspect, sometimes despaired. I remember her at the end of one Cabinet meeting commenting to somebody talking about his post-Election plans, 'After the Election none of us may be here.'

John Major's arrival at No. 10 caused a sharp rise in Conservative support. From then on sometimes we were marginally ahead of Labour, and sometimes behind, but the gap narrowed. When would be the best time for the Prime Minister to call the Election? Michael Heseltine subsequently said that if he had won the election for leader he would have called a General Election immediately. Perhaps, with his strong personality and flair, such a bold move would have worked. As Prime Minister, he would have been an even stronger campaigner than he was as a member of a team and he had great confidence in his own abilities as a communicator. One of the Whips told me that after the leadership election, Michael had gone into the Whips' Office and explained how he would have called the Election, announcing, 'I can electrify this country'.

That may have been true, but it would not have been right for John Major, and I don't think he seriously considered it. The timing remained difficult. Some deep thought was given to the idea of an Election in autumn 1991. Other voices had even suggested a 'khaki election' in the spring of 1991 in the glow of the successful British campaign in the Gulf War. John was adamant that he did not want to fight an Election on the back of a war. I think he found this distasteful and I respected him for that.

It was not an easy decision for John, especially as our support fell back and at times it looked as though he had missed his opportunity. To his credit, however, he never succumbed to doubts and seemed quite comfortable playing a waiting game.

This suited me, as I was in favour of putting off the Election, if necessary, until the last possible day. I felt the country would grow to like and respect the new Prime Minister the longer they could compare him with Neil Kinnock. I also thought the economy was likely to improve the longer we waited. It did, but barely perceptibly. The indicators of confidence improved a little from a low base, but people were reluctant to recognise what was happening and there was still plenty of gloom around.

In the end John Major decided to go to the limit, but not quite. He felt that if he went to the wire, it could look as though he was afraid to face the electorate and there would be an impression of clinging to power. When he did call the Election, for 16 March, we were behind in the polls, and he was the first Prime minister to call an Election voluntarily while behind in the polls.

Planning the campaign

Douglas Hurd, Ken Clarke, Michael Heseltine, Chris Patten, Sarah Hogg and myself were formed into a Committee called the 'A team' to consider ideas for the Manifesto. We had our first meeting on 9 January. It was doubtful whether the A Team achieved very much and there were plenty of arguments, not least between myself and Michael Heseltine over his proposals for an English Development Corporation.

We would never have got anywhere had not Sarah Hogg wisely decided to take matters into her own hands. She put herself in charge of writing the Manifesto after she had become fed up with the disagreements, which included that between Malcolm Rifkind, myself and the Prime Minister, over different forms of privatisation for British Rail. The Manifesto that Sarah produced eventually was too long, some 27,000 words, and lacked shape, but it was full of policy ideas. Indeed, there were too many of them, and some were rather minor, such as the Hedgerows' Inspectorate!

The Conservatives: the low tax party?

I had no doubt that the big idea had to be tax. We were committed to reducing income tax, while Labour would undoubtedly increase it.

From November 1990 I had been convinced that the key to winning the Election was the issue of tax and spending. It was certainly not an original thought. I had been in the Treasury in 1987, in the run-up to the Election that year, and I had seen how Nigel Lawson had destroyed Labour by painting them as the high-tax, high-spending party. There was nothing unfair about it. It was true and so it worked.

There was no reason why the same tactics shouldn't be applied during the 1992 Election. Labour hadn't changed and were wide open to attack. My first problem, however, was with colleagues. I was well aware that several senior people in the Cabinet were far from being Thatcherites, and I discovered that they were not income tax cutters. Douglas Hurd, Chris Patten, Ken Clarke and John Major had a great deal of sympathy with the view that a high-spending government equalled a compassionate government.

Shortly after John had become Prime Minister, I had been summoned to a meeting at No. 10 attended by Douglas Hurd, Chris Patten and Sarah Hogg as well as the Prime Minister. Ostensibly the purpose of the meeting was to discuss preparation for the Election, the Manifesto, and tactics leading up to the Election. It was one of the first meetings of John Major's premiership and I was taken aback when the discussion suddenly turned to the question of whether the Conservative Party should abandon its long-term commitment to cut the basic rate of income tax to 20 pence in the pound. John floated the idea and sounded as though he wanted to ditch the commitment and Chris Patten was also sympathetic, but the most vociferous was Douglas Hurd. 'My constituents aren't interested in income tax cuts. They are more interested in good public services, and they would be prepared to pay more tax for it.' The others all agreed. I was staggered. Neil Kinnock or John Smith could not have put it more clearly.

Although I was taken aback by John Major's suggestion, I should not have been so astonished. When he was Chief Secretary and I was Financial Secretary he had privately been opposed to Nigel Lawson's tax cuts in his 1988 Budget. He never said so at any meetings of Ministers, but he made it clear to me that he thought money should be spent on improving services rather than on giving tax cuts. He was strongly opposed to the reduction in the top rate of tax from 60 per cent to 40 per cent. He sounded me out on this and tried to get me to join him in an attempt to persuade Nigel to change his mind, but I firmly supported Nigel's reductions. On another occasion, detailed in Mrs Thatcher's memoirs, John Major had challenged Mrs Thatcher as to whether the British public didn't prefer better public services than tax cuts. She recounts that she 'did not treat him or his arguments kindly.'

So it was not a complete surprise that John Major had returned to the charge. In a fairly lighthearted way I said that if they abandoned the pledge to cut income tax they would have to find a new Chancellor of the Exchequer. I was not prepared to drop a pledge that Mrs Thatcher and Nigel Lawson had repeatedly made. I didn't feel I was making much progress with my argument, but I then went on to make a point that I knew was much more likely to persuade the Prime Minister. I said that we risked dividing the Party. The pledge to carry on cutting the basic rate of income tax had been repeated so many times by every backbench MP in his constituency that they were committed to it. For the leadership to drop it now would cause a major division in the Party. Furthermore, I said that cutting income tax and painting Labour as the party of high spending and high taxation was the way to win the Election.

Somewhat unsatisfactorily this issue was not resolved at the meeting, but I subsequently spent some time with Chris Patten convincing him that another campaign on taxes and spending was our best hope for the Election. I also had discussions with Maurice Saatchi on the subject. In general I am not a great admirer of spin doctors and PR men in politics. It seems to me that their contribution is somewhat exaggerated, not least by their own propaganda. They don't understand the issues, and because they don't really want to understand the issues they try to make the policy correspond to the presentation they want rather than the other way around. Maurice was a different sort of spin doctor, who understood that the presentation had to follow policy. And he was extremely keen to make tax and spending the central point of the Election campaign.

One problem was that other Ministers thought that the Election could be fought on a wide range of issues. Each Minister thought that his Department was the most important one. I never changed in my conviction that there was only one issue that was going to matter in this Election, and that was taxation.

Preparation for the 1992 Budget

I had more time to prepare the Budget in 1992 than in 1991, but the planning was complicated by the imminence of the Election. Right up to the very day of the Budget I did not know for certain the date of the Election, though it was always clear that the Budget measures were unlikely to be enacted in a Finance Bill which would be completed before the General Election.

The economic background to the Budget was not encouraging. It was still a case of waiting for the dawn that never came. Even by February 1992 there was little sign of the recovery that I had suggested would arrive in late 1991. Impatient with my increasingly circumlocutory utterances, the PM had at one point announced that the recovery had started, but there was little evidence for it and he was lucky that in the pre-electoral excitement his remarks were not subject to more criticism. GDP had only levelled off in the second half of 1991, and in the fourth quarter of the year was at much the same level as in the second quarter.

When I was questioned at a meeting of the National Economic Development Council (NEDC) in January about the vanishing recovery and the errors of the forecasts, I observed in my reply, 'The policy would not have been different had we known the outcome.' I was puzzled at the reaction to this remark. It reinforced my view that in general commentators did not understand that forecasts were not the basis for the making of economic policy. We were not attempting to 'steer' or to 'fine tune', let alone to 'manage' the economy through its ups and downs. Interest rates obviously could not have been different as long as we remained within the ERM. That left fiscal policy, where we were allowing the automatic stabilisers to operate. But we certainly could not have had an additional fiscal stimulus, even if we had known the economy was going to linger in the doldrums for such a long time.

On the other hand inflation had continued to come down further than expected. Inflation by February 1992 on the headline measure had fallen to 4.1 per cent and on the underlying measure to 5.6 per cent. My expectation was that the headline rate would be below 4 per cent by the end of the year.

All the forces that should have made for recovery were in place: the automatic fiscal stabilisers, lower inflation, a levelling off in the rundown of stocks, and the fall in interest rates, which were now down to 10.5 per cent. As a result of falls in interest rates, net disposable income for a typical family with a £30,000 mortgage had risen by over 15 per cent since October 1990, but these positive influences continued to be more than offset by conditions in the housing market. The huge build-up in personal debt in the late 1980s had been followed by a sharp retrenchment, which was persistent throughout 1991.

Alan Greenspan phoned me on 6 January and said because of the overhang of household debt in the United States he thought there would be no growth in the next two quarters. But at least he was able to cut his interest rates. We could not. Instead of the usual problem of a shortage of savings, people were saving too much. Our problem was that although we were in much the same situation as the United States, we were linked by policy to Europe, where the circumstances were very different.

The failure of the recovery to take hold in the second half of 1991 was also part of a weakening of activity in many of the major industrialised countries. I was struck at the G7 meeting how some other countries had similar experiences. Canada in particular had, like ourselves, experienced the appearance of a start to recovery in the autumn but it then petered out. In the United States figures for retail sales were the worst for twenty years. In Continental Europe output was weakening and Germany had formally moved into recession after two quarters in succession of falling growth. The world recession had been led by the English-speaking world and Scandinavia and peripheral Europe: in addition to ourselves, the United States, Canada, New

Zealand, Australia, Sweden and Switzerland and now Germany were all in recession.

The PSBR increases yet again

Another consequence of the delayed recovery was a further deterioration of the public finances. The actual out-turn for the PSBR for the current year was now expected to be £13.8 billion, 2.25 per cent of GDP, compared with the £7.9 billion forecast a year earlier. This was likely to be a shock to the financial markets, particularly when it followed four years of debt repayments. For the year ahead, 1992/93, Treasury officials expected that the PSBR would probably be around £30 billion.

It should be added that, even with this increase, the borrowing requirement was still expected to be lower than Germany's and half the level reached in the recession of the 1970s. Our policy still remained, and crucially so, to balance the Budget over the cycle. Just as the surpluses of the late 1980s reflected the strength and dramatic growth of the economy then, so the move into deficit reflected the subsequent recession. Thus a substantial move into deficit was to be expected and the Budget, it was believed, would return to balance as activity recovered, though this process would obviously take time because of the lagged impact of the recession on both revenue and expenditure. Looking further ahead it was expected that the PSBR would peak at 4.75 per cent of GDP in 1993/94 but then decline gradually to 1 per cent of GDP in 1996/97. Nigel Lawson had defined a 'deficit of around 1 per cent of GDP' as the equivalent of a balanced Budget, in the modern world: a world of growth and inflation, albeit low inflation.

At our special pre-Budget Chevening meeting with Ministers and senior officials on the weekend of 10 January there was discussion about how to interpret the balanced Budget rule over a cycle. There were various interpretations. The tightest was that surpluses in the boom years should equal the sum of deficits in recession. But all the Ministers – Portillo, Maude, Maples and Shephard – agreed that it was sufficient to argue that when output corresponded to the longer-term growth rate then at that point the Budget should be in balance. Robert Culpin, Head of Fiscal Policy, tartly observed that the rule itself was probably less important than sticking to it.

There was considerable argument between myself and Bill Robinson on the one hand and officials on the other about the appropriate level of the PSBR it was right to forecast for 1992/93. Officials believed that the out turn for 1992/93 would be about £32 billion while Bill and I found it difficult to believe that, if the recovery that the Treasury continued to forecast took place, the PSBR could be anything like as high as that, even after making allowances for the timelags. The PSBR is the residual item between two much larger numbers for expenditure and taxation, and as such is liable to huge error, as usually happens. Bill and I were genuinely convinced we had a good case.

The Treasury were forecasting that growth would be almost 2 per cent a year to the second half of 1992 and would be close to 3 per cent per annum by the middle of 1993. It was also noticeable that outside forecasters were looking towards a lower PSBR figure than the Treasury. We discussed this at great length and also with the PM, who was shocked by the figures and thought that the forecasts should not be much more than £20 billion.

Treasury officials, I think, were nervous that they would have to justify whatever figure was chosen to John Smith if he became Chancellor after the Election. The disputes between the Treasury and myself at one point became quite acrimonious. In the end we agreed to publish a figure of £28 billion, 4.5 per cent of GDP, which was £2–3 billion lower than the central case put forward by officials. This was the only occasion during my time as Chancellor that I ever insisted on substituting my own judgement for a forecast by officials. As Chancellor John Major frequently altered the forecasts for inflation and growth or exports that were put to him by officials. I did so only once – and on that one occasion was proved wrong.

The prior decision to be taken was whether we could afford tax cuts at all in this Budget. Opinions at Chevening were divided. Despite the deterioration in the public finances, I was of the opinion that it was acceptable to have a small discretionary fiscal relaxation and I was determined to have one, despite some

Treasury misgivings. It was also important that the Budget was helpful to industry, so the theme was to be 'a Budget for recovery'. But what was the best way of helping industry? Some people advocated increases in capital allowances. I was less attracted to measures to boost investment than to measures that would cut industry's costs and help it to survive.

During this period industry was preparing to deal with the consequences of the change-over from locally set business rates to the nationally determined uniform business rate. Although I was confident that in the longer term the uniform business rate would help industry, the transition was awkward in parts of the country and for certain sectors. It was going to produce both winners and losers, and some companies would experience an increase in their rates bill. By means of a grant from the Treasury into what was called the Non-Domestic Rates Pool, I managed to minimise the losses of the losers and increase somewhat the gains of the winners to ensure that no business would face an increase in its rates bill greater than the rate of inflation: some businesses had reductions of up to 27 per cent in their bills. This measure, though thinly spread, helped some 900,000 business premises throughout the country.

Nigel Lawson had developed the admirable habit of abolishing a tax in each of his Budgets. I was keen to find a candidate for abolition in 1992 and found one surprisingly inexpensive candidate: inheritance tax on family businesses. There had always been partial reliefs from inheritance tax for family and private businesses and over the years these had been progressively increased, so much so that I found the total abolition of inheritance tax on business assets – that is, shareholdings over 25 per cent in private companies – cost only £25 million. I was surprised that it was so cheap to ensure that family businesses could pass from one generation to another without the business being broken up.

Having spent much of my life before politics working for Rothschild's, I had a strong sense of the value and the ethos of medium-sized private businesses. A strong economy benefits from strong public companies, but there is also a role for the medium-sized private business that may be sometimes paternalistic but may also take a longer-term view than shareholder-driven public companies.

I had one other proposal for removing a provision from previous Finance Acts that I knew would not go down so well with Conservative backbenchers. The Business Expansion scheme had become a much loved relief for higher-rate taxpayers to invest in smaller companies. Schemes for utilising the relief had grown ever more ingenious and more and more money had gone into wine bars and stud farms. I felt the relief no longer justified its existence. It had done a useful job in highlighting the opportunities in smaller companies and in helping to bring into existence a British venture capital industry, but its task was essentially done.

The other measure which I had in mind to help industry was to halve the discriminatory tax on motor cars known as Car Tax, which had been introduced in 1973 to bridge the gap between VAT and the old higher rate of purchase tax that it replaced. On the average car the tax could amount to as much as £400. Ever since I had been a Minister in the DTI responsible for the motor industry and the struggling British Leyland, I had been aware of the resentment towards this tax. And, in truth, there was no fiscal justification for a tax to be levied on one item of consumer spending alone.

The Prime Minister was eager to have extra help for pensioners in the Budget. I was not at all in favour of expenditure measures in the Budget, which under our still unreformed non-unified system was meant to be only about taxation and not about spending, which would be increased in the autumn. However, in the end I had to agree there should be further increases in income support for poorer pensioners, and payments of £2 extra for single pensioners and £3 for pensioner couples. But I insisted that this should be done within existing public expenditure plans.

Although I was prepared to see a small discretionary reduction in taxation it was plainly necessary to raise some taxes in order to pay for the reductions in business rates and the halving of Car Tax. I managed to raise over £1 billion by increasing the duties on cigarettes by 10 per cent and on leaded petrol by 7.5 per cent and by increasing vehicle excise duties by 10 per cent.

The move to a unified Budget

I was keen that the 1992 Budget should be the occasion for what I saw as one long overdue reform. In Britain we had a strange fiscal practice whereby the income and expenditure parts of the country's Budget were considered separately. Tax was dealt with in the Budget in March and public spending in the Autumn Statement announced at the beginning of November. Many people had criticised this uniquely British way of doing things. Elsewhere in the world and indeed in the private sector the meaning of the word Budget is perfectly clear: it is a schedule showing where the money is coming from and where it is going to be spent.

In my view our system was not only illogical but also had a number of highly undesirable consequences. It could not be right to consider expenditure proposals completely unrelated to income, and thus the system, I believed, tended to encourage unrealistic expectations on expenditure. I also felt that the announcement of tax proposals in isolation created a tremendous pressure for gimmicks and innovative special tax reliefs. I wanted to avoid the mass of minor tax changes that were now necessary and it would be far better to have a Budget with fewer changes. The old system had contributed to the extraordinarily complex tax system that we had build up over the years.

I had first discussed the need to bring the two parts of the Budget together with Peter Middleton and Treasury officials shortly after I became Chancellor. But in the rush to frame the 1991 Budget there was hardly time for such radical measures.

When I returned to the issue in late 1991 and early 1992, I was slightly surprised that Treasury officials were so hostile to the idea. Part of their concern was over the sheer burden of work that would fall on a relatively small number of officials in a crowded period of the year, but they also feared that the Treasury's power and position within Whitehall would be very much weakened and that taxation would become a subject for collective Ministerial discussion.

Regarding the fiscal consequences of the proposed reform, one Treasury view was that borrowing would be lower but that spending and taxes would both be higher. The argument was that Ministers would prefer higher spending plus higher taxes to any other outcome that would leave the PSBR unaffected. Treasury officials also knew that by negotiating spending separately they had sometimes been able to frighten Ministerial colleagues with threats of consequential tax increases to come later in the spring.

Despite the Treasury's opposition, I pressed on with the idea and received strong support from the Prime Minister, who had a number of ideas of his own for further reform, such as dividing the accounts into capital and current. In the end we decided to press ahead, but in view of the work required, to defer the first unified Budget until 1993.

This decision meant that the March 1993 Budget was expected to be the last spring Budget. From then on the annual budget would be in December, covering not just taxation but also public spending. There would be a White Budget in December, when indirect taxes would be implemented, and other taxes would be introduced from 1 April. Roy Jenkins once made an observation to the effect that it is more difficult for a Chancellor of the Exchequer than other Ministers to leave a lasting impact on history since their much prized fiscal reforms tend to be wiped out by their successors, like sandcastles by an incoming tide. When I introduced this change I did believe it was one likely to last, not least because it was so rooted in common sense. As long as it worked for the first few years, I thought its appeal would be irresistible. It fell to Kenneth Clarke to deliver the first unified Budget and, from what I learned from Treasury officials, the new system worked well and was even welcomed by them. Although it continued for the Budgets of 1994, 1995 and 1996, Gordon Brown, for short-term internal Labour Party reasons, decided to return to the system of separating spending and taxation. I rather suspect one day another Chancellor will revert to my idea.

Costing Labour's Programme

Groundwork for the Election was being done at the same time as preparations for the Budget. There was an immense task

ahead in carrying out the costing of Labour's programme. I had
the advantage of having seen how Nigel Lawson had organised
and masterminded the costing of Labour's programme before the
1987 General Election. Andrew Tyrie, who had done the exercise
in 1987, was no longer formally a paid advisor but was able to
give guidance to Warwick Lightfoot, the special advisor in charge
of the operation this time.

There was the delicate issue of the sort of work it was proper
to ask civil servants to do, but guidelines had been laid down and
confirmed by Sir Robin Butler from the previous exercise. It had
been agreed that if the political advisors did the work of identifying Labour's pledges it was quite proper to ask an individual
civil servant in a particular section of the Treasury to cost a
policy. Civil servants were, after all, costing policy options all the
time.

The first task was to identify Labour's programme before
adding up all the pledges and costing them as a whole. Labour
were wide open to attack. For the last four years their frontbench
spokesmen had travelled the country making speeches and
appearing on TV and radio, making promises of increased spending in response to different interest groups. There was a huge list
of promises made by spokesmen all over the country, but Labour
tried to deny that such speeches amounted to pledges and argued
that its programme was only what was to be contained in its
Manifesto. But what were these promises, then? Labour maintained they were merely 'aspirations'.

After the General Election, and indeed during it, Labour complained that it had been misrepresented in a dishonest campaign
and had been cheated in the Election. But this was not sustainable.
Labour had been quite prepared to let audiences and pressure
groups believe that promises and speeches were exactly what they
appeared to be. It was entirely legitimate to cost Labour's programme in this way.

Warwick Lightfoot, under the supervision of David Mellor, the
Chief Secretary, set about the immense task of going through all
the speeches and broadcasts of Labour frontbench spokesmen
and seeing what promises they had made. Sometimes we had to
make various assumptions about the nature of the pledge and its

precise meaning. No pledge was included unless it had been uttered as an apparently firm commitment. If any assumptions had to be made, they were specified.

When all the pledges had been assembled, they were individually costed and then listed together with the relevant dates and places. This was then published by Conservative Central Office as *Labour's Programme*. This booklet was originally launched with a press conference I chaired on 21 June 1991. The total cost of Labour's pledges turned out to be £35 billion, the equivalent of 10 pence on the basic rate of income tax. David Mellor revised it to £37 billion, having found various other pledges. Later in the Election I recalculated it as £38 billion.

One of Labour's mistakes was to have published so many long-winded policy documents between 1987 and 1992. They were packed full of expensive pledges and Central Office had an easy task adding them up. One of the things that made the exercise work so well was that Labour spokesmen had repeatedly been trapped into saying that such-and-such an item of spending was a 'priority', or 'first-term commitment'. This enabled Central Office to show that the Beckett Rule (named after Margaret Beckett) – that only increases in pensions and child benefit were priorities – was a sham.

When Labour published their Manifesto it demonstrated how justified our Treasury exercise was. Nearly all the pledges we had costed were included. I offered to adjust the figures if John Smith withdrew any of the pledges.

Labour's reaction was one of fury, but this was merely the beginning. I had discussed what we would do next with Maurice Saatchi and Chris Patten. Maurice had worked up a number of designs for posters, and after looking at several alternatives it was decided that the most effective was the tax bombshell. This poster had a crimson background dominated with the silhouette of a bomb that had the figure £1,250 painted on it. This, we had calculated, was the cost per household of Labour's spending pledges.

The war of the posters started several weeks in advance of the General Election. Indeed it was one of the signs that the Election was imminent and the political battle was hotting up. The first tax bombshell poster was unveiled by Chris Patten and myself in front of a battery of TV and newspaper cameras.

Some people have wondered how effective such posters are. My own experience is that people certainly notice them and they were placed at a surprising number of prominent sites in towns up and down the country. But posters are only one part of an over-all campaign, raising a theme that is repeated in similar advertisements in the newspapers and also in speeches and broad-casts. Posters are just one way of reminding the public what your message is. Labour obviously thought a poster was an effective weapon, because they responded in kind with their own cam-paign. I was startled one morning to find a picture of myself with a mask, disguised as 'VATman', across every national newspaper.

Until that moment I had no idea my mouth and chubby lower jaw were regarded as so distinctive. Indeed, I was astonished that people recognised it as me. Some people thought the poster was rather personal, but I can't say that it worried me. I was amused by it, and wrote to Peter Mandelson asking if I could have a poster. Sadly he never replied, and to this day I do not have one.

Last-minute decisions on the Budget

The final touches were now being put to the Budget. As is often the case, the biggest decisions still had to be taken. To frame a Budget in a pre-Election period is a difficult task for any Chancellor, and this was particularly the case in the circum-stances of 1992. Roy Jenkins was later to write, 'No Chancellor must ever be put in this position again.' The pressures were intense. Many on the right of the Parliamentary Party, together with papers such as the *Daily Express*, were clamouring for large tax cuts. At the very least the Party was looking for some-thing to boost their chances at the Election. But the public, I believed, would react badly to anything that appeared cynical and irresponsible.

As normal, we had the Budget Cabinet on 20 February. By that time many of the smaller decisions had indeed been taken, but there was still time to decide whether or not to cut income tax or whether there should be any overall tax cuts. Kenneth Baker argued for 2 pence off income tax, which was not surprising. He is a gifted and inspired politician, but he is always in favour of cutting taxes and spending more money and against what he calls 'Treasury parsimony'. Some Cabinet Ministers argued against any tax cuts at all, but they were in a small minority. I outlined the background to the economy, but did not say much beyond that. In fact I had long ago come to the conclusion that there had to be some relatively modest tax cuts to demonstrate our intention for the longer term. But could this be done in a way that was not too expensive and not too blatant?

Some colleagues favoured an increase in personal allowances, which would remove many of the lower paid from paying tax, but it had little visibility compared with a reduction in the basic rate of income tax. Experience showed that when allowances are increased, the beneficiaries were rarely aware of it. A penny off would certainly be visible, but for many of the electorate it would strike the wrong note.

But my mind was turning towards a more novel option which was not discussed at Cabinet, and which could be a big surprise. This was the idea of a new rate of income tax, a reduced rate band, so that a taxpayer would only pay 20 pence on the first £2,000 of income. It would also mean that four million low-paid people would pay tax at only 20 pence in the pound. For those taxpayers it would be more valuable than a penny off the basic rate, and a significant reduction in the tax burden. It also had the added attraction that it had been Labour policy as well. Labour, I believed, would face an impossible choice: to agree with us and have to raise taxes higher to pay for their commitments, or to reject it, thus revealing that their rhetoric about helping the low-paid was empty.

It is true that some tax specialists did not like the idea of a reduced rate band. It did not give as much help to the poor as an increase in allowances and it was said to be administratively complex. I was not impressed by these arguments. I had always doubted whether the two-band income tax structure introduced by Nigel Lawson could last for ever. It is interesting that my successor, Ken Clarke, maintained the 20 pence band as did Gordon

Brown, until he performed a similar trick of his own and replaced it with a 10 pence band.

John Smith and Neil Kinnock had made it clear that they were opposed to reductions in the basic rate of income tax and would vote against a cut. But what would be their reaction to a measure that would give considerable advantage to the lower paid, even if it were also of some limited benefit to all taxpayers?

There was a further attraction in the idea of the 20 pence band. It opened up a second route for moving towards the 20 pence basic rate. On the one hand, the tax band at which the 20 pence rate applied could be widened in future years; on the other hand the 25 pence rate might be cut. It was a step-by-step approach that could reduce the costs of marginal progress towards the 20 pence target in future years. By this time the Prime Minister, Hurd and Patten had all accepted my insistence that we would maintain a 20 pence basic rate as a long-term objective of the Conservative Party. I debated the idea of the 20 pence rate within a restricted group of advisors. Alastair Ross Goobey was one of its early supporters. The final decision to go for the reduced rate band was not made until the last possible moment.

The overall 'give-away' in the Budget was £1.5 billion for 1992/93, an amount equal to less than 0.25 per cent of GDP. Although that would still offend some purists, it was very much less than the markets were expecting. I was sure the markets would be more interested for once in the political consequences of the Budget and whether it would help us win the Election. If it did that without being irresponsible, it would win the markets' approval.

Once the decision on the reduced rate band had been made, I was extremely worried that it might leak. The only discussions I had had were with the PM and very tentatively with Chris Patten, but news of these matters tended to spread. On this occasion surprise was essential if we were to reap the full benefits.

One story about a reduced rate band by Bruce Anderson appeared in the *Sunday Express*. At first I thought this might have ruined the Budget presentation, but no other paper followed it up. Whether Bruce's story was a leak or intelligent guesswork, I never discovered.

On Tuesday 25 February the PM had a big wobble about the Budget. At a meeting of backbenchers some had argued that tax cuts were now less of a priority and they were more worried about the public finances. The PM began to get cold feet about the Budget, the 20 pence tax band, and the reduction in car duty. I might have been more impressed if I thought it was a genuine concern with the deficit rather than anxiety to avoid a rebellion by backbenchers. It was now only a fortnight until the Budget and it was far too late to alter the arithmetic and the big decisions.

Fortunately he calmed down, but only after he had his own way in getting an expenditure package for poorer pensioners.

The Budget speech: Kinnock flounders

Budget day was fixed for 10 March. It was a strange experience, solemnly presenting a Budget in the usual way, even though there was a very real possibility it might never be enacted. There was intense excitement and speculation about its contents. At that time it was not certain whether the Prime Minister would go to the end of the Parliament or somewhat sooner or call the Election immediately after the Budget. No matter: I knew, and everyone knew, that the Budget was the send-off for the General Election campaign.

I began the speech with the announcement of the unified Budget, and that in 1993 there would be two Budgets. That took everyone by surprise, but was well received.

There was quite a lot of raucous laughter when I announced that the Budget was a 'Budget for Recovery'. I pointed to the delayed recovery that had also been experienced in North America. Yet again most forecasters, not just the UK Treasury, still foresaw the resumption of growth in 1992, and growth in the year to the second half of 1992 was now expected to be almost 2 per cent followed by 'more rapid growth as the recovery gains momentum'. This was received sceptically by the House. No one was unkind enough to point out that a year before I had forecast

growth of 2 per cent over the twelve months to the first half of
1992 followed by faster growth as the economy recovered further.
It was almost the same words, only the 2 per cent growth had
moved a further six months away. It was always six months away.
On inflation I forecast that it would fall decisively below 4 per
cent by the end of the year. That was more optimistic than the
Autumn Statement, and was to be proved correct, falling below 3
per cent. For mid-1993 I said it would be close to 3 per cent and
it turned out to be below 2 per cent. So on one front my forecasts
were far too pessimistic, though on the other hand they were too
optimistic again on growth.

But the interest in the speech was not in economic forecasts. No
one thought that forecasts won any votes. What everyone was
waiting for was the announcement on income tax.

I left the announcement of the income tax changes for the end,
as is usual in the Budget speech. When I said that there would be
no change in the basic rate of income tax I could sense the disappointment of Conservative backbenchers behind me and I could
see smiles on the face of Opposition Members.

But when I announced the lower rate band, I could see frantic
conversations taking place between Neil Kinnock and John Smith,
who were plainly very discomfited and confused. When I sat
down there were strong cheers and waving of Order Papers from
Government backbenchers. It was clear from Neil Kinnock's reply
to the speech that he had not anticipated the announcement and
was completely at a loss how to respond, speaking as though
there had been a basic rate cut. After Bruce's article in the *Sunday
Express*, I was surprised he had not prepared any comments on a
reduced rate band. As it was, he ignored the most important
measure in the Budget Speech and was unable to answer
Conservative MPs' questions whether he was for or against it.
Later that day Smith did announce that they would vote against
it, but in the Commons Kinnock's dithering was there for everyone to see.

My purpose was not just to score a Parliamentary debating
point, but to emphasise the different attitudes of the Parties to
tax. That was the purpose of the Budget.

Philip Gould, the marketing and advertising guru and later an advisor to Tony Blair, at that time was working closely with Kinnock and Smith. In his book *The Unfinished Revolution* he wrote: 'In a brilliant move just before the campaign started, the Tories destroyed us in the Budget of Tuesday 10th March . . . By introducing a 20 pence band, Lamont had presented us with an impossible dilemma. The meeting in the Shadow Cabinet room went on until the early hours of the morning, but could find no escape.' Gould quoted from his diary for Budget day: 'By the time Lamont got to tax David Hill and I were pacing nervously at the back of the Shadow Cabinet room, waiting for the knock-out blow. I was saying: "2p (tax cut). It's got to be 2p." David said: "No way. They're not going to do it." And then at the end, when there had been absolutely nothing, David said to me, "You're right, it must be 2p." But Lamont announced: "There is going to be no cut in the basic rate of income tax. We are going to introduce a 20 pence band." John Eatwell, who had been glued to the screen in silence throughout, looked up, flung his papers over the table and said, "We can't respond to that. That's it. It's all over. We have got no money to spend. Neil's got no speech."' Gould comments in his book: 'And he was right. The Budget totally undermined our strategy. The Tories had looked at our figures, and worked out that the way to kill us off on tax was a 20p band. No one had any idea how to respond. The room was in chaos.'

Political reaction

The excited headlines in the press the next day tended to emphasise the wrong-footing of Labour: 'Lamont ambushes Labour', *Daily Mail*; 'Norman's box of goodies has Labour reeling': *Sun*; 'Lamont steels Labour's thunder', *Financial Times*. Only the *Express* was simpler: 'Tax cuts for all'.

The *Daily Express* was one of the papers that thought the Budget could have delivered larger tax cuts: 'The Chancellor did not perhaps deliver the Budget of every tax cutter's dream.' However, most newspapers thought the Budget politically well judged. The *Daily Mail* in its front page story wrote: 'In an

audacious yet shrewd political Budget, Chancellor Norman
Lamont yesterday lifted Tory Party morale to fighting fitness on
the eve of the General Election . . . He did it by trumping all
Labour's aces . . . leaving them with virtually no cards to play.'

Matthew Parris in the *The Times* was more balanced: 'It was
68 minutes of boredom, and 2 minutes of magic, or was it con-
juring?' Sam Brittan in the *Financial Times* reacted against the
alleged 'cleverness' of the budget and sarcastically wrote:
'Promising to enact the whole of Labour's manifesto would have
been a cleverer move still.'

Reaction to the increased PSBR

What most concerned me was not just the political reaction, but
also the response to the announcement of the large PSBR figures.
The markets took it in their stride. The FTSE 100 rose slightly, as
did the pound against the mark. On the other hand, the long-
dated gilt fell slightly. But generally, as I expected, the markets
were more interested in whether the Budget would help the Tories
to win the Election, though that is not to say there was no concern about the PSBR figures.

Most of the broadsheets thought the Budget in the circumstances fairly responsible. The *Financial Times* commented: 'Mr
Lamont has presented a Budget that . . . possesses a number of
clever touches. He has in the end bribed the electorate much less
than some hoped and others feared. But the main reason for his
frugality, the UK's rapidly deteriorating fiscal position, should
give all observers pause.'

Some of the commentators pointed out that the Budget deficit
for the year after next, 1993/94, was expected to be even higher
than the £28 billion for the year ahead, and that the return to balance in 1996/97 was based on quite optimistic assumptions about
growth. The *Independent* wrote:

Although the new PSBR forecast of £28 billion is quite
high enough the Government can just about hang onto its
claim to be the Party of fiscal rectitude. A Budget deficit

which is 4.5% of GDP at the bottom of a recession is justifiable and is underpinned by the healthy underlying state of the public sector's finances. Nor will the charge quite stick that the Chancellor was borrowing to finance tax cuts. The total package of measures is worth the net Exchequer cost of £1.6 billion which is relatively little given the depressed state of the economy, let alone the temptations of electioneering. The Treasury can also claim that with net public sector capital asset formation, next year projected at about £30 billion, investment is still at a higher level than borrowing. By erring on the side of caution he may be blamed for doing too little, as was Roy Jenkins in 1970, if the Tories are defeated.

On balance his Budget should do the Government some political good, above all because he has made the case for tax cuts morally respectable while underlining the difference between the Tories and Labour on one of the few remaining issues which genuinely divide the Parties . . . He has also passed the test which we set him on Friday, which was to deliver a Budget which might have been the same if the Election was four years rather than four weeks away.

The Times wrote: 'The Cabinet has made him [the Chancellor] concede one spending increase after another in the past six months. Faced with that awesome £28 billion, he has rightly resisted any further excessive bribing of the electorate . . . Mr Lamont kept his fiscal credibility and cleverly avoided any reasonable accusation of Election bribery.'

The economic position after the Budget was perhaps most shrewdly, if chillingly summed up again by the *Financial Times*: 'Should growth prove to be as constrained by ERM membership as some fear, tax increases are inevitable. That possibility depends on the British consumer on the one hand, and the German wage bargainer on the other. The Chancellor insisted that recovery is dependent on the behaviour of the private sector. He is right, but the most important private sector is the German, and the institution that will channel its response is the Bundesbank'. That was the reality, which few appreciated.

Election date announced, Parliament dissolved

The next day, 11 March, there was a short Cabinet meeting. Everyone seemed pleased by the reaction to the Budget. Then the Prime Minister told Ministers the General Election was to be on 9 April and Parliament was to be dissolved on 16 March. He went straight from Cabinet to Buckingham Palace to see the Queen.

I felt a curious sense of anti-climax after the Budget. The preparation had been as hard work as ever. All the different press releases for the hundreds of tax changes had been prepared as usual. Normally after a Budget there would be meetings with interested parties, a Budget debate and eventually a Finance Bill to be taken through the House by the Chief Secretary and the Financial Secretary. This time, the day after the Budget the House of Commons was virtually deserted as everyone was preparing for the Election. The Finance Bill proper, if there was one, would not come until after the Election. In the meantime the non-controversial items that could be agreed with Labour could be passed through the House. The Budget Debate was limited to two days. I made the closing speech on the Thursday instead of the Monday in reply to Tony Blair, then Shadow Employment Spokesman, who tried to make out in his speech that the Budget had not been well received.

At one point John Smith interrupted me with a challenge to a face-to-face debate on television. Although John Smith was an amusing, scintillating debater, dare I say it, I had never ever felt he had actually won any arguments with me in the House of Commons. He amused, but he did not convince, so I accepted immediately. I was sure that tax could only play to my advantage. I think Smith was surprised I accepted there and then. I later discovered that No. 10 were annoyed with me because the PM had turned down a debate with Kinnock.

We were now moving straight into the Election. On 12 March the Manifesto was approved by the Cabinet. On Saturday 14 March I went to the Conservative Party Central Council meeting, a sort of mid-year mini Party Conference, at Torquay. I received a warm welcome and I particularly noticed the popularity of the abolition of inheritance tax on family business with the Party faithful. I couldn't imagine why we had not done it before.

Labour tax proposals

The good sense of the Budget was underlined by John Smith's foolish Shadow Budget on Monday 16 March. Common sense seemed to desert John Smith at this moment. While I liked John, I always suspected that economically he was something of a flat earther, out of touch with the realities of life in much of the country and overly influenced by conditions in his Lanarkshire constituency. He not only opposed our tax cuts but advocated tax increases. Furthermore, he proposed to do it in a way that would hit hard the skilled worker in the South of England: by abolishing the National Insurance contributions ceiling for those earning more than £22,000 to pay for increased child benefit and pensions. In other words everyone earning over £22,000 was going to be worse off.

Labour had done their planning for the Budget on the assumption that I would cut at least one penny off income tax. Advised by Philip Gould, their main proposal in response was going to be to reverse the tax cut, but to drop National Insurance by 1 per cent which would have been the equivalent of an income tax cut of 1 pence. This would have had two consequences: it would have softened the blow of abolishing the upper earnings limit for National Insurance contributions for those earning over £22,000, and it would have meant an effective tax cut for those earning below £22,000. When I introduced the 20 pence band I gave them a very awkward choice. If they reversed the 20 pence band and cut National Insurance by 1 per cent, higher income earners would be slightly better off but people earning between £3,000 and £10,000 would be worse off. On the other hand, if National Insurance was not cut and personal allowances were increased to help lower income earners, middle income earners, earning around £22,000, would be hit. In the end Labour decided they had to drop their idea of a cut in National Insurance contributions.

John Smith was nonetheless extremely confident about his Shadow Budget and oblivious to the damage he was doing to Labour. The Shadow Budget was presented at a press conference at the Institute of Civil Engineers with a great fanfare, accompanied by detailed documents spelling out the damage. John Smith then compounded his error by marching round to the Treasury with Margaret Beckett and the rest of his team to be photographed at the front door. It was the first hint of the triumphalism that was to do Labour much harm. The irony was that John Smith's Shadow Budget undermined his own Party and Neil Kinnock; through his own incompetence he paved the way for his own rise to power. Of course there was a fiscal argument for tax increases to reduce government borrowing, but there was not a case for tax increases to go straight into more public spending.

That same day I did my televised debate with John Smith on BBC Television. The debate was not enough on taxation and too much on the economy, but I didn't think I had done badly, though there were some unfavourable press comments about the lighting and my waving my hands too much. Others, including Woodrow Wyatt, told me I hadn't done well, and they must have been right. Anyway I was convinced the message on tax would get through to the public.

John Smith was uncharacteristically rather pompous and arrogant during the debate. As we had a drink in the studio afterwards he said to me, 'It must be hard to be about to lose both your job and your house.' That was not typical of him.

To win the argument on tax we had to have the material. Although John Smith had presented his Shadow Budget with figures, they did not, of course, tell the whole story. It was important that the Conservative Party presented a detailed analysis of Smith's proposals and their effect on different family groups by income level, so I immediately asked Bill Robinson to prepare an analysis that the Prime Minister and I could use. He had spent some time thinking how it could be done and I imagined that Bill would do his final work within twenty-four hours. Uncharacteristically, he seemed to be having difficulty and I had to keep pressing him. At the same time the Prime Minister was becoming impatient with me. Eventually, on Thursday Bill showed me some statistics about how different income and family groups would be affected and the next day at the 7.30 a.m. meeting before the press conference I said that Bill had now completed his study. When I proposed a discussion of his figures, Bill interrupted, 'I am sorry, I don't trust my figures. You can't use them today.' He had given me no warning that he was going to say this. You could have heard a pin drop. The Prime Minister was furious, and Chris Patten didn't know where to look.

Bill, of course, had done the work, but such is his own intellectual honesty and modesty that he was worried there might be some slight mistake that would land the Party in deep trouble. At the press conference we were asked repeatedly why we could not produce the detailed figures we had promised. We lamely replied that they would be available very soon. Bill eventually produced the figures by Friday and they were published in the next day's newspapers. Although by this time the press were extremely critical of me for having been so slow to reply to John Smith, we were now able to show how every household in the country would be affected by Labour's proposals.

The campaign takes off

From the start of the Election, as in his leadership campaign, John Major was remarkably confident. If he had moments of self-doubt, I did not see them, and I saw him regularly throughout the Election, both at Central Office and late at night when he returned to No. 10 after a hard day's campaigning.

I cannot say that I was always as confident as he was. I felt we deserved to win and that Labour were unfit to govern. I also felt that our message must eventually get through. I tried hard not to pay too much attention to opinion polls. I know that, contrary to what they claim, they are often wrong and even the margin of error that pollsters themselves allow can be the difference between victory and defeat. Nonetheless it is difficult to ignore them.

In order to bolster my spirits I had typed out on a sheet of paper the opinion poll predictions on polling day in every General Election since 1945 for the share of the vote of each party. In a second column I had typed up the share that each party actually received. Although polls have often got the overall result right – it would be difficult not to sometimes – their predictions for the share of the vote, which is what they claim to measure, has frequently proved unreliable. I then stuck the table with Sellotape to the top of my desk in No. 11. Every day when I opened the newspapers and saw the Tories behind in the opinion polls I looked at this sheet of paper and reminded myself that they were probably wrong. I needed it most days because the polls showed us behind almost all of the time.

John Major didn't really need any such props. His political antennae were always much better than mine. One night he and Jonathan Hill, his Political Secretary, arrived back at No. 11. John was excited and elated by a rowdy rally at which he had spoken in Bolton and also by his walkabout in the day. At this stage the polls were showing something of an upsurge in support for the Liberal Democrats and I asked him how well he thought they were doing. 'There aren't as many orange badges as there ought to be in the crowds,' he said, 'and the faces behind the badges don't look at all confident.' I could only marvel at his self-confidence.

My daily routine was to go into Central Office early in the morning for strategy meetings, followed by the press conferences in which I participated on several occasions. After that I would usually drive down to Kingston if I was not required to visit other parts of the country. While I was keen to participate in the press conferences I was quite anxious about Liberal Democrat opposition in my own constituency and so wasn't particularly keen to do a lot of travelling around the country if I could avoid it. Nevertheless, each week of the campaign I did some travelling.

I was luckier than Chris Patten. My own constituency, outside the rush hour, was a half-hour's journey away. Chris had to be at Central Office for at least most of the morning and then had to be flown down to his constituency, Bath. This placed a considerable burden on him, and it was not an ideal situation for a Party Chairman in a General Election. Chris was a brilliant Chairman, and his defeat was a great loss to politics.

Some newspapers tried to suggest that I was being sidelined in the Election Campaign. I did not feel so. My main aim was to make sure that tax was at the centre of the campaign, and I believe I achieved that. I attended all the press conferences on tax and spending, and Chris told me that I did more press conferences than any other member of the Cabinet with the exception of himself and the Prime Minister.

These sniping stories nonetheless persisted in the press, and some of them were definitely inspired by people in Central Office. On one occasion I accidentally overheard Shaun Woodward, the Director of Communications, on the telephone criticising my performance at a press conference to a *Financial Times* journalist. I was puzzled, but said nothing to him. The next day I read the unattributed comments knowing precisely from where they had come. We were all meant to be on the same side, and if the polls were to be believed, it looked as though we were behind. What good could it do the Party for an official at Central Office to run down a key member of the team in the middle of the Election?

I was worried that our campaign would lose focus when we talked too much about subjects other than tax. Every time I saw the PM or Chris Patten or a Minister on TV failing to make our points about tax I would be on the telephone to Central Office immediately. I think Chris Patten and Maurice Saatchi became quite irritated with my constant calls telling them that we should stick to tax and nothing else, even though Maurice had agreed with this from the start. At times I thought we were still not doing enough on tax. On one occasion, when I decided to write to Kinnock about Labour's tax proposals, I telephoned David Cameron at Central Office, and got him to organise a press conference of my own.

The *Daily Mirror* and its political editor, Alastair Campbell, ran a campaign each day, under the heading 'Where's Norman?', suggesting I was being excluded. One day when I was in Kingston Alastair Campbell's car drew up alongside Alastair Ross Goobey's and he asked where I was. Alastair Ross Goobey was not naïve enough to tell him; instead he pointed vaguely in some direction. Campbell, returning empty-handed, sat in his car waiting for the other Alastair to make a move. Ross Goobey realised that Campbell thought if he kept him in view I would eventually come to him and he would be able to make some mischief about the Chancellor wandering the streets of Kingston alone and unrecognised while a General Election took place. Ross Goobey drove off suddenly, and sure enough Campbell's car followed. There followed a spirited car chase through the streets of Kingston.

The next day the *Mirror* carried a story about how I had escaped from their grasp by being driven away at high speed in my 'powerful Government Rover', which was actually Alastair Ross Goobey's.

Disagreements with the PM on tax

Although initially I had had difficulty in persuading John Major that we should make tax an issue at all in the Election, as the campaign went on I found it harder to restrain him from making almost wild promises on cutting taxes. Two incidents particularly worried me.

At a morning press conference, Tony Bevins, political correspondent of the *Independent*, pointed out from a table in the Budget Red Book that the tax burden had risen since 1979. Major at first denied this, but it was, however, true. The tax burden, the ratio of taxes to GDP, is very difficult to control, because the ratio is affected by the state of the economy and whether, for example, it is growing or shrinking. Even though tax rates themselves may have been cut, when the economy grows rapidly revenues and thus the so-called 'tax burden' may increase. The opposite is equally true. In a recession, tax revenues may fall and thus the tax burden may appear to fall. I was sitting next to John Major and whispered to him that Bevins's statement was correct and that we should not make any commitment because the tax burden was difficult to control. Nonetheless Major insisted on saying that in the course of the next Parliament the tax burden would be reduced. That would have required a drastic reduction in the size and role of the state. I was somewhat uneasy about this promise, particularly given John Major's views on public spending.

The next incident was more serious. At another press conference John was asked about the 20 pence tax band in the Budget, and he promised that the Government would expand the band of income to which this applied year by year. This commitment to cut taxes every year was certainly something that no party in power could responsibly promise. He and I had in fact discussed this very point, and I had emphasised that no government could possibly commit to cutting taxes every year. I was even more surprised that someone who had been opposed to the principle of tax cuts was now prepared to promise them every year.

Incensed by the PM's remarks, I made it clear that I would refuse to repeat them. I received a written note from Sarah Hogg insisting that I should use words identical to those of the Prime Minister. This was followed up by a telephone call in which she said that it was essential there was no disagreement between us. I said that I thought the words were completely unacceptable. It was the only disagreeable telephone call that I ever had with Sarah the whole time she was in Downing Street. In fact I managed to avoid ever using the same words as the Prime Minister, but I felt my concern was justified when I saw the *Evening Standard* carrying the front page headline 'Tax cuts every year by Major'.

Not surprisingly, hints of these tensions reached the press. The *Guardian*'s front page headline on 31 March was 'Major and Lamont split over tax'. It commented: 'John Major virtually pledged "year on year" tax cuts towards his 20 pence goal, only to see Labour claim the PM's promises were being undermined by his Chancellor. Lamont admitted there was "very little room for manoeuvre at all either on the tax side or the spending side" in the years ahead. Mr Major insisted he saw no reason at all for spending cuts this year while John Smith said Mr Lamont "had blown apart Mr Majors claims on his own Budget".'

I had wanted to make tax the main issue, and I had spent much time and effort persuading the Party that we should campaign on tax, but I had wanted to do so responsibly, restricting ourselves to two main points: firstly that Labour would put up taxes massively, and secondly that we would reduce the rate of income tax. Of course, over the longer term we wanted to reduce the tax burden by reducing spending, but we had first to get borrowing under better control.

As I expected, John's words about the lower-rate band became converted in the campaign into a promise to cut taxes every year. After the Election these words were thrown back at me repeatedly. I was frequently asked by Gordon Brown when he became Shadow Chancellor about my promise to cut taxes 'year by year'.

Another problem area was VAT. Even before the campaign had started, Labour was trying to persuade voters that VAT would be extended to food, public transport, children's clothes, and fuel and power, as shown in its 'VATman' poster. At that time the extension of the scope of VAT was not in my mind, but it was all too easy for Labour. All they had to do was to go through every tax in the tax system, one by one, and ask if we were planning to increase it. If we replied 'No' to every such question, no future Chancellor would ever be able to put up any tax again; it was an easy game for them. Each time we had to reply with the time-honoured formula that we had 'no plans and no need' to extend VAT or whatever tax they were referring to. Such replies did not sound as firm as some of our supporters would have liked. In fact we faced the worst of all worlds because after the Election we were accused of having misled the British public, even though what we had said was correct at the time.

I kept looking at those figures Sellotaped to my desk. It was possible that the polls were all wrong, as they had been before, but I also felt I ought to begin making some preparations in case I had to move out quickly. I cleared my desk both in the Treasury and in the study in No. 11. Rosemary decided we had better not put any sacks outside No. 11, as they would surely be noticed by the press. On 31 March Alastair Ross Goobey, Rosemary, Sophie and I had a gloomy supper in No. 11. We discussed how the transfer of power would go, how long we would be given to move out and where we would go to live, since our house was still rented.

The next day, 1 April, I went on a tour of Yorkshire, including Huddersfield and Colne Valley. In the evening, after my meetings, I went back to my hotel in Huddersfield and watched part of the Labour rally at Sheffield. Neil Kinnock attacked me as a 'lounge lizard' and the whole tone of the rally was astonishing in its triumphalism. It was very distasteful, although I did not immediately appreciate quite how much harm it was doing to Labour.

But the following day we detected a general distaste for the Sheffield rally and the trend seemed to improve, helped by some beautiful weather which raised everyone's spirits for the moment.

On Saturday 4 April I telephoned Terry Burns in response to a call from him. He had wanted to talk to me about movements in the Portuguese escudo that were affecting sterling. This seemed rather incongruous in the middle of the Election, and I had difficulty getting my mind round the problem. I told Terry I was planning to plug away at the tax issue right up to the end, even though Central Office was not wholly persuaded it was a big issue. But I was gloomy about the result.

On the Tuesday of the third week of the Election I had another TV confrontation with John Smith on *Channel 4 News*, although this time it was not actually a debate. We turned up to be greeted with the news that the latest poll had shown the largest Labour lead in the campaign to date. I went off to be made up. Smith and his entourage, including Helen Liddell, turned up. The Labour team were so cocky, one of them actually asked Alastair Ross Goobey where he would be sitting in the Treasury.

At the end of the third week of the campaign, with the polls still showing us trailing, John Major changed his campaigning style and also the issues. Firstly, in a visit to Luton he used his famous soap box and started to talk about constitutional issues such as devolution and proportional representation. I strongly agreed with his views and was pleased to discover that he held these strong opinions because up until then I had not known it. Major's entourage were later to claim that this was the turning point in the campaign, but this was an exaggeration. Although the Prime Minister's soap box may have contrasted with Sheffield, just as his natural courtesy and modesty were very different from the personality of Neil Kinnock, I did not think that the soap box was a good way to convey a clear message. And I have to say, although I agreed with the PM's views on the constitutional issues, I did not find that they brought any response on the doorstep.

If there was a dominant issue in the campaign, it was that of tax. The tabloids, particularly the *Daily Express* and the *Sun*, continued to hammer away and Alastair Ross Goobey and Bill

Robinson fed all the papers with much material. At the morning press conferences Central Office used to choose a theme, such as the environment, but in my opinion this was a waste of time. Questions never addressed the subject of the press conference but were always on something more topical. We would have done better to have held more press conferences on tax.

At one point in the campaign, Major rather despairingly said to me that we didn't appear to be making any progress in the opinion polls on the tax issue. It was the only moment in the Election he appeared at all unsure. I replied that I couldn't believe our message was not getting through, despite the polls. 'It is the only message we have,' I said. 'It must get through.'

That was my instinct. There was no evidence for it, but there was no alternative other than to battle away on the issue. I continued to make a nuisance of myself to Major, Patten and Maurice Saatchi. The theme was to some extent reinforced, but not as much as I would have wanted, in party political broadcasts.

On the day of the Election the newspapers showed a Labour lead in the opinion polls of between 4 and 7 per cent. That morning I went into the Treasury, imagining it might be my last in my brief period as Chancellor. I went around to Terry's office for a chat and a cup of tea, and he immediately said, 'You've won, haven't you?' He felt there had been a tangible movement of opinion, particularly in response to tax. He thought the Conservatives would be at least the largest party, possibly with about 315 seats. I was more pessimistic and started to discuss having a farewell party if I failed to come back.

I spent most of the day in Kingston touring committee rooms and having cups of tea with Party workers. As I normally did on Polling Day, I then returned to London in the late afternoon, as there was nothing much more I could do. I rested, had supper, and then returned to Kingston with Rosemary and Alastair Ross Goobey at about 9 p.m. We listened to the car radio and heard the news of the BBC exit polls, which I had expected to indicate a large Labour lead. When I heard they showed only a marginal lead for Labour I suspected it would be a hung Parliament. Alastair, on the other hand, was from then on confident we had won.

Normally elections in Kingston didn't attract the media, but on this occasion the Guildhall was surrounded by television cameras and TV vans. There was a large corps of journalists, including Peter Jay. In previous elections I had sometimes found the count at Kingston a frustrating experience. Sometimes we had been effectively locked up in the Guildhall without access to TV or radio and so were without any idea of what was happening in other parts of the country. Rumours tended to gather pace, with Party workers occasionally whispering alleged bits of information to each other. On this occasion, however, the officers of Kingston Council had provided a room with a TV set, and I was able to see the results from Basildon and Billericay come in. It was clear that we were going to win. Typically, the BBC kept saying the result was uncertain and there might be a hung Parliament.

My own result at Kingston was slightly disappointing. I was comfortably returned with a majority of 10,153, but with a swing rather worse than the national average. I put this down to being Chancellor of the Exchequer during a recession.

We returned to No. 11 at about 1 a.m. By now even the BBC were beginning to accept that there would be a Conservative Government. No one had invited me, but I decided to go to Central Office and to see what was happening. Walking from No. 11 to Smith Square, I witnessed an amazing scene. The square was packed with supporters. Inside No. 32 you could hardly move. Young people were hanging out of every window, waving Union Jacks and drinking beer. When I first arrived the PM had not yet come back from Huntingdon, but when he did so there was a massive cheer. Shortly afterwards, various journalists showed up, including Nick Lloyd, the editor of the *Daily Express*, who patted me on the back and said, 'It was tax that did it.'

On the stairs the PM made an elegant little speech thanking everyone in Central Office and particularly Norma, who also received a great cheer. The sad news of the night was the expected defeat of Chris Patten in Bath.

The next day, when the final figures came through, the Conservative Party had 336 seats, Labour 271 and the Liberal Democrats 21. We had an overall majority over all other parties (including Nationalists) of 21.

The Election was seen as a personal victory for John Major. He had been Prime Minister for only sixteen months, but he had managed to present the Government as a new one and he was a fresh face. Although Neil Kinnock had done much to change the Labour Party, he had never quite shaken off his left-wing past and his reputation for being unpredictable. Surprisingly, the recession had not hurt us much in the Election. Voters seemed to blame the Thatcher Government and did not connect the recession with the new one. There was also evidence that voters thought the Conservative Party better able than Labour to deal with any economic crisis.

If there was an issue that swayed the 1992 Election, it was undoubtedly tax. A poll by Anthony King in the *Daily Telegraph* showed quite clearly that tax was the number one concern. Maurice Saatchi commented that the only issue the Tories had was tax and that Labour gave it to them: 'If they'd dealt with it, we had nothing else.' Bryan Gould, the Labour MP for Dagenham, said the Election was on 'tax, tax, tax'. Strangely, the PM never once acknowledged in my conversations with him, then or subsequently, that tax had played any part in the Election at all.

The importance of tax was confirmed to me after the Election by the many letters I received from MPs saying how much the Budget had helped to highlight the issue. I would say the Election was won by a combination of Major's attractive personality and the issue of tax. Of course, we had little idea of how soon we would be forced to eat our words on tax and how we would be embarrassed by some of the more carefree words of the campaign. The newly returned Government would have to decide which was more important: the commitments for a large increase in public spending or the Conservatives' reputation on tax. One thing was certain: it would be impossible to preserve both.

8

How Victory Turned to Dust,
April–September 1992

It may be vain now in the midnight of their intoxication to
tell them there will be an awakening of bitterness, it may be
idle now in the springtime of their economic frenzy to warn
them there may be an ebb of trouble.

Benjamin Disraeli

The day after the Election there were large crowds outside
Downing Street all day. I didn't want to go outside until after I had
seen the PM, but I needed to go to a local shop and as I emerged
through the door the crowd waved and cheered. I went over and
shook hands with some of them. Elinor Goodman described this
on TV as a 'bizarre victory march'. Actually, it was only a walk to
the tobacconist.

Reappointment and reassurance?

Elinor Goodman's comment was part of a slot in a news
programme speculating on changes in the new Government,
including my own position. She reported that she had been told by
someone in Central Office that if I was reappointed Chancellor it
was only because I would otherwise have to be dragged kicking
and screaming out of No. 11. Upstairs at the window Sophie, then

fourteen, with one eye was watching the TV with fascination and with the other could see Elinor Goodman, who was actually standing on our doorstep. Not surprisingly, Sophie was extremely upset and came down to tell me. The *Financial Times* that same day had also carried a story speculating that I might not be reappointed. The stories came from the usual unnamed sources in Central Office and No. 10. By now I was getting rather fed up and decided that I would raise it with the Prime Minister.

Later that morning I received the expected telephone call from No. 10 asking me to come and see the Prime Minister. We met in his study upstairs. No official was present. The PM immediately said that 'of course' he wanted me to continue as Chancellor. I told him I had read all the stories in the press that he wanted to move me and went on to say that he owed me nothing and that if he wanted to offer the job of Chancellor to another colleague then he should do so. I also said that I did not want to remain as Chancellor for long, merely to see through the unified Budget.

The PM professed himself baffled and said, 'I have no idea where these stories come from. They are not true.' He continued that no one else in the Government could do the job so well, and insisted he had never at any time had anyone else in mind. I was conscious, and embarrassed, that my voice was cracking a little as I repeated that he owed me nothing and in no circumstances did I want to be Chancellor unless I had his full confidence. He repeated that I did, and went on to say that he wanted Rosemary and me to have Dorneywood for our weekends, since Kenneth Baker was leaving the Government. He was going to announce this to underline the confidence he felt in me. When I returned to the Treasury my Private Secretary said I looked as though I was upset and I told him about the conversation. It was one that weighed heavily on my mind and that I was to recall several times after the events in the autumn.

Later that day Peter Lilley telephoned me to say he had been removed from Trade and Industry and had been offered the job of Chancellor of the Duchy of Lancaster, in charge of the Citizens' Charter. I was surprised John had offered Trade and Industry to Michael Heseltine because he had frequently expressed his opposition to Michael's interventionist views on industry. Undoubtedly

Peter was upset at his demotion, particularly as he had been such a strong defender of the PM. During the Election he had rung me up and said we ought to make a contingency plan to keep John Major as Leader if we lost the Election. I didn't feel I was in any position to help Peter at this time, although I advised him to follow his own instinct and refuse the job. He stuck it out and was offered the much better job of Social Security Secretary, of which he made a huge success.

There were other changes in the Cabinet. I was particularly sorry that Kenneth Baker, a good friend, should have left the Government. I felt we could ill afford to lose his flair and enthusiasm. But the Prime Minister's changes were designed to provide a more youthful as well as a more feminine image, with the average age coming down from fifty-four to fifty-one. I remained just under the average age. Gillian Shephard at Employment and Virginia Bottomley at Health joined the Cabinet. John had been particularly stung by the criticism of the absence of women in his Cabinet in 1990. To compensate he was always pressing me to appoint women to posts and was persistent about having a woman Director of the Bank of England. Eventually I was able to find a very able one in Frances Heaton of Lazard's.

In my own team at the Treasury, Francis Maude and John Maples had, alas, been casualties in the Election and I missed their considerable talents. Stephen Dorrell became Financial Secretary, Tony Nelson, a friend from Rothschild's, Economic Secretary and John Cope, an old colleague from Conservative Research Department days, Paymaster General. David Mellor moved across to become Heritage Secretary and Michael Portillo Chief Secretary. I was particularly pleased to have Michael, who was more my sort of Treasury Minister than David. Lastly, Gyles Brandreth was our Whip, and a highly amusing one, too.

I was somewhat surprised that John Major did not ask my opinion or consult me about my new team. It seemed a strange way to treat a senior Minister. As it was, I was happy with the team, which was a strong one. In naming the team John made it clear that he regarded Stephen Dorrell as a possible successor to himself.

In my team of political advisors I persuaded David Cameron, a

brilliant old Etonian with a taste for the good life to come across
from Central Office and replace Andrew Tyrie, who went off to
the City. Jacques Attali had offered Andrew a job at the EBRD,
where I was sure he would do well. Alastair Ross Goobey also
departed to manage the Post Office Pension Fund, a job for which
he was extremely well qualified.

Jeremy Heywood had replaced John Gieve as my Principal
Private Secretary after the Budget. He had been my Private
Secretary when I was Financial Secretary and Chief Secretary. After
that he had gone off to a glittering job with the IMF and World
Bank. Before he went we had half-jokingly agreed that if I ever
became Chancellor he would again be my Private Secretary. At the
time that possibility looked remote. But when I became Chancellor
I telephoned him and reminded him of our arrangement. His
return to London meant giving up a well-paid job in Washington,
but I knew him to be one of the brightest and the best, and I was
keen to have him. I was not surprised when he subsequently
became Private Secretary to Tony Blair as Prime Minister.

An early decision: rejection of ERM narrow bands

One of the first pieces of paper on my desk after the Election was
a document raising the question of whether we should announce
that Britain was going to join the narrow bands of the ERM.
When Britain and Spain had joined the ERM we had been
allowed different permitted fluctuation bands from the other
members, 6 per cent compared with 2.25 per cent for everyone
else. But we had given the undertaking that we would join the
narrow bands when circumstances were right. In addition, the
Maastricht Treaty had specified that a country had to spend two
years in the narrow bands of the ERM as a condition of joining
the single currency. The Prime Minister was always pressing me
on when we would join the narrow bands and thus become full
members of the ERM, but I disliked the idea intensely. I felt the
extra room for manoeuvre, the little bit of floating we were
allowed, was valuable and I personally would have been quite
content never to give any undertaking to join.

I rejected the suggestion, and told the PM that I did not think the time was right. Surprisingly there was little reaction. The decision was very significant. If I had not made it, Britain would have faced a currency crisis far earlier than it actually did. Opinion will differ on whether that would have been a good or bad thing.

The new Cabinet met on the Wednesday following the Election to discuss the Queen's Speech. There was a very full programme: the Asylum Bill, which had been abandoned because of the Election, fresh trade union reforms, the Bill to establish the Lottery, expected to raise billions, and a Criminal Justice Bill.

A new style of Government?

I very much hoped that the new Government would herald a change of style and that John Major would feel more secure after his remarkable Election victory. For the last year and a quarter I had understood that politics had to be at the front of his mind, but there were moments when I thought politics had predominated too much. There was too much sugar and not enough pill. Now I hoped we could be a government concentrating on governing well.

The first signs were encouraging. There was a change in the Prime Minister's mood. He became more relaxed. On one occasion I rushed round to No. 10 late at night on some matter I considered very important. When I went up to the flat there was the PM eating crisps and watching a video, flown over from Australia or New Zealand, of the fastest cricket hundred ever scored. 'Sit down,' he said. 'It only lasts another six minutes.' So I did. He was also more relaxed about the economic recovery. Instead of poring minutely over every economic indicator, the Prime Minister began to talk more about the medium-term prospects for the economy, the merits of a really low level of inflation and how it was better to have a sound recovery even it was slow. Unfortunately, it was very slow: there was still little sign of the upturn he had announced unilaterally to the world in January. The economy stubbornly refused to move.

One of the arguments that had been put forward for an early Election was that it would end the uncertainty that was preventing the economic recovery from happening. Something other than policy was always to blame: if it wasn't presentation it was the Election, or the Banks. Some people must have believed this and John frequently made the point during the campaign that the return of the Government would in itself bring about recovery.

Rates come down again after eight months

Immediately on my reappointment there were more calls for cuts in interest rates. This was unsurprising since they had not moved since September, the previous year. As the *Financial Times* had rightly foreseen at the time, we had all but exhausted our room for manoeuvre against German interest rates. The differential had been squeezed and at the same time the problems of the German economy, far from improving, had grown worse, with public sector strikes and a surge both in money supply and the fiscal deficit. There was a risk German rates might move up yet again.

In Britain the need for a rate cut, if it could be delivered, was very clear from the state of the housing market. The package of measures I had introduced before Christmas did not appear to have had any visible effect. The stamp duty suspension was due to end in August and there were predictable calls for its continuation. House prices in London were estimated to have fallen 8 per cent in the year to March. People who had borrowed at 11 per cent to buy larger properties had suffered losses on their capital values sometimes of up to 20 per cent. In fact houses were now more affordable than they had been since 1984 because of a combination of falling interest rates and lower house prices. The ratio of house prices to average earnings had fallen to the lowest point for many years. If affordability were the problem, the housing market should have been taking off like a rocket. Instead the fear of unemployment and further falls in house prices were preventing recovery.

On 30 April I met with the Governor and the Deputy Governor

of the Bank of England to discuss when we could cut rates. Paul Gray, Under-Secretary for Monetary Policy, and Terry Burns outlined the monetary situation at a pre-meeting. The pound had risen on the back of our victory at the Election. On monetary grounds there seemed ample scope for a cut, and although the differential in favour of sterling against the Deutschmark was only a small one it made sense to try to reduce it further. The Governor and the Deputy Governor agreed, but wanted to wait a week. They felt the market was not expecting a cut. Expectations should be conditioned and the delay could be used to sell more gilts.

On 5 May interest rates were duly cut by 0.5 per cent down to 10 per cent. Continuing my tradition of tedious circumlocution, I said on ITN: 'Britain is now well placed for recovery.' I was running out of phrases.

Unsurprisingly the rate cut received only a grudging welcome and the general reaction was 'too little, too late'. Sir John Banham, the Director General of the CBI, said the reduction 'was not before time' and added that 'real interest rates remain very high for manufacturing'. Housing analysts said the rate cut was insufficient to revive the moribund market.

There was a curious aftermath to the May rate cut. A belief spread that Britain was beginning to decouple itself from German interest rates. There was talk of cutting rates unilaterally below those of Germany. The interest rate differential was now 0.25 per cent, the lowest in a decade, while sterling remained trading apparently comfortably within its ERM band, but this was largely wishful thinking. It was true there appeared little risk that the May rate cut would need to be reversed, but that was a different matter from cutting below German rates. I suspected such wishful thinking came from No. 10.

But these matters were temporarily banished from my mind on my fiftieth birthday on 8 May. Rosemary had suggested we should hold a dance in No. 11. As far as I or anyone else knew, there had never been a dance there. Treasury officials became worried and official memos were exchanged questioning whether the floor in the State Room at No. 11 was strong enough to support the weight of Conservative politicians dancing through the night. But we went ahead and it was a wild success. We had a

dinner party for twenty friends, including Michael and Sandra
Howard, Leon and Diana Brittan, Evelyn de Rothschild and his
wife Victoria, and other friends gave dinner parties for guests in
their homes. After dinner Treasury Mandarins, Conservative
politicians and a few mercifully few representatives of Fleet Street
and their wives danced all evening. Rosario de Mandat-Grancey
gave a demonstration of the tango and Petronella Wyatt sang
'Lili Marlene' brilliantly at midnight. Later on Gordon Brown
amusingly referred to this in the House of Commons when attacking my strained relations with the Bundesbank.

Dancing went on until breakfast at 2 or 3 o'clock in the morning, when kedgeree was served: the floor hadn't fallen in. The
doors upstairs and downstairs were open to the garden and outside, the song of a nightingale could be heard. This was rather
surprising in the somewhat sparse garden of Nos. 10 and 11, but
it was only a tape recording put there by Rosemary.

The Danish referendum: plucky little Denmark

But 'Events, dear boy, Events', in Harold Macmillan's phrase,
continued to surprise. On the evening of 2 June I dined with
Christopher Hogg, the Chairman of Reuters, in their headquarters in Fleet Street and had an interesting evening hearing how
financial publishing was helping to develop the market economy
of the Soviet Union. As I was getting into my car Chris Green, my
driver, said to me, 'Have you heard that the Danes have voted
against Maastricht?' I leapt into the air, punching it with my fist.
It was an incautious reaction of sheer delight, but fortunately no
passer-by saw me. I could not believe it. Could this, I wondered,
be the end of the single currency?

The next morning I thought the Prime Minister would ring
me, but he didn't. So I rang him. I was a bit surprised when he
said to me, 'I don't know whether to laugh or cry.' I said I was
quite clear which I was going to do, adding, 'Well, you have
always insisted to me that it would never happen. You have been
proved right more quickly than you could have imagined.' I
remember clearly what I then added, vaguely misquoting some

line of Stephen Potter: 'If a house falls down and becomes a rock garden, it is best left as a rock garden.' The Prime Minister did not tell me that, as we were speaking, the Foreign Secretary was on the *Today* programme discussing how Maastricht could be rescued. Douglas also said that Britain would proceed to ratify the Treaty.

A few minutes later I was invited to a meeting at No. 10 with the Prime Minister and others. Before attending I popped into the Treasury and had a brief discussion about the events overnight. Political advisors and officials were of the view that there was no point in continuing with the Maastricht Bill. Pressing ahead with it when it was without purpose would bring out more opposition than we had met so far. That was one senior official's view. Politicians are meant to know more about politics than officials, but his analysis was spot on.

I assumed that the meeting at No. 10 was being held to discuss the implications of the Danish vote, but found that it was, as usual, just to discuss 'presentation'. I tried to open the issue, but was told firmly that the policy decision had been made and already announced by the Foreign Secretary.

I was dismayed, but the PM and the Foreign Secretary strongly argued that Denmark was too small to derail Maastricht and that even if Britain didn't ratify the Treaty the other countries would go ahead, if necessary signing a replica treaty. Although we tried, it was difficult for people like myself, Michael Howard and Peter Lilley to maintain our position, when the Danish Government itself indicated that they wanted a second referendum. Of course, they had been encouraged to do that by the British and French Governments.

My instinctive reaction was identical to that of many Conservative backbenchers. The pent-up frustrations over Maastricht now burst into the open. Within twenty-four hours of the Danish referendum, seventy Conservative MPs signed a motion calling for a fresh start on European policy. Mrs Thatcher made her views known. Kenneth Baker, using his new freedom of the backbenches, warned John Major of the need for changes. Eventually the Government bowed to the inevitable and for the time being stopped progress on the Maastricht Bill.

My problem was keeping my reactions to myself. Unfortunately, during John Major's statement to the House of Commons on the Danish referendum, one eagle-eyed journalist noted that at one point I nodded vigorously after an anti-European intervention from Tony Benn. Douglas Hurd shook his head. The canny John Major revealed nothing in his reaction.

Backbenchers were up in arms. Many of them equated Maastricht, the ERM and the recession and they made a dangerous cocktail. Reports began appearing for the first time about damaging splits within senior Government ranks. The previous Friday I had delivered what I hoped was a blistering attack on the centralising ambitions of the European Commission and stated that there was nothing inevitable about the development of the European Union. I hoped I was in a strong position to try to calm the sceptics and on the radio I asserted that the Government was united on the question of Maastricht. It was more or less true. Some of us had misgivings but the divisions that were to become a chasm in a few years' time were not yet there.

For the first time, criticism also began to appear about John Major's style of government. An article in the *Independent* on 11 June stated: 'One Cabinet Minister complained the PM was too lax in the way he ran Cabinet meetings. "He lets everyone have their say, then he winds up, but he doesn't give a clear line sometimes. It is more collegiate, but it has gone too far."' There was further trouble when it was discovered that Peter Lilley and Michael Portillo had attended a meeting of Junior Ministers organised by Edward Leigh to discuss their worries about Maastricht. I was amazed that Michael Portillo could be so rash as to attend a meeting whose existence was likely to leak out.

But it was only a meeting of Ministers. No doubt No. 10 grew more nervous when Bill Cash, the Eurosceptic MP for Stafford, claimed that there had been contacts between Ministers and rebel MPs. He declined to name names, so no one – at least I didn't – knew whether it was true or not.

An article in the *Evening Standard* on 11 June tried to identify the Eurosceptics within the Cabinet. The author wrote: 'Norman Lamont does not share Douglas Hurd's faith in the perfect ability of Brussels. Unlike Mr Hurd who patently revels in the European game, the Chancellor deeply dislikes the whole business. Whereas Europe gives the Foreign Secretary a chess player's pleasure, Norman Lamont is irritated by the folly and futility of it all. Friends say that after gruelling sessions at Brussels policy meetings Norman Lamont heads wearily for home saying how awful he finds them.'

I don't know who talked to the *Evening Standard*. It certainly wasn't me. But the article encapsulated precisely my feelings about business with the European Union. Not that I experienced any difficulty working with Douglas. I liked him and found him an agreeable colleague, with a mind not necessarily closed to others with different views.

The Government set about rescuing the Danish Government and trying to find Treaty alterations that could be portrayed as significant concessions to Denmark, allowing the issue to be put to a second referendum. John Major's considerable diplomatic and negotiating ingenuity found full scope. But was it the right strategy?

The effects on the markets of the Danish referendum

The Danish referendum and the announcement on 1 July by President Mitterrand of a French referendum had serious consequences for the financial markets, which had assumed that the exchange rates in the ERM were going to remain stable because, for those countries that wanted it, we were now on the glidepath towards the single currency. Markets had bet on falling interest rates, lower deficits and firm exchange rates. Immediately after the Danish referendum huge amounts of money began to flow out of the lira and peseta as convergence plays were unwound. There was a big move into the Deutschmark. If there was not going to be a single currency, then the Deutschmark would be the real store of value. Amazingly, the politicians had contrived to introduce the prospect of turbulence in the markets continuously right up to 20 September, the date of the French referendum.

Initially the pressure was on the lira, understandably so since the fundamentals of the Italian economy were weaker than our own, particularly the public finances. But if the lira went down, we would be next in the firing line.

Much hinged on the progress of the recovery, which still seemed as far away as ever. The recession had ended in the sense that things had stopped getting worse, but there was no real recovery. If the economy remained weak then high rates of interest to defend the pound would be necessary, but would lack any credibility since they were plainly inappropriate.

The June Treasury forecast was not particularly encouraging or credible. The prospects for the whole of 1992 were presented as little different from the January forecasts, but what had been expected to happen in the first half of the year had already failed to materialise. The interest rate cuts had failed to move either the economy or the housing market, which in turn was a drag on the wider economy. GDP had fallen by 0.5 per cent in the first quarter compared with the slight rise anticipated at the time of the Budget. Slightly hedging their bets, the authors, with refreshing candour, entitled the forecast *Recovery at last, or another false dawn?* But where did that leave us? It was clear to me that what we needed, but could not deliver, were lower interest rates.

For many businessmen the worst depths of the recession were still with them. In June figures published by Trade Indemnity showed that business failures continued to rise in the first three months of the year. The company announced that any significant improvement in the rate of failures would lag well behind any recovery. Failures notified to the group were up 10 per cent from the last quarter of last year.

On 11 June the *Sun* ran an article with the heading '180 reasons why Lamont has to act now': 'Every three hours 180 people lose their jobs . . . the economic alarm bells are ringing loud and clear, the Chancellor, Lamont can't hear them. For God's sake wake up, Norman, the economy is crumbling around us and yet you still do nothing.' There was nothing unusual about this article: it was one of many.

The day before a journalist from the *Sun* had taken me out to a lavish lunch at the Gay Hussar. He was exceedingly flattering to me, and I wondered why. Suddenly he pulled out of his pocket a reproduction of the front page of the next day's *Sun*. 'I thought I had better show you this. It is nothing personal of course,' he said. What startled me somewhat was that the whole front page was in the form of a dartboard made out of my face.

EU Presidency and tax harmonisation

At the end of June Britain took over the Presidency of the EU from Portugal. I was not looking forward to this, not because my Finance Minister colleagues were disagreeable – on the contrary, they were overwhelmingly agreeable and on the whole rather realistic about Europe – but because I disliked the razzmatazz. The Foreign Office luxuriated in the Presidency, and arranged endless PR gimmicks: logos, badges, press packs and especially packs for schools on Britain's place in Europe. None of the publicity quite matched that of the Blair Government for its Presidency in 1998, but considerable effort was made.

Ministers were issued with special ties, a little white lion on a tasteful dark blue background, to mark the EU Presidency. They were not unattractive and John Major and Douglas Hurd wore theirs for every meeting. Mine remained firmly within its Cellophane cover, where it remains today in a top drawer. If anyone had offered me one of the more attractive blue golfing umbrellas I might have been tempted, but no one did.

The four main aims of the British Presidency were: firstly, to reach agreement on the future financing of the EU, which had to be done as the present arrangements were coming to an end; secondly, to complete the single market, which is the perpetual aim of every country's Presidency; thirdly to reduce the scope for fraud, which is a perpetual British objective; and fourthly and most importantly, an early settlement of the General Agreement on Tariffs and Trade (GATT) negotiations on world trade. This was an urgent task and had it been left to the Europeans would probably never have been achieved. Fortunately the Americans were our main negotiating partners and they were determined to bring matters to a conclusion.

As Chairman of the Council of Finance Ministers, I had another awkward item: EU proposals for the harmonisation of indirect taxes. Unsurprisingly I was strongly opposed to the principle of the harmonisation of taxes. It seemed to me that market forces, namely cross-border shopping and the mobility of capital, would tend to bring about some convergence of tax rates within the economic area of the EU. There was nothing wrong with that, but such a result would be very different from government-imposed harmonisation. The latter meant harmonisation of taxes upwards and would also deprive national governments of their ability to set tax rates: a right of governments that lies at the heart both of sovereignty and democracy.

Slightly to my surprise Nigel Lawson and Mrs Thatcher had made one partial but significant concession to the idea of the harmonisation of indirect taxes. Because Britain had higher taxes on alcohol and tobacco than in Continental Europe, they had agreed to the principle of legally binding minimum rates of tax on alcohol and tobacco being set by Brussels. They hoped this would prevent other countries from undercutting our taxes on alcohol and tobacco. This approach to indirect taxes had been developed during 1988 as an alternative to the Commission proposal for harmonisation of the main rates of indirect tax and took the form of a paper, *Taxation and the Single Market: A Market-Based Approach*, which Nigel Lawson presented to an informal Ecofin on 17 September 1988.

The paper argued that as frontier controls were lifted market forces operating through the increase in cross-border shopping would bring about a natural convergence of tax rates, as national governments had to balance fiscal expedience against other priorities. Trade distortion was not something to be avoided but rather the engine of change. However, the Lawson paper noted one exception: for health and social policy reasons, the free play of market forces would be limited, either by restrictions on personal imports or agreed minimum excise duty rates in respect of tobacco and alcoholic drinks.

This seemed to me the surrender of an important principle. Perhaps the agreement of minimum taxes was not strictly speaking harmonisation, but it was a move in that direction since legally binding minima would force some countries to raise their taxes in the direction of British taxes. This may have been in the short-term interests of the British Treasury, but it nonetheless was the establishment of a hugely important principle.

I was faced with two immediate decisions: firstly I was asked to agree the minimum rates for duty on alcohol and tobacco, and secondly I had to agree the same principle of a minimum binding rate of tax applied to VAT.

On the first point it was impossible for me to go back on the agreements that had already been made. Furthermore the whisky industry and other parts of the drinks industry were anxious to see continental taxes increase nearer to British levels. Sensing my reluctance on the issue, the whisky industry complained to the Prime Minister that I was not zealous enough in protecting their interests.

It had been intended to resolve these issues during the Portuguese Presidency, and there was a long meeting on 27 June, in its dying days, to see if agreement could be reached. A number of other issues on the agenda relating to financial services were also discussed and Leon Brittan, who attended the meeting, was extremely helpful in protecting British interests.

On alcohol taxation, however, the meeting reached an impasse, with the Southern wine-producing countries not wanting taxation on wine and the Northern EU countries wishing to tax alcohol irrespective of its origin. Proposals were made at the meeting that would have made the situation of Scotch whisky even worse, and the problem was further complicated by the issue of that most unattractive of all British products, British sherry. The problems were not resolved and passed to the British Presidency.

In spite of the acceptance of the principle by Nigel Lawson and Margaret Thatcher, I was deeply reluctant to extend the idea of a legally binding minimum rate further to VAT. I discussed the matter with both the PM and others. John Major was not very interested in the issue, and Ken Clarke pressed me saying, 'I don't know why you are so worked up about this,' urging that I should support a legally binding minimum rate. It was rather like the arguments I had with the PM and Douglas Hurd over whether the ERM should have been made by Maastricht into a legally binding commitment. They saw my objections on these issues as theoretical, and thought that all that mattered was 'fighting for Britain's interests'.

My officials from Customs and Excise were not much support either. They too thought I was being 'hard-line', and 'doctrinaire'. But I refused to agree to the recommendations of officials, who thought that I should accept the suggestion from the EU that the legally binding minimum rate for VAT should be 15 per cent. Since I had increased the standard rate of VAT from 15 per cent to 17.5 per cent in 1991, as they pointed out to me, we would plainly not be affected in any practical sense. We had a problem with an overlarge borrowing requirement and were most unlikely to be in a position to cut VAT in the near future. But in my view it was not as simple as that. It was quite conceivable that at some date in the future a Government might want to restructure VAT at no revenue cost so that a lower standard rate was combined with various reduced rates for goods and services such as children's clothes or public transport.

The problem was that this issue was intertwined with other apparently unrelated issues, such as the completion of the single market. Although it is regularly announced every year, it never actually seems to reach completion. This year's 'completion of the single market' was meant to be finally achieved on 1 January 1993 and involved the liberalisation of financial services. Quite rightly, I was reminded that this was of enormous importance to the City.

I offered to make a statement on behalf of the Government that we would give a commitment not to reduce the standard rate of VAT for four or five years, but this was opposed by other countries, particularly the Italians and the Belgians.

The second meeting of Ecofin under my Chairmanship was fixed for 27 July to consider the abolition of fiscal frontiers and the remaining issues of indirect taxes, which had not been dealt with by the Portuguese Presidency. I spent much time in advance of the meeting lobbying other Ministers, and in the end legal minima were agreed for spirits and British sherry at levels that protected British interests. On VAT the other countries refused to accept a mere declaration of intent not to cut VAT. I then thought up the idea of a time-limited minimum rate of VAT. Eventually we agreed that there would be a legally binding minimum rate of VAT, but that it would last only until 1996, when it would lapse if there was no agreement among Ministers that it should continue. In one sense I had conceded the principle, but only for a limited period of time, and in any practical sense our freedom to set our own tax rates was not infringed. The legally binding rate would lapse if we wanted it to do so.

It is difficult to overestimate quite my isolation on this one issue, in the Treasury, in the Cabinet and indeed among my Treasury Ministerial colleagues. But I thought I had salvaged something and I was taken aback when I returned to London to find myself the subject of fierce criticism from Norman Tebbit for having given away Parliament's right to set our own taxes. He seemed to be ignorant of the ground that the Thatcher Cabinet of which he had been a member had already surrendered, or of the battle I had been waging for the very principle that he rightly held dear. He was quickly joined by other Eurosceptics, who rushed to attack me.

Another attempt at tax harmonisation in my time as Chancellor was the idea mooted by the Commission of a carbon tax to be levied on energy producers, which would have savaged British industry. Needless to say it was strongly supported by the Liberal Democrat Party, which was so opposed to VAT on fuel and power, even though the carbon tax would have increased energy prices more than VAT on fuel. Despite the urging of Michael Heseltine and Treasury officials, I saw to it that the proposals were quietly buried. I firmly resisted them every time they were raised.

The Eurosceptics were quite right to be deeply concerned on these issues. Creeping tax harmonisation from Brussels is a real threat. The single market does not require uniform taxes, and it would be far better if market forces were left to bring about a degree of downward convergence of tax rates. In the large single market of the United States sales taxes vary considerably and some states have no local income taxes at all. It is one of my strongest objections to the single currency that it is likely to lead to greater pressure to harmonise taxes and thus deprive both governments and voters of their freedom to make choices. I was greatly intrigued by the efforts of Oskar Lafontaine, Gerhard Schroder's Finance Minister, to push tax harmonisation to the top of the European agenda. As an issue it will certainly return, and it should be resisted.

Frustrations with the ERM

There has been much speculation about my own attitude to the ERM, enlivened by myths such as the story that I sang in my bath on 16 September when we finally ended our membership of it. As has been stated, I accepted the policy when I became Chancellor. It was not my preferred policy, but I had no reason to think it would become unworkable.

For a while the policy seemed to have more advantages than disadvantages, but by the end of 1991, when the Germans put up rates, I was beginning to doubt its sustainability. After the Election my doubts intensified and by the late summer of 1992 my worries had reached the point where I was highly sceptical of my own policy and began to feel intensely frustrated.

But I knew that withdrawal was extremely difficult. It would be not just a dramatic U-turn that would be controversial in Britain and strongly opposed by senior colleagues; it would be profoundly disruptive of the politics of other countries. The ERM had become embroiled with Maastricht, yet soldiering on seemed to condemn us to at best a flat economy for as far as the eye could see, or at worse something much more alarming. What was the answer?

I endlessly debated the issue with officials. My usual method of making decisions in the Treasury was 'destructive dialogue'. I would frequently question the fundamentals of an issue to test it. I think officials enjoyed that; I can recall at least six or seven occasions when I had fierce arguments about our policy, but the policy remained unchanged.

There was only one person responsible for making decisions, and that was myself. If policy remained unchanged, that was my decision. It would be wrong also to give any impression that

Treasury officials were strong propagandists for the ERM. There is a myth in the press that the Treasury foisted the ERM on the politicians, but it was the politicians who took the decision to join. Once the momentous decision had been made, officials backed it and tried to make it work, which meant not giving it up at the first sign of trouble.

I was very careful to keep my doubts on these matters to myself, and to make sure my discussions were extremely restricted. I don't think I ever discussed them with my Ministerial colleagues, but the special advisors, particularly Bill Robinson, knew. Nothing would have been more damaging than a leak that a highly controversial Government policy was doubted even by the Chancellor of the Exchequer.

I only put my doubts to the PM, or more accurately attempted to put them to him, on one occasion. After that was rebuffed, I came to the conclusion that I must soldier on with the policy until the end of the year, when I planned to reopen it.

On 5 May, the day we cut interest rates, I had a meeting with officials in the Treasury. I asked at what stage we would conclude that our policy stance was wrong. What were the alternatives? Realignment, international co-operation, under-funding in the gilts markets or, I asked, leaving the ERM? I suggested that countries like Australia, with no exchange rate regime, had been able to have lower interest rates and had not experienced such a deep recession. Again, we came to the conclusion that depreciation within the ERM would not make much impact. It might increase external demand, but if anything it would reduce domestic demand and was likely to put up interest rates.

Leaving the ERM was a huge step that could not be divorced from other aspects of policy. Lower interest rates might lead to a sharp fall in sterling, leading to higher inflation and back to higher rates. I think officials were overinfluenced by the period in the 1980s when rates were reduced from 17 per cent to 12 per cent and then had to be put back up again. That was a recurring nightmare in their minds.

On 24 June I had another long discussion about alternatives to the current policy. I said that we were locking ourselves into German interest rates when it was clear to everybody that the UK economy was in quite a different phase from the German economy. The question was raised whether it was clear that to leave the ERM would deliver any significant benefits. I felt officials were continually emphasising that trying to manage the economy within a floating exchange rate regime brought difficulties of its own. They argued that the only realistic alternative to the current policy was devaluation. Over the long term this might not necessarily be damaging, but the short-term consequences would be higher interest rates and higher inflation.

Despite my doubts, it was not really open to me to make a decision to leave the ERM. Terry Burns once put it very calmly to me by pointing out that the decision to join the ERM had been made by the present Prime Minister, the previous Prime Minister and the present Foreign Secretary, and had been Conservative policy since 1979. We had been arguing about this policy for a decade. What did it say for the determination of British Government, if after less than two years of a policy about which it had argued for ten years, it simply abandoned it. This was a powerful argument.

The pound: too high?

Conventional wisdom, that oxymoron, frequently asserts that Britain joined the ERM at too high a rate. I have no knowledge of the circumstances in which we chose the rate because I was not involved in John Major and Mrs Thatcher's discussions. Some said the Germans had thought the rate too high, and Michael Heseltine rather provocatively once alleged that Mrs Thatcher had imposed a high rate. I myself suspect it was just as likely that John Major or the Treasury would themselves have wanted a reasonably demanding rate, since the perception in 1990 was that joining would lead to a fall in interest rates which could push up inflation.

But was it too high a rate in reality? I certainly examined that question but could see little evidence that it was too high, nor did officials in the Treasury. The central rate was close to the current market rate and the average of the previous decade, and making the adjustments for differential inflation rates did not suggest it was overvalued (see Table 1 in the Appendix). Sometimes it was suggested that the deficit on the balance of payments at a time of recession was clear proof that the pound was overvalued, but that was not so. What mattered from this point of view was the trade account with Europe, where the deficit was shrinking quite fast.

There was no convincing evidence that the level of the pound against the Deutschmark was the problem. Arguably, the level of the pound against the dollar was a far bigger one. The economy was stuck in recession, but not just in the export sector. It was the domestic economy, particularly the housing market, that was not moving. Interest rates, not the level of the pound, were the main problem, and interest rates could not be lowered below the levels of the anchor currency in the ERM, the Deutschmark. Devaluing without leaving the ERM would not have produced lower interest rates, but higher rates. If a currency is devalued within a fixed exchange rate system, inevitably holders of that currency will believe it is likely to happen again and will demand higher interest rates as an insurance premium. Such was the experience of both the French and the Dutch for years after their devaluations within the ERM.

The European Policy Forum speech

At the same time that I was feeling increasingly trapped by the ERM, I had to carry on arguing in public for the policy, constantly assuring MPs that there was no alternative. To recount this now must make me appear schizophrenic; indeed, at the time I felt schizophrenic. But in my mind there were only two alternatives: being in, or being out. As long as we continued to remain in, I had to continue to argue for the policy. Politicians do not have the luxury of airing their doubts in public. If you haven't changed the policy, it is unchanged and you have to defend it without any ambiguity and that is what I did.

In late June the pressure on sterling had returned. For the first time we had fallen out of the narrow bands of the ERM.

Although I had firmly rejected the idea of joining the narrow bands, sterling had continued nonetheless to trade within them, which had put some space above the floor that was the absolute bottom. Our reasoning was that if we only responded when we hit the floor it would be too late.

The Prime Minister, understandably, was concerned at what was happening to sterling. He kept pressing me to be more 'convincing' and to use 'tougher' language about our commitment to the ERM. In response to his urgings I agreed to make a speech to the European Policy Forum at the Queen Elizabeth Centre on 11 July.

In early June I asked officials for a paper reviewing all the options for our policy, including the options of either devaluing or leaving the ERM. This sounds open-minded, but it was not so much a fresh look as a rationalisation of all the arguments in favour of our existing policy. This paper formed the basis of the most important policy speech of my time as Chancellor.

The date of the speech coincided with some dramatically good inflation figures. I hailed these and reminded the audience that the objective of the ERM was to break the cycle of inflation. I had a new statistic that two-thirds of Britain's exports went to countries with inflation rates lower than our own. Our inflation improvement had been dramatic and I concluded, 'I cannot believe we would have achieved all this outside the ERM.' I then continued along the lines of our paper to examine all the alternatives to our present policy. These were:

(1) Cut interest rates immediately. That was not possible within the ERM.
(2) A German realignment. Other countries, particularly France, had ruled that out.
(3) Devaluation within the ERM. I repeated the view that currencies that devalued within a fixed exchange rate system would pay an interest rate premium. A devaluation would only put interest rates up, not down. The Deutschmark was able to have low interest rates because it had never devalued, which was why no country had lower rates than Germany.

(4) Leave the ERM, cut interest rates and let the pound find its own level. This was the option that caused me the greatest difficulty. I said that this would cause a fall in the pound 'unprecedented in the last forty years' and called it the 'cut and run option'. From past experience devaluation – which is what this would be, in effect – simply did not work for Britain because the temporary gain in competitiveness from devaluation was usually wiped out by Britain's inability to keep its inflation consistently down.

(5) Leave the ERM and set interest rates according to domestic monetary targets. This was really a variant of the fourth option, but I acknowledged the unreliability of monetary targets. That was a point that genuinely bothered me. But essentially the fifth option was the same as the fourth.

I concluded: 'So we have five options, five ways we could try to change the current monetary policy. What they all have in common is that each is a plea for a free lunch. As the Russians say, only mouse traps have free cheese. The result of attempting to implement any of them would be either higher interest rates, higher inflation or most likely both.'

Reading the speech today, the arguments against cutting interest rates and devaluation still, I think, stand up to analysis. To me it is clear that devaluation would not have produced lower rates but would have put them up. But in the light of events since 1992, the arguments against the different versions of floating were clearly overstated. And at the time they were in fact the options that, given a free hand, I would have considered, but they were not available to me at that time.

The speech, along with the inflation figures, received a very good press. Even Anthony Seldon in his book on John Major commented 'for a committed Eurosceptic it was a brave speech'. The *Financial Times* saw it as an attempt to persuade Conservatives that 'the gain which lies in the future was worth the present pain'. They saw the speech as starting the process of persuasion. It added: 'Mr Lamont, who has shown greater courage and persistence under pressure than most of his post-war predecessors, has until now been slow to perceive that you cannot hope to lead the British public on a long march towards permanent near zero inflation unless you explain the benefits of such an endeavour.'

As I said on the day of the speech, the underlying rate of inflation fell spectacularly from 5.3 per cent to 4.8 per cent: a four-year low. But on the same day it was reported that a group of Britain's leading house builders were expected to write to me warning of a deepening crisis in their industry. Six leading economists, including Sir Alan Walters, Patrick Minford and Tim Congdon, wrote to *The Times* advocating withdrawal from the ERM. John Townend, Chairman of the Conservative Backbench Finance Committee, went on BBC television to announce that if there were no signs of an economic recovery soon there would be intense pressure for a devaluation. Obviously the speech had failed to impress him and other Conservative MPs.

The *Daily Telegraph* was also fulsome and described the speech as 'courageous, articulate and important . . . In one of the frankest statements of policy by a Treasury Minister for years he proclaimed the Government's determination to maintain its course towards a low inflation economy . . . implicitly adding: "at whatever costs".' The paper went on, however, to add quite rightly that there were certain flaws in some of the points and that it was no easier for the Chancellor than for anyone in the markets to predict the value of the pound outside the ERM.

Lex in the *Financial Times* pointedly added: 'The alternatives are dismissed with such determined precision he would have to resign rather than switch course.' Samuel Brittan put it more gently: 'Mr Lamont is enough of a politician to know he is putting himself out on a limb, and that the official Treasury would not hesitate to leave him as a scapegoat if it changed its mind about the appropriate policy.'

I am not sure that at the time I did fully appreciate the significance of the speech. Looking back today it is quite clear that from the moment I uttered those words I would eventually be forced to resign if the policy were changed.

Weekends at Dorneywood

It was a depressing and exhausting time. I was relieved to slip away at the weekends to Dorneywood. Because I had sat for a London constituency for twenty years I had never had a house in the country and I enjoyed the opportunity to walk in the ancient beech woods owned by the Corporation of the City of London.

Dorneywood as a house is comfortable rather than grand. It is largely Edwardian, appropriate to the industrialist who gifted it to the nation. It was too small to be used for the pre-Budget Treasury weekends that continued to be held at the Foreign Secretary's grander residence of Chevening.

The house had a lightly panelled drawing room, where guests could play bagatelle and compare their efforts against the scores carefully recorded in a book by previous occupants of the house, such as Winston Churchill. I was surprised to see from the book how often he had played with his advisor Professor Lindemann, even at the height of the war, but as my own concerns with the pound mounted, I found I too increasingly played.

The entrance hall doubled as a dining room. It had a spectacular mural by Rex Whistler of the 'Silvae Dorneywood' in a neo-classical style. Although not a proper dining room, it had a large dining table that we used for a party for Carla Powell's birthday, to which she invited a number of her friends, including Stephen Fry.

The extensive gardens had a lot of fruit, too much for the use of the household. Not all of it was picked and some of it rotted on the trees, which was a scandal. I was told that Dorneywood had three types of woodpecker: the green, the greater spotted, and the lesser spotted, though I never saw the lesser spotted. There was also a dovecote, occupied by a dozen and a half pure white, fantailed doves. I was surprised how much I enjoyed watching them manoeuvre in flight, never colliding and all simultaneously managing to disappear into their individual roosts in the dovecote. One day a hawk, presumably a sparrow hawk, pounced, and killed several of them, leaving white feathers everywhere.

Problems in Germany

Britain's inflation may have been tumbling spectacularly, but in Germany the opposite was happening. Germany was beginning to pay the price for policy mistakes following reunification, particularly the one-for-one conversion of the ostmark. The Federal Government had also been pumping huge amounts of money into the East German economy. As industry proved incapable of satisfying the rising demand, in March inflation reached 4.8 per cent, which was high by German standards. There was also a planned VAT rise for the beginning of 1993. To compound the problem, much Federal Government assistance to the East was in the form of subsidised credits, which forced the Bundesbank to have higher rates than it otherwise would have needed.

The Bundesbank needed to curb the increase in money supply and inflation, yet other members of the ERM wanted it to prevent Europe falling into recession. Germany's money supply had ballooned by nearly 40 per cent in the previous two years. Just when we thought sterling might be earning some respite, our hopes were shattered when the Bundesbank on 17 July put up its discount rate by a hefty 0.75 percent to 8.75 per cent. The discount rate is the floor of the corridor within which the Bundesbank influences money market rates and normally the Lombard rate is the more important when rates are rising. However, all the markets noticed that Germany had raised its rates when most of the countries in Europe desperately needed lower rates. It was interpreted as a sign that monetary co-operation within Europe was non-existent, and it was hard to deny that was the case. Sterling fell below Dm 2.85 again, even lower than its level when the polls closed on 9 April.

Though the German move was decidedly unhelpful, I was not surprised that they put their own interests first, but the Bundesbank's justification of its action was unnecessarily unaccommodating. There were several careless remarks in the weeks that followed. A senior official of the Bundesbank was quoted as saying that countries that were suffering from Germany's monetary policies could take the initiative of seeking a realignment within the EMS. Incredibly, the same spokesman indicated market forces might eventually force weaker currencies towards devaluation.

The tension increased further when the Bank of Italy also raised its discount rate by the surprisingly large amount of 1.25 per cent. Unfortunately and to its surprise the lira did not strengthen. The markets knew that much Italian debt was short-term and had to be refinanced and rises in interest rates exacerbated the already serious budgetary problems of the Italian Government.

I did not believe in the ERM at any time as a step towards monetary union. I had accepted it as a monetary device for lowering British inflation, but I had imagined that such a system involved a modicum of co-operation between members. Germany's actions seemed to indicate an absence of any interest in co-operation. Of course I was aware that Schlesinger had reservations about the single currency and for that reason many people also believed he would be quite happy to see the ERM disintegrate.

Although sterling was weakening, it was not in the front line; the concern of the markets was more with the lira. But we were also caught in the crossfire between the dollar and the Deutschmark. Alan Greenspan had cut rates aggressively to a very low level to cope with the US banking crisis, so there was an unprecedented yield gap between German and US interest rates and money flowed from New York to Frankfurt. As the markets bought marks, the pound weakened further.

On 28 July there was a seminar at No. 10 for the PM to discuss economic policy. This took the form of a presentation by officials of much of the material used for my European Policy Forum speech. The PM said we must think the unthinkable. But he tended to make that sort of remark. His idea of the unthinkable was usually more public expenditure.

Most of the talking was done by Terry Burns and Alan Budd, and the discussion also covered the housing market. The question of withdrawing from the ERM was raised briefly, only to be dismissed. Introducing the discussion, I said we had to accept that the flatness of the economy would continue, but we had to tough it out with our eyes open.

The PM said if we left the ERM, Maastricht would be dead. That, he made clear, was unthinkable, even though it might make the ERM more acceptable to some Eurosceptics. The discussion led on to action we could take to get the economy moving, such as cuts in National Insurance contributions, a housing package or, perhaps in time, limited tax reliefs. The PM wanted a package before the Party Conference.

As July moved into August the pressures on the pound continued, so when I picked up my *Sunday Times* on 2 August I was amazed to read the headline on the front page: 'Major aims to make sterling best in Europe'. Unknown to me, the Prime Minister a few days earlier had attended a dinner at the Kensington flat of Andrew Neil, where he said the pound would become the strongest currency in Europe, stronger even than the Deutschmark. It was a ludicrous and ill-timed claim. I later discovered that without telling me he had been peddling this line to journalists for some time. I could not see how the Prime Minister could say such an extraordinary thing without mentioning it to me. A comical postscript to this episode came a year later when Sir Edward Heath attacked me for having, he claimed, undermined sterling by making extravagant claims that sterling would be the strongest currency in Europe!

Before going on holiday I had one last discussion of our ERM policy with officials. Although my European Policy Forum speech had made a strong case for the ERM, I still felt we faced an unusual combination of circumstances. It was possible we might be forced to suspend our membership of the ERM. I said we were coming to the end of the road. My confidence in the Treasury's ability to see what was happening had been diminished. Repeatedly we had been told recovery was about to take place, but perhaps we now faced a slump or a 'double dip' recession.

As I saw it, there were two scenarios under which we might be forced to leave the ERM:

(1) If the French said 'No' to Maastricht.
(2) If the Germans put up rates. It seemed to me there was no way that we could follow and put up rates when the economy was still languishing.

In both cases UK membership of the ERM would be suspended, rather than terminated.

It was agreed that leaving the ERM was not completely

unthinkable. Indeed, if the French rejected Maastricht there might be no other option. It was argued that pulling out in response to an increase in German rates might be difficult since any such increase would probably be small. Another option was to leave the ERM and to say we would only rejoin and ratify Maastricht once German rates had come down.

The best rationale for suspending membership was that the conditions prevailing and likely to prevail in Germany were not foreseen at the time of entry and had become irrelevant to our circumstances. It made no sense to persist for the moment. We would leave and return once Germany had sorted out its problems.

I said that under any of the scenarios it would be worth thinking again about the issue of Bank of England independence. We agreed that no work should be done at present on a contingency plan to leave the ERM, but that we would talk again about the subject in early September when, in any case, we needed to consider how to deal with a possible French 'No' vote. I would talk through some of the options with the PM.

At this stage I still believed that we could probably survive the pressures to 20 September, the date of the French referendum. After discussing the matter, the Prime Minister and I both decided it would be right for us both to stick with our holiday plans. Not to have done so would have given a bad signal to the markets.

9

The Glidepath Towards Disaster

History is the natural selection of accidents.
Leon Trotsky

Summary holidays in France and Italy

Ironically at the very top of the Lamont family suitcase for the summer holiday were no fewer than three mobile telephones. Arrangements had to be made for me to keep closely in touch with the Treasury. Even in Burgundy and Tuscany I was now no more than a dialling line away from the Bank of England and the Treasury. It was a new experience, as I had always resolutely refused to have a mobile telephone. A Treasury spokesman was reported to have said, 'After his holiday I think he will be even less keen . . . Do not be surprised to see a hike in the tax on mobile phones next Budget.'

We holidayed first with the de Mandat-Granceys at Grancey near Dijon and then drove on to Port Ercole, where Woodrow and Varushka Wyatt had taken the same house as the year before. But our holiday this year was less peaceful. Friends who holidayed in other parts of Tuscany told us they had been accosted by journalists seeking our whereabouts. Since we had holidayed at the Wyatts for several years, and had never made any secret of the fact, I was surprised it took the press so long to track us down, but soon we were besieged in the house by photographers. The Villa Safir was halfway up a hill covered in cypresses and olive trees. Some of the photographers and reporters at the back of the property would occasionally come over the garden fence trampling on the vegetables and flowers, but the main body were further up the hill with long-range telephoto lenses. Every time I ventured out of the house to go to the swimming pool the sun caught the reflection of the lenses in the woods. I decided it was wiser not to be photographed at the poolside in my not very flattering swimming trunks.

One day we went out to lunch at the Pelicano Hotel at the invitation of the owner, Roberto Shaw. We had a very pleasant lunch and afterwards I played table tennis and won against one of the Agnelli sons. The next day one of the tabloids had a picture of me eating my spaghetti and added, 'While UK businesses were going bust, Norman Lamont tucked into a £150 lunch yesterday.' We were also invited out on the yacht of a local businessman. One of the papers reported that I had hired the boat for £10,000. The businessman was very annoyed. 'They think my boat only costs £10,000 to hire.'

There were other lighter moments. We went with Woodrow, Varushka and Petronella to a party given in the Arboretum of Count Corsini, where I met Prince Bernhardt and Queen Juliana of the Netherlands. For some reason Prince Bernhardt thought I was a competitor from the Tour de France and engaged me for several minutes in a conversation about cycling. It was a relief not be known by some people.

Meanwhile the strains on sterling continued, but they were largely caused by the dollar, which was falling against the Deutschmark, which it was pushing up against the pound. At the beginning of August sterling closed above $2 to the pound as the dollar came under renewed pressures. Now I was in touch not just with the Treasury and the Bank of England but also with the US Treasury. Whatever reservations I had about the insensitivity of the Germans, they were nothing compared with the strong feelings held by Nick Brady as the dollar plunged in the foreign exchange markets.

A Treasury spokesman at the time commented, 'It's a funny

sort of crisis with the pound at $2.' He pointed out that both sterling and the lira were about 17 per cent stronger against the dollar than a year ago. The irony was that if the ERM had not existed this would not have been a crisis at all. There was in fact no sterling crisis, only an ERM one.

On 14 August sterling, pushed by the dollar, plunged to its lowest level ever in the ERM, down to DM 2.815, 3 pfennigs above its floor. 21 August was a very significant day, when eighteen central banks tried to prop up the dollar with massive support-buying. At one point, when these plans were being finalised, I had to telephone Nick Brady from the depths of a yacht belonging to the Italian representative of Schroders and had to take great care that the other passengers, several of them bankers, did not hear my conversation. The importance of the intervention on 21 August was that it failed. It demonstrated to the markets just how powerless central banks really were and paved the way for later events.

My attitude towards intervention in the foreign exchange markets was one of scepticism. Its value was limited. I accepted it was possible; if the timing was skilful or there was a 'thin market', that is low volume, then central banks might temporarily change sentiment and move a currency. But if the fundamentals were wrong no amount of intervention by central banks would make any difference. I was never keen to advocate intervention in the foreign exchange markets, and contrary to what has been written I was never one for flinging money into the foreign currency markets to support sterling

I had a three-way call with Terry Burns and Eddie George, the Deputy Governor of the Bank of England. We discussed the prospects of further intervention. Eddie George said he thought the pressure might last several weeks and would come on the French and the Italians. He was doubtful whether there was any solution short of Germany cutting interest rates.

I suggested our best card might be to put up rates; the French would have to do so too, which would threaten the referendum, so that Kohl would be encouraged to intervene. Eddie thought it was odds on that interest rates would have to rise.

Half an hour later I telephoned the PM in Spain, with Terry

Burns and Paul Gray listening from the Treasury. I told the PM we had spent some $3 billion – the pound was down to DM 2.80, but up against the dollar at $1.96. The odds were against avoiding an interest rise.

The PM was worried about the impact of a rate rise on European policy. There were thirty or forty 'irreconcilables' on Maastricht in the House of Commons. Higher rates would increase that number and might lead to a double dip recession. I said I thought I should come back. The PM was not keen, but said if I did I should play it as a routine matter.

Return to London and a growing crisis

I returned early from holiday on 24 August, though since the planned date for my return was not known this went unnoticed. Within hours of my return I again talked through with officials both the alternatives: suspension of our membership of the ERM, or the damage that would be caused if we had to put up interest rates to defend our membership of the ERM.

I questioned whether suspending our ERM membership now would be so damaging. Given the weakness of domestic demand, even a 20 per cent depreciation of the pound against the Deutschmark might not have any serious impact on inflation. On this point, as it turned out, my view was more realistic than the Treasury's. Again, we agreed that the option of leaving the ERM was clearly available but in the circumstances it might be potentially extremely damaging. A difficult situation didn't mean that another policy would make it easier.

The important issue was whether we would be able to reduce interest rates. Some doubts were expressed about whether a cut in interest rates would be sustainable in anything other than the short run. The Government's nerve might crack as the pound went into free fall, and interest rates would be forced up to defend the exchange rate. Officials argued that if we ended up with unchanged interest rates, plus a 20–25 per cent devaluation of the pound and a return to the ambiguities of a floating exchange rate regime, that would not be satisfactory.

We debated whether a depreciation on its own would boost activity. A lower nominal exchange rate might improve the current account, but it could also reduce domestic demand. We agreed that the only basis on which leaving the ERM would clearly benefit the economy would be if it led to 'sustainably lower interest rates'. Many people in the Treasury and the Bank were not persuaded that this would happen. Our inflation performance when floating had not been impressive and it was important not to underestimate the difficulties involved.

I accepted that the initial impact of withdrawal from the ERM would test the Government's nerve. My view was that it would probably lead to a depreciation down to DM 2.20/2.30 as the market overshot. However, once sterling began to steady and as inflation continued to fall, investors would gradually regain confidence in sterling. Other countries, I pointed out, had successfully pursued a strategy of allowing their exchange rates to float; indeed, Britain had lived for years with a floating exchange rate before joining the ERM.

We returned to the narrow question of how we would handle a 'No' vote in the French referendum. Again I argued, if a 2 per cent increase in rates was necessary, would we really soldier on regardless of the damage to the UK economy? Surely we could not carry on indefinitely with continuously falling GDP? There would come a point when we would have to say too high a price was being paid. We considered the view that we should be prepared to respond by putting up rates by 2 per cent, provided the increase seemed likely to be temporary. We also considered the case for a modest devaluation if higher interest rates had to remain in place for a fairly lengthy period or a further increase in rates was necessary. This might provide the basis for getting interest rates back down to German levels. My concern was that this could end up with the worst of all worlds, a modest devaluation and a major loss in confidence. To me it seemed there wasn't much logic in putting up rates followed by an ineffective devaluation to get them down again. It would be better to withdraw from ERM membership.

However, I did not believe we could acquiesce in a further year of continuing recession. If there was a French 'No', the appropriate first step would probably be to put up rates, and then it would be necessary to re-examine the whole issue of membership. In the meantime we would have to consider a package of measures to help the economy. I intended to speak to the Prime Minister about tax measures for the housing market, including a public expenditure package designed to take a large number of empty houses off the market.

I was informed that the PM did not want to retreat from the ERM as soon as our resolve was tested. He was therefore resigned to putting interest rates up early 'but not too soon'. The PM was prepared to write or speak to Kohl.

Having considered all the arguments and knowing the Prime Minister's views, I concluded once again that I had no option but to carry on with the current policy. Nonetheless if we got through the French referendum I thought that by the end of December I would reopen the whole question of whether we should remain within the ERM, a conclusion that was minuted by my Private Secretary. I would support the policy and continue with it, but only until the end of 1992.

This was a fateful decision on my part. Later I was to reflect it might have been better if I had followed my own instincts. However, I was not convinced that this was the right course to follow at that point and there was little ground for believing that I would have been able to persuade either the Prime Minister or other Ministers to accept a change in policy. We were trapped. Some might say that I should have forced the issue by threatening to resign. If I had resigned, it would have made sterling's position in the ERM untenable. To have forced a change in policy that way would have been dishonourable, and would have fatally damaged the Government. I would have got precious little thanks, since no one would have known in those circumstances what was going to be the result of staying in the ERM.

Of course, I did not discuss this only with Treasury officials. Earlier I had made one attempt to persuade the PM himself that we should consider suspending our membership of the ERM. I had approached Sarah Hogg outside the Cabinet Room about the subject very tentatively, beginning by saying that I had been thinking about what we could do and that I felt that if there was no recovery soon we should consider suspending membership of the ERM.

She interrupted me before I could complete the sentence. I thought she would dismiss the idea, but to my surprise she disclosed that she had been thinking along exactly the same lines. She then talked to the PM and I talked briefly to him too, and we agreed that we would meet to discuss the subject of withdrawal from the ERM. I was both surprised and excited. A meeting was set up with the PM to discuss the matter, but it had to be done in the greatest possible secrecy. Alex Allan, the PM's Principal Private Secretary, knew about it, but Mary Francis, the No. 2 Private Secretary, was told it was a meeting to discuss the Honours List.

I spent some time with Jeremy Heywood discussing the pros and cons and how we could manage the presentation. On the day I turned up for the meeting, I slipped into the sitting room and sat down. The Prime Minister began with a few pleasantries and started talking about the political situation, which went on for perhaps ten minutes or a quarter of an hour. I felt a little anxious that we were never going to get to the point. No doubt the Prime Minister would have other meetings, so we needed to get a move on. I gently reminded him that we had come to discuss the highly sensitive subject of our withdrawal from the ERM. The PM looked up with a surprised expression. 'Oh no, I don't want to discuss that at all, I want to discuss my speech for next week.'

I was stunned and appalled that such a vital discussion should be shoved to one side simply to discuss a political speech for the following week. But the PM was quite firm. 'I don't want to discuss leaving the ERM,' he said. Completely puzzled, I went back to the Treasury. My Private Office could see that I was in a furious mood. I told them what had happened, and said I would return to the subject at the end of the year. I was not to know that events would overwhelm us before then. I have not been able to find a record of that meeting. Since it turned out to be a non-meeting it is not surprising there is no record.

An attempt to co-ordinate policy

Shortly after my meeting with officials on 24 August I had a meeting with Eddie George. The pound had had a fair day and remained in touch with the DM at 2.80, doing better than the franc or the lira. The dollar had continued to fall and was now DM 1.40. We had intervened to about $640 million and had now taken a total of $5 billion out of the market to support the dollar. After that I telephoned Michel Sapin, the new French Finance Minister (Bérégovoy having become PM) and asked him to arrange a G4 Meeting with France, Germany, Italy and ourselves for Wednesday, in advance of the Ecofin meeting scheduled for Bath. Sapin was desperate for us not to put up rates.

The next day, Tuesday 25 August, I talked to Brady. He said he would get George Bush to call Helmut Kohl. An independent bank, he said, should not mean that it was indifferent to other countries' interests. That observation was chillingly reinforced by a call from Eddie George, who had visited the Bundesbank that day. The Germans, he said, were sympathetic but showed no inclination to help. Hans Tietmeyer, the number two at the Bank, had said lower interest rates would send the wrong signal, and had noted that many Germans would welcome the end of Maastricht. It seemed the Bundesbank was not too concerned about the wider implications of high German rates. When I reported that to the PM he was incandescent.

Sterling closed above DM 2.79, but slipped back later. Both the lira and the French franc were stretched. Two polls in France suggested that the result on Maastricht would be extremely close.

During these two days I and officials were in contact with nearly all my opposite numbers in Europe, trying to find common ground and a way forward. It was not easy, but as Chairman of Ecofin I tried to organise a statement by all the EU Finance Ministers that we were all committed to existing parities.

The Prime Minister was keen that I should again try to talk up sterling on my own. Some senior Treasury officials were opposed, and I was not keen. What would it add? But No. 10 pressed very strongly for a statement. On the morning of Wednesday 26 August I appeared on the steps of the Treasury and explained I wanted to remove any 'scintilla of doubts about the pound'. I added, 'We are going to maintain sterling's parity and we will do whatever is necessary.' My statement was followed by overt intervention by the Bank of England, as had been planned, then as

Chairman of Ecofin I issued the statement from all the Finance
Ministers that they remained committed to existing ERM parities.
'A change in the present structure of central rates would not be
the appropriate response to the current tensions.' It was not just
a British statement, but a European one.

I had spoken on the telephone to most of the Finance Ministers
and none, not even Waigel, had disagreed. Most were enthusiastic supporters. But amazingly again this agreed declaration was
undermined by public destabilising remarks by the Bundesbank.
This time it was Mr Jochimsen, a member of the Bundesbank
Board, who said there was 'potential for realignment within the
ERM'. The EU Ministers' remarks had no effect on the markets,
which could see clearly for themselves the wide interest rate differential between the US dollar and the Deutschmark that was
one of the root problems, and of course the continuing public disagreements between the Bundesbank and the rest of Europe.

A hurried G4 Meeting

That afternoon I flew to Paris for the G4 Meeting of Sapin,
Waigel, Barucci and myself, together with the Central Bank
Governors, LaRosière (France), Tietmeyer deputising for
Schlesinger (Germany), Ciampi (Italy) and Leigh-Pemberton (UK).
Just before I left there was a message from Eddie George who said
the Italians were furious with the Germans. Eddie felt that we
might get somewhere with the Germans if all three countries put
pressure on them. The Germans had plenty to be shamefaced
about. This morning's statement had worked until the Germans
had messed it up.

But the meeting did not get very far. Building on what
Schlesinger had said earlier, we tried to put together a package
that included a statement that German rates would go no higher,
activating the Basle-Nyborg agreements on mutual support, and
saying there would be no realignments. But Tietmeyer was very
difficult and Waigel not helpful. I had pointed out that Germany's
subsidised credits to the East, effectively lowering interest rates,
were exacerbating the problem.

The question then arose of whether the United States might make a statement that it would not reduce its rates further. That might help the Germans to agree to a statement on their rates. I was always struck on these occasions how the Europeans assumed I was able to speak for the Americans. Of course I could not, but I agreed to telephone Nick Brady about whether he would make a statement that there would be no further interest rate reductions by the United States. When I called him he said he could not make such a commitment, not least when they were about to fight an Election. I duly reported back the conversation but I did not mention that Brady had also said that he did not trust the Germans.

That night Jeremy Heywood reported to the Prime Minister. He was upset, and said we had supported the Germans over reunification and were now paying an excessive price. He wanted me to be as tough as possible with them.

It seemed like a complete breakdown in international co-operation. It was a case of each man for himself and the devil take the hindmost. What struck me was the hostility of the Bundesbank to Maastricht. Chancellor Kohl might be committed to it but Tietmeyer was openly hostile to it and Waigel at times distinctly cool. In some ways I sympathised, but this was not a graceful exit but a road to disaster.

We scratched around trying to find other ways to persuade the Germans to move, but there seemed no escape. The Germans would accept a unilateral Deutschmark revaluation. So would we. But the French wouldn't and if Britain was left with what appeared like a unilateral devaluation of sterling we would be lumped with higher interest rates.

One possibility was to persuade the Dutch and the Belgians to cut their rates, which would have the effect of pushing the Deutschmark to the top of its band in the ERM, possibly giving the Germans an incentive to cut rates. On the other hand it might increase German pressure for a unilateral revaluation. The Belgians, after feelers were put out to them, made it clear that they did not want to be seen as the fall guys.

Every day seemed a nail-biting eternity. A pattern emerged that outside European market hours sterling fell dangerously lower. In theory that did not matter as we were not obliged by the rules of the ERM to intervene or maintain the parity outside European market hours, but these sharp dips in the pound in the New York market were worrying and one always wondered whether sterling would open the next day within its bands in Europe.

A fiscal package?

All this time the domestic economy was not moving and that was the real problem which the markets could see and underpinned the weakness of sterling. The Monthly Monetary Assessment delivered by the Treasury at the beginning of September made grim reading. There were fears that manufacturing output would fall again. Growth in the United States had checked, Germany and Japan were slowing fast. The case for an interest rate reduction on domestic grounds was entirely persuasive and carried no risks, but we had no room.

The housing market remained the biggest source of worry. The temporary removal of stamp duty and the Election had not produced the expected results. Particulars delivered (contracts completed) were running at about an annual rate of 1 million against an annual average in the 1980s of 1.6 million. The nightmare scenario was that the weakness of the market would interact with consumption to cause output to fall further. A further fall of 10 per cent in house prices would be worrying. Talk in the newspapers of a slump or a 1930s-style depression was, of course, wildly exaggerated. Or was it?

Since the PM's Seminar at the end of July, we had been considering measures that might be included in another package, particularly if interest rates went up. These included bringing forward some items of public spending for next year, not a very practical idea given the speed at which Whitehall operated. The PM was keen on workfare on the US model, whereby the unemployed would be given community work to do in exchange for benefit. We also looked at possible time-limited increases in mortgage interest relief. This would have been a U-turn after my 1991

Budget and the PM rightly observed that it was the sort of policy that had got us into this mess in the first place.

Actions speak louder than words, particularly words uttered on the steps of the Treasury. My next move was to utilise an idea devised by the Bank of England and Eddie George. On Thursday 3 September we announced that the Bank was going to supplement the reserves by borrowing 10 billion ecus (£7.25 billion) selling them on the foreign exchange for sterling. The significance of this was that firstly it added to the reserves, secondly it underlined the government's determination to maintain the parity because the loan would have to be repaid in foreign currency. It was a clever idea, well received by the press, and it impressed the market. Sterling did rise quickly above DM 2.80 for the first time in two weeks.

The Seguin/Mitterrand debate

That evening, 3 September, was the occasion of the televised debate between Philip Seguin, then leader of the anti-Maastricht campaign in France, and President Mitterrand. Chancellor Kohl was participating in the pre-debate jamboree. John Major had declined to do so, but sent a message and tried to influence French public opinion by announcing that Maastricht would be withdrawn in the House of Commons in the event of a French 'No'.

The tone of the French Government's referendum campaign was distinctly odd. Both Pierre Bérégovoy and Michel Rocard, the former Prime Minister, adopted a tone that could only be described as xenophobic as they continually referred to the 'dragons' and 'tigers' of the Far East. More offensively, there were some none too oblique references to the teutonic demons in the German soul. Some of their comments drew protests from German politicians.

Mitterrand mustered all the glitterati to beat the drum for Maastricht. Thanks to Jack Lange, the former Culture Minister, the government was able to round up a public endorsement from many singers, musicians and film-makers, including Catherine

Deneuve, Gerard Depardieu, Charles Aznavour and Placido
Domingo. Elton John and Clint Eastwood warmed up the audience; what Clint Eastwood had to do with it was not clear. The
debate with Philip Seguin was relegated to after 11 o'clock, and
before that Mitterrand was interviewed by three pro-Maastricht
journalists.

I watched the debate between Mitterand and Seguin from the
small TV room in Wellington Square, where we were living while
No.11 was being refurbished after the IRA bombing. I had never
met Seguin, but I admired him greatly and still do. That night he
seemed the embodiment of a certain type of provincial Gauloise-
smoking Frenchman. Mentally I wished him luck. I was both
impressed and depressed by his elaborate courtesy to Mitterrand
and admired his respect for the institution of the Presidency, but
I was appalled at his failure to correct Mitterrand on some blatant misrepresentations, particularly about the European Central
Bank. Mitterrand stated quite untruthfully 'the technicians of
the European Central Bank are charged with applying in the
monetary domain the decisions of the European Council . . .
One hears it said that the European Central Bank will be the
master of the decisions. It is not true . . . The people who decide
economic policy of which monetary policy is no more than a
means of implementation are the politicians.' Six years later I
asked Charles Pasqua, the former Interior Minister in Balladur's
Government, whether Mitterrand was ignorant or deliberately
lying. He replied, 'Probably a bit of both.' I was puzzled by
Seguin's failure to expose this rewriting of Maastricht to the
French people.

Mitterrand's misleading description of Maastricht did not go
unnoticed in Germany either in the Bundesbank or in the German
press. The French President's remarks reopened fears in the
Bundesbank that they were being led up the primrose path by the
politicians. Schlesinger himself a few weeks later expressed doubts
whether European countries other than Germany would appoint
genuinely independent figures to the Board of the European
Central Bank. His determination to maintain the independence of
the Bundesbank even if it undermined Maastricht must have been
strengthened.

The Bath Ecofin: an angry meeting

On Friday 4 September the Bank of Italy, in a desperate attempt to safeguard the crumbling lira, now increased its discount rate again by 1.75 per cent to a hefty 15 per cent. It was scarcely credible. Italian industrialists, including the Europhile Giovanni Agnelli, complained strongly. No one could say the Italian Government hadn't done almost everything to maintain their commitment. The Italians were now looking for help from the Germans and hoping something might be achieved at the informal Ecofin meeting to be held under my Chairmanship at Bath that weekend. I had already had many talks with Piero Barucci, Michel Sapin and Carlos Solchaga, the Spanish Finance Minister, and there were other talks at official levels. Our strategy was agreed and planned well in advance.

Much has been written about that weekend, criticising my Chairmanship and the strong pressure that I put on Dr Schlesinger and the Germans. It has sometimes been alleged that in some way I broke the unwritten rules of the Chairmanship.

My Finance Minister colleagues had made it very clear to me that the last hope was a cut in German interest rates. On the Friday evening at Bath we had a G4 pre-meeting – France, Germany, Italy and the UK – at which the need for a cut in German rates was emphasised by Italy and France. The word 'realignment' was not mentioned. Whatever difficulties Germany was experiencing, only political intervention could save the ERM from a real crisis. Countries like Italy felt they had done everything they could within the rules; the French were also unhappy with the Germans and the same was true of the Irish and the Danes. Across the Atlantic, Nicholas Brady was bitterly critical of the Bundesbank. After hearing what other Finance Ministers and officials thought, I had discussed the situation at length with the Prime Minister. Far from urging caution, he was one of the keenest that I should put maximum pressure on Dr Schlesinger and throughout that weekend in Bath I received several messages from the PM reminding me that it was essential to put pressure on the Germans to cut interest rates.

I agreed completely. It was a long shot but it was not entirely without hope. There were some tensions between the German Government and the Bundesbank. Both Kohl and Waigel themselves were known to be somewhat impatient with it. On previous occasions, such as the Plaza and Louvre Agreements, the Germans had, in the interests of international co-operation, decided to alter their interest rate policy. To raise the question of doing that again within a European policy that they themselves so strongly advocated did not seem unreasonable. Nor was it unprecedented.

We stayed in the Royal Bath Hotel in the Royal Crescent. It was a delightful setting. On the Saturday morning when all the Finance Ministers and Central Bank Governors came out to have a group photograph, there was a small demonstration taking place. It was an anti-Maastricht, anti-ERM demonstration. One of the demonstrators carried a placard with the words 'ERM – the *Extending Recession Mechanism*'. I thought to myself that it was not just clever, but quite right. I wished I could say that.

In my heart I thought attempts to persuade Dr Schlesinger to cut interest rates were probably in the end unlikely to succeed. European co-operation was not high on Dr Schlesinger's agenda, and he deeply disliked Maastricht. Most of all he was an old style monetarist, determined to maintain the independence of the Bundesbank, doubly so after Mitterrand's remarks during the televised debate.

Early on the Saturday morning I held a meeting with Sapin and Barucci to discuss tactics. The Italians did not want to devalue and the French did not want them to do so either, as they would be next in line. They wanted us to be tough with the Germans, and if necessary said we might have to keep the meeting going until Sunday.

At the same time there was a series of telephone calls between myself, the PM, my Private Secretary Jeremy Heywood, and Terry Burns, who was not due to be at the meeting and who was going off to play golf. The PM prophetically said that it was a choice between a crisis now and a slow death later, and his inclination was to have the row now. The PM was anxious that the Italians should say at the outset that they had to sort out their position. The best option was a reduction in German interest rates now. If that did not happen we would have to have an Italian devaluation which, of course, would impact not just on the franc but on the French referendum and thus the whole of Maastricht. The PM said he was happy for me to be as tough as I wanted with the Germans and to keep them there for as long as it took.

The meeting began with a very gloomy assessment of the European economy by Henning Christophersen of the Commission. He presented the latest forecasts, slashing growth, indicating that those countries that were in recession showed no sign of coming out and that other countries, including Germany, were possibly going to slow down. Everyone agreed that the prospects for the European economy were exceedingly gloomy.

We then moved on to the ERM. The discussion was opened by the Italians, who did not want to devalue but stressed the need for action and agreement. Sapin, for France, had followed with a strong plea for German action and suggested four points: no realignment; more co-ordination; at least a token reduction in German rates; and further budgetary measures by the Italians. Tactically this was poor, as it was probably not enough. He was, however, strongly supported by the Danes and the Irish. The Germans insisted they could not loosen further, but it became clear there were differences between Waigel and Schlesinger. I continued to press and said we could not leave without a solution. At this point I asked Jeremy to ask Terry Burns, who was just completing his nine holes of golf, whether he would come down and join us, which he did at about 3.30 in the afternoon.

A draft communiqué prepared by the central bank Governors contained some words about there being no case for further German rate increases. The feeling of the meeting was that this was still not enough. The PM was telephoned; he was keen for us to try for a better outcome.

I too doubted whether the draft communiqué would satisfy the markets. I went round the table and asked for views as to whether we should continue for longer or into tomorrow. The Italians, French, Danes and Irish argued for a stronger communiqué, even if it took longer. The Dutch, Belgians and Germans said the longer the meeting lasted the bigger the problem, which was a point. The Germans made it clear that in their view an Italian realignment, in reality a devaluation, should be one of the possibilities. There was also a suggestion made that instead of a communiqué there should be a statement of conclusions by the Chairman. We then took a break. There was a problem in going on after 7 p.m. as the room was required for a dance! I said to Barucci and Ciampi, the Governor of the Bank of Italy, that it was clear that the Germans would go no further; the choice lay between holding a realignment meeting tomorrow or reaching an agreement tonight and Italy taking its chance with the markets. Piero said they would take their chance. A revised draft in the form of the Chairman's conclusion appeared from Jacques LaRosière, the Governor of the Banque de France.

I am told that I put my request to Dr Schlesinger to cut rates four times in all. Of course, that was after a long discussion and analysis of the situation, but apparently he later complained that no one had ever spoken to him in his life like that before. Well, perhaps he had not lived very fully. Perhaps our tradition of argument is more robust than in other countries. Other Ministers, such as Piero Barucci, Michel Sapin, and Bertie Ahern, on whose behalf I was talking, said much the same, and to a lesser extent it was also true of George Macedo de Braga of Portugal and Carlos Solchaga of Spain. It is true that the central bankers, who wanted to support the professional independence of the Bundesbank, said relatively little. Nevertheless, as Ciampi was to show in an outburst later, some of them were also exasperated with the Germans. He knew, as the Finance Ministers knew, that if there was no change in policy the ERM was going to come under intense pressure. Much has also been written about how a 'realignment' of the ERM, that is, a devaluation of several currencies, could have solved all the problems, and how an opportunity was lost. I have already indicated that the French had told me unambiguously that they were adamantly opposed to a revaluation of the Deutschmark and they were also reluctant to see a devaluation of the lira. The British Treasury had also concluded that a unilateral devaluation of the pound or a devaluation of the pound alongside the lira and the peseta would put up interest rates rather than reduce them.

In the light of what subsequently happened to those currencies and their interest rates, The Treasury analysis seems valid even today. As we now know, some currencies did devalue and Germany did revalue, but interest rates did not come down significantly in the countries that devalued, and for some they went up. Without a rate cut Britain would have been stuck in recession.

But the fact is that there was no easy solution on offer at Bath. Why people should imply there was I cannot imagine. I can only conclude they wished to blame other people or to explain away their own failure to address the crisis that was staring us in the face.

The Chairman's conclusion ended with a sentence that Schlesinger somewhat reluctantly had agreed to: 'In the light of a slowing of the growth prospects of their economies, and in so far as the disinflationary process allows it, they have decided to take advantage of any opportunity to reduce interest rates.' This was followed by the critical sentence: 'They [Ministers and central bank Governors] welcomed the fact that the Bundesbank in present circumstances has no intention to increase rates and is watching closely the further development of the economy.'

The phrase 'in present circumstances' had been inserted at the insistence of Schlesinger, as was the phrase 'in so far as the disinflationary process allows'. But the communiqué reflected the overwhelming sense of other Ministers, not just myself, that the minimum co-operation in the European project demanded political action.

The few sentences on interest rates did not really add up to much. Michel Sapin rather pounced on it and said to the press, 'The Bundesbank is no longer in a frame of mind to raise rates.' I was more circumspect, merely drawing journalists' attention to the last sentence and observing it was the first time such an observation 'had been made openly and publicly'. That was true. However, Schlesinger quickly and unhelpfully made it clear that the communiqué represented 'no change in our policy'.

Later that evening all Ministers, central bank Governors, officials and their wives had dinner in the Pump Room. Later, when I had a late-night drink with Terry, he told me that after dinner Schlesinger and Wim Duisenburg, the Governor of the Dutch central bank, approached him separately and said we should have opted for parity adjustments. This was more than they had said at the meeting. Terry, and others to whom the conversation was reported, reacted sceptically. It was difficult to know what weight to give to it.

I said that my view was that the meeting demonstrated all too clearly that there were opposing and irreconcilable national interests. The French and Italians had their reasons and so did we, but the Germans also had a case from their point of view. I again said we should leave the ERM and look after our own interests. We needed an easier policy stance. I felt a fall in the UK exchange rate was unlikely to do much damage to inflation and would reverse itself as the economy recovered.

The next day just as we were departing Schlesinger gave my wife a gift of a presentation case with thirty silver Deutschmarks in it. I have to confess that unkind phrases about thirty pieces of silver reverberated in my mind.

Despite all that has been written subsequently, at the time the Bath Ecofin did not receive such a bad press. *The Times* wrote that Finance Ministers and central bank Governors 'were pleased that Mr Lamont's conducting of the chorus resulted in the German saying that at least they would not put up interest rates for the moment'. In *The Times* business section the headline was 'Bath Finance Meeting signals short term relief for the pound.' Gavyn Davies wrote in the *Independent*: 'It has been an unreservedly good week for the Chancellor.' The pound on Monday morning rose above DM 2.85 but fell back in the afternoon after unexpectedly strong consumer borrowing figures. Analysts said the figures represented a rush to beat the deadline for the ending of the suspension of stamp duty.

Italy in the front line, but Finland falls first

Despite the attention of the English press on the pound the main focus was elsewhere. Hamish McCrae wrote in the *Independent*: 'The problem is not sterling, but the lira. The lira will have to be devalued within a matter of months, not so much because it is overvalued but because the high interest rates needed to defend it are increasing the cost of funding the country's debt.'

We were following the lira but the next unexpected news came from a distant part of the battlefield. On Tuesday 8 September Finland, having exhausted a large part of its reserves, floated the markka against the ecu and the result was an immediate depreciation of 14 per cent. They had already devalued by 12 per cent the previous year. Strictly speaking, the markka was not part of the ERM, but the Finnish Government had made a policy decision to link the currency to the ecu and to operate interest rate policy as though it were part of the ERM. The Finns had now decided they could not afford to go on defending their currency.

The implications for the markets were clear. Intervention could not continue indefinitely. The move intensified immediate fears for the lira and the pound if the French voted 'No' in the referendum. Schlesinger once again unbelievably added to the tensions by stressing that Germany could still in theory put up rates, but now the crisis was spreading to other Scandinavian currencies including the Norwegian krone and the Danish krone and also the Swedish krona, like the Finnish markka not in the ERM but pegged to the ecu. The markets saw it as the next domino. The Swedes pushed overnight interest rates up to 24 per cent and mortgage rates went up 5 per cent in a week. On Wednesday the Swedes shoved short-term rates up again to 75 per cent. They were at this stage hoping currencies under siege might receive some political support from the Germans, but a Bundesbank source was quoted as saying, 'The lira, the peseta and the pound were all candidates for devaluation.'

The *Daily Telegraph* had commented the day before: 'Even the hardest Landesbanker must now be feeling a few pangs of guilt at the Euro misery he is inflicting on Europe from North to South.' There were few signs of German guilt. Ciampi, the Governor of the Bank of Italy, who had said little at Bath, revealed his true feelings when he said German interest rates 'were excessively high and needed to be brought down'.

The markets continued to dump the lira and on Friday 11 September it actually closed below its ERM floor. This caused huge problems for the Germans, who under the rules of the ERM were obliged to satisfy the demand for Deutschmarks from holders of lira at the official parity. Dr Schlesinger later said that the Bundesbank had taken in DM 24 billion, which swelled Germany's money supply. Of course, under the rules of the ERM the Italians would have to repay the Germans, but it caused problems for Germany and Schlesinger felt it necessary to draw it to the attention of Chancellor Kohl. The closure of the markets at the weekend was a relief, but with five trading days to go it was still possible that we could get through to 20 September. We had, after all, remained above the official floor despite everything.

My view, stated on several occasions, was that if there were a French 'No', as seemed quite possible, we should leave the ERM. We should say German rates were not suitable for the United Kingdom, and leave for the time being. Officials tended to think that we should raise rates and try to realign before actually leaving.

The Germans to the rescue: too little, too late

On Saturday night the Treasury team was dispersed. I went to the Last Night of the Proms with Rosemary and Bryan Gould and his wife, as guests of John Birt and Joel Barnett, Director-General and Vice-Chairman of the BBC. It had been an exhausting and draining week. I have to say that the singing of 'Land of Hope and Glory' and 'Rule Britannia' matched something in my mood. Bryan and I competed to see who could sing the most heartily. At one point I turned to Bryan and shouted against the din, 'No ecus here.'

At the same time Terry Burns was at Dulwich College for the twenty-fifth wedding anniversary of Andrew Turnbull and his wife. There Terry received a call from Nigel Wicks. Terry reminded Nigel it was a 'squidgy line'. Nigel then said, 'Remember our sick friend. Well, I think he is going to have an operation tomorrow, and our strong friend shows signs of moving.'

When I returned to our temporary house in Wellington Square, I quickly found Nigel Wicks on the line. He told me he had been rung by Jean-Claude Trichet, the Director of the French Trésor, and told that the Italians had decided to devalue. At the same time there would be a 0.25 per cent reduction in the Lombard rate and 0.5 per cent reduction in the discount rate. Nothing had been said about any other currency. Our conversation was brief. From our point of view it was not bad news. Whether it would do the Italians any good was a different matter, but the German cut, albeit small, might take some pressure off the pound. I arranged to meet early the next morning with Eddie George, Nigel Wicks and other officials.

Normally an emergency meeting like this would have been held in Downing Street but because it was still under reconstruction we met in the Treasury at 7 a.m. on Sunday. The Treasury building, great though my affection for it is, is not a very welcoming one and on that Sunday morning seemed bleaker than ever. We had some croissants brought in. Nigel reported on the conversations he had held with Mario Draghi of the Italian Treasury and Jean-Claude Trichet. The latter had assured him that reductions were 'guaranteed'. Nigel said this decision to cut rates had been made after a huge row between Schlesinger and Kohl.

Eddie George was worried that the devaluation of the lira would be announced before the reduction in German rates was known and after the beginning of trading in the Far East. It was agreed that it would be a good idea if the Germans could at least announce that the Bundesbank would be meeting to discuss an interest rate change at the same time as the Italian devaluation was announced. It was decided Eddie would telephone Tietmeyer, the Deputy to Schlesinger, to press them to be as forthcoming as possible. We assumed the Germans themselves would not want sterling to come under pressure, because under the rules of the ERM they would be forced to intervene in support of sterling on an even larger scale than they had been required to with the lira. Eddie George phoned Tietmeyer, who agreed to announce that the Bundesbank Council would be meeting to discuss an interest rate reduction.

My worry was that a 7 per cent devaluation would do nothing for the Italians. It hardly seemed enough, but this was probably the maximum they could get away with. The convention was that realignments should be by small amounts, particularly now that the ERM had become a precursor to the single currency and a sort of 'hard ERM'. One could only hope that the markets would particularly notice the interest rate cut and come to the conclusion that Germany had finally decided to reduce interest rates in order to reduce tensions between currencies.

In the event the reaction in the markets was moderately favourable, at least initially. This was helped by the fact that the Dutch and Belgian central banks also cut rates by 0.25 per cent. The lira went to the top of its new band and unsurprisingly sterling was at its lower limit against the lira, but at 10.30 a.m. it was at DM 2.81, comfortably above its floor of 2.7780. By 12.15 p.m. we had spent $700 million. The Swedes, responding to the rate cut, reduced their overnight rates from 75 per cent to 25 per cent. Sterling closed higher than at any time since the Bath Ecofin.

On Monday night, 14 September, I again met with the Prime Minister, Terry Burns, Alex Allan and Sarah Hogg to discuss contingency plans for the French referendum the following weekend, which was going to coincide with a G7 Meeting. The official record of the meeting appears to be missing. According to both Anthony Seldon, Major's biographer, and Philip Stephens, I raised the question of sterling's suspension from the ERM. They imply that this was not done seriously, but with a view to putting down 'a marker'. That is not the way I thought. I imagine Seldon and Stephens have been fed this line by the same source. Stephens also reports that Major said that if there was no easing of the tensions in the system, the Government might well have to suspend the ERM before Christmas. I can categorically say that the Prime Minister never at any time in my presence made any such remark implying any sympathy with the idea of leaving the ERM. The only remarks he made about withdrawal to me were to the effect that he wasn't prepared to discuss it. If he had made such a remark I would certainly have seized on it and remembered it.

Stephens, in his account of this meeting, also says that the Prime Minister and I were forced to recognise the growing conviction among officials that the link with the Deutschmark could not be sustained indefinitely. He adds, 'Eddie George was certain that a change in sterling's parity was unavoidable.' Neither I, nor, I imagine, John Major ever had any reason to think that that was the opinion of Eddie George and I do not believe it was. Philip

Stephens also says that Sir John Kerr thought it might be possible to negotiate a 10–15 per cent devaluation of sterling. At no time did Sir John ever suggest that to me.

In his book Anthony Seldon says that I made a point of recalling this meeting in my resignation speech, implying that I exaggerated the seriousness of the remarks I made about suspending our membership. But it was not this meeting to which I referred in my resignation speech, but the earlier meeting in which I had tried unsuccessfully to raise the question of withdrawal from the ERM but the Prime Minister would not discuss it.

Although the meeting was really about the French referendum I said that if we reached next year and there was no recovery we should reconsider our membership of the ERM. In the short run we should defend our position, even if it meant we had to put up interest rates. I said I was prepared to put them up aggressively if there was a French 'No', even though that would be very unpopular, but if we continued to be locked into zero growth the policy would have to be reconsidered in January. We could not go on for another year without recovery.

The PM took the meeting back to the immediate subject and we discussed the reaction in Westminster to a French 'No' vote. John Major said that Kohl wanted to salvage Maastricht even if there were a 'No'. I do recall that I was quite adamant that a 'No' must be the end of Maastricht, and Major agreed.

The PM said we were not looking for an exit from the ERM. That would cause chaos. Even if the problems persisted, he would not be keen to come out. He then added prophetically that it wouldn't happen like that. 'Great policy changes are brought about by events.'

It was agreed that I should be in touch with EU Finance Ministers. They would all be in Washington. We were going to meet in the IMF Board Room, and would try to co-ordinate both our words and our actions after the French referendum.

On Tuesday 15 September the markets had second thoughts and concluded that the Bundesbank cut was insufficient. The peseta, the lira and the pound all fell sharply in the ERM. The pound closed at DM 2.7812, only a third of a pfennig above its

DM limit. In New York that night it traded below the DM limit
for the first time. That was in one sense ominous, but it was outside the formal European trading times.

That evening Rosemary and I were due to have dinner with
Ray Seitz, the US Ambassador, at his residence in Regent's Park,
but first I had an evening meeting with the Governor of the Bank
of England, the Deputy Governor and Terry at the Treasury.
Robin said that, despite the pressure, the Bank had decided
against overt intervention that day because there was a danger of
bringing the spotlight too much on sterling. The attention had
been focused on the Swedish krona and the lira.

I discussed whether we should put up interest rates. Robin said
he thought we should be prepared to undertake substantial overt
intervention first before contemplating interest rate increases.
Eddie George said that if higher rates did not succeed in holding
the pound, the only option would be to float. I agreed, and added
it would be very difficult if that happened to re-enter the ERM.
Our plan, as agreed that night for the next day, was that overt
intervention should begin between 8 and 8.30 a.m. If that did not
succeed, we would put up rates. If that failed to hold the rate, we
would have no option but to suspend our membership.

We were at the point of breaking up when the Governor said he
had just been informed that Schlesinger had been reported by the
news agencies as saying that a wider realignment than the previous weekend's would probably have been a good thing. I was
stunned. I could not believe that after all that had happened we
could have yet more comments from the Bundesbank, let alone
from its President. I asked the Governor to speak to Schlesinger.
He was worried about interrupting Schlesinger's dinner, but he
did so and came back to say that Schlesinger had given a joint
interview to the *Wall Street Journal* and to *Handelsblatt*. With
amazing complacency, Schlesinger said he would be given the
opportunity to see and comment on any quotation attributed to
him but he had not yet done so. He would make sure there was
no quotation of the sort rumoured to be in the article. He complained bitterly that the UK press often made up quotes and
attributed them to him. This seemed all too leisurely a response,
and I asked the Governor to talk to him again. A direct denial was

the minimum we needed. I had to go off to the Embassy, but I said I would talk to the Governor again later.

The dinner at the US Embassy was quite a large one and the party was divided up into a number of separate tables. One of those present was Richard Lambert, the editor of the *Financial Times*. According to accounts I have read I berated him for the coverage I had heard his paper was giving to Schlesinger's remarks. I may have overdone it, but it was hardly surprising in the circumstances.

Ray Seitz is one of the suavest and most entertaining of diplomats and I was embarrassed that I had to leave my table several times to talk on the telephone to the Governor. At 8.45 p.m. I had my first telephone call to Robin, when I emphasised that it was necessary to have a complete denial from Schlesinger. Robin was reluctant to go back to him again and I had to insist that he did so. At 9.15 p.m. I had my second call, when Robin said that Schlesinger had said that the remark attributed to him was in fact part of the journalist's question. The press office of the Bundesbank said the quotations were from an 'unauthorised version' of the interview, since no official version had yet been approved. Schlesinger said that when he reached his office in the morning he would check the article and issue an appropriate statement. He was unwilling to issue an immediate denial. Accordingly, all the Bundesbank was prepared to say that night was that it was an 'unauthorised disclosure'. I knew that the markets would be deeply troubled by Schlesinger's remarks.

That night, when I went to bed, I thought the next day would be a very difficult one. But I did not in any way foresee the scale of what was to happen, let alone that the next day would see the end of our membership of the ERM. It simply did not cross my mind.

10

Black or White Wednesday?

Everything looks stupid when it fails.
Fyodor Dostoyevsky

Storms produce lightning, and in these flashes we see men as
they really are.

Raymond Asquith

In the morning's papers Schlesinger's remarks were widely publicised and were every bit as bad as I feared, although
unsurprisingly only the so-called 'unauthorised version' of his
remarks was published. He was quoted as having said, 'the situation in the EMS could have been further eased if there had been
a more comprehensive realignment', words that could not have
been more deliberately calculated to damage our position. It was
difficult to believe that anyone, let alone the Governor of a central
bank, could have behaved in such a cavalier way. The effects
were bound to be devastating.

The avalanche began immediately. Sterling plunged to the
bottom of its band. By 8.30 a.m. the Bank of England had done
two shots of £300 million of intervention, each to no great effect.
This had taken us initially to about DM 2.7850, but we had
fallen back to DM 2.7795. It intended to do another burst of
£400 million. The Bank said we were staring a base rate increase
in the face.

At 8.40 a.m. I had a meeting with Terry. By this time the Bank had spent £1 billion. The French were not under pressure and it was clear we had to put up rates. The Bank would say it was just for the next few days to get through to 20 September and draw up a schedule of tapered daily rates to give the impression we thought it would be short-lived. The Bank thought if the rate rise did not work we should then float, leaving base rates at their new level, requesting a decision from me by 9.45 a.m. when money market operations began. I told Terry he must ignore everything I had said in our private chats. We had to do what was necessary.

At 8.50 am I telephoned the PM and said I believed we should increase interest rates, describing to him the plight of sterling. The PM said he was not keen to do so. Amazingly, he told me that some good economic indicators were to be publicised later on that day. I was taken aback. I had accepted the PM wanted to stay in the ERM, but there was no way we could do so if he was unwilling to put up interest rates.

At 9 a.m. I summoned a meeting with Terry, the Governor, Eddie, Andrew Turnbull, the Deputy Secretary, Treasury, Paul Gray and Bill Robinson. The Governor reported that already there had been three tranches of overt intervention totalling £1 billion. The first two had not been very effective because a large number of traders had bought sterling out of hours in New York and Tokyo and they had been able simply to turn up and get their money converted at the official rate. Money markets were anticipating a rise of 1 per cent or possibly as much as 2 per cent that morning. Eddie George said that the Bank would continue to intervene to see if the situation improved, but he expected the position to worsen and the pressure to increase after 10 a.m.

We discussed a proposal from the Bank to act on very short-term interest rates. The danger was that the markets might think such a move indicated a lack of resolve or simply might be thought too clever. In any case a rise of a few percentage points in the rate for three days would not offset the potential for capital gain if sterling were devalued. We then discussed by how much we might put up rates. Eddie said he favoured an increase of 2 percentage points, although 4 was more likely to work. I said I thought the markets would regard 4 as excessive and so would lack credibility. After some discussion we settled on 2.

We agreed that, subject to the PM's views, the pound should be allowed to remain at the floor. If the marginal intervention required of the Bank was too heavy, then rates would be increased by 2 per cent. If that did not work we would have to consider a further rise in rates or suspension of our ERM membership.

It should be emphasised that by now the purchase of pounds by the Bank was not 'intervention' in the conventional sense of the word. We were not trying to support sterling with the reserves, but under the rules of the ERM if the pound fell out of its bands holders of sterling are able to demand payment at the official rate from the Bank of England. There was no discretion in the matter. By now every commercial bank and corporate treasurer was short selling sterling and demanding to be paid at DM 2.7780 at the bottom of the band. People subsequently observed that we wasted billions trying to support sterling, but we did nothing of the sort. We had to abide by the rules of the ERM and match all demands for foreign currency that were made. That should have made it all the more important to move quickly and arrive at clear decisions early on.

At 9.45 a.m. money market operations began, and the market absorbed the fact that there was no move in interest rates. This was the first bad mistake of several. Not to have put up rates as soon as the markets opened revealed a reluctance to do what was necessary and the markets sensed weakness behind the delay. Nonetheless it was the case that the Minimum Lending Rate (MLR) could go up at any time.

At 10.30 a.m. I spoke to the PM for a second time, informing him that sterling was still firmly stuck on the bottom and that we were haemorrhaging badly. I recommended again, and this time he agreed, that we put up rates by 2 per cent at 11 a.m. At that moment precisely the minimum lending rate was increased, and I put out a statement saying that I was prepared to take 'whatever measures were necessary'.

I went into the outer office in my room at the Treasury and looked at the Reuters screen, waiting for the announcement to be made. When it was, the pound did not move at all. From that moment, I knew the game was up. I later told a journalist I felt like a TV surgeon in *Casualty* watching a heart monitor and realising that the patient was dead; all we needed to do now was to unplug the system. I wanted to suspend our membership of the ERM as quickly as possible and stop the haemorrhaging of our reserves. I asked Jeremy to arrange for me to see the PM at once, and to tell him that we were suspending our membership. I assumed that a meeting would happen immediately.

The Governor and Eddie George, who had gone back to the Bank, returned. They said that after the increase in interest rates there had been no decline in the rate of 'intervention', that is to say the demand to convert sterling to foreign currency at 2.7780. They felt there was no point in another increase in rates unless it was huge. I agreed with them completely. The Governor was quite ready to speak to the other Governors and to inform them, rather than ask them, that we intended to suspend our membership of the ERM.

I said I would recommend to the PM that we would suspend our membership and that the Governor would inform all other central bank Governors. I would tell Finance Ministers. But still there was no reply from the PM's office. I had asked Jeremy to ring repeatedly to say that I needed desperately and urgently to see the PM. The minutes were ticking by and I was conscious that we were losing hundreds of millions of pounds every few minutes, but still there was no sign of any meeting or indeed any indication when there might be one. I was quite unable to understand it.

Eventually Terry, the Governor, the Deputy Governor and I then went round to Admiralty House to see the PM, but even when we arrived we had to wait because the PM was in a meeting chatting with backbenchers. We sat on a sofa in a corridor and I asked the Private Secretary to go in and to tell him we were there, but still he didn't come out. I could not fathom what could be more important than to make the decisions we had to make and to announce our withdrawal from the ERM. It was somewhere between quarter and half an hour before the Prime Minister emerged, joking with Tory MPs and looking extremely relaxed.

Over the years there have been repeated reports that the Prime

Minister had a nervous breakdown on Wednesday 16 September. To my considerable annoyance, the PM's own supporters often accused me of spreading these rumours. I certainly never did. I am happy to confirm, as I always have done, that the PM was perfectly calm then and for the rest of the day. My criticism was precisely the opposite: he was far too calm, and slow to take the difficult decisions that we needed. He seemed unwilling to face up to the issue.

Our meeting with the Prime Minister didn't start until 12.45 p.m. I said I felt we had no alternative but to suspend our ERM membership. We had been defeated by a combination of Schlesinger and the French referendum. Temporary suspension was the last option and we should do it immediately. I suggested we give other countries fifteen minutes' warning. Speed was of the essence.

The PM wondered whether we could ask the Germans to do more; perhaps the French could do some intervention on their own account. He also referred to the damage that withdrawal could do to Maastricht. At this point both Sarah Hogg and Alex Allan, the PM's Private Secretary, said they thought we should try and put up interest rates further. I did not believe this would work now.

My irritation at being kept waiting was increased when the PM said we would shortly be joined by Douglas Hurd, Kenneth Clarke and Michael Heseltine. I was astounded. I could not see why it was necessary to involve all these Ministers. What could they contribute to discussions? There was an obvious danger that it would make it much harder to reach decisions, and in a financial crisis speed was of the essence. It was only a long time later that I realised the Prime Minister had probably felt that he would safeguard his own position if the decisions were shared with other people. That may have been a wise precaution, but the way our discussions continued was not at all businesslike.

I outlined the situation once more when the others arrived, making it quite clear that in my opinion we had no real option but to withdraw from the ERM there and then. The Governor said that was also the clear view of the Bank of England and Terry Burns said a further 2 per cent would not help. Then the

PM repeated what I said but elaborated upon it at great length. To my dismay, he put forward withdrawal as just one of several different options including various sizes of interest rate increases. Clarke, Heseltine and Hurd, unfortunately, were not at all inclined to agree to withdrawal from the ERM and I became increasingly exasperated, pointing out that every minute we wasted talking we were losing reserves. Every minute was 'costing' us millions. Still the discussion went on with little sense of urgency.

At one point in the meeting the PM referred to the humiliation of withdrawing from the ERM and said that there would be demands for my resignation, adding 'and my own as well'. We then continued the discussion, and there was a break as we waited for some communication from the Bank. When we sat down again the PM passed me a note he had written. It said, 'I am not going to resign and you must not consider it either.'

The Governor and I wanted an immediate suspension, but the discussion became bogged down on whether we could withdraw or whether we needed the consent of our partners. Douglas Hurd became agitated, insisting that everything was done according to the rules so as not to offend our partners. The Governor and I had envisaged an immediate announcement whatever the legal niceties, but even an announcement would have stopped the short selling of sterling. I found it very difficult to believe that colleagues could go on with this leisurely discussion, turning things over endlessly while the crisis continued.

Later on Kenneth Clarke claimed, 'The whole thing was taken out of the hands of the politicians by the technicians. We were just there to sign on the dotted line.' The opposite was the truth. It was the politicians who had interfered with the technicians and only succeeded in making things even worse with their amateur and bungling intervention. Later on Kenneth Clarke also claimed the meeting had no information from the outside world and that we were cut off from the markets. In fact Eddie George had with him a pocket Reuters monitor that told him the value of sterling every minute. In no way were we cut off from the markets. But you didn't need a TV to know what was happening: the pound, having been in free fall, was now stuck at DM 2.7780, at which we were obliged to pay out to all those speculators who had sold sterling short. We were bleeding to death, and all we were doing was talking. We had clearly lost the battle but the generals refused to recognise it.

Then we turned to the option of putting up interest rates. Michael Heseltine, supported by Kenneth Clarke, thought that we should increase interest rates once more. They didn't really give any coherent reason for this except that they wanted to stay in the ERM. I said that the pound was firmly out of the bands of the ERM and that in my opinion an interest rate increase would have no effect and certainly would not appear credible given the depressed state of the economy. An increase would have a devastating effect on business confidence and, because it so obviously could not be maintained, it would not deter short selling.

There followed a discussion as to whether the further increase should be 2 or 3 per cent. I continued to express my opposition, but I was also desperate to bring matters to a conclusion, and I finally said that if this was what they insisted I would put interest rates up by a further 3 per cent to 15 per cent, but I was quite certain it would make no difference. If that was the only way to demonstrate that we had no alternative but to suspend our membership, then I would do it. It was agreed that if the rate increase did not work, we would then be prepared to consider suspending membership. After Hurd's intervention, the view was that we had to do it by the book, consulting both other countries and other central banks one by one. The long and stubborn discussion at least demonstrated to me that if I had ever taken the option of leaving the ERM to the Cabinet I would have got nowhere, as it would have been fiercely opposed by those Ministers.

At 2.15 p.m. it was announced that MLR would be increased to the skyscraping level of 15 per cent with effect from Thursday. Again I watched the news reach the Reuters screen, and as before, the patient showed no signs of life. This time I was relieved.

In the outer office, where my diary secretary sat, was an ordinary television and I was able to watch the reaction of the public to the announcement. We did not normally turn the TV on, but that day it was on all the time. One of my constituents was interviewed after a late lunch at the Villa Pasta restaurant in Kingston.

The interest rate rise had not helped his digestion as he spat out his views about his MP who was also the Chancellor of the Exchequer, 'God's teeth. Another 3 per cent. That's staggering . . . are you sure? It was only 2 per cent before lunch. Have you got your telephone in your bag so we can confirm this.' Another businessman said, 'I think it's April 1st.'

We now had to continue with the consultation process that the Admiralty House meeting had insisted on. I spoke in rapid succession to other Finance Ministers. Sapin was naturally concerned about the effect on the French referendum, and was keen that suspension was temporary. Solchaga in Spain thought that now the pound had gone, the peseta would go. In Germany Waigel suggested I consider a realignment! This was the first time he had ever mentioned the word, but it was a bit late. I told him we had lost billions of pounds and it would be highly unlikely we would be able to maintain any new parity any better than the Italians, who we could see were now on the way to falling out of their new lower limit. Waigel also asked whether it would make any difference if the Germans now cut interest rates. As John Major used to say, 'I didn't know whether to laugh or cry.' I said that it would be of no use unless it was a really big cut.

My last call was to my closest friend among the Ministers, Piero Barucci, who was deeply depressed at the plight of the lira. He asked me whether I thought I might suspend the markets and then discuss a realignment over the weekend. I repeated what I had said to Waigel, and pointed out that it was not within my powers to suspend the markets all over Europe. At the same time the PM was talking to Bérégovoy, who said that we were now at 'the hour of truth with the Germans', and the PM knew what his view was. Whatever we decided, he would support us. Bérégovoy said he would talk to Kohl about a reduction in interest rates and when he rang back stressed that he wanted to avoid a realignment at any cost, presumably because it would affect the Maastricht referendum. France could not accept a realignment, even if one were on offer, and floating was in his opinion the option we should pursue.

The PM then spoke to Kohl, who astonishingly expressed surprise at the reaction in the markets to Schlesinger's remarks. From the reports he appears to have been somewhat out of touch with what was happening. He claimed that the Bundesbank had intervened massively. It had, but as the PM pointed out under the rules of the ERM all the intervention had to be repaid to the Bundesbank by the Bank of England by the fifteenth day of the third month following the intervention.

The Governor and the Deputy Governor were also ringing round the European central banks. Some of them were talking about a realignment, while others emphasised the need to act strictly within the rules. When the Governor and Deputy Governor came back to the Treasury they reported that £14.5 billion had flowed out of the reserves, not, as I have stressed, from discretionary intervention or so called 'support operations', but because of traders presenting currency to the Bank of England and demanding to be paid at the official rate. They had had a licence to print money while the politicians argued.

But our obligations ended at 4 p.m. when the markets closed. The Governor, Eddie, Terry and I returned to Admiralty House to see the PM, who for the first time began to talk about 'faults' in the system of the ERM and of the need to correct them. I could not understand what 'faults' he meant. It was the policy that had been wrong. Hurd, Clarke and Heseltine joined us at 5 p.m. I told them of the day's developments, and reported that the higher interest rates had not worked. A meeting of the Monetary Committee in Brussels that evening was going to consider suspension. The Governor and I reported on my conversations with other Finance Ministers and central banks, who had been appreciative; our proposals were better received than I had expected. But the Germans had been unwilling to help with their own reserves. Reluctantly, colleagues gave their formal agreement to suspending our ERM membership. It was hours too late.

John Major insisted that I announce that the second interest rate rise would be reversed. I did not want to do this. I felt I had been made to look a complete fool with the second rate rise and I thought it would look even more ridiculous to reverse it. But in his insistence he was quite right and I was wrong – though not wrong to think I had been made to look a fool.

The consultations with central banks were still continuing. At one point we thought we might get the whole ERM suspended, and not just British membership. The Italians and the Portuguese were sympathetic to that, but most argued for UK suspension alone.

I returned to the Treasury and with officials drafted a statement, then went out into the central courtyard of the Treasury which, as far as I know, had never been used for an announcement before or since. In front of a massive battery of TV cameras from around the world I said, 'Today has been an extremely difficult and turbulent day. Massive speculative flows continued to disrupt the functioning of the Exchange Rate Mechanism. As Chairman of the Council of European Finance Ministers I have called a meeting of the Monetary Committee in Brussels to consider how stability can be restored in the foreign exchange markets.

'In the meantime the Government has concluded that Britain's best interests can be served by suspending our membership of the Exchange Rate Mechanism. As a result the second of the two interest rate increases that I sanctioned will not take place tomorrow. The Minimum Lending Rate will be 12 per cent until conditions become calmer.

'I will be reporting to Cabinet and discussing the situation with colleagues tomorrow and may make further statements then. Until then I have nothing further to say. Thank you very much.'

I felt no emotion of any kind as I made the statement. I simply felt I was playing a part in some drama that had been written for me. This was how it had to be and this was my predetermined role.

There was nothing more I could do and I returned to No. 11 exhausted. Somewhat selfishly, I did not even think about Nigel Wicks, who had flown to Brussels for the meeting of the Monetary Committee, which continued haggling until nearly midnight. As always, Europe would be as difficult as possible, but now it would make no difference what they decided. In the end the Monetary Committee decided shortly before midnight to agree to the suspension of sterling that I had announced at 7.30 p.m.

That night I did not feel immensely depressed about what had happened. Indeed, I felt that some good would come of it. I knew I had done everything I could to sustain a Government policy about which I had become increasingly unenthusiastic although powerless to alter. It had been too tight, as the critics had said, and we would now have more flexibility. Above all I saw it as an international and not a particularly British crisis. What I did not appreciate was the scale of the political disaster that had hit the Government. Not for the first time I lacked an ability to stand back to see either myself or my situation as others did.

Our exit from the ERM

I give elsewhere my views on the overall economic consequences of the ERM experience, but what of the immediate crisis? Could the events on 16 September itself and in the weeks leading up to it have been handled differently or better? There has been no shortage of people suggesting so.

Bank of England tactics

Some critics have suggested that the Bank of England should not have allowed the pound to sink to its ERM floor at the opening of business on 16 September, a point made in a note given to the Foreign Office by the Bundesbank. In fact sterling only fell to its floor or below on the evening of 15 September after the disastrous comments of Dr Schlesinger in the advance release of the *Handelsblatt* article. Up to Tuesday evening it had been possible to keep sterling, in European trading hours, above its ERM floor with the Deutschmark without an interest rate rise.

The Bundesbank also suggested that the Bank wanted to raise rates from the beginning of business on Wednesday 16 September and that these moves were blocked by the Treasury. But it certainly was not the Treasury that blocked any moves to act in the money markets, as I have already related. There is some point in this criticism by the Bundesbank, but given the scale of the speculative attack on sterling there seems no reason to believe that bringing forward the interest rate rise would have made the crucial difference to the outcome. After all, sterling had been above its ERM floor all the time up to then.

Then there have been suggestions that we might have followed the Swedish strategy of pursuing extremely high overnight interest rates, though significantly that did not prevent Sweden from having, in the end, to float the krone. People have focused on the extremely high interest rates in Sweden, quoted as being 500 per cent or thereabouts, but these rates applied only to overnight money. The increase in three-month interest rates was a good deal lower. In fact we had a similar spread between our overnight rates and other money market rates. Overnight rates at one point went up to 180 per cent, but this was still insufficient to stem the tide, any more than it did in Sweden.

A rise in interest rates?

The one area where I believe our actions could have been significantly different was interest rates. We could have raised rates significantly some weeks prior to 16 September, before sterling came anywhere near hitting its floor. Again, one has to point out that the Italians and others attempted this without success, so could it have worked in the case of Britain? A rise in interest rates of say 2 or 3 per cent in July or August might have seemed incredible given the absence of recovery in the economy, the crisis in the housing market and the large pressure that there already was for lower interest rates. In my view a 2 point rise in July or August would have appeared unbelievable and therefore counterproductive, but I agree that this is more arguable and it might have worked at a cost. At best it would have been a French solution, permitting us to remain in the ERM until the next crisis the following summer, with higher interest rates, which at the very least would have wiped out all prospect of recovery. But what would have been the gain from this?

The losses to the reserves

Much of the comment on 'Black Wednesday' has concentrated on the massive loss of foreign exchange reserves. They were unprecedented, although the scale suffered by the Bank of England was no different from those of the central banks of Italy, Spain, Portugal, Sweden, Norway, Finland and Ireland. France also lost a large part of its reserves, and would lose even more later, when the whole crisis reignited again in the summer of 1993.

Newspapers particularly criticised me for 'throwing money

away' in a futile attempt to keep the pound in the ERM, but as I have explained we intervened in the strict sense of that word sparingly in the period leading up to 16 September. The haemorrhaging was not caused by 'intervention' designed to support the pound. Once it had reached the bottom of its band we were bound by the rules to buy sterling at the official level as long as we remained within the system. Much of the loss of reserves resulted from the demand from sellers of sterling that we convert to other currencies once we were at the bottom of the ERM bands. Those who had 'shorted' sterling made huge profits selling pounds to the Bank of England at DM 2.7780 and then buying sterling at lower levels. The losses would have been significantly less if the PM the other Ministers present in Admiralty House had accepted the recommendation of myself and the Governor to suspend membership at 12.45 p.m., or even earlier, as I had wanted.

Some of the newspaper comment implied that the loss of reserves meant the loss of money that could have been spent on schools or hospitals, but that is nonsense. Foreign Exchange Reserves are there for official use in the markets. The so-called 'loss' of foreign exchange reserves is a transfer of assets between a foreign currency and sterling. The sterling that is acquired in place of the foreign exchange reserves can be used either to replenish the reserves by buying more foreign currency, or it can reduce the need to sell government stock to fund government borrowing. The loss consists not of the transfer of assets but of the change in the exchange rate. For that reason it is genuinely difficult to calculate at any one time the extent of losses experienced by the Bank of England since it depends when the foreign currency has been bought and at what rate. Many of the Deutschmarks in the Bank of England's reserves were acquired around 1988 at around 32 or 33 pence each and were sold for around 36 pence each. Regarding the use of borrowings, it is also difficult to know at what rate those who went short of sterling on 16 September were able to buy it back.

But the total value of movements out of the reserves is known. By the close of business on 16 September we had drawn down only half of the 10 billion ecu loan (that is to say $6.5 billion) negotiated by Europe. We also drew to a large extent on VSTF

(Very Short Term Credit Facility), made available on a temporary basis by other central banks to support each other's currencies. The published reserves at the end of August 1992 stood at $44.4 billion. Intervention by the Bank of England amounted to $22.6 billion of which $19.9 billion was financed by the VSTF. Intervention by other central banks amounted to $4.1 billion, of which $3.8 billion was financed by the VSTF and had to be repaid by the UK. This means that the movement out of the Bank's reserves amounted to roughly $27 billion gross.

Reserves can be, and were, rebuilt. The fact that sterling was to be volatile over the next few years gave the Bank of England many opportunities to use the sterling it acquired on 16 September to buy foreign currency. Initially it had to do so with depreciated pounds, but it would have been possible to make a profit on these transactions when the pound strengthened to above DM 2.80, as it subsequently did. Kenneth Clarke, when Chancellor, made a conscious decision not to rebuild the reserves to the previous level. He considered it unnecessary. That may have been right, since sterling was no longer in the ERM, but it could easily have been done on the back of sterling's subsequent rise.

The Conduct of the Bath Ecofin?

Clearly this was a key, and ill-tempered, meeting, but the basic tension was not just between Britain and Germany, but between Germany and several other EU countries, particularly the French, Italian and Irish, as well. It would be quite wrong not to recognise that there was frustration all round with the behaviour of the Germans. Immense pressure had been put on me by other countries to make these points as forcefully as possible to Germany and, as Chairman of Ecofin, it was my job to reflect these views. If I was more open about it at the meeting than some other governments, then that is how it frequently is at EU meetings. Other countries are sometimes afraid to speak bluntly to the Germans, and often expect the British to do it for them. Although Dr Schlesinger claimed to have taken offence at the pressure exerted on him, I don't believe that his subsequent remarks about the pound were made out of malice. He is a bigger man than that.

For all its mystique and deservedly high reputation, the Bundesbank is a strangely parochial institution. Its federal constitution makes it, in a literal sense, provincial, and it has often proved indifferent to the international consequences of its actions.

Dr Schlesinger's remarks were irresponsible and inexcusable. Although there was indeed a fundamental problem in the ERM, the evidence suggests that we might have got through to 20 September, the French referendum day, if he and other members of the Bundesbank had refrained from commenting. His remarks were one of a whole series made by officials and members of the Board of the Bundesbank over a period of weeks. It is difficult to imagine how they could have been more unhelpful, but for all that I do not believe for one minute that they set out deliberately to undermine our position, although they very effectively did just that. Dr Schlesinger was also unused to dealing with the British media and on many occasions expressed his bitterness towards them.

It should also be noted that in addition to the tensions between Germany and the rest of Europe, there were also considerable strains between the Bundesbank and the German Government. This probably explains some of the mysteries of misunderstandings and confused communication. Dr Schlesinger did not share Helmut Kohl's devotion to the European cause. He was not an enthusiast for the single currency, and his main concern was to prevent the monetary consequences of other countries' problems in the ERM undermining his own monetary control.

Devaluation of the pound?

The suggestion persists to this day that sterling had joined the ERM at too high a parity and it required only a devaluation to have avoided a crisis. The subsequent devaluation of sterling after its departure from the ERM, at one point amounting to nearly 20 per cent, for a while appeared to support this idea. However, the right level for a currency at one point may sometimes be different from the level appropriate at another. The subsequent strengthening of sterling over several years back up to its ERM levels then made it appear that the market had changed its mind and did not think sterling had been overvalued.

As I have mentioned, the evidence on grounds of differential inflation, past parity rates and purchasing power parity did not lead me to conclude that the rate at which John Major had joined the ERM was wrong (see Table 1). The rate chosen was close to the market rate at that time and also to the average rate for the last ten years, adjusted for inflation. It is worth stressing the last point: that it was adjusted for inflation, and inflation differentials are one of the main determinants of exchange rate movements.

However, even if sterling were overvalued it does not follow that a unilateral devaluation of the pound would have helped. The recession in the UK was not primarily caused by the exchange rate, and high interest rates were a far greater problem. In the ERM we could not get our interest rates below the level of those in Germany, though the differential was very successfully narrowed. Had we devalued the pound but remained within the ERM we would certainly have had to increase interest rates and reverse the cuts we had so painstakingly made over two years. Time and time again it has been shown that a devaluing country within a fixed exchange rate system loses credibility because the markets think that at some point the devaluing country will do it again. They therefore perfectly logically demand an interest rate premium, as the French and the Dutch experienced for many years after their earlier devaluations.

This analysis is confirmed by the experience of those countries that did devalue in 1992. The lira devaluation initially was 7 per cent, which proved unsustainable. There seems no reason to believe that we would have been allowed by the French to devalue by any more than that because of their fears of 'unfair competition'. After the Italian devaluation, the respite proved very temporary and they were quickly under pressure again and had to devalue a second time and float. The experience of the escudo, peseta and the punt also appears to confirm the analysis. None of these countries, despite their devaluations, succeeded in getting lower interest rates, which was what Britain needed. Starting from August 1992, and leaving out the immediate pre-devaluation crisis hike in interest rates, those countries did not manage to cut interest rates after their devaluations. After ten months interest rate differentials eventually returned to their position before the Deutschmark itself got into trouble. But for the whole of that ten-month period they had substantially higher interest rates.

For all these reasons there seems force in what Matthew Symonds wrote on 17 September in the *Independent*: 'At least Norman Lamont did not compound earlier tactical errors, by seeking an inadequate devaluation within the Exchange Rate Mechanism last night, which would only have given the markets something new to aim at.'

A *wider realignment?*

Rumours also persist that at Bath and afterwards an opportunity for a wider realignment, not just of the pound but also of the lira and other currencies, was available and somehow missed. Several questions arise here. Firstly, was such an opportunity available? Secondly, what is meant by 'wider realignment', and would it have worked? I have seen several television programmes in which Horst Kohler, of the German Treasury, and Wim Kok, the Dutch Prime Minister, have suggested that a wider realignment was offered but frankly I am baffled by these suggestions. No suggestion was ever made to me, either at the meeting or any other time, and all my officials at the Treasury denied that any such approaches were made to them. Both Schlesinger and Wim Duisenburg made comments to Terry Burns in an informal way, but only after the meeting had ended.

The Bundesbank note delivered to the Foreign Office on this point was frankly as absurd as it was untruthful. It appeared to suggest that I refused to put a German proposal on the agenda at Bath and had chaired the meeting to avoid the subject coming up. It even implies that Kohler spent half an hour trying to persuade me to put realignment and German rate cuts on the agenda. I can state here that this is completely untrue and I am astonished that this suggestion has been made.

If the Germans had wanted to press this issue, Waigel or Schlesinger could easily have done so and I could not have prevented them putting forward proposals of the kind suggested. In the event, there was a strong majority of Ministers at the meeting in favour of ruling out any realignment.

I would have been prepared to accept a unilateral revaluation of the Deutschmark against all the other ERM currencies, which would have taken some heat out of the German economy, and in theory it might have allowed them to reduce interest rates. But whatever the arguments for and against a German revaluation, the French were adamantly opposed to it. They did not wish to abandon the *franc fort* policy, and also thought that to do so would lose them the Maastricht referendum. I had privately explored this with Bérégovoy and was left in no doubt about their opposition. A German revaluation was never a runner.

That leaves the one remaining option of what is called a 'negotiated realignment', in fact a devaluation, of all the division two currencies – the lira, the peseta, the escudo, the punt and at that time the pound. The argument that a devaluation would lead to lower interest rates seems just as implausible when applied to four currencies as opposed to one, but when the Deutschmark was effectively revalued after 16 September against the pound, the lira, the peseta, escudo, and the punt, not to mention the Scandinavian currencies, there was no significant change in German interest rates. The reduction of 0.25 per cent in the Lombard rate at the same time as the first Italian devaluation was only extracted from the Bundesbank after massive political pressure from Kohl and German rates did not move again until February the following year. Plainly the Bundesbank did not consider a revaluation against the pound of around 12–14 per cent and more against the lira as sufficient to justify a significant cut in the Lombard rate, yet that revaluation by the markets was far larger than anything that could have been negotiated by governments.

The currencies that devalued but remained within the ERM had to put up interest rates. Even the lira, which left the ERM, also put up rates to stop a complete collapse.

I do not believe that what is euphemistically called a 'realignment' would have worked, and at the time I had no reason to believe that it was proposed in the way that some people have suggested. But why do these rumours persist? They were seized on by supporters of the ERM, who perhaps wanted to believe that the system only crashed because of some policy mistake, but it is also possible that between the German Government and the European Union there was some breakdown in communication.

On the weekend before 16 September there were several developments of which I was at the time completely unaware. On Friday 11 September Kohl had secretly visited the Bundesbank. Kohl would have been made aware of the large amount of lira that the Bundesbank had taken in by that time. It seems likely that Schlesinger may have invoked what was called the 'Emminger letter'. In 1978, when the Bundesbank had been persuaded to accept the ERM but the exchange rate remained a responsibility of the Federal Government, Chancellor Schmidt and Otmar Emminger, then Bundesbank President, had agreed that although the exchange rate regime was a matter for the Government, the Bundesbank had the right to ask for a realignment if intervention distorted domestic monetary policy. Certainly, on the following Monday Schlesinger appeared to confirm this when he said, 'The solution to the exchange rate trap lay in the hands of the Governments – we have the Federal Government to thank for extricating us.'

I do not know for sure what happened, but according to some accounts that I have heard Kohl seems to have taken on board part of the message from Bath. He insisted that the Bundesbank fulfil its intervention obligations and that the French franc must be safeguarded at all costs. This was what Bertie Ahern was later to call the 'sweetheart deal'. Kohl also agreed to the Bundesbank's suggestion of a devaluation of the lira, but insisted on at least a token movement in internal rates.

On Saturday 12 September, Kohler, from the German Treasury, and Tietmeyer, the Vice-President of the Bundesbank, had flown to Rome to negotiate the realignment, via Paris, where they saw both Trichet, the Governor of the Banque de France, and Sapin, the Finance Minister. Trichet was, of course, also the Chairman of the EU's Monetary Committee, but if they were consulting him in a European capacity, why did they not consult British officials, since we occupied the presidency? And if Trichet was acting in a European capacity, why was Sapin, who had no European position, involved? According to some accounts, arrangements were agreed to put a floor below the franc to make sure it survived until the referendum with, if necessary, unlimited support.

The Germans subsequently publicly stated that the Bundesbank had asked the German Government to negotiate a realignment, but one that involved more currencies than the lira. Not one word of this ever reached me. Nothing in that sense, I am assured, was ever said by Trichet to Nigel Wicks, let alone by Nigel Wicks to myself.

I have now, however, learnt some of the details of that meeting. Initially, I am told, the Germans put forward a proposal for an Italian devaluation, which was not enthusiastically received by the French. They feared this might lead to pressure on the franc, but in the end they agreed. Kohler and Tietmeyer than mentioned the possibility of other currency adjustments, without naming names. Again the French were reluctant, because of the possible effects on the franc. But in the end it was agreed there should be a meeting of the Monetary Committee in Brussels to discuss it. At least one of the Germans present altered his travel plans so as to attend. To their surprise, no meeting of the Monetary Committee was called by Trichet.

It is clear that, for whatever reason, there was a breakdown in communications between the Germans and the EU. As I have argued, I do not believe anything would have prevented the events of 16 September, but why this happened remains a matter of speculation.

The Bundesbank paper presented to the Foreign Office (discussed in the next chapter) also claimed that the Bundesbank sought a realignment of several currencies on the weekend of 11–12 September, but neither the German Finance Ministry nor the Bundesbank contacted London during that weekend. Eddie George did talk on his own initiative to the Vice-President of the Bundesbank on Sunday 13 September, but there was no mention of any of these issues.

Arrangements had been made for a visit on Monday 14 September of senior Treasury and Bank of England officials to the German Ministry of Finance and the Bundesbank. That visit took place and one of the British participants recalls a Bundesbank Council Member remarking that there was no point in raising the possibility of a sterling devaluation because the Prime Minister had definitely ruled it out the previous Thursday.

The Prime Minister also spoke on Sunday 13 September to Prime Minister Amato of Italy. Probably he would have hoped we would devalue with the Italians to make his situation appear less embarrassing, but what passed between the two hardly amounted to a proposal for a realignment and there was no mention of any larger German rate cut.

If the Bundesbank's attitude during these events can be partly explained by its dislike of monetary union, it failed to achieve its objective of preserving its own position. Throughout the 1980s and 1990s, it had been Europe's most powerful central bank, setting the floor for interest rates for all the members of the ERM. With the launch of the euro at the beginning of 1999, it lost this power. As a result, it is now a shadow of its former self. Ironically, in so far as it precipitated Britain's departure from the ERM, the Bundesbank helped put the Bank of England on the path to independence and to becoming a Bundesbank for Britain. And it gave Britain the opportunity to have a financial framework for its own conditions, which previously Germany, of all the ERM members, could have inside the ERM. The opportunity this gave Britain was one I grasped with both hands.

11

Rebuilding – Policy Out of
the Ashes

The dogmas of the quiet past are inadequate to the stormy
present. The occasion is piled high with difficulty and we
must rise with the occasion. As our case is new, so we must
seek anew and act anew. We must disenthral ourselves.

Abraham Lincoln

Contrary to legend, I didn't sing in my bath the day after Black
Wednesday. But it is true that I had a strong feeling – indeed
more than that, a certainty – that the economy would now turn.
We would be able to cut interest rates, and the economy would
now begin to grow. I remember remarking to Peter Lilley as I
went into Cabinet that morning, 'Now I have got the economic
policy I want, I don't see why I should resign.'

Why I did not resign

That was to beg the question. I did, of course, consider very carefully on the day after Black Wednesday and the following days
whether I should resign. I took soundings from colleagues such as
Michael Portillo, Michael Howard, William Hague and Terry Burns
and I had even given the matter thought before 16 September. On
one occasion in the summer I had raised with Terry the subject of

whether I should resign if we were forced to devalue. He thought I should not.

There is no convention that a Chancellor who devalues resigns. Cripps, in the Attlee Government, devalued and remained in post. Callaghan devalued and then skilfully changed jobs. The Callaghan devaluation was also very different in that it had been a purely British crisis.

This last point was important in my mind, and was one way in which I saw the ERM differently from other people. Viewed from the Treasury or the Bank of England, the collapse of the ERM did not seem a particularly British event but the collapse of an international system under the strain of its own contradictions. No British policy decision had brought about the collapse of the ERM. Six other countries had gone through at the same time exactly the same experience as ourselves, 'losing' billions of dollars of their reserves and all being eventually forced off their fixed parity. Others were to follow, some quickly, some as the months went by. The humiliation, if humiliation it was, must have been just as great in every one of those countries as it was felt to be in Britain.

In Britain the press were convinced the ERM was a purely a British catastrophe and that the Government was to blame. In none of the other devaluing countries did the Finance Minister or the Governor of the central bank resign or, as far as I know, even come under pressure to resign. Ironically, in one country the Finance Minister, and in another the Governor of the central bank, went on to become Prime Minister. In France Edouard Balladur, the Prime Minister, in his efforts to support the franc had promised to resign if France was forced off its parity, but he did not do so in the event, nor was he even pressed on the point.

In addition, although it was a reverse, I did not believe that I had technically mishandled our membership of the ERM in any way, though I did feel that the manner in which we had collectively suspended our membership was a shambles. As I discussed in the previous chapter, I remain unconvinced that there were alternative decisions that we could have made which would have kept Britain in the ERM. If John Smith or Ken Clarke had been Chancellor the result would have been exactly the same.

Finally, the decision to join the ERM originally had not been mine. I had played no part at all in the formulation of the policy and had never attended a single meeting in my entire Ministerial career about joining the ERM. It was inherited, and it was a collective policy.

But what is logical is not always politically right. I knew that the world would not see it that way, particularly after my European Policy Forum Speech. And there were other considerations. The PM had made it emphatically clear that he did not want me to resign, saying so in his note to me and repeating it to me in public and in private many times. 'You are a lightning conductor for me,' he said. I believed the PM. I also remembered how, after the election, when I had said he need not reappoint me, he had been emphatic about the confidence he felt in me and that any rumours otherwise were unfounded. In Cabinet he went out of his way to defend me and to say it was the policy of the whole Cabinet that I had been operating.

Of course, as people pointed out I could have insisted on resigning, despite the PM's opposition, but what would have been the consequences for him? It would have been inevitable that the pressure would move to him, not just quickly but immediately, since he was the author of the policy. This was the point mentioned to me frequently by colleagues. As one Treasury civil servant pointed out, if I had resigned on Wednesday 16 September, and it had then got out that the Prime Minister had overruled me, both about withdrawing from the ERM early in the day and also about the second rate increase, where would that leave the Prime Minister? I could see that from my own point of view, resignation, perhaps to become Home Secretary, as Callaghan had done, would have had advantages. As Peter Jay, ironically Callaghan's son-in-law, put it, 'To resign would have been tactically right, but morally wrong.' It certainly would have been immensely damaging to the PM. I do not believe he would have survived if I had resigned that day.

However, looking back on it now, my departure from the Government appears inevitable. I should have seen the pressure was going to mount, but I was not motivated by a desire to cling to office. The consequences for the PM were a large part of my decision, and so, rightly or wrongly, having made a decision, I put the matter to one side and decided to get on with my job as best I could.

The calls for my resignation were widespread. Tory MPs such as Bill Cash, Andrew Hunter, Richard Shepherd and Geoffrey Clifton-Brown all called on me to resign. An exception among Eurosceptics was Michael Spicer, MP for South Worcestershire, who rang from France to tell me not to resign. The press was pretty unanimous too. Among the tabloids, the *Sun*, *Today* and the *Mirror* were brutal, and did not mince their words. Among the broadsheets the *Daily Telegraph* was particularly strong in its criticism. The *Mail*'s headline was 'the devalued Chancellor'. Its editorial was a little kinder, but firm. 'We have much sympathy for Norman Lamont. He is a courageous man and he has done his best. But it was not good enough. He must go.'

Somewhat surprisingly in the *Guardian*, Michael White claimed to detect 'a discernible surge of sympathy for his plight among Tory politicians'. MPs, he wrote, did not want to 'dump the Chancellor of the Exchequer in a way that would leave his compromised Prime Minister exposed'.

Most of the papers had hour-by-hour accounts of the events of the preceding day, with talk of billions of pounds being flung to support the pound as though it was money taken from pensioners. Apart from the *Financial Times* and the *Guardian*, most papers gave little coverage to the fact that the ERM crisis was an international one enveloping so many other countries. For the British press this was a British crisis caused by stupid British politicians, particularly myself.

On one point the newspapers were unanimous: the worst decision of the day had been the second interest rate rise to 15 per cent. The *Daily Express* called it 'economic madness' and Sir Brian Hill, President of the Building Employers' Confederation, had said the second rise in rates had been 'a total disaster for the British construction industry'. Years later, Sir John Nott, former Defence Secretary and chairman of Hillsdown Holdings, the food company, asked me how I could have been so mad as to put interest rates up to 15 per cent. He said that the moment they went to 15 per cent confidence in his business shattered and didn't recover for months, even though the second rate rise was quickly reversed.

Some articles highlighted the exposed position of the Prime Minister if I were to resign. Matthew Symonds in the *Independent* compared Major and Wilson as Prime Ministers who had presided over devaluations, pointing out that while Wilson had inherited both an exchange rate system and a parity, John Major had not only fought to take the pound into the ERM, but also himself fixed it to its 2.95 central rate against the Deutschmark. Bernard Ingham wrote in the *Express*: 'If there is any justice in this world, every man on the Clapham omnibus would argue that Mr Major should precede Mr Lamont out of Downing Street.'

I knew the press would continue to be extremely hostile. I read the papers in the immediate aftermath of 16 September, but then gave up reading them, though I wasn't allowed to escape that easily. Shortly after 16 September, Max Hastings, editor of the *Daily Telegraph*, asked if he could come to see me. In my office in the Treasury he asked me if I was going to resign, and I told him that I was not. He said that that was not good enough, making comparisons with the Falklands and the resignation of Peter Carrington and saying someone must accept the responsibility. He told me the *Daily Telegraph* had run a poll about whether I should resign and a majority had said I should not, but they intended to run another. He added, 'We will go on until we get you out. I will have to clear it with Conrad, but that's no problem.' I took this statement perfectly calmly, telling Max that I was grateful for his past support and that he was entitled to take whatever line he wanted. He confirmed my reaction in a conversation he had with Sarah Hogg, though some time later he claimed that I had responded angrily.

Cabinet considers the aftermath

There were an unusually large number of reporters and TV cameras outside No. 10 that Thursday morning as Ministers arrived for an extended Cabinet. David Mellor must have quite enjoyed it when reporters yelled, 'Are you going to resign?' For the first time in weeks they were not shouting at him. The meeting lasted nearly three hours. The Prime Minister opened by informing the Cabinet that the interest rate rise to 12 per cent had been cancelled. He then went on to praise me, saying that I had acted with 'courage and speed' and that he was not prepared to see me treated as an 'air raid shelter'. It was a somewhat curious and inelegant way of putting it, but its meaning was clear. He also said, as he did to me on many occasions, that he regarded attacks on me as simply coded attacks on himself. When he had finished speaking other members of the Cabinet, including Kenneth Clarke, voiced their agreement.

We then discussed future economic policy and Britain's future relationship with the ERM. Michael Howard expressed the strongest opposition to any idea of rejoining the ERM. In fact, I think he considered resigning on this point. However, I supported the Prime Minister's line that we had suspended our membership but would not consider rejoining until the German economy and German interest rates were more closely synchronised with our own. With every hour that passed, as I raised my eyes from the wreckage of the policy I had struggled to preserve, it was obvious that it would be a long time, if ever, before those theoretical conditions would be met. In other words, we would not rejoin the ERM in any timescale shorter than the politically infinite. Meanwhile we could decide our own policy. I had no intention of rejoining the ERM.

I had one other reason for supporting this line. I was very worried about the possibility of a complete collapse in the exchange rate preventing us from cutting interest rates, so I was happy to emphasise anything that gave an appearance of continuity to policy. My concerns were ones that were widely held, even though they were later shown to be exaggerated.

After Cabinet I went back to the Treasury and did a large number of interviews with different TV and radio programmes. In the interests of speed, the Treasury had arranged for TV and radio crews to set up temporary studios in different rooms in the Treasury, so I moved rapidly round the building meeting them. Later the myth grew up that I had somehow retreated into a bunker and did not go out and explain on TV what had happened, when in fact I appeared on every main news programme and gave extended interviews to many other programmes. Of course, having done them once, there wasn't a great deal of point doing them again and again the next day and the day after that. This wasn't, as the PM seemed to think, a crisis we could talk our way out of or finesse with superior presentation. But it was not true that on 16 September or on the days following that there was a silence or an absence of comment.

I particularly remember the interview with Peter Jay for the BBC, and his opening question: 'Are you still the Chancellor of the Exchequer?' I was somewhat startled and mumbled, 'Yes, of course'. In the same interview, when I quoted some words of Jim Callaghan on inflation, he muttered *sotto voce* to himself, 'I remember writing those words.'

Although I continued to consider my position, when I was asked about it in interviews of course I had to say firmly that I was not resigning. The result was a series of newspaper headlines rather firmer than the reality. The *Guardian* headline on Friday was: 'Chancellor I won't quit'. And in *The Times*: 'Defiant Lamont shrugs off calls to resign'. I was far from shrugging it all off. In its editorial *The Times* was somewhat gentler than I had expected. It called for interest rate cuts and measures to reduce the deficit, and added: 'This policy happens to be far closer to Mr Lamont's heart than his membership of the ERM. He may have been temporarily persuaded by his officials and his Prime Minister of the virtues of fixed exchange rates, but they have never been his natural inclination . . . Once the French referendum has resolved the market's uncertainty, Mr Lamont should have the courage of his old convictions. He may even keep his job.'

On Friday morning I first appeared on the *Today* programme and said clearly that the UK would not rejoin the ERM quickly. Of course, as I well understood, many backbenchers were pressing for a firmer rejection of rejoining. I had two meetings with the PM that day, who was worried that the press would blow up stories of differences between us. There were reports that the PM had told Kohl that we would rejoin the ERM quite quickly. In fact he said that he agreed with me, and that we needed time to reflect on what had led to this situation. The PM said he would write to Kohl to make it clear there was no prospect of rejoining quickly. I told the PM that while I had accepted being in the ERM as a means of bringing inflation down, now that we were out it would not be sensible to rush to rejoin. I also stressed that a floating exchange rate was not necessarily that easy, and it was not a free lunch. We could not be wholly indifferent to the level of the exchange rate and the dangers for inflation if it collapsed. Thanks to the ERM, we had massively and rapidly reduced inflation more than we had anticipated. Having got it down, at a price, it would be madness now to throw it away when it could give us such strength over the medium term. But now we were out of the ERM we had scope to reduce interest rates. I suggested that we should cut 1 per cent off the following week and a further 1 per cent before the Party Conference.

Rebuilding policy

When we were forced out of the ERM we lost not only credibility, but also a policy. The urgent task was immediately to begin the construction of a new policy. I wanted to show the aims of Government policy remained the same although we needed different means for achieving them. The object of policy had always been low inflation and recovery.

To newspapers it all seemed simple – cut interest rates and get on with it. But it was more complicated than that. The ERM, as I had explained in my European Policy Forum speech, was much more than an add-on to policy: it was the total framework for policy. The theory, as first put forward by Nigel Lawson, was that if the British and German exchange rates were locked together eventually their inflation rates would converge. Interest rates were set to maintain the exchange rate link, which was chosen to produce a lower rate of inflation.

Many people at that time, not just in the Treasury, thought that there was a great risk that inflation would rise again through the sudden depreciation of sterling. That fear turned out to be exaggerated, but based on past experience it was at the time entirely rational. The ERM exit had been a humiliation but to have compounded it with a return of inflation would convert a disaster into a catastrophe.

The ERM was also what economists call a 'rules-based system'.

It was mechanistic; if the exchange rate threatened to fall out of its bands, governments had to put rates up. Of course, no system is entirely rules-based and there is always an element of judgement; monetary policy outside the ERM was inevitably going to be much more discretionary. This meant there was a risk that the policy would not carry credibility and that we would be seen to return to a judgemental policy of the kind we had exercised in the mid-1980s, which had been largely discredited. It was necessary to demonstrate to the markets by what criteria decisions were being made so that they themselves could judge the consistency or otherwise of our decisions.

The great danger I foresaw was that outside the ERM, particularly as we were a Government under pressure, decision-making would now be seen as entirely political. One solution would have been to make the Bank of England independent, but I knew the PM would not go that far. The steps I was proposing would ultimately lead to independence for the Bank of England.

Thus began a rapid search for a new policy. It had to be done quickly, because politics demanded that, but it also required care. The reconstruction of policy was done step by step: first, four days after Black Wednesday, there was my speech to the Interim Committee at the IMF, followed by a letter from me to the Chairman of the Treasury Select Committee, then my appearance before the Select Committee itself and finally the Mansion House Speech. Peter Jay was kind enough to describe the period after Black Wednesday as 'a period of rare enlightenment in economic policy-making'.

The centrepiece of the new policy framework was the inflation target. Underlying inflation – that is retail price inflation minus the effects of mortgage interest rates – had fallen to around 4 per cent in September 1992. I decided to set a range of 1–4 per cent with the aim of reaching the lower half of the range in the second half of the Parliament, an ambitious target that, if achieved, would be a departure from Britain's past performance. In the previous decade underlying inflation had been in the range of 3–7 per cent in nine out of the last ten years. The British have lived with relatively high inflation for so long that the moment inflation drops below 5 per cent or so newspapers tend to think it is not worth a second thought. Although it sounds wonderful to say that our inflation level is lower than the EU average, and we were able to say that in 1992, inflation in the EU included countries like Greece and Portugal, which raised the average figure considerably. I was keen to see Britain's inflation rate well below that of the average of the G7 countries, which would be a much more demanding challenge. I wanted to get it down permanently to a lower level.

If inflation is consistently higher that that of one's competitors, British goods gradually become uncompetitive and lose their markets. Even if the margin of uncompetitiveness is only 1.5 per cent each year, that cumulatively builds up over a five-year period to become a significant problem, when pressures would increase for a devaluation of the pound. But perpetual devaluation is not a way to prosperity but a lowering of living standards. In Britain we have continually altered our exchange rate to our poor productivity rather than trying to adjust our productivity to our exchange rate.

Inflation itself is a lagging indicator of the economy. Inflation may fall, rise or stabilise, but it will not tell you what is going to happen in a year's time. For that reason it was necessary to define the role of monetary aggregates in policy. Some monetarists would have liked us to have had only a series of targets for the money supply, such as M4, broad money (bank deposits plus money in circulation) and M0, narrow money (notes and coins in circulation). I attached considerable weight to M0 and regarded it as proxy for retail spending, but it was only a contemporaneous indicator, not what economists call a 'leading indicator'. It too did not forecast the future, only the present. Broad money was meant to be a leading indicator, although it had proved somewhat unreliable in the past.

I therefore continued to set a target for M0 of 0–4 per cent for 1992/93. For M4 I set what I called 'monitoring ranges', but I also indicated that we would take asset prices and inflationary expectations derived from market instruments and house prices into account in interest rate decisions There was no easy answer. Policy would also give weight to the exchange rate. In no sense would there be an exchange rate target. But I did not think it was right to be completely indifferent to the level of the exchange rate, even with our new freedom. Movements in the exchange rate themselves constitute an easing or a tightening of monetary conditions under which businesses operate. Fears of inflation returning in autumn 1992 may have been exaggerated after a 14 per cent or so devaluation, but that did not mean we could have allowed a 25 per cent fall, let alone an unlimited one.

It was important to indicate clearly why we were making decisions so that the markets could judge whether we were being consistent or not. I wanted to give them as much information as possible, so I gave an undertaking to publish a monthly monetary assessment covering asset prices as well as technical monthly data and a document giving the reasons for any changes in interest rates. I also asked the Bank to produce a quarterly inflation report assessing the Government's progress in reaching its inflation target. This novel and unprecedented outburst of *glasnost* would act as a discipline on the Government and make it more difficult for interest rate decisions to be political. Some saw it as leading naturally to Bank of England independence.

Lastly, in order to buttress the Treasury's capability and to demythologise forecasting, I decided, as I had long wanted, to create an outside independent panel of forecasters. This would demonstrate the uncertainties of the future, as seen not just by the Treasury but also a wider group of people.

I believe that all these changes were well received both by the markets and by professional economists. The PM thought I was taking too long about it and that I fussed too much about the details, but I believe the care taken was worth it. The policy framework that was established in that period has lasted and indeed delivered very impressive results. It is essentially the framework under which the newly independent Bank of England now operates.

The autumn IMF and World Bank meetings

That Friday I was due to fly out to the autumn IMF and World Bank Meetings in Washington. I always enjoyed them, but on this occasion I was naturally looking forward even more to getting away. One result of living in Wellington Square was that we were exposed to the press banging on the door or window or following Rosemary as she went shopping, shouting at her, 'Is he going to resign?'

I flew with Rosemary and officials in a Concorde, which was half empty. I don't recall anyone making a fuss about the cost of our going in Concorde. I have to confess that I never find it a very comfortable means of travelling, particularly because it is so noisy. I remember that Nigel Wicks, Jeremy and I were all shouting to make ourselves heard, as we discussed some of the details of 16 September. Occasionally our shouting became audible and I wondered what the few other passengers made of the details of Black Wednesday. Any journalist could have had a great scoop.

We all stayed in the Embassy, where Sir Antony Acland and his wife Jennifer made us very welcome. The weather was warm and close, but it was pleasant to walk in the extensive gardens. They were under the route of Vice-President Dan Quayle's helicopter, which occasionally interrupted the calm. We had tea and tomato sandwiches on the terrace and discussed the forthcoming meetings with Antony who, at the same time, walked up and down hitting a tennis ball with his racket deep on to the lawn for his black labrador to retrieve. Margaret Thatcher was also staying at the Embassy, though I didn't bump into her. I rather regretted that, as I would have liked to have discussed the events of the previous week with her. She wrote in her memoirs that she heard 'no singing in the bath'.

Because of the rush, we had had little time to prepare for the G7 and IMF Meetings, but as usual my officials in difficult circumstances had done a magnificent job. We expected the weekend to be dominated by the French referendum, whose result was to be declared on Sunday. Even at the IMF and World Bank the ratification of Maastricht was the subject everybody wanted to discuss. Wherever I fled I couldn't avoid it.

One of the most important occasions at these semi-annual Meetings of the IMF is the gathering of the so-called Interim Committee, where Finance Ministers normally report on developments in their own economies. These speeches are often drafted for domestic rather than international consumption. I outlined the circumstances of sterling's departure from the ERM and the strains that had been imposed on the whole system by German reunification. I then moved on to discuss future UK policy. At that time I had just begun the process of reconstructing new monetary policy, but I outlined a few of the principles that would guide us.

At the G7 Meeting we again discussed Russia, and G7 Finance Ministers met George Bush who pushed the idea of a new international monetary system, based on commodity values. It was an interesting but rather puzzling exercise, and at a time when the Europeans were all reeling from the collapse of the ERM it scarcely seemed relevant. George Bush was much exercised by the level of interest rates worldwide, but especially in Europe. He thought American rates were too high, even though they were low by European standards. I did wonder a little about the real nature of central bank independence when, in a White House meeting with Alan Greenspan, George Bush remarked, 'Now Alan over there is independent. But I want those rates down.'

I also had the opportunity to discuss the forthcoming November Presidential Election with US Secretary of State Jim Baker and Nick Brady. All the indications and all the polls were against George Bush, but Jim Baker professed to believe that he could still win. My impression was that there was no longer the hunger for victory that there should have been. At one point Nick Brady asked me if we could send across some bright young man from Central Office to explain how we had won the 1992 Election in the UK. There were only weeks to Election Day and at that moment I became convinced the Republicans were going to lose.

On Sunday morning I gave a press conference covering some the points from the G7 Meeting, my Interim Committee speech and Russia. It was a glorious day and I had had a much needed breath of fresh air in the Embassy garden. At the end of my conference, Hugh Pym from ITN said to me, 'Chancellor, you do seem in a very good mood this morning. Just why are you so cheerful?' I replied, 'Well it is a very beautiful morning, but it is funny you should say that. My wife said she heard me singing in the bath this morning.' That was the basis of the story that became widespread that I claimed that I sang in my bath on Black Wednesday.

The French referendum on Maastricht

The evening of 20 September was the occasion of the French referendum result. I had telephoned the PM during the day and found him extremely low. I could tell he was very depressed and to my surprise he told me that he was desperately hoping for a French 'No'. He had spent months persuading the Danes to vote 'Yes'. Now he wanted the French to say 'No'.

I watched the results of the French referendum in the White House with other Finance Ministers and Bank Governors. I was sitting next to Alan Greenspan as the results came in from the different French regions. He had done some detailed calculations and was quite convinced that the final result would be 'No'. However, as the figures swung towards the smallest possible 'Yes' to Maastricht he became quite suspicious. When the final result was announced, – 13,162,192 'Yes' votes to 12,623,582 'No' votes – one French diplomat, later a close aide to Lionel Jospin, remarked that he saw how my 'face fell'. From that moment, he said, he realised Britain would never be part of Europe.

Chancellor Kohl later complained to John Major that it had been reported to him that it was quite obvious from my demeanour that I was hoping for a French 'No'. The PM ticked me off for showing my feelings. I did not reply, as I might have done, that I merely wanted the same result as he did.

Kohl may have been annoyed by my facial expression, but I found the task of chairing the ad hoc Ecofin meeting at which I had to congratulate the French truly difficult. After the meeting, as Chairman, I had to make a statement saying how satisfied Ecofin was that the ratification process had overcome its last obstacle. I am sure my face on that occasion told a story too.

Back to the UK and a cut in rates

The trip to Washington seemed all too short. When I returned it was as though I had never been away. All the time I was still pressed by reporters as to whether I was going to resign. My political advisors, including David Cameron, told me it was clear

I couldn't believe how well we were doing in the Leadership Election. With John Major and, in the background, Terence Higgins, Bob Hughes and Ian Lang.

You could practise putting in the Treasury office.

My team at home at No. 11

As Master of the Royal Mint. Disraeli tried to sell his Chancellor's robes to Gladstone.

The 1991 Budget: the press can be intimidating.

Talking to Mikhail Gorbachev at the Russian Embassy.

How I liked to see myself.

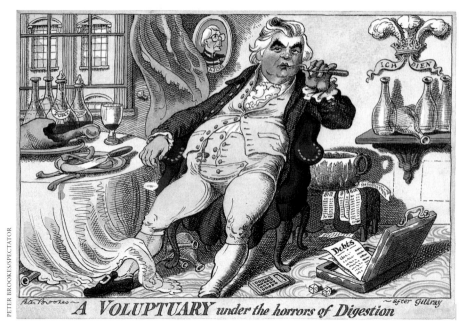

How others saw me.

John Smith and Margaret Beckett present the way Labour liked to see me.
But I was surprised people recognised me.

LEFT: The 1992 Budget: William Hague had more hair then. And the Budget Box didn't have a whisky bottle in it. RIGHT: Theo Waigel (right) made me drink white beer at breakfast.

John Major, Douglas Hurd and me being escorted by Chancellor Kohl at the G7 Summit in Munich in July 1992.

OFFICIAL WHITE HOUSE PHOTO

BRISTOL UNITED PRESS LTD

LEFT: Meeting George Bush at the White House on the night the result of the French referendum on Maastricht was announced. RIGHT: European Finance Ministers at the stormy Ecofin meeting in Bath. Rasmussen (Denmark) and myself, and behind us, from left, Kok (Holland), Barucci (Italy) (with spectacles), Waigel (Germany), Junker (Luxembourg) and Solchaga (Spain).

SEAN DEMPSEY/PA

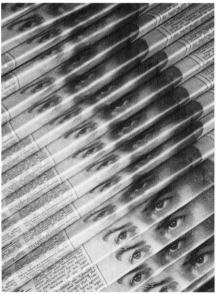

LEFT: Announcing Britain's withdrawal from the ERM.
RIGHT: Hitting the headlines again.

ABOVE: My senior Treasury advisors: Peter Lewis of the Inland Revenue, Alan Budd, Andrew Turnbull, Terry Burns and Tony Battishill, Chairman of the Inland Revenue. RIGHT: With Jeremy Heywood: the best ever Private Secretary. BELOW: My ministerial team at a Budget overview in 1993: Tony Nelson, John Cope, Stephen Dorrell, Michael Portillo and me, flanked by Bill Robinson (far left) and Jeremy Heywood (far right).

Brave rebels or loonies? Back row: Bill Walker, Edward Leigh, David Evans,
Christopher Gill, Barry Legg; Teresa Gorman; front row: John Redwood,
Hywel Williams and the author.

This was how most voters wanted to remember me, but actually it was another
Norman Lamont, MP for Wells in the nineteenth century.

that colleagues were positioning themselves to replace me. I did
not believe that, although both Kenneth Clarke and Michael
Howard were doing a large number of broadcasts on the economy. I did point out to both of them and to No. 10 that even
when I was away there were other Treasury Ministers, such as
Michael Portillo and Stephen Dorrell, who were well able and
better informed to handle any interviews on economic policy. I
did eventually speak to Michael Howard and he agreed to stop
doing broadcasts.

Rates cut outside the ERM

On Tuesday 22 September I made the first interest rate cut, as discussed with the PM the previous Friday. It was the first time we
had cut by a full percentage point in nearly two years. It was necessary to avoid any impression the cut was political. Obviously it
would help in the debate scheduled for that week in the House of
Commons, but it was overwhelmingly justified – the underlying
rate of inflation was now only 4 per cent, the economy was still
shrinking, interest rates were 9.5 per cent and it was only the
second cut in twelve months. It had been a long time. Fortunately
the cut was well received by the markets and I was able to tell that
to the PM when I met him with Terry later that day.

The emergency debate

The debate in the House on Thursday 24 September was not
technically a censure motion, since the motion had been tabled by
the Government. Indeed the motion before the House expressed
support for the economic policy of the Government, but it was
difficult to disagree with John Smith when he observed there was
a certain vacuity about the motion, since no one now knew what
the Government's economic policy was. It was John Smith's first
House of Commons appearance as Leader of the Opposition, and
the Prime Minister had to start his speech by welcoming him in
his new role.

The Prime Minister got off to a bad start by making an unnecessary attack on Norman Tebbit. He mocked him for having suggested that he, John Major, had somehow persuaded Mrs Thatcher against her will to join the ERM. 'Ah yes,' the PM said sarcastically, 'I remember it well.' He referred to Tebbit as a man who 'likes to bite your ankles, even if you are not walking up his pathway'.

It was a mistake because Norman Tebbit was widely admired and most MPs believed that Mrs Thatcher had indeed been persuaded against her will by John Major. The PM was barracked and interrupted repeatedly. He ducked a question from Teddy Taylor about whether the Government would rejoin the ERM.

John Smith mercilessly ridiculed my European Policy Forum speech, going through all the alternatives to ERM membership that I had so precisely rejected. After each one he asked whether it was Government policy. He went on to argue that at the time of the lira devaluation we could have had 'an orderly realignment' instead of the chaos that followed. But he had no convincing reply when the PM intervened to point out that Italy's devaluation had brought them little benefit since they had had to leave the ERM almost immediately afterwards.

Ted Heath was generously supportive of the Government, and added his warning of the dangers of a complete collapse of sterling, reflecting the widespread view at the time. Paddy Ashdown, as vapid as ever, said the whole crisis was about the 'fundamental long-term weakness of the UK economy'. Gordon Brown, now Shadow Chancellor, rose to speak at 9 p.m. He directed more of his fire at me than John Smith had done: 'The Chancellor is entirely consistent. We can rely on him always to get it wrong. There are two possible explanations for the Chancellor's behaviour. The Chancellor can choose between them. He has been seriously wrong for the past two years or he has been seriously wrong for the past two weeks.' He quoted my description of devaluation as 'fool's gold'. 'The Chancellor has no shame, makes no apology and gives no hint of remorse for damaging the stability of people's lives.'

As I rose I was conscious that this was possibly the most crucial speech of my life. I remembered how I had seen John Nott shouted down in the emergency debate on the Falklands, and early on I said, 'Provided that I can be given a hearing, I want to answer the questions . . .' I need not have worried. There was an air of expectation, and the House of Commons is usually a fair place. My speech was unvarnished, but did attempt to address the precise points Smith and Brown had made. I decided there was no point in being defensive. Indeed I didn't feel defensive; nothing said in the debate had made me feel uncomfortable. I felt confident I had a good case and I believed the House of Commons would hear me out. If a speaker is confident, it usually shows and counts.

I went over all the actions I had taken to safeguard our position within the ERM. Whatever my private impatience with the policy, I believed I had done everything I could to maintain it. The only thing I hadn't done was to put up interest rates, which might have been the right thing to do, but no one wanted me to do that. In any case I was able to quote Smith and Brown's endless calls for faster and deeper interest rate cuts coupled with simultaneous calls for us to remain in the ERM.

I described the unique combination of events we faced: never before had the foreign exchange markets had a specific date against which to speculate; the combination of the French referendum and German reunification had produced the strains. But I knew I had to address convincingly the question of a 'missed opportunity' for 'an orderly devaluation'. I repeated that a German realignment was never on offer. As for the idea that the pound should have been devalued with the lira, I was able to point out that Brown himself at the time of the Italian devaluation had specifically gone out of his way to rule out devaluation as emphatically as I had myself. By the time of the debate the lira had already left the ERM and the peseta was still struggling to stave off its second devaluation, so the arguments for a unilateral devaluation didn't look good. I was also able to ridicule Gordon Brown's endless calls for concerted interest rate reductions.

I rehearsed all the options and stated what I believed. 'I have read much about those events and I have listened to what people have said. I can only say that on the matter of the events of last week, and the week before, I have not heard of anything that might have been done or handled differently that would have produced a different outcome.'

I felt the tension as I spoke. Sometimes when one makes a speech, one is able metaphorically to stand back and say to oneself, 'Is this going down all right?' Sometimes one can tell, sometimes one can't. On this occasion I couldn't tell as I spoke. The House remained quiet, and there were surprisingly few interruptions, far fewer in my speech than in the PM's. But when I sat down there was a tumultuous cheer and stamping of feet from the Tories, which is unusual in the House of Commons. I was surprised. It was obvious it had gone down better than the PM's speech, largely I think because its points had been better directed at MPs' anxieties.

It was too late for the next day's papers, but it received strong praise at the weekend. An article in the *Independent on Sunday* (which I didn't read at the time) contrasted my speech and John Major's and said that I had rescued my position and that some Tory MPs were saying I was a candidate myself to replace John Major. That was nonsense. But there was no doubt that its success, for the moment, had taken the heat off me and transferred it to the Prime Minister. I hadn't intended that. When I spoke to a meeting of backbenchers I received a warm welcome. At one point I appealed to MPs to remain loyal and support the PM. I don't know whether I was more hurt or astonished when I found out that No. 10 later suggested that I had been attempting to destabilise the PM in my remarks. They were out of touch if they did not know what was being said about him, and they were wide of the mark if they thought I would ever have done anything to undermine him. To this day I am deeply puzzled at their reaction.

Developments in the currency market since Black Wednesday certainly helped in the debate. The chaos in the markets had continued, with currencies falling like dominoes. The lira had been first devalued and then had to withdraw from the ERM. The Portuguese and the Spaniards devalued twice, the Finns, the Swedes and the Norwegians had all floated. The Irish at the time of the debate were under the pressure that was in the end to force devaluation on them too.

Even the French franc was under pressure, and France had to

put interest rates up to 13 per cent, the very last thing that its economy needed. But perhaps that was the difference between the two countries' attitudes towards Europe. The French were prepared, for political reasons, to stick to 13 per cent interest rates, which in Britain would have been utterly unacceptable and inappropriate. But the most important point was what was happening to the Deutschmark, which soared to unprecedented heights against all currencies. The Germans had won their realignment on a far greater scale than they could ever have anticipated and yet they still refused to make any further cuts in interest rates – so much for the argument that a realignment would have brought about a reduction in German interest rates.

John Major after the debate

I have already made it clear that it is completely without foundation that Major ever had any sort of breakdown on Black Wednesday. However, in the following weeks his mood did become one of deep depression.

The Prime Minister never actually said to me that he was considering resigning, but he seemed close to total despair. I could not see that my leaving the Government would have helped him.

One evening in the flat in Admiralty House he explained to me how he felt his whole Premiership had been ruined by our exit from the ERM. Above all he thought that it was a political disaster rather than an economic one. I think that was an accurate analysis. The experience was much more damaging politically than economically. He listed to me several goals he had set himself for his Premiership. They included removing some of the blots of poverty in our society, creating a classless society (by which I always thought he really meant an opportunity society) and being 'at the heart of Europe'. Now that had gone. He asked me how I managed to remain so cheerful. I told him that I had stopped reading the newspapers. I knew what they were saying, and that several were calling for my resignation daily. I know the fact that I didn't read the newspapers for some weeks infuriated certain editors. But John Major could never have done that. He always looked at the first editions of every paper every night before he went to bed.

I felt very sorry for him. The real difference between our moods was that I was more comfortable with the new policy that events had forced upon us.

So-called 'fault lines' in the ERM

The Prime Minister and I discussed in several meetings a question that had been referred to in the House of Commons debate, namely the alleged 'fault lines' in the ERM. I regarded this as a bogus excuse, implying that the ERM had broken up because its rules were flawed and so the ERM had not worked properly. According to this line of thought there was nothing wrong with fixed exchange rates, merely the way in which this particular regime had operated.

The 'fault lines' argument focused on issues such as intra-marginal intervention, that is intervention in the markets before a currency actually hits its floor within the ERM. Another question was the obligations of stronger currencies to help the weaker currencies. The way the ERM operated, the cost of intervention ultimately was borne by the weaker currencies. Tendentiously this was sometimes described as 'asymmetric', but it always seemed to me there was no convincing reason why a strong currency should spend unlimited amounts of its money to support a weaker currency. If a weaker currency wanted to become a strong currency, it had to help itself, probably with interest rates.

The Prime Minister at times maintained that the ERM in which we had existed was not the ERM he had intended to join. There were frequent hints that the Germans had not helped as much as they should. The Prime Minister was keen that I, as Chairman of the Council of European Finance Ministers, should commission an official report into the alleged 'fault lines' and come up with recommendations for changes in the ERM. It would have been highly convenient if I could have done this. It would have exculpated us and made it easier for him to rejoin the ERM.

But I was uncomfortable with the idea and did not believe that the failings of the ERM lay in any technical 'fault lines'. The problem was more fundamental. Although I was annoyed by the remarks of Schlesinger and others before Black Wednesday, I did not feel that in their support for the pound they had behaved other than correctly. They had fulfilled all their legal obligations. It may be true that they gave much more help to the French franc for political reasons, but that did not mean that they had not satisfied their obligations to us or that the ERM had 'fault lines'. To me, the detailed operating rules of the ERM were entirely logical, if you wanted a fixed exchange rate system at all. The problems had not been in the rules for intervention but in the underlying tensions between the different economic conditions in Germany and other parts of Europe. I couldn't see how any changes in the technical rules would have bypassed that problem.

Nevertheless I was instructed to press ahead with Treasury officials in the first instance, then with officials from other Treasuries, and to come up with a report to be presented to the Birmingham European Council to be held in four weeks' time. Treasury officials were as embarrassed as I was. There was a predictably disappointing Ecofin meeting on 28 September, when there was no support from other countries about 'fault lines'. The Spaniards queried the help they alleged the Germans had given to the French, but no one wanted to change the operating rules of the ERM. Clearly other countries thought the British were wasting people's time, trying as usual to find an excuse for ourselves. When the report was finally produced, to the PM's annoyance it identified no 'fault lines' and we had some difficulty explaining this to newspapers, which had been fed the No. 10 line about them.

The Bundesbank paper

The Germans were on strong ground in saying that they had behaved correctly in the markets, but they were on weak ground when it came to defending the verbal comments they had made. On Tuesday 29 September I had received a letter from the German Ambassador attempting to rebut the criticisms that had been made of the Bundesbank. The day before, the German

Ambassador had called on the Permanent Under Secretary at the
Foreign Office and handed over a paper from the Bundesbank,
attempting to rebut criticism. Two days later, without warning, a
copy was made available to Peter Norman at the *Financial Times*.
The paper was to put it politely, 'economical with the truth'. But
the *Financial Times* decided to print everything the Germans said
as though it was gospel, and very little of what we wanted to say
in reply.

Firstly, the note asserted that Dr Schlesinger, in his interview
with *Handelsblatt*, was supportive of sterling on 17 September.
One wondered how they could have dared to make that point –
sterling had left the ERM on that date. What did the damage
were the remarks before Black Wednesday on the 15th, not the
corrected comments after the disaster on the 17th. Later Hans
Tietmeyer told me he could not believe Schlesinger had said what
he did.

Then the paper claimed the Bundesbank substantially supported sterling. That was correct. It was obliged to do so, and I
never suggested otherwise. But it did not mention that the Bank
of England had to repay the Bundesbank for all its support in
accordance with the operating rules of the ERM. The support
complied with its legal obligations, and nothing more. The article had a number of other ill-informed points about the Bank of
England's handling of the crisis and argued that sterling should
not have been allowed to fall to its floor. But it only fell to its
floor on the evening of 15 September, after the comments of Dr
Schlesinger. Prior to that date the Bank had succeeded, as was its
objective, in keeping sterling above its floor. Lastly the paper
repeated the allegation about the Germans seeking a revaluation.

Of all Eurosceptics, I think I am probably the least anti-
German. I admire German culture and modern Germany deeply. I
have never made an anti-German speech or sought in my
Euroscepticism to appeal to anti-German feeling. But I have to say
that the Bundesbank's paper strained my regard for Germany
almost to breaking point, and momentarily made me wonder if
some of the harsh things sometimes said about Germans might not
have a grain of truth.

My failure at the Party Conference

The Party Conference in Brighton on 6–9 October was always going to be difficult. Party members were obviously still deeply unhappy and bewildered and it was important that the Prime Minister and I gave good accounts of ourselves. As well as preparing my own speech, which was important, I was also busy with meetings on our new framework for policy. Terry Burns and Alan Budd came down to join me for meetings with the PM who, perhaps understandably, was impatient with the time we were taking to fill in all the details as it was now two and a half weeks since the ERM debacle. While I understood his concern, a number of decisions, both big and small, were difficult. I had decided the best way to make a statement about policy was for me to write a letter to John Watts, MP for Slough and Chairman of the House of Commons Treasury and Select Committee (CTCSC), as my speech to the Party Conference would not be a suitable vehicle for a mass of detail mainly designed for the financial markets. I was due to appear before the CTCSC on 12 October, so a letter could be both a statement of policy and also part of my evidence to the Committee.

The Prime Minister and I met several times in his suite in the Grand Hotel, Brighton. One of our meetings was continually interrupted by a loudspeaker van driving up and down the front. Just when the Prime Minister was pressing me to cut interest rates, the loudspeaker bellowed, 'Cut interest rates.' This was followed by 'End recession, restore growth', and I think the Prime Minister rather felt this reflected his impatience with his Chancellor of the Exchequer. Finally came the shout, 'Rebuild Britain's economy.'

As we talked it became clear that there was a division between us. I felt quite confident that the cuts in interest rate that were now in prospect would themselves be quite enough to get the economy going again, but the PM still talked in terms of stimulating the economy by fiscal measures. I felt we had had more than enough of that experiment while we had been in the ERM and we were now lumbered with the catastrophic consequences. He kept returning to the subject of 'a strategy for industry' and said that the Thatcher idea that the Government's only role was to create the framework for growth was inadequate. We needed more than that. He talked about export subsidies and help for manufacturing industry but I couldn't see why we needed to help exporters when they had been handed a huge devaluation on a plate. It was a not a good meeting, and others were equally tense, but it was agreed that my letter would go off to John Watts and be released to the press.

That was also the day of the debate on Europe at the Party Conference. Douglas Hurd was speaking from the platform and Norman Tebbit spoke from the floor, making a fierce attack on Maastricht and receiving a big ovation. He went out of his way to defend me, turning to the rostrum and looking at Major, saying 'Don't sack your Chancellor.' In front of the whole Conference, he reminded Major that it was he who had made the decision to join the ERM.

That afternoon I bumped into Norman on the stairs of the Grand Hotel, and I thanked him for what he said. He replied, 'I'd find an issue on which to resign if I were you. The two-faced bastard will push you in the end, when he feels safer and it is more convenient for him,' and then walked off. I didn't believe him, and gave it no thought.

My speech was not until Thursday, but on the Wednesday night I was due to give the Conservative Political Centre (CPC) lecture on Europe and Maastricht. David Cameron had given me a lot of invaluable help. It was Eurosceptic in tone, but strongly defended the Government's policy. I emphasised the Government's opt-out from the single currency, which I stressed gave us complete freedom to run our economic policy for ever as we wanted without any interference from Europe, which was why I said, Maastricht as a Treaty was acceptable to me as a Eurosceptic. But I made clear my opposition to moving to a single currency, and in some depth I criticised the increasing moves towards a highly integrated Europe. It was very different from Douglas Hurd's speech to the Conference because I acknowledged and indeed described the threat to Britain's independence from Europe. The speech was very well received, and I was given a warm standing ovation, which made me more optimistic about my speech to the Conference on Thursday.

I had a few difficulties with No. 10 over my CPC speech. They objected to my remark: 'No one would die for Europe' – an observation on Europe's ambition to become a state. But I ignored their advice.

I was not able to do the same with my Conference speech because the Prime Minister demanded to see every draft and kept objecting to passages. It was even worse than the previous year. He and Sarah Hogg felt my speech did not emphasise enough his theme of 'going for growth'. I was more concerned to emphasise that the policy remained the same and was worried that the markets would take fright if we talked all the time about 'going for growth'. My view was that governments didn't stimulate growth but allowed it to happen. There was no doubt we were now going to get growth because we were going to have a looser monetary policy. Another disagreement was over references to Mrs Thatcher. I put in my speech a number of references praising the economic policy of the 1980s but the PM wanted me to take out all references to Mrs Thatcher. In deference to him, I did modify one or two of them, but I was incensed.

Curiously, he also objected to a quotation from Churchill that I wanted to use with reference to the public finances: 'If we do not face reality, reality will face us.' This, he thought, was too bleak. But I wanted the Party and the public to understand that we had some very tough decisions ahead.

An enormous amount of work had been contributed to my speech by David Cameron, Bill Robinson, David Hart, a business friend, and William Hague. It was necessary to produce a speech that gave hope and inspiration to the dispirited Party faithful without unsettling the markets. If my speech in the Commons debate had been the most important I had ever made, this speech was the most important I would ever make at a Party Conference.

One of the points in the speech was that from now on we would be pursuing 'a British policy for British interests'. That was what I felt. It seemed to me a not unfair summary of a situation where for the first time in years we were uncoupling our interest rates from those of Germany, setting them for the British economy and doing so when we had been told it could not be done. My emphasis on a 'British policy' brought vitriolic condemnation from Sam Brittan in the *Financial Times* and later from Helmut Kohl. John Major wasn't very keen on it either.

Rereading today the carefully crafted draft, I think it was quite a good speech, but it undoubtedly did not go down well. The debate on the floor of the Conference was fractious, and although there were no direct attacks on me, some of the representatives who spoke were unsurprisingly very unhappy.

When it came to my turn to reply to the debate, I stood up and looked at the teleprompters on to which my speech was to be projected. I had done a number of rehearsals with the equipment; I didn't like using it, but on this occasion I thought it was necessary. The Conference waited for my opening words as I discovered that I could hardly read the text, which was extremely faint and difficult to see. The problem was that two bright lights on the platform immediately behind me were beaming down directly on to the Perspex teleprompters.

It was a nightmare. Here was a highly important speech and I could hardly read the words we had spent days drafting. I had to keep moving my head from side to side, and up and down to particular positions so that the lights were not shining so directly on to the words. Eventually I got the knack of it, but it completely destroyed the delivery. The moment I returned to the hotel the telephone rang and David Hart asked, 'What was the matter?' I knew the next day's papers would be bad. 'Lamont fails to lift the Conference' was a fairly typical headline. Even the *Daily Express*, with whose editor I had dinner the night before and who was very supportive, was critical. I am quite sure they were only reflecting what others said.

I left the Conference in low spirits. It seemed as though one day it was up a ladder, and the next down a snake. But the failure of the speech was not all. There was a postscript to the Conference in the *Sun* newspaper, which reported in front-page headlines that I had left the Grand Hotel after the Conference without paying my bill. My bill was described as very large because I had consumed a combination of big breakfasts and champagne. According to them, I had simply departed. One would have thought the average reader would have considered it improbable that a Chancellor of the Exchequer would be able to avoid paying his bill by simply walking away from a hotel. In fact, like several other Cabinet Ministers, I had arranged with the hotel that my bill would be sent on to me. The *Sun*, I was told by the hotel manager, had obtained the information by telephoning and pretending to be Conservative Central Office, asking for a list of those whose bills had not been paid, but writing the story only about me. The manager of the hotel had made it clear to the *Sun* that the story was nonsense, but they paid no attention.

The week after the Party Conference on 12 October I appeared before the Treasury Select Committee. They had my letter outlining my proposals for the reconstruction of monetary policy outside the ERM. It had been useful to be able to publish the letter so that it could be studied both in the press and in the markets, but alas the Committee were not much interested in the letter and wanted to hold yet another post-mortem on the ERM and the arguments about devaluation and realignment. The appearance went smoothly enough, despite Nick Budgen's attempts to create some sensations. I had John Major's words that the recession would be 'short and shallow' thrown back at me, not for the first time.

Crisis over the coal mines

One issue that added greatly to the Government's problems was the future of the coal industry. British Coal wanted to close down thirty-one pits with a loss of 30,000 jobs. The industry would thus be left with only twenty deep mines and a workforce of 20,000–30,000 people. It would have been British Coal's biggest closure programme since the mid-1980s, and would shut eleven of the twenty-one Yorkshire pits and eight in Nottinghamshire. But the logic was inescapable, not least after the privatisation of the electricity-generating industry in 1990. Increasingly the electricity industry wanted to move to gas for power generation, but John Wakeham as Energy Secretary had vetoed all pre-Election large-scale closures.

When Michael Heseltine brought the plans to a Cabinet Committee he had done so without any heavy pressure from myself or Michael Portillo. I say that because when the episode later became a great public-relations disaster there was something of an attempt to shove the blame on to the Treasury for being too hawkish and pushing too hard. Of course Michael and I wanted the closures, but what else did the DTI expect the Treasury to do if they presented us with proposals that made industrial sense, cut electricity prices, raised competitiveness and saved taxpayers' money? In a Government where it was increasingly difficult to get hard-headed decisions, it was hardly the job of the Treasury to suggest that the rational decisions should be scaled back or abandoned. Of course, Michael Portillo, supported by myself, also argued against the DTI to keep compensation terms and the package of assistance for closure areas to the lowest possible figure. That was Portillo's job. If there was to be a compromise for political reasons, it was up to the Prime Minister to say so.

The announcement on Tuesday 13 October caused a storm of protest. Strong Labour opposition was to be expected, but they were joined by normally loyal Conservative MPs such as Elizabeth Peacock and Winston Churchill. Many Tories were, not surprisingly, angry because the closures included pits represented by the Union of Democratic Mine Workers (UDM) that had stayed open despite the threats of Arthur Scargill during the NUM strike of 1984–5. One of the problems was that the DTI was none too sure of its own costings for the viability of individual pits. The PM became irritated by the constantly shifting statistics offered by Michael Heseltine and Minister for Energy Tim Eggar. The figures for the number of pits that were viable, their coal price and their level of orders constantly kept altering. One of the reasons I was surprised when Major subsequently made Michael Heseltine Deputy Prime Minister was that I remembered vividly how angry this made him and what little confidence he had in him at that time. Anthony Seldon in his book says that the Prime Minister 'possessed great faith in Heseltine'. That was certainly not the case then.

The Government's handling of the pit closures received an extremely bad press. Many people thought it even worse than after Black Wednesday. Certainly the popular outcry was much worse, with marches, demonstrations and denunciations by churchmen. It was a much easier issue for the public to understand. What made the reaction so fierce was that all this was happening at a time when unemployment was already high and it was not easy for people to find alternative jobs. Anyone with uncertainty about their economic future could sympathise with the miners.

Opposition in the Conservative Parliamentary Party was such that in order to get through the House of Commons debate we were driven into making a dramatic and unconvincing U-turn. The closures were modified and even more money was thrown at them. Twenty-one of the pits were subject to a full review of their viability to be carried out by independent consultants. Michael, as usual, saved the day in the House by turning in a bravura performance. No one else could have done it. Without his speech the Government might not have survived the vote.

The climbdown itself further damaged the Government and led to increased criticism of the Prime Minister personally. Peter Riddell was not alone when he talked of the 'impression of shambles' and the absence of 'firm Government'. The *Independent on Sunday* called on the PM to resign, while the *Sunday Express* called the pit closure fiasco 'the most maladroit piece of government this country has seen for many years'. The episode also played a key role in hitting business confidence, already weak after Black Wednesday, and undermining political support for the Government.

Interest rates come down to 8 per cent

The issue of interest rates then got muddled up with the pit closures. I had postponed the rate cut until after the Party Conference because I thought that to do it before would look too political and too much as though I was trying to bolster my own position. The Prime Minister tried to persuade me to make the rate cut on the same day as the announcement of the pit closures so as to lessen the impact of the bad news. I was appalled, and refused. Firstly, it would again make the rate increase look political. Secondly, it wouldn't work. No one would be fooled by such a crass tactic. In the end it was agreed that the rate cut would take place on Friday 16 October and so on that day rates were cut again by 1 per cent, down to 8 per cent. Now we had rates near to a level that would bring about real recovery.

The cut was well received in the markets, but not so well by our European partners. By this time sterling had now drifted down 14 per cent against the Deutschmark and fallen from 92 to 82 against the trade-weighted basket index of currencies. Our interest rates, the lowest they had been since 1978, were the lowest in the EU. The French were getting particularly nervous and Bérégovoy attacked the 'short-sighted' nature of UK policy. Kohl, picking up my Conference Speech, warned the UK against the illusion of any country trying to go its own way. Despite his words, that was precisely what we appeared to be doing rather well, and continue to do so.

The Mansion House Speech: a panel of independent forecasters

The next engagement in the Chancellorial calendar was the Mansion House Speech. The preparation for that was a repetition of the arguments the Prime Minister and I had during the Party Conference. The PM wanted me to put forward 'a strategy for growth' and an industrial strategy, whereas my arguments remained the same as at Brighton.

A few days before the Mansion House Speech the PM himself went on TV and announced, 'A strategy for growth is what we need, a strategy for growth is what we are going to have.' It might have looked as though the remarks were aimed at me, but that would be to underestimate the PM. The interview diverted attention from the growing crisis over pit closures and earned him some good headlines. That was the main intention. Another, unintended, consequence was a sharp fall in sterling in the markets.

The Mansion House Speech is normally an opportunity for the Chancellor to make a fairly technical speech. This year it therefore seemed the ideal opportunity to outline the new ideas on which I had been working. I also talked at some length about the role of forecasting, because I had never successfully been able to get across the point that forecasting does not occupy nearly as central role in policy-making as most people imagine. I announced my intention to have a panel of independent forecasters whose assessment we would publish. This was something less than a full-blown American Council of Economic Advisors, but it would enable my judgements to be compared with other people's. A few weeks later I was pleased to be able to invite on to the panel people such as Wynne Godley, Professor of Applied Economics at Cambridge, Tim Congdon and Patrick Minford. All of them had been among my fiercest critics, but they were all people for whom I had a high regard.

I had resisted any remarks about 'a strategy for growth', all too reminiscent of Reggie Maudling, but in the speech I stressed that 'though the aims of Government policy remained the same, we are now in an entirely different policy environment'. I then went on to say that 'the goal of the Government's macro-economic policy has never been simply to defeat inflation. Lower inflation is not just an end in itself.' The key words then followed: 'But just as prosperity can be jeopardised by too lax a monetary policy and too high a rate of inflation, so too we have always recognised that policy can become too tight.' This was public acknowledgment of the fact that during the last few months of our membership of the ERM we had an inappropriate policy. I wanted to signal to the markets that, without jeopardising inflation, we were moving into a new situation. 'Leaving the ERM was a setback, but it has given us the opportunity to rebalance our policy and to take greater account of the risks to the world economy. This does not mean that the Government has gone soft on inflation. But the dramatic progress we have made in getting inflation down does allow me now to give greater weight to securing an early resumption of growth.'

The return of growth, of course, depended on the return of confidence. That, I added, 'cannot simply be drawn like a rabbit from a conjuror's hat. I may be dressed as a magician, but I am in face just the Chancellor of the Exchequer.' All the cartoons the next day were of me in white tie and tails producing a white rabbit out of a hat.

The speech was well received in the financial markets and in the City press which was what had most concerned me. I was not best pleased, though not entirely surprised, when I read in other papers that the speech had been substantially rewritten in No. 10.

Nonetheless I had established a new, durable basis for the conduct of monetary policy. By targeting inflation rather than a specific monetary indicator such as the exchange rate or some measure of the money supply, I believed I had found a solution to the problems that had led to past breakdowns, whether in the ERM in the nineties or targeting broad money ten years previously. At the same time I had to allay the markets' concern about the wider discretion this could imply. Unless this was done, policy would carry a credibility premium in the form of higher interest than was strictly necessary to achieve a given level of inflation.

My successors as Chancellor further improved the framework. Ken Clarke decided to publish the minutes of his meetings with the Governor of the Bank of England, and Gordon Brown completed the process by making the Bank independent. At last Britain has a structure for setting monetary policy which can compare with the best in the world.

12

Autumn Statement 1992

My official superiors often reminded me of the maxim in
the Treasury that no subordinate can in the long run be
stronger than the Chancellor of the Exchequer. And in turn I
suppose it is true that no Chancellor of the Exchequer can in
the long run enforce a policy which is opposite to the prevailing current in the Cabinet.
John Maynard Keynes, in a letter to Beatrice Webb, 1918

In the summer I had announced an entirely new system for controlling public expenditure, which came to be known as the
'top-down approach'. I recognised that the high level of public
expenditure agreed in the 1991 Autumn Statement was too high,
although there was a striking contrast between the intended
public expenditure outcome and the actual out-turn. I have
described this problem in Chapter 6.

I had harboured some hope that, after the Election was out of the
way, we would be able to revisit the public expenditure figures and
reduce them, as John Smith accused us of wanting to do. Alas, his
accusations had no substance. This option had been effectively pre-
empted when John Major said without warning in the Election
campaign that the public expenditure figures in the Red Book would
remain sacrosanct. After the Election I had suggested to the Prime
Minister that since inflation was lower than expected in the 1991
Autumn Statement, and programmes therefore overfunded, we had
every justification for cuts. But he would not contemplate that.

The top-down approach

Reflecting on these problems, I concluded that the traditional mechanisms for settling the public expenditure round were wrong in several ways. The Treasury regarded the ratio of public expenditure to GDP not just as some political objective but actually as a criterion for controlling public spending. As long as this ratio was declining, any increase in public expenditure was acceptable.

Of course, it was right for a Conservative Government to aim to reduce public expenditure as a proportion of GDP. That was a political objective. It meant the state was doing less and interfering less. But using that same ratio to judge whether particular increases in spending in any one year were affordable was not right. In the late 1980s, when the economy was growing very fast, large public expenditure increases were judged acceptable because the economy was growing even faster than public expenditure, and so the ratio was falling. This was a false reassurance. The Conservative Party persuaded itself that it was achieving a hat-trick of a growing economy, a falling ratio of public spending to GDP and increased spending on programmes such as health and education. When the music stopped, however, it was likely to go wrong. Everything was all right as long as the economy carried on growing, but if it slowed down or even contracted one would be left with unaffordably large increases in public expenditure.

When I first became Chief Secretary in 1988, new to the job though I was, I thought the remit for public expenditure increases that I had been given by the Cabinet was surprisingly generous. The year-on-year increases were large in real terms and I remember arguing this with the Treasury officials then in charge of public expenditure. But it was argued that as long as the ratio of spending to GDP was falling it didn't matter, and we expected the economy to carry on growing. As Terry Burns later said, 'You should never target a ratio.' This approach went disastrously wrong in 1991, when the Treasury misread the economic recovery. The economy did not grow but public expenditure did.

After that experience my view was that we had to go back to the simple idea of looking only at the year-on-year increase in public spending in real terms. The rule ought to be that public spending should grow no more quickly than the average long-term growth of the economy.

One problem with this approach is that public expenditure itself is cyclical: recession increases public expenditure in areas such as unemployment benefit and nationalised industry losses, so in a recession public expenditure tends to grow faster than the economy, breaking the 'Lamont rule'. For this reason I decided to separate out public expenditure into 'cyclical' expenditure, such as unemployment benefit, and 'non-cyclical expenditure,' which covered the remainder and would be subject to a strict 'new control total'. The aim should be that the 'new control total' would not grow faster than the long-term rate of growth of the economy as a whole. At the same time the 'cyclical' expenditure would automatically shrink in boom years in order to offset its rise in recessions. This approach I believed would give us much better control of public expenditure over the longer term.

The second area of public expenditure control that needed rethinking was the whole idea of what was called the 'public expenditure round'. Every year departments submitted 'bids' to the Treasury for their programmes for the next three years. Except in a very formal sense, none of these bids were seriously considered collectively. The whole burden of reconciling the conflicting demands fell on the lonely figure of the Chief Secretary, who had the task of trying to assess the merits of hospitals against roads, or schools against overseas aid, knowing that each Minister was only interested in his own programme.

The whole process seemed to be deteriorating each year, with more and more drama in the press. Every year the public expenditure round became a struggle, with Ministers seeking to impress their civil servants, backbench MPs and journalists by publicising what they personally had extracted from the Treasury. After each round the newspapers would publish lists of 'winners and losers'.

The crucial point was that, bizarrely, the old system paid no attention to what the total level of spending should be from an overall fiscal perspective, hence the need for a 'top-down' approach.

The old system might have carried on being effective with a Prime Minister like Mrs Thatcher, who was always on the side of the Treasury and had enormous determination to control public spending. It is inevitable that the Chancellor and the Chief Secretary are always in a minority of two in any Cabinet Committee meeting when they want to restrain expenditure, but Mrs Thatcher always made that two even more with her own vociferous support of the Treasury. She illustrated the truth of Lincoln's remark 'One man with courage makes a majority.'

John Major had greater enthusiasm than Mrs Thatcher for 'sensible public expenditure'. He did not believe, as Gladstone did, that the Treasury had to wage a war on 'candle ends'. One of his maxims was that a little extra public expenditure on a small budget like that for the arts could yield huge political dividends. Perhaps, but it is also true the road to Budget deficit is paved with good causes.

To me it was obvious that a new system was necessary. The problem with my proposal was that it involved sharing the Treasury's information, which was its source of power, with other Ministers. My proposals caused great heart-searching and anxiety among Treasury officials.

The creation of EDX

I proposed that instead of the annual public expenditure round, the Cabinet should collectively agree a total for public expenditure in line with the new control total. Individual departments, instead of making bids to the Treasury, would do so to a new Cabinet Committee, EDX, which would be chaired by the Chancellor. The other members would include several senior Ministers, the Chief Secretary and some non-departmental Ministers such as the Leader of the House of Commons. By volunteering to share the decisions I hoped we would persuade the Cabinet to be more realistic and to understand the conflicts in bids for scarce resources. My changes were designed to make the public expenditure round into a zero-sum game.

There were risks in my proposals. Firstly, EDX members might try to involve themselves in wider discussions of economic policy, particularly taxation, a danger that would be increased in future years now that I had decided to have a unified Budget with taxation and spending considered together. I persuaded John Major to emphasise to the members of EDX that they were only to consider expenditure and nothing else, but this still proved to be something of a problem in the first year of operation.

The second problem was, simply, time. EDX and the top-down approach were likely to be immensely time-consuming, involving more Ministers and many more hours of collective discussion. Treasury officials did not hesitate to point out to me that it placed a huge extra burden on the Chancellor, who normally left the public expenditure round, in its detail, to the Chief Secretary. Now the Chancellor would be involved, albeit only as Chairman.

The new system had been agreed by the PM and then by the Cabinet on 23 July. The members of EDX were to be myself; Michael Portillo; Michael Heseltine, Secretary of State for Trade and Industry; Kenneth Clarke, Home Secretary; John Wakeham, Leader of the Lords, and Tony Newton, Leader of the Commons, with Sarah Hogg also present.

The target for non-cyclical expenditure was set at an average growth rate over three years of 1.5 per cent per annum. This figure was well below the Treasury's estimate of the long-term rate of growth of the British economy, which was 2–2.25 per cent per annum. Since the PM refused to consider spending cuts for the coming year, I had demanded as a quid pro quo that the average growth over the three years be reduced to 1.5 per cent per annum.

This meant for the first year there could be no addition at all to the increases already planned. To have a public spending round with a zero addition to existing plans was something that had not been achieved for many years.

The Committee met in the summer, but started work in earnest after the Party Conference. A draft package of budgets for each Department was put before the Committee for consideration and each departmental Minister then appeared before the Committee for sessions of around three-quarters of an hour to an hour to defend the estimates of their Department's needs. It was a heavy workload which needed to be completed in time for the Autumn Statement, usually made some time in early November. The process did give the Cabinet via EDX a much greater sense of the inevitable trade-offs in public expenditure. I believe it also encouraged greater realism, although there were a number of very difficult decisions.

I walk out of EDX and 'resign'

A few teething problems were to be expected. Michael Heseltine and Kenneth Clarke did, as feared, try to extend the remit into taxation. Michael, in particular, wasted a huge amount of time considering impractical ideas such as cutting the basic retirement pension. There was no way the Conservative Party could do that, having said clearly in its Manifesto that we would increase the pension in line with inflation.

At one point I thought I had made a terrible error. Against the advice of my officials, I had surrendered a Treasury monopoly of decision-making for a Committee that was behaving unrealistically and apparently did not want to face up to the issues. I became a little depressed. I was convinced we needed to get the public finances in order, but my colleagues showed no sign of wanting to take their new responsibilities seriously.

On Friday 16 October there was a dreadful meeting of EDX. That was the day I had made the interest-rate cut described in the last chapter after a row with the PM over whether the cut would be used to draw attention away from the announcement of the pit closures. I felt we were in danger of losing all credibility as a Government.

Kenneth Clarke was particularly unhelpful, saying he was not necessarily going to accept the public expenditure total given to the Committee without looking at tax. Michael Heseltine also wanted to discuss the future of mortgage interest relief and continued to push his point on pensions. It went on a very long time until I simply picked up my papers, said I had had enough, walked out of the meeting and went home to Wellington Square. I telephoned Jeremy Heywood and said I was resigning. I was not prepared to go on being Chancellor when there was no support from anyone for controlling public expenditure. We were in great danger and nobody was prepared to face up to the facts.

The PM was informed of my walk-out. Eventually I was telephoned and asked if Sarah Hogg could come round to see me. I said I didn't want to see her, but she turned up and was, as always, charming and helpful. Eventually, after much talking, she assured me that EDX was going to accept what I wanted. This incident was leaked and there was much talk of my being 'emotional' and 'erratic'. It was all taken as evidence that I was an unstable and very prickly colleague, who couldn't bear interference with his department. I certainly could not. I was feeling more and more angry at the drift and the way the Government made its decisions, but I confess there was an element of calculation in my walk-out. Without it there would never have been agreement on the proper target for the new control total that year. I had had to resort to these tactics to get the backing that I should have had from the start from the PM.

EDX resumes

The negotiations and work of EDX resumed and went much more smoothly from then on. Kenneth Clarke was quieter and more constructive. Michael Portillo was a clear and skilful advocate for the Treasury view. But there were some difficult decisions. The Jubilee Line extension, which the PM was keen on, did not to me look affordable. Michael Howard put forward proposals for an expensive package to soften the introduction of the new Council Tax, which was really bad news. It was scarcely believable that we had had to fling large amounts of public money at the Poll Tax to make it acceptable, even in its dying days, and then when we had abolished it chuck more money at its replacement.

One area that I would have liked to tackle more strongly was defence spending. We were planning to take £570 million out of the next year's defence budget, though in truth I thought we could take much more. Defence is always a sensitive subject in the Conservative Party, but surely now the Election was out of the way was the time to be tough.

I felt we were not sufficiently acknowledging the great changes that had taken place. With the break-up of the communist empire, Russia, even if it wanted to, was not in a position to offer the threat it had in the past. Britain alone, out of all the European countries, insisted on maintaining senior positions and a very large capability in all three NATO commands, air, sea and land. Surely we could reduce our commitment in one of them? Some of the MoD's pet projects, such as troop carriers to reinforce the coast-line of northern Norway, never particularly convincing at the height of the Cold War, looked ridiculous now. We had, of course, the cuts from the MoD's 'Options for Change'. Britain wanted to play a leading role in NATO and also elsewhere. As the threat in Europe diminished, we also seemed keen to assume a possible wider global role. I was never enthusiastic about that. The proposed cuts were small compared with those being made in other countries, but the PM turned down flat my proposals for radical reductions. Sarah Hogg tried to help me, but even she could not persuade the PM.

EDX did manage to agree a limit on public sector pay of 1.5 per cent, which was tough by any standards. Immediately after the Election, Portillo and Dorrell had proposed a wage freeze, which I felt would guarantee that the Government would be drawn into conflict with the public sector. Mrs Thatcher, in my opinion wisely, had always refused to have an explicit norm for public sector pay on the grounds that it would become a target at which to aim, and there had not been a specific pay ceiling for thirteen years. The policy was undoubtedly risky, because we had now made ourselves the direct target for all protests about low public sector pay. But it did enable us to make savings of £1.5 billion which were transferred to capital projects. In addition we decided that Cabinet Ministers, judges, senior civil servants and senior military officers would have no increase. There was ample justification for the policy as earnings in the public sector had risen much more rapidly than in the private sector in the last few years.

This helped to fill in one of the themes of the Autumn Statement, which was that economies would be made on current spending while capital programmes would be safeguarded as far as was practical. This sounded good, but was actually rather specious. The definition of what is capital and what is current in the public sector is never as simple as in the private sector. Is £1 million spent on a school toilet really more of an investment than £1 million spent on training teachers? And, of course, any claims that increasing capital spending helped employment, though frequently made, were spurious.

The Prime Minister was still keen to have another package to aid industry. To me this was the more cosmetic than real. If we cut interest rates at the time of the Autumn Statement, as we were planning to do, that would be another addition to the already massive easing of policy. Rates would have fallen to become the lowest in the EU, falling 3 points since leaving the ERM. They were now at the lowest level for fifteen years, so it was not easy to see why a further stimulus was needed. A recovery was now inevitable.

Because of the need to take the initiative and to be seen to be reconstructing policy after the ERM, the Autumn Statement inevitably became more of a mini budget. As part of our package of capital projects we decided to announce a £1.8 billion extension of the Jubilee Line to Docklands and £700 million extra aid to exporters through ECGD (Export Credits Guarantee Department), and local authorities were to be allowed to spend more of their accumulated capital receipts than before. A £6.3 billion road programme was to be emphasised, although in reality this was largely a reannouncement of existing plans. What particularly made the statement more like a Budget was the inclusion of some 'time-limited' tax measures, such as a temporary increase in capital allowances from 25 per cent to 40 per cent. I decided to abolish the special car tax of 5 per cent, which I had already halved in my Budget. I was delighted to kill it off. I had never been able to justify why cars, alone among consumer expenditure items, should suffer a special tax on top of VAT.

We also decided we could not avoid yet another package to help the housing market. Despite the reduction in interest rates, which should in theory have moved the housing market, there was still a large debt overhang and negative equity remained a massive contributor to the lack of confidence and the failure of consumer spending to recover. I proposed to make available an extra £170 million to be used, before the end of March, to buy up through Housing Associations some of the empty properties on the market. I wanted to persuade the housing movement as well to put up some matching private finance, which I estimated would reduce the overhang of empty properties holding back the market. Many people saw this as a return of Keynesianism.

The Private Finance Initiative

A striking innovation of the Autumn Statement was the announcement of the start of the Private Finance Initiative, which lasted and is still with us today, under a Labour Government. It has had a significant impact on the country's stock of capital and undoubtedly has made possible capital investment that otherwise would not have happened. I had touched on this subject in my Mansion House Speech.

Much of the credit for this belongs to John Major as he kept pushing me on this subject. I was initially, I confess, suspicious of his motives, since I thought he just wanted to avoid the rules defining the PSBR and to get public spending increased by the back door and put off the balance sheet. But the idea eventually opened up a whole new dimension for privatisation. And it was needed. Traditionally, the public sector is hopeless at running large capital programmes.

The concept was a simple one: capital projects in the public sector could easily be financed by private capital, with the private sector providing management, purchasing services, or leasing assets. In theory such private finance deals had always been possible, but only under Treasury rules of Byzantine complexity that had ensured that nothing ever happened. At the Prime Minister's urging I set about trying to simplify these rules and set up a panel to assist in this task and encourage proposals from the private sector. As a result, a number of important projects were brough forward, many in the NHS.

Ironically the Private Finance Initiative turned out to be very important for the new Labour Government, anxious to improve public services without putting up taxes, though it is still too early to judge its real long-term success. The PFI is not a 'free lunch'. For private finance to work properly it has to provide greater value and efficiency to make it worthwhile. The Government itself can always borrow money more cheaply than any other private sector borrower, so the efficiency test for a private finance project has to be real. Secondly, it is essential that the risk in the project really is wholly transferred to the private sector, otherwise privately financed public expenditure ought to count towards Government borrowing. Lastly, there is the risk that the private sector may provide finance up front but that the long-term consequences will be the silting-up of public expenditure with a stream of never-ending rental payments. I suspect that in the long run some of these projects will go wrong and appear again on the Government's balance sheet, adding to public spending. We shall see.

In the autumn of 1992 I remained deeply concerned about the level of Government borrowing. Despite the tough settlement and the limits for future years that were achieved, we were still not doing enough to bring down borrowing quickly enough. The longer we delayed, the greater the risks. Although the PM was more worried about the effects on the recovery, I was feeling increasingly confident provided we kept interest rates down. We were most likely to do that if we acted to reduce the deficit.

The PM, I felt, wanted the interest rate cuts before we had earned them, which we needed to do by cutting the deficit. He pressed me to cut rates by 2 per cent at the time of the Autumn Statement. I was reluctant but volunteered to do so if I could, at the same time increase revenue by putting up National Insurance contributions. I suggested that we increase them for both employers and employees by 1 per cent. This would have raised £4 billion at a stroke, making a decisive contribution to deficit reduction and firmly demonstrating our seriousness. We discussed a number of variants on this, such as whether it should apply to employees above the upper earnings limit, but the PM would not contemplate it so we compromised on a 1 per cent reduction of interest rates to be announced on the day of the Autumn Statement.

We were now entering the final stages of the new-style public expenditure settlement. The conclusions of EDX were discussed before a special Cabinet on Monday 9 November that lasted for four hours. At one point it looked as though the negotiations might stretch on for days of never-ending meetings, but further meetings on the Tuesday and Thursday finally brought the negotiations to a conclusion.

By coincidence, Thursday 12 November was the day for Treasury Questions as well as the day for the Autumn Statement. Just a few minutes before I rose to give the statement, Nigel Evans, the young MP for the Ribble Valley, stood up to call for an immediate cut in interest rates. Stephen Dorrell assured him that his idea would be carefully considered. He could not have guessed he was going to get quite such quick results.

The Statement

The Autumn Statement was definitely well received in the House, the country and the Conservative Party. Some of the points John Major had made strengthened and improved, as he had intended, its politics and presentation, but I still had my economic doubts. When I sat down Conservative MPs stood and cheered, many waving their Order Papers, though many of them saw it as a successful attempt to draw a line under the past. Nicholas Winterton, one of my main critics, said I had restored my credibility. Terry Dicks, another critic, said, 'You could measure the success of the Chancellor's statement by the long faces on the Labour benches.' Another Tory MP called me 'Franklin D. Lamont'. Gordon Brown described it as a set of 'half measures'.

The front pages of the tabloids were definitely enthusiastic. The *Daily Mail*'s headline was 'Lamont Moves Into Top Gear', with a cartoon of me driving a racing car. The *Express*'s headline was 'Tories cheer Lamont tonic'. The *Sun*'s headline was 'Go, Go, Go', its editorial beginning, 'Well done, Norman.' I suppose I had John Major to thank for many of these plaudits.

The pundits in the broadsheets were in my view rightly more cautious. Tim Congdon in the *Daily Telegraph* was scathing: 'The

Chancellor followed Keynes and made a grotesque £50 billion mistake. His next Budget must explain how he proposes to correct it.' He was not to know I was thinking along the same lines. The *Daily Telegraph* in its editorial said it was politically shrewd but deserved in economic terms a somewhat cooler reception.

Peter Riddell in *The Times* said, 'So the Chancellor is likely to have to be tougher on taxes for at least the next year or two . . . Taxes may even rise next spring in the Budget.' I did not disagree.

The reaction from industrialists like David Lees of GKN, Clive Thompson of Rentokil and Chris Haskins of Northern Foods, was also strongly favourable. They all thought that in the difficult circumstances following 16 September it was a good new beginning.

I do not think the Autumn Statement could really be described as 'Keynesian' or an 'attempt to kick start the economy'. It gave no discretionary stimulus to the economy and for the first time for very many years stuck to existing plans. Of course, it was only one side of the correct policy response to the problem of the large budget deficit. But the Autumn Statement had a number of targeted measures aimed at particular areas that I felt influenced the economy as a whole, such as the housing market. It was necessary to recognise that confidence had been exceptionally badly dented in September. But the main aim was to regain control of the public finances to make the reduction in interest rates possible.

It was the first Autumn Statement since 1988 that made no additions to the following year's public spending. The rate of increase in spending for the next three years was to average less than 1.5 per cent, half the rate of the last three years. It was not enough, but it was the beginning of a new way of doing things.

On the economy I forecast it would grow by 1 per cent in 1993, following a fall of 1 per cent in 1992. It was a pessimistic forecast compared with most and privately I thought it would probably prove overpessimistic. On inflation I confirmed the inflation target of keeping underlying inflation (Retail Price Inflation minus the effects of mortgage interest) below 4 per cent. I said I expected it to be below 4 per cent by the end of 1993, and in fact it turned out to be below 3 per cent. We were still continuing to beat all our inflation targets.

The PSBR was forecast to be £37 billion for the current year 1992/93, up from the forecast for the Budget. That was alarming. I had said to the House in my statement: 'As the economy recovers it is absolutely vital that borrowing is brought back towards balance.' What I didn't mention was that the following year's deficit was likely to be worse, even if the economy recovered. It was crystal clear to me was that further action was necessary to reduce the deficit.

13

Muddling On

Forsan et haec olim meminisse juvabit
(In time even these things will appear amusing)
Virgil, The Aeneid

After the success of the Autumn Statement I thought the pressure on me might abate, but I was quickly to find I could not have been more wrong.

'Threshergate'

I had been concentrating hard for some months on the country's finances, but now the country was given the opportunity to examine mine. The *Sun*, or someone acting on their behalf, decided to break into my credit card account. It announced on its front page to an expectant nation that I had exceeded my Access credit card limit of £2,000 by £470, and in the past 'no fewer than 22 times over 8 years' (that is, an average of three times a year). I rather suspect the *Sun* was looking for something more dramatic in my credit card account, but it printed this story as the best it could find.

For what it was worth, the allegation was true. For some years I had simply paid my credit card bills every two or three months in order to save myself the bother of writing endless small cheques, and naturally I had regularly received word-processed reminders about this. However, it had never bothered the National Westminster Bank, of which I had been a valued client for thirty years, as I am today. Some people may have thought this was not a very sensible way for me to run my own affairs, but the cost was marginal and seemed to me an entirely private matter. It did not seem to me that it had any bearing on my ability or otherwise to look after the country's finances.

I was rather annoyed when John Major shoved an *Evening Standard* headline in front of me and said, 'What shall I say about this?' I replied, 'Tell them it is nobody's business but mine.' I was grateful to a group of Labour MPs who were rather more robust than the Prime Minister and tabled an Early Day Motion condemning the invasion of privacy involved in breaking into and then publishing details of a person's bank account.

It didn't seem to matter very much, but the press hadn't finished. In a further twist it was revealed that I had used my credit card last at a branch of a chain of wine stores called Thresher, in a seedy area of Paddington. According to the papers I had bought a bottle of Bricout Champagne, a brand of which I had never heard, at a knock-down recession-busting price of £15.45, together with 20 Raffles cigarettes, another brand of which I had never heard. This last piece of information was gleefully relayed around the lobby by so-called serious journalists like Philip Stephens of the *Financial Times*. This story was told to the newspapers by a man who claimed to have both served me and recognised me. The press thought this was wonderful. 'What was he up to?' yelled the *Star*. 'Eyebrows were raised at where the Chancellor does his shopping.'

The newspapers all said I had overreacted to the stories about my sex therapist tenant, so I decided to take their advice and ignore the story, but unfortunately the press would not leave it or me alone. In Brussels, at a press conference with Douglas Hurd and Jacques Delors, where I was meant to be talking about the EU budget, all the British journalists wanted to ask was about

'Threshergate' and where I did my shopping. Not for the first time, Jacques Delors was completely bemused by the British press.

I was a little bemused myself. I remembered being driven back from Dorneywood on a Sunday night and buying a couple of bottles of wine in some shop. I had a relief driver that night and asked him to stop where it was convenient, but I didn't take in the name of the shop or the street. Eventually the Treasury got a copy of the receipt from the company and it showed indeed that I had bought two bottles of wine, though not, as claimed, in Praed Street, but in the rather more upmarket branch of Thresher in Connaught Street. The press had assumed I had shopped in Praed Street because it was the only Thresher listed in the W1 area and my credit card statement had given the address only as W1. The pack had all descended on the wrong shop, but why had the staff claimed I had been there?

Even when the receipt was produced, the press were still sceptical. The *Daily Mail*, I was informed, visited a large number of different branches of Thresher, comparing prices in different shops, trying to prove that my receipt could still have been used for Bricout and Raffles. The staff who said I had visited the shop eventually owned up to having invented the story. Precisely why they did so, I do not know, though the Treasury were told by the management of Thresher that reporters had offered money for the receipts. When it was discovered that one of the people involved was an illegal immigrant from Nigeria, he was unfortunately forced to return there and inevitably I was accused in the *Observer* of having had him deported.

Even then 'the story' was not over. A few weeks later the Treasury received a telephone call from a North London solicitor representing what he called 'a very attractive client', a woman who lived not far from Praed Street and a Conservative, although she had never met me. For some reason the papers were besieging her house and asking her to admit to her 'affair' with me. The *Daily Mirror* had offered her £100,000 for her story. The lawyer was not without a sense of humour because he added, 'I have advised her to take the money.' His immediate concern was to get the press off his client's doorstep.

These stories, untrue though they were, did further damage to me just as I was beginning to recover from the events of 16 September. Even though the Thresher story was shown to be completely untrue, newspapers continually referred to 'Threshergate' and implied that there was something sinister about the episode. No newspaper ever gave the same prominence to the admission that it had all been made up as was given to the original story. After I ceased to be Chancellor I asked the Press Council to look at the episode, but I was told it was now 'out of time'.

Row over my legal bills

Other problems arose with the newspapers, who, on the same weekend as the Thresher story, also said I had received money from the Treasury 'to evict Miss Whiplash'. The information was leaked to the press by Conservative Central Office, a fact whose significance I did not initially take on board. In fact, as explained earlier, the Treasury payment of £4,700 was not for eviction but partly for handling press enquiries, which would normally have been handled by the Treasury Press Office at the taxpayer's expense, and partly for the cost of the expedited hearing, which was only necessary because of my public position.

There was a great outcry and I was accused of instructing civil servants to use taxpayers' money for a private purpose. An investigation was mounted by the Public Accounts Committee and Terry Burns gave evidence, accompanied by Sir Robin Butler and Sir Peter Middleton, who was summoned back from retirement as it was he who had authorised the payment. It seemed rather incongruous that the Head of the Civil Service, the Head of the Treasury and the former Head of the Treasury should have to spend so much time on this matter. Fortunately the Public Accounts Committee in the end criticised neither me nor the payment, though it made some recommendations about disclosure for the future. Again, though, there was no doubt that the publicity was deeply damaging.

With regard to the help from Conservative Central Office for the remainder of the bill, I found I was then accused of not disclosing the payment in the Register of Members' Interests. It had certainly never occurred to me that help to a Member of Parliament from his own political Party was something that needed to be disclosed. What was I being accused of – being a Conservative? I can understand why a member of the Cabinet should be obliged to reveal financial help from another MP, as in the case of Peter Mandelson borrowing money from Geoffrey Robinson, but how could an MP be compromised by help from his own Party? There were many examples over the years where Members in financial difficulty had received assistance from their Party and I had no idea whether the payment had been made by Central Office funds or by an individual or by a group of individuals. Fortunately this Committee too made no criticism, though it also made some recommendations for the future.

I was sad that John Smith chose to raise the question of the payment of my legal bills at Prime Minister's Questions. The PM, who had been fully involved in the decision, indeed arguably more than I, made, I thought, a rather feeble defence and simply referred to the investigation by the Public Accounts Committee. Afterwards a press officer from No. 10 rang to ask me not to tell anyone that the PM had approved the payment of my legal bills, so that we could keep him out of the row. Naturally I did not tell anyone.

Unfortunately the press curiosity extended not just to me, but also to my children. About this time my son, James, had to go into Canterbury Hospital for minor surgery. The day he was admitted Andrew Hudson, the press officer, received a call from Kelvin McKenzie, the editor of the *Sun,* saying it had learned my son had been taken to hospital as a result of his taking drugs. I told Andrew to say it was quite untrue. Then the *Sun* came back, and said it now knew he was in hospital as a result of alcohol abuse. I told the press office to say on my behalf that this was quite untrue, though I declined to say why he was in hospital. Later that afternoon my Private Office received a request from Canterbury Hospital asking if I could have the reporters removed from the hospital as they were interfering with the work of the staff. There was nothing much I could do. I remonstrated with Andrew Knight of News International, who said it was all my fault because I wouldn't say why my son was in hospital.

The next day my son was pictured on the front page of the *Sun* with coded hints that it might have been something to do with drugs.

The Government drifts

My relations with the Prime Minister were also deteriorating somewhat in this period, partly because of our different views about how to react to the post-ERM situation. But I was also worried at the way in which we were governing. More and more, politics seemed to dominate our decisions. We never stopped discussing presentation rather than issues, and it became more difficult to reach decisions. On one occasion I confessed my frustrations to Douglas Hurd, who agreed that he too was finding it difficult to get decisions from the PM.

When John Major first took over from Mrs Thatcher everyone welcomed the more open consensual approach to Cabinet meetings. As one person said, Cabinet meetings began to matter again. It had been Margaret's habit to open them by expressing her view, almost defying people to disagree with her. Sometimes it was outrageous, but in fact Margaret enjoyed argument and did not mind people openly disagreeing with her, provided it was well argued. But people had become tired of her approach. Now, however, we seemed to have swung to the other extreme.

At one Cabinet meeting during the pit closures crisis, the Prime Minister opened a discussion without offering a view. There was then a 'tour de table', where a number of views were expressed one by one. When everyone had spoken John ended the discussion abruptly by saying, without conclusion, 'We don't seem to be agreed then,' and then moved on to the next item. Perhaps he had in mind to talk to those who disagreed with each other privately?

At the Treasury I had noticed how as Chancellor John very much disliked people arguing in front of him, particularly if he had not be forewarned. On one occasion I had incurred his wrath by taking a very strong line on some obscure point on PEPs and had disagreed with other Ministers. John was white with anger afterwards.

Increasingly, if there was a disagreement between colleagues, the Prime Minister seemed to expect them to settle it themselves without leadership from him. Ian Lang and I disagreed over Scottish Water. I could not see why we could not privatise Scottish Water precisely as we had done with the water industry in England, and reacted against the idea that there should be different economic policies north of the border, as so many Secretaries of State for Scotland seemed to believe. Ian, however, in traditional Scottish Secretary mould, believed that privatisation of the water industry in Scotland would be politically disastrous. He produced some arguments that I did not find particularly compelling and we took them up with the PM, but there was no guidance from the PM, who simply told us to go away and resolve our differences. How could we? We then came back to another meeting, and again were told to settle our differences. We ended up publishing a paper with eight different options for the future of the water industry, six of them retaining Scottish Water and sewerage services in the public sector. No wonder people didn't want to support us.

On other occasions of differences between Cabinet Ministers, the Prime Minister's usual tactic was to refer these to a Cabinet Sub-Committee to be chaired by John Wakeham, who was now Leader of the House of Lords and always a subtle operator. But it was unfair to expect him to solve every problem of Government, and inevitably he couldn't.

One such issue was the administrative arrangements for the payments of pensions. Peter Lilley had put forward a plan to save hundreds of millions of pounds by having people's pensions paid into their bank account rather than being cashed at a post office or sub-post office. The vast majority of the population in this country, including pensioners, now have bank accounts, although there are exceptions and not everyone lives near a bank. So for the minority who would be inconvenienced arrangements had been made for them to continue to draw their pension through the post office. This scheme seemed very attractive from a public expenditure point of view, and would have saved up to £300 million or thereabouts. One consequence was that the sub-post offices would lose business and therefore would be strongly opposed to change. Peter Lilley and I had a plan to cope with that: it could be arranged for other Government business to be put through the sub-post offices to give them replacement revenue.

It was not an easy issue but there were large sums of money at stake. Given the serious nature of Government finances and the fact that it did not involve any cut in a public service, this was just the sort of economy for which we should have been looking. I was surprised that the Treasury did not receive strong backing from the Prime Minister. Once again decisions were deferred and referred to a sub-committee chaired by John Wakeham with the business managers (that is, with members of the Whips' Office or the Leader of the House as additional members). It was no surprise when the latter simply said this would be unpopular with the backbenchers. Needless to say, there was no willingness to explore ways of persuading the backbenchers or of challenging them to find alternative savings, but it was wrong that a decision of this kind should be made by business managers and hundreds of millions of pounds wasted.

Post Office privatisation

Another issue was Post Office privatisation, a saga that dragged on for years after I left the Government. I could never work out what the PM's views were. Somewhat to my surprise Michael Heseltine, perhaps with an eye on attracting support from the Thatcherite Right, turned out to be a great enthusiast and was in no doubt that it was possible to safeguard the universal tariff, keep rural services and give the Post Office the freedom offered by privatisation to become a modern, international, technology-based industry. The management of the Post Office were very keen to privatise. Even the socialist Government in Holland was beginning to draw up plans for a privatisation of their Post Office.

To be fair to John Major, Mrs Thatcher had always opposed privatisation of the Post Office on the somewhat extraordinary grounds that stamps bore the Queen's Head and it was after all 'the Royal Mail'. I had once pointed out to her that we had privatised the Royal Ordnance, but her attitude illustrated that there were such things as Thatcherite policies opposed by Mrs Thatcher. Unreasonable as her opposition was, at least it was clear.

Our discussion on Post Office privatisation went round and round in never-ending circles, occasionally including plans to give the Post Office more commercial freedom or to attract private investment into the industry, but nobody knew where we were going. Later Major was to say, 'Instinctively I was modestly in favour of privatisation. Intellectually when I looked at the case I was much more strongly in favour of privatisation.' He never remotely gave me that impression. If anything I thought him against or inclined to give Heseltine just enough rope to hang himself on the issue. At times No. 10 was openly suspicious about Heseltine's motives.

One day Michael Heseltine, Edward Leigh and I were leaving No. 10 after a particularly futile meeting on the Post Office and we stopped on the steps. Turning to Michael, I said, 'This Government is in office, but not in power.' That was the first time I used those words. I remember it vividly because Heseltine said out of the side of his mouth, 'Be careful, the cameras can lip read'.

A new Governor?

The Prime Minister and I spent much time in this period discussing who should succeed Robin Leigh-Pemberton, who was due to retire as Governor of the Bank of England the following year. I was firmly of the view that Eddie George had been steady under fire and had served us well. The PM differed, but his objections were rather strange. I also canvassed the views of the Court of the Bank and they, having seen him at close quarters, had a very high opinion of Eddie George.

The PM kept repeating that he wanted 'a man of stature'. It seemed a curious attitude from the proponent of the 'classless society'. I wanted the most competent candidate. A number of candidates in investment banking were lined up, although I pointed out that an understanding of corporate finance was no indication of a grasp of monetary economics. I felt uncomfortable that after the events of 16 September the PM and I were proposing to hold on to our jobs, but Eddie George, who had been at the heart of those events, was to be snubbed. People would inevitably draw the conclusion that he carried the blame for 16 September.

In the end the PM agreed to Eddie's appointment, but only after talks had been held with other possible candidates. He would agree to Eddie only on condition that an outsider became Deputy Governor. In the end Sarah Hogg and I agreed on the appointment of Rupert Pennant-Rea, then editor of *The Economist*. I had a high regard for him and knew he had a sound grasp of economics and was an inflation hawk. Sadly his career in the Bank ended prematurely, but not before he had demonstrated what a great contribution he would have made.

Independence for the Bank of England?

Another issue about the Bank was more fundamental. I had come to the conclusion that the logical development of my new policy ought to be to make the Bank of England independent. I had not started out as Chancellor in favour of independence, but a number of factors changed my mind. Firstly, my experiences with the Prime Minister over interest rates convinced me that politicians would always want to interfere with interest rate decisions for political reasons. Even Mrs Thatcher, in my limited observation, was not averse to interfering in the decisions of Nigel Lawson. Secondly, I had over the course of the Maastricht negotiations been able to reflect on the performance of those European central banks that were independent. There was no denying that Europe had become a zone of monetary stability and low inflation. While I disagreed with the idea of a European single currency, I also believed that it would only earn its credibility if it were run by central bankers. The worst of all solutions would be a rainbow coalition of European politicians. The US and Japan also had successful independent central banks, although in their case independence was based on a different model. Britain was one of the few countries where interest rate decisions remained firmly in the hands of the politicians.

Some people opposed independence because they believed monetary policy ought to be about more than the control of inflation, but I did not. I had believed that low inflation combined with effective supply side policies were the most any Government could do to promote growth. Furthermore, sound money was the right of every citizen. The idea of a currency that held its value ought to be above politics, so entrusting the value of money to the technicians seemed to be an idea that ought to be acceptable to all political parties.

The idea of making the Bank of England independent had grown stronger with the passage of time. Nigel Lawson's resignation speech and Sam Brittan's articles made a powerful case. I first raised the issue of independence with the PM in September 1991, when I put forward a scheme based on the model of New Zealand, with the Governor of the central bank being given an inflation target. Failure to meet it could result in his dismissal. But the PM was worried about opposition from the tabloids. He did not believe the issue could be separated from the European debate, or that the House of Commons would stop holding the Government accountable for interest rate charges. My proposals meant that Parliament and Ministers would still have the key role of establishing the objective for the Bank.

I then tried to enlist the support of Chris Patten. We were presenting ourselves as the Party that really was going to break the UK's inflationary spiral, even more than Lady Thatcher had succeeded in doing. Supporting central bank independence in the Party Manifesto would emphasise that and be another way of defining John Major's Government, showing that we were not afraid to embrace radical views that Mrs Thatcher had resisted. But Chris was ambivalent and thought it would annoy the Eurosceptics, which was correct but hardly an argument.

Central bank independence had surprisingly little support in the Treasury. I suspected that some of them too liked having a say in interest rate decisions. Slightly to my surprise, Terry Burns was not at all in favour. All sorts of surprisingly poor arguments were put forward by the Treasury. What would happen to supervision of the banking sector if the Bank were independent? How would there be accountability to Parliament? It was even put to me that no one would want to take on the exposed task of being Governor. None of the arguments was insuperable; some of them were completely unconvincing.

So I decided to make my assault on the Prime Minister without the knowledge of any of my civil servants other than Jeremy Heywood. I drafted a note to the PM, repeating why I believed in central bank independence. Unfortunately Terry Burns discovered it and there was something of a temporary rift between us. He was right, I should have informed him, but stupidly I had not done so because I knew he firmly opposed my views.

The Eurosceptic view of central bank independence has always been atavistic. Because many of the countries in the EU had independent banks, and because independence was a requirement of the Maastricht Treaty, ergo they were against it. But they should have seen that an independent Bank of England would make it less likely that we would be dragged into the single currency because it would ensure that we had a better inflation performance. The Europeans would no longer be able to ask why we clung to our worthless pounds when we could have a decent currency. If Britain is to resist the single currency, it has to demonstrate that it can manage its own affairs competently.

After we left the ERM the case for making the Bank of England independent became compelling, in my view. Now that the lodestar of the fixed parity was no longer available, we needed a framework for our policy and had to make it credible. A monthly monetary assessment, explanations of interest rate changes and an inflation target were all in themselves admirable, but they would be immensely strengthened if managed by a strong independent bank. I saw it as a way of locking in permanently the low inflation that had been delivered by the ERM; whatever else might be said, the ERM had definitely delivered low inflation.

I was not entirely convinced that Major believed in low inflation as much as he claimed. When the ERM turned out to be very disinflationary, my suspicion is that he rationalised it and emphasised the need for low inflation. For all his many speeches about the corrosive effects of inflation on pensioners in Brixton, in conversation he sometimes questioned me as to whether inflation really did matter at all. Deep down the PM also believed it was the responsibility of politicians to run the economy. He quite enjoyed the power involved in making interest rate decisions and thought it perfectly natural that matters such as by-elections should be taken into account in the decision.

In November 1992 I once again put the arguments for an independent Bank of England to the PM. What I had in mind was to publish a White Paper on the subject at the time of the Budget. This time I told Terry what I was doing, but he remained opposed to the idea.

In January I put another paper to the PM on the subject. It seemed to me that if we were outside the EMU and did not have an independent bank we would pay a price in terms of higher interest rates or higher inflation. The French Government had just announced they would make their Central Bank completely independent in the hope of reducing the interest rate premium against the Deutschmark.

But the PM came up with numerous objections. We couldn't give any hint while Maastricht was going through the House. Wouldn't the Government be thought to have lost confidence in itself? The PM also said people were frightened how Labour would handle monetary policy and he didn't want to remove that fear. I said there were some indications that Labour might move in the direction of independence, but the PM wouldn't budge. Reluctantly I had to forget the idea.

My reservations about leaving monetary policy to the discretion of politicians were, I think, amply demonstrated after I left the Treasury. Kenneth Clarke, to applause from Conservative backbenchers, who never really cared much for fighting inflation, overruled Eddie George on interest rates. For a while it looked as though he might have been right for the wrong reasons. Inflation did not increase, as might have been expected, because there was an unexpected strengthening of the pound, but over the longer term those interest rate cuts worsened our inflation performance with the result that we missed our inflation target. This depressed me, because we had paid a heavy price for getting inflation down and now we were getting close to throwing away the one indisputable gain of our ERM membership.

I was careful in public never to give any hint that I supported the idea of independence for the Bank. Once, in front of the Treasury Select Committee, I was pressed quite strongly by MPs about the issue. In desperation at one point I pointed out to Alan Beith, the Liberal Democrat MP for Berwick-upon-Tweed, that independence was no guarantee of low inflation. After all, I said, the Reichsbank in Germany in the 1930s was independent, and few central banks had a worse inflation record. I was a bit too pleased with that reply!

I reverted to the argument when I returned to the backbenches. Many people made the usual comment that Chancellors only favour independence when they themselves have left office. They were not to know that, having failed to persuade the Conservative Party, I then turned my efforts to the Labour Party. I talked to both Gordon Brown and Tony Blair on the subject. I said that it was no purpose of mine to help the Labour Party or to make it more credible but if I were in their shoes I would have seen advantages in supporting central bank independence. I also believed it was in the interests of the country. Both of them were slightly suspicious of me and neither gave any indication that they would eventually support the idea.

The first I knew of Gordon Brown's conversion to Bank of England independence came when he rang me the day he was going to make his announcement. It was during the 1997 Tory leadership election, and I was in Michael Howard's campaign headquarters. When I picked up the phone I heard the Chancellor's voice saying, 'We have decided to take your advice.' It wasn't my advice of course, it was their own decision. I publicly and enthusiastically supported the Government. I regret that the Conservative Party was so slow to support one of the indisputably good things New Labour has done.

The PM and I also had a minor disagreement – and only that – about the lending practices of the clearing banks. Having announced his so-called 'going for growth' strategy, the PM became convinced that the clearing banks were not passing on interest rate reductions and so it was the banks who were preventing economic recovery. After much pointless work our study the year before had cleared the banks of systematically penalising small business customers, and found that interest rate reductions were being passed on. Now, again, I was being pressed by the PM to give more lectures to the clearing banks. The PM himself at the Lord Mayor's Banquet appealed to banks 'to help to bring about economic recovery'. The previous week's 1 per cent interest rate cut, he said, would take a further £1 billion off industry's costs, 'provided it is passed on to borrowers, to small businesses as well as large, which I trust it will be'. I felt such lectures gave an unattractive impression of needing someone to blame.

The Maastricht paving motion

Europe, never long absent, returned to centre stage at the beginning of November, the day after Bill Clinton had stormed to the White House in a big victory. The House of Commons returned to the subject of Maastricht first with a 'paving debate' to be followed by resumed progress on the Committee Stage. Major decided not to speak in the paving debate and Douglas Hurd led for the Government. I presumed I would speak as the other chief negotiator at Maastricht and indeed I was keen to do so since I felt I understood the concerns of the rebels and they would listen to me. Instead Tony Newton was asked to speak. He is an excellent debater, but not someone who had played any role in Maastricht. I was puzzled by this. It was only a long time later that I realised that this probably reflected some suspicion on the part of the Prime Minister about my Euroscepticism. If that was the case, it was absurd. I never ever expressed to any of the Eurosceptic rebels anything other than total support for the Prime Minister's policy.

The rebels at this time were claiming that their strength was hardening. James Cran, the unofficial Whip for the rebels, thirty-five of whom had attended a meeting, told the press that a number who had intended to abstain were now going to vote against the Government. There appeared a real risk of defeat, and there were reports, strongly denied later, that Major was stitching up a deal that might win the abstention or support of nine Ulster Unionist MPs for this make or break Commons vote. There were also implied threats that defeat in the Lobbies would lead to a General Election.

There was much lobbying of MPs, both in the previous week and in the run up to Wednesday 4 November. Much of this was done by the Whips' Office assisted by Heseltine and Clarke. Again, I made the offer to the Prime Minister to talk to groups of backbenchers myself, thinking I was well placed to do so. I might not have succeeded, but I thought I had a better chance than Clarke or Heseltine. In the event I was not asked to talk to a single backbencher about the issues. I was interested when Heseltine, after talking to a group of them, told me he thought they were all quite mad, saying that he felt compromise or sweet talking was useless. The only way to deal with 'these people' was to 'crush them'.

There were two votes that evening. A Labour amendment to delay consideration of the bill was defeated by 319 to 313. The second vote on the paving motion was carried by 319 to 316 votes, with 26 Tories voting against the Government and 7 abstaining. However, to win over some of the potential rebels the Government had to promise that the Third Reading of the Bill would not take place until after the second Danish referendum in May 1993. The rest of the Cabinet, including myself, were completely unaware of this concession.

The Edinburgh European Council

On 12 November, with the agreement of the Bank, rates were cut again by 1 per cent to 7 per cent. The underlying rate of inflation was now below 4 per cent and clearly going down. I felt that we now had a monetary policy that truly suited the interests of the country.

However the last few weeks of 1992 were again dominated by European issues. The European Commission, led by Henning Christophersen, came forward with a European growth package of 50–60 billion ecus to stimulate the European economy. The idea was for Europe-wide co-ordinated measures to stimulate capital investment and the usual 'trans-European networks'. Significantly it had some similarities to the approach the PM and I had agreed for the Autumn Statement. Having had one dose of

such measures I was not keen on another, though it was important to see that the UK obtained a *juste retour* from any
Community expenditure.

I certainly did not feel we needed more deficit financing and I
had no confidence that any European programme would be based
on money spent wisely or efficiently, but it was important not to
appear too negative. Since we were in the Presidency, I had a difficult line to tread between scaling back the Commission's
breathtaking ambitions while making sure that whatever slimmed-
down package was forced upon us was at least of some use to the
UK. Fortunately the Germans were even more fiercely opposed to
the whole idea, so a reforged Anglo-German alliance proved
pretty effective.

Delors, at this stage, was simultaneously pushing his ideas for
a vastly increased European Budget. At an Ecofin meeting on 29
June, he had on behalf of the Commission proposed an increase in
real annual spending of about 20 billion ecus (£14 billion), implying real growth of over 5.5 per cent per year. The own resources
ceiling – that is, the limit on revenue as a proportion of EU GDP –
would increase from 1.2 per cent to 1.37 per cent, which was
clearly unacceptable.

My view was that when public spending in the UK was being
cut back and all countries in Europe were being urged to meet the
Maastricht criteria, it was both contradictory and wrong to
increase European expenditure, which is after all paid for by the
individual European countries. Britain, as one of the larger con-
tributors, would get only half its money back in terms of spending
in the UK. I could not see the case for any increase in European
spending at all, but reluctantly at the Cabinet, in response to
pressure from the Europhiles and pleas not to appear negative, I
had conceded a modest increase.

At one stage I wondered if we would not do better to defer the
whole issue, then we would not have to be constrained because
we were in the Chair and would be able to make a powerful
coalition with the Germans. The argument, however, was rejected
largely at the insistence of Sir John Kerr.

The Budget was one of the items for discussion at the
Edinburgh Summit held on 11–12 December. I had been much

looking forward to going to Edinburgh, a City I knew well from my school days at Loretto at Musselburgh, just to the east of the City. All the Finance Ministers were put up at the Caledonian Hotel at the west end of Princes Street, which despite attempts to modernise it, still had a comfortable old-fashioned atmosphere, just like in the days when I was taken to tea there on Sunday afternoons by my Edinburgh aunt. It was the first time I had been back to the hotel since then. I had also hoped I might manage to slip away from the Summit for a few hours to visit my old school, though sadly that did not prove possible.

There was a lunch at Edinburgh Castle and a dinner on the Friday night on the Royal Yacht *Britannia* in Leith Harbour. Prince Charles made some supportive comments about me to the Prime Minister and said that he of all people understood what it was like to get the sort of battering I was currently receiving from the press. He invited me to lunch as he wanted to talk about handling the press. The Princess of Wales was also there but she kept her distance from her husband. Indeed she seemed utterly alone from all the other Royals. I talked to her at some length and she referred to her husband in very formal and distant terms. At dinner Kohl sat next to Prince Charles; President Mitterrand, as always, got exactly what he wanted, to be seated between the Queen and the Princess of Wales.

I think my fellow Finance Ministers enjoyed Edinburgh too. I was much amused by Michel Sapin, the French Finance Minister, who had gone shopping on the Royal Mile and returned at tea time with some iced biscuits in the shape of Christmas trees. He asked each Finance Minister to accept a present of 'un Sapin'.

The meetings were held at Holyrood House, with Heads of Government in one room and Finance Ministers in another. The Finance Ministers did not have a great deal of work to do as the issue of the Budget was to be handled by Heads of Government. I spent a lot of time hanging around on my own to no purpose in Holyrood House, though it gave me an opportunity to look round the Palace and to contemplate where Rizzio, Mary Queen of Scots' lover, had been murdered.

Apart from the Budget, the main items on John Major's agenda were the beginning of enlargement negotiations with Austria and the Scandinavian applicants, and to reach agreement on Denmark, which had been given opt-outs on defence and EMU which it regarded as legally binding although the other countries did not. This struck me as further evidence of the EU's casually ambivalent attitude to law.

On enlargement the decision to begin negotiations was taken. In my opinion John Major deserves enormous credit for the way he started the whole push towards enlargement in his Paris speech, made early on in his Premiership. When he started there is no doubt France and Germany were quite hostile, but it was difficult for them to make a stand of principled opposition and John Major's persistence paid off. However, less credit is due for the much trumpeted agreement on subsidiarity, which events subsequently proved not to be worth the paper on which it was written.

When it came to the Budget decisions, Finance Ministers were not to be allowed in the room with Heads of Government. Major suggested, however, that I somehow smuggle myself into the room and sit beside him, where an interpreter or a civil servant might sit. I was rather surprised at this, but did what I was told. I was the only Finance Minister in the room and I could see Kohl looking at me displeased and puzzled. However, I sat there quietly.

I couldn't play any real part in the negotiations beyond the occasional whisper in the Prime Ministerial ear. I looked down over his shoulder at his notes and quickly realised why Major wanted me there. What had been agreed at Cabinet had been rewritten. All the figures for the EU Budget growth had been increased further. It was true that there had been intense and intransigent pressure for this from Gonzales, fronting for Portugal, from Ireland and Greece too, but Britain was not without negotiating cards because if Gonzales prevented any agreement he would put himself in the position of the man who wrecked Maastricht. The settlement at Edinburgh moved the ceiling on contributions to the European Budget from 1.2 per cent of GDP to 1.21 per cent in 1995/96, going up to 1.27 per cent by 1998/99. This meant Britain's contribution might increase by £250 million per annum in 1999. These were not huge figures, but given the problems we had, why should the European Budget increase when we were having to go in for retrenchment at home?

I was somewhat unhappy with the increases in spending now proposed, but as a silent observer I was not able to do much about it. The Foreign Office presented the deal that was secured as a great triumph. 'The best ever Summit,' John Kerr called it. I certainly did not agree with that opinion and felt I had been outmanoeuvred.

A year later when I had returned to the backbenches I sat through and indeed spoke in the House of Commons debate on the European Finance Bill agreed at Edinburgh. Kenneth Clarke, then Chancellor, went out of his way to praise my vital role at Edinburgh. It was the only compliment he ever paid me as Chancellor. Backbench Conservative MPs were virulent in their criticisms. I spoke in the debate and, although critical of Europe's attitude to fraud, I did not say anything against the increases in expenditure in the Bill. I voted for them as I felt honour bound to do, but eight Tories refused to vote for the Government and had the Whip withdrawn. Privately, I had some sympathy with their view.

14

The 1993 Budget – The Day of Reckoning

Could man be drunk for ever.
A.E. Housman

In early January 1993 the Treasury team and I met for our pre-Budget weekend at the Foreign Secretary's residence, Chevening, which he kindly lent us. On our first night we had our usual musical entertainment. In the ritual snooker game the officials, represented by Terry Burns and Andrew Turnbull, now No. 2 at the Treasury, beat Michael Portillo and myself. I accused the officials of practising at the Reform Club. Besides, I always maintained, my game was table tennis and Chevening, unlike Dorneywood, had no table.

Officials and Ministers may have been on different sides for snooker, but for the rest of the weekend there was unanimity between us. There was only one subject on the agenda: the level of Government borrowing. Having decided that the fiscal deficit had to be tackled early on, the discussion moved on to where to find the money.

Tackling the deficit: to phase or not to phase?

In the 1992 Autumn Statement I had given no figure for the expected PSBR for the coming year 1993/94, but careful readers of the Grey Book could have worked out that we were assuming it would be in the order of 7–8 per cent of GDP, equal to £50 billion. At Chevening this figure was confirmed. It was very high indeed. If the truth be known, it was getting close to the sort of deficit that had driven Denis Healey to the IMF in the 1970s. It was obvious that, however uncomfortable, drastic action was essential. Although the Autumn Statement had tightened public spending and I had devised a new system that would make sure that it would grow more slowly in future, we were still faced with an immediate and huge problem. Only one thing was clear – to do nothing would run great risks.

The Treasury were now expecting the out-turn for the PSBR in the current year to be £35 billion, £2 billion below the Autumn Statement forecast but comfortably above the £28 billion forecast for which Bill Robinson and I had argued so fiercely with officials just before the Election. We were wrong. Yet again the snail's pace recovery and its effect on tax revenues had well and truly played havoc with the Government's finances. The £35 billion figure probably by itself would not have shocked the markets because by the time of the Autumn Statement I could see it coming and had forecast something even higher. What was really worrying was the figure for the following year.

How had a Conservative Government ended up in a situation where borrowing was so catastrophically high, so soon after we had been running surpluses and repaying debt? The explanation was bound up with our membership of the ERM. Its critics concentrate on the effects on growth and employment, but the effects on the public finances were arguably even more significant.

A number of factors had brought about the situation. Firstly, the depth and duration of the recession proved greater than expected. Apart from adding to the PSBR, the recession itself inhibited the tightening of fiscal policy. If we had not been so worried about recovery, we would have acted earlier. Secondly, the increases in public spending in the 1991 public expenditure round were too high. Politics and the Election played their part here. Thirdly, the Treasury underestimated the extent to which the deficit was structural, that is to say permanent and underlying, rather than cyclical and caused by the recession. Calculating the part of a deficit that is structural is problematic. The longer a recession lasts, the more difficult it becomes. In a 'short, shallow' recession, unemployment costs will cancel themselves out as the economy recovers, but just as a business cannot go on year after year ignoring a prolonged fall in cash flow caused by a recession, so too a government cannot keep on running up debt in the hope that recovery will eventually solve its problems. Even if the debt was originally caused by the recession, the interest on it still has to be paid. What might start off as a cyclical deficit can transform itself into a structural deficit.

Lastly, the Treasury also overestimated tax revenues. Income tax receipts in 1993/94 turned out to be over £9 billion less than projected in the 1991 MTFS (Medium Term Financial Strategy). Corporation tax receipts were £6 billion lower and there were errors in the forecasts of VAT receipts of around £4 billion as well.

At Chevening we discussed papers from Robert Culpin, about to move on from Head of Fiscal Policy, and Alan Budd, the Chief Economic Advisor. Not surprisingly they were unable to define precisely what part of the deficit was structural, but their recommendation was that we needed to tighten policy by at least 1 per cent of GDP, that is, to put taxes up by at least £7 billion. As it turned out, I did more than that, but there was then a discussion as to whether the increased taxes should take effect immediately or whether in the interests of fostering recovery they should be phased in.

The novelty of the 1993 Budget was that it was effectively three budgets in one, in which I announced tax rises stretching three years ahead. Some people dubbed that 'Clintonesque', because it appeared similar to the way in which Clinton had announced public spending savings that were to happen in the future, but my Budget was quite different from Clinton's public expenditure plans. I didn't just announce future tax increases, but legislated for them there and then so that it was certain that the measures would have effect.

One argument for phasing in the tax increases was that the huge increases would hit confidence and abort the recovery. A monetarist might argue that what mattered was not fiscal policy but interest rates, and that even if taxes went up there still might be greater freedom to lower interest rates. I never believed there was such a direct trade-off and although I regarded myself as a monetarist I didn't believe that tax increases would have no effect at all on the prospects for recovery. It seemed to me economically there was an argument in favour, therefore, of phasing in the tax increases.

The arguments in favour of making the tightening immediate were both economic and political. The economic argument was that if a Government announces tax increases but defers the imposition of them, taxpayers may discount the increase, anticipate it, and change their consumption and saving accordingly, so deferring the tax would not avoid damaging the recovery. Personally I was doubtful that taxpayers were that rational or well informed. The political argument was that it is best to get a Government's unpopularity over early in a Parliament. Phased tax increases were likely to bring a Government unpopularity in the latter half of a Parliament, when it was looking towards reelection. In addition, phased tax increases might somehow be overturned in a prolonged Parliamentary process. That alas proved all too true.

The arguments for and against seemed fairly finely balanced. I knew there was no prospect of my being able to persuade the Prime Minister that we should pursue the other alternative and go for public expenditure cuts. I also knew that in any case it would be difficult to get him to agree even on a phased basis to tax increases at all. I do not mean to imply that it was only the unwillingness of the PM to increase taxes that turned my mind towards phased increases.

I put to the PM my view that we had to face up to the problem and put up taxes by at least £7 billion. I acknowledged that it would make us extremely unpopular and we would be accused of breaking promises. The PM's reaction was that the Treasury was always overpessimistic, always refused to cut interest rates and always wanted to put up taxes, which was somewhat unfair, but he thought there was an argument for cutting rates to get the economy moving. It took a number of meetings for the PM to agree to increase taxes. Several of them were pretty tense.

At first the Prime Minister argued that we only needed perhaps a £2–3 billion increase, phased over several years. I felt this was not nearly enough. Sarah Hogg was extremely helpful and when I felt depressed by the PM's attitude said, 'Don't worry, we'll get him there in the end.' So she did and I was grateful to her.

On other subjects the PM seemed determined to go his own way. I was a little surprised when he went on *The Frost Programme* and said that if the ERM was to be reconstructed in anything like its old form, 'We may need to look . . . at some form of relationship between European currencies, the dollar and the yen.' It was the first time I had heard of this and it seemed likely to infuriate not just me, but also backbenchers to whom the ERM was anathema. It also seemed strange that, after we had suffered such a calamity in a fixed exchange rate system, the PM should float an idea of creating a global version of the ERM. I did not know why the PM had done this, and when I was asked about it at the Treasury Select Committee I tried to brush it aside. It did, however, perhaps reveal that in his heart the PM was deeply attached to the idea of fixed exchange rates and would not give up the idea, even after a massive failure. It seemed like wanting to raise the *Titanic*, ram the iceberg, and hope that this time the iceberg would sink.

A disastrous rate cut

The PM and I met several times to discuss monetary policy. We had agreed that another reduction in interest rates of 1 per cent to 6 per cent would be appropriate. It is not true, as I believe John Major on occasions has claimed, that I opposed interest rate reductions after we left the ERM and that he had to force them on a reluctant Treasury, but we quite often had sharp disagreements about market tactics when it came to rate cuts. On one occasion, when I was trying to persuade Major to wait a short while for a rate cut, he turned, in front of me, to a secretary who had come into the room with a piece of paper and asked her, 'Do you think interest rates should be cut?' It was a strange way to conduct monetary policy. Terry Burns had felt it necessary to remind No. 10 that rate cuts couldn't just be conjured out of the air at ten minutes' notice, but on this cut, which was to prove my last, it was true that I was particularly anxious about its handling.

The PM and I had agreed that the cut would take place while he was in India. I had wanted it at the end of the week but the PM for some reason wanted it earlier. I was anxious that it would adversely affect the £2.5 billion auction of medium-dated gilts due to take place in the middle of the week and the Bank was also strongly of that view. I had, therefore, insisted that the cut take place at the end of the week; the PM, furious, telephoned from India to insist that rates were cut immediately. I was certain it would be a mistake and dug my heels in. Then Terry Burns came and told me that, while he agreed with me, it was not possible to carry on this path of resistance. He was, after all, the Prime Minister, and I couldn't just disregard his instructions. And so I gave way.

The cut on 26 January was as disastrous as I had feared. The pound immediately – and this was only the beginning – fell 3 pfennigs against the DM, dropping through an important technical support level. Over the next few days sterling was to fall further, losing 7 pfennigs in all or 3 per cent of its value against the Deutschmark in a further unplanned loosening of policy. Another serious unintended consequence was that the fall in sterling was the kiss of death for the Irish punt which, because it was heavily influenced by sterling, was then pushed out of its ERM bands and had to devalue.

So rushed was the decision that Michael Heseltine, the Trade and Industry Secretary, found himself in the embarrassing position of being unaware of the announcement when asked about it several hours later in a television interview. The PM had announced the rate cut in New Delhi himself, leaving journalists in no doubt that he had ordered it.

It was not just the immediate reaction on the foreign exchange markets but the wider perceptions that politics was dictating monetary policy that worried me. An economist at Midland

Global Markets was quoted as saying, 'Yesterday's move has changed people's perception about UK economic policy and we will see sterling lower from here.'

The *Financial Times* was particularly virulent in its criticism. 'Hopes that it would give a boost to the outlook for recovery were tempered by fears that it reflected an element of panic in Downing Street.' Conservative MPs, according to the same paper, were 'less than euphoric'. Its Lex column said, 'By acting yesterday it [the Government] imposed large losses on gilt-edged market makers who were short ahead of tomorrow's auction. Its disregard for a group whose co-operation is needed in sales of up to £1 billion a week in the coming financial year adds to the sense that the cut was a matter of political urgency, after last week's unemployment data.' In other words the markets saw the cuts as politically inspired. After all our attempts to design a monetary policy that would carry credibility in the markets, it was deeply disappointing to find it undermined at a stroke. The *Financial Times* said we had 'infuriated many gilt market makers' and that they faced losses estimated at £25 million in their operations. In its editorial The *Financial Times* said, 'This government does not just keep on getting its monetary policy wrong. Its determination to be able to do so has become an important reason for its continuing to do so.' To me it all seemed reminiscent of the second interest rate increase on Black Wednesday. The PM's heavy-handed intervention had left me looking less than competent once again. Once again I was 'the air raid shelter'. I decided to write to the PM, and I did not pull my punches. I told him bluntly that his intervention had been wholly wrong and not for the first time he had left me looking extremely stupid. I had said that it must not happen again. I imagined the PM would either drop me a note or say something by way of apology at one of our bilaterals. I was surprised that there was no reply, either written or verbal.

Unfortunately there was another incident not long afterwards which contributed to a further erosion in the relationship between myself and the Prime Minister. A few days after the interest rate cut fiasco, Kenneth Clarke, Home Secretary, the strongest supporter of the ERM in the Cabinet, who had opposed our withdrawal on 16 September, stated on the radio that sterling would not rejoin the ERM within the lifetime of the current Parliament. It was an odd announcement to come from a Home Secretary. His remarks received widespread coverage and were interpreted as removing the one last obstacle to his replacing me as Chancellor.

Despite my own views, I had stuck rigidly to the formula on which the PM had insisted: that we should not reconsider the issue of the ERM until the British and German economies were much closer to being synchronised. I was perfectly comfortable with this formula since it was likely to be a long time before it ever became an issue again. I told the Prime Minister that I did not feel it was right for the Home Secretary to make announcements of this kind. The PM brushed it aside and said he couldn't see why I was so bothered. I did tell Ken that I was annoyed about it, and he said he had not intended to cause me embarrassment. One never knew with Ken. He was like one of those comic characters in a 1930s silent movie who goes around knocking over ladders, leaving everyone else covered in paint. One never knew whether it was deliberate or accidental.

Increasingly I began to think about getting out of the Treasury and returning to the backbenches, but first I wanted to tackle the problem of the fiscal deficit and correct the problem I had helped to bring about. I wanted to deliver what I knew would be a highly unpopular but necessary Budget and I also expected to deliver the first unified Budget in the Autumn as I was spending so much time working out the very complicated mechanics of that exercise. But I certainly assumed that by the end of the year I would no longer be Chancellor.

More tension with the PM

When I returned to England I discovered that reports of splits between myself and the PM were appearing in the papers. John Smith referred to these at Prime Minister's Questions and directly challenged the PM, 'How can people be expected to comprehend the Government's intentions when the Government and No. 10 deliberately brief the press to undermine the Chancellor on Saturday, and then on the other days go into reverse because of the damage done to the economy? . . . The Right Honourable Gentleman supports his Chancellor in public, while undermining him in private. ' I was sitting beside the PM as John Smith spoke. He replied, 'It may be that many people would like to invent divisions between him and I, but there are none.' At the end of the exchanges the PM patted my hand as he left the Chamber. He often did that, and I always disliked it.

The *Daily Mail* reported the next day 'No split with Lamont'. Unfortunately many MPs thought otherwise. I did believe that basically the Prime Minister supported me, but I was conscious of an increasing number of articles saying that Cabinet colleagues, particularly Norman Fowler, now Party Chairman, were pressing the Prime Minister to move me. They had been appearing for many months and there was not much I could do. On one occasion, however, I mentioned to the PM that I did not think that it was doing the Party any good to have articles in which the Party Chairman was reported to be bad-mouthing me. 'Oh, are they doing that again?' said the PM. 'I'm sorry.'

Around this time I became increasingly concerned that policy seemed to be made on the hoof and that ideas were often floated in speeches without adequate collective consideration. There was a sense of a lack of direction. The PM set up a Cabinet Committee on unemployment, but what it was meant to produce I never understood. Unemployment was now plateauing and jobs were going to be created as the recovery gathered momentum. Further special employment measures at this late stage seemed irrelevant and would add to our most serious problem – Government borrowing. In January, when the PM was questioned in the Commons about the economy, he replied, 'I propose to hold a seminar at the beginning of February,' which provoked loud laughter.

On 3 February Major made a speech at the Carlton Club, a strange mixture of nostalgia and a ragbag of policy ideas. He outlined his vision of Britain with its local baker's shops, traditional villages and meals on wheels; he stated that his sort of Toryism had 'an ear for history and an eye for place'. This somewhat incongruously led on to a discussion of the merits of road pricing and a new 'right to buy your council house' campaign. But the idea that caught the headlines was his advocacy of workfare on American lines, whereby the unemployed would be forced to undertake work on projects.

My private office was somewhat startled to receive a copy of the speech only hours before he made it. I was sceptical about the mechanics of workfare, and it seemed dangerous to float such a controversial idea without having come to proper conclusions. We tried to tone the speech down, but No. 10 was insistent. It then turned out that Gillian Shephard, the Employment Secretary, had also been kept in the dark about the speech. She was infuriated. That day No. 10 briefed that work was being done on these measures, while Gillian Shephard had dismissed them to enquiring journalists.

The confusion inevitably forced the PM to retreat. Though it was announced that a small workfare pilot scheme would be launched, to the press there was a clear sense of a climbdown. In the Commons John Smith pointedly asked the PM, 'Can you not get one simple objective and stick to it?'

Trouble for the French in the ERM

The ERM and more monetary turmoil emerged at the end of January. Mysterious grand-sounding talk of accelerated monetary union came from across the Channel between France and Germany as a response to renewed speculative attacks on the ERM. These hints caused some anxiety to John Major and the Foreign Office, who were as usual terrified that Britain would be 'left behind'. Part of the anxiety also arose because we did not fully understand what was happening. With hindsight it is clear that the Foreign Office did not entirely understand what France and Germany were up to.

The events of January and February 1993, were like those of the autumn of 1992, a powerful cocktail of foreign exchange turbulence and politics. The starting point appears to have been my ill-timed and forced interest rate cut of 26 January, which led not just to a sharp fall in sterling but also, in its wake, to the devaluation of the Irish punt. Denunciations of Britain came thick and fast from Irish Ministers; the Irish Labour Minister stated that my British interest rate cut 'was indicative of Britain's attitude to the whole Community'. Michel Sapin declared Britain 'doesn't have the right to solve its own problems'. It was easy to understand the Irish point of view and at least to see the cause of French pique. France was mired in recession and 'the British way' looked increasingly attractive to many French businessmen who asked, 'Why not here?' French politicians purported to see evidence of an Anglo-Saxon conspiracy to break the ERM and frustrate EMU and the challenge to American domination.

After the Irish devaluation the markets moved on to the Danish krona and even the Belgian franc looked wobbly. If they went, the French franc would be the next in line. At this point the German Government seems to have moved decisively in the way it did not do, and denied it could do, in the weeks before 16 September. On 1 February Horst Kohler, the State Secretary at the German Finance Ministry, criticised the Bundesbank in an interview in *Der Spiegel*, singling out 'its political comments', and not before time. He also implied the independence of the Bundesbank was not irrevocable and called for lower interest rates on the grounds that it was impossible for Germany to ignore the situation in other countries. It was, he said, the responsibility of the Bundesbank to ensure 'monetary stability' but that 'does not confirm the obligation that stability be achieved through a deep recession'. If only he had said that at Bath.

On Thursday 5 February the Lombard rate was cut by 0.5 per cent and the discount rate, the more important one at that moment, by 0.25 per cent. For the first time a signal was sent to the markets that the Bundesbank was prepared to defend the ERM, or perhaps more accurately the French franc. Delors greeted the rate cut as 'a much needed signal that it [Bundesbank] recognised it had a responsibility not just to the German economy, but to the rest of the Community'. But the franc was not out of the woods by a long way yet. On the same day, amid increasing fears that speculation would succeed in toppling the franc, French Government sources predicted that France and Germany would leap ahead to full monetary union if the ERM collapsed. At a special briefing for British journalists, an authoritative French source said, 'If the EMS [European monetary system] explodes then France and Germany and Benelux will be obliged to do something.' French officials also expressed displeasure with John Major for some disparaging comments he had made about monetary union.

The French flirtation with accelerated monetary union, if it was serious, had a dual purpose. Firstly, it helped to hold up the franc, and secondly, if the franc went under the only way France could maintain its policy of having a French input into European monetary policy was via this route.

All this talk was anathema, however, to the Bundesbank. Schlesinger stated quite clearly that bringing forward monetary union would clearly be against the Maastricht Treaty. He was now coming more and more into conflict with both the German Government in general and Kohl in particular. The interest rate cut was a defeat for the Bundesbank, both in its struggle with the German Government and with France. It felt it had become a prisoner of an ERM constraint forced on it by Mitterrand and Kohl.

During the preparations for the Budget, the usual round of international meetings continued in Brussels and elsewhere. Lloyd Bentsen, who had replaced Nick Brady as US Treasury Secretary, asked me to host a G7 Meeting at No. 11 on 27 February. Bentsen, an eloquent, patrician Texan, had become famous as a result of his strong attack in a television debate on Dan Quayle ('You're no Jack Kennedy'). I knew him from the Senate and was an enthusiastic fan, but I had been surprised at his appointment. He was a conservative Democrat and didn't seem to have much in common with Clintonistas. At our meeting he made it clear that fiscally the Clinton Administration was going to be conservative, and so it was.

The final stages of the Budget preparations

My energies were entirely focused on what looked like being a very unpopular Budget. The PM had been reluctant to increase taxes, and continued to argue the Treasury was overpessimistic and that tax increases would depress the economy. Sarah Hogg, however, had continued to encourage me in my efforts.

The decision to increase taxes was both a top-down and a bottom-up process. When I had got the Prime Minister to agree initially to at least about £3–4 billion of tax increases I then kept putting to him different individual tax increases, which eventually increased the total towards the £6 billion which I regarded as the absolute minimum. The PM would only agree to taxes being put up for 1994/95, and only reluctantly to the idea that we should legislate for the subsequent tax increases in the current year.

I reverted to the idea that I had put to the Prime Minister, but he had rejected before the Autumn Statement, of an increase in both employers' and employees' National Insurance contributions. It was necessary to find a few large, simple revenue-raising measures. We couldn't put up the basic rate of income tax, since the reduction over the longer term to 20 pence was a fundamental aim to which the Party was strongly attached, but the PM would not agree to an increase in employers' contributions because he was afraid that it would harm employment. In the end we agreed on a 1 per cent increase for employees and the Class 4 rate for the self-employed, which together would bring in £1.8 billion in 1994/95 and £2.2 billion in a full year. It was a useful start, but there was still a lot more to be found.

Bill Robinson was the inventor of one ingenious and complex idea that enabled us to solve two other problems at once. He earned his salary several times over with it. In discussion with businesses in preparation for the Budget, the problem of what was called in technical terms 'stranded, advance corporation tax' had come up over and over again. Without going into the technical details, British companies with a high proportion of overseas earnings found themselves paying excessive taxation and felt they had an incentive to move activities such as headquarters or R&D overseas. With Bill's help we devised a new way of taxing dividends paid out of overseas profits and at the same time also decided to reduce the rate of tax on dividends. This had the added advantage of giving industry, still suffering from the recession, a cash flow benefit of about £2 billion. And paradoxically the reduction in the rate of tax on dividends also raised money for the

Treasury, because those who paid no tax on dividends, like pension funds, were able to claim back the advance corporation tax which was paid out on their behalf by companies. It is one of the curiosities of taxation that sometimes reducing a tax or even abolishing one can bring in more revenue. This is because of those who reclaim a tax, or claim a deduction against a tax. In this case reducing the tax on dividends brought us in £1.2 billion a year in a way that also was going to delight manufacturing industry, though not pension funds.

Another opportunity to abolish a tax and bring in more revenue was offered by Petroleum Revenue Tax. This hideously complex tax levied on North Sea oil companies had for some time become a device for keeping several chambersful of tax barristers in Jaguars. Ironically, because of the generous regime of reliefs it had become a drain on the Treasury rather than a source of revenue. At its peak in the 1980s the Treasury raised £2.3 billion from PRT but in 1991/92 the Treasury had paid the oil companies £200 million net. I decided to cut the rate of PRT on existing fields in the North Sea and to abolish the tax completely for new fields, which brought in the tidy sum of £400 million in 1995/96. It also prompted a furious reaction from Michael Heseltine, who came to my office complaining I was insensitive to the needs of industry and the oil companies. It is one of the few occasions when businesses lined up to complain about the abolition of a tax.

The 1993 Budget was preceded by the most careful and extensive consultation exercise ever before a Budget. It was necessary because it was going to be deeply unpopular. Every Conservative MP was invited to offer his or her suggestions to a Treasury Minister in an intensive series of meetings, either in the Treasury or in my room behind the Speaker's Chair. Groups of between six and twelve arrived for tea with myself or Michael Portillo. Other Ministers, senior backbenchers and ex-Ministers were seen individually, usually by me.

During these meetings MPs were softened up and told about the need to fill the gaping cash hole in the public finances. I could not actually reveal to them any figures, which were market-sensitive, but at the end of these sessions no MP can have been unaware of the seriousness of our situation. In general MPs accepted the situation. Sometimes the suggestions that were made were somewhat unrealistic, such as calls for swingeing cuts in pensions. Many advocated putting VAT on newspapers, largely because of the intense dislike for the press that had grown up on the backbenches. Few advocated increases in income tax, but opinions were sharply divided on what areas of indirect taxation could be increased.

The VAT decision

I was also having parallel discussions within the Treasury and with the PM. It was clear that we had to increase VAT. I had always been in favour of taxes on expenditure rather than on income and in favour of broadening the tax base on consumer spending. The structure of VAT in Britain was and is one of a relatively high standard rate, but with a much narrower coverage than in other European countries.

It was clear that the choice narrowed itself down to two or three options. We could extend VAT with a reduced rate to a whole series of items that were currently zero-rated, which would have meant, for example, VAT at perhaps 7 or 8 per cent being extended to items such as children's clothes, public transport, food, newspapers and books and fuel and power. Another alternative was simply to extend VAT at the standard rate of 17.5 per cent to other items, the most obvious being fuel and power. It would be controversial, but would it be more controversial than VAT at a reduced rate on food, transport, children's clothes and newspapers? The press would certainly have reacted strongly against VAT, even at a reduced rate, on newspapers.

It was possible to play different tunes with different packages and to raise much the same amount of money. In the end it was a matter of politics. Not only did VAT on food, public transport, books, newspapers and children's clothes look just as politically dangerous as VAT on fuel and power, but it had the added risk that the House of Commons might decide to knock out one or two of the items. The greater the number of individual items, the greater the risk was. As events were subsequently to prove, this risk was very real, but by imposing VAT on fuel and power alone we were advocating a simpler measure with fewer votes in the House of Commons.

There were also compelling economic reasons for taxing fuel and power. Electricity and other energy prices had been falling in real terms for several years, so whatever the political reaction the real hardship was likely to be relatively modest. At the June 1992 Rio Conference on Environment and Development we had also committed the Government to bring forward measures aimed at tackling the problem of global warming and reducing greenhouse gas emissions to 1990 levels by the year 2000. This was an ambitious target and at the time of the Conference I personally thought it had gone too far, but we were now saddled with this obligation. Britain was unique in the European Union in not having VAT on fuel and power. Green campaigners tend to think energy can be conserved without the use of the price mechanism, but that is unrealistic. Rationing, either overtly or covertly, is both inefficient and undesirable. The most reliable means of reducing energy consumption is the price mechanism, and some of the more intelligent Greens recognise this.

Part of our Rio target could be met by increasing road fuel duties, since it was the transport sector that made the largest contribution to the growth in carbon dioxide emissions. I was already intending a hefty increase in the 1993 Budget and a commitment for future years to increase duties by 3 per cent above the level of inflation in future years. But the Rio target could not be met simply by measures on the transport sector. It was necessary to encourage greater energy conservation across the whole economy and in every household.

I was surprised that people later thought that the environmental argument for VAT on fuel and power was somehow bogus. It wasn't. The arguments were genuine, as was courageously recognised by environmental groups such as Friends of the Earth. The Labour and Liberal Democrat Parties, who had previously advocated VAT on fuel and power, were not so brave and quickly reversed their policies.

I was interested that in the Budget consultations Conservative MPs were by and large keen to extend VAT and many of them specifically mentioned fuel and power. That, I reckoned, would certainly make its passage through the House easier. I did not, however, expect the Opposition Parties to stick to their policies.

Partly because it was controversial and partly because the Budget strategy was to create a 'wedge' of gradually rising tax revenues, the decision was made to introduce VAT on fuel and power in two stages: at 8 per cent from April 1994 and 17.5 per cent from 1995. It was a difficult decision, but once made it gave the Treasury another £3 billion a year from 1995 onwards. If implemented, this would be the biggest revenue raiser in the Budget and go a long way to solving our problem.

I was determined not to raise the basic rate of income tax, but that did not mean I could not raise some revenue from the income tax system by reducing allowances, and I proposed to do just that with the decision to freeze the personal allowance and the married couples allowance. I also went further and restricted the value of those allowances to 20%, thus raising even more money. I also did the same thing for Mortgage Interest Relief, restricting it to 20 per cent. This carried forward the policy I had begun earlier of phasing out Mortgage Relief, which I believed had done so much to destabilise the housing market and create the problems of 1988 to 1992. These tax increases, later to be criticised as a sleight of hand, raised another valuable £1.2 billion for 1995/96.

It had been a hard slog, but we had now put together by the middle of February a package of increases that would raise more in taxation than at any time since Geoffrey Howe's famous tax-raising Budget of 1981, which had managed to stabilise the economy by reducing borrowing for the rest of the 1980s. I hoped that my Budget would do the same and lay the foundations for low inflationary growth for the rest of the 1990s.

The PM was keen to balance the tax increases with yet another package of help for industry. I was convinced more than ever that this was unnecessary and did not want to give away with one hand money I was raising with the other. While complying with the PM's wishes, I tried to devise as low cost a package as possible. Where I could, I favoured deregulation rather than public expenditure.

Stephen Dorrell and Paymaster General John Cope did much valuable work and a package was assembled that cut red tape and bureaucracy. The requirement for the statutory audit of small companies was removed, penalties for accidental misdeclaration of VAT were reduced, and relief against VAT for bad debts was introduced. All this was rather unglamorous work but it was an important means of getting the Budget welcomed by business. Perhaps the most important business measure was the freezing of the Uniform Business Rate in real terms, so that businesses only suffered a rates rise at the level of inflation: some businesses in the North of England even had reduced bills.

There was also an unemployment package to give part-time work to 60,000 long-term unemployed. Lastly, there were more announcements of private finance deals for infrastructure, particularly the new fast rail link between Heathrow and Paddington.

I would have much liked to have reduced the rate of Capital Gains Tax in the Budget, but as I was increasing so many other taxes it didn't look plausible. Of all the regrets I have about my time at the Treasury, not reducing Capital Gains Tax is one of the greatest. I was convinced that a marginal rate of CGT of 40 per cent, admittedly after indexation, was far too high. Nigel Lawson had aligned CGT and income tax in 1988 when he slashed the top rate of tax. As Financial Secretary I had argued against the decision, though in public I had to defend it. But I was never convinced by it and would have loved to have reversed it.

I could never find the right moment to reform CGT. In my first Budget I had Nigel, my old boss, sitting behind me, and it seemed too soon and I wouldn't have been comfortable. My second Budget was on the eve of the General Election and, although I discussed the idea with John Major, reducing CGT didn't seem to be the best launching pad for a General Election. And in my third Budget I was putting up practically every tax in sight. Nonetheless, in the preparation for each of the three Budgets I delivered, I wasted an enormous amount of officials' time looking in detail at ways of reforming CGT before eventually dropping them. After the 1993 Budget I said to Terry, 'My next Budget will be the reform of CGT.' He replied, 'You've said that before every Budget.'

Despite some improving favourable statistics, at the time of the 1993 Budget, anxieties about the recovery were still widespread. Unemployment was still rising, albeit at a diminishing rate. That was not surprising, and I expected unemployment to lag the recovery. The announcement of the monthly unemployment figures were always a tense moment. In January seasonally adjusted unemployment rose by 22,100, then in February the total rose by 78,726, bringing it to over 3 million for the first time. There were stormy scenes in the House. John Major was shouted down and John Smith told him, 'The country will never forget that it was . . . your Chancellor who told us that unemployment was a price well worth paying. On the day that unemployment has reached the tragic total of 3 million, will you repudiate this heartless approach?' That was humbug.

By the time of the Budget there were signs that the economy had bottomed out and that a gentle recovery was now in progress. GDP appeared to have risen slightly, perhaps 0.25 per cent in the second half of 1992. Once again, this was short of the forecast made in the previous year's Budget of growth over twelve months to the second half of 1992 of 2 per cent. Retail sales had also been on an upward trend for almost a year, and new car registrations in the previous three months were at their highest level for almost a year.

What was really significant was that the basis of the recovery was now shifting away from consumer demand towards exports. However, increasingly it was other countries that appeared to be experiencing the problems. Germany had moved from a boom to a sharp slowdown, and industrial production was down by 6.5 per cent over the year. It was little wonder they were now prepared to cut rates. The mood in Britain still remained sour, but the promised land of recovery with low inflation was definitely now in sight.

The Budget Speech: plain boring

The Budget was fixed for 16 March. At 111 minutes, my speech was one of the longest for years, but a long way short of Gladstone's record of five hours in 1853. The general consensus was that my speech was boring. That may not have been entirely accidental since I was trying to do many unpopular things, and some of the revenue-raising measures were hideously complex. Since the Budget has been televised, the trend has been to make the speech shorter and simpler and to cut out much of the discussion of developments in the economy, both domestic and international. John Major, who delivered the first television budget, liked this development. I did not, and thought the Chancellor ought to explain his measures in full. When I came to the part of the speech dealing with Advance Corporation Tax I was conscious that I would bore and bewilder the House. Rather plaintively I said, 'I hope the House will bear with me, as I am afraid my proposals are complex.' The boredom was indeed palpable, but I felt that if a measure was raising over £1 billion, three minutes was not too long for the House of Commons to be expected to listen. Nonetheless Andrew Rawnsley wrote in the *Guardian*: 'True, it was not a Gladstonian five hours, but some of the speech's more catatonic longueurs made Gladstone seem the soul of brevity.'

William Hague had firmly told me to cut out the jokes, so I made only one when I bracketed sewerage and newspapers together as continuing to be exempt from VAT. The journalists may have been asleep, but they noticed that.

One innovation was that I was able to say I had received the first report of the independent panel of forecasters that I had announced in the Mansion House Speech. This showed that the judgements the Government made were not based on one single forecast. The panel members' forecasts for growth for 1993 varied between 0.25 and 2 per cent, with an average of just over 1 per cent. The official Treasury forecast was for growth of 1.25 per cent for 1993 rising to 3 per cent in the first half of 1994. This time the optimism sounded believable, and in fact the forecast would be achieved. Indeed, by the time of the next Budget the Treasury was able to say for once that its forecast had proved too pessimistic – growth turned out to be 0.5 per cent higher than I had expected. The Treasury forecast of 3 per cent growth to the first half of 1994 was also exceeded. So without being announced the recovery really was under way at the time of the 1993 Budget. Indeed, it was the start of a period of growth that was to go on for a long time.

I made the announcement of VAT on fuel and power about halfway through the speech. If I had made it later I would have run the risk that Labour MPs might have attempted to disrupt the rest of the speech. In fact, although there were some shouts of 'shame' and 'resign' and the Speaker had to call the House to order, the immediate reaction to VAT on fuel and power was milder than I had expected. I was able to move quickly on to the less controversial subject of deregulation and self-assessment, which was itself to become a source of controversy when implemented.

I ended the speech by announcing another extension of the 20 pence band of income tax by £500 to £2,500 and repeated our intention to get the basic rate down to 20 pence, explaining that extending the 20 pence band was another route for moving towards this objective. I then coupled this with the reductions to 20 pence in various allowances such as mortgage relief, and the married couples allowance as being consistent with this objective. These references to 20 pence were designed to play one tune: the future is a 20 pence in the pound basic rate of tax. Even some of the tax increases appeared to anticipate the reduction of the rate to 20 pence. I thought it important to remind the Party of that objective and to do nothing inconsistent with it. I was convinced we could do it in the long term, possibly reducing the overall tax burden too, if we could cut public spending. But, in the meantime, in our situation we had no choice but to put up taxes to reduce borrowing. It was a situation very similar to the early 1980s, when taxes went up. I hoped that in the future, as in the later 1980s we would gradually be able to reduce the rates we had increased.

As Peter Riddell subsequently wrote, 'It now scarcely matters who is Chancellor for the rest of the Parliament. Norman Lamont tied the hands of himself or his successor up to the Election.' But there was no disguising it was also a savage Budget. The strategy was to build up the 'tax wedge' by gradually raising tax revenues. True it was a paltry £490 million in the first year, but the total increase in taxes was £17.5 billion over three years – £6.7 billion and £10.3 billion in years two and three. At least, I felt, no one could accuse me of courting popularity or trying to save my job.

Despite the large tax increases, the more perceptive critics noted that the Budget still left the country with a large PSBR in future years and one also outside the Maastricht criteria. The PSBR was still forecast to be 3.75 per cent of GDP in 1997/98, but this was because the growth assumptions underlying the Budget arithmetic were deliberately pessimistic: minus 1.5 per cent between 1992/93 and 1993/94, followed by 2.25 per cent in 1994/95, 2.75 per cent in 1995/96 and 3 per cent in 1996/97. I was determined this time that the Budget would be based on the worst possible assumptions of growth. In fact they were considerably exceeded, and so even by November the expected PSBR for future years was much lower, and for 1997/98, for example, the forecast PSBR was reduced to 1.5 per cent of GDP.

However, looking at my figures, it was not surprising that some commentators thought I must be planning further tax increases in the second Budget later that year. In fact my view was that any further action should take place on the spending side rather than through taxes. As it turned out, my successor Kenneth Clarke did increase some further taxes in tandem with reductions in public spending made possible by the faster than expected fall in inflation.

The Budget was above all designed to demonstrate that the Government had reasserted its grip on economic policy.

Press reaction

I expected a fierce reaction to the Budget from the tabloids. I was not disappointed. The *Sun*'s headline was: 'Nightmare on Norm Street. £17 billion tax hike: gas electricity shock, home loans blow'. The *Daily Mirror*'s front page headline was 'The Iceman cometh', which had a picture of me looking like a purple-coloured Eskimo. The *Mirror* said: 'He is a cheap and shabby man. And this was a cheap and shabby Budget.' The *Mail*'s headline was 'Lamont tax time bomb', with a picture of me as Guy Fawkes.

The reaction of the broadsheets was more restrained, with most recognising that tough action was necessary, though some understandably questioned whether it might not have been better to have got the pain over immediately. *The Times* on page one said: 'Norman Lamont yesterday presented Britain with the prospect of 3 years of sharply rising taxes as he delivered a make or break Budget that startled MPs by its boldness and toughness.' In its editorial, it said there was 'insufficient contrition in my speech, but [I had] produced some mainly sensible methods of cutting the deficit while keeping recovery alive . . . He succeeded in restoring some sense of determination to a Cabinet that for months seemed to be drifting purposefully from drama to drama. With a rigour not seen since the early days of Margaret Thatcher's medium term financial strategy, the Chancellor of the Exchequer set out a rolling programme that stretched further ahead than Government Ministers have generally been used to raising their eyes.' The *Financial Times* was distinctly cool: 'A package good only in parts'. It thought the tax increases should have been even higher, but this was a rather singular view.

Among economists, opinions were divided. Gavyn Davies said, 'This is almost exactly what I recommended. It is about the best that could be done in very difficult circumstances.' Professor Wynne Godley called it 'absolutely excellent,' while Sam Brittan called it 'an Augustinian Budget' because I had crafted a Budget along the lines of St Augustine's plea 'Please God make me chaste, but not yet.' On the other hand, Anatole Kaletsky called it 'a Budget to pay for Norman mistakes'.

The reaction from business was more positive. Howard Davies, Director-General of the CBI said 'This is close to the Budget the CBI asked for.'

Political reaction in the Conservative Party could have been worse. Some Conservative MPs voiced concern about VAT, and that concern was to grow, but Chris Buckland in the *Daily Express* wrote of MPs: 'The more they looked at his complicated, long range package, the more backbench Tories admired it . . .' Apart from the *Daily Mirror* and *Today* the comments on VAT on fuel and power were surprisingly neutral and dominated neither leading articles nor even front pages. The *Daily Telegraph* praised the measure and *The Times* said: 'It is logical and lucrative to impose VAT on domestic fuels.' Although VAT on fuel and power later came to be regarded as the major feature of the 1993 Budget, at the time it did not dominate the newspapers.

There was criticism that I had not spelled out the full details of the compensation package for those most affected by the VAT increases. I had merely said that the VAT increase would be taken into account in the autumn up-rating of Income Support. This was later regarded, especially in No. 10, as politically inept, but it was quite deliberate, even if somewhat brutal on my part and motivated by my fear of No. 10's constant pressure for more money. In the interests of public expenditure control I wanted to keep the size of the compensation package to the minimum. I knew there would be pressure from No. 10 and I knew I had the best chance with colleagues of controlling the consequences if it was negotiated separately in the public spending round later in the year. Nonetheless my delphic comments caused a certain amount of confusion and Social Security Ministers were not sure what to say.

Subsequently I was horrified by the, in my view, overgenerous compensation package later introduced by Kenneth Clarke as Chancellor. Obviously I have no idea what pressures were exerted on him, but compensation package after package followed, making serious inroads into the yield of the tax. Pensions were also increased by more than inflation to take account of the VAT increase, yet when the second stage of VAT was wantonly lost in December 1994, there was no talk of clawing the compensation back. It was because I wanted to avoid a situation like this that I had kept my comments on compensation to the minimum.

John Smith, for the Labour Party, was quick to condemn the VAT increase but concentrated more on the general tax increases. Normally the Leader of the Opposition's speech in responding to a Budget is a difficult one, because he has no prior knowledge of the measures and sometimes may have difficulty in finding a response, but this time the speech wrote itself. John Smith professed himself 'shocked beyond belief. The Conservative Party has cynically betrayed the pledges that it gave the people of this country. One thing is certain – they will not be forgiven.'

John Smith's verdict was allowed by a supine Conservative Party to become the conventional wisdom. Frequently during the

1992 General Election, in answer to endless questions on the subject, John Major and I had used the well-worn formula that we had 'no plans and no need' to increase VAT or other taxes. That was what we believed, although it was also designed to leave options open. No Prime Minister or Chancellor of the Exchequer could have answered otherwise. It was not a promise never to increase taxes.

Labour rhetoric on this matter deserved little house room. The Conservative Party had been elected in 1992, as it had been in 1979, as the party both of sound finance and lower taxation. In 1981 the Government was forced to put up taxes to satisfy the demands of sound finance and the 1980s vindicated the Party's claim to be the party of low taxation. The same could easily have been true both of the 1992 Budget and the rest of the 1990s.

The Labour Party was profoundly committed to significantly higher levels of public spending. Its programme for the 1992 Election was not just for increased spending, but for increased spending on top of that planned by the Government. This was a respectable position, but it was not respectable to fail to acknowledge that the inevitable consequences were much higher levels of tax.

But the question remains – would it have been better to have implemented the tax increases all at once? My own view is that the blow to confidence of implementing the measures might have delayed the recovery that gathered strength in 1993/94. But the strongest argument against my Budget was political. The stringing out of the tax increases meant that criticisms of the Conservatives 'breaking their Election promises' were trotted out throughout the rest of the Parliament and were still fresh in voters' minds by the time of the 1997 General Election. The agony of phasing in VAT eventually broke Conservative MPs' nerves. I had intended the full 17.5 per cent to be voted on in the 1993 Finance Bill, but through a clever amendment Labour contrived to secure another vote on the second VAT increase in December 1994. By that stage backbenchers and the Government had lost what little nerve they had and the second stage was lost.

Looking back at the 1993 Budget now, it did go a long way to achieving its objective of a massive switch of resources back towards reducing the deficit. It was the largest increase in taxation for years. Obviously I wasn't pleased about that, but it had to be done. Far from promoting recovery, if we hadn't increased taxes that really would have aborted the recovery. Ken Clarke didn't have to do much more. As I expected, by 1996/97 the Budget deficit had come down more than the 1993 Budget Red Book suggested (£5 billion for 1995/96). The 1993 Budget, controversial and unpopular though it was, put the public finances back on a sound footing, and so kept the recovery going on a sustainable basis for the rest of the 1990s.

15

Resignation and Exit from the Government

Out of the night that covers me,
Black as the pit from hole to hole,
I thank whatever gods may be
for my unconquerable soul.
                    W. E. Henley

Obloquy is part of glory.
                    F. S. Oliver

On the day of the Budget the PM had issued a statement saying that it was 'the right Budget from the right Chancellor at the right time'. It had taken a long time to get him to the starting gate for the tax increases, but in the end he agreed. It was obvious that it would be an unpopular and highly controversial Budget, but I was prepared for that mentally and I assumed that he was too.

The PM's fears over Newbury

Quite quickly after the Budget the PM showed a surprising degree of nervousness. One of his main worries was the forthcoming Newbury by-election, caused by the tragic early death of Judith Chaplin, who had been his political advisor at the Treasury and later worked for him at No. 10. If she had not died so young, undoubtedly she would have had an outstanding career in the House of Commons.

One of my Budget announcements had been about measures to help racehorse owners with the burden of VAT as there was increasing evidence that the bloodstock industry was prepared to move to Ireland. When I made it, cynical observers concluded that it came with an eye on the by-election and the racing industry near Newbury. They were not to know that the decision had been made before Judith's death, and that she herself had been involved in helping me to come up with a solution to the problem. As a former Treasury advisor, Judith had been assiduous in using all the inside levers on behalf of her constituency's racing trainers.

John Major was excessively worried about the by-election, but he told me at one point that Central Office had informed him that they believed we could hold the seat. He asked me several times for my opinion. I told him that it would not be surprising if we lost Newbury. It didn't seem worth worrying ourselves over much. The Budget was bound to be unpopular. It hadn't been designed to win votes but to improve the medium-term prospects and the recovery.

In fact the economic news around that time was not altogether without promise. On the Thursday after the Budget unemployment had surprised us all by falling, which was cheering, especially since Gordon Brown had said in the Budget debate only one thing was certain: on the Thursday after the Budget unemployment would rise. In addition the Economic Optimism Index, measured by MORI, was at its highest level since before Black Wednesday. Inflation had fallen to a remarkably low level of 1.8 per cent measured by the headline rate and to 3.4 per cent on the underlying rate. These figures were better than in any year of Mrs Thatcher's Government. At the same time manufacturing output was 2 per cent higher than a year previously, and retail sales were also higher than a year earlier. Of course it didn't feel so promising and none of these messages were likely to percolate through to the voters of Newbury, but for those prepared to raise their eyes the future looked brighter.

The by-election apart, there were even reasons to be optimistic on the political front. The long agony of Maastricht was drawing to its end. The Committee stage of the Maastricht Bill in the House of Commons was completed on 22 April. When the Bill finally passed through the Lords, surely the Government could look forward to a less turbulent period?

Meeting with Clinton

I dashed across the Atlantic for the spring IMF Meetings together with the usual round of G7 Meetings. The new Clinton administration was by now getting its feet under the table and I was very pleased to discover that I had just as good and close a relationship with Lloyd Bentsen and Larry Summers at the US Treasury as I had had with Nick Brady. The whole time I was Chancellor I found I had much more in common on economic issues with the Americans than with the Europeans.

The US Government was still trying to finalise the last stages of GATT. Clinton had quickly moved away from his campaign hints of protectionism to become an enthusiast for freeing international trade. Bentsen and Clinton, perhaps to the surprise of many, had come forward with a tough deficit-cutting programme, far tougher than anything proposed by the Republicans. I was impressed by their resolution.

At one informal meeting of Finance Ministers at Blair House we were joined by President Clinton, who made his determination to complete the GATT round very clear. I was impressed by Clinton, though puzzled by his taste in clothes. He wore a not very conservative dark blue suit with hugely broad shoulders, very baggy trousers and brown boots – very Kensington High Street. I experienced that famous eye contact, so vividly described in the opening chapters of *Primary Colors*. Talking about him later to John Major I agreed with his verdict: 'I can't imagine anyone not liking him.'

In the White House I also met Bob Rubin, then Head of the National Economic Council, later to succeed Lloyd Bentsen. He had been a friend of Leon Brittan and Michael Howard for many years and I had met him before. I was somewhat startled when we

tiptoed along a dark corridor in the White House to his room and
he paused, pointed at a door and whispered in an awed voice,
'The First Lady's Office.'

I would gladly have avoided another exhausting, long journey
to Tokyo on 15 April for a meeting of G7 Foreign and Finance
Ministers, preparing for the G7 Summit later in the year and discussing Russia, which was represented by Kozyrev and Primakhov.
A new package of assistance for Russia was announced.

The rumour mill at work

There was still much talk in the papers about a reshuffle and a
Lamont replacement. Largely I ignored this. Such talk had been
going on ever since Black Wednesday and nothing had come of it.
Nonetheless I was once again told that the political advisors of
Kenneth Clarke and Michael Howard were actively talking up
their prospects for replacing me. I did not believe this of Ken and
Michael, but I simply didn't know about their political advisors.
However, I was amused to be told by one lobby journalist that
Michael Howard had been telling him his views on the full fund
rule for the gilt market.

But I did notice more reports in newspapers that Norman
Fowler was still pressing for Ken Clarke to replace me. I invited
him to come for a drink in the Treasury and asked him whether
he had any criticisms that he wanted to make of me or economic
policy. I told him that I had read the press accounts, and that,
while he was free to make any points he wanted to the Prime
Minister, it did not seem to me a good idea that there should be
press stories of the Party Chairman being opposed to the
Chancellor. He said he had no criticisms to make of me. Perhaps
it would be more accurate to say that after much beating about
the bush he didn't make any. Furthermore he assured me that he
had never criticised me to any journalist.

Unknown to me at this time, Rosemary, upset by what she was
reading in the press, had gone to see Richard Ryder, the Chief
Whip, in his room in the ground floor at No. 11. She asked,
'Why are you not doing more to support my husband?' Richard,

with his feet up on the table, looked at Rosemary and replied, 'That is a wonderful dress you are wearing.'

Much as I tried to ignore all this tittle-tattle, journalists continued to question me directly. Sometimes I was asked whether I would accept any other job in the Cabinet. I knew that if I ever said that I was interested in being, say, Leader of the House or Defence Secretary, the story would immediately appear that I was about to become Leader of the House or Defence Secretary, so I felt I had no option but to say that I wasn't interested in any other job in the Cabinet. This was then portrayed as 'Lamont digging in his heels'. Much of the press, however, continued to argue that I had one indispensable value to the PM. Peter Riddell wrote in *The Times*: 'Mr Lamont has been a lightning rod for discontent with the Government, an acceptably coded way of criticising Mr Major himself.' Even Alastair Campbell had written in *Today*: 'He is a good lightning conductor, taking the heat and blame that many believe should be directed at Major.' Indeed the PM himself said exactly the same thing with the same metaphor to me on many, many occasions.

My visit to Newbury

Norman Fowler asked me to hold a press conference at the Newbury by-election, which I was much looking forward to doing. David Cameron's family lived in Newbury so we were able to call on his parents, and he knew many people in the area. Part of my time was spent knocking on doors. I can't say the reaction I got was particularly hostile, though I knew the good manners of the British voter could often be misleading.

At the press conference, the candidate, Julian Davidson, made a number of points on local issues and then I talked about the recent run of good figures in the economy and how I had found the reaction on the doorstep. Towards the end I was asked by John Pienaar of the BBC, 'Chancellor, which do you regret most, seeing green shoots or singing in your bath?' How is one meant to answer a question like that? By ponderous self-justification? There was loud laughter when I immediately replied, 'In the words of the singer Edith Piaf, "Je ne regrette rien."'

There was only marginal coverage of my visit to Newbury in the national newspapers although there was a brief account of my press conference on an inside page of the Newbury paper. There was no reference to my remarks about 'Je ne regrette rien.'

I came away from Newbury slightly more optimistic than when I went there and I think I may even have told the PM that I was more encouraged. But I knew that such impressions are often wrong and that by-elections usually surprise Governments with bad news. I had no great expectations. I also realised later that Paddy Ashdown was trying to focus the Newbury by-election on to me and my Budget. 'A vote for the Conservatives will be a vote of confidence in Norman Lamont,' he had said several times.

The day of the by-election, as often happens, had been chosen to coincide with the local elections on 6 May. As always, it was hoped this might increase the turn-out. It was the first real test of public opinion since the General Election.

The results both of the by-election and the local elections were disastrous. Among County Councils the Conservatives lost 500 seats and overall control of Tory strongholds such as Kent and Surrey. Some of the authorities that were lost had never been anything other than Tory. In Newbury the Liberal-Democrat majority was over 20,000 and the swing against the Conservative Party was 28.5% in what was claimed to be the worst by-election result since 1979. Norman Fowler, according to Anthony Seldon, 'to this day' considers it the worst by-election of his time as Party Chairman. I don't know where he was in subsequent by-elections, such as Christchurch, that had worse swings.

This bad result certainly exceeded by far my worst expectations, but I did not see it as a cause for panic. In one sense it was only to be expected after the Budget. There were still three or four years to go before the General Election and everything to play for. Nonetheless I braced myself, as I am sure the PM did, for the subsequent criticism.

Some of it was directed as much at the PM as myself. William Rees-Mogg wrote a strong piece in *The Times* in which he described the PM as 'not a natural leader . . . No sense of strategy or direction . . . His ideal level of political competence would be a Deputy Chief Whip.' A MORI poll showed only 17 per cent of voters thought him a capable leader and only 8 per cent believed he had good judgement. It was a far cry from Major's heady ratings of 1991.

My lighthearted remarks about 'Je ne regrette rien' became the focus of the criticism of me. Newspapers that had not reported the remark claimed that I had stated I had no regrets about economic policy and both the *Daily* and *Sunday Telegraph* wrote editorials criticising my gross insensitivity. The myth grew that my remark had brought about the by-election rout.

I was rather surprised by this, not least since Julian Davidson, the candidate, who himself received a lot of unfair criticism, wrote to me to say he did not think my remarks had any impact whatsoever on the result and he personally thought them very funny. Very stupidly I wrote both to Charles Moore and Max Hastings, protesting at what I saw as grotesque misrepresentation of my remarks, though that was undoubtedly a mistake. Max Hastings wrote back saying I demeaned my office by writing and Charles simply replied saying I should resign.

But the stories about my remarks, despite my efforts, continued to balloon. *Newsnight* did a whole piece about them with accounts of other so called 'gaffes' and references to my alleged unpaid bill at the Party Conference, my tenant and my references to 'green shoots'. Unsurprisingly few people spoke up for me. One who did was good old Woodrow, but he probably made things worse when he appeared on *Newsnight* to tell the viewers about my brilliant ornithological gifts, and how I could do a remarkably lifelike imitation of the call of a Scops owl, which sounds like a tennis-ball emitter. This was something I had learnt to do while staying with him in Italy but I doubt if publicity for it enhanced my reputation as Chancellor.

Another surprising supporter was Matthew Parris, who wrote in the *Investors' Chronicle* about the Newbury by-election arguing that the blame should not be put on me: 'Newbury, say the breathless commentators, was not just another by-election upset. After Newbury nothing will ever quite be the same again. Rubbish, Newbury was just another by-election upset.' Talking of rumours that I might be sacked, he described: 'the sense of shabbiness of making a scapegoat out of the man who is not the architect of the recession and whose unpopularity has arisen from his ability to justify, or in the end hold to, the impossible line he inherited . . . To lurch, all of a sudden into a spasm of breast beating particularly if this were accompanied by the sacking of the Chancellor would be a terrible mistake.' The *Economist* also wrote: 'To sack Norman Lamont now . . . would smack of Prime Ministerial panic and cheap populism.'

A week after the Newbury by-election the PM and I both went to speak at the Scottish Conservative Party Conference and again I made the mistake of making some comments about the press, although the speech in defence of the Government's record was quite well received. Major made an outspoken defence of me and praised my 'determination, skill and guts'. Whether he knew it or not, aides from Central Office were taking a very different line. At the Conference David Cameron overheard an assistant to Norman Fowler, giving a briefing to journalists, presumably on the instructions of his boss, saying that I should be removed.

Sam Brittan gets some good news

When my friend Sam Brittan learnt he was to be knighted, I was delighted. For a long time I had pressed the case for him to be recognised. He is much more than an economist, a great writer on political economy. His thinking had a great influence on Keith Joseph and the economic revisionism of the 1980s. I had raised the question of a knighthood for him several times with Terry Burns and I took up the case in 1992 with the PM several times. At one point it was suggested he should have a CBE, which I considered inadequate. Once, when I was arguing with the PM over some matter, he suddenly said, 'I have some good news for you. Sam Brittan is on the list for a knighthood.' I was delighted, forgot my differences with the PM, and surrendered on whatever point we had been arguing.

A few weeks later, when the next Honours List had been published, Sam's name was not included. Puzzled, I raised the matter with the PM, who replied, 'I only said he was on the list.'

Shortly after Sam was finally offered a knighthood, to be announced in the Birthday Honours List, I had a meeting with the

PM, who told me, 'He's got his honour now. Are you going to ring him up and get him to write something favourable about the Government?' I told the PM, 'He's not that sort of person. He has often been very critical of me.'

Sometimes I suspected that because the PM had been a successful Chief Secretary he had some to believe everything had to be a matter of negotiation.

The Danes vote 'Yes' to Maastricht

On 18 May I felt deep disappointment when the Danes voted 'Yes' to Maastricht on their second vote, but I was hardly surprised after all the pressure that had been exerted on them. This time John Major, after his wobble during the French referendum, had reverted to wanting a 'Yes'. That day I talked about it when I had lunch in the RAC Club with Trevor Kavanagh of the *Sun* and Gordon Greig of the *Daily Mail*. After we had discussed the referendum they told me that Douglas Hurd was also now pressing for me to be removed, which was news to me. But I liked Douglas, as I do to this day. I responded simply by saying that I intended to stay as Chancellor because the new unified Budget was a major challenge, way beyond the normal, and as its originator I was well qualified to tackle it.

Unfortunately the *Sun* the next day somewhat inflated my comments and, anticipating my departure, attributed to me some menacing remarks about knowing where 'all the bodies were buried' from the mistakes leading up to the Election and the ERM. I am sure the reports caused intense irritation in No. 10.

Later, journalists were to express astonishment that I seemed to be the last person in the country to be aware of the direction in which events were moving, but there were a number of reasons for that. Firstly, the Prime Minister had repeatedly said that if he had a reshuffle those affected by it would hear about it directly from him and not from the media. I could not believe he could be planning a reshuffle and allowing all these rumours contradicting what he had said to circulate. Secondly, I could not believe that the PM could have summoned up the courage to back a tough budget designed to deal with the fundamental problems and then very quickly act in a way that would imply the Budget was an error. But that was not how others saw it. That weekend Norman Fowler went on a Party visit to Wigan where apparently I was fiercely attacked and there was much criticism of my decision to put VAT on fuel and power.

Third Reading of the Maastricht Bill

On Thursday 20 May I had to wind up the Third Reading of the Maastricht debate. This, we all hoped, was the beginning of the end of the Maastricht travails. It was an important occasion and a significant milestone. The Whips were expecting a rebellion, but the Bill was not in danger because Labour intended to abstain. On the other hand that meant Tory MPs knew that any vote against the Government was not going to endanger its survival.

I began my speech by noting the end of Gordon Brown's speech: 'Every Honourable Member in this House will have noticed that the Honourable Member for Dunfermline was lost for the last line of his speech. He could not bring himself to utter the words "I urge my honourable friends to abstain."' When I came to describe our opt-out from the single currency I referred to 'our protocol which I negotiated'. I put it that way quite deliberately because I had noticed that the PM had developed the habit all the time of referring to the opt-out which he, the PM, had 'negotiated'.

During the debate Peter Tapsell had raised the question of whether Britain had to rejoin the ERM. I replied, 'There is no obligation in the convergence criteria, or anywhere else in the Treaty, to make Britain rejoin the ERM. There was pressure to include such an obligation in the Treaty. I was wholly opposed to that and I successfully resisted it.' They did not know that among those I had resisted were the PM and Douglas Hurd. Had I accepted their advice we would have been in a very different situation after 16 September, under a public and legal obligation to rejoin the ERM. In those circumstances Maastricht would probably never have received a Third Reading, and never been ratified by Britain.

I addressed my speech particularly to critics on our side of the House. Above all I wanted to draw a line under the disagreements of the past, and I deliberately held out an olive branch to the Eurosceptics. Responding to George Gardiner I said, 'My Honourable friend the Member for Reigate said that he strongly felt that, after the debate was over, there should be no recriminations in our Party, and I strongly agree with him. We must all recognise that there have been strong feelings on both sides of the House, and people have legitimate feelings and every reason to put their views. Recriminations will have to be put aside.' It was not a sentiment I knew was shared by the PM and he had advised me not to say it, but it was well received, as was my speech. The *Independent* commented, 'Lamont is . . . one of the best wind-up speakers in the Commons and it was a good speech.' Possibly, but it had no effect on the Division Lobbies: 44 Tory MPs rebelled, though the Bill was carried by 292 to 112. Labour abstained, so the 112 against was made up of Conservative Eurosceptics and certain Labour MPs, some Eurosceptic but others simply anxious to record a vote against the Government.

It was not quite all over, since there was still the passage of the Bill in the Lords and Labour had secured an amendment to give the Commons a vote on the Social Chapter before Royal Assent. As it was to turn out this would cause problems, but the Third Reading made it much more probable that the Bill would become law and John Major could now hope that the tensions in the Conservative Party would abate. There was a big cheer from Government supporters as the result was announced. John Major put his arm around me, patted me on the back and pointedly looked up at reporters in the Press Gallery apparently to demonstrate the confidence he felt in his Chancellor.

Preparation for the Budget that never was

On the following Monday, fresh from our Ecofin meeting, I had meetings with Treasury officials and Portillo at Dorneywood to start work on the first unified Budget in the autumn. I had chosen the date of 30 November, which was meant to meet Michael Howard's concern that local authorities would not be able to cope with a later one.

The unified Budget was going to be a huge task, especially for the Chancellor of the Exchequer. In addition to making all the usual decisions about tax the Chancellor would, if we continued the new arrangements for public spending, have to chair EDX and be involved in its arguments. I felt I could manage this because I had been involved with Budgets and public spending for so long. I had been in the Treasury for seven years and I knew the routine well. The PM had agreed that it would make sense for me to continue to chair EDX.

The meeting at Dorneywood was fed a diet of gloomy news. Michael Portillo revealed that Whitehall Departments wanted to spend billions more than had been allowed for in the figures agreed. Asked for cuts, Ministers had replied with warnings of the political consequences.

The revenue side of the balance sheet was also again weaker than expected in the March Budget, particularly the yield from Corporation Tax. I was told that I faced the unpalatable prospect once again of raising taxes further in November. I was strongly against that and felt that this time we should look for cuts in public spending. Portillo and I asked for more work to be done on various public spending options and then I said I would reconvene the meeting, which was intended as one of a series.

The next day, Tuesday, I gave an interview to Will Hutton, then economics correspondent of the *Guardian* and later its editor. Despite our sharply different views I always found him interesting and enjoyed conversing with him. Apparently I talked so much I overshot the time for my lunch appointment. That evening Rosemary and I dined with Muck and Donatella Flick in their large house in South Kensington. As always at Donatella's, it was a very hospitable evening and she amused us all by dancing after dinner to the strains of *Carmen*.

Before going out to dinner I had watched the 5.45 p.m. news bulletin. Michael Brunson had said he did not expect a reshuffle, contrary to rumours in the press, but between the early evening

news and the main bulletin at 10 o'clock a senior Minister telephoned Brunson and told him that there would be a reshuffle.
Brunson at 10 p.m. duly and rightly presented this as a great scoop,
announcing that he had obtained the information from a senior
Minister. I dismissed it, since I still remembered John Major's insistence that there would be no leaking of a reshuffle to the media.

The next day, Wednesday, I had to make a speech to the CBI at
Centre Point. As I walked in a reporter shouted at me, 'Are you
past your sell-by date?' Apparently I appeared rather irritated and
I was described as showing 'signs of strain'. That evening
Rosemary and I went to Michael Portillo's fortieth birthday party,
which was held in the Spanish Club. Those present included
Margaret and Denis Thatcher, the Heseltines, the Howards, Enoch
Powell and Clive Anderson, who apparently was an old friend of
Michael's. It did not register with me that the PM, Richard Ryder,
Sarah Hogg and Gus O'Donnell were not there. Peter Lilley and
David Cameron told me the reshuffle was definitely on and
Edward Leigh recalls asking me when I thought there would be a
reshuffle. I said that when the week had passed and there was no
reshuffle we wouldn't get any apology from the press for their inac-
curate stories.

Much of what happened subsequently has been fully reported.
It is true that when I returned to No. 11 from Michael Portillo's
party I happened to look out of the window and noticed that
Richard Ryder's car was still outside No. 10. At that moment I
realised that what David Cameron and Peter Lilley had said to me
must be right and there was going to be a reshuffle. I thought that
I would probably receive a telephone call that night, but there was
none. When I woke up the next morning I thought perhaps I had
been mistaken. At 9 a.m. just as I was preparing to leave No. 11
to go to the Treasury, Jeremy rang me and said in a rather puzzled
voice that the PM wanted to see me.

Resignation

I went through the connecting door between Nos. 11 and 10 and
met Mary Francis, the Private Secretary, outside the Cabinet

Room. I noticed she called me 'Mr Lamont' instead of 'Chancellor'. When I went in to the Cabinet Room the PM rather oddly asked me to sit next to him rather than opposite him. I didn't much care for that. I later read Edward Leigh's article in the *Spectator* describing his similar talk with the PM and I was amused to read that the routine for both of us was identical. Edward, who was sacked from his DTI job, said that when the PM asked him to sit next to him he was worried he might put his hand on his knee.

The PM's opening words to me were, 'Norman, I want you to know how very much I like you.' He then said, 'I am going to have to make some changes in my Government.' He went on to say his respect for me had grown enormously during the last two and a half years and admired the way I had taken rough criticism from the press and how I had made tough decisions for my last Budget. He then added, 'Your place is in the top places in the Cabinet, but for the moment that is not possible.' Whether intended or not, that sounded as though he was suggesting that I might in due time succeed Douglas Hurd. 'I need your advice at the most senior level,' he said, 'but for the moment politics requires something else. I know this will be very difficult . . .' and he went on to ask me whether I would consider becoming Environment Secretary.

The meeting was perfectly calm and courteous. I replied that I appreciated that, as PM, he had a very difficult job and it certainly wasn't pleasant for him. I was grateful for what he had said and for the offer, but I added that if confidence had broken down between us, as it seemed to have done, it was far better for him if I left the Cabinet and that is what I would like to do. The Prime Minister said he would like me to think about it further, and he asked me if I would go into the room next door and perhaps discuss what he had said with Rosemary. He also said he was very happy for me to continue to use Dorneywood and he would even arrange for me to have an official residence, perhaps a flat in Admiralty House instead of No. 11. That seemed improbable, but it was unimportant to me. He then asked me a second time not to make a hasty decision, but to go into the room next door for a few minutes' reflection. I thanked him, but said my mind was already made up. The whole conversation could not have lasted more than five minutes.

I later read accounts emanating from No. 10 of an ill-tempered meeting lasting up to forty-five minutes. That was simply untrue.

I returned to No. 11 through the connecting door, told Rosemary, telephoned my mother and then Jeremy, who refused to believe it. But my main concern was the effect on my son James, who was sitting his A levels that week. I telephoned the school and spoke to him. I was upset that he was so upset himself. He said, 'But you always told me that John Major was much tougher than everyone said.' I promised him that I would come down that afternoon, as quickly as I could.

I then went round to the Treasury just after 11 a.m. I got into the car with all the reporters shouting at me. No formal announcement had yet been made, but by the time I arrived everyone knew I was no longer their boss. I walked into the ante-room to my office, where William Hague and David Cameron were waiting for me.

As I entered I stopped by the Reuters screen at one of the desks to see how news of my departure was being received in the market. The habits of a Treasury Minister die hard. I sat down in the office and mulled it all over for a little while with William and David. A senior civil servant walked in and said, 'It's a terrible moment of weakness on his part.' Michael Portillo, too, was quite upset.

I then went off to lunch at Toto's in Walton Street, a favourite restaurant of mine, with David Cameron and William Hague. We had an enjoyable lunch, but my official car, which I was still allowed to use, got lost and we had to wander around looking for a taxi. By then news was leaking out and workmen on scaffolding on a nearby building waved, half cheering, half mocking.

When I returned Jeremy had prepared a letter for me to sign to the PM in the usual terms, saying what a privilege it was to serve and so on. I decided not to send the letter. It just didn't sound right or sincere. I drafted a statement to be issued at whatever time was appropriate saying, 'I have always been willing to be judged on my record. I believe that the success of the policies I have put in place will become increasingly clear.' Newspaper reports that I menacingly promised 'further comment in a few days' were wide of the mark.

The PM sent me the usual letter. Since I knew such letters were written by Private Secretaries and simply followed a standard format I put it unopened in the waste-paper basket.

We then had an impromptu party in my offices in the Treasury. Having been there for so long I knew a lot of people and about sixty officials turned up. I served the white wine and afterwards made a short speech thanking them for all they had done for me. I said that when things went wrong people often tried to blame the officials, but it was we politicians who wanted the glory when things went right and it was we politicians who should take the blame when things went wrong. I had been marvellously and loyally supported by the Treasury. That was my strong view. The civil servants who worked with me were as remarkable a group of people as I shall ever meet again in my life. Terry made a speech in which he said officials had admired my toughness. No Chancellor, he said, had ever had to put up with so much opprobrium, but to the end I had always been fair and courteous to the officials, even when the going was roughest. After that I shook each of the officials by the hand and left.

I was anxious to get down to Canterbury to see James and Sophie, so we set off, with Rosemary driving. When we arrived outside the gates of my son's school house we put the car into a parking bay and got out. A small boy, not more than six or seven, holding his mother's hand, pointed at me and said, 'Mum, it's that man who has ruined the country.' I shall never forget that moment.

In Canterbury we went out to have a pizza. My daughter wrote in her diary: 'Dad seemed amazingly unstressed about the whole thing . . . Dad turned to James and said, "Look, I've managed to bear this and stay calm, so I am sure you can too."'

My Notting Hill house at this stage was still let, but I had been told I could stay for a few days at No. 11 until we could get our things moved out. I was also to be allowed to stay at Dorneywood until my house was available. We had decided to go down there as soon as possible because at least the press would not be just a few feet outside the front door. When we returned to No. 11 that night the first person who telephoned was Michael Heseltine, who said, 'I more than anyone else in this country know exactly how you are feeling at this moment.' He added, 'When I watched you around the Cabinet table it was not what you said, it was your silences that revealed everything.'

The next day Michael publicly stated I had been dismissed because 'the body politic wanted a scapegoat. Norman Lamont didn't create the world recession. He had made some very unpalatable decisions in order to bring Britain through it . . . He will feel bitter that he didn't get a chance to reap the benefit of that. But politics is a ruthless business.' Some cynics suggested that Michael was angling for my support in a leadership election he saw coming, but that was ludicrous. I am sure he simply said what he felt.

The telephone never stopped ringing. Mrs Thatcher phoned early on to give her support and said I should have been offered the Home Office. Then Bertie Ahern phoned from Ireland saying, 'What is all this?' Quite a number of Finance Ministers phoned from overseas, including Dan Mazankowski from Canada, Piero Barucci from Italy and Jean-Claude Juncker from Luxembourg. I would have been astonished if anyone had phoned from Germany. I also received charming letters from Lloyd Bentsen and Larry Summers at the US Treasury.

The press reaction

The news of my departure leaked out in a strange way. No announcement was made for several hours, but after I had telephoned my mother she, without really knowing what she was doing, told the news to a friendly reporter on the *Grimsby Evening Telegraph*. It was the first time that newspaper had ever been given a 'world scoop', so the news from Grimsby flashed around the world long before any official announcement from No. 10.

The next day's papers were never going to be pleasant reading. *Today* had a picture of me walking out of the Treasury under the headline 'The picture all Britain wanted to see'. The *Star*'s headline was 'Hooray, Hooray we're Norm free today' and the *Daily Mirror*'s was 'RIP, Norman Lamont 1990–1993'. The *Sun* had a massive inside feature going over all my 'scandals' – the tenant, 'Threshergate' and my so-called 'unpaid' bill at the Grand Hotel in Brighton. Trevor Kavanagh wrote: 'The spectacle of Lamont shabbily clinging to office seriously damaged Britain.'

The *Daily Telegraph* was in much the same vein, saying I lacked the weight and personal judgement appropriate to a politician of the first rank and had a 'proneness to rash moments of flippancy'. It welcomed my departure but did add: 'Mr Lamont is a clever man and much that he has done since last September deserves respect.'

The other broadsheets were kinder in their editorials. The *Financial Times* wrote: 'Pity Mr Lamont, a man who has genuine achievements to his credit.' It went on to refer to the low inflation, the inflation target, the unified Budget and 'imaginative fiscal reforms' such as the delayed tax increases, but it added, not unfairly, 'ERM membership, a policy that Mr Lamont inherited from Mr Major, made the Government persist with disinflation. As such it was the source of the Government's principal success and Mr Lamont's downfall. The ex-Chancellor's fate has had elements of irony. Since he had no choice but to reiterate his commitment to the ERM parrot-like, sterling's exit from the ERM, which brought forward the desired recovery, inevitably destroyed his credibility. But it had also damaged that of the man who had chosen both policy and Chancellor.'

Sam Brittan's verdict on my exit was: 'Familiar, predictable, but nonetheless repellent. That is the quick reaction to John Major's capitulation after recent political setbacks to knee-jerk Conservative demands for a reshuffle and a new Chancellor.' Sam had a go at Ken Clarke: 'Another novel feature is the way in which Kenneth Clarke has shoved and bullied his way into No. 11. But most distasteful of all was his semi-public campaign of denigration of Lamont and of his self-promotion to become Chancellor.' He continued: 'Obviously Lamont was not a heroic figure, but history was likely to record him as one of the better Chancellors . . . Above all both inside and outside the ERM he was determined to give priority to securing and maintaining low inflation.'

The Times wrote: 'It was Mr Lamont's enemies who set the rumours of his demise, the media fanned them into a fire storm.' Philip Stephens in the *Financial Times* wrote: 'If the former Chancellor was betrayed it was not by Mr Major but by his Party. That includes many Mr Lamont might still number among his political friends. They found no time to consider the justice of it all as they waited in eager anticipation on Thursday morning for the summons to No. 10 Downing Street. By yesterday Mr Michael Howard, the newly promoted Home Secretary, was dismissing the recriminations as "tittle-tattle".'

If John Major bothered to read the papers that day he might also have noticed a number of articles warning him that my departure left him highly exposed. *The Times* wrote: 'Without Lamont the Prime Minister faces opportunity and danger . . .The PM is now unprotected from his past. During his colourful career Mr Lamont has been given many names, but in No. 10 in recent times, the ones that mattered were "air raid shelter", and "lightning conductor". The former Chancellor was a target not a threat.' The *Wall Street Journal* asked 'Norman Lamont has gone, could John Major be next?'

The next day, Friday, the letters and messages began flowing in. The first I received were from Norman Fowler, Richard Ryder and Kenneth Clarke. Norman Fowler wrote of 'how sorry' he was, and of the 'great deal of respect' and 'affection' for me in the Party. Richard Ryder was only slightly less fulsome, and added that I was quite right to say I should be judged by my record. Ken Clarke wrote to say that he had 'never aimed for your job'. I was relieved there was no letter from Douglas Hurd.

Over the next few weeks I received nearly 2,000 letters, all but a handful of them supportive. No doubt they were utterly unrepresentative of public opinion, the vast majority of which I knew very well, wanted me to go, but it was good to know one had some supporters.

That same day the PM went to Paris to see President Mitterrand and the new French PM, Balladur. The PM announced to the press that there would be no change of policy under Kenneth Clarke, including no change on VAT on fuel and power.

According to the papers the PM appeared irritated by persistent questioning and replied by saying that the timing of my dismissal had been dictated by the start of preparations for the first unified Budget. 'It is necessary to have a new Chancellor in place to see the right way through the preparation and presentation in November.' The PM also said he understood how I felt, and that we shared the same 'vision'.

Some papers suggested his comments were made because he was nervous I might speak out. He need not have worried. I was far too bound up with matters like moving house to think about making any statements.

That Friday night I went down to Kingston to do my usual constituency surgery. Ron Gill, my constituency Chairman, had telephoned to say that if I did not want to do it in the circumstances, everyone would understand. But I felt it would be wrong to cancel and so I ran a gauntlet of photographers and TV cameras outside the Association office. Every person who came to see me about social security or getting a council house was asked on the way out how I looked and what my mood was. Fortunately most of them said I seemed entirely relaxed.

There was other news for me on the constituency front. Almost at the same time that I ceased to be Chancellor the preliminary report from the Boundary Commission indicated I could lose the Commons seat I had held for twenty-one years. Kingston had been targeted for change by the Commission because it had only just over 51,000 voters and was considered too small to be a separate seat so it was likely to be split between neighbouring Surbiton, Richmond and Barnes. I indeed suffered what Chris Patten might have called 'a double whammy' of bad news.

A bit of a backlash

By Saturday a hint of a backlash against my departure was developing in the Tory Party. Eurosceptics such as Michael Spicer, Roger Knapman and Michael Carttiss spoke up on my behalf and indeed called on me to speak out against the single currency.

Michael Spicer complained that the new Cabinet with Ken Clarke as my replacement did not represent the balance of opinion in the Parliamentary Party.

The reshuffle did not appear to have much of a beneficial effect on public opinion. The immediate opinion poll result was that the Conservative Party support fell by 5 percentage points. Gordon Brown said it had been 'a pointless exercise in panic'.

On his TV show David Frost asked the studio audience if the reshuffle would make them more inclined to vote Conservative and only one hand was raised in support. Alastair Campbell wrote in *Today* that he had taken part in a radio phone-in and not one call had supported John Major. He wrote: 'Only John Major could have sacked the most unpopular Chancellor since the War and have people phoning radio stations to protest that Lamont had been treated shabbily.' People were beginning to say there was no point to the reshuffle if policy, particularly on VAT, was going to remain the same. And No. 10 sources made matters worse by indicating, only forty-eight hours after the reshuffle, that there was going to be another one later on.

This change in atmosphere even struck my daughter, who wrote in her diary: 'Everyone is now on our side. Woodrow rang up and said he was voting Labour. But why is everyone on our side now?'

We retreat to the country

We had not yet moved out of No. 11 and there was a rather embarrassing moment when Rosemary was out shopping and Gillian Clarke took the opportunity to come to look around No. 11. Unfortunately they met. It did seem a little insensitive and Rosemary was furious.

We decided to retreat down to Dorneywood for a few days, and it was a relief to get away. Although the press were not outside the front door one was conscious they were in the woods and in the fields several hundred yards away. Occasionally the sun would catch a glint on a camera lens hidden behind a hedge.

I began to turn over in my mind whether I wanted to make a

resignation statement in the House of Commons. Alan Watkins was later to argue that I was not entitled to make a resignation speech as I had been sacked. It is perfectly true that I preferred to use the word 'sacked' when describing my situation, but I had in fact resigned because I had been offered another job in the Cabinet and had turned it down. I was often asked whether I thought John Major really wanted me to take the Environment job or whether it was just one of Richard Ryder's little manoeuvres. Actually my impression was that he would have liked me to have taken the job, but I never gave it a moment's thought. I decided to make a resignation speech. My only purpose was to defend my record and to explain my views on a number of issues, such as why I had not resigned on 16 September, and why we had not devalued, and so on. I saw it as a defence of my record, not as an attack on John Major.

A few friends came down to Dorneywood. David Hart annoyed neighbouring farmers by arriving by helicopter and landing on the front lawn. Woodrow also came to lunch. Again, we all discussed my resignation speech and I outlined to them what I was thinking of saying. There were suggestions later that someone else wrote my speech. In fact I wrote every word myself, though I discussed the structure and points with a number of friends.

While down at Dorneywood I received an unexpected call from David Mellor. He had heard about my worries about my son's A levels and asked if I would be interested in receiving a call from the Prime Minister – would that help? I was rather puzzled by this and thanked him, but said I really thought I could do without a telephone call from the PM about my son's exams. Despite this curious telephone call David Mellor was a help to me on a number of matters. He showed what an *homme d'affaires* he was, much more so than I. A few days later he took me out to a lavish lunch at La Tante Claire and gave me all sorts of helpful advice. He introduced me to a speaker's agency, which resulted in some extra income and also introduced me to a literary agent, since he assumed, he said, that I would, of course, be writing my memoirs.

David kept asking me whether I was planning to make a resignation speech. I suspected he was asking this question on behalf of someone else, so I was very coy. I was unsurprised when I picked up the *Evening Standard* the next day and saw an article about me by him saying that I had assured 'all of my friends' that I would not make a resignation speech.

The difficulty was finding the right occasion, but I soon discovered there was to be an economic debate on 9 June. Although my statement would have to come before the start of the debate, it seemed an ideal time. Michael Portillo later told me that when the business for that week was announced he had said to the PM that there must be a chance that I would speak in the debate. 'Oh, Norman won't cause any trouble,' Major said.

Resignation speech: in office but not in power

I didn't finally and definitely make up my mind to speak until nearer the time. I only notified the Speaker the day before that I would like to make my statement. I was told that when John Major heard on 9 June that I was to make a statement he became quite agitated, cancelled his appointments and started to redraft his speech.

That day Rosemary and I went to lunch with Woodrow at Cavendish Avenue. I tried as best I could to be relaxed. Afterwards Woodrow's chauffeur drove us to the House, with Woodrow in the front of the car. The driver had been instructed to take us to the House of Lords Entrance so that we could avoid photographers. I don't think that Woodrow, good friend to me though he was, was keen to be seen associating with me too much. Unfortunately the driver misunderstood and drove to the House of Commons, straight up to a group of photographers who surrounded the car and photographed a rather furtive Woodrow covering his face with his hands. 'You bloody fool,' he shouted at the driver.

I stood up to make my speech at 3.30 p.m. If anyone reads the speech today, I think that given what people subsequently wrote about it they would be surprised at its restraint.

Some people were later to say that although the speech had an impact it was not as powerful as Geoffrey Howe's after his resignation. But I did not see myself as another Geoffrey Howe.

I was not trying to destabilise Major. If I had wanted to create real trouble I would have played up the attempt I made to get John Major to contemplate withdrawal from the ERM. Instead I downplayed that because I thought it would be unfair to him. After all, I had accepted his decisions. One Treasury civil servant said to me, 'You were more than fair to him on that point.' However, I did refer to the note John Major had passed to me on 16 September telling me not to consider resignation. That seemed an important part of the explanation as to why I did not resign.

I was keen to praise my officials: 'It is we politicians who make the decisions, and it is we politicians who should carry the blame.' I felt sorry for Treasury officials who were blamed both for Britain's entry into and also our exit from the ERM. The entry was a political decision and the exit was forced upon us. I tried to put the recession into the context of getting inflation down and pointed out that Britain was likely to have the highest growth of any G7 country in 1993.

The criticism of John Major was confined to two paragraphs. I said what I felt I had to say, namely that the Government was far too short-termist and paid too much attention to pollsters and Party managers. We spent too much time being politicians and not enough being a Government. 'Too many important decisions are made for thirty-six hours' publicity.' Could I have honourably said less? I had seen it time and time again. I did not feel it was wrong of me to warn the that 'unless this approach is changed the Government will not survive'. Looking back on those words six years later I do not think many people will feel they were unfair or exaggerated. I then repeated the phrase I had once uttered to Michael Heseltine on the steps of No. 10. 'We give the impression of being in office, but not in power.'

I ended by saying how proud I felt still to be an MP and how I felt towards the House of Commons. I was looking forward 'to the great Parliamentary events and battles that lie ahead'. I have always been ridiculously fond of the House of Commons and was saying no more than I felt.

I thought there was very little reaction from either side of the House when I spoke. Towards the end there were some exaggerated mocking 'oohs' and 'aahs' from Dennis Skinner and others below the gangway, and I was convinced the speech had flopped.

Neither John Major nor John Smith responded much. I wasn't surprised by John Major, because he doesn't have much spontaneity in debate and I was sure he would want to avoid confrontation, but I had thought John Smith might have picked up some points. It was Paddy Ashdown who did so, saying to the PM, 'What we have seen is the beginning of the end of your premiership . . . I have to tell you that if you had bothered to turn round you would have seen your fate indelibly written on the faces of Conservative Members.' That was more than I had seen. Immediately after Ashdown's speech I left the Chamber and met up with Woodrow, and we returned to Cavendish Avenue. I said, 'I think I underplayed it. No one reacted, no one was listening.' Woodrow replied, 'Oh, they were listening all right.' I only relate that conversation to illustrate how sometimes one can completely miscalculate the effects of one's words. We watched the TV bulletins and, indeed, the speech received massive coverage and also on *Newsnight* and in the next day's papers.

Norman Fowler on TV attacked my speech as a 'dud, nasty, ludicrous and silly'. He obviously overdid it because there were protests from backbenchers at the 1922 Committee about his remarks. I didn't worry about Norman Fowler, but I was very annoyed indeed after the speech when Gus O'Donnell telephoned me and had the nerve to ask if I still had the note the PM had written on 16 September. It seemed an extraordinary question to ask. Was he implying I had made it up? Was he hinting No. 10 might deny it if they knew I didn't have a copy? I told Gus that I wasn't intending to make further comments on these matters and if he and the PM were wise they would let the point drop.

One person who was outraged by my speech was David Mellor. By making a speech I had made nonsense of his *Evening Standard* article. He took his revenge by writing another, saying no one would bother to read any book that I wrote. It seemed strange he had taken the trouble to introduce me to a literary agent.

The next day it was described as a 'searing attack', 'dripping with bitterness'. The speech is reproduced at the back of this book. Others must judge, but I don't think it bears out any of those descriptions. I did say all the things that one is meant to on

these occasions. I had wished the PM well and went out of my
way to say I had no regrets about having supported him for the
leadership in 1990. But of course what matters is not what was
said, but how it was perceived. I was a little surprised at the reaction.

However, most papers followed the line of *The Times*: 'The fall
of John Major came closer yesterday.' Anthony Seldon in his
book wrote that my speech 'plunged John Major into the worst
crisis of his career'. That was nonsense. Nothing happened after
my speech. The only reason it resonated in the country was
because it confirmed what many people had believed and now
knew. My remarks about decisions being made 'for thirty-six
hours' publicity' and about 'short-termism' were exactly what
people felt about the Government, and the phrase 'in office but
not in power' became an epitaph for John Major's Government.
But they were only words. There was no crisis. The Government
just limped on, much as it always did.

16

The ERM and the 1990–93 Recession

The past has its own uncertainties though on the whole they are not as great as those of the future.

Sir Alec Cairncross

The experience of British membership of the ERM has come to occupy a very special position in the collective guilt of the Conservative Party. One of William Hague's first acts on becoming leader of the Conservative Party was to apologise for 'the mistake' of ERM membership, although he also claimed credit for the Conservative bequest of low inflation and a sound economy. Conservative MPs blamed the ERM for rising unemployment and the recession and Conservative newspapers attributed the Conservative Party's loss of its reputation for economic competence to the ERM. I myself have said that I did not personally believe that we should have joined the ERM and officials in the Treasury were in no doubt about how much I came to dislike it by 1992. On the other hand John Major has sought to make a distinction that while the ERM was a political disaster it also brought economic benefits. His view is not to be dismissed lightly.

The arguments for joining the ERM were both political and economic. I have long suspected, though I do not know, that John

Major was just as influenced by the political as the economic arguments. I suspect that, as Chancellor, he did not like to be excluded from meetings where European Finance Ministers talked about ERM matters. When he said that Britain must be 'at the heart of Europe', he had been describing a personal sense of exclusion. Some people saw the ERM as a stepping stone to the single currency. John Major did not necessarily accept that, though on the other hand he did not necessarily reject it.

The economic arguments for the ERM were much the same as those for any fixed exchange rate system. Businessmen tend to favour such a system because it removes one uncertainty in their lives, namely the volatility of currencies, and this, it is argued, will boost trade. Nigel Lawson was more interested in the monetary theory of fixed exchange rates and developed the concept of what Edmund Dell has dubbed 'exchange rate monetarism'. An exchange rate target was substituted for the erratic vagaries of monetary indicators, so if Britain linked its currency and its interest rates to Germany then, over time, British inflation would eventually converge with that of Germany. Many people in the Treasury had become disillusioned with domestic monetary targets, and had concluded they were too judgemental and unreliable.

The economic arguments against fixed exchange rates were that once you target a particular rate your domestic monetary policy can be distorted. Furthermore, different economies can suffer differential economic shocks, such as oil price changes, that will affect different economies in various ways and make the appropriate domestic response different. Far better, say the monetarists, to set your interest rates for your own domestic conditions and let the exchange rate go where it will. Unfortunately exchange rates also affect price levels, at least in the short term. A more moderate approach is to set interest rates for the domestic economy without being completely indifferent to the level of the exchange rate. This is my own view.

How does Britain's experience of the ERM measure up against these different arguments? Has the guilt of the Conservative Party been overdone? Is there some merit in John Major's argument?

The first point that needs to be made is that the ERM did not cause the recession in Britain. The excess boom of the late 1980s produced a relatively high rate of inflation well beyond Nigel Lawson's 'blip' and made recession in Britain inevitable. In late 1990 the headline rate of inflation was nearly 11 per cent and a period of both below average growth and high interest rates was clearly necessary. It may not have been the most brilliant timing to have joined the ERM just as Britain was about to enter recession and to be hit by the effects of German reunification, although joining earlier would not have overcome the problems caused by German reunification. But in no way can the origins of the recession be found in membership of the ERM.

On the other hand, the ERM did enable Britain to reduce its inflation rate dramatically. The speed of disinflation was remarkable. The headline rate came down from 10.9 per cent in October 1990 to 4.5 per cent in December 1991 and to 1.7 per cent in January 1993, an astonishing fall in just over two years. The progress in the underlying rate was more gradual but equally impressive since it was the real number. Without membership of the ERM it is highly unlikely that any UK Government, let alone John Major's, would have had the determination and consistency to pursue the anti-inflation policy necessary to deliver these results outside the ERM. An independent Bank of England might have, but that was not an option that John Major was prepared to consider.

But did not the ERM lock Britain into a longer recession than otherwise would have happened? The answer to that is yes, but probably not much longer. In 1991 interest rates came down from 14 per cent to 10.5 per cent, much as the Treasury had wanted and forecast. On the other hand, inflation during the first year of Britain's membership of the ERM came down only quite slowly. In the last quarter of 1991 it barely reached the forecast average of 4 per cent that I had made in the Budget, so the immediate success of anti-inflation policy was not that apparent and certainly did not appear guaranteed. A vigorous anti-inflation policy outside the ERM in 1991 might well have had much the same interest rates as those that were in existence at the time.

British interest rates really began to look too high only around the end of 1991, by which stage cuts in interest rates were constrained by the ERM in general and by German rates in particular. The rise of 0.5 per cent in the German Lombard rate in December 1991 effectively put a floor on Britain's interest rates. For eight long months – I remember them well – from September 1991 until May 1992, British interest rates did not move because they could not be moved. Interest rates were definitely higher in 1992 than I thought necessary, but even so GDP rose in the third quarter by 0.6 per cent again, far too soon to have been influenced by the solitary 0.5 per cent cut in base rates in May. At the same time inflation continued to come down and, with interest rates static, real interest rates increased, tightening the noose around the British economy. This gave the fall in inflation further momentum, with the result that inflation subsequently tumbled dramatically to 1.3 per cent by May 1993, much lower than the 'close to 3 per cent' forecast that I made in the March 1992 Budget.

The recession that began in 1990 lasted for eight quarters, and the recovery, in the sense of output moving off the bottom, began in the third quarter of 1992. This was far too early to have been affected by Britain's exit from the ERM, which itself had a severe effect on business confidence. The recession of 1990–93 was longer than that of the early 1980s but was less deep and the loss in output from peak to trough was smaller.

So what would have happened to the recession and inflation if Britain had not been in the ERM in 1990? That is an almost impossible question to answer, because it depends on how determined the Government would have been to reduce inflation. How monetarist or how political would John Major's Government have been outside the ERM? At what point would the Government have decided that the battle against inflation was no longer worth pursuing?

My answer is that the Government would have given up on inflation much earlier than happened, and Britain would not have gained the real advantage of achieving the lowest level of inflation for over twenty-five years. This was the real, decisive break in Britain's inflation record, which enabled the British economy not just to start to grow in 1992 but to carry on growing without interruption right up to the time of writing this book seven years later.

To look at the question another way, what would have happened to British inflation and British output if Britain had *not* been forced out of the ERM in September 1992? That ought to have an easier answer because it does not depend on the determination of the Government: monetary policy would have continued to have been on auto-pilot in the sense that interest rates would have been largely set by German interest rates – and we know what happened to them after 1992.

Many commentators in the press have asserted that there would have been no economic recovery if we had not left the ERM in September 1992, but that is open to argument. Recovery might not have had the same shape, but that is a different matter. Undoubtedly a recovery did start before we left the ERM, but it would not have gathered the strength it did in 1993 and 1994 had we remained within the ERM.

Recovery would not have been held back for ever because we know for a fact that German rates did eventually come down. The Lombard rate peaked at 9.75 per cent on 17 July 1992 but was three points lower by the end of 1993 and down to 4.5 per cent by 1996. Clearly, after an interval Britain could have resumed cutting interest rates without great danger to its ERM position, so if Britain had remained in the ERM the recovery would have been painfully slower. People probably would have continued to call it recession for some time. However, in the circumstances of 1992, staying in the ERM would have required higher interest rates. For how long, no one can say. But the markets judged that the rate increases would have damaged the economy. That judgement was undoubtedly correct.

The other side of the coin was the inflation gain of Britain's membership of the ERM, which was considerable. Indeed, it was precisely because the recovery was prevented that there was overkill on the inflation front, which fell to 1.2 per cent in June 1993. Inflation remained well below the levels ever achieved in the Thatcher years. Critics say that this fall in inflation came at too high a price of greater unemployment and bankruptcies, but if inflation had not fallen so low, growth after 1993 would not have lasted so long, and neither would so many jobs or new businesses have been created in the long upswing that followed.

By making a sharp break in Britain's inflation performance, membership of the ERM brought certain very considerable advantages. These benefits were to some extent accidental and unintended, which was also true of the first great break in inflationary expectations under Geoffrey Howe in the early 1980s, brought about by an unintended, sharp appreciation of the exchange rate.

In some ways fate delivered to Britain a not unsatisfactory outcome from its membership of the ERM. The two years of membership produced a rapid reduction in inflation. Just as the policy was becoming too severe, the markets intervened, and Britain was able to resume growth, unlike its Continental neighbours. The ERM was a tool that broke in my hands when it had accomplished all that it could usefully do.

Obviously it would have been far better if the Government itself had suspended its membership of the ERM in the summer of 1992. Economically that would have been the right course of action, but it would have caused a storm in Europe and would have been strongly resisted by the same Ministers who didn't want to withdraw even on 16 September.

The Treasury forecasters

It has to be asked why the length of the recession was so misjudged by forecasters within the Treasury as well as outside economists, who initially thought the recovery would come in the second half of 1991. Why were they so confident the recovery would happen when the freedom to cut interest rates was so limited?

Economists, like generals, tend to fight the last war. Treasury economists based their view of the future recovery very much on the pattern of the recoveries from previous recessions in the early 1980s and mid-1970s. It was their view that the savings ratio, which had spiralled up with rising inflation and the housing crisis, would fall back as both inflation came down and households rebuilt their personal balance sheets. In this way room would be created for consumer spending to rise. Furthermore, on the face of it the task of reducing inflation from just under 11 per cent appeared much easier than bringing it down from the high teens of the early 1980s and mid-1970s. As inflation fell confidence would be regained and the recovery would start.

Ironically the recovery, when it came, was not the recovery that had been foreseen. The 1993 recovery was a more 'virtuous' one, of the type that appealed to Wynne Godley. It was, for once, export led. That is not to say that consumer spending didn't eventually recover, but the first impact of the exit from the ERM appeared in the export sector. Contrary to the pattern of other recoveries, and contrary to what I predicted, the housing sector lagged the recovery.

It was always recognised that if interest rates were unable to come down then the outlook for growth would be less and the recovery more hesitant. But what the forecasts had not initially anticipated was that German interest rates would continue to rise throughout 1991 and 1992. Indeed, their initial expectation was that they would plateau and then fall.

A real, full-throated recovery would have required real interest rates (after inflation) to have fallen close to zero, which was what happened with the recovery in the early 1980s. But even if German rates had come down they would only have done so slowly and Britain's ability to cut rates within the ERM would still have been constrained and our recovery therefore anaemic. The Treasury forecasts never expected to get rates below 10 per cent in 1991. That would not have been enough on its own to generate a sustained recovery.

Where the Treasury and I particularly underestimated the seriousness of the recession was in the housing market. The effects of negative equity and the debt overhang had a much greater impact than expected. The longer interest rates remained high and the longer the recession lasted, the worse the problem became. The 1990–93 recession was quite different from that of early 1980s because it was more a recession of asset values and property. As I became increasingly aware of this I introduced various housing packages in vain attempts to deal with the problem. The reality was that there was no substitute for a cut in interest rates, which was not deliverable.

But any assessment of the ERM's effect on Britain cannot be judged purely by reference to the impact on output and inflation. The ERM also had a great effect on the public finances and government borrowing and indeed played havoc with them. In saying this I do not in any way wish to underestimate the mistakes made in the 1991 Autumn Statement, which I have analysed separately, but the ERM affected the public finances in several ways.

Firstly, by prolonging the recession, tax receipts were lower and public expenditure and government borrowing higher. These were what one might call the cyclical consequences of the ERM. But there was also another element, ironically stemming from one of the benefits of ERM membership. Because inflation was so much lower than expected, tax receipts were even lower than would have been caused by the recession. At the same time, public expenditure, which was set in cash terms, became higher in real terms. As a result government borrowing was driven even higher.

The correct response to the improved inflation performance should have been to cut public expenditure since it was now increasing more than planned in volume terms. But that was not what happened. The prolonged recession had quite the opposite effect psychologically and inhibited us from cutting expenditure. Since the ERM meant that interest rates could not be used to ease the recession, we saw merits in a slightly more active fiscal policy, hence all the talk about the 'automatic stabilisers'.

In assessing the ERM one cannot, of course, leave out the actual crisis in the currency markets. A crisis happened, but the so-called 'crisis' of 1992 was entirely artificial and self-inflicted by the Governments of Europe. If the pound had been floating outside the ERM, there would have been no crisis. Undoubtedly the same fundamental forces – the reunification in Germany, recession in Britain, high rates in Germany and the need for lower rates in Britain – would have caused the Deutschmark to rise relative to the pound. But that would not have been a crisis.

The artificiality of the situation is illustrated by the fact that the pound, although weak against the Deutschmark, was exceptionally strong against the dollar, touching $2 in the summer of 1992, the highest for ten years. If one had measured the strength or weakness of the pound against a trade-weighted basket of currencies rather than just European currencies, then the pound had hardly moved. Because of our self-imposed restraint, there was a massive 'crisis' throughout European financial markets. Without the ERM this would have been regarded as currencies adjusting themselves both to domestic realities and to each other.

If the ERM crisis was an artificial one, it leads on naturally to John Major's view that, even if the economic damage of the ERM was overstated, it is true that it was a political disaster. I well remember how quickly John Major came to that conclusion. Almost the day after 16 September he said to Douglas Hurd and others that the more he considered it the more he thought that this was essentially a political disaster. What he had in mind was not just the consequences for the Conservative Party but also the effects on the prospects for Maastricht ratification throughout Europe.

Undoubtedly the exit from the ERM was a great setback for the Government, but was it one from which it was impossible to recover? If the overkill of the anti-inflation policy produced some extra, good long-term benefits and if the unintended reversal of the policy had prevented us from further overkill, could not a skilful Government have refashioned policy and presented the benefits in a way that appealed more convincingly to the electorate? As Bruce Anderson has frequently argued, the Government never tried and its explanation of its economic record in the 1997 Election was pathetic. A more sure-footed Government would have seized the initiative. The political counterpart of the domestic monetary framework I was putting in place would have been to make a binding statement to Parliament that the Government would not be joining the single currency. It was the politics that were mishandled, not the economics.

The ERM looms much larger in the minds of journalists, politicians and commentators than in those of the public. I only once heard the subject of the ERM mentioned at all in the 1997 General Election. It is commonly asserted, without any challenge, that after 16 September the opinion poll ratings of the Conservative Party plunged and never recovered. Interestingly opinion polls themselves reveal a slightly different story.

I reproduce the opinion polls during the Major Government in

Table 7. From the Election in April to September 1992, in MORI's monthly opinion polls the Conservative ratings were, with the exception of one month, always over 40 per cent. After Black Wednesday the number intending to vote Conservative fell to around the mid-30s, but it was always above 30 per cent until the end of May 1993. After I left the Government those intending to vote Conservative fell below 30 per cent and remained more or less consistently so throughout 1993 and 1994 when, in July and August of that latter year, support fell even further, to 23 per cent and in December to 22 per cent. In 1995 Conservative support recovered to between 25 and 28 per cent. In 1996 it edged up slightly to just under 30 per cent.

Looking back at voting intentions, as measured by the MORI monthly opinion polls, suggests that it was also events after September 1992, such as the beef crisis and perceptions of weak leadership, that created a serious fall in support. The remarkable thing is that the downward spiral in Conservative support coincided with an almost unprecedented improvement in the economy. If the Conservative Party had only maintained the ratings that it had in the eight months following Black Wednesday it would probably have won about 200 seats at the General Election. Black Wednesday became something of an excuse for the Conservative Party.

Economic historians have not been able to agree about Britain's experience of the gold standard in the inter-war years, and in the same way the controversy over the ERM will continue. A final view will also depend upon what happens to the single currency.

The decision to join the ERM was a mistake. It was foolish to give up the flexibility of the exchange rate, which is also a safety valve for the economy. There is no such thing as the right or wrong exchange rate: at times it may have to be higher or lower to offset domestic economic conditions.

Whatever my doubts, I certainly did not foresee the collapse of the ERM and I did my best to make the policy work right up to the very end. Leaving the ERM was never, alas, a real option available to me. The ERM did generate an unreal currency crisis; it did prolong the recession; it did substantially worsen the public finances; it did damage the reputation of the Conservative Party.

But Britain's experience in the ERM also brought about a savage deflation that brought Britain screaming and shouting against its will into the premier division of low inflation countries. The public finances were quickly restored by myself and Kenneth Clarke and the present Government has enjoyed the twin benefits of low inflation and sound finances ever since. These beneficial effects of the ERM were in many ways accidental, but why should we complain about that? Many things that fail are accidents and so are many things that succeed. We are lucky if anything succeeds.

The French persisted for longer in the ERM at greater cost. But they did achieve something of great importance to them: ultimately they wrested control of European monetary policy from the Germans and the Bundesbank. Viewed in that light, the ERM and Maastricht were a famous Gallic victory – an economic Verdun. The real question is what was gained. Economics is not a zero-sum game. France didn't have to fight in the trenches. It could have followed Britain out of the ERM, taken control of its own policy and set its own interest rates. It didn't need EMU to remove German control over French policy.

So what would a more rational policy for Britain have been? The right answer was that quickly implemented by Gordon Brown. His bold initiative to make the Bank of England independent locked in as permanent gains for Britain the low inflation brought about by the ERM and the new framework established in late 1992. If Margaret Thatcher and John Major had never joined the ERM but instead had made the Bank independent and depoliticised interest rates, they would have achieved the benefits of the ERM without its disadvantages, enjoying a better mix of low inflation and interest rates set for conditions in our own country. Then we wouldn't have had to rely on fate to come to our rescue.

17

Return to the Backbenches

For politicians are an essential part of the ancient system.
They stand the racket and are paid in fame or notoriety.
Most of the blows fall on their heads and when a sacrifice is
required to appease any of the popular critics, it is their
privilege to offer up one of their own numbers.

F. S. Oliver

We are all in this alone.

Dorothy Parker

I ended my resignation speech with the words, 'I have always
been proud to be a Member of this House and not just a Minister.
Today when I walked through Westminster Hall and up the stairs
into the Lobby I felt exactly the same pride and excitement as
when I first entered this House twenty-one years ago.'

It was true that I was looking forward to being on the backbenches again. I felt liberated. I wanted to be an independent-
minded backbencher, free to express my own views, as I had not
been able to do during the eighteen years I had been on the front
bench. I wasn't in any way perturbed by the loss of the trappings
of office, and certainly didn't mind the loss of my chauffeur-
driven car.

Thanks to Derek Conway in the Whips' Office I was given a
splendid office in the new Parliamentary building. The Treasury

had opposed the luxurious building a few years previously, but now I was able to enjoy it. My new office, with floor-to-ceiling glass windows, looked straight out at Big Ben, with a view over New Palace Yard. In the background the Union Jack flew over the Norman Tower of the House of Lords. However down I felt, I never failed to be uplifted by looking out through that window.

Back to the City

I also had to start earning my living now that I had lost my Ministerial salary and had only my MP's salary on which to rely. Fortunately that problem did not last long. Evelyn de Rothschild, the chairman of N.M. Rothschild & Sons, where I had worked before I was a Minister, was quickly in touch offering me a desk there. It was a start. He also invited me to go to the Derby to discuss it further. Rosemary and I met him at Battersea Heliport with a number of other guests including the Begum Aga Khan, and we were all whisked off to Epsom.

Among the great crowds were many of the leading figures of the racing world, such as the Marquess of Hartington, who thanked me for having helped the racing industry over several Budgets. I remembered he had once come to make representations about the racing industry in the Treasury and had had a spectacular nosebleed. I had a long talk with Willie Whitelaw, who told me that John Major should have offered me the post of either Home Secretary or Leader of the House and that I was right not to accept Environment.

All the time we were surrounded by a mass of photographers. I walked down to the paddock to look at the horses with Anita Rothschild, the wife of Amschel, who wore a very large hat. I was amused the next day when the newspapers identified her as Rosemary. But it was a warm, sunny relaxing afternoon. Andrew Neil, the editor of *The Sunday Times* wrote afterwards that he had never seen anyone looking so miserable. That, I am afraid, was just another example of a journalist writing what he desperately wanted to believe.

I found myself every day making the same journey by the Circle Line to Cannon Street, as I had done aged twenty-three, shortly after leaving Cambridge. Just as I did then, every day I walked up the dark narrow confines of St Swithin's Lane to New Court, where the Rothschild's office had been since it first started in London. It never occurred to me to travel other than by tube, so the first time I went I was startled to be accompanied by a posse of flashing photographers who annoyed the other passengers on the rush-hour train.

James Roe, an old friend from Rothschild's, but no longer with the firm himself, introduced me to John Duffield, the chairman of Jupiter Asset Management. John is a remarkable money machine and also something of a philosopher about money and I enjoyed being involved in Jupiter and on the board of a number of their investment trusts. There was also money to be earned on the lecture circuit. In my first year out of office there was a considerable demand for my articles and speeches.

My work in the City gave me plenty of opportunity to travel. No doubt the Whips felt that I would be less trouble away from the House, as they were surprisingly tolerant about that. In the 1980s Rothschild's had developed a formidable expertise in privatisation on the back of the UK's experience. Sometimes, as Financial Secretary, I had found myself on the other side of the table from my old firm, though the faces were not familiar ones, and now I found myself involved in marketing the bank's privatisation expertise. I went off to see Chancellor Vranitzky of Austria, Manmohan Singh, the Indian Finance Minister, the Governor of the Central Bank of Finland and my old colleagues at the Italian Treasury, Piero Barucci and Mario Draghi. I helped to get Rothschild's involved in the privatisation of ENI, the giant energy company. With Jupiter I also travelled widely, particularly in the Far East. John Duffield and I visited Lee Kuan Yew in Singapore, President Lee in Taiwan and Anwar Ibrahim in Malaysia as well as calling on Chris Patten in Hong Kong and visiting Indonesia, the Philippines and Korea. I found it a great relief to get away from the hothouse of Westminster.

I was approached to join some of the Eurosceptic groups in the House of Commons. There was a weekly meeting of backbenchers, chaired by the indefatigable Eurosceptic Bill Cash, where I found it interesting to hear discussed from a different perspective some of the issues with which I had wrestled in Government. While the backbenchers did not appreciate the constraints and lacked detailed knowledge, in many ways they had a clearer strategic vision than Ministers.

Some of the Eurosceptics were surprisingly suspicious of me. I suppose it was only a few weeks since I had spoken on the Third Reading of the Maastricht Bill. Others like Bill Cash and Richard Shepherd were kind enough to say that they were sorry that they had called on me to resign after 16 September.

As a backbencher again, encouraged by friends like Peter Jay and Godfrey Barker, I decided to concentrate virtually exclusively on Europe and to develop my own critique of the European Union. My whole time as Chancellor had strongly reinforced my Euroscepticism. That was unsurprising; as Michael Howard once said to me, 'It is impossible for anyone who actually deals with the European Union to take it seriously.'

My experiences at Maastricht and the proposals for the harmonisation of taxes that I had had to fight had convinced me that the European Union had become a self-serving and ambitious, bureaucratic organisation whose raison d'être was increasingly difficult to see. As Chancellor I gradually came to realise the European Union's contribution to our own prosperity was much exaggerated, but people did not think clearly about it. Above all I thought that, in the not too distant future, certainly within my own lifetime, the House of Commons would be greatly reduced in power to the point where effectively we would be governed largely through European institutions. As Peter Jay used to put it, 'We will become a country called Europe.' This silent revolution was happening without acknowledgement or consultation with the British people.

And so I embarked on a series of speeches on Europe: the single currency, the case for a referendum, the case against the European Parliament and the real costs of the EU. In starting on this speaking programme it was not my intention to challenge Major. I saw myself simply as putting forward a case of which I had become convinced and that I believed should be promoted. I did, however,

think that we would lose the General Election, and I increasingly
saw myself as influencing the thinking of the Conservative Party
on Europe in Opposition and perhaps returning to the front
bench. Certainly I never for one minute seriously envisaged trying
to become Leader of the Party.

Michael Spicer had said to me, 'You will find you get the "bitterness" label. We have all had that.' At the time I didn't
understand what he was saying. It hadn't struck me that he and
other Eurosceptics were always being accused of being 'bitter'.
But I soon saw what he meant. From now on, whatever my arguments, however informed my speeches, no report could appear in
the newspapers without the words 'embittered Former Chancellor'
or 'bitter and twisted'. I noticed this perception was actively
encouraged by No. 10.

What was my frame of mind? I sometimes denied to friends
that I was bitter, but both my children told me bluntly that I was.
I must accept their judgement. I was certainly angry, but not
because the PM had felt it necessary to ask me to resign. I recognised the King had a right to move others to protect himself. My
anger was that I felt I had been placed in a near impossible situation and had endured much criticism, not to mention ridicule.
From the start I had never received the full-hearted backing of a
PM who in turn didn't seem to know what he wanted.

Since I was constantly accused of it I often reflected on the
nature of bitterness. It is a natural but obviously destructive
human emotion which I had never wanted to feel. I remembered
some years previously saying to a friend about Edward Heath that
I hoped I never became bitter like him. A statement by Nelson
Mandela also stuck in my mind: 'Everyone has a right to be
bitter.' He was a man who, remarkably, rose above it.

Bitter I may have been, but in the next few years I never said
anything I disbelieved. Sometimes I was insufficiently conscious of
the impression I created and failed to stand back and ask how
others would see things. The other awkward truth is that I
enjoyed a little too much being mischievous. All my political life
I had had to conform. I thought my new freedom gave me the
opportunity to say what I wanted, or so I naively believed.

One of the illusions I harboured about the backbenches was

that I was going to meet lots of new, young, talented people. But that proved something of a disappointment and I quickly recognised the truth of the phrase, 'the icy wastes of the backbenches'. I did enjoy being able to spend more time with old friends like Peter Tapsell and John Biffen, though.

I had to choose where to sit on the backbenches and eventually forced my way into the already crowded second back row, on the Government side, just below the gangway. At first I was startled at the strength of criticism of the Prime Minister. Whenever he appeared at Prime Minister's Questions there was a strong, audible undercurrent of sarcastic comment, and not just from Eurosceptics.

More trouble over Europe

It wasn't long before I witnessed, this time from the perspective of the backbenches, yet another crisis over Europe. Before the Maastricht Treaty could come into effect, the House was required to have two votes: one on a Labour amendment that there should be no ratification of the Treaty without the Social Chapter, and the other a vote to note the opt-out from the Social Chapter.

The Government were very nervous about these votes, and there were rumours that they would be defeated. I watched the manoeuvres of the Eurosceptics and listened silently to their discussions. I gave them no encouragement. I was firm that I would support the Government and it would have been unthinkable to do otherwise since I strongly opposed the Social Chapter. Nevertheless a number of newspapers linked my name with the expected rebellion.

The vote was on 22 July. In the first vote the result was a tie, Ayes 317, Noes 317. Farcically the next day it was discovered that there had been a miscount and that the Government had in fact won. In the second 'take note' vote the Government was, however, defeated by 316 to 314 votes, with 26 Conservatives voting against the Government. The vote, however, had no legal significance and the next day the Government tabled a vote of confidence that they won by 38 votes, with only Rupert Allason, the MP for Torquay, being absent. As a result he had the Whip removed.

There was a curious incident the same day in which Major was revealed in an off-the-record moment to have called three of his Cabinet colleagues 'bastards'. One of them was thought to be John Redwood, whom he had only promoted eight weeks previously. It must have been a shock for Redwood to hear on TV that was how the PM really saw him, but the PM's remarks did not surprise me at all. I remembered once I had been alone with him and Terry Burns in the Cabinet room. 'One day I am going to have the Cabinet I want,' he had said to a slightly bemused Terry Burns. I wondered whether that would include me.

In July a MORI poll showed that among Tory voters only 25 per cent thought the Prime Minister was doing a good job. Finally on 29 July the Tories lost Christchurch with a 35 per cent swing, considerably greater than that in the Newbury by-election My removal certainly had not yet produced any discernible benefit for the Government.

Another ERM crisis

The summer saw a repeat of the previous autumn's ERM crisis, if anything on a bigger and more extensive scale than in September. On this occasion it would engulf the French franc, which eventually fell out of the ERM bands. Its basic cause was the worsening state of the French economy, and once again the conflict between the needs of Germany and those of other countries, on this occasion particularly France.

The new French Government, elected in March, with Edouard Balladur as Prime Minister and Edmond Alphandery as Finance Minister, had won the Election on a platform of reducing unemployment. Initially the new Government had some success in reducing interest rates and for a while French short-term interest rates were actually below those of Germany. There was heady talk in Paris of the French franc replacing the Deutschmark as the anchor of the system. The fate of John Major so quickly after he had made a similar boast should have made them more cautious. French interest rates may have come down but in real terms they were still far too high, judged by the needs of the economy. In France real rates were over 5 per cent, whereas in Britain they were only 1.5 per cent.

The tensions in the French Government were revealed when Alphondery announced on 24 June that he was summoning Waigel and Schlesinger for a meeting in Paris. The interpretation put on his remarks was that German rates were too high and were damaging the French economy. The franc slumped. The tone of Alphandery's remarks also caused offence to the Germans, and it was announced that Waigel's busy schedule prevented him from coming to France.

Relations between the two countries were patched up. Germany cut the discount rate by 50 basis points, which allowed France to cut by 25 basis points, making French and German short-term rates the same. But the agonies of the French economy worsened. Unemployment was rising and, according to the official forecasting agency, GDP was expected to decline by 1.2 per cent for 1993.

Money started to flow out of the French franc on a massive scale. The ERM looked now as though it was on its deathbed. The Danish krona and the Belgian franc were all under pressure and even the peseta had been devalued for the third time since September 1992. Safe-haven non-ERM currencies like the dollar and even sterling strengthened. The pound went up to DM 2.572, compared with a low of DM 2.30 in February.

No currency seemed immune. It looked as though maintaining the ERM could mean the destruction of any monetary authority in the area. There was talk of the ERM splitting, with Germany, Holland and Luxembourg but not Belgium going in one direction and the remaining currencies in another.

On 16 July, with great fanfare it was announced there would be intramarginal intervention by the Bundesbank to support the franc. Kohl had been busy no doubt behind the scenes, letting the independent Bundesbank know what he thought. But nothing would save the franc and eventually it fell out of its bands, though not, it must be said, by a huge amount. On the day the Banque de

France took in 150 billion francs, about 30 billion dollars, twice the amount the Bank of England spent on 16 September.

It looked as though this was the end of the ERM, but an emergency Ecofin at which Kenneth Clarke played a key role then came up with the idea of widening the bands of the ERM to plus or minus 15 per cent, a clever idea that removed the one-way bet for the speculators.

I watched these events with fascination and horror. It was like a rerun of a bad dream. I noticed that no one insisted on the resignation of Balladur even though he had said he would quit if the franc was devalued.

The widening of the bands brought stability back for the moment, but it could be claimed that, with a total permitted fluctuation of 30 per cent, the ERM hardly existed any longer.

What astonished me was the reaction of the UK Government. The Chancellor said it showed Britain had made 'a judicious choice' in leaving the ERM. Britain hadn't made a choice, 'judicious' or otherwise, but had been chucked out. It was a strange pretence from someone who did everything he could to prevent our departure.

The PM said it showed how right he was to believe there were 'fault lines' in the ERM, but the crisis showed nothing of the sort. It merely showed that the whole concept of a fixed exchange rate system was flawed. The question of 'fault lines' had been endlessly investigated. No one other than the PM thought there were any.

On the first anniversary of Black Wednesday I received many requests for interviews and articles. I turned most of them down, but wrote an article in *The Times* in which I emphasised that I thought our experience in the ERM ought to lead us to reject the single currency: 'As a former Chancellor I believe it is imperative that the evolution of our monetary policy should never again be constrained by political factors . . . To this end we should disengage from the discussions on monetary union, and the Prime Minister should state categorically that Britain will not be participating in the third stage of monetary union.'

In an interview in the *Sun* I also said: 'Unbelievably Jacques Delors wants to accelerate moves to scrap the pound and replace it with a single currency. Fortunately there is now no ERM for us to rejoin and there is not likely to be for some time.'

What better time for the Prime Minister to stand up and say once and for all that Britain should never again have anything to do with a single currency?'

On BBC's *Question Time* that week I had a disagreeable encounter with Roy Jenkins in which he flattened me. When I counter-attacked rather ineffectively, he became angry and refused to talk to me afterwards. I was sorry, as I admired Jenkins.

I denied that I was seeking to challenge the Prime Minister. Indeed I was not. But the PM's position was not strengthened by polls published that showed that Labour now had an 18 per cent lead over the Conservatives. Whatever else Major had hoped for, my departure from the Government had certainly not increased its popularity.

At the end of September Major produced an admirably Eurosceptic article in *The Economist* that emphasised the need for subsidiarity and for a Europe of sovereign nation states. But the most striking passage was where he appeared to dismiss the single currency as having all 'the quaintness of a rain dance, and about the same potency'. I was delighted, but the Prime Minister had made the mistake of asserting that the single currency was something that was not going to happen. I was sure he was wrong about this. Why did he persist for so long in this belief? He knew better than I the determination of Kohl and other European politicians. Sometimes I wondered whether for the PM it was just a way of avoiding coming to any conclusion?

At the Blackpool Party Conference I made a speech to the Selsdon Group on taxes and spending in which I argued that if it was necessary to reduce government borrowing further on top of the measures in my 1993 Budget, it was important that this should now be done by cutting spending rather than putting up taxes. Since inflation was coming down so much further, there was room for reductions in the cash totals for public spending without affecting the volumes of programmes. I had made this point in my resignation speech, so I felt I could repeat it without offence. Ken Clarke, however, did not agree and attacked me. Peter Jay commented: 'The new Chancellor clearly needed to overcome the personal difficulty that, if he was perceived to have inherited an already well-adjusted economic policy, his personal contribution would be hard to appreciate. The opportunity to seize on the deficit, to get off a few lines about how uncomfortable he felt at borrowing a billion pounds a week, and so portray himself as a stern and sound financier come to cleanse the mess bequeathed by a dodgy predecessor was not missed for more than a few hours after his appointment and was duly rehearsed at every opportunity through the summer and early autumn.'

Clarke seemed to tower as a huge figure above the Prime Minister, and seemed to revel in that perception and to encourage it. Never did that seem more obvious than when, with Major sitting beside him, he made what some thought to be a rather clumsy comment: 'Any enemy of John Major is an enemy of mine. Any enemy of John Major is no friend of the Conservative Party.' His comments seemed to exaggerate the threat to the PM and imply that he couldn't look after himself. I thought the PM looked distinctly white around the gills.

But what was the point of Ken's remarks? I may be harsh, but to me they seemed to emphasise and draw attention to the PM's plight rather than strengthen him. There was, at that stage, little serious prospect of a challenge to the PM. But when the House reassembled there was talk for the first time about a challenge to Major as Leader of the Party. This did not involve any of the so-called 'stalking horses'. The rumour was that Major would be challenged by Ken Clarke, backed by Michael Portillo, on 'a dream ticket'.

The unified Budget

The first unified Budget was delivered by Kenneth Clarke on 30 November. I was naturally very interested to see how it would work in practice and ITV invited me to comment on it, throughout Ken Clarke's speech. I enjoyed doing that; I felt more comfortable being in a studio than in the Chamber itself.

Inevitably the fact that the Budget contained measures involving spending as well as tax, made it necessary for Ken to cut out some of the detail, so the speech was not excessively long. But it was excellent, punctuated with humour and brimming with confidence, and I thought the idea of bringing expenditure and tax together looked likely to last. As I did after each of Kenneth's Budgets, I wrote an article in the *Sunday Telegraph* strongly supporting him.

On the tax side Ken announced a slight increase in taxes for 1994/95 and an increase of nearly £5 billion for 1995/96. I was pleased he continued to cut mortgage relief and reduced it further to 15 per cent. The faster than forecast fall in inflation gave him room to cut spending, as I had suggested in my Party Conference speech, and he managed to reduce the New Control Total over three years by £5 billion. The PSBR was forecast to come down in 1994/95 and with the continuing measures of the two Budgets of 1993 the future public finances now looked much more reassuring.

The only mention I was given in Ken's Budget speech was 'the Rt Hon. Member for Kingston's tax increases'. It was his recovery, but they were my tax increases. But some people knew better. Coming back to Notting Hill one evening I passed by one of the local down-and-outs, whom I regularly saw sitting on the pavement with his dog. He raised his spirit bottle and croaked at me through his beard, 'It's all coming right now, Mr Lamont, and someone else is getting the credit.' Clearly he was a careful follower of financial trends.

Troubles with the press for everyone

John Major tried to relaunch the Government himself with his 'back to basics' campaign. I had some sympathy with his feeling that the press deliberately misinterpreted 'back to basics' as about private sexual morality. It was never anything of the sort, but the press were not going to be diverted from ridiculing the whole idea as Tim Yeo, Malcolm Caithness, David Ashby and Stephen Milligan all featured in a series of scandals. MPs wondered weekly whose turn it would be next. The *Daily Telegraph*'s headline on the eve of Parliament's return after Christmas was 'Tory chaos as "back to basics" backfires'. John Major had good reason to feel exasperated, but the 'back to basics' campaign was extremely ill thought out, and an example of his tendency to think he had found a policy when he had merely found a phrase.

At the end of January, both the *Sun* and the *Daily Mail* carried accounts of another outburst by John Major at the leaving party for Gus O'Donnell, the No. 10 Press Secretary and a former Treasury official. The Prime Minister had said, 'I am going to f— g crucify the right for what they have done. And this time I will have the Party behind me.' The remarks were denied, but their publication exacerbated tensions in the Party.

Yet again the Prime Minister had found himself being quoted when he believed he was talking off the record. Any schaden-freude on my part would have been premature, as I had a not dissimilar experience. A journalist from *The Times* had asked for an interview for a lengthy profile, saying she wanted to write a sympathetic piece as she felt I had been badly treated by the press. I agreed and gave a prolonged interview in my office. I was extremely careful not to say anything critical of the Prime Minister. A few days later she rang to say that the interview had gone to print; she had shown it to friends who thought it gave a very positive impression of me. Would I come and have a drink with her and a friend who was interested in becoming active in the Conservative Party? Feeling grateful, I agreed, and the three of us met at the Ritz.

When the profile appeared it was a hatchet job portraying me as both bitter and completely disorientated. It also claimed that I had described the Prime Minister as 'weak and hopeless'. I was certain that I had not said any such thing in the interview, though it was just possible I said something to her later at the Ritz, after the article had 'gone to print'. Significantly the supposed offend-ing words were not actually in inverted commas, even though they were the main selling point in advertisements for that edition of *The Times*. Unfortunately it caused a considerable stir. I felt uncomfortable and denied the remarks strongly, though no one believed me.

I was to learn the hard way that the press were absolutely determined to portray me on all occasions as seeking to undermine the PM. It is indeed true I had little love for him, but many of their reports were wildly exaggerated and based on nothing at all.

On one occasion I attended a party given by Nick Brown, the Labour Deputy Chief Whip and future Agriculture Minister, to mark the end of the Finance Bill. There was nothing strange about my presence there. Nick and I were and are good friends, and I had invited him to similar parties in the Treasury. He had particularly asked me to attend. At one point Harriet Harman made some hostile remarks about the Government. I was embarrassed but did not react. Yet the next day it was reported in the *Sun* that I had enthusiastically applauded her anti-Government comments. It was quite untrue, and both Nick Brown and Peter Kellner, the journalist who was there, offered to support me in court if I took any action. But, of course, I couldn't.

Fiasco over Qualified Majority Voting

Confidence in the Prime Minister was slumping for many reasons quite unconnected with anything I was alleged to have said or done. On 30 January 1994 *The Sunday Times* quoted William Hill, the bookmaker, giving odds of 8-11 that Major would be removed before the Election, with Clarke the favourite to become PM (4-5), followed by Howard (4-1), Portillo (5-1), Hurd (10-1) and Heseltine (20-1). Manoeuvring by Ministers increased. Their actions were watched closely by the press, as with Michael Heseltine's evidence to the Scott Inquiry, to see whether they were furthering their leadership ambitions.

Backbenchers were increasingly bewildered and the splits becoming wider. Europhiles felt they had been let down. Eurosceptics felt the article in The *Economist* was encouraging but they were unconvinced it was Major's real view. Many felt he was merely trying to bolster his own position against potential challengers. His outburst against the 'bastards', Dick Body, MP for Holland and Boston, and the right, scarcely encouraged people to believe him. Then came the fiasco over Qualified

Majority Voting (QMV). It is difficult to over estimate the damage that the Prime Minister did to himself here. It was for many the defining moment.

A consequence of enlargement of the EU to include the Scandinavians and Austria was the need to rethink the weighted voting system and particularly what constituted a blocking minority. In an EU of 12 members, a blocking minority was 23 votes (the equivalent to one small and two large countries). What should be the new figure when the new members were admitted? The issue may seem abstruse, but it mattered profoundly in the European debate. Many Tory MPs suspected that enlargement would be used as an excuse to dilute the national veto and to make majority decisions ever more frequent.

On Tuesday 22 March the Prime Minister went on the offensive on the issue, and was cheered to the rafters by Tory MPs when he said, 'We are not going to do what the Labour Party do, which is to say "Yes" to everything that comes out of Europe, without any critical examination. But we will not be moved by phony threats to delay enlargement.'

The cheers got even louder when he attacked John Smith perhaps a little inelegantly as 'Monsieur Oui, the poodle of Brussels'. The Europhiles were dismayed – how did this square with being 'at the heart of Europe'? – but for the most part they were quiet in the Tea Room.

The Foreign Secretary was extremely exasperated, and according to some, threatened to resign. At the meeting of Foreign Ministers in Greece at the weekend he was unable to deliver anything that remotely matched up to Prime Minister's rhetoric. The best he could do was a formula that gave to any member state whose votes totalled between 23 and 26 the concession that the Council would do 'all in its power' within 'a reasonable time' to reach an acceptable solution. It was just verbiage and a humiliating rebuff, but the Prime Minister and Cabinet accepted it.

When the Prime Minister defended the deal in the House the next week, the contemptuous silence was palpable. There could not have been a greater contrast to the cheers the previous

Tuesday. Tony Marlow, the MP for Northampton North, stood up, pointed his finger at the Prime Minister and called on him to resign and make way 'for somebody else who can provide the Party and the country with direction and leadership'. He was saying what many others thought.

Speculation over a leadership election

Now some Europhiles were calling on the Prime Minister to go. *The Sunday Times* at the weekend had a poll of 100 Tory MPs out of which Heseltine emerged as the favourite to take over. On 3 April an NOP poll in the *Independent* increased Labour's lead to 24 points. Two other MPs publicly called on Major to stand down.

The confusion seemed to be spreading to the Cabinet. On the Sunday before the local elections Michael Portillo in an interview on GMTV blatantly departed from the agreed 'wait and see' line on the single currency and insisted that Britain would never join. This was, unsurprisingly, interpreted as positioning himself for the leadership election.

In the local elections on the following Thursday, 5 May, the Conservative vote fell to 27 per cent, the worst result of the century. As they did in 1995 and 1996, somehow the Prime Minister and the Chairman of the Party managed to present the results as better than they were. Among the more perceptive it did not increase confidence that the Party was facing up to reality.

The speculation continued that there would be a leadership election. John Carlisle, the MP for Luton, offered himself as a stalking horse on the *Today* programme, and added, 'If I do not force an Election others will'. In vain did Heseltine, Clarke and Portillo say they wouldn't stand. Everyone believed what they meant was that they would merely wait until a second round.

To force a leadership election required the public support of 10 per cent of the Parliamentary Party, or 34 MPs, as it then was. This obstacle had not existed during Mrs Thatcher's time as leader and had been put there quite deliberately to deter frivolous challenges. I certainly approved of the change in the rules. With so much grumbling about the leadership one might have thought it would be easy to find thirty-four MPs, but they were wary of falling foul of their constituency parties. It is one thing to sound off in the Tea Room, but quite another to declare publicly and be all over the newspapers.

It was after the QMV debacle that I began to feel that there might be a leadership election. There was certainly a lot of dissatisfaction with the PM on both sides of the European argument. I discussed the matter and what was to be done about it with Edward Leigh and, on the other wing of the Party, Peter Temple Morris. Peter and I consumed a whole bottle of Sancerre one summer evening in my office, but we came to no firm conclusion other than that we would keep in touch.

The *Sunday Telegraph* published a list with photographs of possible stalking horses, which included Kenneth Baker, John Biffen, Edward Leigh, an unknown Cabinet Minister and myself. There were reports that signatures for a leadership election were close to the magic number. As far as I know, there were no signatures at all, let alone 34, and this talk was largely press speculation, but discontent was growing. It might have developed into something.

The death of John Smith

On Thursday 12 May, John Smith died of a heart attack. I heard the news while waiting at Battersea Heliport to go off on a business trip with John Duffield. Unfortunately I had to go, so I missed a remarkable day in the House of Commons including the moving tributes that were paid to him. I felt bad about not being there. He and I had opposed each other in debates for four or five years, and we got on well.

We occasionally had a late-night drink together. He was often very outspoken about his colleagues when he was Shadow Chancellor, and once said, 'Never have anything to do with that bugger Robin Cook.' He wouldn't tell me why. Despite this I noticed Cook was his campaign manager when he stood for the leadership.

We enjoyed debating with each other. He once persuaded me to come up with him to Glasgow University, where his daughter was the Convenor of Debates, and we had a rerun of a debate we had had in the House; we had stayed up most of the night drinking and talking about politics. I remember John saying to me, 'Policies don't matter. Politics is about character.' That remark summed up both his strengths and his weakness. To make up for missing the tributes to him in the House I wrote an article in the *Sunday Telegraph* saying how much I admired him.

John Major made a particularly moving and generous speech. As PM he always did those occasions extremely well. His comments on the death of Anthony Eden were remarkable, considering he had never met him. I had observed that John Smith, at least while he was Shadow Chancellor, disliked John Major with a passion. Perhaps by the time both of them became leaders of their Party they had patched up their relationship. His hostility was based on some row over negotiations on the timing of parts of the Finance Bill when John Major was Chief Secretary. John Smith and Gordon Brown thought he had not behaved in a straightforward way. Gordon Brown felt even more strongly and insisted that in the rest of the negotiations he would never be alone in a room with John Major. Perhaps that was just the rivalry of two young pretenders. Whatever the reason, the remainder of the negotiations were left to me and Nick Brown.

It may seem strange or callous to say the death of John Smith helped Major, but at a critical moment it totally diverted attention away from the Conservative Party and on to the Labour Party. By the autumn Conservative MPs wanted to wait and see what the new Leader of the Labour Party would be like. Quite reasonably they felt it would be premature to think of a new leader until we had seen how his opposite number performed.

The breathing space also gave Major the opportunity to reshuffle his Cabinet. The chief change was that Jeremy Hanley became Party Chairman. I knew Jeremy well as he was my neighbour in Richmond and I liked him. I was, however, struck by the naivety of one of his first newspaper interviews, when he said that our exit from the ERM had been a great achievement and all that was wrong was that we had not presented it properly. Did he really believe that? I thought to myself, 'Here's another politician who thinks presentation is all. He will soon be in trouble.' Sad to say, Jeremy quickly discovered it wasn't quite so easy.

Election of Blair

On 21 July 1994 Tony Blair was elected Leader of the Labour Party. Although I did not foresee how far he would change the Labour Party, I thought he would be an even more difficult leader to defeat than John Smith.

I first met Tony Blair shortly after he had been elected to the House in 1983. I had heard a bit about him because I knew his opponent at Sedgefield, as did Michael Howard. Michael suggested we ought to invite Tony out because he was anxious to try to ascertain why on earth Tony, all appearances to the contrary, claimed to be a socialist. To my surprise Tony accepted an invitation to dinner at Michael's house. We all dined together with our wives and had a very enjoyable evening. At least we enjoyed it, and so did Tony; we weren't sure Cherie did. Later on we all agreed that the reason Tony had joined the Labour Party was Cherie. She was rather more severe then than she is today and also more left-wing than Tony.

I also had the opportunity to get to know him in 1987, when he was my opposite number while I was Financial Secretary to the Treasury. Together we handled the post-Election 1987 Finance Bill. I was very impressed by him, but he was quite a different politician from the one he is today. He was extremely well informed, rather detached, non-partisan and very interested in the detail. He was not at all interested in sound bites or coverage in the media, a taste he seems to have acquired since.

On 7 September Major made yet another apparently Eurosceptic speech at Leiden, where he talked of reducing the powers of the Commission and reform of Qualified Majority Voting system. His words on the latter point sounded particularly hollow after the climbdown earlier in the year. But he also attacked the idea of any inner core of the EU integrating faster than the rest of the EU. Major argued that this risked marginalising Britain. I suspect that this fear was one of Major's strongest convictions on Europe, and was one reason he had been so keen to join the ERM. Unfortunately at other times Major had said he favoured a 'multi-speed', 'multi-layered', 'multi-track' approach to Europe and many people felt confused both with the jargon and the apparent contradiction.

On 13 September the Chancellor increased base rates to 5.75 per cent up 0.5 per cent. Since I thought he had cut rates too much, I welcomed the increase. A number of MPs, such as David Shaw, the Vice-Chairman of the Backbench Finance Committee, were critical, so I issued a statement supporting the Chancellor and saying we were now 'shaping events, not responding to them'.

My Bournemouth speech: could we withdraw from the EU?

There was an air of gloom at the Party Conference at Bournemouth in October. The economy was undoubtedly improving but there was no improvement in the polls and people were increasingly talking about the 'voteless recovery '. The main problem for the 1994 Tory Conference was that it was inevitably overshadowed by the Labour Conference the week before, when Tony Blair delivered his first highly successful speech as Leader.

At Bournemouth I made a lengthy and, I hope, closely argued speech on Britain's relations with Europe to a fringe meeting. With the help of Rupert Darwall, Political Advisor in my last few days as Chancellor, I spent weeks preparing it. This speech reflected all the views I had gradually developed during Maastricht and at the Treasury. The speech was reported as advocating withdrawal from the EU, but it didn't quite do that. It simply attempted to show we could survive outside the EU, and that we were being sucked into a process of political union because we were so scared of being marginalised or losing influence.

I began by observing how different Europe was from the Europe we had been told about in 1972. Maastricht was a successful holding operation, 'a sort of Band-Aid', but there was no doubt where Europe was heading. 'We deceive the British people and we deceive ourselves if we claim that we are winning the argument in Europe . . . There is no argument in Europe. There is Britain's point of view, and then there is the rest of Europe . . . There was not a shred of evidence at Maastricht or since then that anyone accepts our view of Europe.'

I then went on to dispute the argument that the Prime Minister was increasingly using to justify his 'wait and see' policy. 'Because the subject is so difficult and so embarrassing it has been fashionable to say that a single currency will not happen. The Prime Minister has described moves towards a single currency as having all the potency of a primitive rain dance. With respect, I fear that this is wishful thinking. All the signs are that convergence conditions for a single currency are likely in the next few years to be attained in a core group of countries . . . and these countries remain as determined as ever to press ahead towards the creation of a federal Europe based on a single currency.'

Events certainly proved at least this point right. Unfortunately and puzzlingly, John Major refused to recognise that the single currency would happen right up to the point when it did. It was one of his greatest mistakes.

I also took issue with the Leiden speech. 'Recently we have been told that it would not be in our interest to have a two-speed Europe, with some countries integrating faster than others. But what have we to fear if others choose a different destination and different institutions for governing themselves? Far from fearing a two-speed Europe, we should positively welcome it, advocate it and warmly support it. In any case it is not two speeds at all. It is two completely different directions.'

I then moved on to make what might be thought an obvious point, but which I have learnt enrages some people: 'Tempting as it is to think in terms of black and white, Britain's membership of the European Union is not a question of absolutes, it is to do with the balance of cost and advantage of membership compared to the alternatives.' I argued that the modern global economy today was one of low tariffs, and that membership of the institution called the European Union was no longer necessary for access to

Europe's markets. GATT had changed all that. And Switzerland showed life outside the EU was possible. As long as we had market access, we would continue to get inward investment which came here for many reasons.

I went on somewhat provocatively, 'When we come to examine the advantages of our membership today of the European Union they are remarkably elusive. As a former Chancellor I can only say that I cannot pinpoint a single concrete advantage that unambiguously comes to this country because of our membership of the European Union.'

I then turned my attention to the political cost of our membership, which needed to be added to the budgetary and regulatory cost, and made a prediction: 'Lastly, and most importantly of all, our continued membership of Europe means that, reluctantly, we are participating in a process leading to a political goal that most politicians claim they do not want and which is certainly not wanted by the people of this country. Unless this central reality is acknowledged the issue of Europe will continue to dominate our politics and poison the Conservative Party for many years to come.' That certainly proved true.

In my conclusion I stopped short of saying that Britain should actually withdraw from Europe, but was content to underline the problem: 'I do not suggest that Britain should today unilaterally withdraw from Europe. But the issue may well return to the political agenda. Britain is on a collision course with its partners unless we can find a means of resolving the different aspirations. Perhaps in time it will be our partners who press the issue. For they understandably feel that we are frustrating their plans.'

I spoke for forty-five minutes to a packed room. All the TV channels were there and the audience complained that they could not see because of the crowd of journalists. At the end of the speech I was given enthusiastic and prolonged applause.

The reaction elsewhere in the Conference was bitterly hostile. That evening I went to a party given by Maurice Saatchi. As ever the perfect host, he welcomed me. However, the next person I saw was David Cameron, my former special advisor at the Treasury, who cut me dead. Like him, most people at the party didn't want to talk to me, though Michael Heseltine, his face completely expressionless, winked at me across the room as if to say, 'I know what you are experiencing now.'

More unexpected was the reaction of the Eurosceptics, who were furious. Bill Cash attacked me on television for going too far. The real cause of their anger was that the publicity for the speech on TV that night completely wiped out the coverage of the European Foundation's meeting with Jimmy Goldsmith.

The next day the press gave the speech huge coverage and it made the headlines in *The Times*. The reason for the speech's impact was that it said what many people knew to be true and it came from an ex-Chancellor. It made its case calmly without any xenophobia, unlike one Eurosceptic meeting at the conference which showed a film of German tanks and Panzers. It was analytical and logical. That is why it caused such outrage.

One consequence of the Bournemouth speech was that the press assumed that I would stand at some point against Major in a leadership election. That was not why I had made the speech, but from then on it became increasingly difficult to dampen down the press speculation. And I have to confess that I made no attempt to do that. I was quite content to see how events developed.

The House returns: a scandal and a climb down over Post Office privatisation

When the House came back the Government was in trouble almost immediately. A story appeared in the *Guardian* that Neil Hamilton and Tim Smith had taken money to ask questions on behalf of a lobbying company. Smith resigned but Hamilton issued a libel writ. At first Major supported Hamilton and dismissed the allegations as unfounded. On Tuesday 25 October Hamilton was told by Michael Heseltine and Richard Ryder that he ought to resign, which he did. There was a feeling among backbenchers that it was wrong that the Prime Minster should have refused to see Hamilton before he resigned. Yet again the Prime Minister had initially supported a Minister then pushed him out under media pressure.

Next came a row on Post Office privatisation. As I have

already described, I was an enthusiast, as was Michael Heseltine, and after my departure he had continued to push the idea. He wanted to get Post Office privatisation included in the programme for the 1994/95 session and had looked at various options, such as retaining in public ownership the counter division, which ran the sub-post offices. On 19 May the issue had been considered before a Cabinet Committee and Heseltine made a statement launching a consultative Green Paper, but without a firm commitment. The Green Paper favoured selling 51 per cent of the Royal Mail and Parcel Force.

Major was nervous but gave Heseltine five months to show whether he could win over support on the backbenches. It was a typical Major compromise, and cynics suggested that Heseltine was being given enough rope to hang himself. Certainly, No. 10 were suspicious about Heseltine's motives and appeared to suspect he was seeking to advance himself by currying favour with the right.

On 3 November, after a long Cabinet discussion, the Government finally decided to shelve the whole idea of privatisation. The Prime Minister expressed the view that there was nothing for which the Government had to apologise. Consultation had merely revealed that there was not a Parliamentary majority for privatisation. But what sort of leadership was this? Who was governing?

The Cabinet climbdown on the Post Office again intensified talk of a leadership challenge, but this was largely in the press. The election of Blair still made MPs cautious about a leadership election this year and any contest had to come within fourteen days of the new session, which was to begin on 16 November, so newspaper speculation up to that date was guaranteed.

Another Euro rebellion

One of the measures in the Queen's Speech was the European Community (Finance) Bill dealing with Britain's increased contribution to the European Budget, which John Major and I had negotiated at Edinburgh. The Prime Minister said that the Bill was 'inescapably a matter of confidence'. The experience over Maastricht had caused some Cabinet Ministers, particularly Kenneth Clarke, to think it would be a good idea to threaten to call a General Election and put pressure on potential rebels. Many of them, like Tony Marlow, had narrow majorities, so it was thought they might back off. Unfortunately the tactic backfired.

The press wondered whether, if the Government were defeated, only the Prime Minister would resign or whether the whole Government would have to go? However in Cabinet on Thursday 24 November Major secured agreement that the passage of this Bill 'in all its essentials' was to be an issue of confidence. This meant if it was defeated there would be a General Election.

It was an incredible and ridiculous threat from a Government trailing so badly in the polls. And it was unnecessary. It was greeted with derision. The *Daily Mail* described it as 'a mass Cabinet suicide pact': 'Would they . . . could they . . . really go through with it? Would each and every senior member of this cult (sorry, Government) waddle tamely like a turkey towards the Christmas oven?'

The weekend before the vote there were the predictable newspaper stories that I was going to challenge John Major and that Members prepared to sign a leadership challenge were estimated to be between 25 and 30, according to them, so far tantalisingly short of the required number of 34.

On Sunday 27 November Michael Howard, my oldest friend, launched a vigorous attack on me on TV, and said I would 'cut a ridiculous figure' if I stood against John Major. That might have been true, but I was somewhat startled, and Rosemary was particularly upset. Sandra Howard told Rosemary, 'It's just politics. It isn't worth destroying a friendship.' I never discussed the matter with Michael. I understood that he was in the Government and had to be loyal to Major. A few weeks later, on *Any Questions*, I defended Michael strongly against criticism of him as Home Secretary.

Enoch Powell once doubted that such a thing as real friendship is possible in politics. I don't agree. It is true that personal rivalry and differences of view can strain the best friendship. Politics is a cruelly competitive business and these pressures increase in the higher reaches, yet friendship is one of its great gifts, and it is important not to let circumstances separate one permanently from one's friends. It is also important in politics to be able to take some pleasure in the success of others.

The debate took place on Monday 28 November. Although I had made clear my intention to support the Government, I spoke in the debate and began by saying, 'I am told by those who know more about it than I do that the issuing of suicide threats is a classic cry for help. It is in that spirit that I wish to help the Government tonight. In such cases the key is to keep the potential victim talking to prevent his mind from turning to any untoward action.' The loud laughter this provoked was rather more on the Labour side than on ours, but the Conservatives need not have worried: I had no intention of attacking the Government.

I argued that the true scale of the Brussels burden on the British economy was being hidden from the public, and that an accurate measurement of the cost was the gross, not the net, payments that the UK makes to the European Union budget. On this basis we were contributing £8 billion in 1996/97, rather than the net figure of £5 billion put forward by the Treasury. I took the opportunity to describe the difficulties I had experienced in trying to persuade the European Union to take the issue of fraud seriously. On one occasion I had attempted to introduce a discussion on fraud and other Finance Ministers had simply refused to participate. Pierre Bérégovoy just sat reading *Le Monde*.

In fact the Government won the vote quite easily with a majority of 27, but eight Tories refused to vote with the Government and it was announced that the Whip would be withdrawn from them. Sir Richard Body then later resigned the Whip in sympathy with these eight MPs.

The withdrawal of the Whip was a foolish move, because it made martyrs of the rebels and further weakened the Government's position in the House of Commons, when it was already weak enough. It could achieve absolutely nothing. From the day the Whip was removed the Press began to speculate when it would be restored. According to some, Richard Ryder had strongly opposed its removal but Kenneth Clarke had insisted on it.

One consequence of the removal of the Whip was that it ruled

out a leadership contest. The Whipless members no longer
counted as Members of the Conservative Parliamentary Party, so
were unable to add their names to any demand for an election.
Whether this was part of the thinking behind the Government's
move, I don't know.

So the deadline for the leadership challenge, Wednesday 30
November, came and went. Newspapers suggested that there was
a list of about twenty-five names of Members prepared to support
an election, but there was no list.

The Budget and a defeat on VAT

The deadline for a leadership election came the day after the
Budget, which was intended as a low-key affair. Taxes were marginally reduced. The greater than forecast fall in inflation allowed
future spending to be cut by £8 billion. We did now seem to have
created something of a virtuous circle. The recovery was indisputably strong – in the year to the third quarter of 1994 the
economy had grown by over 4 per cent. I certainly envied Ken
being able to preside over such growth. At the same time inflation
continued to fall to record new lows. Surely, backbenchers
thought, this golden scenario must lead to some political recovery.

In spite of the improving economic news, Ken Clarke's personal
popularity fell sharply in 1994. According to a MORI Poll asking
the question, 'How satisfied or dissatisfied are you with the way
the Chancellor of the Exchequer is doing his job?' 17 per cent said
they were satisfied, and 70 per cent said they were dissatisfied.
Oddly, if the poll was to be believed this was a marginally worse
result than the same question asked in 1993 about me.

The Government's agonies in 1994 were not yet over. They
had to face a vote on the second stage of the increase in VAT on
fuel and power. The increase from 8 per cent to the full 17.5 per
cent had already been approved by the House, but for some
reason the Government conceded a second vote. The Whips
warned Ken Clarke that he was in danger of losing. To me, as an
outsider, if sometimes looked as though he was deliberately inviting defeat by the provocativeness of some of his comments. I very

much hoped that was not so. However unpopular it was to have VAT on fuel and power, we wouldn't gain any respect simply by allowing ourselves to be defeated in the House.

On Tuesday 6 December the vote duly took place and the Government was defeated by 319 votes to 311. So VAT on fuel and power remained at the anomalous rate of 8 per cent. The madness of withdrawing the Whip was underlined by the votes of the Whipless MPs: 3 voted against and 5 abstained.

I was deeply depressed and appalled. This was an issue of confidence and a far more important vote than that on the European Community (Finance) Bill. Here was a Government unable to get a key part of its own taxation programme approved by its supporters in the House of Commons. I could not recall when anything like this had happened before.

So 1994 ended with Major still in office, but the Government in a bigger mess than ever.

18

A Vote Against My Party and a Leadership Election

Nowadays most people die of a sort of creeping common sense and discover when it is too late that the only thing one never regrets are one's mistakes.

Oscar Wilde

Major dealt with the Whipless MPs much as he dealt with the IRA. There were threats one moment, the next hints of concessions. There was no consistency, no purpose. It reminded one of Max Beerbohm's description of his tailor making a final demand for payment: 'On his knees, but shaking his fist.'

On Sunday 9 January 1995, on *Breakfast with Frost* Major made some conciliatory remarks towards the Whipless MPs, hoping they would be readmitted to the Party in the weeks ahead. This was only one month after the Whip had been withdrawn. What had been the point of this gesture? Major also talked on the programme about blocking new powers for the European Parliament or any extension of QMV. Many Conservative MPs must have wondered, 'Haven't we heard that before?'

My CIB speech at Oxford

On 17 February I spoke at a meeting of the student branch of the Campaign for an Independent Britain in Oxford. I am always amused when people claim that the young are more enthusiastic for the European Union and the single currency. That is not my experience. I have found the young, because they travel widely, including beyond Europe, have a global view and a suspicion of grand designs for Europe. This meeting demonstrated it yet again.

The meeting was held in the Gladstone Room at the Oxford Union. With its William Morris wallpaper and ceilings, it was a wonderful setting. The room was packed, with many undergraduates also upstairs in the galleries.

I began by referring to my speech in Bournemouth and outlined the reaction. I had been promised a reply, and the Government had said it would embark on a campaign to spell out the advantages of the European Union. But there had been a long silence: 'Last month, the Foreign Secretary replied by releasing an article entitled "The European Union: Why We Are Members". Instead of analysing the costs as well as the benefits of Britain's membership, remarkably the document omitted any reference to the cost at all, either the financial costs or the political costs in terms of the loss of Britain's ability to govern itself. So all the supposed benefits come free – apart, that is, from the sweat on the Foreign Secretary's brow in trying to make the EU work better. This must be the bargain of the century.'

What were the economic arguments for our membership of the European Union? The biggest benefit was alleged to be increased exports, and the implication was that living standards would be lower had we remained outside the EU. But our exports to the European Union had not grown faster than non-EU members. In 1983 Japan's exports to the EU were half the value of Britain's. Ten years later, the proportion had risen to 75 per cent. Between 1983 and 1993, Britain's exports to Europe had grown more slowly than those of Switzerland, Sweden, Japan and the United States, none of them members of the European Union. The fastest growth in exports to the European Union had occurred for Britain during the ten years before we joined. I added: 'A visitor from Mars would find it remarkably difficult to guess correctly from the trade statistics when Britain became a member of the EU or indeed to say whether Britain was a member of the EU at all.'

On the single currency the main problem was how the economy would adjust. 'Before we abolish the pound we ought to ask ourselves: in the absence of flexible exchange rates and domestic interest rates, how are individual economies to adjust to differences in growth, efficiency and unforeseen circumstances? The break-up of the ERM was caused by currency turbulence, which itself was caused by the unexpected effects of German reunification. The unexpected doesn't stop happening because currencies have been abolished.'

But the main objections to monetary union were not economic but political: 'You cannot make a monetary union of the type envisaged in the Maastricht Treaty without political controls . . . The intent and purpose of the Maastricht Treaty is clear. It is to bind the members tightly together, to deepen European political integration.'

The key question surely was: 'When does a state cease to be a sovereign state? . . . There comes a point when if a state has surrendered much of its powers to make its own laws, much of its powers to determine its own taxation, much of its powers to control immigration, and the right to control its own monetary policy then that state has ceased to be a sovereign state. It is difficult to identify the precise moment this happens when those who drive the process will not admit what is happening.'

The speech was well received by the undergraduates and covered widely on the main news bulletins that night and in the papers the next morning. I felt that it was still possible for me to have an influence in the debate, both nationally and in the Conservative Party, and I was determined to make my views heard on this most crucial of all political issues.

Divisions at the top

The economy continued to do well. Unemployment was now falling month by month and real incomes were beginning to pick up. It didn't appear to be making much difference to the Tory Party's popularity, though in the MORI poll at the end of January there was a five-point rise in Tory popularity to the highest level since May 1994. There was still a huge Labour lead, but 'the green shoots' of political recovery were appearing.

On 22 January Clarke repeated his support for the single currency and for Britain to be at the heart of Europe. On 9 February he again returned to the issue and insisted that it was possible to have monetary union without political union, although his example of Ireland and Britain between 1923 and 1972 hardly seemed persuasive. The next day Portillo contradicted Clarke and then Jonathan Aitken, Clarke's new deputy, said that he would wait 'an eternity' before he would ever support a single currency.

It became untidier and untidier. Every time the Prime Minister sounded Eurosceptic, Clarke reasserted his Europhile position. Rumours reached me from the Treasury that relations between the Chancellor and the Prime Minister were no different from how they had been between myself and the Prime Minister. Clarke apparently felt himself to be the subject of adverse briefing, and was increasingly fed up with the indecisiveness.

Clarke became much less popular with backbenchers, who felt he was standing between the Party and a change of policy. On one occasion the PM went to a dining group of MPs where they all suggested to him that the PM should remove the Chancellor. He replied by asking them, 'Do you really think I could do that?'

I vote against the Government

On 1 March there was a Labour motion of no confidence in the Government's European policy. No doubt the Labour Party's intention was to expose another split in the Conservative Party, but neither they nor I quite anticipated what happened.

I wanted to pinpoint the issue that to me was at the heart of the argument about the single currency. It seemed clear that a single currency must inevitably lead to increasing harmonisation of taxation and spending and, once this happened, to the creation of a European Government and a European state. There were many speeches by Kohl and other European politicians to this effect. I also knew that even if it was theoretically possible to imagine a single currency without a single government, as Ken Clarke sought to argue, the European Commission would use the existence of a single currency to argue for more and more integration.

I could never understand why, with the exception of Ken Clarke, neither the Government nor the Labour Party ever addressed this issue. I would have been more content if the Government had said that views such as mine were wrong and indicated why they were wrong, but the issue was always avoided and the argument was always simply about whether the single currency could work or not.

I wanted to be even-handed in the debate, so I made a point of interrupting Blair, but not very effectively. I then put to Major the question that I really wanted to ask: 'Does my Rt Hon. friend agree with Paul Volcker, the former Chairman of the American Federal Reserve Board, and my Rt Hon. friend Lord Lawson of Blaby that monetary union inevitably means political union, or does he agree with the Chancellor of the Exchequer that it is possible to envisage monetary union without political union?'

The PM replied, 'No I do not,' which provoked mirth. 'With one important qualification: I believe that it is possible to move forward to monetary union without necessarily moving forward to political union, but the qualification depends on the nature and style of monetary union and I will deal with that in a moment.' The PM didn't, as far as I could see, return to the issue. To this day I do not know what his reply to me was meant to mean. I didn't know what he intended by 'with one important qualification'. As *The Times* wrote the next day, 'Observers were left none the wiser about what he personally believed.' This was hardly satisfactory and with such blatant evasion I thought that perhaps I might put the question again in the wind-up speech that would conclude the debate.

The wind-up was done by Douglas Hurd at 9 p.m. The House was so packed I couldn't find a seat on my usual bench and had to sit on the front bench below the gangway, which is nonetheless also for backbenchers. It was so crowded I was almost sitting on the knee of James Hill, the burly MP for Southampton.

Again, I interrupted, this time Douglas: 'Will my Rt Hon. Friend address the question that I put to the Prime Minister earlier, to which I do not believe he gave a clear answer? I asked whether the Government believe that monetary union will lead to political union, or whether they believe, as Lord Lawson said the other day, that one cannot have one without the other? I believe that this is the issue of principle. It is two years since we began negotiations on the Maastricht Treaty and that is an issue of principle, not of timing.'

Douglas replied, 'My Rt Hon. Friend is one of the greatest experts on the subject because, with my Rt Hon. Friend the Prime Minister, he negotiated the opt-out. I have always admired the skill with which they both did that. I was sitting in admiration in another room at the time.'

There was loud laughter at this elegant and condescending put-down, as Douglas no doubt intended. He then said the PM had answered my question and went on to another point. One MP said that he saw me physically shake with anger. To me it seemed that there was no way I could say I had 'confidence' in the Government's policy. I felt anything but confidence. I was angry that such an important question as whether or not Britain could exist as an independent, self-governing country was not regarded as legitimate. The fact that Douglas chose to dodge the question so clearly confirmed to me how important a matter it was.

At 10 p.m. when the division bell rang, I rose and walked straight into the Labour lobby. It was entirely spontaneous. Later No. 10 were to brief the press that it was all carefully premeditated. A story appeared that I had announced at the Bulgarian Embassy the night before my intention to vote against the Government. I have never been in the Bulgarian Embassy in my life.

Another story reported that I was drunk. I wasn't drunk, but I might as well have been, because I didn't think and failed to appreciate the enormity of what I was doing. I was just angry.

Later, a friend asked me why I had voted with Labour and said I should have abstained. He was probably right. I didn't see myself as voting with Labour. I had no time for their policy and I voted against their amendment to the motion on a second vote. I was in the lobby with them simply because in all honesty I couldn't pretend any longer I had confidence in the Government's policy. I had no confidence whatsoever in the Government's endless vacillation and evasion, which to my mind amounted to dishonesty.

If I didn't realise what I had done, I soon discovered when I arrived home. Although it was after midnight the house was surrounded by TV cameras. Rosemary was unaware of what was happening and was fast asleep. I woke her up with the words, 'I have really done it this time.'

The next day most of the newspapers covered my vote on the front page. Most put my action down to revenge and bitterness. *The Times* had a cartoon of me playing the bagpipes and wearing a kilt over a grave stone inscribed 'The Political Career of Norman Lamont 1972–1995 RIP'. Simon Heffer drew attention to my need to find a new constituency and wrote what many others did – that no constituency would ever choose me now. The *Daily Mail* referred to the peerage I would now never get. In an elegant phrase, Tristan Garel-Jones said that I had committed 'a rather inelegant political suicide'.

The Times had an editorial entitled 'Lamont votes Labour' with a subheading 'Pique, precision and further proof of Tory decay'. The article said that I was less likely to be selected as a candidate now, but went on: 'In his own days of leisure Mr Lamont has pondered as well as plotted. He has sensed the drift in policy, heard the arguments that it will somehow be all right on the night, weighed up the man in Downing Street, and decided that it will not be all right. His excuse for rebelling is that his interventions during the debate were not answered. His reasoning was that they could not be answered.' That was a not unfair summary of my views, though my decision on the vote was not calculated.

Looking back, that vote probably did end my career in the House of Commons. But I have never for one moment regretted voting as I did. The questions I asked the PM and Douglas Hurd were the heart of the matter, and increasingly became the main issue. The Conservative Party's refusal to face them was the source of all its troubles.

However, my immediate reaction was that I was going to prove all the pundits and newspapers wrong. I decided I would buy the cartoon in *The Times*, then on second thoughts I decided I would buy it only after I had found another seat and won it at the next General Election. So I never did buy it.

The first telephone call I received that morning was from David Hart. 'Congratulations. Now you must go for it,' his voice boomed out. His view was that now I had grasped the nettle and must challenge Major. He had no idea of the spontaneity of my action. Then I had other calls from people such as Godfrey Barker of the *Daily Telegraph* saying much the same thing. The newspapers made it clear to me that by my action I had placed myself, whether I intended it or not, in a situation where I was now expected to challenge Major.

I certainly experienced again what it was like to be cold-shouldered by colleagues. A number cut me dead in the lobby or worse. When I went into the Smoking Room, the younger MPs were careful to sit at the other end of the room in order to avoid being seen talking to me. I did not blame them. But others secretly crept up to me when no one was looking and said, 'Well done, now go for it.'

On 24 April the Whipless MPs were readmitted to the Party, but they returned without any conditions and presented themselves as victors at a press conference. When Blair said at Prime Minister's Questions, 'I lead my Party, he follows his', it was seen by millions in the evening news and must have done the PM great damage.

Once again on 4 May the local election results were catastrophic. The Tory share of the vote was 25 per cent. When it first came on television the percentage of the vote was estimated to be somewhat higher and Tory Central Office, as it always did, managed to add another point or so onto that figure, so that in the morning newspapers the full extent of Tory unpopularity was not really apparent. Even so, no one could deny that the Party had lost over 2,000 seats while Labour gained over 800 and the Liberal Democrats nearly 500. Control was lost in many Tory strongholds and MPs in what had hitherto been considered safe seats became worried. For all the Central Office talk there just was no real sign of recovery.

In response on 12 May the Prime Minister launched a 'consultation exercise' to try to regain the initiative. Labour said it was the Conservative Party's fifth 'fight back' and fourteenth relaunch. The Prime Minister announced that Ministers were going to tour the country, consulting activists over what should be in the Conservative Manifesto for the next Election. To many it merely left an impression that the Government had no ideas of its own any longer.

The Prime Minister landed in further trouble with backbenchers in his handling of the Nolan Report on Members' outside interests. Many thought it unnecessary to set up the Committee in the first place and that it was just another example of the Prime Minister's inability to make decisions. I did not agree with them at all, but Tory MPs were angry that, having had to accept a staging of pay increases, they would also have curbs on their business activities outside Parliament. They resented the implication that they were all crooks. Ted Heath, for the first time in years, was cheered by his own side when he said, 'We have now reached a stage when every man and woman in this House is an object of suspicion.' In reply Major was unable to express any views and lamely said he wanted to listen again to the House before he came to a conclusion.

On 8–11 June I attended the Bilderberg Conference at Birgenstock in Switzerland. Peter Carrington, Dick Holbrooke, Conrad Black and Henry Kissinger were there. The latter made his sympathy for Euroscepticism quite clear to me. Conrad kept urging me to stand in a Leadership Election. I think he wanted Michael Portillo to become Leader, but he was keen for me to open up the process, and promised me that the *Daily Telegraph* would support me if I did so. We continued talking about the subject until about 3 a.m. consuming rather a lot of alcohol. Eventually, according to Conrad, I said I was prepared to go on discussing the matter, but not if he continued to serve me this Swiss wine, about which, he claimed, I made an unrepeatable comment. And so we left it.

PM's meeting with the Fresh Start Group

On 13 June there was a meeting between the Prime Minister and Michael Spicer's Fresh Start Group of Eurosceptic backbench MPs. This was an unusual happening, which had been arranged by Michael and Peter Tapsell, who were anxious to make a positive response to the Prime Minister's apparent increasing Euroscepticism and see whether it was possible to sort out some of the difficulties and find common ground. Unfortunately, the meeting was a disaster.

The Prime Minister was invited to speak, which he did for over ten minutes, but his tone was not quite right. He didn't address the real questions that concerned MPs and merely repeated the arguments he used regularly in the House about the benefits of the opt-out. There were 'hear hears' when Ivan Lawrence said that if we didn't firm up our line on the single currency the Party would not be around to make a decision in 1999 because it would be out of office. Others, like John Townend, Iain Duncan-Smith and Bernard Jenkin, said much the same.

Asked whether he intended to rejoin the ERM, the Prime Minister turned to me and, rather oddly I thought, said that he did not want to have all the pain of the ERM all over again, as he was sure 'Norman would agree'. Some people thought this was a rather cheap jibe, although it didn't strike me as that. I just couldn't see its relevance or logic. He was saying we wouldn't join the ERM again because it might lumber us with inappropriate policies, and yet we might join EMU, which was even more inflexible and also irreversible.

I only intervened to say that all of us knew that the Prime Minister had a very difficult task, but when we had negotiated the opt-out in 1991 it had never occurred to me that we could go into the next Election without having decided whether to use it or not. We had to make a decision some time and couldn't keep putting it off.

But Major got into further problems when, in exasperation at the questions, he snapped that he didn't believe that the public cared much about Europe anyway. The atmosphere changed immediately and the Prime Minister was heckled and interrupted. It was highly embarrassing.

I played little part in the meeting, and had had nothing to do with it being set up. At one point I thought perhaps I would not attend. Needless to say, No. 10 briefed the newspapers and television that I had been one of the leaders of the barracking. As a matter of fact I remonstrated with Bernard Jenkin after the meeting for what I thought was his shockingly discourteous manner towards the Prime Minister.

This meeting probably made a leadership contest inevitable. Many of those who attended were both unimpressed and angry and felt there ought to be an election. What they did not realise was that the PM also drew the same conclusion from the meeting.

Major calls leadership election

In June, John Carlisle, MP for Luton North, declared to the *Today* programme that 'high noon for the Prime Minister is probably approaching in days now rather than weeks'. A few days later Clarke fired back by calling the Eurosceptics 'Right-wing xenophobes'.

Rumours began to circulate that the PM himself would call a contest and put himself up for re-election. When I first heard them I did not believe he would have the courage to do that. I was wrong.

On Thursday 22 June he called the press to the Rose Garden in Downing Street and announced he was resigning as Leader of the Party. I had never heard of the Rose Garden in Downing Street. Every Prime Minister becomes more presidential than the last, but this seemed an unusually self-conscious imitation of the White House.

The first rumours in the House of Commons about the impending announcement had been confused. Some thought that Major was actually resigning as Prime Minister. In fact it was never clear to me how constitutionally he could resign as Leader of the Party and remain PM. Did not his position as PM depend upon his being Leader of the Conservative Party?

That afternoon there was a special meeting of the 1922 Committee at which Marcus Fox read out a letter he had received from the Prime Minister. The next day one Major supporter was quoted as saying that as Marcus spoke I turned 'white as a sheet'. It hardly seems likely – I have quite a pale enough face already – but no doubt Major's team wanted to give the impression that they had wrong-footed the opposition and myself. To some extent they had.

In fact my feelings were of excitement at the events now unfolding. After my vote against the Government, No. 10 assumed that I would be the candidate, although I had not in fact made a final decision. In one sense I was keen to do so. I had tried in my speeches over the previous two years to develop my arguments about Europe and the single currency. I would have enjoyed developing those themes and I knew that Major, Clarke and Heseltine would have difficulty in replying to them. As they had repeatedly shown in the House, their arguments were flimsy.

I knew I would get some editorial support from the broadsheets like *The Times* and the *Daily Telegraph*, who would relish the intellectual argument and support me, if only to prepare the way for Portillo. The question was whether I would even get sufficient support to enable the contest to be opened up. It was quite probable that I would only get around 15 or, if I was lucky, 20 votes and that would be the end of the matter But what if there were a large number of abstentions? Who knows? It was incalculable, and it might have been a gamble worth taking.

If I had stood I would have made it clear that I was doing so only on the basis that I wanted another candidate to present himself in the next round. I also had a more fundamental doubt. If the Prime Minister were forced out of office, could the Conservative Party ever reunite afterwards? On the other hand, I felt Major's ineffective leadership and vacillation were themselves destabilising the Party.

My family were very much against it. Rosemary was cross that I had not ruled the idea out earlier. She was quite right. I had let the speculation in newspapers grow, without even attempting to dampen it down. But Rosemary and the children felt I would be subjected to a very personal campaign, no matter how much I tried to concentrate on the issues. They had all had enough of the intrusions of the tabloids and wanted no more. From what I have learned of the campaign that Central Office prepared against me, their fears were well grounded.

However, I felt I probably had no option. My views about the Prime Minister's leadership were well known, although often exaggerated by the media. I had deployed many new arguments on Europe. Not to stand would make me look cowardly and 'willing to wound, but not to strike'.

At the 1922 Meeting I was sitting next to George Gardiner, who had on many occasions pressed me to stand against Major. He was a Portillo supporter but wanted me to stand first. Immediately the meeting was over I said to him that we must speak. We agreed to meet in a room just off Westminster Hall but to make our ways there separately. I went down the stairs from the Upper Committee Corridor, through the Central Lobby, down the stairs and through Westminster Hall. When I arrived I was amazed to find TV crews in the corridor outside the very room in which we had chosen to meet. I told them to disappear. It is strictly forbidden for TV crews to wander round the House of Commons, but that day was the nearest thing to bedlam that I will ever experience.

I sat down and said to George, 'I would like you to be one of my proposers.' To my surprise George said that he couldn't possibly do that because his constituency would not like it. I was taken aback at his loss of nerve. As events turned out it was a shrewd assessment of his own position because he was later to find himself in serious trouble. But I was surprised, because he had repeatedly urged me to stand. At the time I considered if George was not prepared to stand up publicly it would be very difficult to find anyone who would.

Very soon, several of the Eurosceptics said they were quite prepared to act as proposers or seconders. One possibly unintended consequence of the Prime Minister's announcement was that it was no longer necessary to enlist the support of thirty-four MPs. Since Major had called the Election, under the rules all that was necessary now was a proposer and a seconder. There were press reports that the Prime Minister was annoyed when he discovered this, since No. 10 had not worked it out. Apparently some had hoped that, because of the inevitable difficulty of collecting public signatures from 10 per cent of the Parliamentary Party, there might be no opponent for Major.

That evening Edward Leigh and I went for a drink on the Terrace. We felt in rather an expansive mood and I ordered a bottle of champagne. Later on, back home I was astonished when I turned on the news to see a film of Edward and myself sitting there. Again, it is strictly forbidden to film on the Terrace without the Speaker's permission. An enterprising camera crew had filmed us several hundred yards away from the other side of the river! It was a reminder how careful one had to be.

When I returned to Kensington Park Road the house was again under siege from the press and it remained continuously so for the next few days. I decided to think further about the whole matter, and at this stage to say absolutely nothing. But it was difficult because every time I popped over the road to our Kashmiri newsagent to get a paper or some cigars, I was followed by an army of TV crews and reporters. My creased, cherry summer jacket, which I wore at weekends, became too familiar a sight to millions of people. Friends rudely said I needed a new one, but I was fond of it, even if it wasn't up to New Labour standards.

Redwood enters the lists

Over the weekend newspapers noted that John Redwood, Secretary of State for Wales, was the only Cabinet Minister who had not voiced his backing for the Prime Minister. There was some disagreement whether this was significant. He had managed to absent himself from the Cabinet Meeting at which Ministers had pledged themselves to support Major. An ambiguous statement had been made on his behalf by an aide, and it was claimed he was shocked at the decision of the Prime Minister to call an election and also offended by the failure to consult him.

Immediately I read these reports I suspected he would stand. There was one other interesting development over the weekend. Barry Field, the relatively unknown MP for the Isle of Wight, announced he intended to stand as a stalking horse. This puzzled me, and it took me time to work out its significance.

Over the weekend I received a telephone call from Roger
Knapman, the MP for Stroud, who strongly hinted to me at that
Redwood was going to declare. I had been trying to contact him
and said no one could find him. Knapman immediately told me
that he was in touch with Redwood and gave me a telephone
number. I said that I thought it would be better for me to meet
John at the House of Commons early next week.

I decided to telephone Michael Portillo. From the day of
Major's announcement it seemed to me far better if he stood
against Major. In my view Portillo, though young and sometimes
alarmingly ambitious, was a highly able politician who would
have been a credible candidate. He had belief and great intelligence. If he had boldly declared himself a candidate in round one
he would put himself ahead of all the other possible candidates.
By holding back he was letting Redwood steal a move on him.
Furthermore, I had doubts whether the PM could be unseated by
anyone other than a real candidate. My standing as a stalking
horse would be purely tactical.

I tried as hard as I could to persuade him, but he was adamant
he would not do so, although he made it clear he would stand in
a second round. I said that if I stood or Redwood stood, the
likelihood was that we would not receive sufficient votes to force
Major to resign, so the Prime Minister would then simply say that
he had challenged us and had won. Even if the Prime Minister
only won by 10 votes, he had every right to say that he had settled
it. Michael said that Cabinet Ministers, including himself, would
refuse to serve under Major. He added, 'One way or the other I
am convinced that this is the end of Major.'

Months later over lunch Michael somewhat ruefully observed
to me 'I may never fly so close to the sun again.' He also rather
stupidly said to me 'You should have stood, but you bottled out.'
There was another person who 'bottled out'.

Now it was obvious Redwood was going to stand I concluded
that there was no point in my thinking any longer about the
matter. I felt relief that I had narrowly escaped from what might
have been a unpleasant experience, much as I would have enjoyed
putting the questions on Europe that the Government never
addressed and could not answer.

I issued no press statements, but the following Monday went to the House of Commons to John Redwood's room. He was still using his office on the Ministerial Corridor, where I was ushered into the room by Roger Knapman. Redwood was not yet there but there was much activity. Young men with clipboards came into the room, left yellow stickers on the desk, and picked up phones. They were well organised. What amused me was the air of self-importance; they already seemed to be assuming that they were working for the next leader of the Conservative Party. Then John arrived. He looked different and his whole bearing seemed to have altered. He told me of his decision together with one or two titbits about what had happened so far. He did not ask me whether I was going to stand but simply assumed that I wouldn't. I volunteered that he would be a much more effective candidate than I, and I would be happy to help in any way I could.

The campaign

I realised that the Redwood Campaign had been planned a long time ago, possibly many months previously. I did not believe all this talk that Redwood had been shocked by Major's decision to hold an election. He saw that MPs were dissatisfied and whoever went for it might win. The previous year Roger Knapman had hinted to me that a Cabinet Minister was planning to resign and stand against Major. He was obviously close to Redwood and was in on the campaign from the very first. Barry Field, who had by the Monday withdrawn from the contest, was also a close friend of David Evans, MP for Welwyn, who was Redwood's PPS. It was clear that Field had merely announced his 'candidature' to pre-empt me or any one else from declaring.

John Redwood's leadership campaign was organised differently from others in which I have been involved. Initially he was less interested in identifying individual MPs as supporters and simply wanted to appeal via speeches and articles to 'the electorate'. He seemed to think that it was best done via the media rather than by picking up the telephone or meeting people. As in a General Election, he held a press conference on a different theme every day, although the themes were thin. Amazingly, he produced for MPs a glossy leaflet like a General Election address with a picture of himself on the cover. Its prose style and intellectual level were about the same as a leaflet to be pushed through voters' letterboxes. I was surprised he thought this was fitting for MPs.

But there was an undeniable enthusiasm in his campaign. There were lots of young people. Every day more and more people phoned in wanting to help because they were disillusioned with the leadership or wanted the single currency issue resolved. Individual constituencies showed their support for him, sometimes even when their MPs did not.

I was concerned that John wasn't concentrating enough on direct conversations with individual MPs. I told him that initially John Major had made exactly the same mistake in 1990, and had been equally reluctant to get down to what mattered: methodical telephoning. John took the point and soon we had teams organised to find telephone numbers and make appointments with MPs. I told John and David Evans everything I could remember that was remotely useful from John Major's 1990 campaign. At one point there was a suggestion that I should become the Campaign Manager, but I didn't want to do that again. I had the impression that John's second leadership campaign in 1997 was much better organised and that he learnt a lot from this first attempt.

The campaign was launched on the Monday afternoon in a Committee Room in the House of Commons. It was too small a room and there were too many people. After that they moved to the QEII Centre, which was too large, and there appeared to be too few people. I went along and sat on the platform with John and his political advisor from the Welsh Office, Hywel Williams. Behind us were other supporters, including Teresa Gorman in a bright green dress, David Evans, Tony Marlow, in the famous striped blazer, Barry Legg, Edward Leigh, Bill Walker, Christopher Gill and others. Many people criticised Redwood for including all these people who were said not to be respected in the House and, it was said, put off other MPs who might have voted for John. Frankly I think this is exaggerated. John Redwood, like John

Major in 1990, had to encourage his supporters and make them feel part of his team. However, Redwood took the point because Teresa Gorman was later told not to show her face at more meetings and was offended.

John Redwood gave a sparkling performance at the press conference, answering questions crisply with great confidence. His delivery had improved immeasurably since I last heard him speak. Unexpectedly he revealed a good line in self-deprecating jokes that even had the press roaring. Carla Powell, who didn't know Redwood, watched it on TV and telephoned me later to say she thought he had been brilliant.

I was impressed when Redwood stated that he had always been loyal to the Prime Minister and had never even privately sought to undermine him. He added, 'All of you from the press know that is true.' It must have been true or he would not have risked saying it.

I had made no statements since the election had been called and some papers wondered whether I would run as a second candidate, so I made a statement declaring my support for Redwood.

John Redwood

I had known Redwood slightly ever since we both worked together in the investment division of Rothschild's. He once asked me to All Souls High Table as his guest. I remember the occasion vividly because I was seated next to A.L. Rowse who was memorably outrageous in every way.

I admired Redwood's intellect and I observed during the campaign that he had a great gift for talking about complex matters in a simple way. However, he was very different from that other fellow of All Souls, Keith Joseph. He had political courage but not intellectual courage. Everything was designed to please an audience. His acute brain was seldom deployed to widen people's horizons or to convert them to a new way of thinking. I remembered as Chancellor being infuriated when in the public expenditure round he demanded a large amount of money for local government. When we eventually compromised and gave him much of what he wanted, he told other Ministers that the Treasury had been absurdly generous.

In the campaign my admiration for his strong points grew, but my misgivings about his weaknesses also increased. I found it difficult to support his economic programme and I declined to attend the press conference when he put it forward. Predictably he had advocated tax cuts and increased expenditure, plus the abolition of VAT on fuel and power. When he was asked where the money would come from he took an eternity to come up with an unconvincing reply: 'Across the board cuts and administrative savings.' His budgetary arithmetic did not add up. It damaged him, though not as much as he deserved since most MPs were not sufficiently interested.

I felt particularly uncomfortable with his campaign against the remaining VAT on fuel and power, which was only 8 per cent after the Government defeat in the House of Commons. I cannot believe that John did not recognise that there was an overwhelming intellectual case for this measure. His philosophy ought to have led him to support a broad-based VAT on almost everything. He was also well aware of the need to reduce Government borrowing.

John Redwood's approach had more in common with Ronald Reagan's than with Keith Joseph's. He didn't seem to worry about Government borrowing and thought tax cuts would always pay for themselves. As Reagan discovered, they did not. He could not resist telling people what they wanted to hear. I remember once hearing him say on *Question Time* something to the effect: 'The Tories need to be popular. This is popular therefore I am in favour of it.' He said it with such confidence that he got away with it. I couldn't help admiring him.

One night, after an evening's telephoning, David Evans took John Redwood and me out for supper in the Savoy. David, who was wearing something that looked like a plastic golfing jacket, bundled us into his Rolls Royce. As we drove down the Mall towards Buckingham Palace, David said, 'Just imagine, John, this is what you will be doing next week, driving to see the Queen.' I wondered whether he really believed it? I certainly did not.

One of the key objectives in the Redwood campaign was to win the votes of those who would support other candidates in the second round. This particularly applied to supporters of Portillo. In meetings John Redwood repeatedly stated he greatly admired Michael Portillo. He claimed that he had offered to step aside for him. This was later denied by Portillo.

Unfortunately it proved surprisingly difficult to win over the Portillo supporters. George Gardiner was one who eventually did come, but for the most part they were worried that if John Redwood did too well he would become unstoppable. The Major campaign very cleverly talked up Redwood's prospects with supporters of Portillo. People like Alan Duncan, John Whittingdale and Bernard Jenkin, all of whom had been bitterly critical of Major, wouldn't even abstain, but insisted on voting for the Prime Minister.

I was amazed by Bernard Jenkin, who had been so ridiculously rude to the Prime Minister at the Fresh Start meeting. Alan Duncan, at one point, tried to persuade others to abstain and briefed the press in a remarkable phrase that there was a 'growing momentum for abstentions'. In reality there was not, and Alan was eventually persuaded to vote for John Major by William Hague, his closest friend. Probably the Major campaign picked off the Portillo supporters by using close friends like William Hague or indeed Michael Portillo himself. At one point in the campaign Alan Duncan tried to test the water for Portillo by going on the *Today* programme and hinting that Portillo might come into the race later, but it was too late and there was little reaction to this. Portillo had to be exceedingly careful: he could not afford to be found preparing for the Prime Minister's demise.

Michael Heseltine's followers were in an even more difficult position. They had different views on Europe from Redwood and all regarded him as extreme. They were difficult to approach, but there were some contacts. David Evans certainly talked to Keith Hampson and I renewed the contacts I had had the year before with Peter Temple-Morris. I suspect that many of the Heseltine supporters were speaking without his authority and were really in the dark about what their master thought. It would have been difficult, of course, for Michael to have given any indications of his views. The slightest hint that he was not whole-heartedly backing the PM would have led to bitter accusations against the man who had already disposed of one Prime Minister. Whatever his ultimate motive, I believe that Heseltine behaved impeccably and in no way encouraged his supporters to do anything but back the Prime Minister.

Polling day

On the day of the election, there were reports that the Heseltine supporters had met and had only decided at the last minute to support Major. Many of the stories of the behaviour of different camps were made up by journalists. It would have been very difficult for either Portillo or Heseltine to have had the sorts of conversations with their supporters that journalists so freely described.

Roger Knapman kept the score of pledges for John Redwood. Quite rightly he was secretive about what the state of play was. The night before the ballot we all gave our opinions about the result. My forecast was for between 85 and 90 votes for Redwood. Others were more optimistic.

The date of the election, 4 July, was also a day for Prime Minister's Questions. According to Anthony Seldon, John Major did not do well on that occasion, but that was not how it seemed to me. I thought he gave one of his most effective performances ever, appearing relaxed and as bright as a button. I did, however, sense that Tony Blair for once was asking rather easy questions. I am sure Blair thought it was in his interest for Major to continue in office.

We heard later in the day that when Heseltine had voted he had turned towards the representatives of the 1922 Committee in the polling room and held up his ballot paper to show he really had voted for Major. Some other MPs did the same. I could under-stand Heseltine, because there were so many rumours about what he was really up to, but I thought it was quite wrong for others to do that so that anyone who didn't show their ballot paper to the scrutineers was suspected of voting for Redwood. It was all a bit like an election in Ceausescu's Romania.

In the afternoon I walked through the Members' Lobby and saw Tristan Garel-Jones sitting on a bench talking to Sarah Hogg, who had no right to be there as she was not an MP. Both of them were ashen-faced and looked extremely worried. I do not know to this day what was their concern, but it was clearly real. Perhaps they were worried that Major would resign if his margin was not large enough? By all accounts he had been threatening to do so, and supporters had sent notes urging him to stay on.

I had tea in the Smoking Room with Archie Hamilton, the MP for Epsom, who was a strong supporter of the Prime Minister. He was also concerned. I said to him, 'You needn't worry. You have won easily.'

The poll closed at 5 p.m. While the counting was going on, John, Barry Legg and I retired to Barry Field's office. We had arranged that the figures should be telephoned to us once the result was known. The call came at 5.10 p.m and the result was Major 218, Redwood 89 and Abstentions 20.

I immediately said to John, 'Well done'. It was what I expected and I thought it was a creditable result. He replied, 'It is not good at all.' I think he had genuinely thought he would do better, and force a second round. However his composure was complete and he immediately went out, accompanied by me, to College Green, where there were a host of TV cameras. He read a prepared statement and congratulated the Prime Minister.

I also issued a statement saying it was now time for the Party to unite and we must all back the Prime Minister so that the Party could win the next Election.

The result was not that good for the Prime Minister, and I understand that he felt disappointed. About one third of the Parliamentary Party had failed to support him, but he was helped in claiming a decisive victory by the fact that Redwood and I immediately indicated that we regarded the issue of the leadership as closed. His own campaign team were also very quick to put a positive spin on the figures. They had carefully massaged expectations downwards and persuaded the press to accept that anything less than 100 votes for Redwood would be a convincing victory for the Prime Minister.

One could have disputed this, but I certainly did not feel in a mood to do so. I could not help reflecting that if the Portillo supporters had not almost unanimously backed Major it would have been very a different story.

If John Redwood was disappointed by the result, he had no need to be. His boldness had brought him great gains. From the most junior position in the Cabinet he had made himself into a household name and he had skilfully expressed the concerns of many Conservatives in Parliament and in the country. It is a tribute to the way he comported himself that there was no backlash against him from the constituencies and he became a popular speaker throughout the country. All in all, he was well positioned for the next leadership election after the Election. At that time he had leapfrogged Michael Portillo as leader of the right.

That night Major started the reconstruction of his Government. The main announcement was that Michael Heseltine was to become Deputy Prime Minister, which caused huge depression in the Redwood camp as it hardly seemed to them a gesture of reconciliation or an attempt to unite the Party. But what must the Portillo supporters have felt? People such as Alan Duncan or Bernard Jenkins should have felt very foolish indeed for having supported Major. I too was surprised at the Prime Minister's promotion of Michael Heseltine. All the time I had been Chancellor he had been nervous and suspicious of Michael and had no regard at all for his administrative skills. He thought he had made a terrible mess of the closure of the coal mines.

Inevitably many people concluded that there had been a deal between the Prime Minister and Heseltine. I don't think it was as simple as that, although obviously I don't know. I find it difficult to believe that there could ever be a conversation between a Prime Minister and a Cabinet colleague such as some of those described in newspapers. I suspect that the Prime Minister used his subtle personal skills to finesse Michael Heseltine out of the contest without him ever realising it. By offering him the post of Deputy Prime Minister some time before he told him there was going to be a leadership election, he had locked him in to supporting him. The only way Michael could now ever become leader was by being totally loyal to Major.

At the time there were also intriguing but unlikely stories that Heseltine had been offered the post of Chancellor. I know Michael sufficiently well to say that if he had ever been offered it he would not have accepted it. He hates the Treasury with a vengeance. He thinks it 'anti-growth' and 'anti-public invest-ment'. While he might have been tempted to try to change its culture, he also knows his limitations.

The stories persisted that the Prime Minister wanted to move Ken Clarke from the Treasury after the leadership election, which in many ways would have been logical since the Prime Minister kept complaining in private to MPs that he couldn't move towards ruling out the single currency because of the Chancellor. But there was probably no way in which the Prime Minister could lose two Chancellors in one Parliament. That would have been careless.

My support for John Redwood had one sad consequence for me. Shortly after the leadership election Evelyn de Rothschild said that he felt it was time we severed our connection. Although I was sorry to leave Rothschild's, I understood why he was uncomfortable with a colleague who was controversial and critical of the Government. I was grateful to Evelyn for his kindness, and understood that politics and business didn't mix easily. I knew, too, that one of John Major's Private Secretaries had lunched in the bank with a former Ambassador, also on the Board, who never stopped complaining to Evelyn about my opposition to the single currency.

Evelyn told me, 'I have my views on horses, but I keep them to myself, why can't you keep your views on the single currency to yourself?' I noticed as he spoke he was in front of a picture of General de Gaulle. The Rothschilds were proud of their connec-tion with De Gaulle through Georges Pompidou, who had been Managing Director of the French bank. When it was advanta-geous they liked to parade the connection. I wondered what De Gaulle would have thought of Evelyn's comparison between horses and the single currency, and what he would have thought of me if I had given in to Evelyn's pressure.

19

Why I Am Against the Single Currency

> Men have sometimes been led by degrees, sometimes hurried into things, of which, if they could have seen the whole together, they would never have permitted the most remote approach. The people never give up their liberties except under some delusion.
>
> *Edmund Burke*

The question of a country's currency can dominate politics. In the 1896 presidential election, the Democrat candidate, William Jennings Bryan, campaigned against America's abandonment of silver in favour of gold. 'You shall not crucify mankind upon a cross of gold,' he thundered in one of the most famous sound bites of American history.

To some observers the 1997 General election demonstrated that the Conservative Party had been torn apart on the rack of EMU but it should have been evident to them that the Conservative Party would not support a decision to join. It had only supported Maastricht because it did not commit Britain to monetary union.

The underlying reality was rather different from the stories of splits and divisions. The party was far less divided than it appeared. The real story was the party's uneven but successful transformation from being the party of Europe to being the party of Euroscepticism. In the 1970s and early 1980s, Conservative backing for Europe was reinforced by Labour's opposition. The high noon of Conservative support for Europe followed the settlement of Britain's budget rebate at the Fontainebleau summit in June 1984. At last, it was thought, Britain could play a constructive role in shaping Europe. Britain's task was to export Thatcherite deregulation and liberalisation, unleashing a tidal wave of economic dynamism and unlocking Europe's economic potential. That was the idea.

The European Commission, with its unerring reverse Midas touch, turning everything it touches into dross, seized the initiative and turned it into an engine for spewing out an endless stream of directives. Harmonisation replaced deregulation. Far from leading to faster growth, the 1990s turned out to be Europe's lost decade in terms of economic growth.

Even more decisive than the failed European economic miracle in feeding Conservative disenchantment with Europe was the massive accretion of power to the Commission and the impact of the extension of majority voting. The additional powers Europe gained from the Single European Act were swiftly directed at impeding the Conservative Government's labour market reforms. September 1988 was the turning point when Jacques Delors told the TUC Conference that the trades unions could get from Brussels what they were being denied at Westminster.

The ratification of Maastricht and the impact of the ERM accelerated the Party's transformation to Euroscepticism, isolating the small minority who supported monetary union. William Hague's ballot of party members in 1998 showed massive support for his policy of opposing the euro. The party had reached the other side.

I had started my political career as a supporter of Europe. At my first public rally in Trafalgar Square, I spoke alongside Ken Clarke and John Gummer in favour of British membership of the Common Market. Like most people, I had believed that joining the Common Market was essentially an economic arrangement, although I had always been concerned about the constitutional implications of membership. I recall expressing my fears about Europe's political dimension to Margaret Thatcher in the lobbies as we voted for direct elections to the European Assembly. Were we doing the right thing? I asked. She was then a relatively new Leader of the Opposition. Her reply indicated that she shared my unease but she said she had been advised that it was necessary.

My experience negotiating Maastricht made me realise that these fears were more than justified. It convinced me that Britain's view of Europe was diametrically opposed to that held by everyone else. Britain was alone, without allies on the most important peacetime question Britain has ever faced: Britain's position as Europe developed into a federal state. The public was being deceived. The country was on a conveyor belt to a federal Europe without giving its consent and having been specifically assured that it wouldn't happen. Far from having been settled by the 1975 referendum, the single currency tore open the question of Britain's relationship with Europe.

Like Britain's original decision to join the EEC, the issue with the single currency is portrayed by its British supporters as an economic question: will Britain be more prosperous in or out? In this respect they are out of step with European leaders, who openly acknowledge, indeed celebrate, that the adoption of the euro is primarily a constitutional act involving the transfer of sovereignty to Europe. For them that is the point of the euro. In Britain the economic arguments camouflage the real argument, which is political – the fear of being left out, of losing influence.

The Heath Government's dismissal of the Treasury argument against joining the EEC anticipates the Blair Government's attitude to the bad economics of joining the euro. Gordon Brown's five economic tests are not designed to find out whether the euro would benefit the economy, but rather to show that the euro would not be economically damaging. That is because the real prize is not economic, but the fool's gold of influence, or as Tony Blair puts it, 'leadership in Europe'. As the tests don't have to prove that the euro would be beneficial they can be manipulated to produce the answer the Government wants when the opinion polls look propitious to hold a referendum.

In doing so the Blair Government would be making a characteristic mistake of failing to learn from history. Before EMU, there was GEMU, German economic and monetary union. Ten years on, GEMU has only 'worked' at the cost of high unemployment in eastern Germany, massive fiscal transfers and high taxes. Then there is the experience of the ERM, a softer version of the euro. In France the political consequences of keeping the franc within the ERM propelled two prime ministers, Pierre Bérégovoy and Alain Juppé, to the electoral guillotine. Britain's ERM experience, informally shadowing the Deutschmark and then formally inside it, shows how for economies that are out of phase the ERM led to interest rates that deepened the economic cycle. Denmark also had a similar experience in the 1980s.

What is striking about EMU is the meagre economic benefits even claimed by its proponents before taking account of the full economic costs and risks. If Britain were inside EMU we would have greater exchange rate stability with the rest of the euro-zone, but our exchange rate with the rest of the world, accounting for around 50 per cent of our trade, would become less stable, as non-euro-zone trade accounts for only a relatively small part of Euroland's GDP. Insofar as exchange rate instability influences long-term trade, it would make Britain more dependent on Europe's low-growth markets.

Then, it is argued, the euro would force down prices by a mysterious process newspapers like the *Financial Times* call 'transparency'. Apparently prices will be the same all across Europe when they are denominated in the same currency. The argument is repeated over and over again, no doubt because it is one of the few benefits consumers might have. Perhaps people who make these arguments assume people are too dim to use a calculator or a bit of mental arithmetic. Prices are set by supply and demand, not the denomination of the currency. A Coca-Cola costs more in the Savoy than in a supermarket. Some countries have more dynamic and competitive markets, while others have higher costs, protected markets and high taxes. It is these that determine costs and prices, not the £, $ or € on the price tag.

The euro, it is said, will bring us lower interest rates. Long-term interest rates, which are set by the market, are very close. Britain's higher short-term rates partly reflect the different positions of the cycle, but very low short-term interest rates are a flashing warning sign, indicating chronic economic distress. Following the logic of seeking low interest rates, Britain should join the yen, with rates at 0.1 per cent, rather than the euro and plunge into Japan's intractable financial crisis.

Elimination of transaction costs for changing currency within the euro-zone has to be set against the costs of converting the whole of the British economy to the euro. There are enormous economic costs from losing the pound. Unless Britain's economic cycle is aligned with the euro-zone – and, anyway, one cannot speak of a single euro-zone economic cycle with rapid growth in Ireland and Spain and weak growth in Germany and Italy – interest rates set in Frankfurt will be inappropriate for Britain's needs, setting off successive waves of damaging credit gluts and credit crunches. A one-size-fits-all interest rate means bigger booms and deeper busts and increases the returns from successful financial speculation. The higher risks from increased economic volatility would raise the costs of providing goods and services. Against the reduction in transaction costs, which an accountant can add up, must be set the enormous damage in terms of lost output, bankruptcies and higher unemployment, because Britain could not calibrate interest rates for the demand and supply of credit in the UK. For anyone other than a euro ideologue, the choice is obvious.

It is possible that over many years – decades, centuries even – the economies of the various European countries will converge so that it is meaningful to talk of a single European economy, not an aggregation of national economies, with a similar level of labour mobility as in the United States. Before that stage is reached, there is not a rational economic case for considering a single currency. What is certain is that such an economy does not exist in Europe today and shows no signs of emerging in the near future. The hubris of EMU is believing that a single European economy and a single European economic government can be forged with the hammer of the single currency on the anvil of the convergence criteria and the Stability Pact.

The monetary order created by Maastricht will not produce a stable currency. Like a producer cartel, currency unions suffer from what economists call the free rider problem. For a price-fixing cartel such as OPEC, it pays all members to limit production in order to raise prices. It pays an individual member even more to break his quota and sell more oil at the higher price, but if all members do this, prices fall and the cartel breaks down.

The euro has a similar problem. Members with weak public finances benefit from lower interest costs on their borrowing. Convergence of bond yields across the euro-zone members show that the markets expect that countries like Italy and Belgium would be bailed out if they ran into difficulties. Because their own currencies no longer exist, it removes direct pressure from the markets on individual governments to take unpopular decisions and stabilise their public finances. Market discipline has been replaced by the peer group pressure of European Finance Ministers, few of whom are in a position to lecture their colleagues on sound public finance.

The absence of direct market pressure on individual countries and the one-size-fits-all interest rate means that Europe's currency arrangements are at the polar extreme from the pre-1914 gold standard, to which it has on occasion been wrongly compared. The gold standard can claim to be the most successful international monetary regime the world has known. For all today's talk of globalisation, the gold standard era saw the greatest international capital flows relative to the size of economies in history.

Unlike EMU, the gold standard was not created by international treaty. It wasn't even a system of fixed exchange rates. Its stability derived from it being fundamentally a domestic system of organising money with the central objective of preserving the domestic purchasing power of the currency. International currency stability was the automatic outcome of the success of the leading economies in achieving domestic stability. Interest rates between countries could vary. Economic imbalances between countries led to differential movements in interest rates, which triggered self-adjusting capital flows, providing a relatively painless adjustment mechanism. By contrast adjustment under Maastricht is painful, for prices, output and jobs, as there is only one interest rate and one monetary policy.

Under the gold standard, the role of Finance Ministers was to ensure fiscal stability, to balance their income and expenditure. There was no committee of Finance Ministers poking their noses into other countries. The markets rewarded virtuous countries and those that had weak finances had less success in maintaining their domestic parity. Central banks controlled monetary policy, which in the case of the Bank of England was privately owned.

Britain's post-ERM framework, which I introduced and essentially remains the regime for the independent Bank of England, is much closer to the precepts of the gold standard. It is a domestic system with the objective of stabilising the domestic price level. There is clear accountability. The Bank of England has freedom to decide interest rates to achieve the price stability objective defined by the Chancellor. The Government's task is to ensure that public finances are stable over the economic cycle. By keeping the pound as a freely traded currency, Britain is exposed to the markets, which promotes self-discipline, which is much better and more durable than the erratically imposed rules of the Stability Pact. Interest rate differentials with other countries and capital flows between them help smooth the effects of the cycle or shocks, whether adverse or benign.

Britain's system is similar to those of Australia and New Zealand and to the policies pursued by Alan Greenspan in the United States. It has delivered good results for nearly seven years – a long time by previous British standards, with no sign of any deterioration in performance. As the Monetary Policy Committee of the Bank of England gains experience and the confidence of the markets increases further, long-term interest rates could fall further, removing the final legacy of Britain's inflationary past. What more could one want?

Yet the Blair Government's objective is to throw all this away by joining the euro. I strongly supported Gordon Brown's decision to make the Bank of England independent but the Blair Government's objective of joining the euro shows that it does not understand the economic philosophy underpinning the success of the post-ERM framework. Its motivation in joining the euro is not to improve economic performance. It is political. If the Government wanted Britain to be exposed to virtually the full economic impact of the euro without any loss of sovereignty, there is a simple answer to hand. It could turn the Bank of England into a euro currency board. The pound would have a fixed and mechanical link with the euro, just as the Hong Kong dollar has with the US dollar. The reason why this has not been proposed reveals the true motivation of those wanting to join the euro. It would throw in to sharp relief the pitiful nature of the economic case for joining the euro.

No one in their right minds would wind up the Bank of England's Monetary Policy Committee and turn it into a currency board to act as a *de facto* branch of the European Central Bank. Yet the economic consequences of joining EMU are even worse than this. At least with a currency board Britain could unilaterally break the link with the euro, as Hong Kong did with the pound in 1972, and switch to another currency, such as the dollar, or revert to having its own central bank. With EMU this option has been signed away for ever. There is no legal way out except by getting all the members of the European Union to ratify a new treaty to let Britain out. The absurdity of this proposition is self-evident.

The purpose of joining EMU is expressly to disenfranchise Britain from having responsibility for its own economic affairs. The underlying motivation is not economic. It is a manifestation of the modern British disease, which combines a view of Britain as weak, unable to thrive as an independent nation state, with a post-imperial delusion about Britain's mission in the world, which can only be accomplished by ending Britain's independence.

Britain, it is alleged, cannot survive with its own currency. As the fifth largest economy in the world, logically this means that 162 smaller countries around the globe that also have their own currencies cannot survive. It would mean Australia and New Zealand joining the yen, with disastrous consequences for them. No one says Canada, with just over one-tenth of the population of the United States, should give up the Canadian dollar, yet Britain, with a population one-fifth of the euro-zone, is too weak to keep the pound.

Such sentiments are not the result of rational economic thought. They are psychological in origin, a product of the fear of being excluded, of not being at Europe's top table. British supporters of the euro want a voice in the government of Europe, even at the cost of Britain's ability to govern itself. It shows the fundamental weakness of the pro-euro case. Although its proponents keep denying that Europe is becoming a federal state, they want Britain to join precisely because the single currency is a decisive step to creating a federal Europe. If EMU did not result in the centralisation of economic policy in Europe, there would be no purpose for them in Britain being at the top table, because nothing of substance would be decided. The identical arguments used by those wanting to join the euro could equally well be deployed to justify Britain joining a federal Europe. They do not put their arguments into an explicitly federal frame because they know that if they did they would be instantly rejected by the public. This fragile tissue would be blown away in the gale of a referendum campaign.

So the fundamental issue is whether Britain should formally renounce its independence and participate in the creation of a United States of Europe. The key question is: Do the objective conditions exist to create a peaceful, democratic federal union of Europe? Put another way: Would Britain gain more than it lost by belonging to a federal Europe?

The United States of America is the supreme example of a great federal democracy. It is therefore worth examining why the United States was successful in establishing itself as a viable democratic entity and whether these factors exist in Europe today. By the time the American Constitution was being decided, twenty-one years after the Declaration of Independence, Americans thought of themselves as a people and a nation. This was expounded with great eloquence by John Jay in the second Federalist Paper: 'Providence has been pleased to give this one connected country, to one united people, a people descended from the same ancestors, speaking the same language, professing the same religion, attached to the same principles of government, very similar in their manners and customs, and who, by their joint counsels, arms and efforts, fighting side by side throughout a long and bloody war, have nobly established their general Liberty and Independence.'

Jay then spoke of Americans being 'a band of brethren, united to each other by the strongest ties': 'To all general purposes we have uniformly been one people, each individual citizen everywhere enjoying the same national rights, privileges and protection. As a nation we have made peace and war, as a nation we have

vanquished our common enemies.' Jay could have added that
before independence, the American states were ruled by one
power, the British crown, and had a system of law based on
English common law.

Not one of these factors is present in Europe. There is not a
nation called Europe. There is not a European people. It is easier
to list the factors that Europe does not have in common than
those it does. The prerequisites for a genuinely democratic state
do not exist. As the Spanish philosopher, Miguel Herrero de
Miñón has argued: 'There is no such thing as a "European
people". The lack of "demos" is the main reason for the lack of
democracy. And the democratic system without "demos" is just
"cratos", power. The European institutions have structures and
functions which pretend to be a reproduction of national democratic institutions whilst being a mock counterfeit.'

In the words of General de Gaulle, the nation state and democracy are in the final analysis the same thing. Democratic
accountability – the ability of the governed to hold to account
those who govern them – can only function effectively within a
nation state. The steady erosion of national sovereignty as a result
of European integration is thus a loss of democracy.

But, say those who favour this development, sovereignty in the
modern world is a fiction. Globalisation means the end of the
nation state. This is only true in the limited sense that if countries,
such as the members of the European Union, give up their sovereignty, there will be fewer nation states. It is not the case that
more trade, cross-border investment and the Internet mean the
demise of the nation state. These developments give individuals
greater opportunity. The sovereignty is dead argument confuses
sovereignty with power. The growth of markets does circumscribe
the discretionary executive power of government. It reduces the
power of governments to tell people what to do, which is a very
good thing, and reinforces liberal constitutions that limit the
power of the state.

Sovereignty denotes the supreme right to make and interpret
laws. Law is definitive of liberty. Free societies require the rule of
law; otherwise there is anarchy or despotism. In democracies,
laws are made with the consent of the governed. Proponents of

the globalisation argument do not assert that the making of laws is redundant, only that the supreme right of nation states to make and adjudicate laws should be replaced by supra-national bodies such as the European Union.

The argument against national sovereignty is therefore an argument against democracy. The greatest loss from Britain joining a federal Europe would be democracy. Some people, while acknowledging this as an unfortunate loss, might say that it is a necessary price for continued prosperity, but freedom and the rule of law are the fundamental requirements for capitalism to thrive. 'A brave people will certainly prefer liberty, accompanied with a virtuous poverty, to a depraved and wealthy servitude,' as Burke put it.

Democracy and the competition between parties for office results in good government. Governments that can't be removed by the voters start to govern for themselves, not on behalf of the governed. Corruption takes root. Identical policies are more effective when they result from democratic decision than by bureaucratic fiat. The success of Margaret Thatcher and Ronald Reagan was because they had to persuade their countries that they needed tough economic reforms. Winning arguments and gaining popular consent requires getting people to understand the reason for the policy. A decree just requires a signature.

Selling Britain's democracy and self-government is meant to procure 'influence' in Europe. Even in its own terms, the deal won't work. To influence Europe requires being in the vanguard of European integration. The ceaseless forward momentum of European integration is resented by a large majority of the electorate. After more than a quarter of a century of membership, barely half the country wants to remain in the European Union. The absence of a solid pro-European domestic base constrains the ability of any British government to lead Europe, even if France and Germany permitted it. Like his predecessor, Tony Blair made a speech in Germany pledging to put Britain at the heart of Europe. Neither his greater fervour nor his popularity have had any more impact than John Major in reducing popular opposition to European integration.

The Blair Government made two decisions shortly after coming into office that will create insuperable difficulties for it to win a referendum on the euro. The first was making the Bank of England independent. Britain's monetary arrangements are now superior in every respect to those of Maastricht. It also made it much harder for the Government covertly to shadow the euro and engineer a big cut in interest rates to buy off public opposition. The second was the Prime Minister's decision not to have a quick referendum while the Conservative party was in disarray, exploiting the euphoria surrounding Labour's victory and its early months in office.

Tony Blair hesitated and missed his best chance to get Britain into the euro. Delay will work against him. The longer Britain keeps the pound, the more difficult it will be to persuade people to give it up on the grounds that switching to the euro is inevitable or necessary. The passage of time will simply show that this is untrue. If there is a referendum, it will be a difficult campaign for the Government. The case for the euro is that Britain is too weak to have its own currency. Voters always prefer politicians who have confidence in their country over those who tell them that their country has had its day.

Why do so many politicians want to push Britain into the euro and into a federal Europe against the wishes of the people? Part of the answer is that politicians are the real victims of the inevitability argument. They want to be on the winning side of history. It is partly vanity. Europe is a bigger stage that gives politicians a sense of self-worth and relevance. Building Europe is more exciting than being at the coal face of politics reforming the welfare state. But I've come to realise that the most powerful reason is a sense of cultural dissatisfaction with Britain, which is shared by many businessmen, civil servants and commentators. They want Britain to be something else. Britain would be better if it wasn't British. They wish it were a European country, the West Midlands covered in olive groves and vineyards, the south coast to have the sophistication of the Côte d'Azur, their countrymen speaking with the tongue of Dante and thinking with the mind of Descartes. They want a fantasy to compensate for the end of Empire.

But they miss what makes Britain great, its tolerance and sense of fair play, public life that is uncorrupted, a constitution that underneath an old skin evolved to provide a highly democratic form of government, while preserving a sense of authority derived from antiquity.

The British people have more sense than the politicians who want them to give all this up – and all for a botched currency called the euro. I look forward to the time when Tony Blair announces a referendum on the euro, and to hearing the people speak.

20

The Countdown – The Wasted Years, 1995–7

The hour is great and the honourable Gentlemen, I must say, are small.

Thomas Carlyle

The period of almost two years between the leadership election and the 1997 Election should have given John Major a golden opportunity to rebuild the fortunes of the Conservative Party. He had won a victory that he had claimed as 'decisive' and John Redwood and I had accepted the result and were serious in our intention to do all we could to help to win the Election. The Prime Minister's authority and standing should have been vastly enhanced.

In fact, between 1995 and 1997 the fortunes of the Conservative Party at first hardly moved at all and then plunged disastrously again. How could such an opportunity have been squandered? How could it go so wrong?

For much of this period the European issue was likely to be in abeyance. There was no major European legislation. There was to be another Inter-Governmental Conference (IGC) beginning in 1996, but that was not expected to conclude until after the Election, and the prospects of the single currency starting in 1997 were certainly receding. That should have made the PM's task easier.

Predictably there was muttering on the right about the role of Michael Heseltine. This first crystallised when Michael Howard allowed it to be known that he was infuriated by the Deputy Prime Minister interfering in his Department. There was also increasing friction between the PM and Gillian Shephard at Education, but none of these problems would ever have led to another leadership challenge.

Party Conference 1995

In the autumn the Party Conference went off well enough, though it was initially overshadowed by the unexpected defection of Alan Howarth, MP for Stratford upon Avon, to the Labour Party. A clever piece of news management by Alastair Campbell led to this dominating the weekend's press before the Conference.

That week Portillo made an explosive speech in which he accused Brussels of wanting to interfere in defence matters, invoking the SAS motto 'Who dares wins'. It went down extremely well with the Party faithful, but the reaction of much of the press was unfavourable. Nonetheless Major also had a success, speaking from the heart without an auto-cue in a highly personal speech. It was one of his best performances. Was this the beginning of the recovery?

Events continued to dog the Government. Nothing seemed to go right in this period. In the week after the Party Conference there was the row in Parliament over the sacking of the Director-General of Prisons, Derek Lewis, which led to some press criticism, though Michael Howard had another Parliamentary triumph over Jack Straw in the debate.

The feeling that the Government was still not getting a grip was highlighted by the resignation of Hugh Colver, the Head of Communications at Central Office, on 8 November. He felt the Party were not exploiting the new situation and wrote in the *Sun*: 'The Prime Minister's remarkable leadership victory should have put the Conservative Party on course for a dramatic comeback against Labour . . . Instead everything has turned sour and Ministers have seemingly been unable to do anything to stop it.' A Gallup poll that day gave Labour a skyscraping 39.5 per cent lead. It was almost unbelievable. If the Tories were going to recover, they were leaving it late indeed.

The Budget

Neither the Queen's Speech nor the Budget in November left much of a mark. The Chancellor cut income tax by 1 penny to 24 pence in the pound from April 1996. This disappointed many on the right who said he should have done more. I did not feel their criticisms were realistic.

Further tax cuts would only have been possible with further cuts in spending. Oddly Major had said in his speech at the Lord Mayor's Banquet that he wanted to reduce public spending to way below 40 per cent of GDP. He went further at the Conservative Political Centre in January and said he wanted to cut public spending to 35 per cent of national income. I found that bold aim even more astonishing as the Prime Minister had always been adamant to me that 40 per cent was the absolute rock bottom level to which spending could practically be reduced. Thirty-five per cent would have required radical surgery of welfare and the National Health Service, a measure to which he was instinctively deeply opposed. Substantial tax cuts would only have been possible with controversial policies. If that was what John Major now believed, he had come a long way since he had opposed the idea of the Conservative Party as the party of low taxation.

John Major seemed unable to believe that he was now secure in No. 10. There was an over-reaction to a speech by Lady Thatcher on 11 January, when she delivered the Keith Joseph Memorial Lecture and criticised Europhiles as standing for 'no-nation conservatism'. and said of the aspiring middle classes, 'They feel they no longer have the incentives and the opportunities they expect from a Conservative Government.' She also praised Howard, Lilley, Portillo and Redwood. No. 10 reacted furiously, seemingly believing that Lady Thatcher intended to stir up talk of another leadership challenge. This was paranoid nonsense.

Emma Nicholson, MP for Devon West and Torridge, announced on 29 December 1995 that she would join the Liberal Democrats, and then in February Peter Thurnham, MP for Bolton North-East, announced that he had resigned the Whip. On top of that there was the row over the Scott Report, brilliantly exploited by Robin Cook, but the most unexpected event of all was the row over BSE. Evidence of a link between the spread of BSE among Britain's beef herd and new cases of CJD in humans led to British beef being banned by a European Committee. This applied not just in EU countries but worldwide. The last point infuriated the many MPs who already felt the matter had not been well handled.

I found myself in the unlikely position of urging restraint on the Eurosceptics. Bill Cash had set up a monitoring group that met once a week to consider the issues in the new IGC. He and others still wanted to press the Government publicly to rule out the single currency. I felt that the Government was at this stage unlikely to move further. Also I felt that after the leadership election we had to accept the PM's decision. We were in far too deep political trouble to risk further splits on the floor of the House of Commons. Little did I know that arguments on the single currency were continuing within the Cabinet. Perhaps I was too cautious.

The impression of a lack of self-confidence was increased when Marcus Fox announced on 1 February that the Executive of the 1922 had decided there could not be another leadership election during this Parliament. It was puzzling why the Executive had made this decision. There wasn't the slightest chance that anyone would have contemplated another election. I did not object to the decision, but thought it unnecessary. I did object to the way the Committee simply made up the rules for the Party without con-sulting the members, rather like Arthur Scargill did in the NUM.

U-turn on a referendum

On 7 March 1996 the Cabinet considered the White Paper that Malcolm Rifkind, now Foreign Secretary, was proposing to publish on the IGC. Unexpectedly prompted by Douglas Hogg, the Minister of Agriculture, and to Kenneth Clarke's intense irritation, there was a discussion on the idea of holding a referendum on the single currency. I had discussed this subject with the PM while Chancellor and had the impression that he was not wholly opposed, even though he did rule it out publicly. After I left the Government I campaigned strongly for a referendum and pressure for it had subsequently increased. Now the PM had become openly more sympathetic to the idea. In the Cabinet not just Howard, Forsyth and Lilley but also moderate Europhiles like Newton and Shephard supported the idea, though I am told the policy was still furiously opposed by the Chancellor.

In the House that afternoon Marcus Fox asked the Prime Minister a planted question. The Prime Minister replied in a rather tortuous way, 'I have made clear to the House on previous occasions that I believe a referendum on a single currency could be a necessary step . . . At present the Government are considering the circumstances in which a referendum might or might not be appropriate.' It was classic Major. Obviously it was the intention of the Prime Minister gradually and publicly to nudge Clarke away from his position. It was the first time I understood what was happening in Cabinet. From my knowledge of the Prime Minister I could see how he was finessing Clarke and I had no doubt how he would react. Not long afterwards there were reports in newspapers that Ken Clarke was close to resigning.

Trouble on Europe

On 21 March 1996 Malcolm Rifkind's White Paper on the IGC was debated in the House. There was no vote but I have never seen a Minister so interrupted and, as *The Times* put it, 'mauled by his backbenchers'. I respected Malcolm and did not want to make his life more difficult, so I did not intervene. The White Paper argued that the 'pillared structure' for the EU, as at Maastricht, should be retained with Foreign Affairs and Justice continuing as matters for inter-governmental co-operation. There should be no new powers for the European Parliament and majority voting should not be extended. It was not a bad White Paper, but its title *A Partnership of Nations* was subtly different from the idea of a partnership of nation states.

But the Government's move in a Eurosceptic direction continued. On 4 April there was an important Government statement: 'Because we will be keeping [the Maastricht single currency opt-out] open at the next General Election we have decided to make a commitment in our manifesto, that if the Government decided to join a single currency during the course of the next Parliament that decision would be subject to confirmation in a referendum.' Kenneth Clarke had extracted a concession that the promise only applied to the 'life of the next Parliament' and that the referendum would only come after a recommendation and decision by the Government. Many MPs were pleased because they thought it would help them to deal with the Referendum Party, but then Rifkind, in his statement at Central Office, amplifying the Cabinet's agreement said, 'The government made quite clear some considerable time ago that we are not going to rule out the possibility of joining a single currency in the next Parliament.' That somewhat took the gloss off the announcement.

Enter Jimmy Goldsmith

Jimmy Goldsmith's Referendum Party was getting increasing publicity, even after Major's volte-face on the question of a referendum. That increased the nervousness of backbenchers and also the Government. No. 10 seemed to be suspicious that there might be some plot between Redwood, myself and Goldsmith. Others suggested I was considering standing for the Referendum Party. These were fantasies.

I did see Goldsmith later for exactly the same reason that many other MPs went to visit him. In January 1996 I had already been selected as the candidate for Harrogate and Knaresborough and I wanted to be sure that he didn't put a candidate up against me in the General Election. He was rather erratic in deciding against whom he would put up candidates. In the Election, Referendum

Party candidates stood against David Heathcoat-Amory, who had resigned from the Government over the single currency, as well as other strong Eurosceptics such as Michael Howard and Michael Spicer. However, I needn't have worried. I had been chosen at Harrogate when Carla Powell was staying with Goldsmith in Mexico and she told me he had woken her up to tell her the news.

I was also interested to hear Goldsmith's views on Europe. I first met him at his suite at the Dorchester and then on another occasion at Wilton Place. It was obviously necessary for these meetings to be kept secret, and he was very good about that. No leak ever appeared.

I told him that while I agreed with many of his views, though not on free trade, he must not interpret my talking to him as indicating any support on my part for him putting up candidates against the Conservative Party. He replied, 'You can attack me publicly, I quite understand. That is no problem.'

I admired Goldsmith much more than most Conservatives did, particularly as he was prepared to use his own money for a cause. I could not have disagreed more with Douglas Hurd's attacks on him as 'a rich man dabbling in politics'. Why, I thought, should politics be the preserve of established political parties? What better use could there be of private wealth than a political cause? One of the justifications for private wealth is that it encourages independence and the freedom of individuals to question the view of the establishment. And what was wrong with the fact that he lived partly in France, partly in the UK and partly in Mexico? He seemed like the model twenty-first century international citizen that the Europhiles always talked about.

Goldsmith was much more thoughtful about politics than most people realised, and his opposition to the single currency and the political direction of Europe was cogent and coherent. I was grateful to him for introducing me to a remarkable essay about nationalism in the modern world by Isaiah Berlin, 'The Bent Twig'. In it Berlin argued against the inevitability of globalisation and suggested there was no reason why nationalism had to be a destructive, aggressive force. A benevolent non-aggressive nationalism could be a constructive force. I had a more selfish reason to be grateful to Goldsmith when he ordered 500 copies of a book of mine on Europe and sent it to all his candidates.

Goldsmith assured me that he would not put up a candidate against me. He told me he had decided to stand against David Mellor in Putney because Mellor 'can't attack my sex life'. He went on to say that when Mellor learnt that Goldsmith would be his opponent, he had commented, 'At least Goldsmith can't attack my sex life.'

I was amused to note that, despite his deep dislike of Goldsmith, David Mellor saw which way public opinion was going and himself decided to oppose the single currency.

I remembered Goldsmith's interview on *The Frost Programme* well. I had talked to Lady Thatcher about it and said to her, 'I watched Goldsmith on *The Frost Programme*, and I thought he was rather good.' She replied 'Good? He is the only leader in any political Party.'

Emotionally I had a lot of sympathy with the Referendum Party. Their attitude to the referendum and the precise nature and wording of its question was very muddled, but I found it impossible to share the deep hatred of some Conservatives towards it. But then I wasn't going to be opposed by a Referendum candidate.

My own view was that if Goldsmith had wanted to succeed he should have done much more to get daily coverage for the Referendum Party in the newspapers and on TV. He tended to give few interviews and yet there was hardly a week in politics in which there wasn't some Euro row or crisis. He should have commented on them all, but he seemed to want to make only occasional interventions and to communicate with the voter via free newspapers, videos and the occasional slightly glitzy conference.

I hoped the Referendum Party would at least ensure that the European issue was brought to the forefront of British politics. I thought that it was possible they might win 10 per cent of the vote. But it never really took off, as it could have done. Perhaps that was because Goldsmith's health was failing, a fact he bravely concealed as he battled on.

The local elections

The next tests for the Government were the Staffordshire South-East by-election on 11 April, 1996, caused by the resignation of Alan Howarth, and the local elections on 2 May. The by-election was lost to Labour on a 22 per cent swing, a devastating result in what had always been a safe Conservative seat. The local election results on 2 May were not quite as bad as some had expected, but the Party won only 27 per cent of the vote. Doorstepped by a television crew next day, I managed to say, 'The fight back begins now.'

The *Daily Telegraph* went to town after the by-election: 'Get off your knees . . . Overall the Government is a disaster. The fact that Mr Major does not stand for anything is an invitation for everyone else to fight!!' That was indeed the problem for many people. The Government's refusal to make up its mind did invite others to attempt to make it up for it.

In April Iain Duncan-Smith introduced a Private Member's Bill to give Parliament power to overrule certain decisions of the European Court and 66 Tory MPs, including myself, supported it. In many ways I would have preferred to have avoided a vote, but Iain was determined to have one. It was described as a 'rebellion' although it was not actually a vote against the Government but a vote for a Bill on which there would be no Government comment. Nevertheless the episode didn't help.

In the run-up to the local elections the Prime Minister referred to politicians calling for withdrawal from the EU as living in 'cloud cuckoo land', merely reinforcing the impression of a rattled PM. No one had publicly called for a withdrawal from the EU. I had not publicly referred even to the possibility since my speech at the Conference two years previously, so why was the PM so determined to tilt at windmills? Why was he spending time attacking imaginary opposition in the Conservative Party?

Whitehall had been considering a range of ideas for retaliation against the EU because of the beef ban. These included leaving an empty seat at EU meetings, withholding budget payments, restrictions on imports and the obstruction of decision-making. Rifkind, the Foreign Secretary, publicly warned the EU that these options were being considered to increase pressure and his speech excited the newspapers and backbenchers. Then, to Rifkind's annoyance, the Deputy Prime Minister appeared to contradict him. Euro-sceptics concluded it was another QMV climb down.

On 20 May the EU's Veterinary Committee voted against lift-ing the ban on British exports of tallow, semen and gelatine. The Prime Minister appeared outraged and announced that Britain would pursue a policy of non co-operation with Europe, but the impact was lost when press stories emerged of Britain continuing to participate in certain meetings. The *Daily Mail's* headline – 'Major goes to war at last' – seemed ridiculous.

On 17 June, after agreeing to slaughter 167,000 cattle, there was agreement between Britain and the EU for a progressive lift-ing of the beef ban though without a precise timetable. Backbenchers were silent but the press voiced what they were all thinking. 'After British bravado comes a hasty retreat,' said the *Independent*, while Peter Riddell wrote: 'The ill-judged beef policy leaves Major with lasting damage.' Robin Cook too called it a 'massive climbdown'.

On 22 July, my former PPS, David Heathcoat-Amory, the Paymaster-General at the Treasury, finally resigned because he felt he could not continue to support the Government's 'wait and see' policy on the single currency. David was a Junior Minister to Kenneth Clarke and therefore knew exactly what his thinking was. He must have argued about it frequently with him. At the same time, many in the press took the line that only the Chancellor now stood between the Prime Minister and a change of policy.

But was this true? Not if the words of the Prime Minister are to be believed. In an interview in *The Times* on 25 July he argued passionately that a decision on the single currency should be delayed. Once again we were told Britain's interests would suffer if we walked away from the negotiating table, and that to opt out of the argument now would be a dereliction of responsibility. This argument was utterly unconvincing and I had difficulty accepting the Prime Minister believed it. But I just didn't know.

It was nonsense because all the important decisions about the single currency had been taken at Maastricht: how the ECB was to operate, the convergence criteria, the composition of the Board, and, of course, Britain's own opt-out. It was true that the relationship between the euro and non-participating countries had not been settled, but that could not be settled unilaterally by EMU participants. Nevertheless the PM continued to argue this line right up to the General Election. If it had ever been true, and I doubt it, it had long ceased to be true.

The Government was now beginning its campaign for the next General Election, which could hardly have got off to a worse start. Central Office produced advertisements featuring Tony Blair with a black strip across the demon eyes and again the slogan 'New Labour, New Danger'. Predictably there was a fierce reaction beyond protests from the Labour Party. Unfortunately it confirmed the impression that the Conservative Party had not the slightest idea how to tackle New Labour.

Disagreements at the top

The myth has been established that John Major's Government was destroyed by backbenchers, but the divisions over Europe that were most evident after 1995 were those within the Cabinet and it was headlines about quarrels between Ministers that dominated the newspapers.

In a speech in Zurich Rifkind adopted an unusually Eurosceptic tone and said that the single currency would be divisive within the EU. Not surprisingly, this was interpreted by newspapers as Rifkind positioning himself for a leadership bid after the Election.

The Chancellor apparently had not been consulted by Rifkind and retaliated when asked about the 'wait and see' policy. He said that it would be 'pathetic' for Britain to stand back and only join the single currency later. Then Sir Nicholas Bonsor, the Minister of State at the Foreign Office, had his go and announced on BBC Radio's *World at One* that the Chancellor was 'out of line with Government policy'. Finally Nicholas was rebuked by the Prime Minister.

The autumn brought a false dawn for the Government, but at least a little light was better than never-ending darkness. The

1996 Party Conference went well, and an NOP poll in *The Sunday Times* on 20 October showed Labour's lead dramatically tumbling from 23 to 14 points. There was still six months to go until the last possible date of the Election so defeat, even now, was not inevitable. Surely recovery was possible, as the PM had said?

But then war broke out between the Chancellor and No. 10 again. Shortly after his successful Conference Speech, Clarke learned that Central Office were briefing that it was the Chancellor who was preventing a change in policy on Europe. There would be a different policy for the Election and the Prime Minister would announce it. The Chancellor himself was quoted as saying, 'It put me in a very bad frame of mind.' My sympathy, perhaps surprisingly, was with Clarke since it was far too late now to keep changing policy. And understandably Clarke felt that every time he made a concession he was asked for another, and none of them did any good.

One reason the Major Government was so accident-prone and experienced so many rows in its own ranks was that there were far too many aides from No. 10 and Central Office, some of them barely out of short trousers, who were allowed to run around briefing on the Prime Minister's view on this or that. One of Major's greatest mistakes was not to get a grip on the No. 10 machine. Frequently very junior individuals, eager to impress journalists, overinterpreted the PM's views and betrayed confidences, and sometimes invented things or denigrated Ministers. The PM seemed virtually unaware of the problem.

The next row was one between the Chancellor and Tory backbenchers. No fewer than 150 backbenchers had signed a motion calling for a debate on the Stability Pact on the floor of the House. The Stability Pact was a later addition to the Maastricht Treaty, designed to impose extra fiscal discipline on the single currency countries and make them liable to fines if they had excessive Budget deficits. Eurosceptics feared that the Pact meant that Britain could not pursue its own fiscal policy. I did not agree with the Eurosceptics. I was sure we were protected by our opt-out. The Stability Pact would only affect us if we joined the single currency. But I understood their fears and thought it was quite legitimate to ask for a debate before the Chancellor went to Ecofin to discuss the matter.

Instead of agreeing to this request the Government panicked, thinking this would lead to a rebellion. The Whips, as usual, only made things worse with a crude attempt to put pressure on the Committee that had to decide the form of the debate. To its credit the Committee recommended by one vote a debate on the floor of the House. The Prime Minister was furious. But why? It was entirely reasonable to want a discussion on the floor of the House. Temperatures rose. The *Sun*'s headline – 'Major Out in Ten Days: Will Force Election, Warn Eurorebel MPs' – was as absurd as the Whips stand.

When the debate took place, Clarke, as I expected, was able to give a 'copper-bottomed' guarantee that there would be no interference in British economic policy as long as we didn't join the single currency, so there was no rebellion. Why the Government had so little confidence in its ability to state its own strong case was incomprehensible to me.

In November there was another avoidable incident when a No. 10 aide to Major told Charles Moore, the editor of the *Daily Telegraph*, that the PM was about to announce that he would rule out Britain joining the single currency in the next Parliament. On 2 December Moore ran a story to this effect and wrote that the Prime Minister wanted to persuade Clarke that it was now time to ditch the 'wait and see' policy. The Chancellor, in Brussels at the time, went on to the *Today* programme and denounced the article as 'quite preposterous', saying that the Prime Minister and he were united behind 'a sensible policy'. The newspapers, however, kept on with the story, and even the sober *Financial Times* predicted a change of policy. Then Michael Heseltine went on *The World at One* and categorically ruled out any change of policy either in the Parliament or during the Election campaign. Backbenchers were angry, and so was Clarke. Both sides had good reason to feel let down.

At Prime Minister's Questions that week, Blair quoted Heseltine's *World at One* remarks and asked Major whether he supported them. The Prime Minister replied tersely, 'My Rt Hon. Friend said that that is our position.' This left the impression that the Prime Minister was unhappy and had been overruled by his own Chancellor and Deputy Prime Minister. It appeared a strange thing for a Deputy PM and a Chancellor to do to a Prime Minister, and it seemed even stranger for the PM to want to admit it.

The row wasn't over yet. Clarke was subsequently overheard in Chez Nico telling two BBC journalists that the remarks from No. 10 had been 'a boomerang laden with high explosives' that would rebound in the Prime Minister's face. These words were repeated on *The World at One* the next day.

Whoever was causing the Government problems, it was not backbenchers. Ministers had only themselves to blame, though the machine in Central Office and No. 10 never stopped spreading rumours about plots or threats from backbenchers. The Prime Minister could have done himself a lot of good if he had simply told the staff in No. 10 and Central Office to calm down. With the Government in chaos it was not surprising a Gallup poll showed Labour's lead, which had fallen, had now shot back up again to 35 points.

Within the Cabinet the single currency issue refused to lie down. A Treasury paper made the obvious point that serious thought would have to be given to making the Bank of England independent, even if the Government wanted to maintain the 'wait and see' policy. If the Government wanted to retain the option of joining the first wave of the single currency, work on making the Bank of England independent would need to start before the Election in order for the Bank to become independent after the Election.

Lilley and Howard once again tried to get the policy changed. Clarke disagreed but the Prime Minister wasn't happy to rule out any change in the policy and said he would like a further paper from Clarke after Christmas. MPs wondered which was the real Major. He had denied the *Daily Telegraph* story, then he had appeared unhappy denying it in the House of Commons, and then here he was, unhappily flirting with changing the policy. The Government seemed unable to decide to stay undecided. To add to the pressure on Clarke, Maurice Saatchi favoured a change of policy and wanted to convey the 'Big D' message: 'The European Danger'.

The bookies continued to offer odds on who would replace Major after the Election. One candidate who wasn't usually mentioned obviously felt that he had to get his name into circulation. Astonishingly, Stephen Dorrell, the Health Secretary, published on New Year's Day some remarks calling for a renegotiation of Britain's relationship with Brussels. This was something a Eurosceptic like Cash might have said, but from Dorrell it was utterly incredible.

I knew Dorrell well, since he had been my Financial Secretary, when he did a very good job. He was no Eurosceptic but one of the keenest and most long-standing Europhiles. Cabinet Ministers now seemed to be jumping over each other to put themselves in the best position to succeed Major. When someone as sensible and as level-headed as Stephen Dorrell joined in, things must have been getting pretty desperate.

Yet another line on Europe

The Cabinet disagreements continued. A meeting on 23 January 1997 resulted in a wholly unconvincing fudge. Major and Clarke apparently met before Cabinet and agreed that there should be a change not in policy but 'in tone'. The Government would say it was now 'very unlikely' that the single currency itself would start in 1999.

But it wasn't up to the British Government to speak for other countries. It was an extraordinary position to adopt. Admittedly Major had always tried to convince himself that the single currency wouldn't happen and all his difficulties would disappear, but Clarke must have known perfectly well that there was every likelihood that the single currency would begin in 1999. Chancellor Kohl was hardly likely to be diverted by the opinion of the British Cabinet.

Nonetheless the Chancellor and Prime Minister agreed that if they could say the single currency was unlikely to proceed this would do something to satisfy backbenchers and critics within the Cabinet. Clarke and Rifkind announced this change in Downing Street and the Prime Minister in the House of Commons that afternoon said: 'On the basis of information currently available, it is very unlikely but not impossible that the single currency can proceed safely on 1 January 1999, but if it did proceed with unreliable convergence we would not of course be part of it.' The 'not impossible' qualification added to the impression of a Government twisting and turning. It must have been one of the most unconvincing statements ever made by a British Prime Minister.

This was hailed as the most sceptical stance yet towards EMU, but it was all built on sand. Increasingly Clarke blamed Major rather than the Eurosceptics for putting pressure on him and there were further disputes between Central Office and the Chancellor, particularly about advertisements on the theme of Europe for the Election. Clarke wouldn't agree to posters with the slogan 'Euro Labour, Euro Danger'.

The Cabinet did however manage to pull itself together to make one decision. They decided to commission a new Royal Yacht at a cost of £60 million, nearly two years after John Redwood had offered to make the decision for them.

In February Clarke and Rifkind had yet another row. On 19 February Rifkind announced that he was 'hostile to a single currency' and the Chancellor replied that the Foreign Secretary's comments were 'obviously a slip of the tongue under pressure from a very skilful interviewer'. Major predictably was asked about it by Blair at Question Time and said the Government was 'not hostile in its attitude to a single currency – the position remains that we have an open option'. His reply only deepened the sense of gloom among backbenchers. The Cabinet increasingly looked like a Punch and Judy show. Many backbenchers felt it was ludicrous to go into a General Election knowing that weeks afterwards we would have to make a decision on the single currency. During the Election we were not prepared to give any clue to what our policy would be on an issue the Prime Minister had described 'as of immense constitutional significance'.

Redwood deserved a prize for the understatement of the year. When calling for clearer leadership, he said, 'Sometimes confusing messages were being given.'

21

Adoption at Harrogate and Defeat

Wherever life leads, there one must follow.
Oscar Wilde

My support for Redwood and my vote against the Government greatly increased the problem of finding a seat to fight at the General Election. Kingston was to be split and merged with the two neighbouring constituencies of Surbiton and Richmond Park, but both seats had sitting MPs, Dick Tracey and Jeremy Hanley, who wanted to stand again. Since these existing constituencies would make up the larger part of each of the two new seats my chances of getting the nomination in either were not great.

A reverse at Surbiton and Kingston

The Officers of my own Association, who did not want to lose me, encouraged me at least to make an attempt to get the nomination for one of the seats. In the end I decided to challenge Dick Tracey. I was initially reluctant because we had over the years cooperated amicably on local matters. Relations between neighbouring MPs can often be strained, but ours had never been. Dick was understandably cross with me, but since just under 40 per cent of the new seat came from my constituency I was, under Central Office rules, well within my rights.

Dick need not have worried as, although I won over quite a proportion of his constituents in the vote, I narrowly lost. However, the newspapers chose to interpret the result as meaning that I had been rejected by my own constituents. That was not the case. After the result had been declared Dick made a victory speech in which he gave a lecture on 'loyalty'.

The publicity over this rejection at Surbiton made my problem even more difficult. Why should a seat want someone who had been rejected by his 'own constituency'? In the autumn I was rejected by several seats without an interview, though not by quite as many as the press said, but I reached the semi-final in North West Hampshire. I felt encouraged to think that I would eventually be successful, and I received a number of overtures from several different parts of the country. Lady Thatcher wrote to me, 'Don't worry about the constituency, you will find one when you least expect it'.

Despair was beginning to set in again when in December 1995 I received a letter inviting me for an interview at the vacant seat of Harrogate and Knaresborough in Yorkshire. In many ways it appeared ideal, close to Rosemary's mother's home at Thorp Arch, so I had visited the area frequently.

Politically it had a somewhat troubled history. The sitting MP, Robert Banks, had had some disagreements with the local Association and had decided not to offer himself for reselection after it moved to open up the selection of a candidate. Furthermore the boundaries had been altered so that it lost its rural hinterland and now consisted only of the towns of Harrogate and Knaresborough. It was less safe than it had been, and it was difficult to know how at risk it might be.

Central Office put the theoretical majority at 9,700 over the Liberal Democrats on the basis of the same vote as 1992. While I was pessimistic about the General Election I thought the Liberal Democrats would not do well if Blair was going to win. Looking for a constituency, my rule of thumb was to rule out any with a

Conservative majority of less than 15,000 over Labour or less than 10,000 over the Liberal Democrats, so Harrogate was just on the border line. But I decided, after consulting several people, including William Hague who sat for neighbouring Richmond, to let my name go forward.

Selection at Harrogate

The selection procedure was unusually prolonged, with three stages. I passed through the first two rounds fairly easily and the final meeting of the whole Association was fixed for a date in January at the Majestic Hotel, on the top of the hill on the Ripon Road in Harrogate.

Inevitably during such protracted procedures, my name leaked out and there was some adverse local reaction. At lunchtime in Thorp Arch, on the day of the selection meeting, I turned on the television and saw people being interviewed at a Yorkshire Post Literary Lunch in Harrogate. Asked what they thought about me, they were unanimously rude. At that point I said to Rosemary, 'I really don't want to be chosen. If that is how they feel, they can keep it.'

I was in a rather aggressive mood as Rosemary drove me to the Majestic Hotel, where there was chaos when we arrived. As I got out of the car I could hardly see because of the TV lights. In the dark I heard a woman screaming, 'Mr Lamont, what do you say to those who say you are liability?'

The meeting itself was not large, only about 200 people, because the Association had been badly run down. By this stage I didn't care about the result. When I was asked about loyalty to the Party and my vote against the Government I pointed out that I had voted only three times in over twenty years against my Party. I said that perhaps the criticism should be that I hadn't been independent enough. I considered that the very existence of Britain as an independent country was at stake with the single currency and I couldn't imagine any issue that was more important. It had to come before Party loyalty. The Government didn't seem to know whether the existence of Britain as a self-governing country was or was not at stake. I was sorry, but that to me was unacceptable. My reply was greeted with applause.

I didn't expect to be chosen and was now quite relaxed. I could not have been more surprised when Estelle Edwards, the elegant Chairman of the Association, walked into the room, looked at me and said, 'Lamont it is.' I had won by a small majority.

Colin Brown from the *Independent* told me that when people went into the meeting they were making hostile and critical remarks about me. When they came out they were all saying, 'He's quite different from how the press write about him. You should have heard him.' One lady even added the final accolade, 'He hasn't got piggy eyes at all!'

The *Yorkshire Evening Post*, under the predictable headline 'Norman Conquest', wrote: 'Former Chancellor Norman Lamont has shocked the pundits . . . Observers at the Selection Meeting . . . said Mr Lamont gave a stunning performance which won over the doubters.' One lady who preferred not to be named said she was 'spitting feathers'.

I was indeed pleased to get Harrogate. John Major congratulated me when we bumped into each other in a corridor and said he was pleased. I think he was. There were comments in some papers that he was glad I had not got too safe a seat, and thus would be kept busy, but that was too Machiavellian.

There were other suggestions in the press that he had helped me get the seat. It was true that Central Office had, after talks between myself and Party Chairman Brian Mawhinney, made it clear to constituency Chairmen that there was no reason why I shouldn't be chosen, but neither Central Office not anyone else could influence a meeting of two hundred people.

There were few ripples of dissent in the Association after my selection, which were played up by the press, but these quickly died down and I was warmly supported by all the branches of the Association for the next year. Switching from one constituency to another is never easy. Voters tend to be suspicious of newcomers, and that is probably even truer in Yorkshire than anywhere else.

Harrogate and Knaresborough

I hugely enjoyed my year and a quarter as a candidate for Harrogate and Knaresborough. I was keen to win the seat, not simply to return to the House of Commons but because I liked the idea of representing a place of real character and elegance. While I had enjoyed being the MP for Kingston and had many good friends there, sadly it had become a somewhat anonymous part of London. Its history had largely disappeared from view. I always used to say of Kingston that the people who worked there didn't live there and the people who lived there didn't work there. You could only meet your constituents in schools and churches. If they were unmarried, not religious and not retired they were difficult to find.

The constituency was not just Harrogate, but Harrogate and Knaresborough. The latter was a delightful market town which was older than Harrogate and, at the time of King John, had been an important financial centre. Knaresborough was on the edge of a spectacular gorge, and in the back streets there was a wonderful stillness and feeling of timelessness.

Harrogate itself was once described rather insultingly to me by a Yorkshire MP as 'the Chelsea of the North'. I don't think that is accurate, but I could see what he was trying to say. Originally a village in the Forest of Knaresborough, the town developed into an international spa visited by royalty from many countries in the nineteenth century. It had wonderful antique shops and bookshops as well as the famous Betty's tea room, with its cinnamon toast. Such is the extent of globalisation that this English institution was now owned by a Swiss gentleman. I also enjoyed retiring to the Swan Hotel, where Agatha Christie had once disappeared. Occasionally I wished I could disappear. Alas, the world in which one could 'disappear' in a hotel in Yorkshire has itself vanished.

I went up to Harrogate almost every weekend. I had promised the Selection Committee that I would come 'so often they would be quite dismayed' and I nearly reached that point. I accepted invitations to every function to which I was asked. Harrogate had innumerable local societies: literary groups and conservation groups, and an excellent art gallery. Whenever there was spare time I was happy simply to wander round the town, exploring and taking in the architecture. I enjoyed going to Harrogate so much I once said to Paul Meyrick, the new Chairman of the Association, 'I can't believe this is work. I enjoy it so much.'

All the time I was the candidate in Harrogate I still had to carry on as MP for Kingston and deal with my constituents' problems. The Kingston Association Chairman, Ron Gill, a good friend, wanted me back in the House of Commons and made it quite clear that the local Tories did not require my presence at Conservative functions. For them it was important that I won Harrogate. But I continued to hold surgeries and deal with the regular mail from my constituents.

The General Election: the local campaign

I gradually came to realise that the seat was not quite as safe as William Hague had led me to believe. The Liberal Democrats dominated the council and the Liberal Democrat candidate was the Leader of the council as well as being a local teacher. He was not much liked, but well entrenched. The Liberal Democrats were massively targeting the seat and had poured money into it many months before the General Election. For the fifteen months while I was the candidate they bombarded households with mailshots, often letters from Paddy Ashdown, referring to 'London-based sacked Chancellor Norman Lamont' and contrasting me with their candidate, the local teacher. These letters, in my view, should have counted as General Election expenses since they were promoting one candidate and attacking another by name.

Although I recognised it would be a tough fight, I still expected to win. Nationally I thought the Conservative Party would be massacred. Privately I had actually taken a bet with Bob Worcester, the Chairman of MORI, who did not believe his own opinion polls and thought Labour would win only by about 50 seats. I bet him £100 that Labour's majority would be over 100.

I thought the Conservative Party would poll around 30 per

cent of the vote and that, in an Election fought largely on TV, the Blair effect would be felt in Harrogate as much as elsewhere. Although Harrogate had a strong Liberal Democrat Party I thought many dissatisfied Tories would nonetheless make the complete jump to Labour and the anti-Tory vote would be split between the Liberal Democrats and Labour. I was also sceptical about tactical voting. In every election I had fought in Kingston people had always predicted tactical voting and it never happened.

During the Election campaign I tried hard to keep myself out of the national news, turning down requests for interviews on TV and radio unless they had some constituency angle and I even declined many of those to discourage national TV programmes from running special programmes about the 'expected close result at Harrogate'. I also tried to do the same with journalists from the national press.

The Liberals Democrats' campaign had the opposite objective. Every article in a magazine, such as *The Economist*, that suggested Harrogate might go Liberal Democrat was reproduced locally. They tried to encourage the national press to come to the constituency and profile it. For visiting journalists they produced a press pack about me that reproduced in lurid detail all the tabloid stories about Thresher, Miss Whiplash and my credit card. These were then put alongside disparaging comments from 'local voters', so the press were given the impression the voters of Harrogate were very opposed to me. Actually the people couldn't have been friendlier.

On one occasion the Liberal Democrats went too far and I was forced to take legal action against sixteen Liberal Democrat Councillors and the Liberal Democrat candidate when they circulated a leaflet alleging that I had been accused of bribery by the Parliamentary Commissioner for Standards. I was amazed at their reluctance to apologise. Eventually, after I had shown my determination to sue, a few councillors conceded, and then a few more, and then all of them, but the Parliamentary Candidate hung on until we were about to go to court. He was forced to make an apology in court and to undertake that he would circulate literature withdrawing the charge. In fact he made his apology in a leaflet in such small print that it is no exaggeration to say it required a magnifying glass to read it.

John Major had planned an extra long campaign for the 1997 Election, believing that Labour's policy weaknesses would be exposed. That was a reasonable view, but unfortunately the extra week was lost as it was dominated entirely by sleaze. The leadership couldn't make up their mind whether to veto Neil Hamilton as a local candidate or to say that it was entirely a matter for the local Association and the same uncertainty characterised the handling of the problems of Piers Merchant, MP for Beckenham. Both Brian Mawhinney and Michael Heseltine veered from one position to the other and helped to keep these matters alive.

Our campaign lacked a strategy. Michael Heseltine had believed for the last year that rising real disposable incomes would assure rising real popularity for the Conservative Party. This may have happened in the past, but rather like iron laws of monetary policy, so-called political laws also have a habit of breaking down when they are followed too closely. This belief also resulted in the Conservative Government spending a whole year sitting in office waiting, not knowing what it was wanting to do.

In Harrogate I deliberately tried to campaign as much as possible on local issues. Some people in my Association were doubtful of the wisdom of this, but I felt it was important to show that I was genuinely interested in the constituency, as I was, and to try to neutralise the local domination of the Liberal Democrats. I also felt there were no national issues, other than Europe, that I wished to emphasise. Party workers were enthusiastic about making Europe the issue.

Most of the time during the campaign was spent simply canvassing. Rosemary did a huge amount of work every day. I was also helped by Rupert Darwall, my former advisor in the Treasury, Wendy, my hard-working secretary, whose family came from Yorkshire, and Peter Fullerton. A group from Kingston also came up, as well as Eurosceptics from different parts of the country and elsewhere in Yorkshire. Other friends like William Astor came up for odd days, as did a number of students and other young people who felt strongly about the single currency.

Europe and the Election

I had no doubt, and have no doubt today, that the Yorkshire voters were strongly Eurosceptical. When I became the candidate the membership of the Association rose as people who were opposed to the single currency joined. All the time I was there I had a large number of letters supporting my position on Europe.

Many academics, such as Tony King, have written that the 1997 Election showed that Europe did not matter. My experience was quite different. It was mentioned more frequently than any other issue, with the possible exception of the National Health Service. One night my canvassing team and I were watching *Newsnight* when Peter Kellner explained that the polls showed quite clearly that Europe did not matter to voters. The whole room spontaneously exploded with laughter. My impression was confirmed by visiting journalists who had visited seats throughout the country.

The Conservative Party was in no position to exploit the European issue since its own position was formally no different from that of Labour. Tony Blair moved to a more Eurosceptical position and wrote articles in the *Sun* newspaper to give the impression that he was opposed to the single currency. It was noticeable that when Major mentioned Europe at the morning press conferences there was an immediate rise in the temperature on the doorstep. Other candidates told me they had exactly the same experience.

In all my literature I stressed my opposition to the single currency. We had one superb large poster with that message in a prominent site in Knaresborough. A remarkable feature of the Election was that at least 150 Conservative candidates in winnable seats stated in their Election addresses that they were against the single currency. Since official policy was not to rule out the single currency, this was a remarkable show of independence. Some were no doubt motivated by a desire not to be opposed by a Referendum candidate.

The Conservative Party leadership rather surprisingly seemed completely unprepared as to how to react to this extraordinary situation. Before the General Election Clarke had stated that it would be absurd if Conservative candidates maintained their own policy position on the single currency, but once again this issue had been blurred and Major had given a more ambiguous answer to Blair at Question Time on this matter.

I had warned the Party over a year before the Election that this problem was inevitable. At lunch at the *Spectator* I had told Maurice Saatchi that in my opinion at least 80–100 MPs would have their own policy on Europe. That was something of an underestimate. I pointed out that it would be embarrassing and we ought to work out how to handle it.

But the Party got in a dreadful tangle over this and some Ministers even joined the rebellion. This was something I had not anticipated. One of the first was Angela Browning, a junior Agriculture Minister, who stated that she was against the single currency if it meant that control of our reserves was transferred to Frankfurt. Major managed to present this as a position that was consistent with not ruling out the single currency, but that was unbelievable. Angela was then followed by John Horam, a junior Health Minister, who simply stated that he was against the single currency. He appeared somewhat sheepish on TV about this and there were great cries from the press for him to be sacked, but Major had little choice but to accept his position. What was the point of sacking a person who probably wouldn't be a Minister in a few days?

John Major's considered response to these difficulties was to make an impassioned plea at a morning press conference for the Conservative Party not to 'bind his hands' in future negotiations. Apparently it was unscripted and spontaneous. It came across well on TV and several newspapers described it as an impressive performance.

So it was, and it increased interest on the European issue immediately on the doorstep. But it was nonsense. It was disingenuous, because the important details of the single currency had long ago been settled. Major was merely rehearsing the same old line that he had used for the last few years in order to avoid a decision. But the indisputable absurdity of Major's appeal was that by the time he made it Conservative candidates' Election addresses had long ago been written and sent to the printers. He knew that perfectly well. If Conservative candidates had ever wanted to respond to his appeal, there was nothing they could have done.

I did not wish to add to the Party's national problems. Whenever newspapers rang up and asked for a copy of my Election address my agent was instructed to tell them it was in the post. It was never sent to a single paper. The journalists never noticed that it didn't arrive. When papers like the *Daily Mail* printed long lists of those who had made specific pledges in their Election addresses I was always listed as 'position unknown'!

A visit to William Hague

The Conservative campaign nationally lacked the sort of clear theme we had in 1992. Maurice Saatchi would have liked to have made the single currency the main issue, but that was not allowed. I know he felt there was a lack of direction.

Much has been written about how the ERM debate cost the Conservatives their reputation for economic competence but I was struck by the fact that during the whole election only one person ever mentioned the ERM to me. As I state elsewhere, I suspect the ERM was more an inhibiting factor in the minds of Conservative politicians than for ordinary voters. The ERM exit was, after all, something that had happened all of four and a half years previously. Much had gone right with the economy since.

If Conservative MPs had wanted guidance on how to deal with questions about the ERM they wouldn't have got much help from the *Campaign Guide*, the fat volume written to assist candidates. A glance at the index showed that the ERM was hardly mentioned. It didn't seem to make much sense to provide Conservative candidates with no briefing at all on the matter, even if it was for defensive purposes only.

Michael Howard was one of several Ministers who came to help me at Harrogate, giving a press conference and joining me on a walkabout in Harrogate shopping centre. I was delighted to see Michael, who, within a few minutes of arriving offered the opinion, 'This is the best atmosphere in any constituency we have visited anywhere in the country!'

Another welcome visitor was William Hague, who didn't have far to come; he did much the same as Michael but then spoke to Party workers in the headquarters. It was interesting to watch his effect on the audience. Most of them knew him as a neighbouring MP but had not met him in person. William made a short, but highly effective speech. When he left the room the reaction was warm and several of the audience were heard to say, 'He ought to be Party Leader.' It was not surprising that during the subsequent post-Election leadership consultation exercise the Harrogate constituency voted for William.

I also talked to William several times on the telephone during the campaign. I was getting increasingly nervous about how things were going and was keen for his opinion, since he knew the constituency well. William and I expected the Conservative Party to lose the election but he thought the Party would get a rather higher percentage of the vote than I expected. He was quite confident that the effort I had put into Harrogate in the last year was having a big impact. He had heard many favourable comments and thought I would win fairly comfortably.

On another occasion I went over to William's home on a Saturday night. When I arrived he was still in his gym downstairs and I chatted to Ffion, then we drank a bottle of wine between us. We briefly discussed the leadership election that might follow an Election defeat. At that stage William thought that Michael Portillo was the most likely candidate to win, but he did significantly add, 'Unless I decide to go for it myself.' As soon as I heard him say that I thought he probably was going to stand. I later learned that he had mentioned the matter to other MPs during the Election.

On 10 April *The Times* in an editorial entitled 'Endangered species' urged Harrogate voters to support me because I would influence the European debate in the next Parliament: 'He has, braving criticism from above, been the most intelligent and articulate figure suggesting fundamental renegotiation or outright withdrawal are options worthy of consideration . . . Mr Lamont's continued presence in the Commons would help steer the Conservative debate in the right direction.' I was grateful, but how many people in Harrogate follow the recommendations of *The Times*?

Our canvassing returns in Harrogate continued to show us clearly in the lead. One evening I was canvassing in a not very prosperous street that I would have expected to be a Liberal Democrat area, but to my astonishment the result was overwhelmingly Conservative.

I became sceptical about the figures and the replies that people were giving. I suspected voters were just being polite and wondered whether perhaps we should knock 30 per cent off the total of pledges we had gathered. That would make it much closer. I was also uneasy that the Labour Party appeared to be making no effort at all and I wondered whether their voters were switching to the Liberal Democrats.

Another evening, again canvassing in a modest street, I came across a house with a Labour sticker in the window. I was rather pleased, as there were very few of them. The owner of the house came out and congratulated me on the hard work I had been doing. He then introduced himself as the chairman of the Labour Ward Committee. I said, 'Well, at least you will be voting Labour,' but to my dismay he replied, 'I didn't say that.' If the Labour Ward Chairman with posters in his window was switching to the Liberal Democrats, then how many others must be doing the same?

The Liberal Democrats had organised a tremendous poster campaign. All the main roads, many of the minor streets and apparently every tree were covered in orange posters that swelled up in size like balloons as polling day got nearer. Their expenses budget must have been enormous. They also continued to send selected households letters from Paddy Ashdown blaming me personally for the recession and referring endlessly to VAT on fuel and power. It was pointless to point out that the Liberal Democrat Party had been the first to call for a tax on energy use, but their campaign was organised and designed to reinforce the point that a Labour vote was wasted and the only way to get the hated Lamont out was to vote Liberal Democrat. They also had an intensive telephone canvassing campaign. We managed to trace several of the calls and were not surprised to find that many of them came from London. I wondered what the expense of that was.

Later I learned that the Liberal Democrats had given up canvassing in neighbouring constituencies and had flooded into Harrogate. At the same time Labour had flooded out, making no effort in Harrogate and going to Leeds. My agent, having been very optimistic in the last few days of the campaign, suddenly became pessimistic and said he thought the result might be very close, possibly a recount.

I decided to ask Peter Fullerton if he could telephone recorded Labour supporters from our canvass to see if they were still intending to vote Labour. His conclusion was grim. He told me they were nearly all going to vote Liberal Democrat. From that moment I knew I had lost.

Fortunately I only came to that conclusion two days before Election Day, and we continued to work hard right up to the end. On Polling Day, 1 May, as in my Kingston campaigns, Rosemary and I toured the Committee Rooms and polling stations. I was struck by the absence of any evidence of a Labour campaign. Again following the Kingston pattern, I went home to Thorp Arch in the early evening for supper. I told Rosemary I did not want her to come to the count. She had been present at every count in every Election I had fought since 1972. I felt it was quite likely to be an unpleasant occasion and I did not want her to see it. I decided to take James.

Defeat

In telling Rosemary not to come to the count I had in mind the dreadful scenes at Bath in 1992 when Chris Patten, defeated by the Liberal Democrats, had been appallingly shouted down. I knew that Lavender had been very upset. However, my fears were overdone, largely because the Harrogate Conference Centre, where the count was taking place, was so huge that the crowd was lost in the sheer size of the room. There was no atmosphere. I arrived before the other candidates, which was bad planning. When my Liberal Democrat opponent arrived he immediately gave a great victory salute.

My agent told me he thought I had lost by 3,000. In fact it was worse – I lost by 6,000. I felt resigned and quite relaxed. I had been through so many crises in recent years that it was difficult to feel any great sense of shock at this latest turn of events. I joked and chatted with Liberal Democrat Party workers. Inevitably, however, the television news managed to catch one momentary shot of me looking very gloomy and chose to broadcast it.

When the result was declared I congratulated my opponent and said that it was a very great honour to be an MP, but it was a very special honour to sit in the House of Commons for a place as glorious as Harrogate and Knaresborough. I said that I envied my opponent, and that I wished him luck.

Immediately after the declaration the TV cameras and journalists thronged around me. I had no particular interest in giving any interviews, especially when the shouted first question was, 'Don't you agree you were the wrong candidate for this seat?' My son and Peter Fullerton, who tried to clear a way for me to get to the door, were described by one journalist as 'heavies from London' trying to protect me.

I then went back to Party headquarters. Many of the Party workers were very upset both by my defeat but also the scale of the Labour victory. Paul Meyrick made a short speech. I then went back to Thorp Arch with James and watched the results for the rest of the country. I was sorry when Michael Portillo was defeated and admired the typical grace with which he accepted it. I did not feel any great wish to go to bed and at about 5 a.m. I telephoned Michael Howard. I was pleased that he had at least survived. He was kind enough not to complain about the hour. I also saw my opponent on TV proposing a toast 'to Norman Lamont'.

Inevitably some commentators put the loss of the seat down to me personally. I did not feel there was much that was personal about the defeat, although the Liberal Democrat campaign had attempted to be personal. The swing against me in Harrogate was above average for the country and Yorkshire, but it was not as high as the swing in Sheffield Hallam, the other Yorkshire seat targeted by the Liberal Democrats.

The appearance of an above average swing was caused by tactical voting. Swing is a two-party concept and becomes meaningless with three parties. I was interested to note that my

Conservative vote and Michael Howard's Conservative vote fell by exactly the same percentage amount, but he won by 5,000 and I lost by 6,000 because in his case many voters switched to Labour, whereas in my case they went overwhelmingly to the Liberal Democrats.

Others argued that my result, and Michael Portillo's, showed that Europe as an issue did not matter. Pollsters like Anthony King and Peter Kellner argue this strongly. I can only say, and I know that many other Conservative MPs agree with me, that voters were deeply interested in the European issue. Once, when I put this to Anthony King, he suggested that perhaps voters talked to me about Europe because they knew I had views on it. But it was the experience of my canvassers as well. Europe did not become a decisive issue because both parties had on the surface identical policies. In British elections voters make their choice for parties rather than individuals. Every time Europe looked as though it might become an issue there was a strong almost tangible response on the doorstep.

The next day I had the satisfaction of hearing on the lunchtime TV news that 'the defeat of the former Chancellor, Norman Lamont, in Harrogate has been warmly welcomed in the European Commission and in Brussels'. That cheered me up a lot. At least I knew I had got to them.

22

The Major Years, 1990–97

Yet all experience is an arch wherethro'
Gleams that untravelled world whose margin fades
For ever and for ever when I move.
                                    Alfred, Lord Tennyson

In any circumstances, John Major would have faced a difficult task in the 1997 Election. The Conservative Party had been in power since 1979 and the country had grown tired of its stale rhetoric. In some ways the country had voted repeatedly for Mrs Thatcher in the 1980s against its own instincts. Mrs Thatcher was lucky, except in 1979, in that she faced weak opponents as alternative Prime Ministers. She had been able to impose radical government on a slightly unwilling country because there was no obviously acceptable alternative Prime Minister. Tony Blair was both acceptable and electable. Even Mrs Thatcher would have had difficulty in defeating him.

In 1992 John Major's fresh face had unexpectedly won a victory for the Tories against the odds. Sometimes one had the feeling that the country and the newspapers had not really wanted a Tory victory in 1992. This was the victory we were not meant to have. Certainly the newspapers seemed to feel so, and they were determined to prove their point. Major had to put up with some unprecedently unpleasant personal attacks. But nothing can take away from him the credit for his victory in 1992. And it is ludicrous to argue, as some Conservatives do, that it would have been better to have lost the 1992 Election. You cannot pick and choose which victories you will accept in politics.

There were important achievements in the Major Government. The enlargement of the EU owes much to John Major. The Council Tax was a better tax than the Poll Tax that it replaced. I was one of the strongest critics of the Northern Ireland peace process and I still feel uneasy about its contradictions, but thanks to Major's perseverance it at least produced a respite from never-ending violence. The privatisation of the railways was not a popular measure, but it was an extension of Thatcherism. I am convinced that it will endure and in time provide a revival of the railways.

The economic inheritance of the Blair Government from the Major administration was also undeniably a strong one. The public finances were sound and there was a ratchet movement downwards in the level of inflation, which Labour's move to an independent Bank of England locked into a permanent achievement. Britain now has European levels of inflation that look like persisting. Unfortunately, all the political benefit has gone to Blair.

The verdict of history will be kinder to John Major than the tabloid newspapers of that time. Even so, there will be a sense that the hopes and opportunities of victory were never realised but needlessly thrown away. Drift and indecision turned the country virulently against the Conservatives.

And so, on 2 May 1997, there was a palpable sense of release. The country was happy with what it had done. The new Government got off to a bold start, rising in the opinion polls. If voters had known on election day what they would later feel about the new Government, they would have given Tony Blair an even larger majority.

This was no ordinary defeat for the Conservative Party. Its scale cannot be accounted for by policy failure. After all, in 1974 Ted Heath only narrowly lost although the country was in a deep crisis as a result of his policies. Neither can it be explained, as many commentators would like to, as just a result of Black Wednesday. The country's humiliation following the Suez fiasco in 1956 was followed three years later by a massive Conservative election victory. The real plunge in John Major's Government's popularity ratings came in late 1993 and 1994, not in 1992.

Unlike the 1979 election, the 1997 election was not a repudiation of the status quo but a confirmation of it. For Labour could only become electable by promising not to reverse what the Conservatives had achieved since 1979. The only thing the electorate wanted to change was the Government. They wanted the Tories out. Labour's most potent weapon was to exploit the fear of a Conservative fifth term. The prospect of five more years of the same was unendurable. Conservatives had put themselves into a position where the country felt it could not move forward until they were out of the way. Tony Blair's task was to project reassurance and to minimise the risks associated with having a Labour Government while appearing fresh and energetic. He did this brilliantly. It was too late for the Conservative Party, and hanging on purposelessly until almost the last moment made the eventual outcome even worse.

The mandate won by the Conservative Party in 1979 had been delivered. The Party had to renew its mission while in office. This would have been hard to achieve at the best of times. What added to the difficulty was that the Government divided between those who enthusiastically supported Thatcherism and those who were still Heathites at heart.

The success of Thatcherism through the mid-1980s depended on the partnership between Margaret Thatcher and Nigel Lawson at the Treasury. It was a cause of great sadness to me to see that partnership fall apart. I greatly admired both of them, and they were crucial to each other's continued success. Ironically, each of them was right in their criticism of the other. Nigel Lawson, allegedly the less political of the two, was absolutely right in predicting that the Poll Tax would be the disaster it was. At the same time, Margaret Thatcher's instinct that something was going wrong with monetary policy turned out to be correct. Their rupture, which became final in 1989 with Nigel's resignation, spelt the end of the Thatcherite dominance of the Government. It would be only a matter of time before Margaret herself followed.

By then the senior ranks of her Government were bereft of her supporters. The generation that had led the Party's intellectual revival in the 1970s was no longer in front-line politics. Keith Joseph had gone. Nick Ridley had been forced to resign. Norman Tebbit and Cecil Parkinson, for different reasons, were no longer candidates for the leadership. Younger Thatcherites such as Michael Howard, Peter Lilley and myself were on the fringes of the Cabinet. Mrs Thatcher had been careless in ensuring that her philosophy would thrive by bringing on her natural supporters. By the time she fell, the Cabinet was dominated by Heathites such as Douglas Hurd or weathervanes who would follow the prevailing wind. The younger generation of Ministers was more Thatcherite and anyone who knew the Party outside Parliament understood that its heart beat on the right.

Despite their dominance of the Cabinet, the left could not gain complete ascendancy over the right because of the colossal success of Thatcherism, yet the right could not prevail unless its candidate became leader.

In this situation, John Major turned out to be the ideal leadership candidate in a way that I had not fully appreciated at the time. With hindsight it is clear. He had cultivated to quite an extraordinary level of execution the ability to encourage people on both sides of any question to believe that he was one of them. This facility was the secret of John Major's political success and his rapid rise. Vital as it was to getting him into No. 10, it was the opposite of what was required in leading a Party that needed reinvigoration and fresh impetus far more than an image makeover.

It meant imparting a clear sense of direction, but that would have required choosing one side and upsetting the other. His reluctance to do this meant there was no fixity of purpose. It was difficult to know where he stood on any of the big issues. At the beginning of his Premiership he was in favour of higher public spending. By the end he said he wanted to get public spending down to 35 per cent of GDP, a level not seen since the 1950s. In public, he would talk about his hatred of inflation and the need to have zero inflation. He claimed his view was a reaction to inflation destroying his father's gnome business. I found this strange, as there was little inflation after the war. But in private he would tell me when I was Chancellor that he couldn't see what was wrong with a bit of inflation.

Governments need a sense of direction. Decisions have to be made and they determine whether the Government has a coherent programme that can be sold to its supporters and defended against attack from its opponents. If done well, it results in a political achievement greater than the sum of its parts. If not, it results in confusion and muddle. The Government lacked a big idea. The emphasis continuously placed on the National Lottery or the Citizens' Charter and the Cones Hotline merely served to underline the absence of one.

Early on there was an attempt to spin a philosophy of Majorism around some fairly innocuous ideas. But it didn't last long. Anthony Seldon, Major's biographer, argues that Major's difficulty in fashioning a coherent programme arose because he didn't have enough time to think. But this misses the essence of John Major as a politician. His whole success had been based on not being categorised. But events wait for no man, least of all a Prime Minister who didn't like making up his mind. Eventually it led to deep distrust on the part of colleagues in Government, the press and the electorate.

Although Europe came to dominate the Major Government the economy and Europe were linked. The ERM, if we were to have it, should simply have been a tool of monetary policy, similar to targeting M3. There was force in the Treasury's argument that part of Britain's record of poor inflation was the inability to stick at a consistent policy for any length of time, although that generalisation overlooked the impact of German reunification and the nature of the recession. For the first time since the depression between the wars, economists were talking about debt deflation.

However, for John Major the ERM wasn't about monetary policy but part of the Government's European policy, which made disengagement from the ERM politically impossible except by being forced out. It was a heavy price to pay to be seen as Good Europeans. Except for the embarrassing and trivial attempt to find 'fault lines' in the ERM, the Government never publicly addressed the reasons why the ERM failed. This added to the

Government's difficulties. The clear lesson was the need to keep
monetary policy entirely separate from European policy.

Following in the wake of the ERM, the Government had to
start paying the bills for greater public spending. By 1990 planned
spending increases were vulnerable if the economy slowed down
and two pre-Election spending increases overlaid them. The recession further intensified pressure to spend. As John Major told
Anthony Seldon, 'I followed Keynesian policies. If I had not let
government spending increase, unemployment would have been
much higher.' Higher spending also reflected his political prefer-
ence, as well as those of other senior Ministers such as Chris
Patten and Douglas Hurd. At a fundamental level it appeared as
if John Major did not understand the basic connection between
increased spending and taxation. During the 1992 Election, the
Prime Minister said that Britain had never been in such a good
position to borrow. Debt has to be serviced and higher spending
meant higher taxes. During the Election the Prime Minister
insisted the spending increases were sacrosanct. The cost would
be paid in terms of the Conservative Party's reputation for being
trusted on taxes.

With my departure from the Treasury and the ensuing reshuffle, Michael Portillo was the only Thatcherite left in any of the
Cabinet's economic posts. The change was to have important
consequences. There was a second large tax-raising budget. Given
the windfall the public services had received from lower inflation,
there was ample scope for cutting public spending but, more
important than any single action, senior Ministers no longer
believed in tax cuts. There was a certain relish in raising taxes.
The Conservative party vacated the moral high ground that it
had occupied since the 1970s. When Ken Clarke did cut the basic
rate in November 1996, it seemed like a grudge cut – opportunistic, against his instincts, and done for electoral reasons rather
than belief. In the battle of ideas, the Conservative party stopped
fighting and switched sides.

Thus the convergence between Labour and Conservative gathered pace. There was one big winner – Tony Blair. Labour's
traversal across the political spectrum to acceptance of the big
Conservative reforms was made easier by the Major Government.

In 1992 the announcement of the 20 pence lower rate band high-lighted the difference between the two Parties on taxation. By 1997, there was no difference. It would have needed a bold move, such as doubling the threshold for the 40 per cent tax band, to win back the tax agenda, but that was far from anyone's thinking. Instead the Blairite hegemony was demonstrated by Labour's clever campaign alleging that the Major Government was lurching to the right. Nothing could have been further from the truth. But it worked, and the Major Government kept rigidly to the centre.

John Major and Europe

Europe was the issue that destroyed John Major's Government. Even if other issues mattered more to the voter, because of its effect upon the Conservative Party, Europe became the most important one.

Of course John Major's position was unenviable and extremely awkward. The party was divided, but his approach of trying to bridge the splits by keeping options open was only ever going to work for a limited time.

When a decision has to be made by a specific date, the nearer that date comes, the less convincing it sounds to say that you haven't made up your mind. And when passions run as high as they did over the single currency it is in the end necessary to come down on one side or the other. Persisting with ambivalence merely invited both sides to push their case even harder up to the last moment.

John Major's formal position in 1997 was that we might actually join the single currency in 1998, when half his party was against it.

It is difficult to see why Major was so determined in trying to keep his options open on the single currency unless he really did think that a Conservative Government needed to join. Most of his rhetoric from 1993 onwards was Eurosceptical in tone. I myself could never work out on which side John Major's convictions really lay. That may have been a tribute to his skill. Sometimes I thought he simply wanted to be on the side that history would judge the winner. As that varied from time to time, so his opinion varied. John was never the sort of person for whom lost causes had any attraction, which is perhaps the ultimate irony of his Premiership.

He made life more difficult for himself when he appointed Kenneth Clarke rather than Michael Howard or Peter Lilley as Chancellor in succession to me. He then compounded the problem by making Michael Heseltine Deputy Prime Minister. This is not to say that Ken Clarke and Michael Heseltine did not do their jobs well. But they had clearer views than he on the issue and so made it impossible for him to move from his position. He became their hostage. At times in conversation he seemed to relish being in that position. He was always telling backbenchers he couldn't change his policy on Europe because the Chancellor wouldn't let him.

In exactly the same way he seemed to relish having a small majority. I remember listening to him telling a manifestly bored Chancellor Kohl in Munich in 1992 about the problems of his small majority in the House of Commons. Of course the small majority made life more difficult, but a determined party with a small majority responds to leadership. The problem of the small majority was intensified rather than lessened by the style of the Government and the way it made its decisions.

Even if John Major thought it unwise to rule out the single currency for ever he could easily have ruled it out for the next Parliament, which was what most of the Cabinet and the Party wanted. William Hague did just that, and as a result led a more united, though not, of course, more unanimous, Party. It is difficult to see why Major did not do the same, because in reality no Conservative Government ever could have taken Britain into the single currency in the 1997 Parliament. If he had not appointed Clarke and Heseltine that would have been an option for him.

A decision against the single currency would have invited opposition from some committed Europhiles, but both Mrs Thatcher and William Hague have shown that firm decisions create fewer problems in the long run than a policy of being merely decided to be undecided and to be adamant for drift. It would not have been a painless choice, but Major's position would have been stronger. In his heart I suspect he did not want to make up his mind because part of him told him that one day the single currency might happen.

Britain only negotiated at Maastricht so as not to be isolated. Having a difficult hand does not remove the need to define the end goal. The opt-out was a tactical device to buy time.

Although the conclusion of the Maastricht negotiations had been warmly praised, the Treaty's ratification proved very different. For the first time MPs and the press were faced with the unwelcome reality of European integration. Up until then it was possible for mainstream MPs to reassure themselves that the logic of European integration was a spectre conjured up by those with overvivid imaginations. Maastricht changed all that. The mainstream became Eurosceptic, yet as the Conservative Party became radicalised the Government clung to the Treaty and the opt-out, elevating a tactical device into a principle on which the Government would stake its whole survival.

The truth was that the aims of Maastricht and the single currency were not in Britain's interest, as seen by most Conservatives. Britain would never have created the single currency. It became an issue because other European countries wanted monetary union and to create a European federation. The dilemma was whether Britain would join one that did exist. The Government never analysed the issue in these terms. If it had, such analysis never informed its actions. Instead the Government was to hang itself on the Foreign Office line of accommodating Europe, which was only to be suspended for an instant over the far less important beef ban. Nothing better demonstrates the inside-out nature of our membership of the European Union, where European considerations override domestic priorities in defining the national interest rather than the other way round.

The Danish referendum on 2 June 1992 rejecting the Maastricht Treaty was an important moment for the Major Government. By the time of the Danish referendum, the bulk of the Parliamentary Party was moving decisively away from Maastricht, which meant the weak hand we had had while negotiating the Treaty had been strengthened. The Danish 'No' then gave the Government an ace.

Why did the Prime Minister not welcome the 'No' in the Danish referendum? Part of the answer is pride of ownership. The other reason is that he had not yet become thoroughly exhausted and weary of the arguments in the Conservative Party. The PM always had a high regard for his own negotiating skills. Maastricht was his achievement and it had not yet inflicted political pain on him as it was later to do.

An opportunity was missed here. The survival of the Treaty could only have been in Britain's interest if it was thought that Europe having the single currency and Britain joining it were in the national interest. Otherwise the right action after the Danish referendum would have been to take all the steps necessary to kill off the Treaty. Instead John Major and Douglas Hurd colluded in the charade of getting the Danes to approve the Treaty, the text of which remained in many ways identical to that which they had rejected earlier. In so doing they elevated the interests of Europe above those of the country and their Party. It was the beginning of the Conservatives' agony.

Europe's devastating effect on Party unity derived from the role of truth in politics. A dispute can be contained and measured if both sides are honest. Respect for the integrity and motives of each side should not be at issue. The arguments deployed by the Eurosceptics were designed to reveal an important truth, namely that the single currency represented a decisive move for Britain becoming part of a European State. By contrast, the arguments the Government used were designed to obscure this truth. They did not argue that Britain should belong to a federal Europe, but denied that it was happening. Their favourite defence was to argue that Mrs Thatcher had conceded more control to Europe in the Single European Act than Maastricht would. Whether or not this was the case, it demonstrated the cumulative nature of European integration.

The dispute proceeded with increasing frustration on the Eurosceptic side and a pattern of evasion and half-truths on the other. Like an artichoke, Eurosceptics peeled off leaf after leaf of evasion and obfuscation to reveal the contradictions at the heart of the Government's European policy. It was immensely damaging for the Government's public standing. For it was plain for everyone to see that the Government could not give straight answers to straight questions. On radio and television, Ministers mumbled complicated formulae that defied common sense and persuaded no one, least of all those who uttered them.

Ministers justified the policy of remaining undecided about whether Britain should join on the grounds that they needed more information and did not want to leave the negotiating table. This was nonsense. The negotiations were over. Logically this involved accepting the principle of joining. There could be no answer to this, as confirmed after the 1997 Election, when Gordon Brown announced that the Labour Government had accepted the principle of joining and John Major said that had been his policy too.

The evasion at the heart of the Government's policy, the one that led me to vote against my party, was that the single currency was not a step towards federalism. The cover-up took a number of forms: 'Maastricht was the high tide of European integration', 'Britain was winning the argument in Europe', 'Subsidiarity meant Europe was decentralising'. Douglas Hurd pronounced that Eurosceptics were trying to frighten themselves with imaginary phantoms and spectres. Worst of all were the apparent safeguards. 'If Europe goes federalist, a Conservative Britain will not,' John Major told the 1995 Party Conference. But Europe was going federal, and he wasn't going to let on. He had no excuses for ignorance. Eurosceptics used to pore over Helmut Kohl's speeches to extract quotations demonstrating that Germany wanted a federal Europe. John Major knew that already. It was clear from discussions with the German Government in preparation for Maastricht. As Anthony Seldon recounts, 'Major exploited his good relationship with Kohl to extract concessions for Britain as the price for not sabotaging Kohl's domestic need to present Maastricht as a big step towards a federal Europe.' Who was kidding whom? The Government knew full well what was happening but decided to obfuscate the truth to the Party and the country.

A Prime Minister can naturally expect to have the trust of his Party. His high office commands the respect of his Parliamentary colleagues and the country but both were casualties in the Government's battle to sustain its European policy. The 1995 Leadership Election was precipitated by Europe. With Ken Clarke at the Treasury and Michael Heseltine as Deputy Prime Minister, John Major locked the Government into keeping open the option of joining EMU, but Europe pursued the Government right to the very end, with Parliamentary candidates at the Election taking their own stand.

Europe ruthlessly exposed the weaknesses of John Major's style of governance. The electorate saw what was happening and came to its own conclusion. Whatever Conservative Ministers said or promised made no difference.

23

After the 1997 General Election

I am dead, dead but in the Elysian Fields.
*Benjamin Disraeli on going
to the House of Lords*

For the first time in twenty-five years I found myself outside Parliament. I returned to my desk at Jupiter, but felt reluctant to retire from politics at the relatively young age of fifty-five. Too often with politicians the roar of the crowd and the smell of the greasepaint overwhelm common sense. It is difficult to know when to get off the stage. Even when you have been pelted with tomatoes and rotten fruit, walking away from a lifetime's toil is never easy.

I kept complaining to Michael Howard about how miserable I felt outside the House of Commons. Michael wasn't very sympathetic; he thought it was just as bad to be in Opposition. In many ways he thought I was better off outside.

But unlike him I had been looking forward to Opposition. I remembered clearly the glorious freedom of Opposition in the mid-1970s, and how I had enjoyed not being encumbered by boxes and responsibility. Politics in Opposition largely consisted then of speeches, media appearances, attacking the Government and participating in academic seminars and discussion groups about future policy. It can be more fun asking awkward questions than giving careful, cautious Ministerial answers. I had found the prospect of Opposition quite attractive.

I had another important reason for wanting to continue in the House of Commons, namely that I wanted to argue the case against the single currency. I had devoted a large part of the last four years to the subject and I like to think that I had contributed to the debate. In 1995 I had published *Sovereign Britain*, a series of articles and speeches about the EU and it had been quite well received. Obviously I could continue to contribute in that way, but it would be far easier to do so from within the House of Commons.

To go to the Lords?

Going to the House of Lords was one course urged on me by a number of friends, particularly Kenneth Baker and Michael Howard. On the other hand, Alan Clark argued with me that I could go to the House of Lords at any time. Why not hang on and see what happened, as he had done? I rather agreed, and was reluctant to think about the Lords. It always seemed to me a civilised but essentially duller place than the House of Commons. But was there a real alternative? By-elections would be few and far between; the risks of being defeated were high and the chances of being selected slim. To hang around for five years outside the House of Commons, kicking one's heels, did not seem very enticing.

Usually former Cabinet Ministers who lose their seats or retire from the House of Commons are offered a seat in the House of Lords on the recommendation of their Party Leader. I was, however, sternly warned by Alastair Goodlad, the then Chief Whip, that this was not automatic. It is, however, pretty well automatic for a former Chancellor of the Exchequer. Nonetheless I was intrigued to discover that Peter Thorneycroft, Chancellor under Harold Macmillan, had been recommended for a peerage, not, as many assumed, by Macmillan, but by Harold Wilson. This had been necessary because of Macmillan's resentment at Thorneycroft's resignation from his Government.

The thought did cross my mind that Major's attitude might be the same as Harold Macmillan's, but on the whole I thought probably not. While I could see that John Major would consider I had caused problems for him between 1993 and 1995, I had studiously avoided saying anything that would be interpreted as criticism since the 1995 leadership election. He had in fact had a clear run in the last two years to lead the Party as he wanted.

I was still reluctant to go to the Lords, and I was also unsure, even if I did decide to go, how to indicate my wish in the appropriate quarter. Kenneth Baker had advised me that I had no alternative but to write to John Major myself indicating my wishes. I was reluctant to ask him for anything and was quite sure my request would appear as ironic to him as it did to myself. But Kenneth insisted there was no other way.

A few days later I had a cup of tea in the Treasury with Gordon Brown, now Chancellor, to discuss a quite separate matter. Gordon was very kind and said how sorry he had been that I had lost my seat. I think he meant it. He also said that if I wanted to go to the House of Lords and if John Major caused any problems, he was quite sure that Tony Blair would help. If necessary he would talk to him, and if I foresaw any difficulty I should talk immediately to Nick Brown, the Chief Whip, to whom he would mention the matter. In some ways the thought of being recommended for a peerage by a Labour Prime Minister appealed to me; perhaps I could have sat on the cross benches in the House of Lords? Nevertheless, as Kenneth Baker advised, I sat down and wrote a letter to John Major, making it clear that I had been advised that the only way in which I could make my wishes known was through a letter. I also took the opportunity to congratulate him on the dignified way on which he had accepted defeat at the Election. I hoped that did not sound too grovelling, but it seemed a reasonable thing to say and it was what I thought.

I did not hear from John Major for many weeks, but I kept reading little diary pieces in the newspapers about how he had been both angered – or, in other accounts, amused – to read my letter. I could imagine it and I didn't entirely blame him.

As the weeks passed I did not know what was happening and wondered whether I should contact Gordon Brown again. On one occasion, at a party of Jeffery Archer's, I bumped into Robin Butler, the Cabinet Secretary, and explained to him my conversation with the Chancellor of the Exchequer. I asked him whether he had seen John Major's resignation list and whether he could give me any guidance as to whether or not I should contact Gordon Brown. Robin said he had seen it but could not tell me its contents. He also said that Gordon Brown had no business saying what he had, which seemed a little unhelpful. At the same party, both Brian Mawhinney and Norman Fowler came up to me and said to me that if I was not on John Major's list it had absolutely nothing to do with them. From all this I gathered that I had been omitted from Major's list.

I was embarrassed by the whole grubby business. Not long afterwards, on 26 July, I received a strange handwritten letter from John Major. He began by saying how sorry he was that I had lost my seat and that it was 'a poor reward for your contribution on behalf of the Party and the Country'. He then went on to say that he and I had had our disagreements in the past and it was now time for us both to put them behind us. That sounded encouraging. I turned over the page expectantly. Instead he said that a very long list of people had indicated their wish to go to the House of Lords and there was no room for me. He did, however, go on to say that he had discussed the matter with William Hague and he was minded to include me in a list of working peers at an early date in the Parliament. It was vintage Major; there was a bit of the Maastricht opt-out about it. He wanted to say no, but could not quite bring himself to do so, or perhaps it was the other way round. Who could tell? It would have been far better if he had simply said he did not feel it was appropriate. I was slightly surprised that he obviously still harboured strong feelings.

When John Major's list was published the press obviously noted the absence of my name. The *Daily Telegraph* ran an editorial attacking John Major's 'pettiness' and 'vindictiveness'. I also noted a number of stories planted by someone in other papers suggesting that I had only been excluded from John

Major's list because I had indicated I did not want a peerage. Someone somewhere was trying to obscure matters.

Actually I felt no great resentment towards John Major about the matter. Perhaps it was a blessing in disguise? I thought perhaps it was better not to go to the Lords. At least I could reconsider the matter.

European Parliament?

I also harboured the ambition of becoming a candidate for the European Parliamentary Elections. That may seem curious when I have always been bitterly hostile to the idea of a European Parliament, but if I couldn't be in the House of Commons perhaps the European Parliament would be an ideal platform from which to campaign against the single currency. I would also have much enjoyed cross-examining Commissioners about waste and corruption.

I thought, in my innocence, that I would find it relatively easy to get adopted as a candidate for the European Parliament. Competition was likely to be much less strong than for a Parliamentary seat and, after all, I had managed to get the candidature for a Parliamentary seat for the last Election when I was perceived as a critic of the Party leadership. Now the leadership and policy had changed, and William Hague, the new Leader, had adopted a Eurosceptical line very much in tune with my own views. But my confidence was seriously misplaced. Part of the reason was that after the Election disaster the constituencies were very strongly opposed to all former MPs. Furthermore the new selection procedure that William Hague had introduced, although more democratic in its final stages, left a huge amount of power in the hands of constituency Chairmen in the preliminary stages and by and large they were Major loyalists. I did manage to get to the final stages of the run-off in the North-East of England Region, and came second. Under the new regional list system it would not have given me a winnable position so I withdrew.

At one point William Hague, who was sympathetic, asked me about the difficulties I was experiencing. I firmly told him that I did not want him to try to help me in any way. It was up to me to succeed or fail on my own. I did not want him to be embroiled in any controversy. Anyway, it was not to be.

John Major had quickly resigned as leader of the Conservative Party after the Election defeat. There had been suggestions that he might hang on until the Party Conference and some interested parties had argued that this would give the Conservative Party the chance to study the form of different candidates. For others it was a ruse to see if Chris Patten could get back in time to join the lists. But John Major wisely disregarded these siren voices and quit.

The 1997 Leadership Election

Since I was not in the House of Commons I was unable to play much of a part in the leadership campaign, but I did what I could to help the bid of my friend Michael Howard, telephoning some MPs for him. In addition to Michael, Peter Lilley, John Redwood and Ken Clarke had all quickly announced their intention to stand. Initially William Hague had thought he would stand on a joint ticket with Michael, with the plan being for William to become Party Chairman if Michael became leader. Champagne bottles were opened to clinch the deal. Later on, the very night that deal was agreed, after pressure from Alan Duncan, William changed his mind and decided he could win on his own. I was not altogether surprised as I remembered our discussion during the Election and comments William had made over meals when he had hinted that he might stand. In previous conversations I suspected he was testing my reaction, as I know he had done with other MPs. It reminded me of the way Margaret Thatcher had decided she could win against Ted Heath and boldly gone for it.

William said he would welcome my support, but he knew from our conversations that I felt I had to support Michael. I would in fact have been happy with any of the candidates of the right or with William, who I knew from his time as my PPS would move the Party more towards opposition to the single currency.

My assumption was that whoever won between Michael Howard, Peter Lilley and John Redwood, which would probably be either Michael Howard or Peter Lilley, would gather the core right-wing vote and eventually emerge as the winner. In the event Michael was badly damaged by Ann Widdecombe's attacks, and unexpectedly, at least to me, John Redwood by a whisker won the most votes of the three right-wing candidates. To his dismay, Peter and Michael decided that they did not want to back him and switched their votes to William Hague. From that moment on it was highly likely that William would win.

John Redwood had campaigned in the first round for firmer opposition to the euro, strongly attacking the Major and Clarke line of 'wait and see' on the single currency. His subsequent decision to form an alliance with the euro-enthusiastic Ken Clarke appeared utterly incredible. As soon as I heard the first hints of a Redwood-Clarke axis I telephoned Margaret Thatcher to inform her and urged her to publicly back William Hague. She was fond of John Redwood and simply could not believe this unlikely alliance had been formed. She felt it would discredit both individuals equally, but after some consideration decided to come out for William Hague. I do not think she would have done this without the provocation of the Redwood–Clarke alliance.

I made some critical comments at the time about John Redwood's turnabout. It seemed astonishing that John was now prepared to say that he would 'wait and see' how the disagreement between himself and Clarke would be resolved at a later date. I rather regret having criticised John Redwood, even though I was astonished at his decision. I can see now that he must have felt badly let down by Michael and Peter. If either of them had been the winner among the right, I am sure he would have backed them and I can understand why he felt he was entitled to make whatever alliances he wanted. But it was far too opportunistic to be credible. I felt sorry for John, who had bravely put himself forward in 1995 for the leadership and now looked likely to have the prize elude him for a second time.

From the conversations I had with him, William Hague was pretty confident that he would win. I was more than happy now to declare my support for him and again to telephone wavering MPs to persuade them to back William. I watched him give a speech to an assembled audience of supporters and journalists at

the Atrium Restaurant in Millbank. The occasion was very pro-
fessionally managed by his campaign team, and the speech, like
all of William's, was very polished and poised, punctuated by
resounding sound bites.

William Hague

William's was as meteoric a rise as any in recent years. He had
only reached the House of Commons in 1989 and became my PPS
in 1990. Seven years later, after zooming up the Ministerial ranks
to become a very youthful Cabinet Minister, he was now the
leader of the Party aged thirty-six. It was an astonishing achievement, but if anyone's talents deserved it they were William's. I had
always thought he had great qualities and could easily become
Leader of the Party. But I had not expected it to happen quite so
swiftly. The only reasons I had not backed him in the first round
were because of my friendship with Michael and my fear that perhaps he was still too young. But he was right to go for it when he
perceived he could win. If Michael Portillo had shown a similar
decisiveness in 1995, the history of the Conservative Party would
have been different.

William is probably the best orator to have led the Conservative
Party since Churchill. Because everyone knows that, it tends to be
discounted. His brilliant performances at Prime Minister's
Questions go unremarked and somewhat unappreciated, but to his
irritation people remember his extraordinary oratorical triumph as
a schoolboy at the Conservative Party Conference. I know that
William finds the endless repeats of that precocious performance
on TV highly embarrassing. At the first Conservative Party
Conference where William appeared as leader I gather that there
was a possibility that a schoolboy even younger than William at
the time of his triumph was going to make a speech from the
floor. William was enthusiastic for this, hoping that the event
might completely wipe out the memory of his schoolboy speech,
though unfortunately, in this case, the young man withdrew and to
William's disappointment the speech was never made.

But there is much more to William than his ability as a speaker.

Again, everyone is aware of his intelligence and outstanding academic record, so that too is discounted. What people do not realise is that he also has great steel and reserve and is very cool under pressure. I saw all these qualities when he worked for me.

Not long after William became leader I said to Gordon Brown, when William was having a difficult period, 'I wouldn't underestimate Hague if I were you.' He replied, 'We don't. I remember when he was your PPS you told me that one day he would be Prime Minister.'

At the time of writing William Hague has had a very difficult period as leader and endured much criticism, although no more than Mrs Thatcher did as Leader of the Opposition. I know William well enough to know he will not be deflected or depressed. He is far too resilient. He has suffered by comparison with a rather glamorous Prime Minister, but in time the British public will grow to see William's very considerable qualities, which are rather more durable than the superficial glitz of our Prime Minister.

When William became leader he asked me to help him with one or two of his speeches, and I was delighted to do so. I enjoy writing, and I enjoyed writing speeches. Five years previously he had been helping me with mine, now I was helping him with his, and greatly enjoying it. But he needed far less help than I did. He has a truly remarkable instinct for the phrase, pause or rhythm that will appeal to an audience.

Back to business

In the year after I lost my seat, and not knowing whether I would be going to the Lords, I spent more time on my business activities. In 1995 I had joined the board of the Balli Group, a private trading company owned by the Alaghband family, who after the Revolution left Iran to settle in the UK. Vahid Alaghband, the chairman, is a remarkable businessman whose professionalism, quiet modesty and courtesy show you do not have to be a megalomaniac to be a successful entrepreneur. Balli has worldwide investments including subsidiaries in the Black Sea and Caspian Sea areas and thanks to them I was able to visit these regions. I made a particularly memorable trip with Vahid Alaghband and David Owen to Turkey, Azerbaijan and Romania and, thanks to Balli's activities, found myself in the improbable position of becoming an advisor to the Romanian Government on privatisation, spending a lot of time in that strange and sad country. I don't think my advice was of much value, but I was struck by the sheer enormity of the privatisation task in Romania compared with the modest programme that we carried out in Britain in the 1980s. I fear greatly for the future of Romania. I believe the EU has been criminally indifferent to what is happening there, as it has been in so much of Eastern Europe. It will be the fault of the West if political instability or socialism return to these countries.

The Lords at last

In the early summer of 1998 I received a letter from the Prime Minister saying that he was minded to recommend me to Her Majesty the Queen as a peer. This was, of course, on the recommendation of William Hague, and by this time I was delighted to accept.

So many new life peers have been created during the Blair Government that I was unable to get to the front of the queue to take my seat in the House of Lords until October. My sponsors were Lord St John of Fawsley, to whom I had been PPS when he had been Minister of the Arts and who has been a generous and kind friend to me for decades, and my predecessor as Chancellor, Lord Lawson, to whom I owe a great deal. I did not feel I could have had two better supporters.

What with writing this book and other activities, so far I have not been quite as active in the House of Lords as I would like to be and intend to be in the future. The House of Lords is very different from the House of Commons. Former MPs can easily make mistakes there because they are more impressed by the similarities to the Commons than they are by the differences. To former MPs the House of Lords can be infuriatingly polite, yet that politeness can also be lethal. I find I miss the gales of controversy and nonsense of the House of Commons. It is true the speeches are better in the Lords, but that is because they do not matter so much as they are not part of the competition for power. People offer their personal opinions more in the Lords.

It has been interesting to be in the Upper House while the Bill to reform it has been going through. The Conservative Party has made much of the iniquity of abolishing the right of hereditary peers to sit before deciding who should replace them. But from the Labour Party's point of view it has been a sensible move. Every attempt to get rid of the hereditary peers in the past has floundered because of disagreement about this question and Labour has learnt the lessons of the past.

I have felt ambivalent about the hereditary principle. It is difficult to rationalise in the twenty-first century, even though it works. As a Tory I feel once the hereditaries are removed the House of Lords will become an empty shell of meaningless symbolism, a stately home with no family living there any longer. Something of value will be lost. The House of Lords, I suspect, will change much more in style than is now apparent. Many of the hereditary peers are interesting and intelligent people and they are also the only ordinary people in the House of Lords. Everyone else is there because they are a placeman or a person of achievement or distinction. Which is which can be a matter of argument.

I am pleased to have had the opportunity to sit for a short while in an unreformed House of Lords. I was amused to discover when I arrived there that I had been at school, although I did not realise it, with a duke, the Duke of Montrose, the descendant of the supporter of Charles I. When I am older I shall enjoy telling my grandchildren how I sat in the unreformed House of Lords along with the Dukes of Norfolk, Marlborough and Montrose.

Although now on the sidelines of politics, my appetite for politics remains undiminished. Debates in the House of Lords are even less reported these days than those of the House of Commons, but being there at least gives me the opportunity of going along to the 'other place' on Wednesday afternoons to watch my former PPS regularly beat up the Prime Minister and then pour cream over him.

I hope that now I am in the Lords I will at least be able to play a part in the referendum against the single currency, which is the greatest issue in British politics today. Tony Blair and Gordon Brown have accepted the single currency in principle while saying that they see no constitutional impediment to Britain joining the euro. The Government has tried to create a bandwagon effect with the impression that the euro is inevitable, but they have failed. Many prominent and successful businessmen remain doubtful. There is still a long time to go. I was delighted but not surprised when David Owen added his voice to the opponents of the euro. He will considerably widen the appeal of the anti-euro campaign.

When I speak at schools and universities I am often asked whether I would recommend a young person to enter politics today. It would be a very sorry state of affairs if a person who has spent his whole life in politics were to warn young people against it as a profession. I always encourage them to participate, although today it requires a very thick skin. University students, I find, are sometimes inhibited from pursuing a political career by the sheer aggression of today's media. I hope that this will not always be the case.

The nature of politics has changed dramatically in my lifetime, and I am only fifty-seven. I often wonder how Keith Joseph, an intellectual giant who altered the history of Britain in the 1980s by sheer force of argument, would cope with today's politics. It is true that Keith was often mocked in his lifetime, but his arguments were listened to and were influential. How would he fare in a world in which the media are interested solely in the trivial or the scandalous and in which every political pronouncement has to be reduced to a single sound bite? How would he get a hearing?

One of the least attractive aspects of the Blair Government is that its great skill with media manipulation has further trivialised political debate and 'the medium' has truly become 'the message'. I never used to understand what Marshall McLuhan meant by this until Tony Blair came along.

When Rab Butler famously described politics as 'the art of the possible' he meant that a politician can't simply be an executive or a Minister. Politics involves persuasion or sometimes concessions to public opinion. Sometimes you have to eat your words. On other occasions the issues are so vital you may have to defy public opinion and risk the ending of your own career. These are the noble moments. Politics often demands skill in the baser arts of compromise and obfuscation or the need to dissemble, yet on other occasions it demands leadership and clarity. Different politicians have different mixes of the skills required, which is why there are different politicians for different moments: executives and persuaders, hedgers and ditchers, intellectuals and those who are good at what Whips call 'practical politics'. The life of the politician is an exciting one. Thatcher's law is that 'the unexpected always happens', and that is why the politician is never his own master. The events are always great, the problems huge and usually impossible to solve. As J.K. Galbraith put it: 'Politics is not the art of the possible. It consists of choosing between the disastrous and the unpalatable.' There is no money to be made in politics, and it requires a huge commitment. If a politician succeeds the only reward he will receive from the public is half-hearted and grudging recognition. In the more probable event of failure he will have to seek consolation in himself that it was all worthwhile.

'Politics is a dangerous profession,' was well said by F.S. Oliver.

It is this uncertainty, with its various consequences, that makes politics the most hazardous of all manly professions. If there is not another in which a man can hope to do so much good to his fellow creatures, neither is there any in which, by a cowardly act or by a mere loss of nerve, he may do such widespread harm. Nor is there another in which he may so easily lose his own soul. But danger is the inseparable companion of honour. The greatest deeds in history were not done by people who thought of safety first. It is possible to be too much concerned even with one's own salvation. There will not be much hope left for humanity when men are no longer willing to risk their immortal as well as their mortal parts. With all the temptations, dangers and degradations that beset it, politics is still, I think, the noblest career that any man can choose.

I still think that, too.

The Resignation Speech

This is not an easy statement for me to make today, but I am sure that the House will understand that and that I can rely on the traditional tolerance and generosity of Hon. Members.

To give up being Chancellor of the Exchequer in the circumstances in which I did is bound to be an uncomfortable experience, but I have also been a Treasury Minister for almost seven years, a longer continuous period than anyone else this century. Indeed, I have been the only person ever to have held the three offices of Financial Secretary, Chief Secretary and Chancellor of the Exchequer.

I should like to pay tribute to the officials with whom I worked all those years. In my opinion, they are equal to the best in the world, and I am astonished how, when things go wrong, often it is the civil servants who are blamed when it is we politicians who make the decisions and it is we politicians who should carry the blame.

When the Prime Minister told me two weeks ago that he wished to make changes in his Government, I of course told him that I appreciated that he had a very difficult task. He generously offered me another position in his Cabinet, but, in my opinion, it would not have been right either for him or for myself if I had accepted. If he wished to change his Chancellor, it was surely right that I should leave the Cabinet. Perhaps I can make it clear that I wish the Prime Minister well and hope that his changes will produce whatever advantage for him and the Government that he intended.

It has not been easy being Chancellor of the Exchequer in this recession, continually and wrongly described as the longest and deepest since the war or, even more inaccurately, since the 1930s. It is certainly not the deepest recession since the war and, when the figures are finally revised, it may turn out not even to have been the longest. But it is a recession which has affected many areas which have not experienced such severe recession before; and that was bound to have an adverse effect on the fortunes and popularity of the Government.

This recession was not caused by Britain's membership of the exchange mechanism. The recession began before we joined the ERM – and, incidentally, before I became Chancellor – and a large part of the fall in output occurred in late 1990 and early 1991, far too soon to be influenced by our membership of the ERM. No, this recession has its origins in the boom of 1988 and 1989. That boom made the recession inevitable.

But the recession is now behind us, and so I am able with confidence to wish every success to my Rt Hon. and learned friend the new Chancellor. He inherits, I believe, a fundamentally strong position. As Mr Lloyd Bentsen, the United States Treasury Secretary, said in a generous letter to me last week, Britain is the only European country likely to experience any significant growth this year; and inflation is at a thirty-year low. Since the war only two Conservative Chancellors have been responsible for bringing inflation down to below 2 per cent. Both of them were sacked. In my view, that tells us a great deal about the difficulties of reducing inflation in a democracy as lively and disputatious as ours.

I am delighted to hear from the Prime Minister that policy will not alter. My Rt Hon. and learned friend the Chancellor will understand if I say that he thus comes to the Treasury at a most favourable time. Much of the hard work has been done and he should be able to enjoy increasingly encouraging trends for a long time to come. I am sure that my initiative in bringing the autumn statement and the Budget together into one December Budget is a reform that will last, and I wish my Rt Hon. and learned friend well with what is a massive task.

I have been privileged to present three Budgets. All three achieved the objectives that I set for them. The first drew the sting of the Poll Tax; the second, by introducing the 20p income tax band, helped us to win the election; the third, unpopular though it undoubtedly was, made a significant step towards reducing our budget deficit. That, as I have frequently observed, is the greatest threat to our long-term position.

Having put up some taxes, it is vital that the Government now turn their attention to public spending. Last year I set up a new system for controlling public spending. I believe that it gives my Rt Hon. and learned friend the means to do what is necessary. I am sure that he has the will. We do not want more tax increases. We need tight control of public spending. My Rt Hon. and learned friend will have my full support if he is robust in tackling that problem.

I should now like to say a word about Britain's experience of membership of the exchange rate mechanism. Although many people are either for or against membership of a fixed exchange rate system, there are many others, including, for example, Alan Greenspan, the chairman of the United States Federal Reserve Board, whose views about fixed versus floating exchange rates have never been theological. My views are not theological either. I have always believed that one could run an economy on either a fixed or a floating rate basis, although at times one might be more appropriate than the other.

I tried to persuade my noble friend Lord Lawson that it was not worth resigning over the ERM in 1988. Although I probably would not have joined in 1989, I did not believe then that a fixed-rate system was doomed to break up. Presumably those who hold that view blame my noble friend Lady Thatcher for committing us to a policy that was bound to fail. But I do not take that view now, and I did not take it then. When I accepted the office of Chancellor, I accepted the policy, believed that it could be made to work, and did all that I could to make it work. It certainly enabled us to get inflation down dramatically. Indeed, without the ERM, I doubt whether the Government would have had the courage and determination to get inflation down; that is a point to which I shall return.

The reason why our policy on the ERM ultimately broke down was that German policy developed in a way which, in my view, was mistaken and which was not anticipated – not least when German interest rates were put up last year. As members of the ERM, we were forced to respond in a way that meant that our own policy became increasingly over-tight. I became increasingly concerned last summer that our policy was too restrictive and that our membership of the ERM was impeding recovery.

I raised with the Prime Minister the idea that we might suspend our membership temporarily at some future date if recovery were being prevented. He made it clear that he did not want to do that. Probably he was right. I accepted it. In any case, it would not have made any difference. We were talking about the distant future and we would have been overtaken by the same events in September that ultimately hit us. But I would not want the country to believe that these matters were never under consideration or that we were not aware of what was happening in the economy outside.

That perhaps explains why I did not do one thing that some have argued and urged might have enabled us to remain within the exchange rate mechanism – to put up interest rates in the summer of 1992. Because of the position of the domestic economy, I did not believe that that was an option. Furthermore, I did not believe that it would have been credible, and I am sure that I was right.

People have frequently asked me why we did not devalue within the system. I did not devalue because it would have meant higher interest rates at a time when we needed lower interest rates. One solution might have been a revaluation of the mark against all other currencies in the ERM, thus making room for lower German interest rates. I was not opposed to that, but, unfortunately, my friend and colleague, the late Pierre Bérégovoy, the French Finance Minister, was, despite my efforts at persuasion, implacably opposed to such a move.

I do not believe that any question of rejoining the ERM should remotely be on the agenda during this Parliament. Fortunately, my Rt Hon. and learned friend the Chancellor has already announced his policy. I am only thankful that, despite the residual doubts of some of my colleagues, I insisted on getting my own way and on keeping the ERM out of Maastricht as a treaty obligation. I need hardly remind the House how difficult our position would be today if the Maastricht Treaty obliged us to rejoin the ERM.

Some argue that the credibility of the Government was destroyed on 16 September. But once I had reconstructed our policy, that was not the view of the markets, or of the stock exchange, which touched an all-time high not so long ago, or of the foreign exchange markets, where the pound's recovery has been strong enough to worry some businessmen – nor was it supported by that crucial indicator, long bond yields, which are lower than for some time and lower today than in September.

Markets and businessmen are cynical. They know that, in a fixed exchange rate system, there are certain things that Finance Ministers have to say. Credibility and confidence depend not on words but on objective conditions. I am glad to say that those objective conditions today are better than they have been for many years.

On the crucial question of credibility, I want to take this opportunity to give my Rt Hon. friend the Prime Minister and my Rt Hon. and learned friend the Chancellor some advice. Nothing would be more effective in establishing the Government's credibility than if my right hon. friend would have the courage to establish an independent central bank in this country. The time has come to make the Bank of England independent. It is my greatest regret that, after two and a half years of trying, I failed to persuade the Prime Minister of this essential reform.

Now that we are outside the ERM, the need is even more urgent. Britain is one of the few countries where monetary policy remains firmly in political hands, and the pressures on politicians to take policy decisions for political reasons can be quite irresistible. With an independent bank, we could have lower interest rates for a given exchange rate. Policy would be more credible and it would give us the necessary discipline for keeping inflation down on a permanent basis.

While my Rt Hon. friend the Prime Minister and I have been in general agreement on interest rate policy, I do not believe that even the timing of interest rate changes should ever be affected by political considerations. Interest rate changes should never be used to offset some unfavourable political event. To do so undermines the credibility of policy and the credibility of the Chancellor.

When my resignation was announced ten days ago, the reaction of many was that it was a delayed resignation, a resignation that should have happened on 16 September. On that day, and during the subsequent days, I did of course consider my position carefully with friends and colleagues. I was anxious to do what was right for the country and for the Government. Sir Stafford Cripps, who is rightly regarded as an honourable man, did not resign after devaluing the pound. On the other hand, Lord Callaghan, also an honourable man, did.

There are three principal reasons why I decided to stay in office. First, the events of last September were very different from those of 1967. They affected not just this country, but most of Europe. The Finance Ministers of no fewer than nine countries were forced to eat their words and either devalue or float. Five floated; four devalued; one both devalued and floated. In none did the Finance Minister resign or, to the best of my knowledge, come under any pressure to resign. Indeed, in one country the governor of the central bank was actually promoted: he became Prime Minister.

Secondly, membership of the exchange rate mechanism was the policy of the whole Government; and as the Prime Minister said, I was implementing Government policy. Our entry was not a decision in which I myself played any part. It was, however, a decision made after a whole decade of fierce public and private argument – a decision made by the previous Prime Minister, the present Prime Minister and the present Foreign Secretary.

Thirdly, I did not resign because that was not what the Prime Minister wanted. When the Prime Minister reappointed me after the general election, I told him two things: first, that I did not wish to remain Chancellor for very long; and, secondly, that he did not owe me any debt or any obligation. On 16 September he made it clear to me in writing that he had no intention of resigning himself, and that I should not do so either.

Of course, I discussed the question further with the Prime Minister subsequently. In all those discussions he emphasised that he regarded the attacks on me as coded attacks on himself, so I decided that my duty and loyalty was to the Prime Minister and that I should remain in office.

Two and a half years ago, I did play some part in helping the Prime Minister into the position that he occupies today. I have always believed, and still believe, that in supporting him then I made the right choice, and I now wish to say one thing to him; it goes to the heart of the way in which the Government conduct themselves. There is something wrong with the way in which we make our decisions. The Government listen too much to the pollsters and the party managers. The trouble is that they are not even very good at politics, and they are entering too much into policy decisions. As a result, there is too much short-termism, too much reacting to events, and not enough shaping of events. We give the impression of being in office but not in power.

Far too many important decisions are made for thirty-six hours' publicity. Yes, we are politicians as well as policy-makers; but we are also the trustees of the nation. I believe that in politics one should decide what is right and then decide the presentation, not the other way round. Unless this approach is changed, the Government will not survive, and will not deserve to survive.

It is a great change to return to the Back Benches after fourteen years in Government, Madam Speaker, but I have always been proud to be a Member of this House and not just a Minister. Today, when I walked through Westminster Hall and up the stairs into the Lobby, I felt exactly the same pride and excitement as when I first entered this House twenty-one years ago. I look forward with anticipation to the great parliamentary events and battles that lie ahead.

Source: *Hansard*, 9 June 1993

Bibliography

Anderson, Bruce, *John Major, The Making of a Prime Minister*, Fourth Estate Limited, 1991.

Connolly, Bernard, *The Rotten Heart of Europe: The Dirty War for Europe's Money*, Faber and Faber Ltd, 1995.

Dell, Edmund, *The Chancellors*, HarperCollins, 1993.

Kavanagh, Dennis, and Seldon, Anthony, *The Major Effect*, Papermac, 1994.

Seldon, Anthony, *Major, A Political Life*, Weidenfeld and Nicolson, 1997.

Stephens, Philip, *Politics and the Pound: The Conservative Struggle with Sterling*, Macmillan, 1996.

Thatcher, Margaret, *The Downing Street Years*, HarperCollins, 1993.

Quotations from the work of A.E. Housman reproduced by kind permission of the Society of Authors as the literary representative of the estate of A.E. Housman.

The publishers have attempted to observe the legal requirements with respect to the rights of suppliers of photographic materials. Nevertheless persons who have claims are invited to apply to the publishers.

Appendix

Table 1
UK Base and Exchange Rates

	Base rate (%)	Sterling ERI	DM/£	$/£
1990				
8 Oct	14.00	103.0	3.03	1.97
1991				
13 Feb	13.50	102.9	2.91	1.97
27 Feb	13.00	102.7	2.92	1.90
22 Mar	12.50	101.5	2.94	1.79
12 Apr	12.00	102.5	3.00	1.78
24 May	11.50	101.3	2.96	1.73
12 July	11.00	98.9	2.95	1.65
4 Sept	10.50	100.2	2.94	1.70
1992				
5 May	10.00	101.3	2.94	1.79
16 Sept	12.00	99.5	2.75	1.81
17 Sept	10.00	99.2	2.64	1.78
22 Sept	9.00	91.7	2.55	1.72
16 Oct	8.00	89.7	2.45	1.66
12 Nov	7.00	85.8	2.43	1.54
1993				
26 Jan	6.00	88.5	2.39	1.49
23 Nov	5.50	90.2	2.53	1.49
1994				
8 Feb	5.25	91.5	2.61	1.48
12 Sept	5.75	87.3	2.39	1.55
7 Dec	6.25	89.2	2.46	1.56
1995				
2 Feb	6.75	88.7	2.41	1.58
13 Dec	6.50	82.8	2.22	1.53
1996				
18 Jan	6.25	83.2	2.24	1.53
8 Mar	6.00	83.7	2.26	1.53
6 June	5.75	86.4	2.37	1.55
30 Oct	6.00	89.1	2.43	1.61

Table 2
National Income 1990–93

Quarter	GDP at constant market prices			Non-oil GVA at constant basic prices			GNP at constant market prices		
	Index 1995 = 100	Change on previous year	Change on previous quarter	Index 1995 = 100	Change on previous year (a)	Change on previous quarter (a)	Index 1995 = 100	Change on previous year (a)	Change on previous quarter (a)
1990 Q1	92.8	1.6%	0.7%	93.2	1.9%	1.0%	91.6	1.0%	0.8%
1990 Q2	93.2	1.5%	0.5%	93.4	1.5%	0.2%	92.2	1.3%	0.6%
1990 Q3	92.1	0.1%	-1.2%	92.8	0.9%	-0.6%	91.8	0.8%	-0.4%
1990 Q4	91.6	-0.6%	-0.5%	92.4	0.1%	-0.4%	90.6	-0.3%	-1.2%
1991 Q1	91.5	-1.4%	-0.1%	91.6	-1.7%	-0.9%	90.5	-1.3%	-0.2%
1991 Q2	90.9	-2.5%	-0.6%	91.5	-2.0%	-0.1%	90.4	-1.9%	-0.1%
1991 Q3	90.8	-1.4%	-0.1%	91.3	-1.6%	-0.2%	90.6	-1.3%	0.2%
1991 Q4	91.0	-0.7%	0.2%	91.3	-1.2%	0.0%	91.3	0.7%	0.8%
1992 Q1	90.9	-0.6%	0.1%	91.2	-0.4%	-0.1%	91.3	0.9%	0.0%
1992 Q2	90.7	-0.3%	-0.2%	91.3	-0.2%	0.1%	91.0	0.6%	-0.3%
1992 Q3	91.2	0.4%	0.6%	91.7	0.4%	0.4%	92.1	1.7%	1.2%
1992 Q4	91.6	0.7%	0.5%	92.0	0.8%	0.3%	92.5	1.4%	0.5%
1993 Q1	92.1	1.3%	0.5%	92.6	1.5%	0.7%	92.4	1.2%	-0.2%
1993 Q2	92.6	2.1%	0.6%	93.0	1.9%	0.4%	92.9	2.1%	0.5%
1993 Q3	93.5	2.6%	1.0%	93.8	2.3%	0.9%	94.2	2.3%	1.4%
1993 Q4	94.5	3.2%	1.1%	94.4	2.6%	0.6%	95.0	2.6%	0.8%

Note: (a) Calculated from rounded data
Source: ONS–CSDB database series ABMI, ABMM, GDP

Table 3
Manufacturing Output and Retail Sales

Month	Manufacturing output			Retail sales volume		
	Index 1995 = 100	Change on previous year	Change on previous month	Index 1995 = 100	Change on previous year	Change on previous month
1990 Jan	97.9	−0.2%	−0.3%	119.5	1.9%	−0.5%
1990 Feb	97.6	−0.5%	−0.3%	120.2	2.1%	1.3%
1990 Mar	99.0	2.0%	1.4%	121.4	0.9%	−0.2%
1990 Apr	98.8	0.2%	−0.2%	125.1	2.1%	−0.4%
1990 May	98.9	0.9%	0.1%	126.2	1.5%	1.0%
1990 June	98.7	2.0%	−0.2%	126.7	0.5%	−1.8%
1990 July	97.7	0.4%	−1.0%	126.8	2.7%	1.2%
1990 Aug	98.1	−0.1%	0.4%	128.1	0.3%	−1.2%
1990 Sept	97.1	−1.0%	−1.0%	129.3	0.2%	0.1%
1990 Oct	97.0	−0.6%	−0.1%	130.3	−0.8%	−1.1%
1990 Nov	96.3	−1.8%	−0.7%	130.0	−1.4%	−0.7%
1990 Dec	95.8	−2.4%	−0.5%	129.9	−0.9%	1.5%
1991 Jan	95.9	−2.0%	0.1%	130.2	−1.3%	−1.0%
1991 Feb	93.9	−3.8%	−2.1%	130.9	−3.1%	−0.5%
1991 Mar	93.6	−5.5%	−0.3%	131.4	−0.6%	2.3%
1991 Apr	92.7	−6.2%	−1.0%	133.1	−2.2%	−2.0%
1991 May	93.4	−5.6%	0.8%	133.5	−3.1%	0.1%
1991 June	92.1	−6.7%	−1.4%	134.1	−1.3%	0.0%
1991 July	92.2	−5.6%	0.1%	133.8	−1.3%	1.2%
1991 Aug	91.5	−6.7%	−0.8%	134.1	−1.0%	−0.9%
1991 Sept	91.7	−5.6%	0.2%	134.6	−1.7%	−0.7%
1991 Oct	92.2	−4.9%	0.5%	135.1	−0.7%	0.0%
1991 Nov	92.6	−3.8%	0.4%	135.6	0.3%	0.3%
1991 Dec	92.3	−3.7%	−0.3%	135.7	−0.8%	0.4%
1992 Jan	92.3	−3.8%	0.0%	135.6	0.1%	−0.1%
1992 Feb	92.8	−1.2%	0.5%	136.3	0.3%	−0.3%
1992 Mar	92.9	−0.7%	0.1%	136.7	−2.1%	−0.2%
1992 Apr	93.1	0.4%	0.2%	138.8	1.2%	1.3%
1992 May	91.5	−2.0%	−1.7%	139.3	1.3%	0.2%
1992 June	93.4	1.4%	2.1%	139.3	1.1%	−0.2%
1992 July	93.4	1.3%	0.0%	138.8	−1.1%	−1.0%
1992 Aug	92.7	1.3%	−0.7%	138.9	1.1%	1.3%
1992 Sept	92.8	1.2%	0.1%	139.4	2.0%	0.2%
1992 Oct	93.4	1.3%	0.6%	139.9	2.2%	0.2%
1992 Nov	92.4	−0.2%	−1.1%	139.7	2.1%	0.2%
1992 Dec	92.4	0.1%	0.0%	139.2	1.2%	−0.4%
1993 Jan	93.4	1.2%	1.1%	137.9	2.6%	1.3%
1993 Feb	94.7	2.0%	1.4%	138.8	3.6%	0.6%
1993 Mar	94.3	1.5%	−0.4%	139.3	3.8%	0.0%

Month	Manufacturing output			Retail sales volume		
	Index 1995 = 100	*Change on previous year*	*Change on previous month*	*Index 1995 = 100*	*Change on previous year*	*Change on previous month*
1993 Apr	94.4	1.4%	0.1%	140.6	2.2%	–0.3%
1993 May	94.4	3.2%	0.0%	141.1	2.0%	0.1%
1993 June	93.1	–0.3%	–1.4%	141.0	2.9%	0.6%
1993 July	94.0	0.6%	1.0%	140.7	3.8%	–0.1%
1993 Aug	93.6	1.0%	–0.4%	141.3	2.8%	0.3%
1993 Sept	94.1	1.4%	0.5%	141.9	2.9%	0.3%
1993 Oct	93.5	0.1%	–0.6%	141.8	3.2%	0.5%
1993 Nov	94.3	2.1%	0.9%	141.6	3.3%	0.3%
1993 Dec	95.3	3.1%	1.1%	141.9	3.2%	–0.5%

Source: ONS–CSDB database series CKYY & EAPS

Table 4
Retail Prices Index

Month	RPI			RPI(X)		
	Index Jan 1987 = 100	Change on previous year	Change on previous month	Index Jan 1987 = 100	Change on previous year	Change on previous month
1990 Jan	119.5	7.7%	0.6%	116.1	6.1%	0.5%
1990 Feb	120.2	7.5%	0.6%	116.7	6.2%	0.5%
1990 Mar	121.4	8.1%	1.0%	117.3	6.3%	0.5%
1990 Apr	125.1	9.4%	3.0%	121.1	7.9%	3.2%
1990 May	126.2	9.7%	0.9%	122.1	8.1%	0.8%
1990 June	126.7	9.8%	0.4%	122.5	8.2%	0.3%
1990 July	126.8	9.8%	0.1%	122.6	8.3%	0.1%
1990 Aug	128.1	10.6%	1.0%	123.7	9.1%	0.9%
1990 Sept	129.3	10.9%	0.9%	124.9	9.5%	1.0%
1990 Oct	130.3	10.9%	0.8%	125.8	9.5%	0.7%
1990 Nov	130.0	9.7%	−0.2%	125.9	9.2%	0.1%
1990 Dec	129.9	9.3%	−0.1%	125.9	9.0%	0.0%
1991 Jan	130.2	9.0%	0.2%	126.0	8.5%	0.1%
1991 Feb	130.9	8.9%	0.5%	126.7	8.6%	0.6%
1991 Mar	131.4	8.2%	0.4%	127.2	8.4%	0.4%
1991 Apr	133.1	6.4%	1.3%	129.3	6.8%	1.7%
1991 May	133.5	5.8%	0.3%	130.2	6.6%	0.7%
1991 June	134.1	5.8%	0.4%	130.9	6.9%	0.5%
1991 July	133.8	5.5%	−0.2%	130.9	6.8%	0.0%
1991 Aug	134.1	4.7%	0.2%	131.4	6.2%	0.4%
1991 Sept	134.6	4.1%	0.4%	132.0	5.7%	0.5%
1991 Oct	135.1	3.7%	0.4%	132.7	5.5%	0.5%
1991 Nov	135.6	4.3%	0.4%	133.1	5.7%	0.3%
1991 Dec	135.7	4.5%	0.1%	133.2	5.8%	0.1%
1992 Jan	135.6	4.1%	−0.1%	133.1	5.6%	−0.1%
1992 Feb	136.3	4.1%	0.5%	133.8	5.6%	0.5%
1992 Mar	136.7	4.0%	0.3%	134.5	5.7%	0.5%
1992 Apr	138.8	4.3%	1.5%	136.7	5.7%	1.6%
1992 May	139.3	4.3%	0.4%	137.1	5.3%	0.3%
1992 June	139.3	3.9%	0.0%	137.2	4.8%	0.1%
1992 July	138.8	3.7%	−0.4%	136.7	4.4%	−0.4%
1992 Aug	138.9	3.6%	0.1%	136.9	4.2%	0.1%
1992 Sept	139.4	3.6%	0.4%	137.3	4.0%	0.3%
1992 Oct	139.9	3.6%	0.4%	137.8	3.8%	0.4%
1992 Nov	139.7	3.0%	−0.1%	137.9	3.6%	0.1%
1992 Dec	139.2	2.6%	−0.4%	138.1	3.7%	0.1%
1993 Jan	137.9	1.7%	−0.9%	137.4	3.2%	−0.5%
1993 Feb	138.8	1.8%	0.7%	138.3	3.4%	0.7%
1993 Mar	139.3	1.9%	0.4%	139.2	3.5%	0.7%

Month	RPI			RPI(X)		
	Index Jan 1987 = 100	*Change on previous year*	*Change on previous month*	*Index Jan 1987 = 100*	*Change on previous year*	*Change on previous month*
1993 Apr	140.6	1.3%	0.9%	140.6	2.9%	1.0%
1993 May	141.1	1.3%	0.4%	141.0	2.8%	0.3%
1993 June	141.0	1.2%	–0.1%	141.0	2.8%	0.0%
1993 July	140.7	1.4%	–0.2%	140.6	2.9%	–0.3%
1993 Aug	141.3	1.7%	0.4%	141.2	3.1%	0.4%
1993 Sept	141.9	1.8%	0.4%	141.8	3.3%	0.4%
1993 Oct	141.8	1.4%	–0.1%	141.7	2.8%	–0.1%
1993 Nov	141.6	1.4%	–0.1%	141.4	2.5%	–0.2%
1993 Dec	141.9	1.9%	0.2%	141.8	2.7%	–0.3%

Source: ONS–CSDB database series CHAW & CHMK

Table 5
Discount and Lombard Rates of Bundesbank

Applicable form	*Discount rate*	*Lombard rate*
1990 2 Nov	6	8.5
1991 1 Feb	6.5	9
1991 16 Aug	7.5	9.25
1991 20 Dec	8	9.75
1992 17 July	8.75	9.75
1992 15 Sept	8.25	9.5
1993 5 Feb	8	9
1993 19 Mar	7.5	9
1993 23 Apr	7.25	8.5
1993 2 July	6.75	8.25
1993 30 July	6.75	7.75
1993 10 Sept	6.25	7.25
1993 22 Oct	5.75	6.75
1994 18 Feb	5.25	6.75
1994 15 Apr	5	6.5
1994 13 May	4.5	6
1995 31 Mar	4	6
1995 25 Aug	3.5	5.5
1995 15 Dec	3	5
1996 19 Apr	2.5	4.5

Table 6
Deutschmark–Sterling Real Exchange Rate

	Consumer price inflation		Exchange rates	Consumer price levels (1990 = 100)		Real exchange rates
Year	Germany %	UK %	DM/£	Germany	UK	DM/£
1970	3.44	6.35	8.78	47.14	15.45	2.88
1971	5.24	9.45	8.54	46.61	16.91	2.91
1972	5.50	7.08	7.98	52.34	18.1	2.76
1973	7.02	9.19	6.55	56.02	19.77	2.31
1974	6.95	15.95	6.05	59.91	22.92	2.32
1975	5.94	24.3	5.47	63.47	28.49	2.45
1976	4.28	16.7	4.55	66.18	33.25	2.28
1977	3.68	15.83	4.05	68.62	38.51	2.27
1978	2.71	8.64	3.86	70.48	41.84	2.29
1979	4.08	12.61	3.89	73.35	47.11	2.5
1980	5.45	16.85	4.23	77.35	55.05	3.01
1981	6.32	12.19	4.58	82.24	61.76	3.44
1982	5.26	8.51	4.25	86.57	67.02	3.29
1983	3.28	5.2	3.87	89.41	70.51	3.05
1984	2.40	4.45	3.8	91.55	73.64	3.06
1985	2.08	5.16	3.82	93.46	77.44	3.16
1986	−0.13	3.63	3.19	93.33	80.25	2.74
1987	0.24	4.07	2.95	93.56	83.52	2.63
1988	1.27	4.59	3.13	94.75	87.35	2.88
1989	2.78	5.86	3.08	97.38	92.47	2.98
1990	2.69	8.14	2.88	100	100	2.88
1991	3.47	6.76	2.94	103.47	106.76	3.03
1992	5.06	4.7	2.76	108.71	111.78	2.84
1993	4.45	2.99	2.48	113.54	115.12	2.52
1994	2.75	2.38	2.49	116.67	117.86	2.51
1995	1.84	2.83	2.26	118.81	121.2	2.31
1996	1.48	2.95	2.35	120.57	124.77	2.43
1997	1.76	1.73	2.84	122.69	128.2	2.97
1998	0.90	2.66	2.91	123.8	131.61	3.09
Now	0.57	2.68	3	124.5	135.14	3.26

Average real exchange rate

DM/£

1970–90	2.76
1980–90	2.96
1970–98	2.75
1979–98	2.86

Table 7
The Popularity of the Conservative Party

Q: How would you vote if there was a General Election tomorrow?
Q to those undecided/who refused: Which party are you most inclined to support?

	Con	Lab	Lib Dem	SDP	Grn	Other	Con Lead
1991							
18–21 Jan	46	41	9	–	2	2	(+)5
22–25 Feb	44	41	11	–	1	3	(+)3
21–25 Mar	40	40	16	–	2	2	0
18–22 Apr	42	40	15	–	1	2	(+)2
24–28 May	37	43	16	–	2	2	(–)6
21–24 Jun	39	41	15	–	1	4	(–)2
19–22 Jul	38	43	15	–	2	2	(–)5
23–27 Aug	42	40	14	–	2	2	(+)2
20–24 Sept	39	39	17	–	1	4	0
18–21 Oct	39	45	12	–	2	2	(–)6
22–25 Nov	40	42	15	–	1	2	(–)2
27 Dec	38	44	14	–	2	2	(–)6
1992							
17–21 Jan	42	39	16	–	1	2	(+)3
21–25 Feb	39	40	18	–	1	2	(–)1
20–24 Mar	38	41	17	n/a	1	3	(–)3
9 Apr (GE)	43	35	18	n/a	1	3	(+)8
25–28 Apr	43	38	16	n/a	*	2	(+)5
21–26 May	43	38	16	n/a	1	*	(+)5
19–23 Jun	42	39	16	n/a	1	*	(+)3
23–28 Jul	39	43	15	n/a	1	2	(–)4
27–01 Aug	41	44	13	n/a	1	1	(–)3
25–29 Sept	37	43	16	n/a	1	3	(–)6
23–27 Oct	35	45	15	n/a	1	4	(–)10
27–01 Nov	34	47	15	n/a	1	3	(–)13
1993							
21–25 Jan	37	45	14	n/a	1	3	(–)8
18–22 Feb	34	46	16	n/a	1	3	(–)12
25–29 Mar	32	47	17	n/a	1	3	(–)15
22–26 Apr	32	46	20	n/a	*	2	(–)14
20–24 May	28	44	24	n/a	1	2	(–)16
24–28 Jun	28	46	23	n/a	1	2	(–)18
22–26 Jul	27	44	25	n/a	1	1	(–)17
19–23 Aug	28	42	25	n/a	1	4	(–)14

	Con	Lab	Lib Dem	SDP	Grn	Other	Con Lead
16–20 Sept	29	43	25	n/a	1	2	(–)14
21–25 Oct	29	45	23	n/a	1	2	(–)16
18–22 Nov	29	47	22	n/a	*	2	(–)18
9–13 Dec	29	47	20	n/a	1	3	(–)18
1994							
20–24 Jan	28	48	20	n/a	1	3	(–)20
24–28 Feb	28	47	21		1	3	(–)19
24–28 Mar	27	49	20		1	3	(–)22
21–25 Apr	26	47	23		1	3	(–)21
19–23 May	27	46	23		1	3	(–)19
16–20 Jun	24	52	20		1	3	(–)28
14–18 Jul	23	51	21		1	4	(–)28
18–22 Aug	23	56	18		1	2	(–)33
22–26 Sept	25	54	17		1	3	(–)29
20–24 Oct	25	57	14		1	3	(–)32
17–21 Nov	24	55	17		1	3	(–)31
15–19 Dec	22	61	13		1	3	(–)39
1995							
20–23 Jan	27	56	14		1	2	(–)29
17–20 Feb	24	58	14		1	3	(–)34
17–20 Mar	25	57	13		1	4	(–)32
21–24 Apr	26	56	15		1	2	(–)30
19–22 May	22	58	16		1	3	(–)36
23–26 Jun	29	56	13		1	1	(–)27
21–24 Jul	26	59	12		1	2	(–)33
25–28 Aug	25	56	15		1	3	(–)31
22–25 Sept	28	51	16		1	4	(–)23
20–23 Oct	27	56	13		1	3	(–)29
17–20 Nov	26	56	14		1	3	(–)30
1–4 Dec	28	55	13		1	3	(–)27
1996							
19–22 Jan	29	55	13		1	2	(–)26
23–26 Feb	26	57	14		1	2	(–)31
22–25 Mar	28	57	13		*	2	(–)29
19–22 Apr	28	54	14		1	3	(–)26
23–26 May	27	54	15		1	3	(–)27
21–24 Jun	31	52	12		1	4	(–)21
23–28 Jul	29	53	12		1	5	(–)24
20–25 Aug	30	51	13		1	5	(–)21
20–23 Sept	29	52	14		1	4	(–)23
25–28 Oct	28	56	12		1	3	(–)28
8–11 Nov	33	50	12		1	4	(–)17
6–9 Dec	30	51	13		1	4	(–)21

	Con	Lab	Lib Dem	SDP	Grn	Other	Con Lead
1997							
24–28 Jan	30	55	11		1	4	(–)25
21–24 Feb	31	52	11		1	5	(–)21
21–24 Mar	29	50	14		1	7	(–)21
01 Apr	28	55	11		1	5	(–)27
08 Apr	34	49	12		*	5	(–)15
15 Apr	32	49	13		1	5	(–)17
22 Apr	27	48	17		1	7	(–)21
29 Apr	28	48	16		*	8	(–)20

Table 8
Monthly Unemployment Count for the UK 1990–93

| | Not Seasonally Adjusted | | Seasonally Adjusted | |
	Total (thousands)	Percentage rate	Total (thousands)	Percentage rate
	BCJA	BCJB	BCJD	BCJE
1990				
Jan	1687.0	5.9	1612.0	5.6
Feb	1675.7	5.8	1610.4	5.6
Mar	1646.6	5.7	1599.9	5.6
Apr	1626.3	5.7	1593.9	5.5
May	1578.5	5.5	1602.0	5.6
Jun	1555.6	5.4	1614.9	5.6
Jul	1623.6	5.6	1624.5	5.6
Aug	1657.8	5.8	1642.9	5.7
Sept	1673.9	5.8	1672.7	5.8
Oct	1670.6	5.8	1725.2	6.0
Nov	1728.1	6.0	1778.7	6.2
Dec	1850.4	6.4	1852.6	6.4
1991				
Jan	1959.7	6.9	1882.2	6.6
Feb	2045.4	7.2	1977.6	6.9
Mar	2142.1	7.5	2096.0	7.3
Apr	2198.5	7.7	2163.9	7.6
May	2213.8	7.8	2235.0	7.8
Jun	2241.0	7.9	2301.0	8.1
Jul	2367.5	8.3	2364.0	8.3
Aug	2435.1	8.5	2409.8	8.4
Sept	2450.7	8.6	2445.8	8.6
Oct	2426.0	8.5	2483.3	8.7
Nov	2471.8	8.7	2521.9	8.8
Dec	2551.7	8.9	2553.2	8.9
1992				
Jan	2673.9	9.4	2586.7	9.1
Feb	2710.5	9.5	2635.4	9.3
Mar	2707.5	9.5	2658.1	9.3
Apr	2736.5	9.6	2694.5	9.5
May	2707.9	9.5	2723.5	9.6
Jun	2678.2	9.4	2733.8	9.6
Jul	2774.0	9.7	2758.1	9.7
Aug	2845.5	10.0	2802.0	9.8
Sept	2847.4	10.0	2830.5	9.9
Oct	2814.4	9.9	2867.2	10.1
Nov	2864.1	10.1	2909.4	10.2
Dec	2983.3	10.5	2981.1	10.5

| | Not Seasonally Adjusted | | Seasonally Adjusted | |
	Total (thousands)	Percentage rate	Total (thousands)	Percentage rate
	BCJA	*BCJB*	*BCJD*	*BCJE*
1993				
Jan	3062.1	10.8	2962.7	10.5
Feb	3042.6	10.8	2956.8	10.5
Mar	2996.7	10.6	2943.6	10.4
Apr	3000.5	10.6	2952.7	10.4
May	2916.6	10.3	2928.9	10.4
Jun	2865.0	10.1	2918.8	10.3
Jul	2929.3	10.4	2906.7	10.3
Aug	2960.0	10.5	2905.5	10.3
Sept	2912.1	10.3	2887.9	10.2
Oct	2793.6	9.9	2845.2	10.1
Nov	2769.4	9.8	2814.8	10.0
Dec	2782.7	9.8	2783.8	9.8

Index

Entries for Norman Lamont have been placed under the appropriate heading. The subheading NL has been used in some cases, as has PM to denote John Major.

Abbey National 148
Acland, Sir Antony 278
Acland, Jennifer 278
Admiralty House 71, 249, 253–4, 285–6, 372
Advance Corporation Tax 352
Aga Khan, Begum 397
Agnelli, Giovanni 221, 233
Ahern, Bertie 236, 264, 375
Aitken, Jonathan 427
Alaghband, Vahid 513–14
alcohol and tobacco taxation 46, 165, 204–5
All Souls High Table 441
Allan, Alex 226, 242, 250
Allason, Rupert 401–2
Alphondary, Edmond (Finance Minister of France) 402–3
Alyev, M. (President of Azerbaijan) 87
Amato (Prime Minister of Italy) 265–6
American Council of Economic Advisors 297
Anderson, Bruce 393
  Sunday Express 172–4
Anderson, Clive 371
Andreotti, Giulio 111
Anglo-German alliance 274, 329, 340
anti-inflation policy 387
Any Questions 420
Archer, Jeffrey 508
Armistice Day 83
Ashby, David 407

Ashdown, Paddy 282, 364, 383, 482, 489
Asia, great crash 100
Astor, William 72, 484
Asylum Bill 195
Atkins, Robert 19
Attali, Jacques 66–7, 194
Australia 90, 162, 209, 454–5
Austria, EU negotiations 331, 410
Autumn Statements
  (1988) 311
  (1991) 142–6, 166, 174, 299, 392
  (1992) 299–317, 328, 334, 345
Azerbaijan 514
Aznavour, Charles 232

Baker, Jim 279
Baker, Kenneth 137–8, 170, 192–3, 199, 412, 506–7
  and Mary 49
Balladur, Edouard 268, 377, 402
Balli Group 513–14
Baltic States 75, 78
Bangkok, IMF meeting (autumn 1991) 79–82
Banham, Sir John, Director General of CBI 197
Bank of England 103, 107, 150–1, 454
  advice to Russia 84
  Black Wednesday 251, 254, 256–7
  Bundesbank repayments 288
  contact on holiday 220–1
  Deputy Governor 196–7, 322

ERM 248
Governor 196–7, 321–2
independence 26, 121, 219, 266,
    275, 277, 322–7, 387, 395,
    454, 459, 474, 494
intervention 227, 246–9, 254, 286
Monetary Policy Committee 454–5
officials' visit to Germany 265
open market operations 135
reserves 231, 258–9
White Paper on independence 325
woman Director 193
see also George, Eddie; Leigh-
    Pemberton, Robin
banks 97–8, 323, 326–7
Banks, Robert 478
Banque de France 403–4
Barber, Tony 50
Barker, Godfrey 399
Barnett, Joel 240
Barucci, Piero 126, 228, 233–4, 236,
    253, 375, 398
Basildon, election (1992) 189
Basle-Nyborg agreement on mutual
    support 228
Bath 234, 490
    see also Ecofin, meetings, Bath
Battersea Heliport 397, 412
BBC 92
    exit polls 188
    Question Time
        encounter with Roy Jenkins 405
        John Redwood 442
    Radio, World at One 471
    Television
        debate with John Smith 180
        John Townend, devaluation 214
    Wim Kok views 128
Beckett, Margaret 109, 180
Beckett Rule 169
beef crisis 394, 469
beer and spirits, taxation 58
Beith, Alan 326
Belgium 206, 229, 242, 343, 403
Benelux 344

Benn, Tony 200
Bentsen, Lloyd 344, 361, 375, 519
Bérégovoy, Pierre 113–14, 120, 124,
    129–30, 151–3, 253, 296, 421,
    451, 521
    referendum campaign 231, 263
Berlin, Isaiah 467
Bernhardt, Prince of the Netherlands
    221
Bevins, Tony (Independent) 184
Biffen, John 401, 412
Bilderberg Conference 432
Billericay, election (1992) 189
Birmingham
    European Council of Finance
        Ministers 287
    National Health Service 73
Birt, John 240
Black, Conrad 11, 432
Black Sea 513
Black Wednesday 246–66, 253, 339,
    394, 494
Blackpool Party Conference (1991)
    139–43, 154, 405
Blair, Cherie 414
Blair, Tony, (Prime Minister 1997–)
    Bank of England privatisation 326
    Britain at the heart of Europe 458
    Budget (1992) 178
    euro 454, 458–60
    European single currency 516
    Eurosceptical position 485
    General Elections
        (1994) 414–15, 419
        (1997) 493, 495, 498
    Government 203, 450–1, 494,
        514, 516
    monetary union 111
    NL peerage 507
    No. 11 Downing Street 47–8
    PM, Question Time 431, 444,
        473–4, 476, 486
    State Opening of Parliament 53
    Sun 485
Body, Sir Richard 409, 421

Bolton, John Major 182
Bonsor, Sir Nicholas 471
Bottomley, Virginia 193
Boundary Commission 378
Bournemouth, Conservative Party
   Conferences 40, 415–18, 425,
   469, 472
Brady, Nicholas 68, 71, 81, 221–2,
   227, 229, 361
   Bundesbank criticism 233
   Presidential Election 279
Braithwaite, Lady 71
Braithwaite, Sir Roderick 71–2
Breakfast with Frost 424
Brezhnev, Leonid 67
Bright, Graham 19, 21
Brighton, Conservative Party
   Conference (1992) 289–93, 365
British Leyland 165
British Rail 96
   privatisation 157, 494
British sherry 205–6
Brittan, Leon 205, 361
   and Diana 198
Brittan, Samuel 61, 106, 366–7
   Bank of England independence 323
   Budget (1993) 355
   Daily Telegraph 214
   Financial Times 176, 292
   NL resignation 376
Brixton, pensioners 324
Brown, Colin, *Independent* 480
Brown, Gordon 103–4, 198, 413
   Autumn Statement (1992) 310
   Bank of England independence
      395, 451–4
   Budgets 167
      (1993) 360
   Chancellor
      Bank of England independence
         298, 326
      20 pence band 172
   economic tests 450
   European single currency 516
   European Union 503

Maastricht Bill 368
   NL peerage 507–8
   No. 11 Downing Street 47
   PM reshuffles 379
   Shadow Chancellor 282–3
   William Hague 513
Brown, Michael 27
Brown, Nick 409, 413, 507
Browning, Angela 486
Bruges Group, NL speech to 10–11,
   112
Brunson, Michael 370–1
Brussels 116, 201
Bryan, William Jennings 448
BSE 464
Buckingham Palace 69, 178
Buckland, Chris, *Daily Express* 141,
   355
Budd, Alan 93, 217, 289, 335
Budgen, Nick 293
Budgets
   (1853) 351–2
   (1981) 346
   (1991) 31–63, 166, 230–1
   (1992) 'Budget for Recovery'
      155–90, 173
      20 pence tax band 184–5, 499
   (1993) Spring 167, 333–60, 370,
      405
   (1993) Autumn 369–71, 378
   (1994) 406–7, 422–3
   (1995) 463–4
   Red Book 184, 299, 357
   unified 166–7, 173, 303, 340, 367,
      370, 406–7
Bulgarian Embassy 429
Bundesbank 103, 105, 150, 152,
   198, 216, 228, 240, 245,
   259–60
   Bank of England
      independence 266
      and Treasury visit 265
   candidates for devaluation 239
   ERM 264–6, 343
   European monetary policy 395

Foreign Office note 256, 262–263, 287–8
independence 236, 343
interest rates 237, 243
intervention obligations 263
Mitterrand description of Maastricht 232
PSBR increase 177
support of franc 403
Bundestag 123
Burgundy, holiday 220
Burke, Edmund 448, 458
Burns, Sir Terence (Terry) 217, 222–3, 244, 350, 402
    Bank of England independence 323–5
    Bath Ecofin 234–5, 237–8
    Black Wednesday 247, 249–50, 254, 262
    Brighton Party Conference 289
    Chevening (1993) 333, 338
    Chief Economic Advisor 6, 33, 38–40
    Dulwich College 240
    ERM 210
    French referendum 242
    General Election (1992) 188
    Honours List 366
    interest rates 151–2, 197, 281
    NL resignation 267–8, 374
    Permanent Secretary promotion 92–3, 95, 101, 149
    Portuguese escudo 187
    Public Accounts Committee evidence 316–17
    public expenditure 300
Bush, Barbara 69
Bush, George 68–70, 87, 227, 279
Business Expansion scheme (BES) 165
Butler, Rab 516–17
Butler, Sir Robin 48, 94–5, 168, 316

Cabinet
    (1990) 193
    Black Wednesday aftermath 271–4
    Committees
        coal mine closures 294
        EDX 302–8, 370
        unemployment 341
    Maastricht progress review 127
    meetings
        (January 1997) 475
        Queen's Speech 195
    Ministers
        disagreements 319–20
        leadership contest (1990) 17
        reshuffles 367, 371, 379, 413–14, 446–7
    Sub-Committees 319–20
Cairncross, Sir Alec 385
Caithness, Malcolm 407
Call, Mark 32
Callaghan, Jim 268–9, 273
Camdessus, Michel 66, 154
Cameron, David 183, 193–4, 280–1, 362–3, 366, 371, 417
    NL
        Brighton Conference speech 291
        lecture to CPC 290–1
        resignation 373
Campaign for an Independent Britain, speech in Oxford 425–6
Campbell, Alastair 183–4, 462
    Daily Mirror 183
    Today 363, 379
Canada 42, 161, 455
Canterbury Hospital 317
Capital Gains Tax (CGT) 46–7, 350
Capitalism 86, 89
Car Tax 165, 307
    see also company cars
Carli, Guido 76, 126, 153
Carlisle, John 411, 434
Carlton Club, PM speech 341–2
Carlyle, Thomas 461
Carrington, Peter 271, 432
Carter-Ruck (solicitors) 93–4
Carttiss, Michael 378
Cash, Bill 200, 270, 399, 418, 464

Caspian Sea 513
Catherine Place meeting 14–16
CBI 8, 140
  NL speech at Centre Point 371
  surveys 99, 106–7, 109, 141–142
Ceausescu, President 86
Central Statistical Office (CSO), Poll
  Tax 62
Chamberlain, Neville 41, 52
Channel Four News
  confrontation with John Smith 187
  difference with John Major 153
Channel Tunnel 96
Chaplin, Judith 15, 359–60
Charles, Prince 330
Chevening 162–4, 215, 333–5
Chez Nico 474
Child tax allowances 51
Christchurch by-election 364, 402
Christie, Agatha 481
Christodoulou, Effdhimios 126
Christophersen, Henning 116, 235,
  328
Chubais (Russian economic reformer)
  86
Churchill, Sir Winston 17, 41, 215,
  291, 512
  Fulton speech 83
Churchill, Winston 294
CIA 79
Ciampi (Governor of the Bank of
  Italy) 228, 236, 239
Citizens' Charter 497
Civil Servants
  guidelines 168
  Maastricht negotiations 122–3
CJD 464
Clark, Alan 13–14, 23, 506
Clarke, Gillian 379
Clarke, Kenneth 281, 422, 470, 498
  Bank of England 259, 298
  Black Wednesday 250–2, 272
  Budget (1994) 167, 406–7
  Chancellor 298, 354, 356, 358,
    377, 379, 395, 474, 500, 504

  taxes and spending 405–6
  20 pence band 171–2
  Conference speech (1996) 472
  EDX Committee 303–5
  ERM bands 404
  EU membership 449
  European
    Finance Bill (1993) 332
    policy 472
    single currency 427–8, 435, 466,
      475–6, 511
  Europhile position 427
  Eurosceptics 421–2, 434
  General Elections
    (1992) 157–8
    (1994) 420
    (1997) 485–6
  Home Secretary, ERM 268,
    339–40
  interest rates 325
  Maastricht paving motion 328
  NL
    replacement 362
    resignation 377
  Party leadership elections
    (1994) 406, 409, 411
    (1997) 510–11
  proposed referendum 465
  Sam Brittan criticism 376
  Tory backbenchers 427, 472–3
  VAT 205
Clifton-Brown, Geoffrey 270
Clinton, President Bill 327, 335, 344,
  361–2
coal mines, closures 293–6, 318,
  446
Cockfield, Arthur 50
College Green, TV cameras 445
Colne Valley 186
Colver, Hugh, *Sun* 462–3
Commons, House of 53
  Asylum Bill 195
  Autumn Statement (1992) 310–12
  Criminal Justice Bill 195
  debates coal mines closures 295

economy (June 1993) 381
on ERM entry 8
emergency debate on the economy
    281–5
European Finance Bill (1993) 332
European single currency statement
    116
Finance Bills 160, 178, 358
Lottery Bill 195
Maastricht Bill *see* Maastricht Bill
Major leadership campaign (1990)
    22, 24
NL, fondness for 382
Press Gallery 369
Private Member's Bill 469
Select Committee on the Autumn
    Statement (1990) 37–8
Commonwealth of Independent
    States (CIS) 82
Communist Bloc 86, 306
Community Charge 59–60, 96
company cars 46, 58, 61
company chairmens' statements 38
Concorde 278
Cones Hotline 497
Congdon, Tim 61, 214, 297, 310–11
Conservative
Central Office 436
    aides 472, 474
    European single currency 476
    General Elections
        (1979) 495
        (1992) 182, 189
        (1997) 471
    Labour's Programme 169
    NL legal bill 95, 316–17
    recession 91–2, 106–7, 139
    taxation issue 187
Government
    disagreements 471–5
    Euroscepticism 466
    NL vote against 427–32, 435
    in office but not in power 321,
        382
    political disaster 256

splits (1992–) 200
see also Government
Junior Ministers, Maastricht
    meeting 200
Party
    (1995–97) 461
    Backbench Finance Committee
        214
    backbenchers
        European Finance Bill (1993)
            332
        NL meeting 284
    Campaign Guide 487
    Central Council, Torquay 178–9
    child benefit 50–2
    coal mines closures 295
    Conferences
        (1990) Bournemouth 40
        (1991) Blackpool 139–43, 154
        (1992) Brighton 289–93, 365
        (1994) Bournemouth 415–18,
            425, 469
        (1995) Blackpool 462–3, 503
        (1996) Bournemouth 472
        (1997) Blackpool 405, 407,
            510
    EMU 111, 448
    ERM debate 385, 487
    Euroscepticism 448–9
    income tax 44, 158–9
    leadership elections
        (1990) 6–30
        (1994) speculation 411–12,
            422
        (1995) 434–47, 504, 507
        (1997) 326, 510–12
    Major resignation of leadership
        (1997) 510
    Manifestos 323
        (1992) 157–8, 178, 304
        (1997) 432
    MPs 148–49, 385
        Budget 1993; 346–9, 355
        General Election 90
        housing market 149

Conservative Party – *continued*
   Major leadership campaign
      (1990) 20, 25
   motion on European policy
      199
   NL post Black Wednesday
      270
   opinion polls 411
   pay increases 432
   Poll Tax 43–4
   recession 90
   unemployment 102
   1922 Committee 12, 59, 383,
      434–6, 444, 464
   opinion polls 106, 394, 402,
      533–5
   Opposition (1997–) 505–17
   popularity 41
   Shadow Budget (1992) 180
   Whips 20, 473
     withdrawn from PMs 332,
      402, 421–3
  Political Centre (CPC) 463
   NL lecture on Europe and
      Maastricht 290–1
Conway, Derek 396–7
Cook, Robin 412, 464, 470
Cope, John 193, 350
Corporation tax 40, 46, 335, 345–6,
   370
Council of Mortgage Lenders 108,
   · 148–9
Council Tax 61, 305, 494
Covent Garden 71
Cran, James 327
Criminal Justice Bill 195
Cripps, Sir Stafford 268, 523
Crockett, Andrew 79
Crosini, Count 221
Culpin, Robert 163, 335
currency market, since Black
   Wednesday 284
Customs and Excise 39, 206
'cyclical' expenditure 301
Czechoslovakia (1968) 87

Dacre, Paul, *Daily Mail* 103
Daily Express 141
   Autumn Statement (1992) 310
   Black Wednesday 270
   Budgets
     (1991) 60, 175
     (1993) 355
   election (1992) 187
   NL Brighton Conference speech
     292
   tax cuts 170
Daily Mail 103, 106
   Autumn Statement (1992) 310
   Budgets
     (1992) 175–6
     (1993) 354
   Cabinet suicide pact 420
   Election addresses 487
   NL 270, 315, 341, 430
   PM 408, 470
Daily Mirror
   Budget (1993) 354–5
   election (1992) 183–4
   NL 270, 315, 376
Daily Telegraph 98, 106, 142
   Autumn Statement (1992) 310–11
   back to basics campaign 407–8
   Budgets
     (1991) 61
     (1993) 354–5
   criticism of John Major 508
   election (1992) 190
   European single currency 435
   German guilt 239
   NL
     insensitivity 365
     post Black Wednesday 270
     resignation 271, 376
     support 432
   PM European single currency 473–4
   Staffordshire South-East by-
     election 469
Dale, Sara ('Miss Whiplash') 93–4,
   314, 316, 483
Dante Alighieri 459

D'Artagnan, *The Three Musketeers* 131

Darwall, Rupert 415, 484

Davidson, Julian 363, 365

Davies, Gavyn 106
  Budget (1993) 355
  Sun 101–2

Davies, Howard 355

de Gaulle, General Charles 447, 457

de Mandat-Grancey, Rosario 59, 198, 220

de Rothschild, Evelyn 397, 447
  and Victoria 198

Defence
  Ministry of (MoD) 9, 306
    spending 77, 305–6
  'Options for Change' 306
  and Overseas Policy Committee of the Cabinet (DOP) 116, 130

Dell, Edmund 386

Delors, Jacques 113, 116, 128, 314–15, 329, 343, 404–5, 449
  Report 111, 117–18, 120

Deneuve, Catherine 231–2

Denmark 99, 201, 233, 235, 331, 451
  krona 239, 343, 403
  referendums 198–203, 328, 367–8, 501–2

Depardieu, Gerard 232

Departments, draft package of budgets 303

Der Spiegel 343

Descartes, René 459

Desert Orchid (racehorse) 55, 59

d'Estaing, Giscard 126

Deutschmark 90, 151–2, 197, 201, 211, 228–9, 236, 242, 258, 261–3, 285

Dicks, Terry 310

Dijon, holiday 220

Disraeli, Benjamin 191

Domingo, Placido 232

Dorneywood 137, 192, 215, 315, 333, 369–70, 372, 374, 379–81

Dorrell, Stephen 193, 281, 306, 310, 350

Dostoyevsky, Fyodor 137, 246

Downing Street, Rose Garden 198, 434

Draghi, Mario 241, 398

drinks industry 205

Duffield, John 398, 412

Duisenburg, Wim 237, 262

Duncan, Alan 19–20, 443, 446, 510

Duncan-Smith, Iain 433, 469

Eastwood, Clint 232

Eatwell, John 175

Ecofin (Committee of European Finance Ministers)
  ERM bands 404
  European Central Bank 120
    Luxembourg 121
  meetings 33, 116–17, 119, 126, 287
    (1993) 369
    Apeldoorn (September) 128–9
    Bath 227, 233–8, 242, 259–60, 262–3, 343
    French referendum results 280
    (June 1992), Delors 329
    NL, Chairmanship (July 1992) 206, 227–8, 237, 259–60
  Soviet Union 128
  Stability Pact 473
  Taxation and the Single Market: A Market-Based Approach (1988) 204

economic
  forecasters 56
    independent panel of 100, 277, 297, 352
  revisionism (1980s) 366

The Economist
  Eurosceptics 405, 409
  Harrogate 483
  NL, sacking 366
  recession 139

economy 63

ecu 112–14, 450–1
Eden, Anthony 413
Edinburgh 330
  European Council (1992) 328–32, 420
Edwards, Estelle 480
Eggar, Tim (Minister for Energy) 294
Elizabeth II, Queen 178
  and Duke of Edinburgh 75
Emminger, Otmar 264
Employment, Department of 96, 138–9
EMU (European Monetary Union) 110, 118, 134, 153, 433, 451, 453, 455–6, 471
  meetings 33
English Development Corporation 157
ENI (Energy Nuclear Industry) privatisation 398
Environment Secretary, NL, offer 372, 380, 397
Epsom, Derby 397
Erhard, Ludwig 61
ERM (Exchange Rate Mechanism) 91, 99, 103–5, 109, 146, 274–5, 298, 376, 426, 451, 497–8
  alternatives 212–13
  bands 194–5, 197, 404
  Black Wednesday 250–2, 254
  Budget (1991) 35–8
  collapse of 268, 279, 343
  constraints 147, 154
  crises 223–6, 233, 402–6
  devaluation within 262, 268
  economic discipline imposed by 107
  exchange rates 201
  fault lines 286–7
  Finance Ministers' recommended changes 286–7
  fiscal policy 144
  and Maastricht 217
  members, interest rates 266
  membership 33–8, 41–2, 46, 57–8,

    150, 160, 248–9, 283, 325, 334
  framework post ERM 454
  frustrations with 208–10
  joining 7–9, 194, 269
    rate 210–11, 260
  leaving 125, 151, 153, 209, 217–19, 238–40, 243, 245, 249, 254–66, 274, 297
  rejoining 272–4, 368, 433
  monetary union 217
  NL, view 268
  policy 218
  position of pound 151
  realignment 236, 262–6
  recession (1990–93) 385–95
  reconstruction 337
  rules 230, 240, 248, 254, 287–88
  suspensions 250, 254–5
  trouble for France 342–4
euro 451–5, 459–60, 471, 516
  launch (1999) 266
  NL, reservations 123–6, 448–75
European
  Assembly, direct elections to 449
  Bank of Reconstruction and Development (EBRD) 66–7, 70
  Central Bank 120–1, 128–30, 232, 455, 470–1
    Bath Ecofin 234, 237–8
    Black Wednesday 249
    G4 meeting 228
  Commission 134, 449
    carbon tax 207
    centralising ambitions of 200
  Communities Bill, NL, Maiden Speech in support of 123–4
  Community
    (Finance) Bill (1994) 419–22
    report on unemployment 103
  Council 232
    Edinburgh 328–32, 420
    Finance Ministers 123, 126, 453
    Birmingham 287

Black Wednesday 249, 252–4, 253
Chairman (NL) 203–4, 255, 286–7
co-ordination after French referendum 243
co-ordination of policy, attempt 226–8
economic convergence 119
Edinburgh 331
existing ERM parities 227–8
gold standard 453–4
Maastricht meeting 131
single currency 135
see also Ecofin
Court decisions 469
Foreign Ministers' meeting, Greece 410
Foundation 418
Monetary Fund 113
Monetary Institute 129–30
Monetary System (EMS) 216–19, 246, 250, 253–4, 344
Parliament 120, 134
  Committee on Economic and Monetary Union 63
  NL, Election candidate 509–10
Policy Forum Speech (July 1992) 211–14, 217–18, 269, 274, 282
single currency 109, 129–30, 134–5, 322, 324, 426–8, 435, 473, 499, 502, 511
  (1997–) 461–2
  beginning (1999) 475–6
  Conservative manifesto 466
  NL, views 112, 435, 447–75
  opposition to 10–13
  opt-out 290, 368, 471
  proposed referendum 464–5
  see also Delors Report
Summit, Naples (Autumn 1990) 111, 118
Union
  attitude to law 331

beef ban 470
Budget 328–32, 419–22
Cabinet disagreements over 475
central banks 254, 322, 324
common foreign policy 133
debate 149
development of 200, 331
economy 328–9
enlargement 410
expenditure 329
  juste retour 329
financing 203
General Election (1997) 485–7
Monetary Committee 254–5, 264–5
monetary policy 395
Presidency 203–8, 329
single market, completion of the 206
Soviet aid 67
subsidiarity 114–15
tax harmonisation 203–8
Veterinary Committee 470
Europhiles, PM resignation calls 411
Eurosceptics 118, 134, 149, 207, 288, 398–9, 503
  Bank of England privatisation 323–4
  ERM 217
  European single currency 476
  leadership election (1995) 436–7
  Maastricht Bill 327–8, 369
  Maastricht Treaty 401
  NL, resignation 378–9
  Stability Pact 472–3
  within Cabinet 200
Evans, David 439–40
Evans, Nigel 52, 310
Evening Standard 104–5
  Eurosceptics within Cabinet 200–1
  NL 11, 314, 381, 383
  tax cuts 185
exchange rates 274, 276–7, 285–6, 298, 386
  fixed 261, 286–7

excise duty 58
Export Credits Guarantee
    Department (ECGD) 307
export subsidies 290
exporters 307

Falklands War 41
Federal Reserve Board 38
Field, Barry 437, 439, 445
Fildes, Christopher, *Daily Telegraph*
    98
Finance Acts 165
Finance Bills
    (1992) 160, 178
    (1993) 358
financial
    markets, Danish referendum 201–3
    package 230–1
    services 206
Financial Times 37, 90, 176, 183,
    245
    Autumn Statement (1991) 145
    British policy 292
    Budgets
        (1991) 60
        (1992) 175
        (1993) 355
    Bundesbank paper 288
    ERM crisis 270
    euro 451
    interest rates 150, 196, 339
    NL
        European Policy Forum speech
            213
        reappointment 192
        resignation 376–7
        Threshergate 314
    prediction of change of policy 473
    PSBR increase 176–7
    Stephens, Philip 7
Finland 239–40, 257, 284, 398
Flick, Muck and Donatella 370
Fontainebleau summit (June 1984)
    449
foreign exchange

markets 150–1, 222, 231, 255,
    283, 338
reserves 257–9, 258
Foreign Office 72, 75, 78, 342
EU
    Budget 332
    Presidency 203
Forsyth, Michael 27, 465
Fowler, Norman 367
    Major resignation honours list 508
    Newbury by-election 364
    NL 341, 362, 366, 377, 383
    support for Heseltine 21
Fox, Marcus 434–5, 464–5
France 61, 114, 250, 259
    Central Bank 121, 257, 325
    Deutschmark revaluation 229, 263
    devaluations 211, 261
    economy 42, 151, 247, 284, 287,
        296
    ERM 233, 257, 342–4, 395, 451
    EU enlargement 331
    European Monetary System (EMS)
        344
    exchange markets 222
    interest rates 99, 150, 152–3, 222,
        238, 285, 402–3
    Maastricht Treaty 129–30, 227
        referendum 201, 218–19, 222,
            224–5, 231, 235, 239–40,
            250, 260, 263, 273, 278,
            280, 283
    monetary union 344
    NL, summer holiday 220–3
Francis, Mary 226, 371
Franco, Francisco 86
Fresh Start Group 433–4, 443
Friends of the Earth 348
Frost, David, reshuffle 379
The Frost Programme 92, 337
    Goldsmith interview 468
Fry, Stephen 215
fuel and power, VAT 348, 353,
    355–6, 368, 377, 422–3, 442,
    489

Fullerton, Peter 93, 484, 490–1
Fyodorov, Dr 73

G4, meetings (France, Germany, Italy
    and UK) 109, 227–30, 233
G7 74, 81
    Finance Ministers 68, 70–1
    growth 42, 382
    inflation 276
    interest rates 151–2
    meetings 33
        (1991) London 67–71, 68, 76,
            161
        (1991) New York 114
        (1992) Munich 82, 153–4, 500
        (1992) Washington 278–9
        (1993) London 344
        (1993) Tokyo, Foreign and
            Finance Ministers 361–2
    Soviet aid 66
Gaidar, Yegor 73, 81–3, 86
Galbraith, J.K. 517
Gallup poll 463
Gardiner, George 369, 436, 443
Garel-Jones, Tristan 14, 132, 430,
    445
GATT see General Agreement on
    Tariffs and Trade (GATT)
Gayfere Street 19–20, 23
GDP (Gross Domestic Product)
    146–7, 300
GEMU (German economic and
    monetary union) 450–1
General Agreement on Tariffs and
    Trade (GATT) 203, 361, 417
General Elections
    (1974) 494
    (1979) 495
    (1987) 168
    (1992) 90, 137–9, 155–90, 394,
        493–4, 498
        aftermath (April–September
            1992) 191–219
    (1997) 358, 393, 448, 471, 482–7,
        494–5, 499

    opinion poll predictions since
        1945; 181–2, 186
General Government Expenditure
    (GGE) 96, 139, 145
George, Eddie 222–3, 226–8, 227,
    231, 241–2, 244, 265, 325
    Black Wednesday 247, 249, 251,
        254, 322
    Governor of the Bank of England
        321–2
Geraschenko, Viktor, Gosbak
    Governor 79–81
German Ambassador 287–8
German Industry Forum (June 1990)
    113
Germany 216–19
    Bath Ecofin 259
    Black Wednesday 250, 254
    East, economy 216
    East and West, monetary union 63
    economic convergence 118–20
    economy 144, 161–2, 230, 272,
        287, 351, 403, 452
    ERM 240–5
    EU
        breakdown in communications
            259–60, 263, 265
        enlargement 331
    European
        growth package 329
        Monetary System (EMS) 344
    Government, Bundesbank tensions
        260
    interest rates 41, 99, 103, 105,
        140, 150–4, 196–7, 209,
        217–19, 222, 233, 235–7,
        241–2, 261, 263, 272, 285,
        344, 387–9, 391–392
    Lander 153
    Lombard rate 41, 103, 150, 216,
        240–1, 263, 343
    Maastricht Treaty 227, 232
    Ministry of Finance, visit by
        Treasury and Bank of England
        265

Germany – *continued*
  realignment 153, 283
  reunification (1989) 36, 279, 283,
      387, 497
Gieve, John 19, 32, 48, 127, 194
Gill, Christopher 440
Gill, Ron 378, 482
Gladstone, William Ewart 53, 302,
      351–2
Glasgow University debate 413
GMTV, Portillo interview 411
Godley, Professor Wynne 297, 355,
      391
Godolphin School 50
gold standard 394, 453–4
Goldsmith, Jimmy 418
  Referendum Party 466–8, 485
Gonzales (Portugal) 133, 331
Goodhart, Professor Charles
      106–7–8
Goodlad, Alastair 506
Goodman, Elinor 191–2
Gorbachev, Mikhail 64–72, 75,
      77–80, 83, 86–8
  G7, Summit (July 1991) 67–72
  General Secretary of the
      Communist Party 78, 82
  Moscow meeting 74–6, 128
  Presidential Election 87
  Soviet gold holdings 80
  Union Treaty 76
Gorbachev, Raisa 71–2, 77
Gorman, Teresa 440–1
Gorst, John 12
Gosbak 79–80
Gould, Bryan 190, 240
Gould, Philip 179
  The Unfinished Revolution 174–5
Government
  borrowing 47
    (1992) 309
    (1993) 333
  economic policy 274–7, 281–5,
      473
  ERM 388

European policy 427–32, 503
  finances 320, 334, 498
  macro-economic policy 297
  opinion polls 393–4, 495, 533–5
Gray, Paul 197, 223, 247
Greece 118, 120, 276, 331, 410
Green, Chris (driver) 198
'Green shoots' 141, 146–7, 365
Greenspan, Alan 38, 150–1, 161,
      217, 279–80, 454, 520
Greig, Gordon, *Daily Mail* 367
Grey Book 334
Grey, Sir Edward 52
Grimsby Evening Telegraph 375
growth 55–6, 289–90, 297–8, 452
  strategy for 296–7, 326
Guardian
  cash for questions 418
  ERM crisis 270
  NL
    Conference speech 141
    post Black Wednesday 270
    resignation possibility 273
  split on tax 185
Guildhall 142
Gulf War 33, 47, 156
Gummer, John 19, 449

Hague, Ffion 488
Hague, William 51, 500, 512–13
  Conservative Party
    leader 385
    leadership elections
      (1990) 10, 13–14, 19, 28
      (1995) 443
      (1997) 510–12
  European single currency 500
  Eurosceptical line 509
  Harrogate campaign 487–90
  NL
    advice on Harrogate seat 479,
        482
    Brighton Conference speech 291
    peerage 508, 514
    resignation 267, 373

Parliamentary Private Secretary
  (1990) 32, 52–3
Hamilton, Archie 445
Hamilton, Neil 27, 418, 484
Hampshire North West 478
Hampson, Keith 443
Handelsblatt, Schlesinger interview
  244, 256, 288
Hanley, Jeremy 413–14, 477
Harman, Harriet 409
Harrogate and Knaresborough
  477–92
Hart, David 291–2, 380
Hartington, Marquess of 397
Hashimoto, Ryutaro 68
Haskins, Chris 311
Hastings, Max 271, 365
Hayward, Rob 20
Healey, Denis 147
Health Secretary 475
Heath, Sir Edward 218, 282, 400,
  432
  Government 51, 450
    election defeat (1974) 494, 510
  Werner Plan for monetary union
    112
Heathcoat-Amory, David 467, 470
Heathites 496
Heathrow and Paddington, rail link
  350
Heaton, Frances 193
Heffer, Simon 430
Henley, W.E. 359
Herrero de Miñón, Miguel 457
Heseltine, Michael 10, 303–4, 382,
  462
  Black Wednesday 250–2, 254
  coal mine closures 294–5, 446
  Deputy Prime Minister 294, 446,
    500, 504
  EU beef ban 470
  European single currency 435
  Election campaigns
    (1992) 156–7
    (1997) 484

Environment post 42
ERM rate on entry 210–19
EU
  carbon tax 207
  membership 11
  Hamilton resignation 418
  local government taxation 58
  Maastricht 135, 328
  and Mrs Heseltine, Portillo party
    371
  NL 375, 417–18
  Party leadership elections
    (1990) 9–10, 13–15, 17–21, 23,
      25–30
    (1994) 409, 411
    (1995) 443–4, 446
  Poll Tax 42, 44, 52, 61
  Post Office privatisation 320–1,
    419
  Trade and Industry Secretary 192,
    338, 346
  TV interviews 27
  The World at One 473
Heywood, Jeremy 79, 194, 226, 229,
  249, 278
  Bank of England independence 324
  Bath Ecofin 234–5
  Maastricht Treaty 135
  NL, resignation from EDX
    Committee 304
  reshuffle 324, 373
Higgins, Terence 19
Highland Park whisky 52–3
Hill, David 175
Hill, James 428
Hill, Jonathan 182
Hill, Sir Brian 270
Hill, William, leadership odds (1994)
  409
Hogg, Christopher 198
Hogg, Douglas 14–15, 465
Hogg, Sarah 7, 35, 149, 445
  Bank of England Deputy Governor
    322
  Black Wednesday 250

Hogg, Sarah – *continued*
  EDX Committee 303, 305–6
  Election campaign (1992) 157
  ERM 225–6
  French referendum 242
  Manifesto (1992) 157–8
  Max Hastings 271
  NL, Brighton Conference speech
      291
  PM reshuffle 371
  taxation 44, 185, 337
Holbrooke, Dick 432
Holland 211, 229, 242, 261, 320,
      403
  Presidency period 116, 128
Hong Kong 454–5
Honours Lists 366–7
Horam, John 486
Horseguards Parade 48
Housman, A.E. 6, 333
Housing Associations 308
housing market 91–2, 108–9, 142–3,
      161, 196–7, 202, 217, 225, 230,
      257, 307–8, 311, 349
  package for 147–50
Howard, Michael 198, 361, 462,
      467, 474, 496, 500, 505
  broadcasts on economy 281
  Danish referendum 199
  Employment Secretary 96, 107,
      138–9
  ERM 272
  European subsidiarity 115
  European Union 399
  General Election (1992) 492
  Heseltine interference 462
  Home Secretary appointment 377
  local authorities 370
  Maastricht Treaty 133
  NL
    Harrogate 487, 491
    resignation soundings 267, 362
    TV attack on 420
  Party leadership contests
    (1990) 13, 19

  (1994) 409
  (1997) 326, 510–12
  Portillo party 371
  proposed referendum 465
  Thatcher praise 463–4
  Tony Blair 414
Howard, Sandra 198, 371, 420
Howarth, Alan 13–4, 462
Howe, Geoffrey
  Chancellor 8, 57, 346, 390
  resignation as Deputy Prime
      Minister 9, 381
  support for Heseltine 26
  VAT 62
Huddersfield 186
Hudson, Andrew 317
Huhne, Christopher, *Independent*
      145
Hungary (1956) 87
Hunter, Andrew, call for NL to
      resign 270
Hurd, Douglas 372, 377, 410, 496,
      498
  basic rate of income tax 172
  Black Wednesday 250–2, 254, 393
  Brighton Conference debate on
      Europe 290
  Brussels press conference 314
  Danish referendum 200, 502
  Election campaign (1992) 137,
      157–8
  ERM 205–6, 209–10, 368
  European Union 200–1, 203, 425,
      428–9
  G7 Summit (July 1991) 68
  Goldsmith 467
  Maastricht paving motion 327
  Maastricht Treaty 115, 127, 133,
      136, 205–6
  NL, removal 367
  Party leadership elections
    (1990) 13–15, 17–18, 23, 27, 29
    (1994) 409
  PM decisions 318
  Today programme 199

Hussein, Saddam 54
Hutton, Will, *Guardian* 370

Ibrahim, Anwar, Malaysia 398
IMF 56, 100, 140, 334
　Interim Committee
　　Finance Ministers 278–9
　　NL speech 275
　meetings
　　(1991 Autumn) 79–82
　　(1992 April) Washington 81
　　(1993 Spring) 361
　Mission, Moscow 74
　Soviet Union 66–7, 70–1, 74,
　　81–3, 86
　and World Bank meetings (1992)
　　277–9
Income Support 356
income tax 44, 46, 58, 158–9, 172,
　349
　bands 171–2, 353
Independent 52, 109, 238, 411
　Autumn Statement (1991) 143,
　　145
　beef ban 470
　Black Wednesday 262
　Budget (1991) 60
　John Major, style of government
　　200
　NL, Maastricht Bill 369
　PMs who presided over
　　devaluations 271
　PSBR 176–7
Independent on Sunday 284, 295
Indonesia 100, 398
industry, help for 349
inflation 34, 55–6, 62, 145–6, 161,
　274–7, 281, 298–9, 311, 323,
　325, 360, 376
Ingham, Bernard, *Express* 271
inheritance tax on family businesses
　164, 179
Inland Revenue 7, 39, 149
Institute of Civil Engineers 180
Institute of Directors 99, 140

Inter-Governmental Conference
　(IGC)
　(1990) Rome 115, 129–30
　(1991) plan on EMU 113
　(1996) 461, 464
　White Paper, *A Partnership of
　　Nations* 464–6
interest rates 102–5, 202, 211, 222,
　261, 283, 285, 289, 307, 338,
　387–8, 392
　Black Wednesday 248, 250, 252–7
　Budget (1991) 41–2, 62–3
　charges 323
　cuts 196–8, 209, 280–1, 295–6,
　　304, 328, 337–40, 342
　decisions 322
　Germany 41, 99, 103, 105, 140,
　　150–4, 196–7, 209, 217–9,
　　233
　post Black Wednesday 271–2
　post ERM 274
Investors' Chronicle 365
Ireland 233, 235, 257, 259, 331
　devaluation 261, 263, 284, 338,
　　342
Italy 86, 233, 238–40, 257
　Bank of 217, 233
　Bath Ecofin 259
　devaluation 234–35, 241, 244,
　　261, 263–6, 282–4
　economic convergence 118, 120
　economy 42, 202, 217, 451
　ERM 239–40, 255
　exchange markets 222
　German interest rates 233
　interest rates 99, 151, 238, 257
　NL, holidays 77–9, 105, 220–3
　VAT rates 206
ITN poll of Tory MPs 23–4

Japan 230, 322, 425
Jay, John 456–7
Jay, Peter 269, 273, 275, 399, 405–6
Jenkin, Bernard 433–4, 443, 446
Jenkins, Roy 167, 170, 405

Jochimsen, Mr (Bundesbank Board)
   228
John, Elton 232
Jopling, Michael 13
Joseph, Keith 61, 366, 441–2, 496,
   516
   Memorial Lecture 463–4
Jospin, Lionel 280
Jubilee Line extension 305, 307
Juliana, Queen of the Netherlands
   221
Juncker, Jean-Claude 128, 375
Jupiter Asset Management 398, 505
Juppé, Alain 451

Kaletsky, Anatole, Budget (1993) 355
Kavanagh, Trevor 376
   Sun 367
Kazakhstan 76
Keating, Paul 90
Keith Joseph Memorial Lecture
   463–4
Kellner, Peter 409, 492
   Newsnight 485
Kerr, Sir John 116–17, 133, 243,
   329, 332
Keynes, John Maynard 299, 308,
   498
KGB 78, 80
Khrgystan 78
King, Anthony 492
   Daily Telegraph 190
King, Mervyn 152
King, Tom 13–4
King, Tony 485
Kingston constituency 182–4, 188–9,
   378, 477, 481–2, 484, 490
Kinnock, Neil 106, 158, 180, 190
   attack on NL 186–7
   basic rate of income tax 172
   Budget (1992) 174
   Labour's tax proposals 183
   personality 156–7, 187
Kissinger, Henry 432
Knapman, Roger 378, 438–9, 444–5

Knight, Andrew 94, 317
Knowles, Michael 10
Kohl, Chancellor Helmut 68–9, 82,
   119, 121, 222, 225, 227, 240,
   253, 500
   Bath Ecofin 264
   Bundesbank 234, 264, 403
   conflict with Schlesinger 344
   Edinburgh European Council
      330–1
   ERM 344
   European cause 260
   European single currency 405,
      428, 475
   French referendum 280
   German interest rates 241, 263
   letter from John Major 153
   Maastricht Treaty 133, 229, 243
   NL, Brighton Conference speech
      292, 296
   Seguin/Mitterrand debate 231
   speeches 503
Kohler, Horst 262, 264–5, 343
   Der Spiegel 343
Kok, Wim 123, 126, 128–32, 262
Korea 398
Kozyrev (Foreign Minister) 82–3,
   362

Labour Party
   (1992)
      General Election 167–70
      Manifesto 169, 357
      Shadow Budget 180
   (1994) Conference 415
   (1997) General election 495
   Bank of England privatisation 326
   Brussels laws 140
   Maastricht paving motion 328
   MPs' Early Day Motion, privacy
      314
   monetary policy 325
   policy 171
   Private Finance Initiative 308–9
   rally at Sheffield 186–7

tax proposals 179–81
VAT 186
    on fuel and power 348
Lafontaine, Oskar 208
Lambert, Richard 245
Lamont, James 47, 317–18, 373–4,
    380, 490–91
Lamont, Mrs (senior) 373
Lamont, Norman
    articles and speeches 398–400, 516
    backbenches 396–423
    Brighton hotel bill 292–3, 365
    business activities 513–14
    City 397–401
    EDX Committee resignation 304–5
    Europe 200–1
    European single currency objection
        485
    fiftieth birthday dance 197–8
    Harrogate election address 487
    House of Lords 506
    interviews and articles 404
    Je ne regrette rien 363–5
    leadership election speculation
        412, 418
    lecture circuit 398
    Maastricht paving motion 327–8
    Maiden Speech 123–4
    radio interviews, post Black
        Wednesday 272
    resignation 359–84
        possibilities 267–71, 362–3
        statement 380–4, 396, 405,
            518–24
    scandals 365, 376, 483
    Shetlands birthplace 52
    Sovereign Britain (1995) 506
    TV programmes 272, 483
    see also NL under appropriate
        subjects
Lamont, Rosemary 48–50, 53, 59,
    141, 370–1, 379, 381, 420, 435
    Derby 397
    Dorneywood 192
    Gorbachev visit 71–2

Harrogate 479, 484
Kingston constituency 188, 490
Last Night of the Proms 240
NL, resignation 372–4
No. 11 148–9, 186, 197–8
Notting Hill house 94
Richard Ryder 362–3
Washington 278
Lamont, Sophie 47–50, 186, 191–2,
    374, 379
Lancaster House, G7 Summit (July
    1991) 68
Lang, Ian 319
Lange, Jack 231
LaRosière, Jacques 228, 236
Latsis, John 69
Lawrence, Ivan 433
Lawson, Nigel 90, 322
    Budgets 39, 54, 164
        (1988) 158–9
    Capital Gains Tax (CGT) 350
    Central Statistical Office (CSO) 62
    Chancellor 7–8, 34, 40, 45, 90,
        171, 204–5, 387
    Conference speeches 140
    ERM 274, 386
    GDP 162
    Labour Party General Election
        programme (1987) 168
    Lord 428, 514, 520
    NL 26, 55, 61
    Poll Tax 43
    resignation (1989) 36–7, 323,
        495
    support for Heseltine 26
    Treasury office 33
leaded petrol 165
Leader of the House of Commons,
    EDX Committee 302
Lee, President, Taiwan 398
Leeds, Labour Party 490
Legg, Barry 440, 445
Leigh, Edward 27, 200, 321, 371–2,
    412, 437, 440
    Spectator 372

Leigh-Pemberton, Robin 98, 109, 117, 152, 244–5, 321
  Black Wednesday 247, 249–51, 254
  G4 meeting 228
Leningrad, Scottish architects 71
Les, David (GKN) 311
Lewis, Derek 462
Liberal Democrat Party
  election (1992) 182
  fuel and power 207, 348
  Harrogate 482–4, 489–91
  Newbury 364
Lichtenberg, George 87
Liddell, Helen 187
Lightfoot, Warwick 32, 168–9
Lilley, Peter 192–3, 267, 371, 465, 474, 496, 500
  Danish referendum 199
  Maastricht meeting 200
  Party leadership contests
    (1990) 13–14, 19
    (1997) 510–11
  Social Security Secretary 193, 319–20
  Thatcher praise 463–4
Lincoln, Abraham 267, 302
Lindemann, Professor 215
literary agent 380, 383
Lloyd, Nick, *Daily Express* 189
Lloyds Bank 98
local authority expenditure 102
local elections
  (1993) 364
  (1994) 411
  (1995) 431
  (1996) 469–71
local government 43, 58–9, 61
London Business School 92
Lord Mayor's Banquets 327, 463
Lords, House of 506–9, 514–17
Lottery Bill 195
Louvre Agreement 234
Lubbers, Ruud 132–133
Luxembourg 116, 121, 403

Maastricht Bill 83, 199–200, 231, 325, 361
  paving motion 327–9, 420
  Social Chapter 369
  Third Reading 368–9, 399
Maastricht Treaty 110–36, 290, 426, 448, 502–3
  citizenship and passports 133–4
  Cohesion Fund 133
  Dutch draft Treaty 127, 129–30, 134
  economic convergence and the single currency 118–20, 134
  ERM 217, 219
    bands 194
    as a treaty obligation 126–30, 208
  Heads of Government meeting 133
  independent banks 324
  meetings 131–4
  monetary
    order 452
    policy 453
    union 344
  negotiations 115–18, 154, 322, 429
  opt-out, for Britain 122–3, 130–2, 429, 433
  ratification 278, 393, 449, 501
  signing 135–6
  Social Chapter 133, 401–2
  Stability Pact 472–3
  Summit, single European currency 105
McCrae, Hamish 106
  Independent 238
Macedo de Braga, George (Portugal) 236
Macfarlane, Neil 25
MacGregor, John 16–17, 102, 137
Mackay, James 18
McKenzie, Kelvin, *Sun* 317
Maclean, Murdo 149
McLuhan, Marshall 516
Macmillan, Harold 198, 506–7

Mafia 67, 86
Major, John, Prime Minister
    (1990–97) 493–504
  'at the very heart of Europe' 35
  attack on Norman Tebbit 282
  Autumn Statement (1992) 310
  back to basics campaign 407–8
  backbenchers' criticism of 401
  Bank of England 275, 321–5
  banks 97–8
  basic rate of income tax 172
  'bastards' 402
  beef ban 470
  beginning of Premiership 496
  'bilateral' meetings 35
  Black Wednesday 247–51, 253–4,
    273
  British Rail privatisation 157
  Budget (1992) 172–3
  Cabinet
    of choice 402
    meetings 318–19
    post Black Wednesday 271–2
    reshuffles 367, 371, 413–14,
      446–7
  Carlton Club speech 341–2
  Chancellor 7, 33–4, 37, 318–19,
    352
    Autumn Statements 39, 47
    European Finance Ministers
      meetings 386
    Treasury forecasts 163
  Chief Secretary, Nigel Lawson tax
    cuts 158
  Commons statement on Danish
    referendum 200
  Conservative Party 156, 461
    Conferences
      (1992) 218
      (1995) 503
    leadership 409, 496
      elections
        (1990) 9, 11–30, 440–1
        (1995) 434–47, 435–6
      resignation (1997) 510

Conservative Political Centre 463
constitutional issues 187
consultation exercise 432
Covent Garden 71
Danish referendum 367, 501–2
defence spending 77, 306
diplomatic and negotiating
    ingenuity 201
economic policy seminar 217
economy 277, 289
  speech in emergency debate 284
EDX Committee 303, 305, 370
EMU views of 110–12
end-of-term address to MPs 105
ERM 225–6, 258, 261, 269, 273,
    285–6, 290, 342, 368, 385–6,
    393, 395, 404, 497–8
  entry 7–8, 56
European
  Central Bank 120–1
  Community (Finance) Bill
    419–20
  single currency 405, 435, 447,
    470, 475–6, 486, 499–501,
    511
  Union 223, 469, 499–504
    agreement on subsidiarity 331
    enlargement 331, 410
    growth package 329
    integration 458
    Presidency 203
Eurosceptic 414–16, 427, 499
French referendum 242, 280
Fresh Start Group 433–4, 443
The Frost Programme 337
G7 Summit (July 1991) 68
General Elections
  (1992) 156-8, 178, 181–3, 187,
    189–90, 299, 480, 493–4, 498
  (1997) 484–5, 493
German Industry Forum (June
    1990) 113
Gillian Shephard 462
Gorbachev 71–2
Harrogate selection 480

Major, John – *continued*
  Health Service 101–2
  Honours List 367
  housing market 147, 149, 225
  Huntingdon constituency 189
  Independent devaluation 271
  India 338
  industrial aid 307
  inflation 324, 496–7
  interest rates 102, 223, 281, 295,
      309, 322, 325, 337–40
  James Lamont 380
  John Smith 281, 413
  Kinnock debate opportunity 178
  Kohl 69, 153, 273
  Leiden Eurosceptic speech 414–16
  Lord Mayor's Banquets 327, 463
  Maastricht Bill 199, 369
  Maastricht Treaty 110, 127,
      132–5, 205–6, 209–10, 217
  meeting to discuss 'presentation'
      199
  monetary union 112–13, 344, 428
  Newbury by-election 359–61
  newspapers 285–6
  NL
    Brighton Conference speech
        291–2
    Bruges Group speech 11
    Campaign Manager to 9, 20–2
    Conference speech 140
    criticism of 382
    legal bill 95, 317
    meeting and reappointment as
        Chancellor 192
    note to, not to resign 269, 382–3
    offers to 397
    peerage 507–9
    relations with 21–2, 35, 184–90,
        318, 326
    resignation 372, 381, 383
    Threshergate 314
  Northern Ireland, peace process
      494
  Paris 331, 377

  pension payments 320
  personal qualities 22, 27, 91, 182,
      502
  personal ratings 106
  PM Amato of Italy 265–6
  PM's Questions 53
  Poll Tax 42–3, 52
  Post Office privatisation 320–1,
      419
  Premiership goals 285
  Private Finance Initiative 308
  proposed referendum 465
  public expenditure 40, 95–6, 299,
      302, 336
  Question Time 340–1, 431, 444,
      473–4, 476, 486
  recession 90
  resignation honours list 508–9
  Seguin/Mitterrand debate 231
  Seminar (July) 230
  soap box 187
  Spain, holiday 222
  strategy for growth 296–7, 326
  strength of sterling 218
  style of of Government 195–6,
      200, 323
  taxation 184–90
    increases 345, 349, 359
  Thatcherite policies 24
  Treasury 96–7
  TV success 27–8
  VAT 357
  verdict of history 494
  Whipless MPs 424
  workfare 230
Major, Norma 71, 189
Malaysia 100
Mandela, Nelson 400
Mandelson, Peter 170, 317
Mansion House Speeches
  (1991) 142
  (1992) 275, 296–8, 308, 352
manufacturing
  industry 290, 346
  output 360

Maples, John 31, 148, 162–3,
    193
Marlborough, Duke of 515
Marlow, Tony 411, 420, 440
married couples allowance 51
Marshall Plan 66
Maude, Francis 19–20, 23, 29, 31,
    117, 148, 193
    Chevening, pre-Budget meeting
        162–3
    Maastricht Treaty, signing 135–6
Maudling, Reggie 297
Mawhinney, Brian 480, 484, 508
Maxwell, Robert 49
Maystadt, Philippe 126
Mazankowski, Dan 375
Mellor, David 31, 93, 95–7, 101–2,
    138–9, 168–9, 193, 271, 380–1,
    468
    Evening Standard 381, 383
Merchant, Piers 484
Meyrick, Paul 482, 491
Middleton, Sir Peter 33, 39–40, 92,
    94–5, 101, 166, 316
Midland Global Markets 338–9
Millbank, Atrium Restaurant 512
Milligan, Stephen 407
Minford, Patrick 214, 297
Minimum Lending Rate (MLR) 248,
    252–55
Mitchell, Andrew 10
Mitterrand, President François 67–8,
    114, 133, 377
    debate with Seguin 231–2
    Edinburgh European Council 330
    ERM 344
    European Central Bank 232
    French referendum 201
mobile telephones 46, 58, 61, 220
Monckton, Christopher, Evening
    Standard 104–5
monetary
    economics 322
    policy 179, 213, 298
Montrose, Duke of 515

Moore, Charles 365
    Daily Telegraph 473
    Sunday Telegraph 24
MORI
    Economic Optimism Index 360
    opinion polls
        Conservative ratings 394, 402,
            427
        Ken Clarke 422
        PM 364–5
Morrison, Peter 10, 12, 18
mortgage interest relief 45–7, 58,
    60–1, 108, 304, 349
Moscow
    coup 77–9
    visit to 72–6
MTFS (Medium Term Financial
    Strategy) 60, 335, 355
Munich 82, 119
    meeting of G7 (July 1992) 82, 500
Murdoch, Rupert 91, 94

National Economic Development
    Council (NEDC) 160
National Health Service (NHS) 73,
    101–2, 143–4, 308, 463, 485
National Insurance 46
    contributions 179, 218, 309,
        345
National Lottery 497
National Westminster Bank 314
nationalised transport industries 144
NATO commands 306
Neil, Andrew, The Sunday Times
    218, 397
Nelson, Tony 193
Nemstov (Russian economic advisor)
    86
New York 114, 247
New Zealand 161–2, 323, 454–5
Newbury by-election 359–61, 363–6,
    402
News at Ten, economic statistics 138
News International 94, 317
News of the World 93

Newsnight
  economic statistics 138
  Europe and the election (1997)
    485
  NL, gaffes 365
  Wyatt, Woodrow 365
Newton, Tony 14, 16, 303, 327, 465
Nicholson, Emma 464
Nine O'Clock News, economic
  statistics 138
No. 10 Downing Street
  aides 472, 474
  Major 'thank you' dinner (1990)
    22–3
No. 11 Downing Street 47–9, 71, 85,
  374–5
  dance 197–8
  IRA attack 47–50
  Major leadership campaign (1990)
    22–3, 28–30
  NL 47, 186, 379
No Turning Back Group 27
Nolan Report on Members' outside
  interests 432
non-cyclical expenditure 303
Non-Domestic Rates Pool 164
non-oil GDP 42, 142, 146–7
NOP poll, *The Sunday Times* 472
Norfolk, Duke of 515
Norman, Peter, *Financial Times* 288
North Sea oil 147, 346
North-East of England Region 509
Northern Ireland, peace process 494
Norway 239, 257, 284, 306
Nott, Sir John 270, 282–3
Notting Hill house 47, 49, 93–5,
  374, 407, 437

Observer, Threshergate 315
Odling-Smee, John 74
O'Donnell, Gus 49, 371, 383, 408
Office of Fair Trading 98
Oliver, F.S. 359, 396, 517
Onslow, Cranley 12
OPEC (Organization of the

Petroleum Exporting Countries)
  452
Organisation for Economic Co-
  Operation and Development
  (OECD) 56
Owen, David 60, 65, 514, 516

Pankin, Boris 72
Paris 153, 331, 377
Parker, Dorothy 396
Parkinson, Cecil 496
Parliament, new building 396–7
Parliamentary
  Commissioner for Standards 483
  Counsel 149
Parris, Matthew 365–6
Pasqua, Charles 232
Patten, Chris 95, 105, 149, 172, 498
  Bank of England independence 323
  Bath constituency 182–3, 189, 490
  Chairman of Conservative Party
    182
  Election campaign (1992) 137,
    157–9, 169–70, 182–3, 188
  Hong Kong 398, 510
  leadership contest (1990) 14
  Shadow Budget (1992) 181
Patten, John 14–16
Patten, Lavender 490
Pavlov, Valentin 68, 74, 78
Peacock, Elizabeth, coal mine
  closures 294
Pennant-Rea, Rupert 322
pensioners 165, 324
pensions 304, 319–20, 347, 356
  funds 346
PEPs 40, 318
Perestroika 66
Peretz, David 74
Petroleum Revenue Tax 346
Philippines 398
Piaf, Edith 363
Pienaar, John (BBC) 363
Plaza Agreement 234
Plenderleith, Ian 151–2

Pohl, Karl Otto 63, 115, 118, 121
Poland, Catholic Church 86
Poll Tax 42–5, 52, 61–2, 146, 155,
    305
Pompidou, Georges 447
Portillo, Michael 148, 193, 281, 294,
    381, 462, 498
  Budget (1993) 346, 370
  Chevening, pre-Budget meetings
      162–3, 333
  EDX Committee 303, 305–6
  European single currency 427
  fortieth birthday party 371
  General Election (1992) 491–2
  GMTV interview 411
  Maastricht meeting 200
  NL, resignation soundings 267
  Party leadership candidate (1995)
      411, 432, 435–6, 438, 443–4,
      446, 488, 512
  Party leadership odds (1994) 406,
      409
  Thatcher praise 463–4
Portugal 86, 187, 255, 257, 276
  devaluations 261, 263, 284
  EU Presidency 205–6
Post Office, privatisation 320–1,
    418–19
post Black Wednesday, rebuilding
    policy 267–98
post-ERM situation 318
Potter, Stephen 199
Powell, Carla 215, 441, 467
Powell, Enoch 371, 420–1
Press Council 316
Primakhov, Yevgeni 67, 70, 362
Primary Colors 361
Private Finance Initiative 308–10
Private Member's Bill, European
    Court decisions 469
private-sector financial institutions
    84–5
pro-Maastricht journalists 232
property taxes 60
PSBR (Public Sector Borrowing

  Requirement) 56–7, 142, 167
  increases 162–5, 176–7
  1991/92 144
  1992/93 312
  1993/94 334
  rules defining 308
Public Accounts Committee 316–17
public expenditure 146, 301–2, 329,
    334
  Cabinet 97
  control 40, 299–302, 301, 304
  round 95–7, 101–2, 138–9,
      301–3, 334–5
Public Sector Borrowing Requirement
  see PSBR
public sector pay 306
public services 158–9
Pushkin, Alexander 75
Pym, Hugh 279

Qualified Majority Voting system
    (QMV) 409–12, 414, 424, 470
Quayle, Dan 278, 344
Queen Elizabeth II Centre
  European Policy Forum speech
      (July 1992) 211–14
  Redwood campaign 440
Queen's Speeches 195, 419, 463

RAC Club 367
racing industry 360, 397
Radice, Giles 37
RAF Northolt 68
Rawnsley, Andrew, *Guardian* 352
Reagan, Ronald 65, 442, 458
recessions
  (1974) 34
  (1990–93) 89–109, 137–55, 334,
      385–95, 519
Red Book 299, 357
Redwood, John 402, 461, 466, 476
  European single currency 25–6
  Major leadership campaign (1990)
      25–6
  NL support 477

Redwood, John – *continued*
  Party leadership elections
    (1995) 437–41
    (1997) 440, 510–11
  Thatcher praise 463–4
Rees-Mogg, William, *The Times* 364–5
Referendum Party 466–8, 485
Reform Club 333
Reichbank, independence (1930s) 326
Renton, Tim 16
Retail Prices
  Index (RPI) 62
  Inflation 100
retail sales 351, 360
retirement relief 46
Reuters 248, 251–2, 373
Ribble Valley by-election 52
Richmond, Duchess of 116–117
Riddell, Peter 295, 353
  Independent 470
  The Times 311, 363
Ridley, Nicholas 496
  The Times, Autumn Statement
    (1991) 145
Rifkind, Malcolm 133–4, 157,
    469–71, 475–6
  leadership contest (1990) 14, 16
  White Paper on IGC *A Partnership
    of Nations* 464–6
Rio Conference on Environment
    (June 1992) 348
Ritz Hotel 408
road fuel duties 348
Robinson, Bill 32, 148, 209, 247,
    291, 345–6
  analysis of Shadow Budget (1992)
    180–1
  election (1992) 187–8, 334
  PSBR argument (1992/93) 163
Robinson, Geoffrey 317
Rocard, Michel 231
Roe, James 398
Romania 86, 514
Ross Goobey, Alastair 32, 38, 172,
    183–4, 186–8, 194

Rothschild, Anita 397
Rothschild, N.M. & Sons 164, 398,
    441, 447
  Treasury Department 85
Rowse, A.L. 441
Royal
  Mail and Parcel Force 419
  Ordnance 321
  Yacht 330, 476
Rubin, Robert 361–2
Russia *see* Soviet Union
Russian Federation 76, 78, 81
Ryder, Richard 148–9, 362–3, 371,
    418, 421
  leadership contest (1990) 20, 23,
    29–30
  NL, resignation 377, 380

Saatchi, Maurice 159, 169, 183, 188,
    190, 417, 474, 486–7
Sachs, Jeffrey 82
St James's Park 48, 52
St John of Fawsley, Lord 514
Salazar, António de Oliveira 86
Salomon Brothers 11
Sapin, Michel 227–9, 233–3, 235–7,
    253, 264, 330, 343
Savoy Hotel 442
Scandinavia 161, 239, 263, 331, 410
Scargill, Arthur 294, 464
Schlesinger, Professor Dr Helmut
    153, 217, 232–41, 245, 259–60,
    262, 264, 287, 344, 403
  EMS 246, 250, 253–4
  Wall Street Journal and
    Handelsblatt interview 244,
    256, 288
Schmidt, Chancellor, ERM 264
Schroder, Gerhard 208
Schumpeter, Joseph 89
Scott Report 409, 464
Scottish Conservative Party
    Conference 366
Scottish Office 96
Scottish Water 319

Seguin, Philip 231–2
Seitz, Ray 244–5
Seldon, Anthony 213, 242–3, 294,
   364, 384, 444, 497–8, 503
self-employed and sole traders 46
Selsdon Group 405
Sentance, Dr Andrew 106
Shaw, David 25, 415
Shaw, Roberto 221
Shcherbakov, Vladimir 71, 73–4, 78
Sheffield Hallam 491
Shephard, Gillian 31–2, 162–3, 193,
   342, 462, 465
Shepherd, Richard 270
Shetlands, NL, birthplace 52
Shevarnadze, Edouard 78
Silaev, Ivan 76, 79
Singapore 398
Singh, Manmohan 398
Single European Act 449, 502
Skinner, Dennis 382
Smith, Adam 64
Smith, John 31, 72, 103–4, 106, 109,
   146, 158, 342, 351, 410
   basic rate of income tax 172
   Budget (1992) 174, 178, 180
   death 412–14
   ERM 268
   Leader of the Opposition,
      emergency debate 281
   NL
      Conference speech 141
      European Policy Forum speech
         282–3
      legal bills 317
      resignation speech 383
      TV confrontation 187
   Prime Minister's Question Time
      340–1
   public expenditure 299
   Shadow Budget 179–81
   taxation 185
   Treasury figures 163
   VAT increase 356
Smith, Tim 418

social security 143
Social Security, Department of 147–8
   Ministers, Budget 1993; 356
Solchaga, Carlos 233, 236, 253
South American investments 89
sovereignty 457–8
Soviet Union 64–88, 128, 306
   British training scheme 84–5
   Central Committee 78
   dissolved 79, 82, 86–7
   and Eastern Europe, economic
      reform 81
   economy 66, 81, 84, 198
   food aid programme 70
   G7 Meetings 154, 362
   gold holdings 74, 76, 79–80
   IMF 66–7, 70–1, 74, 81–3, 86
   Inland Revenue 84
   London Embassy party 72
   Minister for Electricity 75
   Parliament 78
   seventy-fifth anniversary of the
      Revolution 83–4
   World Bank 67, 70–1
Spain 86, 114, 150–1, 194, 257, 403,
   452
   cohesion fund 130, 133
   devaluations 261, 263, 282–4
   German help for French 287
Spanish Club 371
speaker's agency 380
Spectator 486
   Parliamentarian of the Year lunch
      52–3
Spicer, Michael 270, 378–9, 400, 467
   Fresh Start Group 433–4
Staffordshire South-East by-election
   469
stamp duty 196, 230
Star 314, 375–6
Stephens, Philip 21–2, 242–3
   Financial Times 7, 145, 314
Stephenson, Andrew 93
sterling 221–2, 242, 246, 260–3
   Black Wednesday 256–7, 259

Stock Exchange 148
stock market crash (1987) 34
Straw, Jack 462
sub-post offices 320
Suez fiasco (1956) 494–5
Summers, Larry 361, 375
Sun 101–4
  Autumn Statement (1992) 310
  Blair article on European single
    currency 485
  Budgets
    (1992) 175
    (1993) 354
  economy 202–3
  election (1992) 187
  James Lamont 317–18
  NL
    anti-Government endorsement
      409
    Brighton hotel bill 292–3
    interview 404–5
    post Black Wednesday 270
    resignation 367, 376
    Threshergate 313–16
  PM
    leadership victory 462–3
    Out in Ten days 473
    outburst 408
Sunday Express 295
Sunday Telegraph 365, 407, 412–13
The Sunday Times 91, 97–8, 105,
  218
  Major ratings 41
  polls 411, 472
Surbiton constituency 477–8
Sweden 162, 239, 242, 244, 256–7,
  284, 425
Switzerland 162, 417, 425
Symonds, Matthew, *Independent*
  262, 271

Tapsell, Peter 368, 401, 433
taxation 44, 184–90, 337, 345
  increases 336, 345, 349, 358–9
  press conferences on 183

Taxation and the Single Market: A
  Market-Based Approach 204
Tebbit, Norman 207, 282, 290, 496
Temple-Morris, Peter 412, 443
Tennyson, Alfred Lord 493
Thatcher, Margaret (Prime Minister
  1979–90; Lady 1990–) 449
  Bournemouth Conference 40
  Budgets
    (1990) 55
    (1991) 60
  Cabinet meetings 318–19
  child benefit 50
  Delors Report 116–117–18
  economic reforms 458
  80s 493
  ERM 210, 395, 520
    entry 7–8
    membership 282
  EU taxation 204, 207
  European negotiations 134
  European policy 10, 199
  European single currency 110
  Falklands War 41
  firm decisions 500
  framework for growth 289–90
  Goldsmith 468
  Gorbachev 65
  Hague supporter 511
  inflation 323, 387–9
  Keith Joseph Memorial Lecture
    463–4
  Lawson partnership 322, 495
  Leader of the Opposition 513
  medium term financial strategy
    355
  memoirs 159
  monetary union 111
  mortgage relief 45, 61
  Naples Summit (Autumn 1990)
    118
  NL
    Brighton Conference speech 291
    letter to 478
    resignation 375

No Turning Back Group 27
Party leadership elections
    (1974) 510
    (1990) 12–13, 15–19, 22, 28–9
policy decisions 91
Poll tax 43, 62
polls 155–6
Portillo party 371
Post Office privatisation 320–1
public expenditure 40, 301–2
public sector pay 306
resignation 9–10, 18, 20
Single European Act 502
VAT 205
Washington Embassy 278
Thatcherism 495–6
Thatcherites 28, 449, 498
Third World debt (late 1980s) 68
Thompson, Clive (Rentokil) 311
Thorneycroft, Peter 506–7
Thorp Arch, Yorkshire 478–9, 491
Threshergate 313–16, 483
Thurnham, Peter 464
Tietmeyer, Hans 227, 229, 241,
    264–5, 288
The Times 41, 104, 142
    Autumn Statements
        (1991) 145
        (1992) 311
    Budgets
        (1991) 60
        (1993) 355
    endangered species 488
    European single currency 428, 435
    Harrogate 488
    leadership odds (1994) 409
    letters advocating withdrawal from
        ERM 214
    NL
        Bournemouth Conference speech
            418
        end of political career 430
        ERM 404
        interview 408
        resignation 273, 377, 384

    rumours 363
    votes Labour 142
    PM 364–5
        interview 470
        prediction of fall 384
    PSBR 177
    VAT 355
    White Paper on the IGC 465
tobacco and alcohol duties 46, 165,
    204–5
Today programme 273, 473
    Budget (1993) 354–5
    Carlisle, John 434
    Hurd, Douglas 199
    leadership election speculation 411
    NL 363, 375
    PM support 379
    Portillo, Michael 443
Tokyo 247
    G7 Foreign and Finance Ministers
        meeting (1993) 362
Toto's restaurant 373
Tour de France 221
Townend, John 214, 433
Tracey, Dick 477–8
Trade Indemnity 202
Trade and Industry, Department of
    (DTI) 294
    NL 64–5, 165
trade union reforms 195
Trafalgar Square rally 449
transport section 348
Treasury 33
    Bank of England independence
        323–4
    Birmingham European Council
        report 287
    Chancellor
        (NL) 6–7, 30, 53, 399
            reappointment and
                reassurance 191–4
        office 32–3
    Chief Secretaries
        EDX Committee 302
        Finance Bill 178

Treasury – *continued*
'public expenditure round' 301
economic forecasts 89–90, 99–100,
107, 142, 144–5, 163, 311,
352, 390–5
*Recovery at last, or another false
dawn?* (June 1992) 202
estimates 56
Financial Secretaries, Finance Bill
178
housing market 147
information 302
John Smith and Margaret Beckett
180
Ministerial team 31–2, 39–40, 193
monopoly of decision-making 304
Monthly Monetary Assessment 230
NL
Chief Secretary (1988) 7, 40, 43,
50, 300
contact on holiday 220–1
desk clearing 186
Financial Secretaries 7, 34, 43,
398, 414
legal bill 95, 316
statement on pound 227, 231
political advisors 32, 39–40, 193–4
post election (1992) 193
Press Office 95, 316
Questions 310
and Select Committee (TSC)
289–90
Select Committees
Bank of England independence
326
global version of ERM 337
NL 275, 293
support 374, 382
tax receipts 1993/94; 335
visit to Bundesbank and German
Finance Ministry 265
weekly overview meetings 39–40,
45
Treaty of Rome, amendments to 115,
122

Trichet, Jean-Claude 240–1, 264–5
Trotsky, Leon 220
TUC Conference 449
Turkey 514
Turnbull, Andrew 240, 247, 333
Tuscany, Port Ercole 77, 220–1
Tyrie, Andrew 32, 168, 193–4

Udall, Mo 155
Ukraine 128
Ulster Unionist MPs 327
unemployment 90, 102–5, 333–60,
350, 426–7
Uniform Business Rate 350
Union of Democratic Mine Workers
(UDM) 294
Union Treaty 70, 75–6
United Kingdom
aid to young Russians 142
EU, Budget
contribution 331–2
rebate 449
exports to Europe 425
inflationary spiral 323
policy for British interests 291–3
United Nations, Gorbachev speech
on disarmament 65
United States
banking crisis 217
Congress 67
Constitution 456
dollar 228, 448, 455
domination 343
economy 42, 161, 230
exports to Europe 425
Government, GATT 361
independent central bank 322
interest rates 150–1, 153, 161,
217, 229
labour mobility 452
November Presidential Election
279
single market 207
Treasury, contact on holiday
221–2

VAT 40, 44–6, 59, 61–2, 186, 205–7, 347–51
  see also fuel and power
vehicle excise duties 165
Virgil 313
Volcker, Paul 428
Vranitzky, Chancellor of Austria 398
VSTF (Very Short Term Credit Facility) 258–9

Waddington, David 19
Waigel, Theo 119, 152, 228–9, 234–5, 253, 262, 403
Wakeham, John 139, 153, 293, 303, 319–20
Waldegrave, William 13–15, 139
Wales, Princess of 330
Walker, Bill 440
Walker, Harold, Deputy Speaker 54
Wall Street Journal 244, 377
Walters, Sir Alan 214
War Cabinet, IRA bomb 48–9
Washington
  IMF meeting (April 1992) 81
  lecture on Russia 85–6
water industry 319
Watkins, Alan 380
Watts, John 289–90
Ways and Means
  Chairman of 54
  resolution 149
Webb, Beatrice 299
Wellington, Duke of 125
Wellington Square 232, 240, 277–8, 304
Welsh Office 96, 193
Werner Plan for monetary union 112
Western technology 77
Westminster Abbey 83
Westminster Hall 436

Whips 398
whisky industry 205
Whistler, Rex 215
White Budget 167
White, Michael, *Guardian* 141, 270
Whitelaw, Willie 397
Whittingdale, John 443
Wicks, Sir Nigel 75, 110–11, 116, 132, 151, 240–1, 255, 265, 278
Widdecombe, Ann 511
Wigan 368
Wilde, Oscar 424, 477
Williams, Hywel 440
Wilson, Harold 271, 506
Windsor Castle, Gorbachev visit 75
Winterton, Nicholas 310
Woodward, Shaun 183
Worcester, Bob 482
workfare 342
World at One 474
  Heseltine, Michael 473
World Bank, Soviet Union 67, 70–1
world economy 151, 161
Wyatt, Petronella 198
Wyatt, Woodrow 18, 77–8, 379–81, 383
  Newsnight 365
  NL, TV debate with John Smith 180
  and Varushka 77, 220–1

Xiaoping, Deng, Tiananmen Square 87

Yavlinksy, Grigori 68, 73, 78–82, 86
Yeltsin, Boris 76–80, 82–5, 128
Yeo, Tim 407
Yew, Lee Kuan 398
Yorkshire, campaign trail 186
Yorkshire Evening Post 480